The United States Army and the Making of America

STUDIES IN **CMR**
CIVIL-MILITARY RELATIONS

William A. Taylor, Series Editor

The United States Army and the Making of America

From Confederation to Empire, 1775–1903

Robert Wooster

University Press of Kansas

Published by the University Press of Kansas (Lawrence, Kansas 66045), which was organized by the Kansas Board of Regents and is operated and funded by Emporia State University, Fort Hays State University, Kansas State University, Pittsburg State University, the University of Kansas, and Wichita State University.

Library of Congress Cataloging-in-Publication Data

Names: Wooster, Robert, 1956– author.
Title: The United States Army and the making of America : from Confederation to empire, 1775–1903 / Robert Wooster.
Description: [Lawrence] : [University Press of Kansas], [2021] | Series: Studies in civil-military relations | Includes bibliographical references and index.
Identifiers: LCCN 2020040400
ISBN 9780700630646 (cloth)
ISBN 9780700630653 (epub)
Subjects: LCSH: United States. Army—History. | United States—History, Military.
Classification: LCC E181 .W9145 2021 | DDC 355.00973—dc23
LC record available at https://lccn.loc.gov/2020040400.

British Library Cataloguing-in-Publication Data is available.

Printed in the United States of America

10 9 8 7 6 5 4 3 2

The paper used in this publication is acid free and meets the minimum requirements of the American National Standard for Permanence of Paper for Printed Library Materials Z39.48-1992.

This book is dedicated to my parents.
My memories of you continue to guide me every day of my life.

Contents

List of Illustrations

Foreword

William A. Taylor

In *The United States Army and the Making of America: From Confederation to Empire, 1775–1903*, Robert Wooster, Regents Professor of History at Texas A&M University-Corpus Christi, deftly illuminates the central and enduring element that the U.S. military—in this case the army—contributed to American history from this nation's founding throughout the nineteenth century and beyond. Wooster achieves this laudable goal not by ignoring the military's essential role on the battlefield but rather by augmenting that critical mission with the myriad economic, administrative, political, diplomatic, social, and cultural means that the army interposed to U.S. history in addition to combat. In doing so, Wooster unites the best methods of military history with a nuanced understanding of the many other factors that influenced army development during this formative period and the resulting momentous changes in American society that the army fomented during alternating periods of war and peace.

Wooster deeply researched and meticulously documented this book. He robustly supports his vivid narrative with copious primary sources from numerous archives and libraries and seamlessly integrates them within the broader contours of the prevailing secondary literature, engaging classic works as well as the newest additions to the field. As an added bonus, Wooster includes fifty enlightening illustrations that depict the main characters and major developments throughout his story. The result is a compelling combination of originality and synthesis that will benefit scholars, students, and general readers alike. Wooster elucidates the essence of civil-military relations at its broadest scope, the vital relationship between a military and the nation that it serves. Throughout the period of this study, the U.S. Army played seminal roles in developing America. Balanced and objective, Wooster shows that this bond was significant yet tumultuous and exposes both triumphs and failures. He demonstrates intimate connections between the army and such auspicious trends as nationalism, development, immigration, manufacturing, sectionalism, technology, transportation, expansion, engineering, infrastructure, commerce, and imperialism, among others. In doing so, Wooster uncovers many points where the army as an institution intersected with and interjected into major aspects of American society.

The United States Army and the Making of America highlights the most critical debates at the core of civil-military relations, especially those considerations regarding the army's proper role, appropriate size, and ultimate place in American society. Wooster thus bares the intimate influence of the army on the nation and vice versa in an association that constantly ebbed and flowed for more than 125 years. The ways in which armed forces interacted with the American society from whence they came and for which they fought illustrate a critical pillar of civil-military relations, albeit one that receives far less careful inquiry than merited. Wooster's impressive study goes a long way toward rectifying this scholarly void. He shows how armed forces, once raised, became a tangible manifestation of the will of a particular society and influenced the development of both the army and the nation for better or worse. In many respects, therefore, militaries serve as a reflection of society, albeit an uneven and imperfect one. Even when not wholly representative, however, the debates about a military's role, mission, and place during times of war and peace uncover the values, shortcomings, uncertainties, foibles, and hopes of that society within the context of a particular time and place.

Such a complex relationship was certainly the case with army regulars from the founding of this nation throughout the nineteenth century to its eclipse by the twentieth, as Wooster skillfully establishes in this fine volume. The story of the army thus reveals much about the making of America through a series of crucial dichotomies: militia and regular, liberty and security, citizen and soldier, peace and war, domestic and foreign, state and federal, patronage and professionalism, republic and empire, and civilian and military. The army's ubiquitous presence yet evolving nature within American society tells not only the compelling account of the army but also the larger narrative of America's growth as a nation as well. In *The United States Army and the Making of America*, Wooster adroitly illustrates how these two important stories remained intertwined from the nation's founding to past the end of the nineteenth century.

Acknowledgments

"Several individuals greatly eased the problems concerning this thesis, and acknowledging my gratitude to them is perhaps the most enjoyable aspect of my work." So I wrote forty-one years ago, as I completed my master's thesis at Lamar University. The people have of course changed, but my gratitude to those around me has only grown more pronounced over the years. Financial support has included a College of Liberal Arts research grant, a Faculty Development Leave from Texas A&M University-Corpus Christi, the Joe B. Frantz Professorship, additional faculty grants from the Joe B. Frantz Fund, and a General and Mrs. Matthew B. Ridgway Research Grant from the U.S. Army Heritage and Education Center. William J. Chriss, Patrick J. Carroll, Ariel "Allie" Kelley, and Samuel J. Watson generously offered time, advice, and information. Amanda Hartman helped to enter corrections and changes in the notes, and David Blanke and Peter Moore have been especially trusted friends and colleagues.

In 1994, David Billeaux and I began teaching together in learning communities at A&M-Corpus Christi, and Dave's ideas, lectures, and approach guided me through challenging times as we stumbled our way ahead. The late Dr. Robb Jackson helped me to become a more comfortable, and I think infinitely more successful, teacher. During my career I've been fortunate to have worked with many first-year seminar and composition professors, and Jimena "Chimene" Burnett, Andrea "Dre" Montalvo-Hamid, Allie Kelley, Amanda Hartman, Jen Bray, and Amanda Marquez merit special thanks for their patience, camaraderie, and devotion to our students. I've always been fortunate to have enjoyed teaching, but they've made the past few years especially fruitful.

Catherine I. Cox has been a blessing to my life, and I thank her for her patience, love, support, and understanding. Her kind, generous, and gentle spirit is inspirational; if we only had more people like her on this earth, the world would be an infinitely better place. My parents, Edna and Ralph Wooster, did not live to see the completion of this project, but their memory still brings a tear or two—good and happy ones—whenever I think of them, which is often.

The United States Army and the Making of America

Introduction

The idea for this book originated during the 2000 presidential election. In a bitterly fought campaign between former Texas governor George W. Bush (R) and Vice President Al Gore (D), the Republican hopeful repeatedly chided his opponent for having been part of an administration that had deployed United States military forces in Haiti, Somalia, and the Balkans. In what became one of the most popular lines in his stump speech, Bush exhorted: "I'm worried about an opponent who uses nation building and the military in the same sentence. See, our view of the military is for our military to be properly prepared to fight and win war, and, therefore, prevent war from happening in the first place." Since then, other projects have come and gone, but I've finally gotten back to this one.[1]

The attempt to divorce the American military from nation-building activities other than armed conflict may or may not have been wise or practical policy. Ironically, as president, Bush would dispatch hundreds of thousands of American military personnel to Afghanistan and Iraq, displacing old regimes with new governments entirely dependent for their existence on U.S. support. But what struck me was the ahistorical quality of Bush's premise, for I had become increasingly convinced that the American military—and more particularly the regular army—had played a vital role in the late-eighteenth and nineteenth-century history of the United States that extended beyond the battlefield. Repeatedly, Americans used the army not only to secure their expanding empire and fight their enemies but also to shape their nation and their vision of who they were, often in ways not directly associated with shooting wars or combat. This defends that thesis. To do so, it features a synthesis of existing scholarship with extensive research in primary sources; it also combines traditional military history (commonly the study of battles and campaigns) and so-called new military history, which places military-related issues within broader social, political, and cultural contexts.

Although the existing literature remains badly fragmented, scholars have recognized the army's influence on American life. During the 1950s, Francis Paul Prucha, Forest G. Hill, and William H. Goetzmann wrote pioneering studies on the army's role in developing the Old Northwest, promoting antebellum transportation, and exploring the American West, respectively.[2] A decade later, Marcus Cunliffe explored cultural and social assumptions about regulars, volunteers, and the warrior ethos. Expanding on those themes, Michael Tate examined the dual roles of the "multi-purpose army" in protecting western security and fostering frontier development, a process that I subsequently elaborated on in *The Military Frontiers: The United States Army and the American West, 1783–1900* (2009).[3] Richard H. Kohn, Theodore J. Crackel, and Andrew Cayton have investigated the army's functions during the early republic period.[4] Thomas "Ty" Smith, Mark Wilson, Paul Koistinen, Merritt Roe Smith, William D. Adler, and Andrew J. Polsky have studied its role in the American economy, and a host of scholars associated with the American Political Development school have treated the regulars as part of a dynamic national state.[5] Yet no single work ties these themes together in a comprehensive narrative, helping to explain the continued reluctance by many scholars to recognize the army's significance in building the United States.

It was ironic that regulars would serve as nation-builders. Soldiers obsessed with the warrior ethos—Brian McAllister Linn has dubbed them the "Heroes"—have long eschewed things other than warfighting, and the historian J. P. Clark has recently described the early-nineteenth-century military as "a profession born in war."[6] Moreover, disdain for a standing army ran deep in the American psyche. In drafting the Declaration of Independence, for instance, Thomas Jefferson complained that King George III had quartered "large bodies of armed troops among us" and was "transporting large armies of foreign mercenaries to complete the works of death, desolation and tyranny already begun." A half-century later, Henry David Thoreau reflected similar themes:

> You may see a file of soldiers, colonel, captain, corporal, privates, powder-monkeys and all, marching in admirable order over hill and dale to the wars, against their wills, aye, against their common sense and consciences, which makes it very steep marching indeed, and produces a palpitation of the heart. They have no doubt that it is a damnable business in which they are concerned. . . . Now, what are they? Men at all? Or small moveable forts and magazines, at the service of some unscrupulous man in power?[7]

As Jefferson and Thoreau suggested, relations between the army and civilians remained tenuous throughout the nineteenth century. Confidence in the willingness of virtuous amateurs to grab their firearms to defend home, hearth, and country against tyrannical kings, bloodthirsty savages, and foreign enemies became a staple of American popular culture. Fear that regulars would establish a dictatorship, disappointment that the institution did not unilaterally support expansion (most soldiers sought to maintain order and establish national sovereignty rather than advocating the unrestrained capitalism favored by the public), and controversies associated with the army's implementation of congressional reconstruction and involvement in federal elections loomed large. Some regulars reacted by attempting to completely divorce themselves from national politics, a futile gesture that only diminished the army's ability to shape even the most mundane military affairs.[8] In little-recognized precursors to modern government shutdowns (in 1877 and again in 1879), Congress adjourned without passing army appropriations, leaving the regulars without funding for several months. Yet debates regarding the military's role in shaping and projecting Indian policy, the appropriate division of power between state and federal authorities, and the size of a standing force revealed the inconsistency in the nation's views of the armed forces: the public demanded that the military remain small even as it expected those forces to promote civilian development.

Despite such misgivings, regular troops assumed a crucial role in establishing Washington's authority across North America. Although most federal operations were, as Brian Balogh has observed, "out of sight," such was not the case with the army, whose garrisons, arsenals, armories, and coastal fortifications revealed the government's substantial physical presence. Between 1816 and 1901, regular soldiers comprised between 14 and 48 percent of all federal employees, and war-related matters consumed at least 70 percent of all federal spending.[9] Military roads and telegraphs, along with the assistance regulars provided to railroads, surveys, and river and harbor improvements, involved the armed forces in the "communications revolution" that the historian Daniel Walker Howe identifies as having transformed American life. As Charles Sellers and Robert Wettemann have recognized, officers and former officers had a marked influence on the burgeoning market economy of the 1820s and 1830s.[10] Moreover, the army established ad hoc military governments to provide a modicum of order in newly occupied Louisiana, New Mexico, California, Cuba, and the Philippines. Regulars were also linked to a host of themes associated with the modernization of America, ranging from the burgeoning factory system,[11] the development of modern social policy,[12] the rise of a national state,[13] the preservation of wilderness areas, the growth of accounting and management, and the transformation of the District of Columbia.[14]

Of course, the United States was hardly the paragon of liberty that many hoped it might become, and the army was involved in many of our greatest national tragedies. Territorial expansion usually came through brute force, and the regulars served, as Francis Paul Prucha put it, as "the sword of the republic." Their sense of racial superiority often led them to act against peoples of color in a manner inconceivable had their foes been white, and the army reflected the fissures of race, class, and gender that divided American society. Commissioned officers and their wives jealously guarded access to their privileged positions against promotion from the ranks or social intermingling with enlisted personnel and working-class laundresses; although nearly 200,000 African American volunteers had fought for the Union during the Civil War, the post-1865 army remained segregated. In their zeal to maintain order, many officers were all too anxious to use their power to preserve the status quo, whether that be the defense of slavery or the suppression of labor strikes. Finally, although Gen. William T. Sherman famously voiced his disinterest in politics ("I will not accept [the Republican Party's nomination for president] if nominated and will not serve if elected"), soldiers frequently sought elected office and engaged in deal-making with legislators, government officials, and businessmen that by modern standards would most generously be judged as unethical.[15]

Despite resentment toward a hierarchical institution that seemed inconsistent with American ideals of republicanism and equality, the nation grudgingly came to accept a standing peace establishment. But that army remains, in the words of Gregory P. Downs, "perhaps the least understood government institution of the 19th century." Indeed, as Robert M. Citino ruefully opined in his seminal essay on the state of military history for the *American Historical Review*: "Military history today is in the same curious position it has been in for decades: extremely popular with the American public at large, and relatively marginalized within professional academic circles."[16] In an effort to bridge these divides, this book seeks to reintegrate the history of the American army into the broader story of the nation.

Chapter One

A Standing Army, the Role of National Government, and the Constitution

British colonists in eighteenth-century North America boasted a healthy distrust of standing armies. Weaned on lessons drawn from the classics as well as their own recent past, they feared that unchecked executive control over a regular army might upset the delicate balance of power between king, Parliament, and the people. Particularly in New England, home of religious dissenters, standing forces might also be used to deny their religious liberty. Just as Julius Caesar's legions had transformed the Roman Republic into the Roman Empire, Oliver Cromwell's New Model Army had established military rule over mid-seventeenth-century England, usurping the people's liberties and rendering men vulnerable to even more vulgar vices and corruptions. In 1685, James II had significantly increased the army during his unsuccessful effort to keep the throne. "If any Man doubts whether a Standing Army is Slavery, Popery, Mahometism, Paganism, Atheism, or anything which he please, let him read," warned the commonwealthman John Trenchard in a blistering fusillade. Added to the "frequent Quarrels, Murders and Robberies, [and] the destruction of all the Game in the Country" was "the Indolence of the Officers, and the Debaucheries that are committed both by them and their Souldiers in all the Towns they come in, to the ruin of multitudes of Women, Dishonour of the Families, and ill Example to others."[1]

Seeking to check these evils following the installation of William and Mary to the throne, English lawmakers had codified their fears. As part of the "Act Declaring the Rights and Liberties of the Subject and Settling the Succession of the Crown" (1689), they prohibited peacetime armies without parliamentary consent. Professional soldiers, they believed, would inexorably separate themselves from the rest of society and fall prey to the tyrant's siren call. The widely shared belief that regular soldiers came from the lowest elements of society added to their qualms. Country philosophers thus insisted that national security must be entrusted to the people themselves. As members of organized militias, virtuous citizens would take up arms in their own defense against those who threatened their liberties.[2]

Within this tradition, American colonies initially required militia service of all able-bodied adult freemen. Over time, however, increasing segments of society—Indians, free blacks and mulattoes, and servants and apprentices—came to be excluded from militias, and compulsory training days were often forgotten or ignored. If military requirements demanded long terms of service outside the colony, such as in wars against Spain and France, colonial assemblies raised volunteer units in lieu of traditional militias. From the colonial perspective, the system worked well. White colonists pushed west and taxes remained low. As a bonus, militia gatherings served as lively social occasions near the bucolic village tavern and green. Americans also pointed with pride to the exploits of provincial soldiers during the imperial wars. Especially notable in such lore was the 1745 campaign against the mighty French fortress at Louisbourg, Cape Breton Island, which fell to New England troops after a six-week siege.[3]

Yet British professionals scoffed at the colonials, in part because they failed to recognize the distinction between militias and specially recruited levies. Lured by bounties, promises of relaxed discipline and adventure, or simply steady rations, the volunteers looked and acted differently than the sturdy middle-class yeomen promoted by militia advocates. Provincial military encampments, reported one redcoat, were "nastier than anything I could conceive." As Maj. Gen. James Wolfe, whose victory on the Plains of Abraham at Quebec (1759) sealed Britain's triumph in the French and Indian War, put it, provincials were "the dirtiest, most contemptible, cowardly dogs you can conceive. There is no depending on them in combat."[4]

American concerns about a standing army increased after 1763, when the Crown, seeking to regulate the Indian trade and secure the colonial borderlands by prohibiting white intruders from entering Indian country, resolved to station 10,000 redcoats in North America. Preventing future conflicts would save money, reasoned officials in faraway London. Colonists disagreed; "the MONSTER or a standing ARMY," asserted one writer, signaled "a plan . . . systematically laid . . . for enslaving America." Parliamentary efforts to cajole Americans into paying for the troops exacerbated the dispute, and the decision to quarter four regiments in Boston following the Stamp Act crisis seems akin to waving a red flag before an onrushing bull. Baiting redcoats became a popular sport, and it seems remarkable that incidents like the Boston Massacre, when British troops gunned down five civilians, did not occur more often. Remembering the martyrs became an annual opportunity for Bostonians to vent their anti–standing army rhetoric, which held that any dependence upon professional soldiers ran counter to principles of republican government and liberty. One speaker cited the commentaries of the celebrated English jurist William Blackstone: "It is extremely dangerous in a land of liberty, to make a distinct order of the profession of arms; . . . the laws and constitution of England are strangers to it."[5]

As relations between Britain and its American colonists deteriorated, the perils of a standing army loomed frighteningly real to those who challenged royal authority. Redcoats poured into Boston following the Tea Party; even

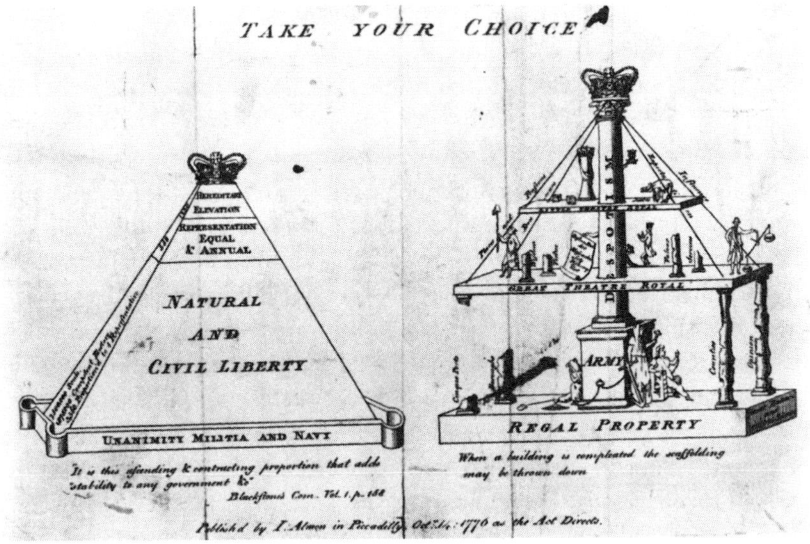

"Take Your Choice." This print, published by John Almon in London in 1776, depicts the choice between "Natural and Civil Liberty," based upon a foundation of "Unanimity, Militia, and Navy," and "Despotism," built upon "Regal Property" and a column of "Army." Library of Congress, USZ62-46310.

as he defended the actions of British soldiers during the Boston Massacre, John Adams recalled that the incident served as "the strongest of Proofs of the Danger of standing Armies." In April 1775, the sight of seven hundred redcoats marching toward Lexington and Concord confirmed suspicions that tyranny was at hand. Proclaimed the Pennsylvania Constitution of 1776: "As standing armies in the time of peace are dangerous to liberty, they ought not to be kept up." Pondering the creation of a new, independent government that summer, Thomas Jefferson proposed: "There shall be no standing army but in time of actual war." Similarly, Jefferson sprinkled the Declaration of Independence with references to the king's abuse of professional armies: George III had quartered in the colonies armies in peacetime without local consent; he had rendered the military separate from civil authority; he was dispatching foreign mercenaries "to complete the Works of death, Desolation, and Tyranny."[6]

Instinctively, most patriots expected their militias and volunteers to spearhead the fight against British and Hessian professionals who sought to enforce London's authority. Liberty could not exist without virtue, and if citizens failed to put aside selfish private interests for public service, the cause itself must die. In truth, militias provided an almost inexhaustible supply of manpower in areas directly threatened by enemy forces. Sometimes, such as at Bunker Hill (June 17, 1775), the amateurs did well; as a fictional British officer in a play usually attributed to Mercy Otis Warren put it: "[Damn] the devils, they excel their very father *Belzebub* for fighting. I had rather engage with a squadron just arrived from the *lower-regions* than with those curst fellows on *yonder hill.*"[7]

Even so, in June 1775 the Continental Congress had sponsored an intercolonial unit of six companies from Pennsylvania, two from Maryland, and two from Virginia (later constituted as the First Continental Regiment), to assist militiamen around Boston. Wearing his Virginia militia uniform to the Philadelphia Congress as if to advertise his availability for military service, George Washington went a step further, insisting that only a "respectable" regular force, the Continental Army, could defeat the British. The dark summer days of 1776 in and around New York City confirmed for many the need for disciplined troops more akin to the hated redcoats than the minutemen of lore. Amid a savage frontier war with the Cherokees, North Carolina delegates to Congress rued the mounting expenses of calling up the militia, preferring instead that the job be done by sturdier (and cheaper) Continentals. Stung by the near disaster at the Battle of Long Island, Maj. Gen. Nathanael Greene lamented "the disorderly conduct of the militia who run at the appearance of the Enemies advance Guard." In his view, "there must be a good army established." Weary of wrangling with Congress and the states for men and material, General Washington warned of "certain, and inevitable Ruin" if he did not get more Continentals. "To place any dependence upon Militia," warned Washington, "is, assuredly, resting upon a broken staff."[8]

Contemporary tactics favored professionals. Infantry dominated eighteenth-century American battlefields, but the inaccurate, single-shot smoothbore muskets carried by most soldiers had a practical range of less than a hundred yards. Volley-firing by lines two or three ranks deep seemed the only way to ensure that someone might hit an enemy target. Absent close supervision by officers and sergeants, musketry could degenerate into ineffective random individual gunfire. With reloading painfully slow and rough terrain demanding more open-order tactics than was the case in Europe, bayonet charges often carried the field. To succeed, such assaults required precise movements and uncommon will, which most observers equated with incessant drill and brutal discipline. In the aftermath of the defeat of Maj. Gen. Horatio Gates's Continental units at Camden, South Carolina (1780), a rout precipitated by the flight of the accompanying militia, Lt. Col. Alexander Hamilton noted: "His [Gates's] passion for Militia, I fancy will be a little cured, and he will cease to think them the best bulwark of American liberty." Washington's fulminations were even stronger: "Regular Troops alone are equal to the exigencies of modern war. No Militia will ever acquire the habits necessary to resist a regular force. The firmness requisite for the real business of fighting is only to be attained by a constant course of discipline and service."[9]

The emerging Continental Army became a breeding ground for nationalism and nationalist leaders. In his study of Pennsylvania soldiers, Gregory Knouff demonstrates that a myriad of local concerns, based on geography, race, class, religion, ethnicity, revolutionary ideology, or the desire to protect one's community, initially inspired men to take up military service. Over time, the appeal of more tangible benefits—land, bonuses, employment, and social advancement—became increasingly significant. Upon joining the army, men became members of an institution, where they found others who fought to defend a diverse array of their own interests. Out of these common causes, argues Knouff, emerged a "popular nationalism" that became a hallmark of the early republic.[10]

Their cosmopolitan experiences and shared sense of suffering, purpose, and accomplishment also left many officers as confirmed nationalists, albeit of a different sort. Their commander, Washington, brilliantly used the specter of selfish politicians and greedy speculators to promote camaraderie among his men. As required by his civilian superiors, he issued frequent status reports, accepted congressional favorites as generals, and assiduously sought out the approval of the latter (through his "council of war") for major decisions. He also pushed for a stronger central government, and his aides included many who did the same: Alexander Hamilton, his de facto chief of staff and future secretary of state; Edmund Randolph, who briefly served as his aide and later his Attorney General; James McHenry, his assistant secretary, a future secretary of war; and Jonathan Trumbull, Jr., another secretary and the future governor of Connecticut. Generals included men who became governor of the Northwest Territory (Arthur St. Clair); secretary of war (Henry Knox); judge of the Northwest Territory (Rufus Putnam); Postmaster General and secretary of state (Timothy Pickering); and a two-time Federalist Party nominee for president (Charles Cotesworth Pinckney). Such veterans voiced their frustrations with a revolutionary vigor. The Confederation, concluded former Maj. Gen. John Sullivan, now representing New Hampshire in Congress, was "a Body without power & the States the Several Component parts of a Monster with Thirteen heads."[11]

General Washington strained to professionalize his troops. Out of the terrible winters at Morristown and Valley Forge rose a more disciplined Continental Army, drilled under the tutelage of traditionalists like Friedrich William Augustus (the self-styled Baron von Steuben). The spectacular success of New England militia at Bennington (1777), over-the-mountain men at King's Mountain (1780), and irregular forces commanded by Thomas Sumter and Francis Marion (1780–1781) notwithstanding, fighting in the set-piece battles at Saratoga, Brandywine, and Germantown (1777), Monmouth

(1778), and most of the Carolina campaigns (1780–1781) featured the Continental units, supplemented by various state militias. Washington and his French counterpart, Comte de Rochambeau, compelled the surrender of Lord Cornwallis and a British army at Yorktown using 15,000 French sailors, 7,800 French regulars, 5,700 Continentals, and 3,200 militia. As contemporary observer David Ramsay's *History of the American Revolution* (first published in 1789) explained, the war's "continued exertions . . . could not be expected from the impetuous sallies of militia. A regular permanent army became necessary." Overreliance on militia, one of Washington's aides later asserted, "had like to have lost our independence."[12]

Even so, many Americans remained skeptical of professional military service. The popular version of history attributed the revolutionary triumph to the American people writ large, not the sacrifices of a relatively small cadre of Continentals. The harsh discipline, undemocratic regimen, and hierarchical nature of military life offended republican sensibilities more concerned with protecting liberty than preserving order. As average Americans avoided the wartime call of recruiters and conscription officials, states had turned to impressment to fill manpower quotas. Although the situation varied from community to community, the profile of Continentals more closely resembled British regulars than the minutemen of Concord and Bunker Hill. As the war dragged on, soldiers in the ranks tended to become younger, less propertied, and more likely to be bachelors. Between 5 and 10 percent were African Americans, and many were immigrants. Their officers typically came from the upper classes, with one observer remarking that they "would not pass unnoticed in the politest court in Europe."[13]

In procuring supplies for the abstract cause of independence, Confederation authorities routinely clashed with local magistrates most interested in defending the properties of their own constituents. Suspicious onlookers saw the inability of officers to comply with strict congressional accounting of their public expenditures as evidence of rampant military corruption. Officers' frequent condemnations of the failures of the states and Congress, arrogant attempts at self-promotion, and demands for compensation—pensions for officers, bounties for enlisted men, and higher pay—grew tiresome, impossibly expensive, and seemed to pose a threat to republican liberties. "I am wearied to death with the wrangles between military officers, high and low," complained John Adams. "They worry one another like mastiffs, scrambling for rank and pay like apes for nuts." With independence secured, truly virtuous patriots should now return to civilian life; the heartfelt thanks of the American people, along with their satisfaction at having triumphed over tyranny, seemed ample reward.[14]

Amid ongoing negotiations with Britain following the triumph at Yorktown, unfolding events alarmed those skeptical of the army's virtue. Congress

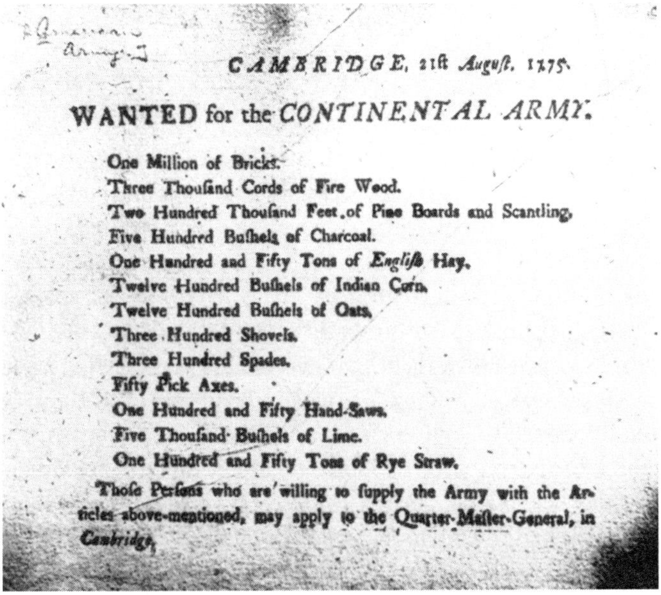

CAMBRIDGE, 21ſt *Auguſt*, 1775.

WANTED for the *CONTINENTAL ARMY*.

One Million of Bricks.
Three Thouſand Cords of Fire Wood.
Two Hundred Thouſand Feet of Pine Boards and Scantling.
Five Hundred Buſhels of Charcoal.
One Hundred and Fifty Tons of *Engliſh* Hay.
Twelve Hundred Buſhels of Indian Corn.
Twelve Hundred Buſhels of Oats.
Three Hundred Shovels.
Three Hundred Spades.
Fifty Pick Axes.
One Hundred and Fifty Hand-Saws.
Five Thouſand Buſhels of Lime.
One Hundred and Fifty Tons of Rye Straw.

Thoſe Perſons who are willing to ſupply the Army with the Articles above-mentioned, may apply to the Quarter-Maſter-General, in *Cambridge*.

"Wanted for the Continental Army." Broadsides like this reflect the army's importance to regional economies, although suppliers often had to endure maddening delays in payment for their services. Library of Congress, USZ62-50145.

had once promised Continental Army officers half-pay for seven years in return for their services, but negotiations concerning the implementation of this agreement had stalled by the winter of 1782–1783. Already having gone without pay for several months, many commissioned personnel felt betrayed by ungrateful politicians. As the historian Charles Royster so aptly put it, long-suffering officers convinced themselves that they were "first among patriots." Fearing that financial insolvency would bankrupt the revolutionary experiment as well as their own personal fortunes, some ardent nationalists and government creditors seized the opportunity to link the army's dissatisfaction with their drive for a stronger government. "The terror of a mutinying Army is playd off with considerable efficacy," the former diplomat Arthur Lee told his friend Sam Adams. "The claims of the army urged with moderation, but with firmness," explained Hamilton, could be put to a "useful turn. . . . But the difficulty will be to keep a *complaining* and *suffering army* within the bounds of moderation."[15]

Incendiary treatises thus circulated among the Continental camp at Newburgh, New York. "Change the milk-and-water style of your last memorial; assume a bolder tone," advised the first of two Newburgh Addresses, which challenged officers "to oppose tyranny under whatever garb it may assume, whether it be the plain coat of republicanism, or the splendid robe of royalty." Should Congress offer "the slightest mark of indignity," it warned darkly, "the army has its alternative." Tipped off by Hamilton, Washington in mid-March 1783 defused the crisis in a dazzling piece of showmanship. Ostentatiously fumbling in his pocket as he addressed fellow officers inside the newly constructed Temple of Virtue, the old Virginian gingerly drew out a pair of eyeglasses and ad-libbed: "Gentleman, you will permit me to put on my spectacles, for I have not only grown gray but almost blind in the service of my country." Sturdy men, these, made harder by the rigors of seven years of conflict against one of the world's strongest powers. But few save his closest advisers had known that their commander now needed assistance in even this simple task of reading his notes. Many wept, and the rest backed away from the abyss as Congress offered officers half pay for five years. The incident nonetheless reinforced suspicions about the links between a regular force and those seeking pecuniary benefits associated with a strong national government. "There seems to be reason to *suspect that* the *intrigues* of the *civil creditors fan* the *discontents* of the *army*," concluded James Madison. Even the venerable Washington cautioned potential conspirators that "the Army . . . is a dangerous instrument to play with."[16]

Enlisted men bore their own grievances. That June, flat broke and out of credit, Congress began furloughing much of the army. Their desire to go home outweighing their desire to get paid, most soldiers trudged away quietly, but about eighty disgruntled Continentals marched from Lancaster to Philadelphia to demand back wages. Their arrival roused several hundred like-minded militiamen, and Congress scampered off to Princeton rather than face down a well-armed mob. Happily, the officers and their men never reached what the scholars James Kirby Martin and Mark Lender describe as a "commonality of purpose"; had they done so, "the army in its bitterness held the potential to become an awesome threat to the very cause that it was upholding and defending."[17]

No wonder, then, that fears of a professional army held strong. The economic mobilization required to win the war had created de facto alliances between merchants, government officials, and soldiers, networks that fostered conditions ripe for corruption. The Articles of Confederation, adopted during the War for Independence, had entrusted the common defense to a "firm League of friendship" among the states, which held responsibility for recruiting, equipping, and supplying the Continental Army. Each state was required to "always keep up a well-regulated and disciplined militia, sufficiently armed and accoutered," but the Articles forbade them from maintaining peacetime armies, save forces needed for frontier defense. Why was there any need for a change? wondered those suspicious of a standing army. Whereas they grudgingly acknowledged that Continentals had been necessary to meet the revolutionary emergency, it was now time to return to simpler republican virtues. Congressman Stephen Higginson of Massachusetts summed up the concerns of those who feared the emergence of a new form of tyranny:

> There are those also among us who wish to keep up a large force, to have large garrisons, to increase the navy, to have a large diplomatic Corps, to give large Sallaries to all Our Servants. Their professed view is to strengthen the hands of government, to make us respectable in Europe, & I believe, they might add to divide among Themselves & their Friends, every place of honour & of proffit.[18]

In 1783, formation of the Society of the Cincinnati added to the sense of unease. Named for the Roman general who gave up his dictatorial powers after an emergency had ended, the Society served as a fraternal organization for former Revolutionary War army and naval officers and their descendants. Its exclusionary, aristocratic nature raised suspicions among Americans fearing that a conspiracy lurked around every corner. Longtime Massachusetts congressman Elbridge Gerry labeled it an "unconstitutional Monster" that would "destroy our Liberties," and in a series of widely published pamphlets, former soldier and South Carolina politician Aedanus Burke (using the pseudonym "Cassius") insisted that "this order is planted in a fiery, hot ambition and thirst for power, and its branches will end in tyranny." With the British beaten, many feared that a peacetime army, led by power-hungry aristocrats and manned by the flotsam and jetsam of society, represented a grievous threat to liberty.[19]

Washington and his compatriots, by contrast, espoused a different narrative of the revolutionary triumph. For these nationalists, the war had confirmed the need for a small force even in peacetime, for the specter of foreign tyranny in a world dominated by monarchies remained very real. To the same end, Congress must have an independent source of revenue, which most assumed would come from the sale of public lands or an import tariff, both of which required protective force. To take up the thorny question of a military peace establishment, the Confederation Congress had in spring 1783 organized an ad hoc committee, featuring three of America's leading Federalists: Alexander Hamilton, James Wilson, and James Madison. Upon the committee's request that he submit plans to "conciliate security with economy and with the principles of our governments," Washington suggested that four infantry and one artillery regiments, consisting of 2,631 officers and men, were necessary to garrison public stores at West Point and "awe the Indians, protect our Trade, prevent the encroachment of our Neighbours of Canada and the Floridas, and guard us at least from surprises." In addition, he recommended that the government erect strategically placed arsenals and establish at least one military academy. To soften anticipated criticism, he made sure to acknowledge the continued importance of "a well organized militia." Predictably, the committee's resulting plan—which reflected their shared belief that an army would strengthen national consciousness and safeguard liberty—closely resembled that of Washington.[20]

Although Congress did not immediately enact these recommendations, pressures in the borderlands remained a powerful factor in considering whether to stand up a regular army. British garrisons still occupied parts of the Old Northwest, for the Crown had no intention of unilaterally ceding its influence. Following a tour of the region, James Monroe, suspicious of a big government but a former officer in the Continental units, recognized the value of permanent military posts in protecting American interests. Opponents of centralization, by contrast, hoped that frontier tensions might mitigate the need for professional soldiers. Maintaining that a standing force "has constantly terminated in the destruction of liberty," Richard Henry Lee, the former president of the Confederation Congress, reasoned that the need for colonists to take up arms to confront Indian threats would produce a cadre of patriotic republicans experienced in the ways of war. "This will always secure to us a hardy set of men on the frontiers, used to arms, and ready to assist against invasions on other parts," he asserted. Otherwise, even patriots might become dependent upon "the Curse of a standing army."[21]

The ideological debate regarding a standing army in a virtuous republic seemed a pernicious abstraction in the backcountry, where racial hatreds transformed the fight for independence into a war to the death. Leading a column against the Seneca Indians of upstate New York in 1779, Maj. Gen. John Sullivan had ordered his men to "totally extirpate the unfriendly nations of the Indians, to subdue their country, destroy their crops, and drive them to seek habitations where they would be less troublesome to us and our allies." Even a traditionalist like Washington acknowledged the ferocity of frontier warfare, warning Passamaquoddy chiefs to avoid the fate of the Cherokees, who had allied themselves with the British: "our warriours went into their country, burnt their houses, destroyed their corn." Although most European observers dismissed the "petite guerre" (little war) of the western frontier, the emphasis on ambush, disruption of supply networks, targeting of enemy homes and villages, and killing and mutilation of noncombatants brought a savagery to the borderlands unknown on battlefields nearer the Atlantic Coast.[22]

The Treaty of Paris (1783) recognized American independence but brought no peace to the contested West. As a veteran of Sullivan's expedition put it: "The nests are destroyed, but the birds are still on the wing." Many rationalized their own cruelties by demonizing their enemies. Indians' resistance stiffened in the face of the Americans' seemingly unquenchable thirst for land; Creek Indians dubbed their Georgia enemies the "Ecunnaunuxulgee," or "people greedily grasping after the lands of the red people." From the Georgia frontier, the retired major general Anthony Wayne, mired in a losing struggle to become a gentleman planter, decried the British alliances with "the Savages, who they indulge in every excess of dissipation, & endeavour to excel them in wanton acts of cruelty, by which means they expect to ingratiate themselves into their favor, as a specimen of their progress in barbarism & inhumanity."[23]

Faced with a crisis, Indian accommodationists joined nativists in agreeing on the need to check American expansion. Sentiment for a pan-Indian confederation ran high; in late 1786 delegates from the confederacy formed by the Six Nations, Delawares, Hurons, Shawnees, Ottawas, Chippewas, Powhatamies, Cherokees, and Wabash confederacy demanded that white surveyors withdraw south of the Ohio River and insisted that "the united voice of the Confederacy" conduct future negotiations. From North Carolina, Agent Joseph Martin reported "constant correspondence" between the Chickasaw and northern peoples. To the north, Indian commissioner and Revolutionary War veteran Richard Butler pointed out that the Six Nations had reached out to Britain and Spain and "laboured exceedingly to form a general confederacy among themselves from north to south."[24]

Ongoing debates about western issues reflected the conflicting agendas of a young Confederation struggling to find its way. Based at Fort Pitt (Pittsburgh), one officer worried that trans-Appalachian white residents would rather accept "a favorable opportunity to submit to a British government than to respect the hell-hounds of the forest." This officer lived in "dreadful apprehension" that the government would withdraw his small contingent of regulars, which seemed to be the only tie between disaffected frontiersmen and the rest of the country. Anxious white borderlanders expected assistance—in the form of offensives unfettered by any eastern niceties—from the American Confederation. Otherwise, they hinted darkly, an alliance with another government that could better protect them offered the only antidote to the savage conflicts. Hamstrung by the requirement that nine of the thirteen states approve significant legislation, however, Congress was at an impasse. Washington's recommendation for a moderate peace establishment went nowhere, and Elbridge Gerry's counterproposal to discharge all but five hundred troops won the support of only five states. Conflicting state claims to potential western empires added to the complex stew: Virginia asserted the most expansive imperial dreams; Massachusetts, Connecticut, New York, and Pennsylvania all professed title to parts of the Great Lakes region; and New York and New Hampshire competed for what eventually became the state of Vermont. Until these issues were resolved, the influence of rival soldiers at West Point, Oswego, Niagara, Fort Pitt, and Detroit would be immense. Predictably, competing states rejected New York's request for authorization to raise five hundred men of its own.[25]

By 1784, the frontiers were aflame, militias were decaying, and stores of government ordnance were badly in need of security. With military expenditures accounting for well over half of the Confederation's budget, the Massachusetts legislature instructed its delegation "to oppose, and by all ways and means to prevent[,] the raising of a standing army of any number, on any pretence whatever, in time of peace." Genuine philosophical differences, regional jealousies, and the lesser angels of human nature obscured the business of government. "Cabaling, Selfishness and Injustice Reign," complained one New Yorker, who chirped that "the Southern Nabob's behave as though they viewed themselves as a Superior order of animals." Gerry reminded fellow members that "standing armies in time of peace are inconsistent with the principles of republican government, and generally converted into destructive engines for establishing despotism." In the end, a less doctrinaire practicality won the day. In a complex series of maneuvers, Congress on June 2–3 defeated New York's request to raise its own troops, discharged the existing army save for two small squads to guard the arsenals, and called on Pennsylvania, Connecticut, New York, and New Jersey to form a seven hundred–strong regiment to serve twelve months for the purpose of "securing and protecting the northwestern frontiers of the United States, and their Indian friends and allies, and for garrisoning the posts soon to be evacuated by the troops of his Britannic Majesty."[26]

Dubbed the "First American Regiment," this would form the nucleus of what became the United States Army. Even so, the Confederation's willingness to maintain a permanent establishment remained in doubt. Explaining the situation to his friend Jefferson, Gerry emphasized that in creating the unit Congress had refused to "*Requisition*" the states for manpower, settling instead on the more palatable "*Recommendation.*" Some hoped that the army's small size would compel the militia, "the dernier Resort of Liberty," to increase their preparations. Hugh Williamson, a genial surgeon representing North Carolina, acknowledged "that a Peace establishm't in the Eastern States is an unpleasing business."[27]

The new regiment's composition reflected the sputtering postrevolutionary economy. Immigrants made up more than half of the command. About three-quarters were artisans, laborers, or semiskilled workers. Economic hard times had led most to enlist, with an outsized number coming from urban commercial centers of New England and the Middle Atlantic states. Fairly high reenlistment rates suggest a certain degree of institutional identification. Officers, nearly 90 percent of whom had fought the British, seem to have viewed themselves as career soldiers. Their commander, Lt. Col. Josiah

Harmar, was a Continental veteran and Society of the Cincinnati member who probably owed his new position to his close ties with Thomas Mifflin, who was president of Congress at this time.[28]

As understood by Harmar, his regiment was to deter conflict with Indians and the British and to prevent squatters from taking public lands, the anticipated revenue from which was crucial to paying the government's debt and making its creditors whole. Situated at the confluence of the Monongahela and Allegheny Rivers, Fort Pitt quartered most of the army. Smaller numbers garrisoned Fort Harmar (present-day Marietta, Ohio). Fort Steuben, erected along the Ohio River, guarded the first federal land office in the Northwest Territory, and Fort Finney overlooked the mouth of the Miami River. But the presence of a few underpaid Confederation soldiers impressed no one. Lacking a permanent garrison, Fort McIntosh (originally established in 1778 thirty miles northwest of Pittsburgh) would "be demolished by the emigrants to Kentucky," predicted one officer. "Previous to our arrival, they had destroyed the gates, drawn all the nails from the roofs, taken off all the boards, & plundered it of every article." British agents whipped up Indian opposition to Americans, and during that autumn a Confederation officer acknowledged that a concerted Native American offensive would pose a "very formidable" danger.[29]

The security crisis boiled over in 1786, with Harmar relaying "truly alarming" reports regarding Indian intentions. One observer concluded that the tiny Confederation forces in the Ohio region "are rather prisoners in that country, rather than in possession of it." In an unauthorized and unsuccessful effort to crush American Indian resistance, George Rogers Clark led 1,200 Kentuckians up the Wabash River, creating a fiasco that only strengthened war factions among the tribes. That summer, long-running negotiations with Spain were terminated when Congress refused to ratify a deal that would have secured the North's much-desired commercial treaty in exchange for giving up the South's hoped-for navigation rights on the Mississippi River. Talk of breaking up the Confederation came from both sides of the Mason–Dixon Line. Adding to the sense of paralysis was the failure of the much-anticipated Annapolis Convention, which had attracted delegates from only five states. That fall's insurrection by Daniel Shays and disgruntled Revolutionary War veterans seeking debt relief in western Massachusetts seemed to be the last straw for many. Some kind of institution must be strong enough to protect the nation from dangers within as well as without and to prevent squatters from despoiling the public lands. After receiving reports that several Northwest tribes and "a banditti of desperadoes" were preparing for war, Congress in October 1786 unanimously resolved that the states "use their utmost exertions" to raise another 1,300 soldiers.[30]

Political movements were also afoot. Thomas Jefferson remained confident that "the good sense of the people is the strongest army our governments can ever have," but many fellow revolutionaries concluded that the situation demanded action. "We are fast verging to anarchy and confusion!" Washington told Madison in the wake of the Shays affair. "What stronger evidence can be given of the want of energy in our governments than these disorders? If there exists not a power to check them, what security has a man for life, liberty, or property?" Security—to protect their liberties and properties from anarchy, European monarchs, and Indians—was clearly on the minds of delegates who gathered in 1787 at the Constitutional Convention in Philadelphia. As war was part of the human condition, nationalists believed that only a more powerful central state could defend a nation's principles and interests from without and within. "Nothing short of a regular military force will answer the end of war, and this only to be created and supported by money," concluded physician and former Washington aide James McHenry. Similarly, South Carolina veteran Charles C. Pinckney insisted that Congress have the right to raise armies, organize militias, and build military roads. Although delegates had agreed to keep their deliberations secret, a "Gentleman in Philadelphia" published a letter claiming that one item for discussion had been a 2.5 percent export duty, to be used "for the expences of keeping up a small land force and navy."[31]

Supportive of a more robust government and the creation of federal structures separate from those of the states, James Madison adopted a slightly different approach to national security. More suspicious of a regular army than most Federalists, he supported during the convention an amendment designed to "discountenance" permanent forces. But Madison was also a realist. Absent a stronger union among states, petty rivalries and foreign threats would inevitably lead some to create the outsized armies that had caused incessant warfare in Europe. "Constant apprehension of war . . . has the same tendency to render the head too large for the body," reasoned Madison. "The means of defence agst. Foreign danger, have been always the instruments of tyranny at home. . . . Throughout all Europe, the armies kept up under the pretext of defending, have enslaved the people." To counter this menace, states must rely on collective rather than individual security, thus necessitating a national military.[32]

With a third of the delegates having been Continental veterans, and a substantial majority of the whole chastened by the dread specter of Shays' Rebellion, proponents of at least a small army at Philadelphia steamrolled their opposition. Only a structure that protected order, rather than naive appeals to public virtue, could preserve liberty. As James Wilson of Pennsylvania put it, no successful government could be "deprived of power to prepare for the defense and safety of our country." In defending the role of small states, William Paterson of New Jersey explained that "there must be a small standing force to give every government weight." A former Continental officer pointed out that "preparations for war are generally made in peace; and a standing force of some sort may, for ought we know, become unavoidable." Attempts by the redoubtable Elbridge Gerry to insert language warning "against the danger of standing armies in time of peace" and to restrict a peacetime regular force to no more than three thousand died quietly. The resulting constitution explicitly authorized Congress to "raise and support armies." But the founding fathers of the new republic were also pragmatists. To decrease the likelihood of military despotism, they divided power among the three branches of the federal government, as well as between the states and the national government. The constitution as approved at the convention made the president commander in chief of the army and navy while also directing him to "preserve, protect, and defend the constitution." Appropriations bills would begin in the House of Representatives, but the Senate reserved the right to confirm officer appointments. Military appropriations were limited to two years. Each state would organize and regulate its own militia, which could under extreme circumstances be used "to execute the laws of the Union, suppress insurrection and repel invasion." Federal authorities, however, would govern those militias when they were "employed in the Service of the United States." Finally, states were prohibited from going to war or maintaining their own armies or navies.[33]

Former Continental Army officers generally backed the proposed constitution in state ratification conventions. Placing the power to raise an army in the hands of Congress, explained Maj. Gen. (ret.) Samuel Holden Parsons, would ensure that the institution remained "the army of the people," whose wisdom could be trusted. All forty-four Continental officers from Pennsylvania whose political opinions are known supported ratification. Former Continentals who stood for election to the New York ratification convention backed the constitution 18–8, whereas less than a quarter of those with only militia experience did so. More narrowly, veterans in Virginia voted 46–35 in favor of the new constitution.[34]

Still, the ratification debate revealed continuing reservations about the army's role in a constitutional government. Maryland's Luther Martin, who had walked out of the Philadelphia convention in protest, complained that the document failed to prohibit the president from taking personal command of the army, through which he might assume tyrannical power. Anti-Federalists still insisted that state militias offered the best means of preserving national security. History, they cautioned, showed that peacetime armies endangered liberty. Acknowledging that "a small number of troops" must garrison frontier posts and guard arsenals, one critic demanded language requiring a two-thirds supermajority of each house to establish an army. "Havoc, desolation, and destruction . . . have been perpetrated by standing armies," proclaimed George Mason of Virginia, one of three delegates remaining at the Philadelphia Convention who refused to sign the founding document. A peacetime army was a tool "of the well-born" to use troops to compel the submission of citizens, thundered "'Centinel.' From Virginia," and "Impartial Examiner" argued that such forces "are generally composed of the dregs of the people . . . wanton in the lap of ease and indolence."[35]

Each side grasped the interdependence of military and fiscal authority in a strong government. Anti-Federalists warned that an oppressive central state would use a standing army to enforce taxation and the resultant tyranny. Ratification opponents in Pennsylvania thus cautioned that regular troops "may be employed to enforce the collection of the most oppressive taxes, and to carry into execution the most arbitrary measures." "Philadelphiensis" predicted that the army would be employed to "protect the tax gatherers in collecting the revenue. . . . Upon the whole I think it is pretty obvious . . . that our *standing army* will have *other fish to fry* than fighting a foreign enemy." "Where and when did a freedom exist," bellowed the mercurial Patrick Henry in the Virginia ratifying debates, "when the sword and the purse were given up from the people." In a series of letters to the *New York Journal*, "Brutus" highlighted a similar theme. The rights to borrow money and to raise and support armies made the constitutional government too strong: "I take these two together and connect them with the power to lay and collect taxes, duties, imposts and excises, because their extent, and the danger that will arise from the exercise of these powers, cannot be fully understood, unless they are viewed in relation to each other."[36]

Federalists countered by insisting that the government must be able to generate revenues to fund the military forces needed to protect its commerce and interests against threats from Britain to the north, Spain to the south, and Indians to the west. "We are not in the millennium," warned Wilson. "Wars may happen." Only with a strong military—which must come from a regular army, not state militias, a distinction made most energetically by Hamilton—could the United States convince other nations to make (and abide by) their diplomatic agreements. As John Jay (soon to become the first chief justice of the United States Supreme Court) explained: "The safety of the people of America against dangers from FOREIGN force depends not only on their forbearing to give JUST causes of war to other nations, but also on their placing and continuing themselves in such a situation as not to INVITE hostility or insult."[37]

Accordingly, a dozen of the *Federalist Papers* stressed the need for some form of regular military establishment. As Hamilton put it in *Federalist* no. 25: "The steady operation of war against a regular and disciplined army can only be successfully conducted by a force of the same kind." In making their case, Federalists strained to alleviate concerns that a professional army would foster tyranny from within. Madison acknowledged in *Federalist* no. 41 that regular forces might threaten liberty: "On any scale, it [the standing army] is an object of laudable circumspection and precaution." But tight checks on military spending and the two-year limit on such appropriations would render a regular establishment "tolerable" to a "united" government and "safe" to the "efficient" one. In *Federalist* no. 46, Madison added that the huge numbers of militiamen "fighting for their common liberties" would overwhelm any standing army that the central government might muster.[38]

Building on Madison, one author pointed out that state militias, "where almost every citizen is a soldier," would counterbalance any threat from a regular force. Hamilton emphasized that, as a practical matter, the nation's immature economy could not support an army large enough to threaten popular liberties; further, the political risks to congressmen of voting for military appropriations every two years "by a formal vote in the face of their constituents" would render any long-term buildup unlikely. Common was the refrain that virtuous citizens, whose representatives held the power of the purse, would not allow such a conspiracy to bear fruit. True patriots, argued Federalists, understood that their government needed money to protect the people's interests; as such, military enforcement of taxation would be unnecessary.[39]

Victorious in the struggle for ratification, Federalists steadfastly rejected any specific limitations against a peacetime army in the Bill of Rights, an indication of the importance they accorded a regular force to the new government's success. Still maintaining "that standing Armies in times of peace are dangerous to liberty," anti-Federalists sought more precise language outlining the circumstances under which such an institution might be used, limiting lengths of enlistment to prevent the formation of a professional class of soldiers, and requiring that a supermajority of legislators authorize such an organization. Although desirous that the obligatory nine states ratify the proposed constitution, Jefferson hoped that the remaining four would refuse to do so, thereby signaling the need to recognize freedoms of religion and of the press, to guarantee the option of trial by jury, and to prohibit monopolies, suspensions of habeas corpus, and standing armies.[40]

Responding to this criticism, James Madison incorporated several measures designed to reduce the potential for military tyranny without unnecessarily limiting a regular army. Confirming the need for "a well regulated Militia," the Bill of Rights enumerated "the right of the people to keep and bear Arms." The new amendments also prohibited the peacetime quartering of troops without the consent of owners. Yet Madison and the friends of a stronger government would go no further. Acknowledging that a peacetime force might be "dangerous to liberty," Madison nonetheless rejected proposals requiring a two-thirds supermajority to form an army. A minority, he explained, must not be allowed to prevent the nation from taking the steps necessary for its self-preservation. "Will it be safe," he continued, "to leave the United States at the mercy of one-third of the states?" Such would destroy the people's freedom by encouraging other countries to prey upon a helpless America. The regular army was an evil, but it was a necessary one. That all sixty-nine electors in the first presidential contest cast a vote for George Washington, former commander of the Continental Army, as the nation's first president suggests that a broad political consensus shared Madison's view.[41]

Chapter Two

The Army and Muscular Nationalism: Nation-building and the Federalists

Determined to forge a stronger government following ratification of the Constitution, Federalists emphasized the interdependence of economic and national security. To this end, the 1787 act renewing the peacetime military establishment explained that soldiers "should be stationed on the frontiers to protect the settlers on the public lands from the depredations of the Indians, to facilitate the surveying and selling of the said lands in Order to reduce the public debt and to prevent all unwarrantable intrusions." Pressed by an impending financial meltdown, international crises, fears of anarchy, and dire threats to the borderlands, Federalists over the next decade repeatedly turned to the regular army to help construct a more powerful national state. The small size of the new government meant that it had few tools for implementing policy, so the army—even a small one, with its attendant arsenals, armories, depots, and contracts—represented its most deployable resource. Deeming regulars more reliable and less expensive than state militias or volunteers, President George Washington utilized them to assert sovereignty over the Old Northwest, execute Indian policies, cement Westerners' loyalties, and build support for the central government. Federalists thus set a pattern for the coming century, in the process changing the nature of debate regarding a standing army.[1] Formerly, those within the political mainstream had challenged the very existence of such an institution; by the mid-1790s, the question was not whether there should be an army, but rather how large it should be.

Driven by his experiences during the War for Independence, Washington remained the peacetime army's most important champion. His secretary of war, the bookseller-turned-artilleryman Henry Knox, shared these views, as did Treasury Secretary Alexander Hamilton. Both had joined Washington as founding members of the Society of the Cincinnati. To fill other national security posts, Washington also turned to other Society members: Arthur St. Clair as governor of the Northwest Territory, and Lt. Col. Josiah Harmar to command the new army. Recognizing the militia's continued rhetorical appeal, the president reminded Congress that an "energetic national militia" remained "the capital security of a free republic." Yet he also insisted on a small regular force, and in September 1789 the Senate rejected a constitutional amendment that would have required a two-thirds vote by both houses to raise an army in peacetime.[2]

The links connecting a regular military establishment, a stronger government, and a healthy economy extended to the frontiers. As Hamilton had explained in *Federalist* no. 24, stationing militiamen in borderlands posts far from their farms and businesses would be "impracticable" and "ruinous to private citizens." But squatters had to be checked if the government hoped to augment its meager revenues through the sale of public lands. Secretary Knox also warned that undisciplined volunteers might precipitate an Indian conflict that the nation could ill afford. "The angry passions of the frontier Indians and whites are too easily inflamed by reciprocal injuries, and are too violent to be controlled by the feeble authority of the civil power," wrote Knox. "In such case, the sword of the republic only, is adequate to guard a due administration of justice, and the preservation of the peace."[3]

Administration officials had ample reason to fear losing the West. As one correspondent observed, backcountry men were "constantly endeavoring to provoke hostilities with the Indians, in hopes of profiting either by a war or a treaty," and reports that the Yazoo Land Company had set aside 200,000 acres as bounty lands for a proposed "Yazoo Battalion" tested the young government's monopoly over national security. Earlier, John Sevier and disgruntled colonists in eastern Tennessee had declared their independence from North Carolina and set up the rump state of Franklin. Doing so, they reasoned, would enable them to secure more direct representation in Congress and conduct unrestricted warfare against the Chickamaugas and Cherokees. By moving into Indian country, reported one government agent, adventurers "from the pretend state of Franklin" threatened to unleash the wrath of three thousand Cherokee "prime gunmen." Reports that Franklin officials were considering an alliance with Spain—always eager to exploit divisions among the expansionist-minded Americans—compounded the threat.[4]

The foreign menace in the borderlands endangered a struggling government that had few dollars, fewer troops, and even less capacity to control the insatiable thirst of its citizens for more land. From Georgia came rumors that Spain had furnished the Creek Indians with six thousand muskets. The federal government, Georgians demanded, must do more to protect the Southwest from Indian depredations. "For Gods sake let us have at least the *skeleton* of an army," insisted the Revolutionary War veteran Anthony Wayne. The War Department's response—that two hundred men were on the way—could hardly have been reassuring. Loyalties in the Kentucky district also remained divided. Angry that their rights to navigate the Mississippi River had not been assured, demanding that Indian resistance be obliterated, and suspecting that the government at faraway New York City

Henry Knox. During the 1860s and 1870s, Constantino Brumidi painted and designed numerous murals for the United States Capitol. Among these was this portrait of Henry Knox (1750–1806), former general and the nation's first secretary of war. Library of Congress, D43-T01-9885.

(and later Philadelphia) had forgotten them, more than a few Kentuckians flirted with Spain. In December 1790, George Nicholas, who would serve as Kentucky's first attorney general, warned his friend James Madison that although "we have every wish to continue united to you . . . this opinion is formed on a supposition that we shall receive from Government that protection . . . of our just rights that we have an unquestionable claim to."[5]

From the outset, the Washington administration believed that a standing army afforded the best means of assuring national security and establishing order in the borderlands. In so doing, reasoned St. Clair, "the People would derive Security, at the same time that they saw and felt that the Government of the union was not a mere shadow; their progeny would grow up in habits of Obedience and Respect—they would learn to reverence the Government." Secretary of War Knox echoed similar themes. Without more regulars, the West "is liable to be wrested out of the hands of the Union, by lawless adventurers, or by the savages." With individual states having transferred their western claims to the federal government, revenue from public lands could do much to restore fiscal solvency. Such would also stimulate the speculation, investment, and migration that seemed essential to upward mobility and economic opportunity; as the historian Andrew Cayton demonstrates, Federalists saw a correlation between patriotism and their own private interests. An army presence would increase the value of these lands and confirm the loyalty of white residents, strengthening the nation while simultaneously profiting investors who had risked much for independence.[6]

Because of his experiences as a surveyor and in the Virginia militia, Washington had long recognized the economic and strategic value of the Ohio River country. For the United States to secure control of the region in an orderly fashion, the president thus calculated that Josiah Harmar's regulars must be deployed there. Seeking reliable agents on the ground, Washington also ascribed leadership positions in the Northwest Territory to comrades in the Society of the Cincinnati. In addition to Governor St. Clair, these included the territorial secretary and five territorial judges. Likewise, Society members held a majority stake in the Ohio Company of Associates, which made the first systematic efforts to colonize what would become southeastern Ohio. These speculators were assured that the army would support their "infant colony" against squatters and Indians alike. Cognizant of the public-private alliance, Harmar promised Knox "that every assistance and protection that is in our power, shall be rendered to this [Ohio] company." The secretary agreed, offering that soldiers could conduct surveys "without any considerable expenses to the public."[7]

In the eyes of the administration, increasing American immigration (soldiers at Fort Harmar reported that 1,019 boats, 598 wagons, 18,761 persons, 8,437 horses, 2,199 cattle, 1,833 sheep, and 33 hogs passed down the Ohio River between 1786 and 1789), the continued British presence at Detroit, mounting tales of frontier atrocities, and Kentucky's uncertain status reinforced the need for a well-disciplined army. Following an abortive effort to push through militia reform, Federalists in March 1790 proposed to more than double the regular establishment. Muttering that "new phantoms for the day must be created," opponents like Senator William Maclay of Pennsylvania saw the move as a craven excuse to justify new offices with which the government could reward its supporters. Echoing traditional republican philosophy, Virginia's Richard Henry Lee warned that "[Gaius] Marius, [Lucius Cornelius Sulla] Sylla, Caesar, Cromwell trampled on Liberty with Armies." In the end, Congress approved a modest expansion to 1,216 rank and file.[8]

The objects of this army were the Indians of the Wabash and Miami River regions of central Ohio, against whom the urbane Harmar was wholly unsuited for command. Many of Kentucky's ablest militia leaders refused to serve under him; rumor held that he was "too apt to indulge . . . to excess in a convivial glass." With contractors delivering inferior supplies, his dispirited officers concluded that any efforts to instill discipline among unruly militiamen would only lead to wholesale desertion. Congress had further undermined morale by halving the pay of privates. In late September 1790, Harmar's motley force of 320 regulars and 1,133 militiamen lurched out of Fort Washington (present-day downtown Cincinnati). Twice, columns blundered into traps laid by the skilled Miami tactician Little Turtle. On both occasions, the militia panicked, allowing the Indians to nearly annihilate the outnumbered regulars. Suffering more than two hundred casualties, the Americans scampered back to Fort Washington.[9]

Confronted by Spain, Britain, and a powerful Indian confederacy, the fledgling constitutional government prepared a military response to the disaster. Rufus Putnam, a former Revolutionary War officer and now prime mover behind the Ohio Company's colonization plans, assessed the situation as being "truly critical. . . . We are in the utmost danger of being swallowed up." Westerners, acknowledged Knox, "request and demand protection; if it be not granted, seeds of disgust will be sown; sentiments of separate interests will arise out of their local situation." Against the opposition of Secretary of State Thomas Jefferson, who opined "that rank and file fighting will not do against Indians," Federalists insisted on more regulars, and in late January 1791 Knox proposed organizing two thousand soldiers into a "legionary corps." In a nod to western sensibilities, Knox also requested a regiment of rangers, to be led by "the best and most popular officers in Kentucky." Two thousand additional levies could be enlisted for up to six months. Administration supporters in Congress pushed through the manpower increase, though shorn of the structural changes Knox had envisioned.[10]

To borrow the money to pay for this army, Treasury Secretary Hamilton found a convenient justification for his National Bank, which the House of Representatives had approved just eleven days before the test vote on the expanded military force. Critics saw these moves—along with appropriations for a larger navy to deal with Algerian pirates and a recently passed tax on distilled spirits—as evidence of creeping federal tyranny. "The Indian war is forced forward to justify our having a standing army," grumbled Senator Maclay. "With these two engines, and the collateral aid derived from a host of revenue officers, farewell freedom in America." Jefferson and Madison encouraged President Washington to veto the bank, the immediate source of funding for the new troops. In a lengthy riposte, Hamilton proclaimed that the pending emergency in fact highlighted the value of the bank's power to loan money. Although the tax revenues that would ultimately pay for the army would not be collected for several months, "the preparations . . . are instantly to be made. The money must therefore be borrowed. And of whom

Fort Washington. Established in 1789 at the mouth of the Licking River as part of Josiah Harmar's attempt to secure control of the Old Northwest, Fort Washington, like many military posts, spurred civilian settlement, in this case Cincinnati, Ohio. Library of Congress, USZ62-1878.

could it be borrowed if there were no public banks?" Convinced by Hamilton's logic, Washington signed the bank bill, which in turn made financing the army's fiscal and manpower increases possible.[11]

Armed with a hard-won legislative victory, Knox in spring 1791 outlined measures "most likely to attach the people of the frontiers to the government of the United States." Several hundred men would garrison a new post on the Tennessee River near Muscle Shoals and, if necessary, "dispossess" private companies that provoked the Choctaws, Chickasaws, and Cherokees. Mounted Kentucky volunteers would raid Indian villages, tying down the enemy and reaping the corollary benefit of "being highly acceptable to the Kentucky district." Regulars would launch an offensive in the Old Northwest, where observers reported considerable British influence among the Indians of the Miami River region. To command the latter expedition, the administration turned to Governor St. Clair, formerly a major general in the Continental Army. Predicting "that disciplined valor will triumph over the undisciplined Indians," Knox hoped to tamper East-West jealousies by instructing St. Clair to "impress the frontier citizens of the entire good disposition of the General Government towards them in all reasonable things."[12]

Such optimism did not extend to the troops assembling outside Cincinnati. Aristocratic, overweight, and periodically disabled by gout, St. Clair did little to inspire borderlands residents already dubious about the national government's inclination or ability to protect them. Charles Scott, a respected volunteer officer, admitted to being "damn skittish" about serving under him. Drawn "from the offscourings of large towns and cities; enervated by idleness, debaucheries and every species of vice," the newly enlisted regulars only confirmed Westerners' doubts. The intermingling of private and public interests further hampered preparations, for regular forces required more logistical support than fledgling frontier economies could provide. Anticipating a bonanza for well-positioned contractors, Secretary Knox saw no reason why he and his friends should not profit from the fruits of their expanded government. Thus in the midst of this security crisis, he and the army's chief contractor, the notorious William Duer (once described by Madison as "Prince of the tribe of speculators"), found time to collaborate on a massive real-estate venture in Maine. The conniving Duer's secret $10,000 loan to Knox was bad enough; worse still, Duer had siphoned off his army contract advances to fund his land schemes, leaving subcontractors without cash to purchase desperately needed supplies for troops at Cincinnati.[13]

Raids by Kentucky volunteers brought back claims of widespread destruction of property but few encounters with Indians. In September, St. Clair's ill-prepared troops staggered out of Fort Washington. Weakened by rampant desertion, the column lumbered into the Ohio wilderness, pausing to erect Forts Hamilton and Jefferson to secure its supply lines. Not even threatened punishments of a hundred lashes could prevent undisciplined militiamen and levies from firing their weapons into the surrounding woodlands, advertising their presence to all who could hear. Just after daylight on November 4, Indians struck St. Clair near the banks of the Wabash River. Although outnumbered by nearly two-to-one, the Indians fought "like Furies" in defense of their homes and families. After a brief stand, the American retreat became a rout, the twenty-nine miles back to Fort Jefferson becoming a bloody reminder of the qualitative superiority of Indian warriors over the regulars, levies, militiamen, packers, and camp followers associated with St. Clair's command. Suffering more than a thousand casualties, St. Clair dubbed this defeat—the greatest Indian victory over the army in United States history—a "melancholy tale."[14]

News of the catastrophe stunned the Washington administration. On December 26, Knox outlined his response: attributing the defeat to a "want of *sufficient discipline*" in St. Clair's command, a regular army of at least five thousand men must spearhead a renewed offensive. Yet in the face of this second embarrassing defeat in the borderlands, even Washington seemed to waver. The same day as Knox's report, the president forwarded to his war secretary a letter from "an influential character in Kentucky" that illustrated "how little confidence the people of it will place in the plan which is proposed by your statement." Washington also suggested that Knox draw up cost estimates for a scheme that relied on volunteers to take the offensive, noting that "the Western people would be endulged" and "Many Members of Congress gratified."[15]

Private misgivings notwithstanding, the administration threw its support behind Knox's proposed army expansion. For two weeks in mid-January 1792, the House of Representatives cleared its galleries to debate the bill in secret. When the doors were reopened, opponents of the Knox plan argued that, rather than increasing the regulars, the government should restrict western expansion, rely more heavily on frontier militiamen and rangers, reduce expenditures, and cut taxes. Maryland's John F. Mercer denounced "this complicated, unauthorized, unnatural, unconstitutional mixture of manufacturing, financial, deficiency, sinking fund, and Indian war ingredients." But when the smoke cleared on February 2, the House backed the expanded army bill 29–19. New England opposed the increase, as did all four North Carolinians, who were frustrated with the government's failure to protect their state's borderlands. Notably, however, states most directly impacted by the army's focus on the Old Northwest—New York, Pennsylvania, and Virginia (including future Republican Party stalwarts James Madison and Albert Gallatin)—backed the measure. As Gallatin explained, those who might otherwise have rejected a larger army were "obliged to join those who have proposed the President's plan in order to oppose those who wish to forsake us altogether."[16]

In something of a surprise, the Senate on February 9 rejected the army increases by a 13–12 margin. Some in New England feared the loss of influence to western migration; North Carolina's Benjamin Hawkins, a longtime Indian agent who had once served on the president's staff, attributed his opposition to the administration's failure to pursue diplomacy more aggressively. Another blamed the setback on a lack of confidence in St. Clair. Eight days later, buttressed by the arrival of the New Yorkers Aaron Burr and Rufus King, new promises that it would renew peace talks with the Indians, and a change of heart by Hawkins, the administration reversed the earlier defeat, winning a 15–12 majority to increase the regulars to more than five thousand men and officers. The new law took effect in early March; to shore up the army's logistical tail, Hamilton's Treasury Department assumed control over purchasing from the poorly staffed War Department.[17]

Two months later, Congress passed a uniform militia act. The administration had for two years advocated without success a standardized militia law that featured mandatory camps of instruction for militiamen aged eighteen to twenty and a "main corps" drawn from men aged twenty-one to forty-five. As an inducement, the proposal also offered vague assurances of federal funding for equipment. The ongoing crisis in the Old Northwest, coupled with the administration's willingness to accept a watered-down version of its initial demands, broke the impasse. The resulting Militia Act of May 8, 1792, required every free, able-bodied, adult male citizen of military age to enroll in his state's militia and equip himself with a musket and suitable military accoutrements. While enshrining the notion of universal military obligation, by failing to provide adequate funding, standardization, or enforcement of its regulations, it essentially reserved to the states control over their own militias, representing a signal victory for republican ideology.[18]

Though disappointing the administration with its tepid militia law, Congress had significantly increased the regular force. To lead the enlarged army, Washington turned to the dashing Maj. Gen. Anthony Wayne, architect of the legendary 1779 midnight assault against British troops at Stony Point, New York. Though Secretary of State Jefferson found him "brave and nothing else," Wayne proved an ideal choice. A Pennsylvania native with a penchant for iron military discipline and marital philandering, he needed the job, having failed in a recent attempt to establish a plantation in Georgia. Wayne would command—for the only time in United States history—a force intentionally tailored to borderlands conditions. Dubbed the "Legion of the United States"—doubtless an effort to market it as something less threatening than a regular army—the new organization featured four sublegions, each composed of a mix of dragoons, artillery, infantry, and riflemen and capable of operating independently. At his camp near Pittsburgh, Wayne encouraged target practice and cavalry maneuvers and organized realistic war games, during which some soldiers donned Indian garb and assumed the role of the enemy. Even so, it would take time to train the men and assemble the supplies needed for a successful offensive; in the meantime, Secretary Knox implored Kentuckians to remain patient and to "exhibit a lively zeal in cooperating with the army."[19]

As Wayne whipped his Legion into shape, President Washington remained sensitive to fears that a standing army threatened the people's liberties. Hamilton's hated excise tax on distilled spirits, passed in March 1791, had generated widespread resistance. Opposition to any tax was second nature to Americans, but this discriminatory toll seemed particularly onerous in frontier districts, where whiskey served not only as a drink but also as an easily marketable commodity. Determined to overawe any organized opposition to the whiskey tax, in September 1792 Hamilton urged the president "to employ those means, which in the last resort are put in the power of the Executive." Siding with Attorney General Edmund Randolph, however, Washington opted for a middle course, ruling that he would use the regulars only as a last resort. "Otherwise," explained the president, "there would be

Alexander Hamilton. This lithograph of Alexander Hamilton (1755 or 1757–1809), steadfast champion of a stronger national government and a larger regular army, was based on one of John Trumbull's portraits. Library of Congress, LC-DIG-det-4a26168.

a cry at once, 'The cat is let out, we now see for what purpose the army was raised.'" In accord with Washington's decision, militia and volunteers, not regulars, would crush the Whiskey Rebellion two years later.[20]

Critics nonetheless charged the administration with using the borderlands crisis as an excuse to expand the federal government. In late December 1792, North Carolina Federalist representative John Steele, citing the militia's purported effectiveness in Indian warfare and the need to avoid new taxes, moved that Congress eliminate two regiments. The standing army brought with it the "usual retinue of political evils," he alleged, and reflected "more of the unnatural spirit of Monarchy, than of the mild and conciliatory temper of a Republic." Madison, who heretofore had not publicly challenged the regulars, spoke in favor of Steele's bill, reckoning that "experience seemed to show militia superior for an offensive war." In the end, the administration fended off Steele's gambit, rallying congressmen from frontier districts to win a 32–26 test vote.[21]

As the historian Richard Kohn notes, the security dispute reflected the increasingly partisan tone of political debate, with the emerging Republican Party opposing the standing army "almost as matter of course." The *North Carolina Journal* explained: "Although Mr. Steele's motion to reduce the army establishment failed, the principal objects are in fact established—the salutary impressions of caution and economy." Angry Federalists fired back, with Representative Fisher Ames of Massachusetts charging that Madison had marshaled his fellow Virginians with party discipline "as severe as the Prussian." General Wayne, now a confirmed Federalist, denounced the failed effort to reduce the legion as "the machinations of a restless junto."[22]

For their part, Indians of the Ohio country were in no mood to concede anything to the twice-beaten Americans. Unfortunately, a sort of malaise now gripped the tribes, who had routed earlier threats to their settlement at the Glaize (near present-day Defiance, Ohio) but lacked the economic resources to conduct sustained warfare. A more vigorous anti-American confederation between Cherokees, Chickamaugas, and Creeks to the south and Shawnees, Miamis, Delawares, Chippewas, Ottawas, Hurons, Potawatomies, and Wyandots to the north never materialized, as reductions in Spanish assistance and deaths among key leaders lessened the influence of the most militant factions. Even so, in summer 1793 they rejected the administration's renewed diplomatic initiatives, demanding instead that the United States abandon settlements north of the Ohio River. "You are now to judge whether your force will be adequate to make those audacious savages feel our superiority in Arms," Secretary Knox told Wayne that September. "Let it therefore be again and for the last time impressed deeply on your mind that . . . a defeat in the present time and under present circumstances would be pernicious in the highest degree in the interests of our Country." Mindful of Knox's warning, Wayne remained on the defensive.[23]

By spring 1794, security challenges were consuming the embattled Washington administration. The radical turn of the French Revolution, the British navy's harassment of American ships bound for France, bellicose statements from Governor General Guy Carleton of Canada, and rumors that the British would occupy the Miami River region also fanned the flames of political partisanship. Whereas Federalists feared the spread of revolutionary anarchy to North America, Republicans accused the administration of turning a blind eye toward British excesses and of using the emergency as an excuse to expand federal powers. With war gathering on the horizon, Congress between March 20 and May 9 authorized construction of six frigates, appropriated $172,000 (roughly $4 million at time of publication) for coastal defenses, increased the corps of artillery by nearly eight hundred rank and file, and added $81,000 to establish as many as four armories (the latter measure serving as the genesis for the creation of the national armories at Springfield, Massachusetts, and Harpers Ferry, Virginia). On May 16, Secretary Knox informed Wayne that "the crucial position of our affairs with some of the European powers" required that he deliver "severe strokes" to force the Indians of the Ohio country to make peace.[24]

Anticipating a European war, Federalists also contemplated the creation of a large auxiliary army. Suspecting that Hamilton would use the troops to enforce his domestic agenda, Madison dismissed this as "the old trick of turning every contingency into a resource for accumulating force in the Government." James Monroe worried that such a force would offer Federalists an unparalleled source of patronage. As a result, the militia "will afterwards become [a] useless and dormant body, scarcely retaining arms in their hands." Accordingly, the House on May 19 rejected a plan to raise 25,000 men in case of war with a European power. In the following two days, President Washington twice asked for the authority to increase military preparations. A week later, the Senate narrowly passed a bill allowing him to raise 10,000 additional troops. Administration opponents rallied in the House, however, handily defeating the Senate measure as well a substitute that would have raised a new regiment of regular troops designated for the Southwest borderlands.[25]

Notwithstanding these political setbacks in the government, Wayne broke camp on July 28 from Fort Greene Ville, Ohio, with 1,500 volunteers and his 2,000-strong Legion. "We have had & shall have a many headed Monster to contend with yet," he complained, fulminating against Congress, negligent contractors, and his uncooperative subordinate, Brig. Gen. James Wilkinson. Fortifying their camp after every day's march, Wayne's troops pushed into the heart of Ohio country. On August 8, they occupied the Glaize, described by Wayne as the "Grand Emporium of the hostile Indians of the West." Pausing briefly amid the wondrous fields of grains and vegetables, they pushed up the Maumee River toward British-held Fort Miamis and Lake Erie. The Indians struck back on August 20 along the north bank of the Maumee River at a site littered with trees uprooted by a tornado. In the resulting Battle of Fallen Timbers, Wayne's regulars won the day with a decisive bayonet charge. Seeking refuge at Fort Miamis, the Indians witnessed a demoralizing sight: not wanting to risk a shooting war with Wayne's army, their erstwhile British allies had shut the gates. The Indian confederacy dissolved as the Legion now laid waste to the lands that had once succored thousands. "Never were the effects of indefatigable industry and perseverance more conspicuous, than in the instance of General Wayne's unremitted attention to the training of the Legion," concluded Quartermaster General James O'Hara.[26]

Force of arms had settled the fate of the Northwest Territory. But the decision to devote resources almost entirely to the Old Northwest (more than 90 percent of the army was still stationed there in November 1794) incensed many Southerners. If not allowed to undertake an offensive against the Creeks, claimed one South Carolinian, "then we may as well dissolve the Union, as to pretend to hold together, because Georgia will be ruined, perhaps this State, and several others much injured." Complaining of the "horrid barbarities" inflicted by the Creeks, Georgia governor Edward Telfair warned in May 1793 that "the people must be protected, and a failure in this juncture will affect the operations of Government in a serious degree." The threat prompted a presidential cabinet meeting; even so, with the army fully committed to the Northwest and the federal budget already overstrained, Washington prohibited offensive operations from Georgia. Although new trading factories along the Creek border fostered an uneasy truce, Georgians remained dissatisfied with a federal government that ranked the needs of the Old Northwest ahead of those of the lower South.[27]

Having placed their bets on the Ohio country, federal officials also scrambled to avoid an expensive conflict in the Southwest Territory (present-day Tennessee). Speaking for many disgruntled Southerners, Andrew Jackson declared that "unless Congress lends up more am[ple] protection this Country will have at length [to break] or seek a protection from some other Source than the present." In spring 1794, Knox acknowledged that although the region's Mero District (present-day Davidson, Tennessee, and Sumner Counties) merited protection, only seventy-five regulars were available for the entire territory. Locals had to be satisfied with a shipment of six small howitzers and two hundred muskets, as well as the authority to raise another 141 militiamen. Impatient Tennesseans took matters into their own hands in September 1794, when 750 territorial rangers sacked the Chickamauga towns of Running Water and Nickajack. As in Georgia, Tennesseans concluded that they must address their problems without federal aid.[28]

In Kentucky, tensions with the federal government over Indian policy and the failure to open the Mississippi River to American traffic threatened still another crisis. Fired by the machinations of the French provocateur Edmond-Charles Genêt and his newly enlisted assistant, the Revolutionary War hero George Rogers Clark, U.S. residents demanded action. The Washington-appointed federal judge Harry Innes urged Jefferson to recognize "the temper & opinions of the western people on the subject of the navigation of the Mississippi." Citizens of Lexington declared that the government's failures constituted "a grievance of the highest magnitude." Fearing that American frontiersmen might invade Spanish territory and ignite a war, Knox ordered federal troops to reoccupy Fort Massac, which overlooked the Ohio River in present-day southern Illinois, where they were to check any "criminal design" without further endangering the tenuous relationship between Kentuckians and the government. Edmund Randolph, who had recently replaced Jefferson as secretary of state, worried that, if blood were spilled, "it will I fear terminate in a revolt of that country, and a separation from the Union."[29]

Faced with multiple complications, Washington redoubled his diplomatic efforts. Northern Indian tribes acceded to U.S. sovereignty over much of Ohio in the Treaty of Greenville (August 1794). John Jay concluded a deal with Britain in November 1794. The resulting treaty, in which the British agreed to withdraw their posts in the Northwest and offered several commercial concessions in return for what amounted to American acquiescence on issues of neutral rights, sparked a public debate of unprecedented partisanship. Less controversial was the subsequent Treaty of San Lorenzo (October 1795), whereby the Spanish crown, fearful that Jay's Treaty signaled an emerging Anglo-American alliance, acknowledged Americans' right to use the Mississippi River and accepted their claims regarding the Florida boundary.[30]

* * * * *

Following the American Revolution, regulars had taken on a significance that few Americans could have imagined. Excluding debt payments, the War Department had accounted for nearly two-thirds of all federal spending between 1789 and 1794. Additionally, the federal armory and arsenal at Springfield, Massachusetts, would emerge as a lynchpin of that region's economy. Likewise, military monies offered a lifeline to struggling western economies: in addition to purchases of food and forage, the army rented boats and wagons, built and maintained roads, and needed oxen, horses, clerks, blacksmiths, and carpenters. In 1794, salaries for the single company of regulars stationed in the Southwest Territory exceeded the total expenses of the civilian territorial government. Federal compensation to the militia there provided an infusion of another $75,000 (roughly $1.7 million at time of publication). Quartermaster stores for the western army that year totaled nearly $200,000, with many of those dollars pumped directly into the borderlands. Military contractors like Pittsburgh's James O'Hara, the army's quartermaster general from 1792 to 1796, also assumed leading roles in developing local economies.[31]

Federalists struggled mightily to consolidate their position amid renewed political challenges to the regulars. Madison feared that the growing military forces would serve personal ambitious of leading Federalists (most notably Hamilton) and provide a lucrative source of patronage for their supporters. "The separation of the power of raising armies, from the power of commanding them, is intended to prevent the raising of armies for the sake of commanding them," Madison lamented. "The separation of the power of creating offices, from that of filling them, is an essential guard against the temptation to create offices, for the sake of gratifying favorites, or multiplying dependents." Recognizing the developing storms, just before his enforced retirement (for having taken a six-week leave of absence to see to his investments in Maine during the Whiskey Rebellion), Secretary Knox made a final plea for checking the unbridled expansion of the past few years. "Some powerful attempts should be made to tranquilize the frontiers," he wrote, urging his countrymen to treat Indians with justice and fairness. Only by preventing "frontier white people" from seizing Native American land could peace come to the borderlands. To establish order, Knox recommended stationing 1,500 regulars in a string of posts separating Indians and whites, taking pains to show that such troops cost a third less than equivalent numbers of mounted volunteers. Arguing that any decrease would weaken its negotiating position, the administration in early 1795 swatted aside attempts to shrink the army to 2,500 enlisted men. A further effort to restrict their use to "the protection and security of the United States against foreign invasion, and against the Indian tribes"—in the process removing any possibility that regulars might be used to quell domestic disturbances such as the Whiskey Rebellion—failed by a 36–44 margin. "I am extremely sorry to remark a growing apathy to the evil and danger of standing armies," wrote a disconsolate Madison.[32]

Still, political winds were shifting amid the furor over Jay's Treaty with Britain. Anticipating the growing Republican influence in Congress, the conniving James Wilkinson seized the opportunity to redouble his efforts to discredit Wayne and secure for himself command of the army. In the meantime, a five-man House committee chaired by the Republican Abraham Baldwin of Georgia, reasoning "that the force to be provided for the defensive protection of the frontiers, need not be so great as what had been contemplated for carrying on the war against the different tribes of hostile Indians," recommended cutting the army's authorized strength from 5,400 to slightly less than 3,000. In a not-so-subtle slap at Major General Wayne, it deemed a brigadier general adequate to command the leaner force.[33]

In spring 1796, the entire House joined the fray. In accord with classic philosophical opposition to standing armies, William B. Giles, Republican of Virginia, argued "that Government would be better without an army, as it was always better for Governments to rest upon the affections of the people than to be supported by terror." Yet even as those opposing any regulars remained an important element of the Republican Party, moderates now focused on efforts to "consolidate" that force and reduce spending, taking pains to distance themselves from more radical assertions that the army "was dangerous to the liberties of the people." The Senate generally demurred to moderate Republican demands, rejecting only larger cuts to the dragoons and the attempt to strip Wayne of his major-generalship. A conference committee split the difference, acceding to the House's smaller dragoon unit but keeping Wayne's position.[34]

On the surface, the resulting Army Act of May 30, 1796, represented a Republican victory. Yet as Richard Kohn explains, the measure affirmed a peacetime standing army in American life. "In defeat," writes Kohn, Federalists "had achieved an objective for which they had long been striving: a peacetime regular army." Defending the regulars before the House Committee on the Military Establishment, newly appointed Secretary of War James McHenry asserted, "it will be taken for granted, that . . . a certain military establishment [was] essential to the interests and peace of the Union. The only point then that remains to be settled, is the quantum of force necessary to be kept up." Mainstream Republicans did not contest McHenry's declaration, focusing instead on the Wayne-Wilkinson feud and the proper size and composition of a peacetime army.[35]

Just eleven days earlier, passage of the Trade and Intercourse Act had recognized the contribution of the regular army to policy making by codifying that institution's participation in Indian affairs. Seeking to maintain order in the borderlands, the United States had since 1790 attempted to restrict physical and economic contact between its citizens and Indians. Federal superintendents licensed traders to deal with the tribes; those who flaunted this law, or trespassed on Indian lands, risked harsh penalties. The House rejected a provision that would have required that these superintendents be army officers, but the implicit links between Indian and military affairs had always been clear: War Department clerks handled Indian department business; the Secretary of War oversaw related matters; and the army tried to enforce government policy and to separate whites and Indians. The new Trade and Intercourse Act made this relationship official by authorizing regular officers to issue passports and providing for use of "the military force of the United States" in apprehending trespassers.[36]

In a span of less than two weeks, a majority Republican Congress had in the process of reducing the army's size implicitly sanctioned a peacetime army and formally recognized that institution's role in implementing Indian policy. Thoughtful Federalists should have been pleased, for the government could use regulars to provide a modicum of order against the anarchy of ungoverned expansion. Yet in a final irony, the budget-minded Congress, even as it codified army engagement in Indian matters, made it difficult for the regulars to carry out the expanded responsibilities. The cuts in appropriations forced the Washington administration to abandon the innovative Legion, which had been tailored to meet frontier conditions. Rather than the combined arms of the sublegions, the army's more conventional organization now consisted of four infantry regiments, two companies of light dragoons, and the Corps of Artillerists and Engineers. Thus a very traditional regular army was tasked with the very untraditional duties of managing the multiracial, multicultural borderlands—a complex assignment it would struggle to fulfill for the next century.[37]

Chapter Three

The Army and the Rise of the Jeffersonians

Thomas Jefferson and his fellow Republicans had long viewed the standing army as a threat to liberty that, in Federalist hands, might be deployed to establish a tyrannical central government. Moreover, the onerous taxes needed to support regular troops would rob the people of the property upon which their freedoms depended. But as Republicans took power, their outlook shifted. In his first Inaugural Address, President Thomas Jefferson evidenced this change: "A well-disciplined militia" remained "our best reliance in peace and for the first moments of war," he explained, "till regulars may relieve them." Even as the army must remain small until the outbreak of war, Jefferson soon came to acknowledge the usefulness of a peacetime force in serving the national interests. Eventually, Jefferson was chastened by his inability to improve state militias, the practical experiences of staking out the republic's claims to an empire for liberty, and a series of international crises; his years in office ended with the first Republican president championing a measure that tripled the size of the regular force. Ironically, Jefferson's use of a multipurpose army reinforced the institution's significance to the early republic.[1]

* * * * *

In December 1796, the death of Maj. Gen. Anthony Wayne, Federalist victor of the Battle of Fallen Timbers, set off a contentious dispute regarding army leadership. With Republican support, Brig. Gen. James Wilkinson retained his star and assumed command despite vocal Federalist opposition. Stressing the need for economy in government rather than traditional Whig fears of military tyranny, congressional Republicans in the following months sponsored several measures to decrease the size of the regular force. The decision to press for reducing, rather than eliminating, the standing force was nonetheless noteworthy. The shift in tactics nearly worked; only after three votes did the House kill a Republican bill to disband one of the four infantry regiments, and a veto by the retiring President Washington was necessary to save the two companies of light dragoons.[2]

The regular army thus remained a major point of contention during the new administration of President John Adams. Concerned with domestic security, Federalists compiled lengthy dossiers on presumed foreign infiltrators and also suspected that many Republicans were serving as pawns for a radical French government. One officer described Kentuckians and Tennesseans as "great friends of the French Republic," and considerable evidence suggested that General Wilkinson was on the Spanish payroll. To counter these threats, regulars probed the Mississippi River Valley, bribing Indian leaders, occupying strategic points, and building armed galleys to patrol the river. In spring 1797, Alexander Hamilton joined Secretary of War James McHenry in pressing for a military buildup that would demonstrate American resolve and deter would-be invaders, most notably France. To shield the nation "against Atheism conquest & anarchy," they called on Congress to pass new taxes to augment the navy, bolster seaboard defenses, expand the regular forces, and create a 20,000-strong Provisional Army. In a May 27 message to a special session of Congress, the president formally requested "an addition to the regular artillery and cavalry, and arrangements for forming a provisional army."[3]

Congress saw things differently. The Senate wanted to add an artillery regiment but decisively rejected the proposed Provisional Army. "More money and more troops was apt to be an increasing passion," warned Georgia's Abraham Baldwin of Federalist proposals for a larger military establishment. "Collect money to raise armies and raise armies to collect money, has been a wheel of fortune to them, and a wheel of rack to their subjects," he added. Convinced that "a British party" dominated the administration, House Republicans pushed an alternative plan to mobilize 80,000 militiamen. Hardline Federalists, reasoning that nine hundred new artillerymen posed no threat to the people's liberties, seemed demoralized by the House's resounding 57–39 vote rejecting even this small addition.[4]

Subsequent events led many Americans to reconsider their positions on security. Less than a month after rejecting the larger army, Congress impeached and expelled Senator William Blount of Tennessee, a former governor of the Southwest Territory, for colluding with a British effort to grab Spanish-held West Florida. Blount's activities served as a vivid reminder of the government's tenuous hold on frontier loyalties. More significant were deteriorating relations with France, which eventually seized more than three hundred American merchant ships and demanded humiliating concessions in the XYZ Affair. In January 1798, Adams queried his cabinet about possible responses. If negotiations collapsed, Secretary McHenry recommended that the nation adopt "a truly vigorous defensive plan," which included arming merchant ships, building dozens of new naval vessels, increasing the regular army to 16,000, and authorizing 20,000 provisional soldiers.[5]

As Adams pondered his options, other Federalists equated military preparedness with patriotism, domestic order, and external security. To protect the nation against enemies from without as well as within, they sought to increase the armed forces, improve coastal defenses, and crack down on aliens and Republican extremists. Demagogues, blinded by their sympathies with revolutionary France (which the president's son, John Quincy Adams, characterized as "the all-grasping, all devouring power that threatens . . . the whole civilized world"), demagogues could easily sway the rabble, rendering state militias allies of anarchy rather than guardians of order. "You see what a reliance may be placed upon the militia here," concluded the three-term Federalist congressman William Hindman, who claimed that "a most bitter French Jacobin" commanded a regiment from his state of Maryland. In a legislative frenzy between late April and mid-July, Congress made it significantly more difficult to become a naturalized citizen, empowered the president to expel aliens he judged dangerous to national security, restricted free speech, created a separate Department of the Navy, commissioned new naval vessels, expanded seaboard fortifications and weapons foundries, authorized an additional regiment of artillery "for the time being," and allowed the president to activate a 10,000-strong Provisional Army in case of invasion. Finally, by a razor-thin 41–40 margin in the House, it expanded the regular force by twelve infantry regiments and six troops of light dragoons (often referred to as the New Army) for the duration of the emergency.[6]

As sailors waged an eighteen-month-long quasi-war against France, the new land formations signaled the centrality of regular troops to the Federalist worldview. "There are three things essential to the maintenance of our proper grade among the powers of the earth," wrote Secretary of War McHenry: "1st an army, and means adequate to its support. 2nd a system calculated to keep its wants regularly supplied. 3d genius in the general who commands it." To fill the latter need, Federalist luminaries coaxed George Washington, sixty-six years old and in declining health, out of retirement. Reflecting on their own experiences as Continentals, many Federalists also hoped that the bonds of comradeship found in a national army might unify their divided countrymen.[7]

President Adams, by contrast, suspected a cabal among his competitors within the Federalist Party. In late July 1798, seeking to avoid the summer heat and fearful of another outbreak of yellow fever, he fled Philadelphia in search of the cooler climes of Quincy, Massachusetts. His wife fell ill during the trip, leading Adams to delay his return to the capital until late November. In the meantime, communications between the president and his new military advisers virtually ended. Washington had agreed to serve on the condition that he could name Charles Cotesworth Pinckney and Adams's bitter rival, Alexander Hamilton, as his chief assistants. As chief executive, however, the president expected to make his own appointments, including the promotion of his son-in-law, William S. Smith, from lieutenant colonel to brigadier general. Washington wanted nothing to do with the irresolute

Smith, who the Senate refused to confirm. The resulting misunderstandings, Secretary McHenry's inability to manage the sudden buildup, and messy disputes about rank—Henry Knox, incensed that Washington did not name him second in command, refused to serve—caused what the former president described as "inconceivable" delays in raising the new units.[8]

In late 1798, Washington, Hamilton, and Pinckney huddled together in Philadelphia for five weeks, straining to create and organize the mechanisms necessary to feed, clothe, equip, recruit, and staff the New Army. In assessing officer candidates, the three Federalists insisted that they must exclude those of "bad political principles—i.e., Democratic-Republicans." "You could as soon as scrub the blackamore white," wrote Washington, "as to change the principles of a profest Democrat; . . . [who] will leave nothing unattempted to overturn the Government of this Country." As Hamilton admitted: "We were very attentive to the importance of appointing friends of the Govern[men]t to military stations." They selected a few Republicans for lower ranks but rejected President Adams's conciliatory proposal to name two Republicans from key states—New York's Aaron Burr and Pennsylvania's Frederick Augustus Muhlenberg—as brigadier generals.[9]

To the chagrin of Republicans, the brilliant, workaholic Hamilton—humiliated by recent revelations of a tawdry extramarital affair—seemed to be everywhere. With minutiae consuming McHenry and the increasingly irascible Washington showing no desire to spend more time away from Mount Vernon, Hamilton used his position as Inspector General to crank out a blizzard of manuals, reports, charts, and directives on everything from military hospitals to the proper square footage of officers' huts. He also speculated about invading Spanish or French colonies in the Americas, drafted legislation on behalf of the War Department, promoted the establishment of a military academy, and urged Congress to make the New Army permanent. Agreeing with Hamilton's contention that a robust military display would deter both external and internal threats, Congress in March 1799 authorized the president to raise 30,000 more troops (dubbed the Eventual Army) in case of "imminent danger" and to deploy Provisional Army units "to execute the laws of the Union [and] suppress insurrections."[10]

Distraught Republicans accused Federalists of manufacturing the crisis as an excuse to raise taxes, expand the grasp of the executive, justify a British alliance, and encourage tyranny. Representative Albert Gallatin of Pennsylvania, a rising star in the Republican Party, dismissed the French threat as "a mere *bugbear*." The French had no means of transporting a large invading force "except [if] they employ balloons for the purpose," quipped Virginia's well-known politician Richard Brent, who served in the House from 1801 to 1803. As the agent of a power-hungry central state, the Provisional Army would "instill a system of terror." Tennessee's newly elected Congressman

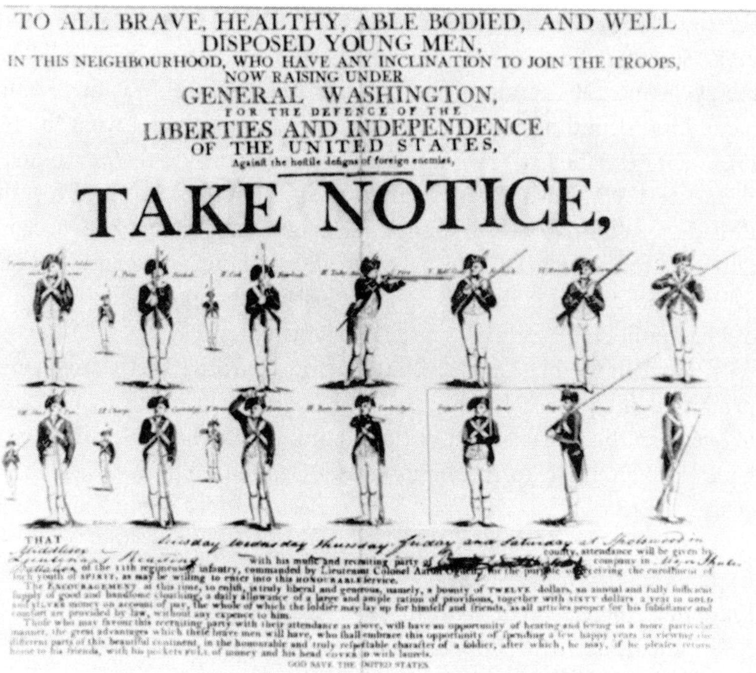

"To All Brave, Healthy, Able Bodied, and Well Disposed Young Men." This recruiting broadside, long associated with the American Revolution, was actually created during the French war scare of the late 1790s, as established by its printed reference to Lt. Col. Aaron Ogden, 11th Infantry Regiment, a Revolutionary War veteran who had rejoined the service in this capacity. Library of Congress, USZ62-35262.

William C. C. Claiborne asserted that the mongrel force "would consist of the refuse of society." Only men "from the streets of large cities . . . and possessed of but little principle" would volunteer for such duty, predicted Republicans. Without the steadying influence of virtuous patriots of the soil in the ranks, Federalists could manipulate the armed forces to fill their lust for power. "An ambitious party may always be suspected of bringing on that state of things which is best calculated to gratify the craving appetites of their selfishness and ambition," wrote Senator Henry Tazewell of Virginia. A prospectus for a new Republican newspaper characterized Federalist rule as "corrupted mazes of funding and banking, stockjobbing and speculating systems, down to the alien and sedition laws, standing army and navy." Another writer claimed that "all Aristocratic governments" created armed forces "to provide some lucrative and honourable places for the 'well born,' and to have that force in readiness to quell their own people in case of opposition."[11]

In 1799, the administration's response to renewed turmoil in Pennsylvania confirmed Republican mistrust. Opposition to the Alien and Sedition Acts and the direct taxes designed to pay for the buildup of armed forces was particularly vociferous in Bucks and Northampton Counties, where John Fries—a Revolutionary War veteran and member of the militia forces that had smothered the Whiskey Rebellion—emerged as a leading resistance figure. Linking these protests to a suspected Francophile insurrection, the Adams administration mobilized Pennsylvania volunteer cavalry and dispatched several companies of the New Army to the infected regions. Reports of the soldiers' misbehavior abounded. "They raged about with drawn sabers and threatened to do unspeakable things" to the wife of a Republican sympathizer, charged one newspaper editor. Fortunately, passions cooled as organized opposition melted away; sentenced to death for treason, Fries was later pardoned by President Adams.[12]

In just over two years, Congress had (including the New Army) more than quadrupled the army, used elements of that institution to enforce domestic order, and authorized the president to raise 40,000 more men through the Provisional Army and the Enrolled Army. But the regulars did not become the destructive force predicted by Republicans, and despite Hamilton's herculean efforts, New Army units never reached more than half-strength. Furthermore, President Adams was uncomfortable with a large standing army, which he had once dubbed "a many bellied Monster." Unlike most within his party, he looked to the militia and the navy to defend national security. Adams also suspected that Hamilton sought to use the situation to regain power, complaining that there was "too much intrigue in this business." The president's resulting decision to reopen peace talks with France split the Federalist Party and signaled the end of the military buildup.[13]

Adams correctly grasped the sensibilities of the American people regarding a large army. A correspondent to the *New London Bee* (whose editor, Charles Holt, was fined $200 and imprisoned for three months under the Sedition Act for printing the letter) condemned soldiers as "useless and burdensome." In his first speech to the House of Representatives, Virginia Republican John Randolph lambasted the regulars: "The military parade which meets the eye in almost every direction excites the gall of our citizens," he shrieked; "they feel a just indignation at the sight of loungers, who live upon the public, who consume the fruits of their honest industry." As the threat of war evaporated, the enlarged standing force became an unbearable political burden for Federalists. Of the eleven known circular letters written by congressmen to their constituents between March and May 1800, ten included significant discussions of army matters, and the eleventh was penned by former captain (and future major general) William Henry Harrison. In late spring, Congress demobilized the New Army, and Republicans subsequently won control of Congress and the presidency.[14]

* * * * *

When crafting a proposed Virginia state constitution in 1776, an idealistic Thomas Jefferson had boldly declared: "There shall be no standing army but in time of war." Just over a decade later, he was still complaining about the federal Constitution's failure to prohibit a permanent force. By 1801, however, newly elected President Jefferson had determined to transform the regulars rather than eliminate them. His actions reflected both his well-known desire to economize and his less-publicized realization that the army could help him to implement Republican policies. If Federalist domination could be broken, small forces of regulars could be trusted to patrol the frontiers, garrison coastal defenses, conduct Indian affairs, and promote expansion. To oversee the necessary changes, Jefferson named Revolutionary War veteran Henry Dearborn as his secretary of war. Also noteworthy was the president's choice of Capt. Meriwether Lewis as his personal secretary. A former army paymaster and special messenger, Lewis possessed what Jefferson described as a "knowledge of the western country, of the army, and all of its interests and relations."[15]

To achieve his goals, Jefferson needed to reduce the army to a size more consistent with republican principles and commence a "chaste reformation" of an overwhelmingly Federalist institution. Military contracts also promised to engender support for his Republican Party. An economic behemoth, the War Department accounted for 70 percent of federal spending (excluding debt service) and provided benefits to more than four thousand veterans, widows, and orphans. Its soldiers consumed more food, shoes, clothing, medicine, and building supplies than any other single entity in the United States. The president thus set Dearborn to work bringing order to the department, still reeling from the challenges stemming from the recent buildup and a November 1800 fire that destroyed its records. Revamping policies and procedures, Dearborn personally approved all expenditures above fifty dollars, cracked down on excessive state claims for militia compensation, and targeted coastal fortification and weapons production for sharp cutbacks. Spending on seaboard defenses, which had averaged more than $157,000 (more than $3 million at time of publication) per year from 1798 through 1800, was eliminated by 1803, when the administration proudly returned $154,000 to the general fund. Dearborn also ended arms contracts for several New England firms and reduced workmen and wages at the Harpers Ferry and Springfield armories.[16]

Republicanizing the army required special care. Whereas Jefferson ruthlessly replaced incumbent federal marshals and attorneys, he acknowledged that he must follow "established process" in removing judges and military officers. A December 1801 message to Congress laid the necessary

Henry Dearborn. Based on a 1796 painting by Charles Willson Peale, this image depicts future Secretary of War Henry Dearborn (1751–1829), once a Revolutionary War general, while he served as a Republican congressman. Library of Congress, USZ62-7659.

groundwork. Ever the republican rhetorician, the president took pains to identify a well-disciplined militia as the nation's first line of defense. He did not, however, use the bully pulpit of his office to recommend abolition of the army; rather, he argued that the existing establishment simply exceeded needs. Secretary Dearborn furnished the supporting documentation: twenty infantry and twenty artillery companies could garrison the necessary posts. In a break from Federalist practice—which had stationed nearly all regulars in the borderlands north of Kentucky—the army would be evenly split between North and South, thus bringing a bigger government presence as well as the accompanying economic spoils to Republican strongholds.[17]

In January 1802, the administration rolled out legislation to reform the army. The four infantry regiments were reduced to two, the two artillery regiments merged into one, and the expensive light dragoons eliminated, thus cutting the army's authorized strength from 5,438 to 3,287 officers and men. Republicans also gutted the Quartermaster Department and abolished the inspector general, apothecary general, and judge advocate general, in the process privatizing most purchases of food and transportation and opening lucrative new military contracts for party favorites. Finally, it established a Corps of Engineers, consisting of seven officers and ten cadets, who were to "be stationed at West Point . . . and shall constitute a military academy." After less than two days of debate, the House approved the package by a 77–12 margin. Following strict party lines, fifteen Republican Senators supported the reductions, with ten Federalists opposed. As Treasury Secretary Albert Gallatin labored to reduce the federal debt, Jeffersonians hailed the results of Dearborn's thriftiness and the 1802 legislation. In a letter to his constituents, Senator Thomas Sumter (R-SC) claimed annual savings of $450,000; Congressman John Clopton (R-VA) rounded the figure up to an even half-million. The smaller regular force, along with cuts to fortifications and other cost-saving measures, slashed army spending from $2.56 million in fiscal year 1800 to $713,000 in 1805. As a percentage of all federal expenditures (excluding debt payments), army appropriations fell from 34.5 to 11.2 percent.[18]

The cutbacks also afforded Republicans the opportunity to make commissioned personnel more closely resemble the government they served. Federalists had packed the officer corps with their friends, and the "midnight appointments" during the final days of the Adams administration had included more than eighty officers. In summer 1801, presidential secretary Lewis quietly assessed each officer's ability (three levels ranging from "1st Class" to "Unworthy of the commissions they bear") and political reliability (eight categories ranging from outright Republican to "Opposed most violently to the administration and still active in its vilification"). Captain Lewis judged that forty-eight of fifty-nine officers with known political sympathies "opposed" the administration, with nine of the former "still active in its vilification."[19]

Jefferson and Dearborn then did just what their fellow Republicans expected them to do: appoint party loyalists. They began at the top. Having once sought to eliminate the position of brigadier general, Republicans now defended it, undoubtedly because Wilkinson was "friendly to the politics of the now reigning party." Secretary Dearborn paid special attention to staff officers, who by virtue of their oversight of routine military activities and contracts wielded enormous influence. With only passing regard for seniority, the administration undertook a carefully calibrated program of outright dismissals, consolidation of offices, and special favors. Thus Dearborn discharged Quartermaster General John Wilkins, an avid Federalist, and divided the position's responsibilities among his own office and three new civilian appointees. The deputy quartermaster (Capt. Bartholomew Schaumburg) and two deputy inspectors (Maj. Isaac Guion and Capt. Edward D. Turner) were removed or sent back to the line. Reestablishing the rank of colonel allowed Republicans to reward three officers, whose promotions in turn opened their former spots to others. As a result, explains the historian Theodore Crackel, each of the remaining ten highest ranking officers in the army benefitted from "Republican largess." Even the avowedly Federalist Maj. Thomas H. Cushing, the respected adjutant and inspector, got a promotion that nearly doubled his pay. Though such baubles would not necessarily sway an honest public servant, Crackel points out that these machinations "could hardly work to the new administration's disadvantage."[20]

When it came to line officers, Dearborn balanced crass political opportunism and professional ability. Overall, the administration discharged 38 percent (88 of 230) of active duty commissioned personnel; of the 41 officers Captain Lewis had rated as "unworthy," 35 were let go. The War Department dismissed Maj. John H. Buell, the only Republican in the latter group, along with 6 of 9 Federalists and 28 of 31 officers with no known political affiliation. Whereas only a tenth of Republicans who Lewis judged as qualified fell victim to the reduction in force, 7 of 33 (21 percent) Federalists were released, along with 18 of the 71 (25 percent) men whose politics were not identified. The ax cut deepest on the 19 foreign-born officers, only 9 of whom survived the cuts.[21]

Even after these dismissals, Federalists still outnumbered Republicans in the officer corps. As a disgruntled engineer put it in 1806: "Democratic officers . . . [who] are independent enough to speak their sentiments will always be prosecuted in a Federal army." To resolve this problem, Jefferson envisioned the new military academy, authorized as part of the 1802 legislation, as a means of preparing right-thinking men free from undue Federalist influence to fill army vacancies. As secretary of state in Washington's cabinet, he had opposed such an institution because the constitution did not specifically authorize it. The context changed when he became president, however, for under his watch proto-monarchists and Anglophiles could no longer endanger the people's liberties. After all, the constitution accorded Congress the power "to raise and support armies," and a school for soldiers was "necessary and proper" for achieving that end. As chief executive, he could appoint the superintendent. Moreover, thinking in the grand terms of great men, Jefferson had long dreamed of promoting education in the new republic, and the military academy could train much-needed engineers.[22]

President Jefferson thus sought to use the Federalist idea of a military school as a Republican tool for transforming the army. Essentially, the academy built on Maj. Henry Burbeck's artillery school at West Point, New York, which had been established in the waning days of the Adams administration. Federalists as well as Republicans seemed comfortable with Maj. Jonathan Williams, a grandnephew of Benjamin Franklin, as the man to establish the academy. Other than brief stints with Pennsylvania militia and volunteers during the Whiskey and Fries rebellions, Williams had until recently been

West Point. This aquatint engraving print, based on a painting by William G. Wall, depicts the United States Military Academy from across the Hudson River, New York. Library of Congress, DIG-ds-10808.

a civilian, a moderate Federalist who had translated French works on artillery and fortifications into English. Just before Adams left office, Williams had accepted a major's commission. Jefferson had known him since the 1780s, during which time the two had corresponded on subjects ranging from the design of agricultural plows to the development of navigational instruments.[23]

Upon becoming superintendent of the new United States Military Academy at West Point, Williams set to work within the parameters of the enabling legislation of 1802, which had directed the institution to prepare cadets for the Corps of Engineers. To attract political support and emphasize the importance of science to the military art, he created the United States Military Philosophical Society, with membership open by election to "any gentleman, whether a military man or not." Shrewdly, Williams (elected the group's president) secured Jefferson's "Countenance and Protection" as the organization's "perpetual Patron." Under Williams's guidance, the Philosophical Society elected a bipartisan pantheon of political luminaries, most notably John Quincy Adams, DeWitt Clinton, Albert Gallatin, John Marshall, James Monroe, and Charles Cotesworth Pinckney. Other notables included Benjamin Latrobe, Robert Fulton, Eli Whitney, and Bushrod Washington. Williams was careful to maintain frequent correspondence with the president, seeking his advice on the design of the Philosophical Society seal, adding a chaplain at West Point, and finer points in the Society's constitution. He also made sure that Jefferson received copies of an anonymous treatise on militias and the Society's translation of Thaddeus Kościuzko's work on light artillery. In turn, the president backed the superintendent's unsuccessful efforts to move the military academy from West Point to the capital, where they hoped it might broaden its influence.[24]

By the end of his first term, Jefferson had concluded that a properly officered regular army could help to secure the territory necessary for a virtuous republic's prosperity. Only with an ample supply of land could citizen-farmers remain free of corrupting urban influences. Furthermore, controlling the Mississippi River was essential to guaranteeing loyalties in the borderlands; as Secretary of State Madison put it, the great river "was everything" to Westerners. If Jefferson the republican theorist had not acknowledged the army's value, as a pragmatic chief executive seeking to claim, explore, and colonize the Louisiana Purchase he most certainly did. Even before that land deal was finalized, the president had set aside money for Captain Lewis to assemble a team of scientists, soldiers, and adventurers to "advance the geographical knowledge of our own continent." Lewis and his colleague William Clark were not alone in fulfilling Jefferson's vision. Escorted by regular soldiers, William Dunbar and George Hunter scouted the Ouchita River region of Arkansas, and Thomas Freeman examined the Red River country of the southern Plains. With Indian affairs embedded in the War Department, military men also played key roles in implementing the Trade and Intercourse Acts, by which the administration hoped to transform Indians into Americanized farmers and husbandrymen. In so doing, wrote the president, "I trust and believe we are acting for their greatest good."[25]

Just as Federalists had used the army to ensure national supremacy over the Ohio River country a decade earlier, regulars in 1803 established Fort Dearborn at the site of what later became Chicago. So, too, did Republicans now deploy regulars to control the lands newly purchased from France. By December 1804, more than seven hundred soldiers and Marines, representing a fifth of the nation's ground forces, garrisoned nine posts in the region. William C. C. Claiborne, who had spoken out against a standing force while in Congress, changed his outlook after being named the first governor of the Territory of Orleans. "I never was an Advocate for a Standing Army," he admitted, and "I wish to God it could be dispensed with in this Territory; But the present state of things will not justify a reduction. . . . I pray that a Reinforcement may immediately come on." Fears of a slave insurrection further fueled the demand for regulars in New Orleans. The city's mayor, John Watkins, though declaring himself no supporter of "standing armies in a free country," noted that "we are in a country of slaves. . . . The Government of the United States must therefore, under such circumstances afford us protection."[26]

Similarly, in moves that earlier Whigs would have found inimical to good government and liberty, Jefferson liberally employed army officers in civil positions. The president named Capt. Amos Stoddard, a Federalist who professed that "as a soldier I have no apparent right to meddle with any concerns out of the line of my profession," to be commandant of Upper Louisiana. From his St. Louis headquarters, Stoddard oversaw both civil and military affairs (he was supposed to keep such functions "separated & distinct") for seven months. To assimilate residents into their new nation, administration officials instructed the captain to "conciliate the feelings" of local leaders and secured slots at the military academy for six members of prominent families. In 1805, General Wilkinson's appointment as governor of the newly organized Louisiana Territory further revealed the president's willingness to blur the lines between civil and military authority. To forestall any international incidents stemming from the disputed American-Spanish boundary in western Louisiana, Wilkinson negotiated the Neutral Ground Agreement with Spain.[27]

The activities of his former vice president, Aaron Burr, greatly complicated Jefferson's use of the army to ensure sovereignty over Louisiana. Whatever Burr's real intent, many believed that he and his supporters were organizing an armed expedition into Spanish-held Mexico. Several regular officers long knew that Burr had something nefarious afoot, but they remained silent. Only in October 1806 did Wilkinson blow the whistle, taking pains to alert officials in Washington about the steps he was now taking to stamp out any treasonous activities. Amid a swirl of rumors, Jefferson gambled that Wilkinson and the army would remain loyal. The president acknowledged the involvement of "many officers of the army" in the Burr affair but threatened with punishment only those who "clearly meant to proceed in defiance of the government."[28]

Jefferson's decision not to go after soldiers suspected of associating with Burr confirmed the Virginian's pragmatism as well as his recognition that regulars could serve the interests of his presidency and the nation. Jefferson also determined to resolve lingering questions regarding his authority to suppress domestic disorder or insurrection. Thus, at his behest, Congress, in the Insurrection Act of 1807, authorized the executive, in all cases where he could legally call up militias, to use "such part of the land or naval force of the United States, as shall be judged necessary." Now aware of the regular army's potential for nation-building, the administration had in January 1807 proposed expanding companies from sixty-four to one hundred privates and adding a third regiment of infantry and a battalion of cavalry. Discouraged by Congress's repeated refusal to undertake genuine militia reform or to grant him the authority to raise volunteers, worried by the continuing presence of Spanish troops along the Louisiana frontier, and with the fugitive Burr still at large, the champion of republican ideals now wanted a larger peacetime military. "I *know* that this additional army-force is what the president *wishes*," explained the bill's sponsor, Samuel Smith (R-MD), to a Senate colleague.[29]

The Senate swiftly approved an army increase, but debate in the House—intertwined with the ongoing furor regarding Burr and the security of the Southwest—revealed sharp divisions within the Republican Party. Matthew Lyon (representing Kentucky) echoed Jefferson's belief that more troops were needed to protect a growing nation. Insisting that the sparse non-Indian population of Louisiana could not muster enough militia to protect itself, even Virginia's John Randolph favored an increase. "After paying fifteen millions for the Mississippi and its delta," wondered an incredulous Randolph, "shall we be so penurious as not to defend this important point—this key to our strong box?" Other Republicans retained their traditional suspicions. Tennessee's George W. Campbell vowed never to raise troops who might "turn their bayonets against our citizens." John W. Eppes of Virginia worried that the measure "gave the Executive the dangerous discretionary power of increasing, whenever he shall think it necessary, the permanent establishment." With its second session set to expire, the Ninth Congress postponed action on the army increase, satisfying itself by appropriating another $150,000 for seaboard fortifications.[30]

In June, the humiliating attack by the HMS *Leopard* on the USS *Chesapeake* rekindled national security debates. Jefferson's diplomacy rested on a controversial—and ultimately unsuccessful—embargo of American ships and goods from foreign trade, which the administration had hoped would force Britain and France to end their restrictions on neutral shipping. Concurrently, the House authorized nearly two hundred of the gunboats Jefferson saw as central to defending American harbors, and it beat back calls to reduce new appropriations for coastal defense from $1.5 million to $500,000. Usually an inveterate opponent of a large standing army, Treasury Secretary Gallatin put forth an elaborate plan for using regulars (whom he admitted were cheaper than militia) to spearhead an invasion of Nova Scotia and Quebec. Secretary of War Dearborn suggested raising 32,000 twelve-month volunteers and 15,000 regulars. Unswayed, William Duane, publisher of the influential *Philadelphia Aurora*, continued to insist that "*the only safe defence of the American republic is the militia*." Jefferson thus proceeded cautiously, taking pains to publicly compliment "the fidelity of the Army" during the recent Burr affair. The fiery Randolph, reverting to his traditional Whig principles and claiming to have received new evidence of Wilkinson's treachery, charged the general (who he dubbed "the most finished scoundrel that ever lived") and the army with having been directly involved in the Burr affair. Jefferson's congressional allies, however, turned aside Randolph's objections.

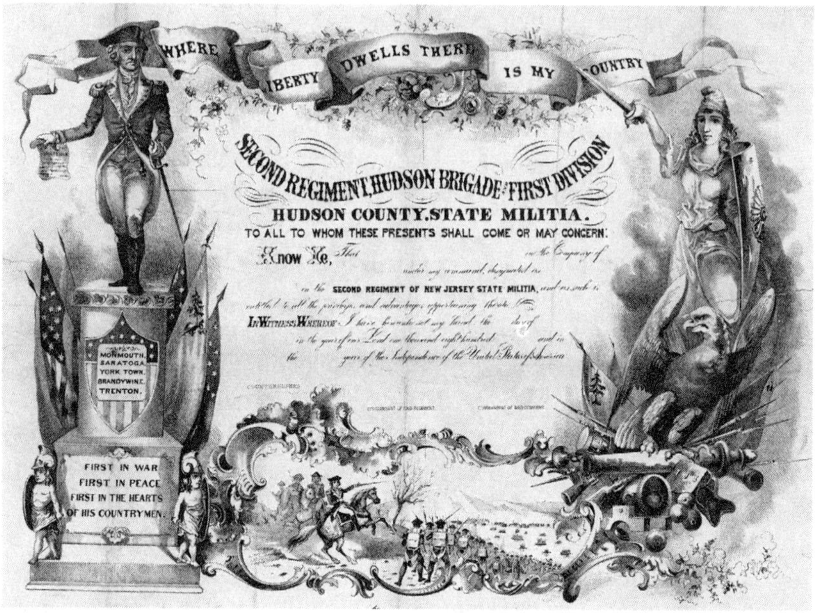

Second Regiment, Hudson Brigade, First Division, Hudson County State Militia. This certificate of membership to a New Jersey militia unit, flanked by George Washington on the left and a sword-wielding Liberty on the right, symbolizes the militia's importance to national lore in the early republic. Library of Congress, USZ62-90653.

Dismissing those who would "denounce the Army as corrupt throughout," Pennsylvania's John Smilie, a Republican and former vocal opponent of a large standing force, proclaimed that the nation "had tried . . . their officers and found them trusty."[31]

His flanks secured, President Jefferson, rather than negotiate with Britain, in February 1808 asked Congress to raise 24,000 volunteers and six thousand additional regulars (five regiments of infantry, one of light artillery, one of riflemen, and one of light cavalry). The new forces would serve as a counterweight to a British threat and ensure the permanent occupation of the lands conveyed under the Louisiana Purchase. Randolph mounted a spirited opposition but was overwhelmed by those convinced that such a force posed no threat to the liberties of a million free men. In a stunning transformation, Congress refused to raise the volunteers but voted 95–16 to triple the standing force. Republicans had backed the larger army by an 85–9 margin. Even Randolph's friend Nathaniel Macon of North Carolina, who had opposed increases in 1798 and again in 1806, supported the measure. "I never regretted differing with him so much in my life as I did on the bill raising troops," noted a remorseful Macon. "He followed his judgment, I mine."[32]

In explaining their positions on the army increase to their constituents, Republican congressmen reflected their party's internal divisions. Edwin Gray of Virginia remained a steadfast Old Republican, placing his faith in a well-armed militia and condemning standing armies as "destructive to liberty." Like his Virginia colleague John Randolph, James M. Garnett had favored the previous year's proposal to enlarge the army as a means of securing Louisiana, but he now maintained that only "actual invasion" could convince him to back the most recent measure. Representative Lyon, for his part, reasoned that whereas regulars raised during the Adams administration would have been "cantoned about in the interior of our country, demoralizing our youth, and threatening the liberty of citizens while they lived on their earnings," he did not dare risk sending militiamen "to that sickly climate" of New Orleans. Regular soldiers, by contrast, would become "inured to the climate in that neighborhood." Other Republicans who supported the newest increase sounded like Federalists during the previous decade. Echoing his old nemesis Alexander Hamilton, Tennessee's George W. Campbell asserted that "the most effectual way to preserve peace, is to be prepared for war." Burwell Bassett of Virginia downplayed the legislation as merely a "precautionary measure"; Benjamin Howard assured fellow Kentuckians that the additional defensive preparations would not necessitate new taxes.[33]

With more than three hundred officers to commission in the expanded army, the Jefferson administration farmed out most of the vetting of candidates to state congressional delegations. Whenever practicable, Secretary Dearborn seized the chance to further Republicanize the army, lamenting the absence of "sound patriotism" and complaining that many applicants "only pretended to be republicans." From Boston, the avowedly Federalist *Commercial Gazette* charged that "beardless boys who belch beer and democracy" were appointed over better-qualified applicants. Among those who secured commissions was future general in chief Winfield Scott, who nonetheless later recalled that "party spirit of that day knew no bounds." With insufficient numbers of "educated men in the dominant party" to draw from, continued Scott, "the appointments, consisted, generally, of swaggerers, dependents, decayed gentlemen, and others—'fit for nothing else.'" Capt. Isaiah Doane, "a good sound republican" from Massachusetts, seems a classic example of the ill effects of such brazen patronage, as he was cashiered within a year.[34]

Not surprisingly, officers who had benefited from the politicized selection process used by both Federalists and Republicans often behaved in a similar manner while in uniform. In vain, orders urged officers to discourage "that little mischievous, quibbling, discordant spirit" and implored them to end their "dispositions to gratify personal revenge." The stench was most odious at the top. In 1809, Wade Hampton, a Revolutionary War veteran, former

Republican congressman from South Carolina, and beneficiary of one of the new brigadier-generalships spawned by the recent increase, was meant to be a counterweight to the equally divisive Wilkinson. Each beholden to competing factions, both refused to cooperate. "Barbarous insubordination . . . prevails too generally throughout the military establishment," grumbled a Wilkinson supporter; by contrast, Hampton complained that "intrigue" and "bitterness of party" rendered it impossible to establish discipline. Such internal backbiting among its top brass served as a forewarning of the army's often inept performance during the crisis to come.[35]

* * * * *

In sharp contrast to his earlier rhetoric, Thomas Jefferson during his eight years as president labored to transform the regular army from a Federalist stronghold to a reliable instrument of Republican policy. After purging dozens of the most rabid Federalists, his administration by 1809 had appointed nearly 90 percent of all commissioned personnel. West Point had the potential to train qualified engineers and to create a pool of officers unstained by Federalist ties. Regulars explored and occupied lands acquired in the Louisiana Purchase and, in the absence of militia reform, won acceptance as an essential element of national defense. Republicans also used the army as policemen. When militias were unable to check the widespread smuggling resulting from the Embargo Act, Jefferson in summer 1808 dispatched a detachment of regular artillery to the Vermont-Canada boundary. The following year, Congress expressly authorized the president to use regulars to enforce the unpopular law. Spending on the army had increased from $1.67 million in 1801 (33 percent of total federal expenditures, excluding debt service) to $3.34 million in 1809 (45 percent). Yet the transition had come with a cost: by eliminating most of the army's staff and by privatizing the purchases of food and much equipment, the Jeffersonian reforms left the institution ill-equipped to mount sustained offensive operations or to expand quickly to meet the challenges of a dangerous world.[36]

Chapter Four

President Madison's Army

On June 29, 1787, thirty-six-year-old James Madison, whose frail appearance masked his stoic determination, intellectual brilliance, and devotion to country, rose to address the Constitutional Convention at Philadelphia. "A standing military force, with an overgrown Executive will not long be safe companions to liberty," he warned. "Throughout all Europe, the armies kept up under the pretext of defending, have enslaved the people." Madison also worried that wars and their accompanying armies could threaten the people's liberties. As he wrote eight years later: "War is the parent of armies; from these proceed debts and taxes; and armies, and debts, and taxes are the known instruments for bringing the many under the domination of the few." By dealing out "offices, honors, and emoluments" during wartime, the Federalist administration could expand its grasp and crush political opposition. In 1799, using the pseudonym "A Citizen of the United States," Madison tempered his rhetoric: although history showed that "there never was a people whose liberties long survived a standing army," he acknowledged the need for a regular force, so long as it remained small, did not necessitate undue taxes, and reflected a balance of legislative and executive authority. A decade later, the newly elected President Madison again struck a more balanced chord. Although "an armed and trained militia is the firmest bulwark of republics," he pledged not to disband the regulars but instead "to keep within the requisite limits a standing military force."[1]

As president, Thomas Jefferson had come to embrace an increasingly Republicanized multipurpose army as a tool for promoting national interests. Upon taking office, however, Madison seemed less inclined to follow the broader path blazed by his fellow Virginian, instead envisioning the regulars in strictly military terms. His 1810 message regarding officer training seems especially reflective of the new president's lack of attention to using the army for nation-building. In calling for more professorships and a second military academy, Madison highlighted the need to prepare cadets in "the branches of military science" rather than in accord with the Jeffersonian emphasis on engineering.[2]

Soldiers could certainly be used as a diplomatic cudgel. Seeking to deter a rumored British move against Louisiana or West Florida, Secretary of War Henry Dearborn, in the waning days of Jefferson's second administration, had instructed Brig. Gen. James Wilkinson to assemble "as large a proportion of our regular troops at New Orleans and its vicinity, as circumstances will permit." As president, Madison inherited a disaster, for Wilkinson's ill-fated decision to camp two thousand soldiers in a swampy, mosquito-infested site below New Orleans killed nearly half his command. Wilkinson's dereliction of duty, complained a Republican congressman, rendered him "a dead weight upon the administration." Despite that calamity, Madison deployed troops to advance U.S. claims to Florida, either as a means of ensuring order in case of the collapse of imperial Spain or in a naked bid for expansion. If circumstances seemed precipitous, regulars were alerted to support the filibustering activities of the so-called Patriot movement. Here the president found a willing ally in the conspiratorial Wilkinson. Promising to "most cautiously avoid wanton provocation," the general nonetheless added that, if the opportunity presented itself, he would occupy Mobile and Pensacola, moves consistent with "the Interests & Honor of the nation, and to the character . . . of the executive." Congress eventually authorized the president to use force against the disputed territory of West Florida, and in early 1813 Wilkinson secured the surrender of Spanish-held Fort Carlota, effectively annexing the Mobile district to the United States.[3]

Madison also depended on regulars to referee escalating tensions along the ill-defined border between Louisiana and Spanish Texas, where smugglers, bandits, and adventurers found the Neutral Ground an ideal base of operations. To chasten the intruders, U.S. and Spanish troops conducted several joint forays into the supposedly demilitarized region but made little effort to deter filibusters. In 1812, for example, Capt. Augustus Magee, a West Point graduate, resigned his commission to join Bernardo Gutiérrez de Lara's ill-fated revolutionary expedition into Spanish Texas. Still, the army seemed decidedly less belligerent than the leading civilian on the scene: Louisiana's territorial governor, William C. C. Claiborne.[4]

Despite Madison's penchant for using regulars as agents of imperial expansion, the choice of William Eustis as secretary of war reflected the president's detachment from the details of military affairs. A former Continental Army surgeon and vice president of the Society of the Cincinnati, Eustis's New England political connections, rather than any military expertise or personal gravitas, had dictated his selection. Earlier budget cuts had eviscerated the War Department's tiny staff, and demands for training, supplies, and equipment stemming from the army increases of 1808 overwhelmed the good doctor. To his credit, Secretary Eustis made at least three requests to create a Quartermaster General's Department (all three were ignored). Otherwise, the burdens of managing the army proved too much, and Eustis allowed recruiting to lag and appointed only twelve cadets to West Point between 1809 and 1811.[5]

Hesitant to expand the executive's powers, restrained by his traditional republican principles, and consumed by the continuing diplomatic furor with Britain, Madison ceded leadership regarding the army's composition to a fractious Eleventh Congress. Eschewing Treasury Secretary Gallatin's plea for reductions, the president in a May 1809 message left any "modifications of the laws relating to the army and navy establishments" to the legislative branch. He took a similar approach that November. Applauding progress in naval production, private arms manufacture, and coastal defenses, Madison asked Congress to give "serious attention" to improving the militia, but he volunteered no advice regarding changes in the regular establishment. Another message recommended renewal of legislation allowing him to call up 100,000 militia and raise 20,000 short-term volunteers.[6]

Shocking accounts of the mismanagement plaguing Wilkinson's ill-fated encampment below New Orleans, combined with Gallatin's demands for sharp cutbacks, lent a surrealistic quality to ensuing congressional debates, already splintered by deep divides over economic embargoes. "The state of that Army is enough to make any man who has the smallest love of country wish to get rid of it," fumed Representative Nathaniel Macon (R-NC). In mid-April 1810, moderates defeated a resolution to disband the regulars, but as the session neared adjournment, Congress directed the Committee on Military Affairs to draw up plans for a smaller force. Hoping to exploit divisions among the Republicans, Federalists now likened Madison's call for 100,000 militia to the much-criticized Provisional Army of the Adams administration. Such a mobilization, complained Rhode Island's Elisha R. Potter, was "inexpedient, oppressive and unnecessary"; regulars, he added, had at a cost of nearly a thousand lives merely succeeded in "ditching and clearing a bog near New Orleans." As had been the case for previous calls to undertake militia reform, Congress failed to enact any substantive improvements even as Madison reminded them of that institution's status as "our bulwark in war, and our safeguard in peace."[7]

By summer 1811, President Madison had concluded that disputes with Britain might lead to war. The flash point came in the Northwest, where the dynamic Shawnee leaders Tecumseh and his brother Tenskwatawa (the Prophet), were laying the foundations for an Indian confederacy that would pose a formidable obstacle to U.S. territorial and economic ambitions. In a preemptive strike that September, William Henry Harrison, veteran of Wayne's Legion and now governor of the Indiana Territory, led more than a thousand volunteers, regulars, and militiamen against the Prophet's community at Tippecanoe Creek. Tecumseh was away seeking additional southern allies. Desultory peace talks having collapsed, a furious battle broke out on November 7. Torching the Indian village, Harrison later claimed "a complete and decisive victory"; actually, the fighting that would later propel him into the presidency had been a very near thing, with American casualties numbering nearly two hundred.[8]

As reports about the Battle of Tippecanoe reached the nation's capital, Madison, with an eye toward a possible conflict with Britain, exhorted Congress to put the nation "into an armor and an attitude demanded by the crisis." To enable the United States to strike quickly in case of war, it must fill the regular ranks, organize a volunteer corps with men of "patriotic ardor," encourage domestic weapons production, reinvigorate the military academy, and engage an auxiliary force for a limited term of service. The president's criticisms of Britain sounded good to a hawkish House of Representatives, whose Foreign Relations Committee put forth an administration-backed report calling for 10,000 additional regulars. Unfortunately for Madison, the Senate lumped foreign relations and military affairs into a select committee headed by his Republican enemy, Virginia's bombastic William B. Giles. Dismissing the administration's proposal as "the plan of a scarecrow," Giles instead put forth a bill calling for 25,000 new soldiers, surely aware that it would be impossible to mobilize that many men in time for an immediate strike into Canada. Vainly seeking to place the genie back in the bottle, Tennessee Republican senator Joseph Anderson cited his own Revolutionary War experiences in arguing that volunteers ("the best military materials in your country . . . the flower of your forests") ought to supplement a more practical 16,000-strong regular force. Giles's insistence upon regulars alone, added Tennessee's two-time Republican senator George W. Campbell, set a dangerous trend. "The people may tremble for their liberties when it is too late," proclaimed Campbell, "when their chains are riveted upon them by a military power." Yet a coalition of administration opponents, Old Republicans, and Federalists soundly defeated an amendment to reduce the number of additional troops to realistic levels, and in early January 1812 the House accepted the Senate's 25,000-man standard.[9]

The House then passed a measure to raise 50,000 volunteers, presumably with the goal of a summer invasion of Canada. Once again, the Senate stymied administration plans. Denouncing the latest measure as "utterly inefficient," Giles secured an amendment that effectively withheld Madison's authority to commission most of that body's officers. In a final spasm of national security awareness that spring, Congress authorized the president to call out 100,000 militiamen for six months of service and appropriated $1.9 million for ordnance. The recent steps looked impressive on paper but would, even under the best of circumstances, take years to implement. Madison fumed at the holdups: "With a view to enable the executive to step at once into Canada they have provided after two months delay, for a regular force requiring 12 [months] to raise, and after 3 months for a volunteer force, on terms not likely to be raised if at all for that object." Moreover, save for reestablishing the Quartermaster's and Ordnance Departments, the House and Senate could not agree on how to respond to repeated entreaties that they authorize a bureaucracy sufficient to recruit, equip, and train the new recruits. "We had made a parade in passing laws to raise twenty-five thousand regular troops, and fifty thousand volunteers," snarled Peter B. Porter (R-NY), chair of the House Foreign Relations committee, "but, in truth and in fact, we had not given him a single man."[10]

Amid talk of war, the continued failure to prepare state militias highlighted the stark difference between revolutionary lore, in which patriots would flock to the national banner in times of need, and the realities of everyday life, where average Americans immersed themselves in the mundane activities necessary to make their ways in a changing world. As Porter noted ruefully, an overconfident American people saw the militia as "the shield of the nation." Mason Locke (Parson) Weems's then-recent book, a wildly embellished (but repeatedly reprinted) biography of the revolutionary partisan Francis Marion, reflected the popular mythos. While acknowledging the problems of militia under poor leaders like Horatio Gates, the author celebrated their achievements under Marion, who had transformed them into "some of as brave and desperate men as ever fought." Abundant evidence suggested a very different reality. Militia musters, complained Harrison, were "generally devoted to riot and intemperance." Local authorities routinely failed to submit even crude estimates of the size and composition of their forces. Lamented one observer: "Our military days of parade are generally considered holidays."[11]

With effective preparations hampered by overoptimistic assessments of the prowess of American citizen-soldiers and sharp divisions over foreign policy, the muddled mobilization legislation was matched only by the War Department's ineptitude in implementing those measures. Secretary Eustis found that immersing himself in minutia was more comfortable than tackling the complex task of organizing a nation for war. Between January and May, only about six thousand men—barely 20 percent of the number authorized—had enlisted. Low pay, equipment shortages, and the lack of cooperation from opponents of the war compounded the difficulties. Finding capable leaders proved just as elusive. Disenchanted with Brigadier Generals Wilkinson and Wade Hampton, Madison toyed with the idea of naming Henry Clay to command the army, but the energetic Kentuckian seemed more valuable as Speaker of the House. Madison's eventual choice of former war secretary Henry Dearborn as senior officer once again demonstrated the president's shaky grasp of military realities. Older than his sixty-one years, Dearborn now found movement difficult and calming his bickering generals impossible. With a Shakespearean flourish, first-term Representative Felix Grundy (R-TN) wondered: "Is there not something rotten in Denmark?"[12]

Commissioning good officers further confounded the Madison administration. There was, admitted one presidential adviser, "a real dearth of capable military men." In a vain appeal to bipartisanship, the president named the Federalist Thomas Pinckney as the second major general, but Pinckney took months to set up his headquarters. Factionalism among the congressional delegations that nominated slates of officers exacerbated the problem. "The appointment of officers in the new army from this state," one New Yorker advised the president, "afford much regret to your friends . . . [for] the minions and sycophants of DeWitt Clinton [a noted rival of Madison] have been taken up [to] the total exclusion of men capable of rendering service to their County. . . . Imbecility, Ignorance, and Vanity, are their chief characteristics." Selections of Federalists also rankled Republican partisans, with Dearborn summoning up enough energy to accuse some Federalist nominees "of Treasonable intentions." Representative John Dawson (VA) complained that commissioning Federalists was causing "grave discontent" among his constituents; another Madison confidante added that such appointments "have a bad effect, because in no quarter is the struggle for supremacy between the parties more arduous, or the opposition more malignant."[13]

Undeterred by the faulty preparations, the United States declared war on Britain in June 1812, with Republicans from the South, West, and Pennsylvania most likely to support the conflict and Federalists lining up against it. Americans imagined that hastily raised columns could seize Canada and force a negotiated peace before the British, embroiled in an epic struggle against Napoleon, could dispatch reinforcements. Unfortunately, the uncoordinated three-pronged U.S. invasion revealed appalling failures in leadership as well as the colossal miscalculations of organizational and logistical realities. At Detroit, Brig. Gen. William B. Hull surrendered 2,500 men to a British/Indian army half that size. At Queenston, a thousand regulars who had crossed the Niagara River into Canada were also forced to raise the white flag when accompanying militia declined to follow. Farther east, Major General Dearborn, who "sauntered away his Time Shamefully," retreated after a halfhearted attempt to take Montreal, defeated by his own timidity and the refusal by Federalist governors of Connecticut, Rhode Island, and Massachusetts to fulfill the president's requests to rally their militias.[14]

Poorly led short-term volunteers and militia had rarely lived up to public expectations. With few exceptions, the militia "consisted of a yeomanry and others accustomed to parade for a few hours each year, some with bad arms, others, without any," recalled a contemporary historian shortly after the war. "Every day's experience tends to force on our minds a conviction that we are unwilling to receive," admitted the *Daily National Intelligencer*. "Volunteer militia are not precisely the species of force on which to rely for carrying on war." Treasury Secretary Gallatin acknowledged that "the series of misfortunes experienced this year in our military land operations exceeds all anticipations made even by those who had least confidence in our inexperienced officers and undisciplined men."[15]

Although Madison won reelection that fall, a loose alliance of Clintonian Republicans and Federalists continued to restrict the administration's efforts to mobilize resources. Clay feared the president might be "unfit for the storms of War." Buffeted by political challenges, military defeats, and the shocking logistical disarray, Madison, Gallatin, and Secretary of State James Monroe tried to right the sinking ship. The ineffectual Eustis was eased out as secretary of war, eventually replaced by John Armstrong, an irascible and polarizing figure who at least brought with him considerable military expertise. Irritated by the lack of cooperation from Federalist governors, the administration in January 1813 won permission to raise another 20,000 regulars for one year's service. Fears of a standing army nonetheless remained a potent rhetorical tool. The new law, cautioned Federalist Lyman Law (CT), meant that militia, the true "defence of the country," would be "overawed and controlled by regular troops . . . [and] dwindle into insignificance."[16]

Troubles in filling the expanded regular ranks (the number in uniform probably never exceeded more than half of the army's authorized strength of 57,000) sparked further rancor. Desperate for manpower but short of cash for the bounties needed to entice recruits, administration supporters in January 1813 sought to divide militias into three classes (ages 18–21, 21–31, and 31–45), with the middle group authorized to serve anywhere in the United States. This suggested to many a dangerous similarity with France, which had turned from republicanism to Napoleonic dictatorship in employing mass conscription to fuel the emperor's armies. "This was a French system; . . . it was a tyrant's system," proclaimed the Massachusetts Federalist Josiah Quincy. "The resulting force might be called a conscription, Imperial guards, or the like, but it was not a militia." Such a body would merely provide the executive with "a disposable force, to . . . do anything for which any Congress might pass a law." Militia reorganization thus died in the Senate.[17]

Events that year reflected the nation's continuing inability to muster either the resources or the leadership necessary to conduct a successful invasion of Canada. In the Northwest, Brig. Gen. William Henry Harrison managed to hold Fort Meigs (modern-day Perrysburg, Ohio) against a siege despite the near annihilation of a 1,200-strong relief force. Following Capt. Oliver Hazard Perry's spectacular naval victory at Lake Erie, Harrison (now promoted to major general) pushed into Canada, where his mounted volunteers, who the *Daily National Intelligencer* described as "an honorable specimen of the yeomanry of the country," spearheaded the rout of British/Indian forces at the Battle of the Thames. Harrison's profligate spending nonetheless annoyed Secretary Armstrong, who wanted to divert resources to eastern theaters; the resulting acrimony led to Harrison's resignation and stalled the offensive. Another stalemate followed initial success on the Niagara Peninsula that summer. Twin thrusts by Wilkinson and Hampton—their bitter personal enmity precluding any effective cooperation—never came close to capturing Montreal. The British also seized Fort Niagara and, after routing two thousand militiamen, torched Buffalo. Summing up the frustrations of a disappointed nation, Brig. Gen. Lewis Cass attributed the failures to the "*criminal neglect*" of officers and "the most cowardly manner" of militiamen.[18]

In December 1813, convinced that bounties, recruiting tricks, and appeals to patriotism would never deliver the needed manpower, Secretary Armstrong unveiled a plan to classify state militias into groups of twenty men, each responsible for supplying one soldier for the war's duration. In effect, this equated to conscription. That same month, using the pseudonym "An Officer of the Army," Armstrong argued that invading Canada would require a larger regular army, commanded by a new lieutenant general (presumably himself). Critics charged that these proposals smacked of military despotism, and Secretary of State Monroe warned Madison that Armstrong would "ruin not you and the admin. only, but the whole republican party and cause." With the reputation of militiamen and volunteers partially restored by Harrison's success at the Thames (where less than 150 regulars had been present out a total force of nearly 4,000), Congress tabled Armstrong's controversial proposals.[19]

Absent meaningful structural reform, the campaigns of 1814 remained problematic. At the beginning of the year, despite an authorized strength of 58,254, only 23,614 men were on the rolls. "We are no doubt a great nation," observed Brig. Gen. Jacob Brown, "but be assured sir, that we shall never have a great army until some of our militia agents die or get hung." Brig. Gen. Winfield Scott, another of the army's rising young stars, declared "that I had rather be without that species of force [militia] than have the whole population of New York and Pennsylvania at my heels." Corruption and mismanagement within the War Department, he claimed, had quadrupled costs.[20]

Despite the difficulties, officers like Brown and Scott gradually forged an army of disciplined regulars whose exploits on the Niagara frontier—often overlooked in the face of more sensational events at the nation's capital—would in many ways establish the postwar identity of the officer corps. At Buffalo, the twenty-seven-year-old Scott established a "camp of instruction" for six regular infantry regiments, several artillery batteries, and a troop of light dragoons, the long drills and camp instruction serving to infuse a spirit of "confidence, the dawn of victory" throughout the command. Crossing the Niagara into Canada, under Brown's leadership on July 5 they clashed at

Jacob Brown. Leading U.S. forces at Chippewa and Lundy's Lane, Jacob Brown (1775–1828) was appointed commanding general in 1821. Based on an 1815 by John W. Jarvis, the print from this engraving by Asher B. Durand was executed after Brown's death. Library of Congress, USZ62-5586.

Chippawa with the enemy, commanded by Maj. Gen. Phineas Riall. "Those are regulars, by God!" an astonished Riall is said to have exclaimed to his staff as Scott's regular brigade checked, then shattered, the center of the British line. Another desperately fought engagement followed at Lundy's Lane (July 25), though only a tactical draw, once again demonstrated that disciplined American forces could stand up to the cream of the British army.[21]

Such accomplishments notwithstanding, humiliating failures soon overshadowed these encouraging developments as Brown retreated to the United States. In August, a British raiding force routed a hastily organized rabble at Bladensburg, Maryland, and then burned the Capitol and most public buildings in the District of Columbia. "Militia simply will never do to oppose British troops," judged one veteran.[22] Desperate to reverse the war's momentum, Madison accepted Secretary Armstrong's resignation, turning again to Monroe, who had temporarily held the post after Eustis. In October 1814, Monroe proposed four different plans for mobilizing 70,000 new soldiers, 40,000 of whom would be devoted to defensive purposes. Drawing on his own experiences as a combat veteran of Washington's Continental Army, Monroe also affirmed the superiority (and cost-effectiveness) of regulars for the offensives required to force Britain to the peace table. Shocked by the battlefield setbacks, several congressmen lectured their colleagues on the need to secure and train reliable troops. "We must have men of some measure or give up the contest," charged Representative Joseph Desha (R-KY), a former major general of volunteers and veteran of the Battle of the Thames. "Militia cannot be deemed an efficient force." Added Charles J. Ingersoll (R-PA): "The fatal doctrine of citizen-soldier (as we adhere to it) has cost us more money, more blood, more mourning, in six months, than a war of six years should or would cost under proper military organization."[23]

Partisan infighting, regional rivalries, fears of a regular army, concerns over conscription, and opposition to the war doomed the new round of reforms. "It is nonsense to talk of regulars," observed Jefferson, who in splendid retirement at Monticello returned to his classical republicanism of days past. "They are not to be on hand among a people so easy and happy at home as ours. We might as well rely on calling down an army of angels from heaven." The brilliant Massachusetts Federalist Daniel Webster characterized the administration's latest requests as "more tyrannical, more arbitrary, more dangerous, more allied to blood & murder, more full of every form of mischief, more productive of every sort & degree of misery, than has been exercised by any civilized Government." Once again, the House and Senate failed to agree upon a remedy, satisfying themselves by authorizing the president to accept 40,000 state volunteers for twelve months.[24]

Only in the Southwest did the performance of citizen-soldiers consistently match popular expectations. For most volunteers in the region, the initial impetus to serve had come in response to renewed conflicts with the Upper Creeks, whose militant Red Stick faction had allied with Tecumseh's short-lived confederation. Like their cousins to the North, white residents in the Southwest were quick to take up the sword when their own communities seemed to be in immediate peril. In 1813, the slaughter of several hundred people by Red Stick warriors at Fort Mims, Alabama, added to the swelling ranks of volunteers willing to fight what one newspaper dubbed the Indian "hell hounds." Bloody engagements by Maj. Gen. Andrew Jackson's volunteers at Tallushatchee and Talladega that November proved inconclusive; frustrated by logistical failures and the lack of discipline among his men, Jackson maintained that the addition of "one regiment of regulars" would have brought complete success.[25]

In spring 1814, the arrival of the 39th Infantry Regiment and several hundred additional volunteers allowed Jackson to resume his offensive against the Red Sticks. On March 27, his mixed force of three thousand volunteers, regulars, and Cherokee and Creek allies struck the fortified enemy village at Horseshoe Bend. The "*carnage* was *dreadful,*" observed Jackson; at a cost of nearly three hundred casualties, his army killed eight hundred Red Stick Indians. Learning of British plans to strike the coast of the Gulf of Mexico, he repulsed a premature enemy raid against Mobile, crossed the border and destroyed a British depot in Spanish Pensacola, then marched to New Orleans, the object of the main enemy thrust.[26]

As redcoats made their way up the lower Mississippi River, Jackson assembled an exotic army of perhaps six thousand men, most of whom were volunteers and militiamen from Kentucky, Tennessee, Mississippi, and Louisiana. Two battalions of free men of color, a detachment of Choctaw Indians, several dozen Baratarian pirates manning cannons, a company of Marines, two regiments of regular infantrymen, several batteries of artillery, and a squad of dragoons rounded out his command, which held a strong position below New Orleans. Following several skirmishes, on the morning of January 8, 1815, Lt. Gen. Sir Edward Michael Pakenham attacked. On the river's west bank, British veterans routed several hundred Louisiana and Kentucky militiamen. The main assault, however, came on the opposite side of the river, where, fighting behind professionally designed earthworks and boasting unusually heavy artillery, Americans threw back the British with astonishing losses: the attacking enemy lost 2,037 killed, wounded, and missing on that day alone, whereas total American casualties for the entire campaign numbered just over three hundred. "It appears that the unerring hand of providence shielded my men from the Powers of Balls, bombs & Rocketts [*sic*]," wrote a thankful Jackson, "when every Ball & Bomb from our guns carried with them the mission of death."[27]

To most Americans the victory of Jackson's makeshift army confirmed the myth of the volunteer citizen-soldier. Patriots had dropped the tools of their civilian trades to drive back the redcoats along the banks of the mighty Mississippi and forced the enemy to make peace. "If ever there was a stain upon 'raw militia,'" wrote one, "it was wiped away on the 8th of January." The British, announced a widely reprinted editorial, "have been met, beaten, and disgraced . . . by a raw militia, hastily collected together from the adjoin-

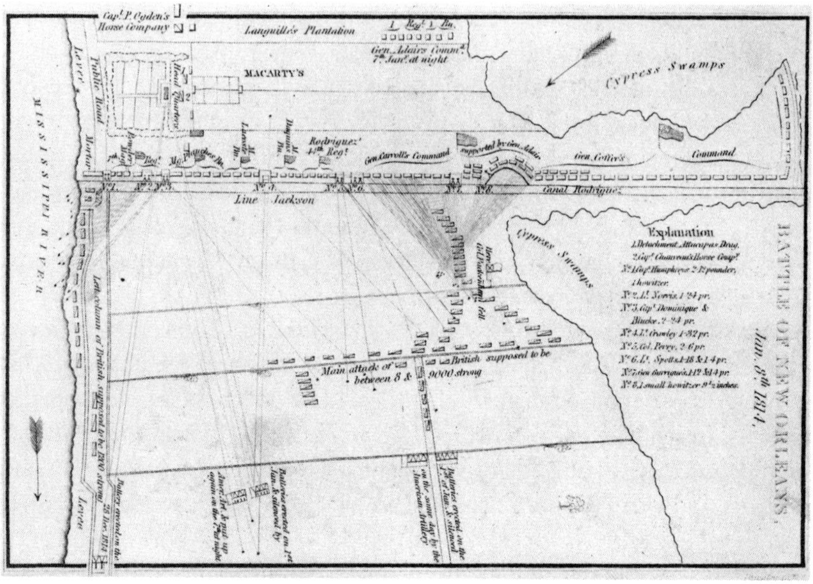

Battle of New Orleans, January 8, 1815. With their flanks protected by swampy ground and the Mississippi River, Andrew Jackson's army, whose cotton barricaded lines are near the top of this map, slaughtered advancing British regulars at New Orleans. Library of Congress, USZ62-132786.

ing country, and commanded by farmers and planters." Jefferson argued that the battle had demonstrated "that our militia are heroes when they have heroes to lead them on, and that when unembarrassed by field evolutions, which they do not understand, their skill in the firearm, and deadly aim, give them great advantages over regulars." Michael Smith, author of a history published within a year of the war's end, proclaimed that the British attackers at New Orleans "were received by the militia, with a firmness and deliberation, unequalled in the annals of *history*." Others credited the victory to divine providence—a sure sign of God's support for the American experiment in republicanism. "His veterans fall before the undisciplined militia of our country like snow before the sun," crowed one newspaper. "We read the account of such victories as we have obtained, with wonder and astonishment, and in no other way can we account for our success, than that the LORD is with us in the hour of battle."[28]

Reality, of course, was very different. Citizen-soldiers had not forced the British to come to terms, for the Treaty of Ghent ending the War of 1812 had been signed more than two weeks before the Battle of New Orleans. The U.S. government had lacked the bureaucratic structure needed to carry out the gargantuan task of mobilizing and supplying a force capable of seizing Canada from one of the world's great powers, even when that enemy was simultaneously fighting a larger war on another continent. Hardened by Jackson's firm discipline and veterans of the savage war against the Red Sticks, most American troops at New Orleans were far superior to typical volunteers and enjoyed a marked superiority in artillery. Moreover, the British had made several tactical errors, and the untested American militiamen on the west bank had broken in the face of the enemy's assault. In his early reports about the fighting, Jackson complained that undisciplined Kentuckians had "ingloriously fled," nearly costing the rest of his command their hard-earned victory. Unsure that the war had been won, Jackson later requested five thousand additional regulars, "the only description of troops upon which reliance can be placed."[29]

Formerly a champion of limited government and the militias, President Madison had by the conflict's end reversed himself. Perhaps he now realized the republic was stable enough to resist any attempts by a standing army to establish a dictatorship; perhaps he simply concluded that external threats demanded more reliable security measures. Chastened by the refusal of some governors to deploy state troops, the erratic performance of raw militiamen and volunteers in combat, the humiliating destruction of the Capitol, and the chronic problems of enlisting and equipping soldiers, the president on February 18, 1815, urged Congress to establish "an adequate regular force," build a larger navy, improve harbor defenses, and add "discipline to [the] distinguished bravery" of the militia. Four days later, a similarly chastened Secretary of War Monroe fleshed out the details, proposing a 20,000-strong permanent force and a $6 million military establishment. To justify the big increases (in 1811, the authorized army had been 9,921 men, the defense budget about $4 million), Monroe cited the continuing menaces posed by the 35,000 British troops believed to be in Canada and the ongoing boundary disputes with Spain.[30]

Backing the administration's proposals, the *Daily National Intelligencer* printed a letter reasoning that "all prejudice must be discarded, and past errors remembered but for the sake of reformation." Another correspondent characterized any risk from a regular army as "truly ridiculous." Borderlands officials also called for a larger military presence. "The late war repeatedly exhibited the melancholy fact," wrote Harrison, "of [a] large corps of militia going into the field without understanding a single elementary principle, and without being able to perform a single evolution." William Theobald Wolfe Tone, son of the leader of the Irish Rebellion and decorated Napoleonic veteran who would soon accept a commission in the United States Army, urged his adopted country to come to grips with reality. To defend itself in a dangerous world, argued Tone, American military forces "require to be improved, organized and augmented. . . . Our liberties can run no danger from such improvements on a moderate but sufficient scale."[31]

Old Republicans and Federalists in Congress, however, saw no need for such measures. Only after considerable debate could the House (which wanted to emphasize the role of the militia) and Senate (which offered more praise to the regulars) even agree on how to word their congratulations to the victors at New Orleans. Similar difficulties confronted the administration's call to set the army at 20,000 men. Kentucky's Joseph Desha—who in the dark days of late 1814 had emphasized the militia's ineffectiveness—now insisted that more recent events had reaffirmed that institution's place as "the bulwark of liberty" and dismissed foreign threats as imaginary. Samuel Farrow, a one-term Republican congressman from South Carolina, found no reason for a large army when "our citizen soldiers have shown themselves capable of defending the soil." The Massachusetts Federalist Timothy Pickering complained of the higher taxes needed to finance the arms buildup. Using language mirroring that of anti-Federalists during the constitutional debates, Richard Stockton (F-NJ) proclaimed: "If there was any one principle which might be called fundamental to our civil institutions . . . it was this—that a standing army was not to be tolerated in time of peace." Thus the House opted for six thousand regulars.[32]

The Senate countered by demanding 15,000 men. As the Madison administration redoubled its warnings about lurking threats to national security, a conference committee agreed on a compromise of 10,000. Although he had originally supported a bigger cut, Louisiana Republican Thomas B. Robertson now informed his House colleagues of his fear that Britain would acquire Florida from Spain and attack Mobile. "Though hostile to a large army in time of peace," he urged his colleagues to accept the compromise. On the last day of the Thirteenth Congress's third session, both houses settled on a 10,000-strong force.[33]

The failure to secure an even larger regular army represented a resounding defeat for Madison, with one officer denouncing the "niggardly and parsimonious conduct" of Congress. Disbanded officers briefly contemplated forming a national organization to represent their interests. "We are Republicans," explained one correspondent, "and have not to be taught that large standing armies, under the control of ambitious and unprincipled men, are dangerous to Republics." When lobbying efforts by active and former officers fizzled, Madison and his cabinet scurried to keep the cuts, as Monroe put it, "within proper limits." As the law referred to "men," the president interpreted the 10,000-man maximum to apply only to privates. This tortured construction, combined with the act's explicit exclusion of the Corps of Engineers from the manpower ceiling, brought the total authorized strength of the army to 12,383—nearly four times that established in the Jeffersonian reduction of 1802.[34]

"Hero's Quick Step." Often embarrassed during the War of 1812, the militia's image quickly recovered, as evidenced by this music cover showing well-dressed citizen-soldiers drilling on Boston Common. Library of Congress, USZ62-69636.

With the war's close, Monroe left the War Department in favor of his full-time service at State, so it fell to acting secretary of war (and Secretary of the Treasury) Alexander J. Dallas to oversee the "difficult and unpleasant" task of reducing the army's nearly three thousand commissioned personnel to less than five hundred. In so doing, the administration showed its increased awareness of military sensibilities as well as an emerging professional ethos within the armed forces. As the war had wound down, then–Secretary of War Monroe had insisted that political affiliation not be a prerequisite for officers, a sentiment that seems to have carried forth in the subsequent reductions. Brigadier Generals Scott, Alexander Macomb, and Eleazar W. Ripley did the heavy lifting, under instructions to retain those of "distinguished military merit and approved moral character." They could also consider an individual's financial situation and potential for securing a civilian job. The generals seem to have balanced sectional and political pressures in a responsible manner, and with Madison expressing "great confidence in the intelligence and dispositions of the Board," they encountered little interference from their civilian masters.[35]

The War of 1812 had highlighted links between regulars, national security, and the economy. The founding fathers had established structures that allowed the federal government to fund the war through long-term loans (if only barely), but enemy occupation forces and blockades could cripple trade. In the past, Republicans had been reluctant to fund seaboard fortifications, fearing that they might legitimize a larger army and explode the federal budget. Now, however, both Madison and his successor, James Monroe, embraced such defenses as a means "to prevent war." Seeking to reenergize coastal defense efforts, Madison appointed a French engineer, Simon Barnard, as a brevet brigadier general to spearhead a new Board of Engineers for Fortifications. Intended to protect strategic points and the intracoastal trade rather than the entire coast, the resulting Third System of fortifications, initially projected to encompass eighteen first-class, fourteen second-class, and eighteen third-class forts costing $18 million (not including armaments), became a cornerstone of national security. By 1851, the program had expanded to 186 works in six classes.[36]

* * * * *

Spending on things military had long influenced the nation's political economy. Creditors who had financed the war for independence supported a new constitution, judging that a stronger government would be more capable of paying debts and fostering economic growth than either the struggling Confederation or the individual states. By positioning Wayne's Legion in the Old Northwest in the early 1790s, George Washington had done much to ensure the region's loyalty by improving security, ensuring control of natural resources, and pumping in outside capital to local contractors. Likewise, the decision to situate federal armories at Springfield, Massachusetts (established in 1794), and Harpers Ferry, Virginia (1798) provided steady jobs and spawned associated artisans, workshops, and businesses. In a similar vein, Kentucky's Richard M. Johnson (D), perhaps the era's most influential legislator in martial matters (he was a two-time representative, senator, and U.S. vice president), long sought to establish an additional military academy in the South or the West.[37]

On a broader scale, the presence or absence of a fort or an Indian trading house—both decisions controlled by the War Department—could make or break a regional economy. Impressed by the sawmills, gristmills, gardens, smithies, and bakeries that often accompanied a garrison, Duke Paul Wilhelm of Württemberg observed: "American military establishments must be looked upon as great industrial centers." Proud of the army's work, one inspector crowed, "the hatchet, the hoe, the pickaxe and the plough, have been with the same zeal and perseverance applied to public uses, whether in constructing barracks and fortifications, or making public roads." Indeed, in the fourth quarter of 1817 alone, soldiers spent 17,400 days building roads; such labor on public works, hoped Lt. Col. John E. Wool, "will convince the nation of their usefulness in peace as well as in war." The transfer of regulars to his state, one congressman assured his constituents, would "have a happy effect on the conduct of our Indian neighbors, while the public expenditures will add to the circulating medium." The War of 1812 had been an economic boon for Philadelphia (where the War Department employed more than three thousand workers to cut cloth for uniforms), New York City, Albany, and the West in general. "Every thing brisk and profitable," reported a visitor to Kentucky in 1813. "The war, so far from depressing the people of the Western States, is making the greater proportion of them rich."[38]

Having internalized the conflict's hard-earned lessons, President Madison now tried to retain the structures required to arm, equip, supply, and manage the nation's soldiers. Congress had during the conflict authorized a significant expansion of the staff, and thoughtful observers recognized the necessity of a supporting bureaucracy. As the Army Act of 1815 had included no provisions for such a specialized structure, the administration showed considerable initiative in retaining the Ordnance, Purchasing, Pay, and Judge Advocate Departments as providing "necessary public service." Madison was particularly keen on keeping the adjutant and inspector-general offices, asking Congress to create a permanent staff required by "the public interests." His latest secretary of war, William H. Crawford, furnished the specifics, insisting that the peacetime establishment have "in time of peace, the organization which it must have to render it efficient in a state of war." With little debate, Congress generally adopted Crawford's suggestions. Although petty and jealously protective of their independence, the resulting staff bureaus met the needs of the army for the next generation. Unrecognized at the time, the division of responsibility and accountability among the various bureaus would also make it more difficult for a lone general to assume dictatorial powers.[39]

In addition to erecting the bureaucratic structure needed to fight and win wars, Madison in late 1815 implored Congress to implement militia reform, fund new warships and coastal defenses, improve facilities at West Point, and erect additional military academies. The president also requested assistance for disabled veterans. The navy, which had performed so spectacularly on the Great Lakes and in individual ship actions, did best, with Congress promising $1 million per annum for eight years to build new warships. Legislators also appropriated more than $800,000 for coastal fortifications and nearly $140,000 for improvements at West Point. A proposal to create as many as three additional military academies enjoyed the support of the influential Kentuckians Clay and Johnson (both of whom wanted such a school in their state) but fell victim to sectional squabbling in the House when it came to identifying specific locations. As usual, militia reform went nowhere, and those advocating small-government ideology and populist class jealousies blocked a proposal to offer land grants to officers let go in the reduction of forces. Georgia's Wilson Lumpkin (R), for instance, complained that many former regulars "were living in luxury and dissipation, spending their time in idleness and pleasure." What about the "brave, patriotic, volunteer militia officers," wondered Lumpkin, who "have achieved far more honor in defending their country's rights?" The House thus refused the land grant bill for discharged army officers by a 77–59 count, with the Senate rejecting a similar amendment 15–10.[40]

Although Congress rejected many of his army-related proposals, Madison's newfound attention to military affairs and security was consistent with the broader nationalistic programs he now espoused. His confidence that a virtuous republic could avoid international conflicts now lay among the ashes left by the British raid on Washington, D.C., so the president had concluded that the United States must take steps to ensure its preservation. To this end, Madison left office with an army nearly 25 percent larger than the one he had inherited. In 1816, nearly half of all federal employees were soldiers; when the navy, Marines, and civilian workers in the War Department were included, that figure rose to 80 percent. To bolster the nation's shield, his Board of Engineers for Fortifications would develop a system of coastal defenses that eventually cost upward of $40 million. Inextricably linked to these steps to defend a truly independent republic were plans to promote economic security. Madison thus urged Congress to re-create a national bank, implement a tariff to protect American industry, and build roads and canals "requiring a national jurisdiction and national means." The new spirit of nationalism was unmistakable: Congress responded to the president's entreaties by establishing a bank with three and a half times the capitalization of the first, erecting a distinctly protective tariff, and appropriating $100,000 to extend the National Road.[41]

Chapter Five

The Army and the New Nationalism

On March 4, 1817, James Monroe became the fifth president of the United States, having won sixteen of the nineteen states and two-thirds of the popular vote. Although he doubted the constitutionality of federal funding for internal improvements such as infrastructure, he did allow that a better communications system could "bind the Union more closely together." Having dropped out of college to join the Continental Army, the former major represented the last of the revolutionary generation, an attribute he often cultivated by wearing knee breeches, buckled shoes, and a tricornered hat. To cement his victory, the president took a triumphal national tour, making sure to include the last Federalist stronghold of New England. He spent July 4 in Boston, visiting Bunker Hill, reviewing local militia units, and attending patriotic celebrations. A Federalist newspaper of that city dubbed it an "era of good feelings."[1]

Political elites joined Monroe in sharing this palpable sense of optimism in the confident times following the War of 1812. Promoters of what the historian Daniel Walker Howe calls the "new republican nationalism" believed that the federal government should help them achieve their visions for America. Whereas Monroe never connected the army with national development as consciously as had Thomas Jefferson, his secretary of war, South Carolina's John C. Calhoun, was eager to use the regulars to effect that end. "In accepting the office which I now fill," wrote Calhoun, long a congressional advocate for a larger army, "I was actuated by a strong desire to contribute as much as possible to the publick prosperity, by giving our military establishment the greatest possible utility and perfection."[2]

Upon entering the War Department, the energetic and ambitious Calhoun, aged thirty-five, hoped to display his administrative skills by reforming a notoriously mismanaged agency where unpaid accounts totaled more than $40 million into an efficient bureaucracy. Calhoun indeed transformed the department, improving contracting systems, reducing 90 percent of its debt claims, and securing legislation that allowed for better management of the bureaus. His reorganized staff featured a quartermaster general, surgeon general, commissary general, adjutant general, chief of ordnance, and paymaster general, all stationed in Washington, D.C. To promote more specialized expertise, the army also established an artillery school at Fortress

Monroe, Virginia. By 1824, the editor of *Niles' Weekly Register* marveled that the War Department was functioning "like clockwork."[3]

John Quincy Adams, Monroe's successor, was an even stronger proponent of the new republican nationalism. "The magnificence and splendor of their public works are among the imperishable glories of the ancient republics," he proclaimed in his inaugural address. "The roads and aqueducts of Rome have been the admiration of all after ages, and have survived thousands of years after all her conquests have been swallowed up in despotism or become the spoil of barbarians." Adams thus urged Congress to sponsor roads, canals, a national university, a uniform standard of weights and measures, and "light-houses of the skies" (astronomical observatories). Sharing none of his predecessor's constitutional qualms about federal support for internal improvements, the new president was limited only by the shortage of personnel to implement them: of the government's 6,526 employees, 4,766 worked for the United States Post Office. The army, realized Adams, could provide much-needed labor.[4]

Partly by design and partly by circumstance, the United States Army was closely associated with this new government activism. Culturally and psychologically, federal aid to Revolutionary War veterans helped to sanctify the suffering of earlier patriots. Fortifications and garrisons promised security and, particularly when placed at sites that possessed inherent economic advantages, encouraged local development.[5] Military contracts stimulated economic growth, and the quest for reliable weapons encouraged new manufacturing techniques. To their traditional duties of implementing and enforcing Indian policy, serving as ad hoc diplomatic assets, threatening foreign outposts, and deterring invasions, regulars in the coming years added efforts to control the fur trade and to promote internal improvements. Of course, the army's high public profile and expanded responsibilities carried some risk; should the political winds turn against the new nationalism, the regulars would become a convenient target.

* * * * *

Wounded during the great Revolutionary War victory at Trenton, President Monroe was sensitive to the needs of veterans. He also benefited from recently published biographies by John Marshall and David Ramsay of George Washington, Thomas Wilson's *The Biography of the Principal American Military and Naval Heroes*, Thomas O'Connor's *Impartial and Correct History of the War between the United States of America and Great Britain*, and fiery publications in *Port Folio*, all of which transformed the popular image of the Continental Army, formerly seen as isolated from American society, into a broader people's force. As the historian John Resch has noted, the "suffering soldier" of the Revolution became an iconic cultural symbol. Responding to Monroe's call for action, Congress in 1818 adopted a comprehensive aid package for Continental veterans. Debates pitted empathy for old soldiers against notions of limited government, memories of a citizen's militia, and equality, as assisting former Continentals would privilege retired regulars over other Americans. Backing the measure, Senator Harrison Gray Otis (F-MA) "drew a picture of the aged hero of the Revolution which drew tears from the eyes of the whole Senate," observed a colleague. Rising in opposition, South Carolina's William Smith (R) declared that Continental soldiers "had not done more than they ought to have done; nor had they done more than fell to the lot of every American devoted to his country."[6]

In this instance, sympathy for suffering soldiers triumphed. The Pension Act of 1818 granted every enlisted man who had served at least nine months in the Continental Army or navy now "in need of assistance from his country" a monthly stipend of eight dollars; commissioned personnel could receive twenty dollars. The political scientist Laura Jensen describes the act as a "watershed event" that moved support for some of the poor from the local to the federal level. That Continental veterans—the nation's first regulars—benefited from such largesse seems a telling indication of the softening public skepticism toward the army.[7]

To the close observer, links between military affairs and economic development were also evident. Between 1816 and 1819, spending on the army, national security, and veterans consumed nearly 60 percent of the federal budget (excluding debt payments). The army's economic significance was especially pronounced in the borderlands, where its purchases, military roads, and physical presence assured those on the nation's geographic peripheries of the government's interest. Further, hundreds of thousands of dollars in annual appropriations for the purchase of weapons for state militias, first initiated in 1808, offered a vital stimulus to private arms manufacturers. By 1810, some two hundred mills in sixteen states were making gunpowder, the most important of which, E. I. DuPont de Nemours & Co., would double its capacity during the War of 1812.[8]

Emphasizing the convergence of technology and national security, modern scholars such as Merritt Roe Smith, Nathan Rosenberg, David A. Hounshell, and David R. Meyer have also highlighted the army's role in modernizing American industrial technology. "The history of virtually every important metalworking industry in nineteenth-century America—machine tools, sewing machines, watches, typewriters, agricultural implements, bicycles, locomotives," writes Smith, "reveals the pervasive influence of military management techniques." A mutuality of interests connected the army, arms makers, and the broader industrial community. Regular officers craved system and order, which naturally extended to weapons and the shops that produced them; soldiers benefited from high-quality weapons; arms contracts promised lucrative profits for private manufacturers; innovations and specialized machine tools used in such production could be mimicked elsewhere. Consistent fabrication, special machine tools, interchangeable parts, and rigid inspection were logical means of improving quality and promoting efficiency. Private enterprise had balked at the difficulty and expense of implementing such a template, but the lure of steady government contracts for standardized arms encouraged cooperation and compliance.[9]

In February 1815, Congress accelerated the process by granting the Ordnance Department authority to negotiate arms contracts, supervise the Springfield and Harpers Ferry armories, and "draw up a system of regulations . . . for the uniformity of manufacturers of all arms ordnance." The mercurial chief of ordnance, Decius Wadsworth, quickly arranged a meeting with fellow Yale graduate Eli Whitney (inventor of the cotton gin and, up to this date, a largely unsuccessful arms manufacturer) and the superintendents of the Springfield and Harpers Ferry armories. They agreed to implement uniform systems of management and manufacturing, with Whitney emerging as the best-known publicist for interchangeable parts. By 1819, Colonel Wadsworth predicted that his department could make Springfield "a credit to the Government and an ornament to the nation." With Ordnance officers scrutinizing operations at government facilities with an eye toward quality control, efficiency, accurate accounting, and uniform procedures, and the Ordnance Department insisting on information-sharing as a condition for awarding contracts, such principles gradually spread through the network of machinists who dominated the small-arms industry in New England. The merger of the independent ordnance bureau with the artillery in 1821 slowed centralized planning, but the re-creation of a separate Ordnance Department in 1832 allowed the group's chief, Col. George Bomford, to make further managerial reforms and to codify a set of regulations.[10]

The army also continued to implement Indian policy. Since 1806, the Office of the Superintendent of Indian Trade, overseen by the secretary of war, had served as a clearinghouse for Indian affairs. By 1818, fifteen agents and ten subagents administered the complex Indian trade laws. Twenty-eight government trading houses (known as "factories") dotted the borderlands, theoretically providing Indians with higher-quality goods and fairer prices than might be obtained through an unregulated market. All but four were situated near military posts, and only regulars could provide the necessary security and labor force. Sadly, such a dependency often left civilian agents and military officers at odds; at Fort Wayne, for example, Maj. John Whistler denounced Agent Benjamin F. Stickney as being "void of understanding, and of all military regulations."[11]

Given the unquenchable American hunger for land, government actions almost invariably favored non-Indians, and virtually every soldier joined

President Monroe in presuming that Indian hunter-gatherers must make way for white farmers. If necessary, force could be used to ensure this transformation. "The savage must be taught and compelled to do what is right," insisted Brig. Gen. Edmund P. Gaines. "The poisonous cup of barbarism cannot be taken from the lips of the savage by the mild voice of reason alone; the strong mandate of justice must be resorted to, and enforced." Such racism notwithstanding, few government officials or soldiers favored outright extermination. Most, including Secretary of War Calhoun, agreed that it was in the national interest to reduce violence by keeping Indians and whites apart; limiting Indian trade to federally sanctioned agents; restricting the introduction of alcohol; showcasing military power; and educating Indians in the ways of the white world. Calhoun accordingly condemned the "disgraceful motives" of those who advocated conflicts with Indians and appointed Thomas L. McKenney, known for his honesty and interest in Indian issues, to head the new Office of Indian Affairs within the War Department.[12]

Forts provided the cutting edge for white expansion, and by the end of the decade more than a quarter of the army was garrisoned along the western borderlands, with another third stationed on the Florida and Canada frontiers. In 1818, Secretary Calhoun expanded efforts to assure U.S. sovereignty over the Great Lakes and upper Mississippi River country into a scheme of transcontinental proportions. Directing that "no pains must be spared" in curtailing British and encouraging American fur trade with the Indians, Calhoun ordered the army to establish a post eighteen hundred miles up the Missouri River at the mouth of the Yellowstone River. His faith in the army's ability to help the nation achieve its destiny never soared higher:

> The remoteness of the post will, in some respects, render it unpleasant to those who may be detailed for the service; but I am persuaded that the American soldier, actuated by the spirit of enterprize, will meet the privations which may be necessary with cheerfulness. Combined with the importance of the service, the glory of planting the American flag at a point so distant, on so noble a river, will not be unfelt. The world will behold in it the mighty growth of our republic, which but a few years since, was limited by the Alleghany; but now is ready to push its civilization and laws to the western confines of the continent.[13]

Although Calhoun soon settled on the more modest goal of establishing a Missouri River post at the Mandan villages (near present-day Bismarck), word of the proposed Yellowstone Expedition electrified the nation. In a widely reprinted editorial, the *St. Louis Enquirer* proclaimed the effort to be "an era in the history of the West." President Monroe also dreamed large, predicting that this move, along with the establishment of Fort Snelling at

John C. Calhoun. Secretary of War from 1817–1825, the steely-eyed, reform-minded Calhoun (1782–1850) represented a break from the political hacks who often occupied the office during the nineteenth century. Library of Congress, USZ62-102297.

the confluence of the Mississippi and Minnesota Rivers, would promote "the great object of their [the Indians'] civilization." Western enthusiasm for a post on the Yellowstone River, added the president in 1819, had convinced him to "take great responsibility to ensure it."[14]

As had Jefferson, Calhoun envisioned army-sponsored surveys as a means of asserting national claims. His directive to Maj. Stephen H. Long was typically broad: "You will permit nothing worthy of notice to escape your attention." In 1819–1820, Long proceeded up the Platte River into the Rocky Mountains, then marched south and east through the modern states of Colorado, Texas, and Oklahoma. Calhoun also saw to it that Henry Schoolcraft, a noted civilian scientist, accompanied regulars as they scoured the regions between Lake Huron and the upper Mississippi. Major Long returned to the field in 1823, conducting a general survey of the upper Red River country along the Canadian boundary.[15]

Maj. Gen. Andrew Jackson displayed an even more nakedly aggressive nationalism in his Division of the South. West Florida's boundary remained in dispute, and hundreds of escaped slaves had used a cache of abandoned British munitions to establish their base along the Apalachicola River. Many Red Stick Indians had also fled south into Spanish-held Florida after the disaster at Horseshoe Bend. Exasperated by the repeated intrusions of white squatters, Seminole Indians likewise opposed U.S. expansion. From Louisiana, Lt. Col. Thomas S. Jesup had in 1816 started to pepper his military and civilian superiors with warnings of an imminent Spanish or British attack on New Orleans, which he predicted would in turn inspire an Indian uprising. In July, a shot from a U.S. gunboat hit the powder magazine at the escaped slave base, setting off an explosion that killed three-fourths of the community's three hundred inhabitants. The following year, Indians ambushed a boat carrying forty-five regulars and their dependents near Fort Scott, leading the administration to order Jackson into the field. Convinced that foreign assistance to Indians and fugitive slaves lay at the root of the problem, Jackson in spring 1818 led two hundred regulars and nine hundred volunteers into Spanish Florida. Exceeding his instructions, he captured St. Marks, executed two British subjects, occupied Pensacola, and appointed one of his officers as governor of Florida. Jackson justified his actions as reflecting "the immutable laws of self-defense."[16]

The Monroe administration scrambled to craft an appropriate response. Jackson had official permission to track Seminole Indians into Spanish-held territory but had violated the order's explicit prohibition against striking Indians who "should shelter themselves under a Spanish post." Secretary of War Calhoun, Treasury Secretary William H. Crawford, Attorney General William Wirt, and the president viewed Jackson's conduct as insubordination. Secretary of State John Quincy Adams, however, pointed out that, by demonstrating Spain's weakness, the unauthorized action could sway ongoing negotiations over Florida. In the end, officials in Washington compromised: the United States returned the captured forts but did not publicly repudiate Jackson. Even so, the Monroe administration could not hide the fact the second-ranking officer in the United States Army had exceeded his authority, executed two British citizens, and invaded foreign territory.[17]

Jackson's high-handed behavior came at an especially inopportune time, for a series of highly publicized disputes was leading Congress to reconsider its confidence in the regulars and Calhoun's War Department. Facing slow promotion and convinced that society did not accord them the respect they deserved, officers held their personal honor to be sacred, often defending it in ways that the public found objectionable. Dueling among officers had been forbidden since 1806, but as Jackson put it, "cases will arise, when honor & every noble sentiment as officers will compel them to appeal to this mode for redress: if they do not, in many cases they will be branded with the Epithet *coward.*" Brig. Gen. Eleazer W. Ripley was associated with challenges involving at least two fellow officers and flouted an official order by publishing a book defending his actions. Brig. Gen. Winfield Scott feuded with Jackson and printed a 150-page denunciation of General Gaines; his attempt to arrange a duel with a United States congressman was averted only by the decision of a quick-thinking aide not to deliver the message. Ignoring his own bad conduct even as he expected increased professionalism from subordinates, Scott admitted that "accusations & cross accusations among ourselves will have the effect of deeply injuring the army in the estimation of the nation."[18]

Widely publicized squabbles at West Point further tarnished the army's reputation. Following Col. Jonathan Williams's resignation as superintendent in 1812, leadership of the academy had fallen to Capt. Alden Partridge, a quarrelsome micromanager who curried personal favor with select cadets, antagonized his academic staff, and had the audacity to suggest that the military academy might train militia. Lacking a standard curriculum or an academic calendar, the school was prey to outside interference, especially among cadets "connected with respectable families." A presidential visit in summer 1817 failed to clear the air, and Partridge was subsequently court-martialed for disobeying orders.[19]

Partridge's ouster allowed the administration to appoint Capt. Sylvanus Thayer (who Partridge had accused of mutiny) as superintendent. Under Thayer's steady hand, the United States Military Academy would eventually flourish, but in the short term his stern discipline—combined with Partridge's public denunciations of the institution—resulted in several ugly incidents. The most spectacular involved cadet protests in 1818 against one of their instructors. The offending teacher was relieved from duty, but Thayer judged that some of the petitioners had gone too far in seeking redress. Smarting from this perceived affront to their honor, five cadets resigned and took their case to Congress, seeking "riddance from tyranny" and publishing their sixty-eight-page protest. A congressional committee backed Thayer, but the charges of arbitrary behavior by officers, coming so closely on the heels of Jackson's unauthorized actions in Florida, boded ill for the army in the court of public opinion.[20]

Internal scandals gave Calhoun's War Department another black eye. In 1818, it was also revealed that Maj. Christopher Van Deventer, the chief clerk and a Calhoun partisan, had a financial interest in contracts supplying stone for Fortress Monroe. More widely publicized were a series of blunders involving James Johnson, brother of Representative Richard M. Johnson (D-KY) and chief contractor for the Yellowstone Expedition. Tasked with providing supplies and transportation for the mission, the contractor counted on the use of untested steamboats to yield a bonanza of profits. To his dismay, the malfunction of the steamboats, the onset of the Panic of 1819 financial crisis, and his overstrained credit paralyzed his operations. Multiple advance payments from the government—some bearing the president's personal authorization—all suggested favoritism to a well-placed insider and overdrew the War Department budget. By September 1819, Calhoun feared that the boondoggle would "render it very difficult for this Department to get through the year."[21]

For two years, the administration had fended off Federalist and Old Republican efforts to limit the government by reducing the army, but members of the House of Representatives would soon whipsaw the federal military bureaucracy in a series of threats, rants, and demands to curtail spending. Anticipating these sharper attacks, Calhoun had in December 1818 taken pains to assert that the regulars were too few and too scattered to threaten American liberties, especially when led by officers "attached to the principles of freedom." The secretary had correctly judged the changing political winds, for 1819 saw a meeting of the minds between anti-Jacksonians and factions seeking to constrain the federal government. New York Federalist and House Member Henry R. Storrs accused Jackson of following in the footsteps of Julius Caesar and Napoleon Bonaparte: "Every tyrant who has succeeded in overturning the liberties of his country first stole away the affections of his countrymen by the services which he had rendered to the State." Philip Reed, a Maryland Republican (serving his first of two terms in the House after being a senator), added Oliver Cromwell and the uprising of American officers at Newburgh to the list. Indications that Spain might give up Florida, and Jackson's dramatic appearance in the capital, temporarily rallied the hero of New Orleans's supporters, who defeated several motions to censure his actions.[22]

Contentious debate about Missouri's application to enter the Union as a slave state did nothing to ease tensions as economizers, conservatives, and those eager to damage their political enemies continued to target the army. North Carolina's Lewis Williams, a Republican House member believed to have a personal score to settle with Calhoun, introduced the attacks by declaring standing armies to be "dangerous to liberty." Backed by fellow North Carolinians Jesse Slocum and James Stewart (both Federalists), Williams charged that the bloated staff was large enough for an army ten times the size of that of the United States. New Jersey representative Ephraim Bateman

(R) broadened the criticism to include all federal spending; others, in a not-so-subtle renewal of the campaign to damage Jackson, sought to eliminate his major generalcy. Treasury Secretary Crawford also seized the opportunity to wound Calhoun, believed to be a future rival for the presidency. A leader among Old Republicans alarmed by the nationalists' use of the federal government, Crawford advocated retrenchment and saw in the War Department—with veterans' pensions ballooning to 16 percent of the entire federal budget and scandalous tales of government handouts to wealthy former soldiers making excellent political fodder—an obvious target. Critics accused Crawford of overstating the impact of the Panic of 1819 on federal accounts to justify reducing military appropriations, but his calls to lessen government gained political traction. Girding for the worst, Calhoun in August 1819 predicted that the next session of Congress would be "the most trying for the Army of any which will probably occur in many years."[23]

Indeed it was, for criticism of Jackson's imperious behavior, West Point arrogance, the Yellowstone fiasco, and the War Department mounted. The army was "uselessly employed," asserted two-time House member Arthur Livermore (R-NH). His colleague, Tennessee's Newton Cannon (R), opined that the regular establishment would soon "become as expensive and oppressive as the Governments of Europe" and lambasted West Point training as "the gratuitous instruction of a privileged class of youth." Economizers passed legislation requiring each revolutionary pensioner to prove his need and eliminating appropriations for the troubled Yellowstone operation. By late April, House members seeking to trim military spending coalesced around a proposal by Virginia's John Floyd (R) to avoid new taxes by reducing the army to six thousand men. Two weeks later, the House directed Secretary Calhoun to prepare a plan that would conform to Floyd's figures.[24]

While Quartermaster General Thomas S. Jesup blasted the attacks "as the miserable cant of more miserable demagogues," Calhoun redoubled his scrutiny of Continentals' pensions and departmental expenses and called on the six generals—Major Generals Brown and Jackson and Brigadier Generals Scott, Gaines, Alexander Macomb, and Henry Atkinson—to craft responses to the House's demand. All warned that such cuts would endanger national security. Brown suggested that ramping up fortifications work in Massachusetts might win support from that state's congressional delegation; with a similar eye to securing political allies, Scott proclaimed "that our troops have always been the pioneers & guardians of expanding civilization." Should cuts be unavoidable, a consensus urged the retention of as many staff and officers as possible, allowing for a smoother expansion in times of emergency. In December 1820, Calhoun proposed what has come to be known as an "expansible" army, which would keep each of the generals, trim the staff only slightly, combine the artillery into a single regiment (thus eliminating

"The Nation's Bulwark." This satirical etching by Edward Williams Clay poked fun at the militia, in this case that of Philadelphia. Library of Congress, USZ62-7752.

twenty-eight line officers), retain each of the nine infantry regiments and their officers, and slash authorized enlisted strength from 11,635 to 6,391.[25]

On New Year's Day 1821, notification that Spain had accepted the Transcontinental Treaty arrived at the State Department. With the United States now in possession of Florida, national security seemed less of a concern. Two days later, Representative Thomas W. Cobb (R), a lame-duck Crawford ally from Georgia, reopened his until-then dormant proposal for "radical retrenchments" totaling $3.2 million in yearly federal spending, more than a third of which would come from the army. Denouncing Calhoun's plan, Cobb saw "no utility in an army of officers." Critics of the War Department paid the obligatory homage to the militia and volunteers, who they claimed could be counted on to defend the country if a crisis arose. Congress had authorized a larger standing army in 1815, explained Floyd, when many "did not believe the peace with England to be a lasting one." Now, however, "all Europe is at peace, tired and exhausted." North Carolina's Williams suggested that an "invasion from the inhabitants of the moon" was more likely than from Spain. Administration allies countered by identifying weaknesses in the militia, emphasizing the need to disseminate military science, magnifying threats from European powers, and defending the need for an outsized officer corps. Such protestations gained little sympathy, and their failure to effectively relate a larger regular force to security in the western borderlands or to highlight the economic benefits stemming from the army's garrisons, contracts, and roads represented a glaring tactical error.[26]

Coastal fortifications took an immediate hit, with annual appropriations falling from $800,000 in 1820 ($20.7 million at time of publication) to $202,000 in 1821. Accompanying the cuts was a change in the procedure for funding seaboard defense, which future Congresses also adopted. In the murky diplomatic waters after the War of 1812, Congress had heeded the advice of Calhoun and army engineers that such works follow "a complete system" designed to defend major harbors and big cities, deprive the enemy of bases for potential invasion, and protect intracoastal trade. But in light of recent diplomatic agreements and Crawford's projected deficits, Congress began doling out appropriations on a case-by-case basis. Line-item approvals of individual projects incited predictable partisan and sectional rancor. Annual funding for coastal forts increased to $814,000 by 1826, but the program had become politicized. Moreover, money for the big guns needed to arm the coastal positions also became more problematic as memories of the War of 1812 faded.[27]

By early 1821, ideology, political opportunism, the financial crisis, improved diplomatic relations, and the imperious behavior of Jackson and other officers formed a compelling narrative for reducing the army. A large House majority passed a measure that shrank the army to six thousand and featured draconian cuts to field officers and staff. "This vote on the army bill beats all I could have imagined," proclaimed a frustrated army engineer. "If reduction was to be made, the project of the Secretary is the only one in which system & science were incorporated." Although it accepted the House's 6,000-man target, the Senate favored an organization more akin to that proposed by Calhoun. The final reduction act retained most staff and provided for one major general, two brigadier generals, four artillery regiments, and seven infantry regiments. The number of authorized commissioned officers fell from 674 to 540 (a 20 percent reduction), and enlisted men to 5,586 (a 52 percent cut). The army was smaller than it had been in more than a decade and now represented only 34 percent of all federal employees.[28]

In the wake of these cutbacks, army officers unleashed a volley of complaints. Second in seniority to Major General Brown, Jackson resigned rather than accept a demotion to brigadier, condemning the "*mania* for retrenchment" sponsored by "the *little* members of Congress who have [made] the reduction of the army their *riding horse* for some years." Striking a similar tone, the *Louisville Public Advertiser* reprinted an editorial that lambasted "the eagerness with which the army have been assailed on the floor of Congress, as a sort of *drum head for political electioneering taps*." The onerous task of overseeing the dismissals of officers fell largely to Brown and Scott. Although they seem to have proceeded according to merit (official criteria were "intelligence, habits, and military skill") rather than political affiliation, several of those forced to resign appealed their cases to patrons in Congress, and the resulting controversies would complicate the army's command structure for years.[29]

Ironically, the 1821 reduction act had significant—if unnoticed at the time—implications for accounting and management, for, in a nod to improving efficiency, it had approved Scott's new army regulations. Stressing personal and financial accountability, the detailed guidelines set forth instructions for virtually all aspects of an officer's professional life. Scholar Charles F. O'Connell has identified the regulated procedures as "the first comprehensive management manual published in the United States." Building on these rules, the sense of responsibility fostered by their shared West Point examinations, and their quest for greater efficiency in weapons production, engineers and ordnance officers developed accounting methods later adopted by private enterprise.[30]

Such unforeseen consequences were of little interest to those seeking to further reduce the army, now led by Tennessee Republicans John Cocke and Newton Cannon in the House. As Secretary of State Adams observed: "Individual personal jealousies, envies and resentments, partisan ambitions, and private interests and hopes" fueled the mania for economy. When the Military Affairs Committee concluded (by a single vote) that the executive branch's implementation of the cutbacks had been constitutional, critics proposed eliminating most staff chiefs, the remaining major general, and one brigadier general, as well as consolidating the army into four infantry and two artillery regiments. Monroe's threat of a veto and Calhoun's demonstration that better War Department management had yielded considerable savings staved off these latest threats, but the secretary and General Brown both recognized that the army needed to do a better job in demonstrating its usefulness to American society. Brown addressed the issue directly in his General Order of June 1, 1821: "It should be the study of officers to cultivate intimate relations with society, and to attach the community to the interests of the army, by mingling, with circumspection and prudence, in those social channels wherein the sympathies of individuals naturally flow," instructed Brown. "The affections of the nation constitute the only certain and permanent basis upon which the military establishment can build its reputation."[31]

Fulfilling such a mandate would be difficult, for the fluid nature of the borderlands made the task of satisfying the public difficult in the best of circumstances. Despite the reductions, regulars were still expected to patrol the newly settled boundary with Texas, check intratribal fighting between the Choctaws, Cherokees, and Caddos, and wrest control of the fur trade from the British North West and Hudson's Bay Companies. As Michigan's territorial governor Lewis Cass insisted, the "moral effect" of the army's forts and roads could outweigh foreign influence and encourage colonization by U.S. citizens. But competing demands meant that the overstrained regulars could not be everywhere. "The truth," confessed Calhoun as he attempted to justify the decision to abandon Chicago (Fort Dearborn), "is that our military establishment is so small compared to the extent of the frontier, that I am often compelled to choose between two evils; and to select that arrangement which is not absolutely good of itself, but which has the fewest objections."[32]

Opportunistic western trading interests quickly capitalized on the War Department's diminished influence. In 1822, John Jacob Astor's American Fur Company flexed its political muscle by convincing Congress to end the government factory system, thereby opening additional Indian business to private enterprise. But if traders were to reap the benefits of more open markets, they needed protection against unfriendly Indians, whether that resulted from military conquest or diplomatic initiatives. The army's weaknesses during the short-lived Arikara War (1823) seemed obvious, when Col. Henry Atkinson admitted that much of the upper Missouri River region was "shut against our traders." Disappointed by the army's inability to stamp out the Arikaras, the Missouri Fur Company's Joshua Pilcher charged that Yankton, Yanktonais, Lakota, and Pawnee observers expressed "the greatest possible contempt for the American character." If the army could not conquer a peace, then alternatives must be found. Never shy about protecting the interests of St. Louis fur companies, Missouri senator Thomas Hart Benton (D) secured $20,000 to make treaties with western Indians. Escorted by nearly five hundred regulars, Commissioners Atkinson and Benjamin O'Fallon from the Office of Indian Affairs advanced up the Missouri in 1825 and concluded treaties with several peoples of the northern Plains.[33]

Attacks on the army and big government continued to enjoy considerable rhetorical appeals, but political winds were again changing. In March 1823, for instance, Congress appropriated $5,000 for a commission to study sites for a western armory. Calhoun had long advocated such a facility, citing cheaper labor costs and the considerable expense of transporting muskets from Springfield and Harpers Ferry to arm western state militias. In January 1825, the commission provided Congress with estimates for eight sites in Alabama, Tennessee, Kentucky, Ohio, and Pennsylvania, emphasizing "the deep interest felt by the people of the Western States." Indeed there was, as evidenced by the torrent of petitions and memorials to Congress. The Tennessee legislature recommended a position on the Harpeth River; citizens of Pendleton County, Kentucky, proposed that the canal, dam, and buildings needed for a working armory there could be had for a mere $230,000. A "large and respectable meeting" at Joseph Bartlett's Inn at Connellsville, Pennsylvania, emphasized the community's "proverbial" health and high-quality beef, pork, flour, timber, and coal. To highlight their "striking advantages" over rival Beaver Falls, residents of Tygart's Valley supplied an auxiliary report from a Virginia civil engineer. Paralyzed by the competition,

Congress failed to act, but the outpouring reflected the enormous appeal of military dollars.[34]

West Point could also promote national development. In 1817, West Pointers had represented 14.8 percent of the officer corps; by 1830, that figure had risen to 63.8 percent. "The institution is the hope of the Army; and it ought to be cherished," proclaimed Calhoun. Although the financial crisis had ended any possibility of establishing an additional school, the military academy boasted the best formal civil-engineering training in the United States, and under the stern hand of Superintendent Thayer its rigorous system instilled in most cadets a sense of individual accountability, duty, and national outlook. The science- and mathematics-heavy curriculum left graduates well prepared for popular civil-works projects. George Ticknor, a Harvard linguist and educational reformer who served on the institution's Board of Visitors in 1826, commended the "thoroughness, promptness, and efficiency in the knowledge of the Cadets which I have never seen before, and which I did not expect to find here."[35]

Similarly, the War of 1812 had demonstrated the importance of transportation to national security. To this end, Maj. Gen. Andrew Jackson urged construction of a military road from Nashville to New Orleans; in 1818, Brig. Gen. Alexander Macomb bragged that regulars were building a "magnificent" road from Detroit to the rapids of the Miami River. Secretary Calhoun aggressively promoted the War Department's road-building, placating a president still wary of federally sponsored improvements by characterizing such projects as being "decidedly of a military character." During the 1820s, soldier labor was responsible for nearly two-thirds of the 1,562 miles of military roads constructed in Alabama, Georgia, Florida, western Louisiana, Arkansas, and the Indian Territory. Contrasting the immense public works and fortifications along the Eastern Seaboard with the untamed western borderlands, Lewis Cass, now governor of Michigan Territory, argued that military roads "would produce an immediate and decisive effect upon the migration to the territory."[36]

Insisting that federal sponsorship of a system of roads and canals required a constitutional amendment, President Madison in 1817 had vetoed a "Bonus Bill" that would have used profits from the newly re-created national bank to fund such projects. Seeking an alternative, the House Committee on Roads and Canals turned to Crawford and Calhoun for suggestions. Crawford apparently demurred, but Calhoun, eager "to make the Army useful and popular," responded in early January 1819 with a proposal of visionary scope: army engineers could draw up a comprehensive plan for a network of roads and canals. Calhoun insisted that such a design would promote commerce and improve national security by enabling troops to reach threatened points more quickly. The clamor for roads and canals eventually trumping fears of big government, in late April 1822 a House committee urged army engineers to develop surveys for "a well-digested and regular system" of roads and canals. On May 4, however, Monroe vetoed a bill to repair part of the National Road (sometimes called the Cumberland Road), using most of his accompanying 25,000-word dissertation to insist on the strict interpretation of the constitution. Yet in a tortured addendum to the original draft, Monroe provided a loophole, allowing that he would not object to using federal monies to improve national defense, expedite the mails, and enhance the value of public lands for "the purposes of general, not local, national, not State, benefit."[37]

The army's thirty-two engineer officers had long responded to local requests for advice on public works, usually assessing the project's national importance as they did. Following a call for assistance on a canal through the ironworking districts of New Jersey, for example, Maj. Joseph G. Totten and Assistant Engineer Simon Bernard suggested dividing projects "made with a view to the general interest of the country" from "those on which the revenue is the principal object." The engineers were never shy about forming political alliances that would allow them to achieve their own ambitions while serving their country. Thus, Maj. Isaac Roberdeau maintained a direct correspondence with Tennessee's John Cocke even as the latter pushed to reduce the regular army, the major reassuring the congressman that his topographical engineers were "entirely free from all local attachments and prejudices." Pleased with Roberdeau's lobbying efforts, fellow engineer Stephen Long added: "I hope we shall be able to convince the public that we can serve them to advantage."[38]

A proposal to sponsor a survey for "a general system of improvements" died in 1823, but later that year Monroe recommended funding for a canal to connect Chesapeake Bay with the Ohio River, "a national object" that would promote commerce, improve security, and "strengthen the bond of union itself." In January 1824, Pennsylvania representative Joseph Hemphill, a former Federalist, took up the broader issue of federal support for internal improvements in the House. Speaker of the House Henry Clay added his support, reminding colleagues of the disparity between Washington's largesse along the coast and in the West, where "we have none of those public works, no magnificent edifices, forts, armories, arsenals, dockyards, &c., which more or less are to be found in every Atlantic State." After considerable debate—featuring especially vocal opposition from New York (which had completed its Erie Canal without federal funding)—the General Survey Act of 1824 provided $30,000 for military and civilian engineers to conduct road and canal surveys that the president deemed suitable. A month later, Congress authorized another $75,000 to the War Department for improvements to the Ohio and Mississippi Rivers.[39]

Over the next fourteen years, Congress would appropriate $424,000 for general surveys, plus more than $9 million for river and harbor improvements. To oversee these projects, Monroe formed a three-man (two army engineers, one civilian) Board of Engineers for Internal Improvements. Within a month of the General Survey Act's passage, the board had drawn up a list of twenty-seven potential canals, each rated according to its military and commercial significance. By the end of the year, surveys were under way for seven canals. Work on a road from Washington, D.C., to New Orleans, would come soon; as Chief of Engineers Alexander Macomb noted: "It is desirable that the Southern portion of the Union should not only see, but feel some of the immediate benefits which will result from a system of internal improvement." In his final annual message to Congress, Monroe pointed out that, through the identification of major transportation arteries, "the military will be incorporated with the civil," in the process eliminating "injurious distinctions and prejudices of every kind."[40]

The 1824 election of John Quincy Adams as president and Calhoun as vice president, with their enthusiastic support for public works and increasing the number of army engineer officers, tasted like fine wine indeed. Of the 708 West Point graduates between 1818 and 1838, 108 would be employed in duties with the Fortifications Board or in internal improvements. Even works that seemed at initial glance to be "purely of a civil character," such as roads, railroads, and canals, allowed an officer to immerse himself "in the practice of his profession, acquiring exact and persevering habits of investigation, improving his *coup d'oeil*, and gathering the most valuable information in relation to the capabilities of self-defence of the locality of the survey, and its ability to aid in the defence of other parts of the country," reasoned one engineer. "The Department continuing to heap work upon us as a miller fills his hopper until it runs over," gloated another satisfied officer as topographers plotted ways of maintaining a high public profile. Congressional delegations advanced a dizzying array of ventures. By 1827, the War Department was overseeing work on thirteen fortifications, a seawall in Boston Harbor, thirty-seven civil-works projects, eight surveys that enjoyed special line-item funding, and twenty others stemming from the General Survey Act. That same year, the Baltimore and Ohio Rail Road Company also applied for army assistance. Promising "the perfect willingness of the Department to accede to the wishes of the company," the new secretary of war, James Barbour, dispatched three engineering teams to advise the B&O, which adopted army regulations to improve efficiencies and evolved into one of the nation's most important railroads.[41]

Barbour's appointment reflected President John Quincy Adams's determination to use the federal government to influence national life, for Barbour, a Virginia-born former congressman, had opposed the army reductions of

1821 and embraced the new nationalism. Much like the president, Secretary of War Barbour supported Indian removal even as he insisted that the nation demonstrate restraint rather than "sordid selfishness." To better carry out its duties, Barbour supported Major General Brown's efforts to concentrate regulars in larger garrisons. "Small and distant commands," insisted the general, rendered military instruction virtually impossible and suggested weakness rather than strength. By late 1826, Barbour had thus transferred nearly seven hundred men to strategically located Jefferson Barracks, just outside St. Louis, where supplies were cheaper and river transport would allow quicker movement during emergencies. The new system received a stern test the next year, when Col. Henry Atkinson led six hundred regulars in response to a flare-up between Ho-Chunk (Winnebago) Indians and intruding white lead miners. Joined by militiamen and Indian auxiliaries, Atkinson averted further violence, but local demands for an army presence prevented the wholesale reorganization of borderlands positions envisioned by Washington planners.[42]

The death of commanding general Brown, along with Secretary of War Barbour's concurrent desire to trade his cabinet portfolio for the ministry to Great Britain, caused Adams much consternation in the final year of his presidency. Next in line to Brown were Winfield Scott and Edmund P. Gaines, but their incessant feuding over seniority had antagonized everyone around them. Secretary of State Henry Clay threatened to resign if Gaines were appointed, and Scott's biting criticisms of Gaines and Secretary Barbour (which flew in the face of the spirit, if perhaps not the letter, of his own army regulations) convinced Adams that he was unsuitable for command. Against the advice of his cabinet and the army's respect for seniority, the president in May instead named the chief of engineers, Col. Alexander Macomb, as the nation's ranking military officer. That same month, Adams accepted Barbour's resignation and, in a nod to political allies in New York, named that state's Peter B. Porter as war secretary.[43]

These controversies notwithstanding, the arm of the government—and the army—seemed to be everywhere. When relations between Georgia and the Creek Indians deteriorated, Adams dispatched General Gaines rather than a State Department diplomat to referee the crisis. The War Department oversaw arsenals in Massachusetts and Virginia, lead mines in Wisconsin and Missouri, and fortifications along the Atlantic and Gulf Coasts. Regulars garrisoned positions throughout the borderlands and provided a flexible tool for imperial advance; engineers compiled surveys for river and harbor improvements, roads, canals, and railroads; Revolutionary War veterans had become important cultural symbols. West Point was the "favorite institution of the nation," wrote one observer in 1826. "The time has past in the United States, when any just fears are entertained of such a standing army,"

Alexander Macomb. President John Quincy Adams's surprise choice as commanding general, engineer Macomb (1782–1841), hero of the Battle of Plattsburgh during the War of 1812, headed the army for thirteen years (1828–1841). This lithograph is based on Thomas Sully's 1829 painting. Library of Congress, USZ62-53013.

he continued. "The army is dependent upon the people, and is mingled with them; it participates in the same habits, imbibes the same sentiments, and regards itself in every respect as part of the great community." Of the army's surveys, Secretary Barbour proclaimed, "there are, probably, no expenditures of the government which come so directly home to the interests and feelings of the great body of the people of the United States, or which are viewed with more lively and unqualified satisfaction."[44]

Events proved both writers wrong, for growing numbers of Americans believed that the government had overreached itself. The champion of federally sponsored internal improvements, Adams had in 1824 won less than a third of the popular vote. Even worse, he had selected Henry Clay, who had engineered the election in the House of Representatives, to be his secretary of state, the traditional stepping-stone to the presidency. Cynics suspected that both men were using the new activism to promote their political ambitions. In a more general sense, the distributive politics of arsenals, armories, fortifications, internal improvements, garrisons, and expeditions rewarded some but not others. "I will not see . . . millions of dollars wrung from the hard earnings of honest industry, in the hands of this Government, be distributed in such places, and for such purposes, as may be selected by those in authority, under the delusive color of internal improvement," vowed House member (in office 1827–1831) William D. Martin (D-SC). The enormous list of public works revealed "the strife between Democracy and Aristocracy," complained another. Finally, the loose constitutional construction recently applied to internal improvements might be employed elsewhere—most ominously when it came to congressional authority over slavery. "If Congress possess[es] the power to do what is proposed by this bill," Virginia's John Randolph had warned during debates in the House on the General Survey Act, "they may emancipate every slave in the United States."[45]

Vice President Calhoun, who had long advocated a multipurpose army and sponsored the use of military engineers to promote internal improvements, now joined those who believed that Washington had gone too far. The process had become, in his words, "merely . . . the means of transferring the capital from one section to another." Having already broken with President Adams, Calhoun on April 9, 1828, cast a tiebreaking vote in the Senate against funding any new projects under the General Survey Act, charging that such works "might be made subservient to political combinations." As that session closed, an exhausted Congress settled on a compromise: the normal $30,000 annual appropriation was continued, but with the stipulation that it "shall not be construed into a legislative sanction of any examination or survey which shall not be deemed of national importance." Along with Calhoun's reversal, the latter proviso suggested the dawn of a new era for the regular army, which, as the historian Robert Wettemann explains, had in many circles become associated with privilege rather than equality.[46]

Chapter Six

Mr. Jackson's Army

Andrew Jackson, first elected in 1828 and styling himself the people's president, well understood the popular appeal of egalitarian rhetoric and criticism of those who used government to consolidate their power. In his first inaugural address, he proclaimed militia to be the "bulwark of our defense," pronounced "standing armies as dangerous to free governments in time of peace," and promised to check the corrupt machinations of the monied elites. At the same time, his own military experiences taught him the value of a disciplined army in advancing his vision of national security. As president, he thus depended on regulars to remove Indians, preserve order, and promote development; even as he promised a "strict and faithful economy," Old Hickory deflected attempts to abolish West Point, deployed army engineers in civic works, and oversaw the expansion of the regulars by nearly a third. Federal spending devoted to the army, which had averaged 40.5 percent during the recent John Quincy Adams administration, rose to 45.8 percent in the Jackson years.[1]

Jackson's handpicked successor to the White House, Martin Van Buren, also used the army to execute Indian removal and deter threats along the nation's northern boundary, supporting measures that increased the regulars' authorized strength from 7,957 to 12,589. The percentage of federal spending on army affairs was consistent with that during the Jackson years. Yet Van Buren, who as a New Yorker had witnessed his state build the Erie Canal without assistance from Washington, opposed federally sponsored internal improvements. With an eye to protecting himself against a revolt by the states' rights wing of the Democratic Party, he divorced army officers from their duties on civil works.[2]

* * * * *

In winning the presidency, Jackson overcame criticisms arising from two enduring themes of American popular culture: fears that an overweening general and chief executive might use the army to destroy the people's liberties, and the belief that militias provided an effective means of national defense. During the 1828 campaign, opponents had highlighted his having ordered the execution of six militiamen during the War of 1812. Editors of the *Daily National Journal* could think of no better means of censuring him than to headline one story "GEN. JACKSON IN FAVOUR OF A STANDING ARMY OF 100,000 MEN!" The *Journal* went on to claim that he had criticized "the militia—the bone and muscle of our country . . . as being 'insubordinate and inefficient!'" Similarly, the *Daily National Intelligencer* reprinted an editorial that had lambasted Jackson's opposition to the army reductions of 1821.[3]

To direct his War Department, Jackson selected men who shared his views on American Indian removal. His first war secretary was fellow Tennessean John H. Eaton, a War of 1812 veteran and senator since 1818. Purging the Indian Affairs office, Jackson within two years had replaced Superintendent Thomas McKenney and more than half of the fifty-six agents and subagents with men who could be relied on to aggressively pursue the expropriation of Indian lands. Upon Eaton's resignation in 1831, the president turned to Lewis Cass, the longtime governor of Michigan Territory, party loyalist, and War of 1812 veteran. While professing a desire to humanize the process, Cass also endorsed removal, declaring that civilized nations "have a right to extend their jurisdiction over tribes of savages living within their limits." Only by moving the tribes into "as favorable positions as possible," then exercising its "paternal authority," could the government save Indians from extinction.[4]

Accelerated white expansion won a significant victory in 1830 when Congress narrowly passed a new Indian Removal Act. Seizure of Indian land had long been a cornerstone of national policy, but this measure explicitly authorized the president to convince tribes to exchange their eastern homelands for sites west of the Mississippi River. In effect, it replaced the piecemeal removals of previous years with a more systematic program that enjoyed explicit congressional sanction. In almost every case, securing an agreement involved bribes, misunderstood promises (or outright lies), threats of military force, and the exploitation of intratribal factions. In the absence of any other bureaucracy to handle the complicated task, Jacksonians turned to the regulars.[5]

Indian removal highlighted the army's institutional strengths and weaknesses. In 1830, for example, nine companies—roughly 10 percent of the army—ejected five hundred white trespassers from Creek lands in Georgia. The blatant disorder, fraud, and inhumanity of expropriation offended the genteel sensibilities of most commissioned personnel associated with the ugly task. Infuriated by the underhanded activities of local officials during the subsequent Cherokee removal of 1836, Col. John E. Wool exploded: "The duty I have to perform is far from being pleasant and only made tolerable with the hope that I may stay cruelty and injustice and assist the wretched and deluded beings called Cherokees, who are only the prey of the most profligate and the most vicious of the white men." Maj. Sylvester Churchill believed that the presence of a regular army escort had at least prevented an

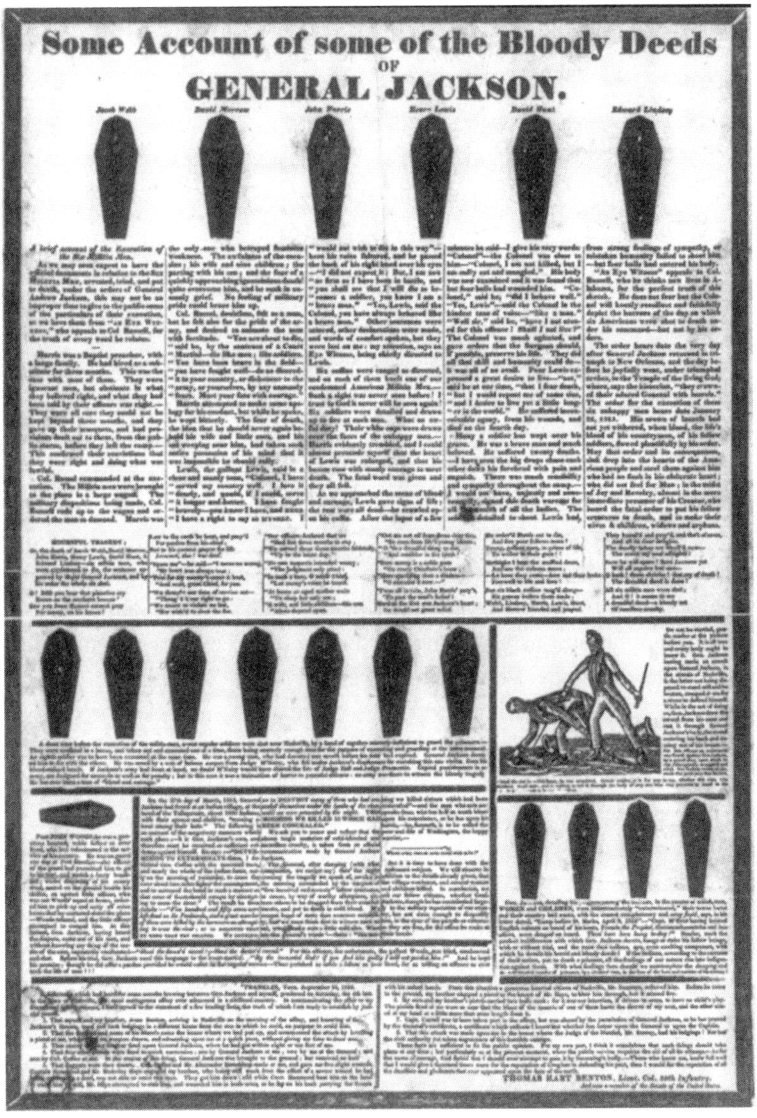

Some Account of some of the Bloody Deeds
OF
GENERAL JACKSON.

"Some Account of some of the Bloody Deeds of General Jackson." This well-known woodcut handbill featuring coffins of militiamen, soldiers, and Indians allegedly killed by Jackson was part of efforts to defeat his 1828 presidential candidacy. Library of Congress, USZ62-43901.

outright massacre of emigrating tribespeople. Enraged by the behavior of white Georgians, Brig. Gen. Edmund P. Gaines, the gruff old frontiersman, reportedly declared: "I tell these Indians the white people will cheat them out of their lands, get all their money and then kick them to hell!"[6]

Empathetic soldiers determined to uphold personal and national honor ameliorated some of the most tragic consequences of Indian expropriation. Yet few regulars accepted Indians as their equals, and the ad hoc nature of their assignments limited any ability to improve removal conditions. Moreover, the army lacked the vision and the planning capacity to smoothly transport tens of thousands of men, women, and children across long distances. Badly hampered by a shortage of capable aides and the incapacity of most volunteers to handle complex logistical questions, senior officers neglected to prepare contingency plans that might have eased the misery associated with Indian displacement. The three captains and seven lieutenants assigned to oversee the removal of more than 13,000 Choctaws between 1831 and 1833, for instance, struggled mightily to secure transportation, locate drinking water, establish and provision supply depots, and prepare roads for the three hundred–mile trek from Mississippi to Oklahoma. Finally, the army's ultimate accountability was to civilian masters who expected removal to be handled with a minimum of expense. So they did.[7]

To the north, the volatile mix of U.S. territorial expansion, white squatters, and intertribal rivalries threatened the delicate peace in the western Great Lakes region. On three occasions, Lt. Col. Zachary Taylor dispatched troops to expel white interlopers from the mineral lands at Dubuque (present-day northeast Iowa), and in spring 1832 Col. Henry Atkinson assembled six companies of regular infantrymen and more than a thousand mounted Illinois volunteers (including a gangly young captain named Abraham Lincoln) in hopes of averting a war between the Menominees and their Sauk and Mesquakie (Fox) rivals. In the meantime, the Sauk leader Black Hawk, an advocate of a pan-Indian confederacy and war captain of the "British Band," crossed the Mississippi River into Illinois with more than a thousand supporters. In mid-May, excited militiamen from Isaiah Stillman's Ranger battalion fired on Black Hawk's emissaries, and the resulting "battle" of Stillman's Run saw the rout of the panicky Illini.[8]

Black Hawk's followers found temporary refuge in the swamplands along the upper Rock River, launching raids into northern Illinois and present-day Wisconsin. When most of the volunteers went home, Atkinson delayed operations until their replacements could be shaped into a semblance of a fighting force. "Here was a fine harvest for the humorous," wrote one bemused regular of the newcomers, "active as a swarming hive; catching horses, electioneering, drawing rations, asking questions, shooting at marks, electing officers, mustering in, issuing orders, disobeying orders, galloping about, 'cussing and discussing' the war, and the rumors thereof." Despite the delays, the noose of fourteen companies of regulars, three thousand volunteers, and seven hundred allied Menominees, Dakotas, Ho-Chunks, and Potawatomies inexorably tightened. After a sharp fight between the British Band and volunteers at Wisconsin Heights, Atkinson caught Black Hawk's starving followers near the mouth of the Bad Axe River. The ensuing battle deteriorated into a massacre, with an estimated 150 casualties among the British Band. Thirty-nine women and children were taken captive.[9]

Black Hawk's War, and the resulting treaties with tribes associated with the conflict, confirmed U.S. domination of the Old Northwest. Yet the regulars had failed to respond in time to avert the crisis. Most companies were "too small for frontier service," observed recently promoted Col. Zachary Taylor. To make matters worse: "Whenever it is necessary to take the field, some of the men from each of the Companies must be left behind under various pretexts, but pretty much for the purposes of attending to families, gardens, & taking care of the horses, cattle, hogs &c belong[ing] to the officers." Once an outspoken advocate of the benefits of using soldiers to build roads and cut military expenses by tilling garrison farms, Colonel Wool eventually concluded that such activities hurt discipline, rendered military instruction virtually impossible, and served "to lesson that respect for the profession, . . . to humiliate the officers, [and] to excite popular prejudices against the army." Col. Abram Eustis, a thirty-year veteran, admitted that "abuses . . . pervade every branch of service." Officers were either "superannuated" or mere "school-boys, who, however much knowledge they may have, know little of men & things."[10]

Desertion posed the army's most serious problem. Twenty-five hundred regulars left the ranks without permission between 1822 and 1825; in 1831, the army estimated that a quarter of all enlisted personnel had done so in the previous twelve months. Some officers attributed the problem to the prohibition against whipping (abandoned from 1812 to 1833, when Congress authorized fifty lashes for desertion) and frequent presidential pardons of accused soldiers. Others believed that their extra duties in what Secretary of War John Calhoun had once trumpeted as "useful works"—road-building, post construction, tilling post gardens, and the like—drove soldiers to desert and rendered the remainder mere "hewers of wood and drawers of water." As did civilian society in an age that boasted some eight thousand local temperance societies, many tied the army's woes to the abuses of alcohol. "The men are so wicked constantly seeking occasion to drink & to get drunk," complained one lieutenant. In 1830, the War Department replaced the whiskey ration with extra cash and—to the delight of temperance advocates who suspected that soldiers simply used the extra money to purchase alcohol from private vendors—later substituted sugar and coffee for the supplemental payments.

But neither ending the whiskey allotment, nor an 1833 act that offered small pay raises, reduced the term of enlistment from five to three years, and held back pay for good behavior, did much to stem desertion, which plagued the army for the rest of the century.[11]

The absence of a mounted force further limited the regulars' effectiveness. As cavalry cost significantly more to train, equip, and maintain compared to infantry, Congress had abolished the last regular mounted units in 1815. Expectations that the federal government support expansion onto the prairies and plains, however, eventually loosened congressional purse strings. In May 1829, Maj. Bennett Riley and two hundred infantrymen escorted that year's Santa Fe trade caravan to the border with Mexico, then waited three months along the Arkansas River until the traders returned. "It was a humiliating condition to be surrounded by those rascally Indians, who, by means of their horses, could tantalize us with the hopes of battle, and elude our efforts; who could annoy us by preventing all individual excursions for hunting, &c., and who could insult us with impunity," recalled one veteran. "Much did we regret that we were not mounted too." Embarrassed by this feeble showing, the Jackson administration made a concerted effort to mount some regulars; pandering to western jealousies, Missouri senator Thomas Hart Benton (D) pointed out that horse soldiers cost but a fraction of the monies spent on fortifying the Atlantic Coast.[12]

The hostilities with Black Hawk lent further weight to calls for a federal cavalry. Even so, the distaste for regulars remained strong, and the House instead preferred to call up a thousand volunteers. Cognizant of the appeal of populist rhetoric, Senator John Upton (D-IN) proclaimed hardy Westerners to be more capable of securing the borderlands than men led by "bar room clerks" or mere "cadets from West Point." Having preempted possible criticism, Upton then pivoted, joining fellow senators in demanding something more permanent than transitory volunteers. In July 1832, Congress thus created the Battalion of Mounted Rangers, whose one-year recruits would supply their own horses, weapons, and equipment in exchange for a dollar a day in compensation. Commissioned personnel in the Rangers would enjoy the same pay and emoluments as those in regular units.[13]

The army sent the Rangers to areas it considered of the greatest national—or political—importance. Three companies were dispatched to Fort Gibson (Indian Territory) and two to the Michigan and Illinois frontiers. A sixth escorted the Santa Fe caravan. Yet the results were decidedly mixed, for rangers had no patience with the dull routines of military life. Though "smart active men at home, good farmers and respectable citizens," one civilian observed, "they seemed determined, to keep up republican equality, by acknowledging no superior." More significant, the Rangers cost twice as much to maintain compared to regulars, offending Jacksonian pecuniary sensibilities. With Congress embroiled in bitter controversies over the National Bank, House Military Affairs Committee chair Richard M. Johnson (D-KY) kept debate on army reform to a minimum. On the last day of its second session, in an act bearing the politically attractive title "the More Perfect Defence of the Frontiers," the Twenty-second Congress scrapped the Battalion of Mounted Rangers in favor of a more orthodox Regiment of Dragoons.[14]

Appointments to the mounted units revealed the administration's enthusiasm for using the army to serve its partisan ends. During the time he was a member of the opposition, Jackson had condemned John Quincy Adams's exhibition of "patronage & power" in commissioning officers; as president, Jackson seized on those very same opportunities. To command the Rangers he selected fellow Democrat Henry Dodge, once described as "a clever man, but not much of a soldier." Twenty-three officers in the new battalion were drawn from civilian life (seventeen from Missouri, Indiana, and Illinois), whereas only five came from West Point. The following year, the administration named Dodge colonel of the Regiment of Dragoons. Seeking a better balance between political patronage and professional expertise, Dodge declared: "I wish the Regiment [of Dragoons] to be serviceable to the country . . . by taking a part of the officers from the Regular Army who understand the first principles of the profession of arms [and] uniting them with officers well acquainted with the woods." Of the thirty-eight officers in the new regiment, twenty-three either came from the regular army or had graduated from West Point, and two others had attended the academy but never graduated. Ten of the thirteen former Rangers drawn from civilian life now commissioned in the dragoons came from slave states (four from Missouri); the other three hailed from Illinois, scene of the recent Black Hawk conflict.[15]

Regulars bitterly resented the civil appointments, which cost them long-overdue chances for promotion. In an anonymous letter to *The Military and Naval Magazine of the United States*, one officer dubbed it "a perfect farce." Capt. Ethan Allen Hitchcock, a West Point graduate who had hoped to secure a transfer to the dragoons, complained that "western members [of Congress] expect the appt. of western people. This is a most preposterous presumption—altogether a new ridiculous species of internal improvement." Gossip held that, in recommending a civilian to become an army paymaster, Vice President Van Buren had proclaimed that the successful candidate "had strong claims on the *party*, but drew his line through that hateful word and substituted government which is synonymous with Jackson."[16]

Others chafed at the government's attempts to use soldiers to regulate public properties. At the request of the Treasury Department, the Ordnance Bureau had in 1821 assumed responsibilities for overseeing lead mining on public lands in present-day Missouri, Illinois, and Wisconsin. Government regulation of such activities would ensure an adequate supply of lead for ammunition and seemed to promise steady revenues for the public coffers. In part owing to the stubborn protest of Senator Benton against what he believed to be an unconstitutional abuse of federal power, the army's efforts to regulate the Missouri lead trade never gained traction, but the 1824 appointment of Lt. Martin Thomas to serve as the Superintendent of United States Lead Mines initially seemed to inject new life into a struggling program. Annual lead production from the Galena, Illinois, district increased from 175,220 pounds in 1824 to 13,343,150 pounds in 1829. More than four thousand lead miners worked on the public lands.[17]

Lieutenant Thomas, however, was replaced in 1829 by Capt. Thomas Legate, who showed none of his predecessor's zeal for the project amid falling lead prices and skyrocketing regional food costs, which made some of the mineral lands more profitable for agricultural use. Moreover, army officers had no special expertise to offer other than routine management skills. That December, "Inhabitants of the Mining Country" (including the powerful Jacksonian Democrat Henry Dodge, who operated a smeltery in Illinois) complained bitterly over the 10 percent tax in kind required by their lease, adding that it was "dangerous to the rights of the people, for an officer of the government, to exercise powers not defined by law," a practice "unusual and unprecedented in this government." Legate, described by one political scientist as "inept and corrupt," had no interest in enforcing regulations against the politically powerful, and smelters had stopped paying their leases altogether by 1834. Legate was replaced by a civilian in 1836, and a decade later the government officially withdrew from its largely moribund mineral leasing programs in Illinois, Wisconsin, Iowa, Arkansas, and Michigan.[18]

Limited government and free-market protestations notwithstanding, many Americans welcomed the benefits of a military presence. Angry over the removal of the Fort King garrison, Floridians reminded Jackson "that we are an integral part of the citizens of the United States." A former territorial governor who better than most knew the value of federal investments, Secretary of War Cass proudly reported in 1831 that soldiers had built 1,902 miles of military roads. During Indian removals, army officers disbursed millions of federal dollars to pay for transportation and supplies, which the *Arkansas Gazette* confessed had provided "profitable employment" for the territory. Federal auditors set the costs associated with expropriating the Choctaws alone at just over $813,000 (roughly $24 million in 2018 terms). Anticipating the subsequent Chickasaw removal, three army officers contracted for 1.1 million rations (costing roughly $176,000) to be assembled at Little Rock, Cincinnati, and Memphis; shipping costs for the rations totaled at least $60,000 and storage facilities another $15,000–20,000.[19]

Alleghany Arsenal. Many American communities longed for the economic benefits they believed would accompany a federal arsenal or armory. This sketch, rendered by former Architect of the Capitol Benjamin H. Latrobe, accompanied a successful proposal for an arsenal near Pittsburgh. By the time of the Civil War, it produced cartridges, and an 1862 explosion killed seventy-eight workers, most of whom were young women. Library of Congress, USZ62-2987.

Similarly, a western armory continued to attract considerable public interest. The Ordnance Department estimated that establishing such a facility would cost $525,000, plus $65,000 in annual operations. Reasoning that Westerners deserved a bigger slice of the federal pie, the House Military Affairs Committee in 1834 reopened the armory debate. The outpouring of petitions, memorials, and resolutions suggests that citizens of the Jackson era believed that their voices would be heard, with Kentucky, Missouri, Mississippi, Indiana, Illinois, Pennsylvania, and Ohio submitting bids. Residents of Pennsylvania's Beaver County filed six petitions featuring 427 names and signatures, promising good rail and river connections, water power, the "best workmen at low wages," and "all kinds of artisans and mechanics." A memorial from Mount Carmel, Illinois, announced that the armory was "a matter of vital and increasing importance to us as a people."[20]

The army also represented a force for order. With the outbreak of Nat Turner's rebellion in 1831, the commander at Fortress Monroe sent three companies of artillery to assist militiamen in the affected area. Commanding general Macomb drew up plans for mobilizing troops against possible slave insurrections; from Louisiana, Gaines boasted that regulars had "contributed to dispel the fears of the inhabitants, and to keep in check the evil disposed blacks." During the nullification crisis, seven companies of artillery reinforced garrisons at Charleston, South Carolina. Brevet Maj. Gen. Winfield Scott, then commanding the Eastern Department, was also dispatched to the scene. Displaying his usual panache for mediation in all matters save those related to his prickly sense of personal honor, Scott helped to soothe local tensions between Unionists and nullifiers. That the Columbia *Telegraph* later denounced passage of an army appropriations bill ("an Army, employed as this one has lately been and is like to be, should not be permitted to exist)" serves as vivid testimony to the institution's role in preserving federal authority. And at Jackson's behest, the War Department in 1834 dispatched two companies of artillerymen to Williamsport, Maryland, where they assisted state authorities in suppressing labor protests against the Chesapeake and Ohio Canal.[21]

In addition, regulars remained a visible projection of national authority. In 1834, as one company of dragoons escorted the annual Santa Fe caravan to the Mexican border, most of the regiment rode out of Fort Gibson to "impress" the Plains tribes "with proper ideas of the power of the United States." The journey took a fearful toll among the green dragoons (of the five hundred soldiers involved, nearly a hundred died of sickness or accidental injury). "Perhaps there has never been in America a campaign that operated more severely on men and horses," admitted Colonel Dodge. Councils with Comanche, Wichita, Osage, Cherokee, Creek, Choctaw, Shawnee, and Delaware representatives, however, failed to make much of an impression. The following year, three companies under Lt. Col. Stephen W. Kearny patrolled the lands between the Des Moines and Mississippi Rivers. A second command, joined by a detachment of infantry, marched up the Arkansas River from Fort Gibson to forestall possible conflicts between Plains tribes and southeastern emigrants. Finally, four companies from Fort Leavenworth led by Colonel Dodge ventured 1,600 miles to the Rocky Mountains and back with the loss of only one man, meeting en route with the Otos, Omahas, Pawnees, Arikaras, Cheyennes, Arapahos, and Gros Ventres. Boasting of the expedition's "*extraordinary*" feats, Gaines judged that it had demonstrated the "*justice*, *magnanimity*, *humanity*, and *power* of our Government."[22]

Keeping peace throughout the borderlands—among Native American tribes as well as between whites and Indians—remained a major army responsibility. Many soldiers saw such duties as being in the interests of humanity as well as the nation; more often than not they were as fair as their class and racial biases allowed. "Constant and rigid deference to the dictates of justice," Major General Brown had ordered, must govern relations with

Indians. An 1832 letter from Gaines was typical: in disputes between Indians, "the calls of philanthropy and justice demand." The army should encourage agitators on all sides to make peace and "warn them at their peril to abstain from hostilities within our limits."[23]

Soldiers blamed most of the problems on white interlopers. "The white people were undoubtedly the aggressors, as is generally the case in all Indian difficulties," concluded one officer after investigating an incident near the Red River of the north. Whiskey smugglers posed a special nuisance, and attempts to check the illegal activities of white frontiersmen could spark expensive and time-consuming legal countersuits. In 1832, Capt. William R. Jouett, based at Fort Snelling, confiscated sixteen kegs of illegal whiskey from boats operated by an American Fur Company trader, who promptly sued Jouett for trespass. Although the captain won his case, his attorney charged him a $600 fee. A year later, while assisting a federal deputy marshal, soldiers under Lt. David Manning killed a white squatter in Alabama; in response, a local court indicted the lieutenant as an accessory to murder. Fearing for his safety at the hands of a civilian mob, Manning requested and was granted a transfer to "some other duty, out of the limits of this state."[24]

Confounded by the complexities and contradictions of the Indian trade laws, officers frequently clashed with civilian agents. "The want of system and regulation for the administration of this branch of the public service, has long been severely felt," Secretary of War Peter B. Porter had complained in 1828, "and has probably subjected the officers to whom it has been intrusted to more animadversion and censure than has fallen to the lot of any other public functionaries." After several false starts, serious reform finally seemed to gain momentum in May 1834, when Congress reorganized the Indian Department, updated trade and intercourse laws, and authorized the president to deploy the army to prevent intertribal wars. In a cost-cutting measure, however, the legislation sharply reduced the number of civilian employees, which placed even more responsibilities on regulars. In another major blow, the House of Representatives rejected what reformers had presumed would be a centerpiece of a new dawn of Indian relations: creation of a Western Territory with limited self-government for Indians. Such a territory, charged critics, might pave the way for the executive to establish military despotism in the West. With its defeat, however, any hopes for genuine change in the course of nineteenth-century U.S.-Indian affairs vanished.[25]

In early 1836, then–Secretary of War Cass unveiled a bold plan to systematize western defense. Supposing that a permanent frontier between U.S. citizens and Native Americans had been reached, separating whites and Indians seemed the best means of securing peace in the borderlands. To do so, Cass recommended construction of a military road from a point high on the Mississippi River (present-day Minnesota), south through Fort

Leavenworth (Kansas), and continuing to the Red River near Fort Towson (Oklahoma). As expropriation continued, Indians would be relocated west of the road. With this road system guarded by nine forts and regular dragoon patrols, the secretary predicted that it "would become a barrier across which parties of hostile Indians would be very unwilling to pass, as they would be liable to be intercepted by a mounted force." With the backing of Richard Johnson's House Military Affairs Committee, Congress appropriated $100,000 for the project.[26]

To the east, West Point's relaxed academic entrance requirements allowed men of modest means the opportunity to become officers. As the historian Ian Hope has noted, the academy served "as a great leveler, where talents of mind were recognized above status of birth." The lure of a free education also made it a popular educational choice among Washington elites. Jackson once described it as "the best school in the world," and in his first annual message he lauded the institution "as one of our safest means of national defense." His nephew and ward, Andrew Jackson Donelson, graduated from the academy (as did Donelson's brother, Daniel), and the general hoped that Lyncoya, an Indian who he had adopted following the Creek War, would also attend. Abraham Van Buren, son of the future president, graduated from West Point in 1827. The son of Jackson's Postmaster General followed suit three years later. Henry Clay's son graduated in 1831; George Washington Cass, Jr., nephew of the war secretary, did so the following year. John C. Calhoun's son Patrick graduated in 1841, and legislators like Representative James K. Polk (D-TN) assiduously solicited appointments for their constituents.[27]

Yet the relationship between Washington and the academy on the Hudson was fragile. Modest entrance standards were offset by a rigorous math and science curriculum, and the high attrition (only 40–50 percent of a class typically graduated) and the politicized appointment process sparked considerable jealousy. Critics accused West Point graduates of "amusing themselves through the country" in works of internal improvement; assertions that the military academy privileged the rich and powerful remained a potent force in American political life, a charge compounded by the army's stubborn reluctance to commission qualified enlisted personnel. In 1830, the embittered former superintendent, Alden Partridge, published a scathing condemnation of the institution whose "military dandies" prevented common men from becoming officers. Representative Charles A. Wickliffe (D-PA) deemed it a monopoly closed to all save "the wealthy and politically influential." Tennessee's colorful David Crockett (W) attacked it as "not only aristocratic, but a downright invasion of the rights of the citizen." In January 1834, a measure to abolish West Point mustered 87 out of 189 votes cast; two months later came another effort to suspend House rules to allow the full body to consider a select committee's blistering attack. Although friends of the academy fended off the challenges, the protests reflected the intensifying populist resentment.[28]

Amid such inflammatory rhetoric, differences between the White House and Superintendent Sylvanus Thayer boiled over. Whereas Thayer insisted on enforcing iron discipline, Jackson's inner circle was more prone to forgive cadet misdeeds (one of which involved the planting of a hickory pole on the parade grounds). Thayer complained in February 1832: "The President . . . is in the habit of dispensing with the most important regulations of the Academy in favor of his friends." Fed up with the interference, Thayer resigned from the superintendency eleven months later. His insistence on standardization, order, and academic rigor was firmly implanted in West Point culture, but word of Jackson's meddling spread like wildfire. "The evils flowing from this case have not been confined to the cadets," wrote Chief Engineer Charles Gratiot, "& a spirit of criticism of the general & local administration of the affairs of the academy, subversion of discipline & good order, has become so prevalent, as to be the subject of common remark in the bar-rooms and other public places." Although Jackson eventually admitted that his interference had hurt the institution, his actions added to the backlash from regular officers against his administration.[29]

Jackson's populist rhetoric extended to internal improvements. As the historian Charles Seller argues, Jacksonians saw an "active capitalist state" stemming from a centrally planned transportation system and a Second National Bank as endangering premarket liberties and equality. Jackson evinced his most famous opposition to internal improvements in his March 1830 veto of the Maysville Road Bill, when he insisted that federal support for projects "of purely local character" would foster corruption by encouraging a "scramble for appropriations." His desire, the president explained later, was to reestablish "equality in the condition of the people."[30]

But Jackson's rhetoric often differed from the actual practices of his administration, for he used the army to aid roads, railroads, canals, navigation improvements, and coastal defenses on a scale as grand as John Quincy Adams. Having long supported increasing the number of engineers, Jackson continued to do so throughout his presidency. In addition to the twenty-two engineers (who focused on fortifications and navigation projects) and ten topographers (who worked on internal improvements) in the Corps of Engineers, four dozen other officers were typically reassigned from their line units, along with at least a dozen civilians. Annual appropriations for harbor enhancements, which had averaged $187,650 (roughly $5.2 million at time of publication) during the Adams administration, ballooned to more than $400,000 during Jackson's two terms. By 1835, soldiers were assisting eleven railroads, two canals, two roads, and two river surveys, in addition to their longer-term assignments on the Potomac Aqueduct, the U.S. Coastal Survey, harbor improvements, and coastal fortifications. "There is no peace for the wicked," quipped one engineer.[31]

Traditionally, army engineers had taken considerable pains to connect their projects with national concerns. Canals in the Mississippi River Delta designed to encourage sugarcane production, for example, would "render our population still less dependent on foreign markets." The three-man Board of Engineers for Internal Improvements explored various means of systematizing these plans, and their surveys featured the best that early nineteenth-century science had to offer. But such a board, whose appointed experts sought to centralize control over the army's civilian works projects, seemed the antithesis of freewheeling Jacksonian democracy, and the administration's June 1831 decision to place the Topographical Engineers under a separate bureau in the War Department (which separated them from regular engineers and their navigation projects) removed any semblance of truly comprehensive planning for national improvements.[32]

Others charged that army engineers were cashing in on their associations with recipients of federal favor. Dennis H. Mahan, West Point's most influential professor, acknowledged that "the practice has . . . infused into the service a spirit of extra-duty-seeking which is often more liable to be swayed by a view to private interest than the public good." Making matters worse, engineers often lost sight of practical economics. Perhaps most important, an experienced soldier like Jackson knew that the prolonged absence of officers from their units hurt discipline, a point he emphasized in two annual messages. A May 1833 directive thus prohibited officers from visiting Washington, D.C., without the commanding general's permission. Their absence from their proper stations had "been injurious to the public service" and negatively impacted "public opinion."[33]

In 1835–1836, a revolution in Texas threatened to involve the United States in a shooting war. Fearing that the conflict between Texans and the Mexican government of Antonio López de Santa Anna would spill over into Louisiana, Western Department commander Gaines called on the governors of Arkansas, Louisiana, Mississippi, Tennessee, and Alabama to mobilize volunteers and moved his headquarters from Memphis to Natchitoches, Louisiana. Although officers were instructed to observe strict neutrality, more than a hundred deserters from the United States Army joined the Texas ranks. Responding to calls from newly independent Texas for assistance against a potential Indian uprising in late 1836, seven companies of regulars from Fort Towson crossed the Sabine River and occupied Nacogdoches for several weeks. Cautioned by the president not to intervene, Gaines exacerbated the problem by allying himself with anti-Jackson partisans in Tennessee. But war did not come, for Gaines, despite his unabashed sympathies for

American expatriates in Texas, neither attacked Mexican forces nor violated his discretionary orders.[34]

Florida was a different story. An uneasy peace with the Seminole Indians there, complicated by white demands for expansion and fears that the tribes offered a haven for escaped slaves, was shattered on December 28, 1835, when the Seminole leader Osceola ambushed an army column under Maj. Francis L. Dade near the Great Wahoo Swamp. Only two of the 108 officers and men escaped with their lives. President Jackson dispatched General Scott, commanding the Eastern Department, to take over operations, but petty disputes regarding lines of authority between Scott and Gaines confounded efforts to assemble the men and supplies required for operations in the Florida Everglades. Scott's refusal to implement Jackson's suggestion that he strike the camps of Seminole women and children added to the warrior-president's fury at the lack of decisive military action, and the failure to crush fugitive slaves who had joined the Indians loomed large in the eyes of many white Southerners. "This, you may be assured, is a negro, not an Indian war," proclaimed Maj. Gen. Thomas S. Jesup in December 1836. "If it be not speedily put down, the south will feel the effects of it on their slave population before the end of the next season."[35]

As the challenges mounted, the administration lobbied for more regulars, but opposition to any national project that smacked of big government or privilege ran strong, especially in light of the army's listless performance in Florida and the bitter partisan struggles over nullification, the National Bank, and the Senate's censure of the president. "I must say that the representatives of the sovereign people are a pretty randy lot," wrote one officer after observing congressional debates. Deliberations on appropriations for coastal fortifications vividly reflected the discord. The South Carolina nullificationist Henry L. Pinckney complained that Americans "had enough of tyranny from the Federal Government." Asserting that the West had not received its fair share of federal spoils, Kentucky representative Albert Hawes (D) characterized seaboard defenses as "an organized system of plunder." Unable to agree as to where federal dollars should go, Congress killed appropriations for fortifications in 1835 and again in 1837.[36]

Condemnations of the army's association with internal improvements also escalated. House member Abijah Mann, Jr. (D-NY) accused cadets of entering West Point "with the secret design in their hearts of devoting themselves to the civil pursuits of society." Critics commonly asserted that army officers saw themselves as superior to the citizens they were assisting. A travel writer complained that army engineers "with white vests and pantaloons and an eyeglass dangling at the button hole of their coats" intentionally overstated cost estimates, the profits from which they shared with their contractors. Another charged that the superintendent of the Springfield Armory

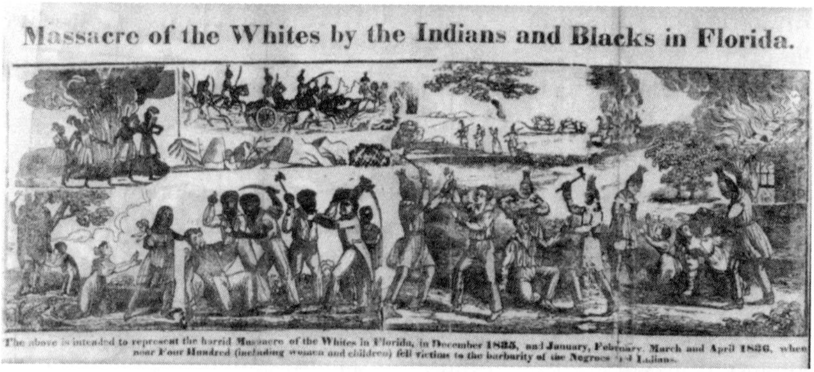

"Massacre of the Whites by the Indians and Blacks in Florida." Appearing in 1836 in *An Authentic Narrative of the Seminole War*, this wood engraving appealed to the racial antagonisms that fueled U.S. fears during the Second Seminole War. Library of Congress, USZ62-366.

had caused "political disasters to the friends of this administration." A third told Jackson that army officers and federal workers on the National Road "are all said to be political opponents of your administration, obnoxious to the people, and unworthy [of] the public confidence."[37]

Cognizant of the choppy political waters but desperately needing additional manpower to fight the war in Florida and to carry out the ethnic cleansing of Indians east of the Mississippi River, War Department officials in March 1836 unveiled a plan to raise the regular force from its legal limit of 6,301 enlisted men by nearly 60 percent. Balking at such a move, Congress instead created the Second Dragoon Regiment and authorized the president to raise a thousand volunteers for service against Indians. Accepting half a loaf, the administration feasted on the political spoils offered by the new dragoons. Col. David E. Twiggs, a twenty-four-year veteran of regular service, was shifted from the Fourth Infantry to take command, but thirty of the remaining thirty-three openings for officers came from civilian life. Particularly galling to graduates of West Point, four of the newly commissioned personnel had failed to complete their studies there. The appointments also reflected a strong sectional bias, with twenty-four coming from the South (including five from Missouri).[38]

In addition to demonstrating the Jacksonian distribution of federal patronage, the refusal to reward more regulars with assignments to the new mounted regiment reflected the administration's growing dissatisfaction with the army. Jackson suspected that "the Tyranny of a monied aristocracy" infected some commissioned personnel, and the savage punishment meted out to enlisted personnel for minor offenses rightly offended his egalitarian sensibilities. Charges that West Pointers used their government-sponsored educations to further their private interests also had merit. In a particularly egregious example of the marriages between public and private interests, Capt. James D. Graham (an 1817 graduate of West Point), who had surveyed a route for the Alabama, Florida and Georgia Railroad, was also listed as the company's engineer under its president, William H. Chase, a fellow West Point graduate (class of 1815). Disgruntled by low pay and slow promotion and attracted by lucrative private offers for their engineering talents, officers began resigning in droves, from 15 in 1830 to 117 in 1836 (an astonishing 18 percent of all commissioned personnel). Facing chronic manpower shortages in the contested Southeast, the Adjutant General on June 28, 1836, again attempted to force officers to return to their regular stations. When that failed to do the trick, another missive came in October, featuring Jackson's ultimatum that "this condition of the Army must no longer be permitted to exist."[39]

With the war against the Seminoles showing no signs of ending, removal of the Creeks and Cherokees further tested relations between President Jackson and the army's high command. Eager to disassociate himself from the quagmire in Florida, Scott avoided open warfare with the Creeks through a massive show of military force. Regulars blamed the troubles on the unprincipled actions of local "land speculators and defrauders." In June 1836, the administration dispatched Inspector General John E. Wool to expedite the expropriation of the Cherokees. Wool soon concluded that unscrupulous whites represented the greatest danger to peaceful dispossession and public order. Proclaiming that the Indians "look to the military and the military alone" for justice, he clashed with civilian commissioners and had the temerity to suggest that the 1835 Treaty of New Echota, whereby a nondescript group of Cherokee leaders agreed to relocate west to Indian Territory (and upon which the administration's policy depended), might be fraudulent. Brooking no protests, the War Department ordered the arrest of any officer who might "countenance resistance or opposition to the treaty." Stung by what he later described as the "degrading orders of the President of the United States," Wool switched his political allegiances to Whig and, after several requests for a transfer, was finally replaced in May 1837. Censured by the Alabama legislature for violating the property of white citizens, Wool demanded a court of inquiry, whose four officers implicitly challenged the administration's handling of the crisis by vindicating the general's actions.[40]

Wool's successors in overseeing Cherokee operations, Col. William Lindsay and General Scott, shared their predecessor's ethical quandaries. But when the time for final Indian removal came in May 1838, the army duly rounded up 11,000 Cherokees and moved them to temporary deportation camps. To avoid the malaria season, the long trek to Oklahoma was delayed until October. Short of food and medical supplies, perhaps a thousand

Cherokees died in the camps. In contrast to the earlier Choctaw removal, the army did not manage this final removal to the West. That task fell to John Ross and other Cherokee leaders who, lacking the resources and bureaucratic expertise to move thousands of men, women, and children over two thousand miles through unfriendly territory in the dead of winter, had to endure the Trail of Tears, which cost another two thousand lives.[41]

As the Creek and Cherokee removals continued, the stalemate in Florida fueled support for an even larger regular army. Annoyed by the unprofessional squabbles between Scott and Gaines, President Jackson in summer 1836 had given Florida governor Richard K. Call, a former aide during the Creek conflict of 1813–1814, command of military operations. Call did no better, so Jackson soon replaced him with Maj. Gen. Thomas S. Jesup. An exasperated president described the inability of nearly five thousand regulars, volunteers, and allied Indians to catch and defeat several hundred Seminole warriors burdened with their families as "humiliating to our military character." Debilitating field operations, marked by occasional truces and savage if sporadic fighting, had little strategic impact. "They have literally out ran all that could whip them, and overwhelmed all they could whip," observed one disenchanted veteran. As usual, regulars bemoaned the misbehavior of civilian contractors, land speculators, and volunteers, as well as the failure of their countrymen to recognize their sacrifices. "This is a service which no man would seek with any other view than the performance of his duty," wrote Jesup. "Distinction, or increase of reputation, is out of the question." Overruling Jesup's calls for a negotiated truce, the incoming Martin Van Buren administration poured in more reinforcements and insisted that removals continue.[42]

By late 1837, Jesup commanded nearly nine thousand men in Florida, just over half of whom were regulars. Converging columns meant to force the Seminole to fight were too slow to be very effective. "We travel like gophers," confessed one discouraged officer. The army won a few hard-fought victories, most notably Col. Zachary Taylor's triumph at Lake Okeechobee (Christmas Day 1837), but a final military conclusion to the war seemed out of reach even as Taylor endured a firestorm of criticism for having had the temerity to reproach volunteers under his command. Reflecting the almost universal consensus among the dispirited regulars, Capt. George Nauman sighed, "God knows I am tired enough of Florida."[43]

To the north, violence along the Niagara River border with Canada compounded national security concerns. On January 4, 1838, officials in Washington learned that British authorities, seeking to check unauthorized foreign assistance to "Patriot" rebels, had destroyed the ship *Caroline* in U.S. waters, killing an American in the process. With no troops to spare, President Van Buren ordered Scott to go north and "use your influence" to prevent illegal border crossings. "Whenever possible," he must employ regular officers. Fed up with "peace societies, antimasonry, nullification, Mormon difficulties & abolitionism" (which he dubbed "'cankers of a long peace & a calm world'"), Scott privately muttered that "a good hot foreign war only could save the Union & our free institutions, by effectually curing our people of those moral distempers." But he harbored no sympathy for the "borderers" who might start a conflict without the sanction of legitimate authorities. Buttressed by Colonel Wool, Maj. William J. Worth, and several companies of militia and regulars, the general's adroit diplomacy soothed tensions, and his insistence that three thousand regulars were needed along the northern frontiers buttressed the case to increase the size of the army.[44]

Infuriated by the high number of officer resignations and the fumbled prosecution of the Seminole War, those opposed to the regular army, federally sponsored internal improvements, and perceived corruptions in Washington lashed out. "Standing Armies are a standing curse," complained editors of *The New Yorker*. "They consume every thing and produce nothing." A House of Representatives study revealed that actual costs of public-works projects often exceeded the "fallacious" estimates provided by army engineers. Citizens of Louisiana groused that work on the Red River raft (a series of log jams that clogged the Red River north of Natchitoches) was being done "for the personal benefit of the superintendent"; Indianapolis residents grumbled about the slow progress on the Cumberland Road. Taking his case directly to the president, another critic denounced "the enmity existing on the part of a large portion of the officers of the army, towards the late and present administrations." In addition to hiring too many Whigs to work on civil projects, most regular officers were "in the constant habit of sneering at the mass of the people."[45]

Despite fierce partisanship, sharp criticism of the Seminole War, resistance from House Military Affairs Committee chair James McKay (D-NC), and the administration's futile attempts to deal with the ongoing impact of the Panic of 1837, a bill to increase the army crept forward. Testimony that volunteers cost four times more than regulars helped, as did popular amendments to extend the required service time for West Pointers and to prevent army officers from working on civilian improvement projects. In the end, supporters of a larger army formed an unlikely coalition with those seeking to reduce the privileges afforded select communities thanks to the work of army engineers. In a key procedural victory that June, the bill's supporters, led by New York's Gouverneur Kemble (D), fended off a House proposal to eliminate a new infantry regiment, then trounced a measure abolishing West Point. Passed on July 5, the army bill of 1838 represented the largest augmentation of the regular army since the War of 1812. It created a new infantry regiment, tacked on an additional company to each of the four artillery regiments, increased the number of soldiers in infantry and artillery companies, added engineer officers, granted the Topographical Bureau's wish that it be separate from the Corps of Engineers, raised pay and emoluments, and augmented the staff. Finally, it obligated West Point graduates to eight years of military service (four at the academy and four after graduation) and forbade the employment of commissioned personnel on internal improvement projects. For this larger army, the new nationalism—in which a larger regular army might oversee a comprehensive program of internal improvements—had ended.[46]

Chapter Seven

An Uncertain Future

In contrast to Andrew Jackson, Presidents Martin Van Buren, John Tyler, and James K. Polk came to office either indifferent to or suspicious of the regular army. Van Buren admitted that his knowledge of military affairs was "very limited." A fiscal conservative and advocate of federal retrenchment, he insisted that army officers divorce themselves from the internal improvements programs that had consumed so much of their time during the previous decade. Tyler, a courtly Virginian who supported territorial expansion, fancied himself a representative of Old Republican values and defender of state rights, slavery, and a small regular army. "Our chief reliance must be placed on the militia," he lectured Congress in June 1841, as "they constitute the great body of national guards, and, inspired by an ardent love of country, will be found ready at all times and at all seasons to repair with alacrity to its defense." Similarly, Polk, who once promised to oppose "large standing armies of any kind," showed little regard for the regulars.[1]

Despite these presidential reservations, the army remained the federal government's most visible agent of expansion, whether that be the acquisition of new territory or the occupation of existing lands by U.S. citizens. Dominated by an increasingly institutionalized officer corps that enjoyed unequaled job security in middle-class society, most regulars, fired by ambition and what the historian William Goetzmann aptly calls a "self-conscious nationalism," backed efforts by white Americans to occupy the West. Privately, younger officers—most of whom saw martial accomplishments against a conventional enemy as their only means to fame and promotion—often expressed their willingness to enter battle. "Our swords are getting rusty in their scabbards," rued Cadet James Schureman, "and we want something to do to brighten them." But the overwhelming majority now acknowledged that expansion must come through a lawful, orderly process rather than the deeds of rogue, nonstate actors. As an officer stationed at Fort Towson explained in response to suggestions that he rush to the aid of newly independent Texas: "The people of Texas should be left to fight their own battles."[2]

Civilian officials had generally come to trust the army's reliability in implementing the will of the federal government. While disagreeing on its pace, the trio of modern scholars William B. Skelton, Robert Wettemann Jr., and Samuel J. Watson all emphasize the increased professionalization of the officer corps during the 1830s and 1840s. The shared West Point experience (64 percent of officers were West Point graduates in 1830) and codified Army Regulations encouraged officers to develop self-discipline and a shared corporate identity. By the early 1840s, the median career length of the lowest commissioned ranks had risen to fourteen years. More and more officers tried to separate their private sensibilities from their public duties and recognized that it was in their institutional self-interest to disassociate themselves from ever-changing party factions. "Should ever the army become a clamorous band of active politicians, it will cease to be that calm, deliberate, and faithful arm of government," explained one correspondent to the *Army and Navy Chronicle*. "It would be an armed mob, dangerous in its nature to the vital interests of the government, and subversive of the honor belonging to the profession of arms." West Point graduate Lt. Benjamin Alvord acknowledged that being sent to Florida might help him achieve his personal ambition through feats of martial glory. "But I do say, nonetheless, that my first thought in accepting the offer to come here, was that it was my duty professionally to do so," he added.[3]

Job security and the desire to avoid what they viewed as the less attractive traits of nineteenth-century American society kept many officers in the service. Despite the hardships of the Second Seminole War, newly minted Lt. Rowley S. Jennings proclaimed: "I am daily growing more & more fond of the army & conceiving a deeper & deeper disgust for those things most valued in the world, wealth, fame &c. . . . The army is a certain & genteel living." Frequently complaining of his lot, Lt. John P. Hatch nonetheless confessed that the fear of being otherwise unable to support his family kept him in the service. And Lt. Edward L. Hartz, dissatisfied with "the papers! papers!! papers!!! and red tape which constitutes the constant and most common enemy of our army," nonetheless took comfort in having a career that rendered him largely immune to the economy's periodic crises. He was, Hartz continued, removed from "the money changing, money bragging world . . . not in danger of losing my reward by the breaking of some treacherous bank or the failure of some individual employer." Having contemplated retirement, Lt. George W. Cullum also opted to remain a soldier. "Good quarters, good society, plenty of books, no fear of ennui, and when sick a good physician to attend me without expense. These are not the only advantages. I am associated with very intelligent men and my buttons are a passport to the best society everywhere."[4]

Yet the increased institutional loyalty did not translate to a universal adherence to professional ethics or principles. As Watson acknowledges, "professionalism was still a work in progress"; stressing a similar theme, J. P. Clark insists that officers of the post-1815 generation "subscribed to a guild-like conception of professionalism that granted all members some degree of deference and left those at the middle or higher ranks largely unfettered in how they practiced their trade." Sensational cases of irresponsible behavior by officers—whether fueled by their own personal weaknesses or inflated sense of honor—continued to color public perceptions. Even as he acknowledged that most officers treated him well, a British traveler observed "that drunkenness and gambling are but too often the results of their habits of intimacy with some of the settlers." Inspector General George Croghan, who owed his appointment to the influence of Henry Clay, Richard M. Johnson, and William Henry Harrison, long battled alcoholism and was, by admission of his sister, "disgraced by his habits." In a particularly spectacular example of tawdry behavior, Lt. John F. Lane, Fourth Artillery, accosted Representative John Ewing (W-IN) on Pennsylvania Avenue just outside the Capitol Building, apparently in retaliation for the congressman's critical remarks about a family member. Lane struck Ewing just above the left eye "with a slender iron cane, of less than six ounces in weight." The affair turned into a brawl as Lieutenant Lane, having satisfied his personal honor, remained largely on the defensive against Congressman Ewing's retaliatory strikes. A board of officers expressed its "deep regret" over a West Point graduate's having accosted a member of Congress but elected not to recommend a general court-martial.[5]

Some officers continued to make little effort to hide their political activities. Lobbying for personal or professional advantage included not only correspondence with government officials and representatives but also elaborate campaigns to secure favorable press coverage. Their party affiliations seemed evenly divided. Of the seventy-eight officers with known political preferences during the second party system (roughly 1828–1852), forty-one were Democrats and thirty-seven National Republicans or Whigs. Winfield Scott, named commanding general following the death of Alexander Macomb in 1842, housed political correspondence in his official military office and openly worked to become the Whig Party's nominee for president. Alternately identified as a Democrat, then a Whig, then again a Democrat, Brig. Gen. John E. Wool mounted a concerted effort to gain the Democratic nomination in 1852 and was seen by at least one observer to be a potential candidate as late as 1860.[6]

The majority of regulars nonetheless limited their partisanship to curious observation or private correspondence. In Washington, watching debates among the great congressional triumvirate of John C. Calhoun, Daniel Webster, and Henry Clay became almost compulsory. Still, most concluded that engaging in partisan politics was off-limits. "We must serve all parties," declared Brig. Gen. Edmund P. Gaines, "and in return we must expect *help* from all parties." Soldiers must be "free from all political and party prejudices," added Lt. Braxton Bragg; Cadet John A. Thomas believed that the president "should strike every officer from the Army List who engages in politics." Having earlier scolded a junior officer for allying with certain factions in Florida, Quartermaster General Jesup in 1842 and 1843 rejected entreaties that his name be placed on the Democratic presidential ticket. Capt. Edwin V. Sumner, commanding a detachment of dragoons at Carlisle Barracks, refused Pennsylvania lame-duck governor Joseph Rittner's [Anti-Mason] call to intervene in disturbances associated with the state's 1838 elections (the so-called Buckshot War), explaining that the controversy was "entirely a political affair," a position backed by the War Department.[7]

President Martin Van Buren's natural talents for party politics stood in sharp contrast to the career interests of most of the soldiers he commanded. Yet like so many of his fellow executives, Van Buren, once in office, found military affairs to be more important than he had formerly assumed. He had supported the big army increase of 1838, and several diplomatic crises along the Canadian border required a military presence. Always the practical politician, Van Buren awarded commissions to 102 civilians (43.4 percent of the total available positions) from 1837 to 1839, although an examination system for candidates reduced the overt partisanship of the process. Largely overseen by regulars, Indian expropriation consumed 11.5 percent of all federal spending between 1831 and 1842, and more than 40,000 Indians were moved west of the Mississippi River during Van Buren's administration.[8]

The most expensive of the removals, the Seminole War, continued to confound the government and embarrass the army. Having cost $50 million by 1840, the conflict affronted Van Buren's fiscal sensibilities, limited his political options, and offered fine rhetorical fodder for rivals. The army has "lost the confidence of the nation," screamed Representative William Montgomery (D-NC), who charged that officers spent their time enjoying "city dinners . . . sparkling champagne . . . [and] evening walks and dances" instead of serving in Florida. Former president Andrew Jackson admitted that "it has been a disgraceful war to the American character, and its army." Desperately seeking a way out of the quagmire, the usually sober-minded Col. Zachary Taylor even backed Florida territorial governor Richard K. Call's request to deploy packs of bloodhounds against the Seminoles. The bloodhounds caused the administration no end of grief and resulted in a public relations bonanza for abolitionists, who linked the army's prosecution of the Florida war to the conspiratorial forces of the slave power.[9]

For their part, virtually every regular in Florida advocated some form of negotiated peace. With sick lists claiming nearly half of those present, soldiers resented what they perceived as the ingratitude of their countrymen and the misconduct of civilians and volunteers. Florida was nothing but "a howling wilderness, the proper abode of owls and bats and snakes and centipedes and scorpions, and so up along to an Indian—savage things

"The Secretary of War presenting a stand of colours to the 1st Regiment of Republican bloodhounds." This 1840 parody, highlighting the use of bloodhounds during the Second Seminole War, was especially powerful among abolitionists, who viewed the tactic as chiefly designed to track down fugitive slaves. Secretary of War Joel R. Poinsett is with the flag; prominent Democratic editor Francis P. Blair is on his knees, showing the hounds a map of Florida. Library of Congress, USZ62-91404.

in a savage land," complained Assistant Surgeon Lewis A. Birdsall from his sickbed. "All is confusion, contradiction & humbug!" added Lt. Edward J. Steptoe. Lt. Andrew A. Humphreys dismissed militiamen as a "swarm of locusts." Scores of officers—including Humphreys—requested transfers. Col. William Jenkins Worth, who assumed command of Florida operations in 1841, admitted the "utter impracticality" of a complete military victory and convinced his civilian superiors to declare an end to the war in May 1842. Worth's replacement, Col. Josiah H. Vose, later rejected, "for the good of the country," a Washington directive that would have reopened the fighting. Less than 250 Seminoles were believed to remain in Florida; by army calculations, 2,833 of the tribe had been relocated to what is present-day Oklahoma. Deaths among the regulars totaled 1,466, of whom 328 had been killed in action.[10]

As usual, officers blamed politicians for their woes. "Is there outside of the penitentiaries an equal number of men as careless of the welfare of the country as in the present Congress?" wondered the Fifth Infantry's Alexander

Johnston. Lt. Montgomery Meigs denounced the Democratic Party's use of patronage; upon being transferred out of the capital, Capt. George W. Cullum was glad to leave "the scene of filthy politicians." Critical of Van Buren for commissioning so many civilians, the irreverent Cullum described his commander in chief as "his highness the famous Mr. Vanderfool, the hero of Kinderhook."[11]

Van Buren had initially offered the War Department secretary position to a Virginia party stalwart, William C. Rives, as a means of reinforcing his Southern political flank. When Rives rejected the post as insufficient to his ambitions, the president settled on Joel R. Poinsett. A South Carolinian noted for his steadfast unionism during the nullification crisis, Poinsett exhibited a keen interest in improving the army. Reforming the federal government had long been a Jacksonian mantra (the State and Post Office Departments had been substantially reorganized during Old Hickory's second administration), so Poinsett sought to do the same for his area. Within months of taking office, the secretary endorsed the creation of a separate Corps of Topographical Engineers, lobbied to renew appropriations for coastal defenses, called for establishing a national foundry and a western armory, and supported the 1838 army increase—taking pains to reassure Congress that such additions presented no threat to democracy.[12]

As his tenure continued, Poinsett worked hard to improve the army's efficiency. Although he failed to convince former superintendent Sylvanus Thayer to return to the military academy, Poinsett helped to secure funds for new construction at West Point, introduced equitation to the curriculum, and assisted with the creation of a new professorship of chemistry, mineralogy, and geology. In 1839, detachments of dragoons and infantry joined the Fourth Artillery Regiment for joint drills at Camp Washington, New Jersey, the most significant combined arms training in a generation. Poinsett also backed a proposal to establish a company of "sappers and miners" to improve instruction in field engineering and seacoast defenses. The secretary sent six officers to the French cavalry school at Saumur, dispatched another four-man team to study European ordnance facilities, and selected Capt. Samuel Ringgold to lead a new light artillery battery, which would later distinguish itself in the war against Mexico (1846–1848). With much justification, Capt. George H. Pegram, First Infantry Regiment, concluded: "We shall not get a better friend."[13]

Given Van Buren's lack of familiarity with military issues, it is ironic that Poinsett's War Department also undertook the most systematic peacetime security planning (other than that for coastal defense) in nineteenth-century U.S. history. A champion of internal improvements and the cofounder of the National Institute for the Promotion of Science and the Useful Arts (a predecessor to the Smithsonian Institution), the erudite Poinsett condemned as

Joel R. Poinsett. Secretary of War during the Van Buren administration, Joel R. Poinsett (1779–1851), a South Carolina Unionist and cofounder of a predecessor of the Smithsonian Institution, brought an unusual vigor and interest to the post. Library of Congress, DIG-pga-06456.

"entirely inefficient" former secretary of war Lewis Cass's plan for a north-south military road that did not include the Texas-Louisiana boundary. Such a road would be exposed to attack, argued Poinsett, who insisted that lines of communication be perpendicular, rather than parallel, to the frontier. Six or seven new forts should be built west of white settlement to protect emigrant Indians and to display U.S. power. Eight interior posts would provide points of refuge in case of hostilities. War Department staff estimated the costs of Poinsett's western defenses at between $700,000 and $900,000 (roughly the cost of one ship-of-the-line and one frigate). Although it enjoyed the president's backing, Poinsett's vision for western defense never gained much attention. Buoyed by the previous $100,000 federal appropriation, bureaucratic inertia, pressure from western politicians, and the support of Quartermaster General Jesup, soldiers continued their work on surveys and roads linked to the original Cass proposal. By the time of the plan's completion in 1845, however, the inexorable expansion of non-Indians had rendered the defenses obsolete.[14]

Not to be outdone was Brig. Gen. Edmund P. Gaines, commander of the Western Division. A veteran of four decades of borderlands service, Gaines proposed erecting eleven massive square fortresses—each capable of quartering fifteen companies of soldiers and protected by stone or brick walls sixteen feet high and four feet thick, and studded by two powerful towers at the opposite corners—to guard the frontier from Minnesota to Texas. Four thousand miles of railroads should be laid to connect these positions with the rest of the country. For $50 million (he later increased it to $64 million), Gaines promised a system capable of defeating all enemy threats in the interior West for the remainder of the century. Dismissed as impractical, his grandiose plans were quietly relegated to the War Department's files.[15]

Renewed turbulence along the Canadian frontier evoked an even broader flurry of strategic planning. Longstanding disputes between the United States and Britain erupted into violence in the winter of 1838–1839, when lumberjacks clashed in the Aroostook River region. Maine and New Brunswick both called up militiamen and arrested rival civilian officers. Scott, then in Vermont as he continued to try to smooth tensions stemming from the patriot outbreak, hustled back to Washington for emergency meetings with Van Buren. On March 3, the last day of the Twenty-sixth Congress, that body appropriated $500,000 for northern defenses and, in case the crisis worsened, authorized the president to call up 50,000 militiamen and augment existing naval forces to the tune of another $10 million.[16]

Four days later, Secretary of War Poinsett ordered his staff to draw up contingency plans for a war with Britain. The disjointed responses of the tiny bureaus, immersed in the minutia of daily operations, reflected poorly on the army's preparedness for conflict. The day after meeting with Poinsett, Inspector General Croghan whipped out a short response, which assumed "as a premise that irregulars at no time [are] to be confidently relied on, [and] are deplorably inefficient in all offensive movements entrusted to themselves alone." Commissary General George Gibson followed with a similar warning the next day. Taking the matter more seriously, Jesup submitted a fourteen-page report, supplemented by a ten-page appendix. If the nation went to war with Britain, advised Jesup, it should be a fight "for nothing short of the commercial and naval supremacy of the globe." Col. John J. Abert, leading the Corps of Topographical Engineers, cautioned "that our efforts must of necessity . . . be unequivocally defensive." Adjutant General Roger Jones also ruled out immediate offensive operations but urged that the nation assemble militiamen along the Canadian frontier to make it "*appear*" that an attack was forthcoming. Chief of Ordnance George Bomford offered a plan for using regular officers to train militiamen and volunteers, rounding out his report with a detailed accounting of the nation's manufacturing capacity, which could produce 250 cannons and five thousand small arms every month. Scornful of any bookish Washington competitors, General Gaines weighed in with at least four missives of his own, lambasting "the outrageous conduct" of his army rivals and suggesting the construction of three ironclad floating batteries to protect the Mississippi River outlets to the Gulf of Mexico. In addition, Gaines offered to march against Quebec with 50,000 volunteers from "the two great military states" of Kentucky and Tennessee. Another floating battery could block the St. Lawrence and force Canada's surrender.[17]

In the absence of any strategic consensus, Van Buren continued to rely on Winfield Scott, who emerged as a key administration lobbyist among congressional Whigs. Appropriations for defending the Canadian border included a secret fund that the general used to develop a network of spies and sources designed "to *prevent* the mischief" and to ferret out threats "of a warlike, marauding, or incendiary character." Under the watchful supervision of the senior officer on the scene, Brig. Gen. John E. Wool, regulars dispatched to the Canadian boundary stood firm for "preserving order and quiet" against those who threatened the peace. "The history of this strange affair," observed one Vermonter, "will show what can be effected through the vigilance and promptness of our experienced military officers." The administration's faith paid off as regulars gained the confidence of local authorities and Scott worked with his British counterpart, Sir John Harvey, to tamp down the crisis. Three years later, the Webster-Ashburton Treaty formally settled the dispute.[18]

Secretary Poinsett also proposed substantive militia reform, which had eluded every previous president. Knowledgeable observers recognized the difference between the citizen-soldier of myth and reality. "The militia system of our state is in a miserable condition," acknowledged the quartermaster general of Illinois. As one English onlooker explained, infrequent militia drills were "a perfect farce." Bent on improving the system, Poinsett unveiled his recommendations in November 1839. In place of the phantom militias, which theoretically numbered 1.5 million men, Poinsett envisioned a genuine force of 200,000 divided into active and reserve categories. Active militiamen would undergo mandatory drills for four years, then be rotated on a rolling basis into the reserves for a similar period. Regular officers would oversee training.[19]

Poinsett's reality-based proposals challenged cherished traditions, and

"The New Era or the Effects of a Standing Army." Poinsett's plans for militia reform brought about widespread criticism that it would produce a tyrannical military. In this 1840 cartoon, uniformed soldiers are seizing civilians; the second soldier from the left says, "The bayonet is the instrument what we use old boy." Also note the assembled bloodhounds in the background, a reminder of another public-relations disaster. Library of Congress, USZ62-91424.

Whig propagandists joined conservative Democrats in pouncing on the scheme. The *Raleigh Register and North Carolina Gazette* denounced it as "RECOMMENDING A STANDING ARMY OF ONE HUNDRED THOUSAND MEN!!!" The *Natchez Daily Courier* claimed that Poinsett's plan would provide the president with a huge standing army, warning "that short would be the life of liberty, if an ambitious and unscrupulous Chief Magistrate should ever have at his command, a body of soldiery." By May, Democrats admitted that Poinsett's proposal was hurting Van Buren's reelection chances. "Even if it were sound policy to organize the Molitia," wrote one, "our people hate to muster and will oppose any thing of the kind. . . . The sooner the Molitia Bill is buried the better." Thomas Ritchie, head of the Democratic Committee of Virginia and longtime editor of the *Richmond Enquirer*, warned of the devastating political effects of a measure widely perceived as "tyrannical and oppressive."[20]

As the 1840 elections neared, Whigs smelled blood as Democrats vainly attempted to disavow Poinsett's reforms. "SKULKING AND DODGING—THE ARMY SCHEME," screamed a headline in one Virginia newspaper. The *Cleveland*

Daily Herald condemned Van Buren's "smooth disclaimers" of "Poinsett's monstrous Army project." Whig speakers broadened the attack to include the administration's mishandling of Indian removal and the Second Seminole War. "No plan was ever so misrepresented as yours," rued one correspondent to Poinsett. Ritchie ascribed the Whig victory in early Virginia elections to the militia debacle; in a telling reminder of the continuing power that fears of a large standing army had in American politics, Horace Greeley's opposition newspaper, *The Log Cabin*, led its October 24 edition with a denunciation of the plan "endorsed by the President for drafting 200,000 men from the Militia of the several States." Likening Poinsett's militia to a Praetorian Guard that would oppress the people's liberties, Greeley used selective quotations from the Army Regulations to highlight the executive's military power.[21]

Ultimately, William Henry Harrison's triumph in the 1840 presidential race reflected the public's ambiguous views of the regular army and military affairs. As a young man, Harrison had been an officer for seven years before resigning to pursue more promising opportunities in government and politics. While governor of the Northwest Territory, he had attacked a nascent Indian confederacy in the Battle of Tippecanoe; appointed a general at the outset of the War of 1812, he recaptured Detroit and defeated a mixed British-Indian force at the Battle of the Thames. Although Harrison was born to Virginia aristocracy (his father had signed the Declaration of Independence), Whigs successfully marketed him as a frontier warrior from a log cabin who drank hard cider, rather than as a regular army officer. "What a grand channel the Army is to the Presidency!" marveled Capt. John R. Vinton. Whereas Americans distrusted politicians, as the captain recognized, "old generals stand forth for the country and not for a party, and the people take them up with confidence & even enthusiasm."[22]

Upon Harrison's death just a month after taking office, John Tyler acceded to the presidency. Consistent with his belief in the limited reach of federal authority, Tyler on four occasions rejected appeals from Rhode Island governor Samuel W. King (W) to dispatch troops to fend off Thomas Wilson Dorr's challenge to the state's outdated colonial charter. Early in the controversy, the War Department had doubled the garrison at Fort Adams to four companies, but only when the post commander indicated that a display of regulars was needed to prevent an armed confrontation between state militia and Dorr's insurgents did the president authorize troops to occupy Providence and "defend that city from assault." Fortunately, passions cooled before the regulars deployed; some Democrats in Rhode Island excoriated Tyler for what they believed to have been his unconstitutional intervention, but the United States Supreme Court ruled that he had acted legally in its *Luther v. Borden* decision.[23]

"Matty's perilous situation up Salt River." Another cartoon of the 1840 election in which Martin Van Buren (*right*) is neck-deep in treacherous political waters. Among the boxes weighing him down is one marked "Standing Army of 200,000 Men." William Henry Harrison is rowing atop a barrel of hard cider. Library of Congress, USZ62-91413.

In an administration marked by frequent cabinet turnover, Tyler had four war secretaries. Harrison had appointed Tennessee's John Bell, who joined several other holdovers in resigning in protest to Tyler's vetoes of popular Whig legislation. John C. Spencer, a War of 1812 veteran and New York attorney, was an efficient administrator, but he shifted to the Treasury Department in 1843. The Senate refused to confirm the nomination of his successor, Pennsylvania Democrat James M. Porter. Porter's replacement, William Wilkins, another Pennsylvania Democrat, was noted for his support of Texas annexation rather than any military expertise. Whereas his predecessors had used the army to further the cause of territorial growth, Tyler saw more potential in the navy, especially for developing an American presence throughout the Pacific Rim. He also lobbied successfully for increased appropriations for coastal fortifications.[24]

By mid-1842, resolution of the Second Seminole War, warmer relations between the United States and Great Britain, and negative perceptions of regular soldiers (who still comprised 30 percent of all federal employees) opened the door for a new round of army cutbacks. Enlisted men were overwhelmingly recruited in urban areas (in 1840, for example, stations in New York, Philadelphia, Boston, and Baltimore accounted for nearly half of all enlistments), and many were immigrants. As such, they scarcely resembled the virtuous American farmers and citizen-soldiers of revolutionary lore. One officer admitted that the poor behavior of many troops seemed "to show that our ranks are filled with the refuse of the jail." Branding the standing army as "Day Police," leaders of an increasingly vocal labor movement characterized regulars as the tools of "landlords and capitalists" seeking to prevent honest workingmen from organizing. The mind-numbing drudgery of garrison life seemed to many the antithesis of the nurturing of entrepreneurs. Democrats also criticized the growing social chasm between officers and enlisted men. Anne Newport Royall's rambunctious magazine, *The Huntress*, insisted on "the absolute necessity for reform in both army and Navy—they are all officers—we mean a parcel of high fed, insolent upstarts . . . eating, drinking, and lolling about in silk gloves and silk stockings." That summer, the House and Senate Military Affairs Committees both recommended sharp cutbacks, and the resulting bill jettisoned nearly three thousand infantry and artillery privates, converted the Second Dragoon Regiment into a dismounted rifle regiment, abolished the office of Commissary General of Purchases, reduced officer emoluments, and eliminated several inspectors, paymasters, and surgeons. "A strict system of economy has been introduced into the service," proclaimed an exuberant Tyler.[25]

At the same time, Tyler championed expansion under the guise of American exceptionalism, once describing himself as "an instrument of Providence." Although Congress refused to sanction such steps, the president backed proposals to establish a line of military posts from Council Bluffs to Oregon. In the absence of permanent garrisons, dragoon patrols had ventured out from Fort Leavenworth in 1839 and 1840; three years later, four dragoon companies under Capt. Philip St. George Cooke were dispatched to protect merchants along the Santa Fe Trail. Just inside U.S. territory they encountered Jacob Snively and a hundred Texan freebooters. The aristocratic Cooke branded Snively's followers a "ruffian crew" and dismissed their commission from the Republic of Texas authorizing them to seize Mexican property as being in violation of "all the rules of modern warfare." Cooke's troopers disarmed the Texans, who scampered back across the Red River. The following year, dragoons escorted another merchant caravan without incident.[26]

Mounted regulars having proven their worth, Tyler in December 1843 asked Congress to remount the Second Dragoons. Enthusiastic Westerners rallied behind the push to enlarge the mounted forces, which the House Military Affairs Committee described "as an act of justice to our western people." Arkansas governor Archibald Yell claimed that 50,000 Indian warriors threatened the Southwest; several hundred citizens from western Louisiana signed petitions lauding mounted men as "the only species of troops that can give the permanent security required." Concurrently, army officials emphasized the high costs of militia and volunteers. Overcoming critics like now-Representative John Quincy Adams (W-MA), who condemned the "magnificent appropriations for both the army and the navy," Congress approved the bill by a comfortable margin in April 1844.[27]

The increase in mounted troops enabled the War Department to expand its forays into the Plains. As Scott announced in 1844, it was "standing policy . . . *to prevent Indian hostilities by the exhibition of military force on and beyond our frontiers.*" The First Dragoons conducted three expeditions that summer, with two more the following year. Capt. Edwin V. Sumner's two companies contacted the Wahpeton Dakotas; whereas Sumner tried to impress upon the tribes "that there was no part of the Indian country in which a criminal could not be reached," he acknowledged that their disposition was not "very friendly." Leading five companies and two mountain howitzers, Col. Stephen W. Kearny marched from Fort Leavenworth along the Oregon Trail to the Continental Divide, encountering several parties of Pawnees, Sioux, and Arapahos. Disinclined to establish a permanent post so far from what he considered to be civilization, and skeptical of the Midwest's agricultural potential, Kearny instead recommended strong mounted expeditions every two or three years to remind Plains tribes of Washington's power.[28]

Although federal spending before the war against Mexico represented less than 2 percent of the nation's gross domestic product, at a regional level the army remained an economic powerhouse. Excluding debt payments, 37 percent of federal expenditures had gone to the army between 1789 and 1811; between the War of 1812 and the war against Mexico (1846–1848), that figure fell only slightly, to 34 percent. As urban cores expanded, older military centers were sometimes viewed as impediments to economic growth, but Americans were usually happy to profit from federal dollars. Frankford Arsenal, established in 1816 just outside Philadelphia, serves as a prime example. Initially, locals resented the intrusion, only to become more appreciative as the depot became the testing ground for all gunpowder purchased through the Ordnance Department. In addition to security, western garrisons offered excellent markets for commercial centers such as Pittsburgh, Cincinnati, and St. Louis. On the Gulf Coast, demands for materials to erect seaboard fortifications fostered development of the brick-making industry at Pensacola. Hundreds of skilled seasonal laborers came to Key West each year to build Forts Jefferson and Taylor, and the government's lease of hundreds of slaves explained why the number of slaveholders there more than doubled between 1840 and 1850.[29]

Consisting of thirty-six officers when it secured independent status in 1838, the Corps of Topographical Engineers occupied an outsized influence over economic development, public policy, and the popular imagination. Its

Frankford Arsenal Steam Engine. The regular army's role in encouraging technological development is illustrated here in the specially designed steam engine, built by Philadelphia's Franklin Iron Works for that city's Frankford Arsenal. Library of Congress, DIG-ppmsca-39604.

head, West Point graduate Col. John J. Abert, was a clever veteran of War Department infighting, fiercely protective of his branch, supportive of transportation improvements, and anxious to foster western exploration. With the army's regular engineers now focusing exclusively on fortifications, his topographers assumed responsibility for navigation improvements, boundary and lake surveys, mapping and road-building in the borderlands, and projects in the capital. Accordingly, in 1842 Lt. John J. Frémont led an expedition to the Rocky Mountains that did much to reshape public perceptions of a "Great American Desert" into a more complex land of romantic possibilities. Handsome, flamboyant, and ambitious, Frémont benefited from the patronage of his powerful father-in-law, Senator Thomas Hart Benton (D-MO). Even at this early stage in his career, the lieutenant demonstrated a willingness to exceed his orders. In 1843–1844, a second great reconnaissance—during which he violated his instructions by venturing into Mexican territory—went all the way to Oregon. In the process, Frémont confirmed his reputation as the "Pathfinder" whose reports and maps would help to guide thousands of emigrants across the Oregon Trail.[30]

Seeking security, markets, and better communication, Americans continued to lobby their government for military and post roads, forts, and army garrisons. Between 1839 and 1845, for example, Iowa Territory secured

$60,000 for roads. Upstate New Yorkers petitioned to fortify the Canadian border, as did residents of Erie, Pennsylvania. Citizens of Platte County, Missouri, denounced efforts to replace local suppliers for nearby Fort Leavenworth with outside contracts as "injurious to the farming interest of the country." Arkansans were especially busy, with Democratic senator W. S. Fulton requesting $120,000 to improve southwestern defenses and the state legislature calling for federal roads to Fort Smith and the Red River. While they were at it, Arkansans also asked for $100,000 to expand the arsenal at Little Rock and fended off the army's repeated efforts to reduce or abandon Fort Smith. Not to be outdone by their neighbors, the General Assembly of Missouri demanded a military road from New Madrid to the St. Francis River. Four big new military posts, linked by a well-patrolled road, were also deemed essential to protecting the state's frontiers, as was a road from the mouth of the Des Moines to the Missouri River.[31]

Weapons production also remained a target of considerable jousting. Though bent on reducing federal spending, President Van Buren had backed a national artillery foundry, a gunpowder plant, and a western armory, all of which would "extend throughout the country the improvements which exist in establishments of a similar description in the Atlantic states." With local leaders sensing an opening, within three years resolutions, petitions, and memorials for a national foundry poured in from Virginia, Maryland, Vermont, Connecticut, Pennsylvania (five locations), New Jersey, New York, and Tennessee. Memphis city officials (who also wanted an arsenal and a naval depot) warned of the "disasters" that would befall eastern sites in case of a war with Britain; a "large and respectable" group that met at William Smith's hotel at Havre de Grace, Maryland, countered by reasoning that the devastation they had incurred during the War of 1812 "entitled [them] to the preference of the General Government."[32]

The deluge of applications for the western armory featured appeals from Alabama, Kentucky, Illinois, Indiana ("the sun shine of government favor has yet to shine upon her borders"), Ohio, Tennessee, and Mississippi (Vicksburg as well as Natchez). Seeking to cut the Gordian knot, President Tyler formed a three-man committee of officers whose 346-page report (a dissenting opinion of encompassed another 74 pages) supported a site on the Ohio River at old Fort Massac, Illinois. Predictably, the recommendation sparked petitions of support from nearby Kentucky, Ohio, and Indiana, all of which stood to profit from an armory there. But promoters of rival sites refused to back this competitor. In 1844 and again in 1846, frustrated by congressional sluggishness, members of the House Military Affairs Committee exhorted (unsuccessfully) their colleagues to support the proposal, emphasizing the need for "equalizing the expenditures" on national works—but to no avail.[33]

Amid the clamor for military facilities, War Department efforts to impose greater efficiencies at the Harpers Ferry and Springfield Armories continued to meet spirited resistance. By tradition, skilled craftsmen had dominated weapons manufacture. Workplaces opened at sunrise and closed at sunset, with armorers coming and going as they pleased so long as they met their monthly production quotas. Keener on maintaining their independence than in becoming cogs in a depersonalized system, many artisans worked part of the day in the armory, then spent the rest of their time farming or operating their own businesses. Frequent breaks for whiskey, conversation, visitors, and rough-and-tumble entertainment punctuated their schedules. The preindustrial culture was especially prevalent at isolated Harpers Ferry, where local politics and investments in slavery stymied development of the network of machinists who were fostering creativity and the exchange of ideas with Springfield. The arsenal's longtime superintendent, James Stubblefield, enjoyed the support of Virginia's political establishment and sympathized with skilled craftsmen who resented efforts by outside interlopers to transform their workplaces. Back in 1830, under sharp criticism from Ordnance officers and with the accession of the new Jackson administration in Washington, Stubblefield had resigned. The replacement appointee worked hard—too hard, as it turned out—to break the old system and was murdered by a disgruntled former employee.[34]

Despite such obstacles, the seeds of modernization slowly sprouted, aided by varying doses of entrepreneurial vision, government contracts, and habits of mind learned at West Point. Especially favored was John J. Hall, whose Rifle Works (which operated as a separate department at Harpers Ferry) served as a pilot plant for advancing the cause of uniformity in arms manufacturing processes. In the Springfield region, arms manufacturers like Eli Whitney, Simeon North, and Stephen Jenks employed networks of upwardly mobile machinists prodded by Ordnance pressure to exchange ideas, drawings, machinery, and patterns in return for contract renewals. Their mutual efforts made it clear that rifles and muskets could eventually be produced with largely interchangeable parts.[35]

Firmly in the hands of Democratic operatives, civilian superintendents nonetheless frustrated Ordnance officers eager to complete the uniformity of arms manufacturing. By enabling common workers to produce the weapons needed to safeguard American liberties, regulars were confident that they would encourage efficiency, and the Whig triumph of 1840 gave them their opening. In April 1841, seizing on President William Henry Harrison's denunciation of political patronage, they convinced Secretary of War Bell to replace civilian superintendents at the arsenals with army officers. Armorers and citizens of Harpers Ferry howled that, by introducing "rules revolting to the spirit of freeman," the new military managers had created a situation "unproductive of public good." A three-man War Department panel nonetheless endorsed the new military superintendents, condemning the "great looseness in the management" and "strong local influence" that had hampered efficiency under civilian regimes.[36]

Congress addressed the issue in 1842 during its drive to cut military spending. The Senate Military Affairs Committee recommended retaining Ordnance officers at the federal arsenals, claiming that doing so would increase efficiencies. Echoing the fierce protests from Springfield, the Massachusetts Whig Isaac Bates spearheaded a spirited opposition on the Senate floor, winning a preliminary vote by a 23–14 count. Aided by personal lobbying from Assistant Chief of Ordnance George Talcott, Military Affairs Committee chair William C. Preston (W-SC) convinced members to reverse course. As part of a larger compromise package on army reorganization, a House-Senate conference committee reaffirmed the military superintendents.[37]

The election of Democrat James K. Polk in 1844 brought another confirmed expansionist to the executive office. Democrats had demanded "the reoccupation of Oregon and the re-annexation of Texas"; less publicized was Polk's determination to also secure a foothold in California. Consistent with his past doubts about the army, his inaugural address advised that the nation must rely "mainly on our citizen-soldiers, who will be ever ready, as they have ever been ready in times past, to rush with alacrity, at the call of their country, to her defense." As had been the case for most of his predecessors, Polk's choice of New York's William Marcy as secretary of war reflected his determination to reward political friends and balance his cabinet rather than any special interest in the regulars.[38]

Though wary of Polk, soldiers naturally took great interest in the bellicose talk of expansion. A number undoubtedly agreed with Col. Stephen W. Kearny, who hoped that an international conflict might heal internal partisan divisions. "A War would tend to unite the feelings of our People & of our Public Men," wrote Kearny in 1842, "who would then be willing to put the Country in a state of Defence, when they will not do, in these times of Peace." Anxious to achieve glory for their nation and to fulfill their own martial ambitions, most regulars focused on a potential war arising from the quarrel over Oregon, as Britain posed a conventional threat of arms considered far more legitimate than Indians, widely believed to be "an unprofitable business" in terms of career advancement. Capturing this sentiment was William T. Sherman, a recently married artillery lieutenant. "War as such is to be deprecated," he told his wife, "but if it is necessary for the interests or honor of the country of course I may with perfect propriety rejoice at the opportunity of being able to practice what in peace we can only profess."[39]

The drums of war also beat loudly in the Southwest. Despite the narrow margin of Polk's victory, his election was taken as a popular referendum supporting the annexation of Texas, and a lame-duck Congress passed a

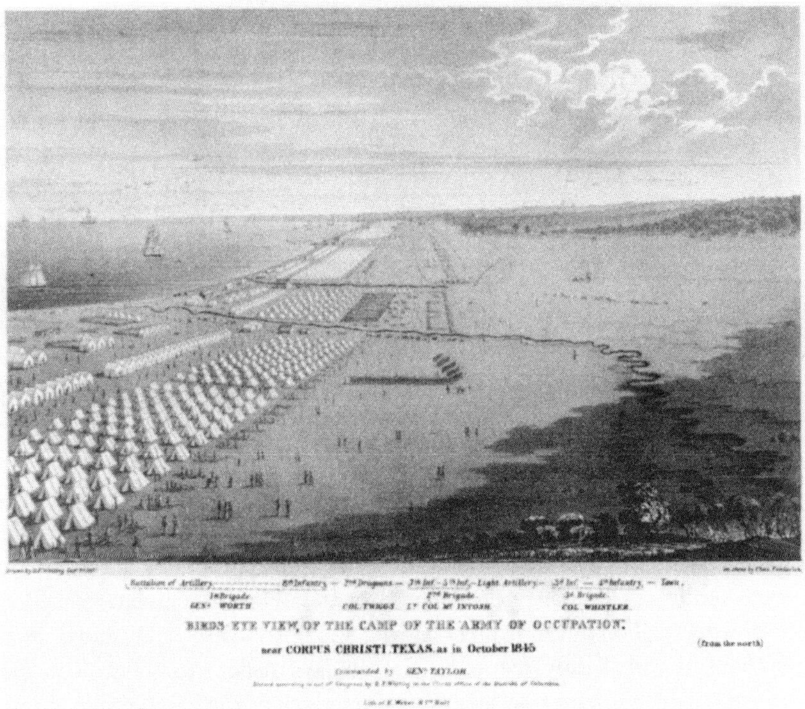

Camp of the Army of Occupation, Corpus Christi. On the eve of the war against Mexico, Zachary Taylor's Army of Occupation gathered at Corpus Christi, the largest assemblage of regular army units since the War of 1812. Following a popular contemporary genre, this bird's-eye view of that encampment was drawn by Capt. Daniel P. Whiting, a West Point graduate, who also created pictorial representations of the army's subsequent advance to Monterrey. Library of Congress, DIG-pga-06718.

joint resolution to that effect. Hoping that a display of military muscle might convince Mexico to come to terms, the administration in June 1845 ordered Col. Zachary Taylor to assume a position "on or near the Rio Grande." By mid-October, Taylor had assembled 3,500 regulars—half of the entire United States Army—on the southern banks of the Nueces River, transforming the sleepy village of Corpus Christi into a bustling boomtown. "Many old officers have never before seen so many troops at one time," observed one, as long-scattered units undertook battalion and regimental drill. By late March 1846, Taylor had begun to establish a camp on the Rio Grande across from Matamoros, Mexico.[40]

Several months earlier, with an eye toward promoting immigration to Oregon, Polk had asked Congress to fund a line of stockades to the Rocky Mountains and "an adequate force of mounted riflemen." As tensions heightened, Secretary Marcy also wanted to increase existing companies to eighty men. In early January 1846, the Senate agreed, but attempts to push through a bill expressly empowering the president to appoint officers to new units met stiff opposition. Whigs rejected the move as a ploy to allow Polk to stack the army with Democrats; after treating listeners to a dissertation praising the feats of militiamen at Bunker Hill, Ohio's House member Daniel R. Tilden charged that "there was not anywhere a more lawless set of puppets than those [regular] soldiers." Maverick Democrats, including Southerners leery of federal spending and Northerners who saw a larger army as a tool for acquiring new lands for slavery, pointed out that ninety-five brevet second lieutenants had no formal positions in line units. These men were, according to Maine congressman Hannibal Hamlin, allowed simply "to loaf upon the community." By early April, the unlikely coalition had bottled up all legislation to raise more troops.[41]

Considering Polk's aggressive diplomacy, failures to adopt measures augmenting the regular army (which numbered just 6,562 officers and men) illustrated the era's fierce partisanship as well as the continuing appeal of the citizen-soldier. On May 9, 1846, the president and his cabinet determined to ask for a declaration of war against Mexico. Unbeknownst to the administration, fighting had already begun, for sixteen days earlier Mexican troops had ambushed two companies of U.S. dragoons north of the Rio Grande. News of the defeat arrived just in time for Polk to alter his war message, which on May 11 asserted that Mexican invaders had "shed American blood upon the American soil." Congress agreed.[42]

Chapter Eight

Manifest Destiny and the Regular Army

In his last annual message to Congress (1848), President James K. Polk argued that the war against Mexico had demonstrated that "without cost to the Government or danger to our liberties, we have in the bosom of our society of freemen . . . virtually a standing army of 2,000,000 armed citizen soldiers." Architect of the victorious invasion of a foreign country, Polk had overseen the mobilization of volunteers and wartime regulars in numbers large enough to supplement the standing army and capture the enemy capital, forcing Mexico to cede the greater Southwest in the Treaty of Guadalupe-Hidalgo. The treaty concluded a decade of expansion, featuring the forced removal of most Seminole Indians from Florida (1835–1842), the annexation of Texas (1845–1846), a boundary settlement with Britain that acknowledged the U.S. possession of the Pacific Northwest south of the 49th Parallel (1846), and the admission of Iowa (1846) and Wisconsin (1848) as states. Characterized as the republic's "manifest destiny," this surge of territorial expansion had been highly controversial (with Democrats typically more supportive than Whigs), further plunging the regular army into partisan and sectional quarrels. But the United States, through it all, would rely on the army to establish, govern, and promote newly acquired territories.[1]

The historian Samuel Watson, whose exhaustive research has produced the definitive study of regular army officers before the Mexican–American War, suggests they adopted a more nuanced approach to the conflict than once thought. Col. William J. Worth saw a war against Mexico as "a glorious chance" to fight a conventional army, for, as Maj. Philip St. George Cooke put it, "fame, glory, are not accorded to the conqueror of Indians!" Some officers were unabashed in their criticism of all things Hispanic, and class and race clearly influenced their perceptions of so-called common Mexicans. Capt. Robert Anderson observed that the latter could be easily assimilated into American society if they were educated in the ways of the white world. Unfortunately, he concluded that "they bend their necks to the yoke of the Spanish dons, without thinking of their miserably degraded state." Officers generally supported expansion but preferred that it be done honorably; many suspected that the war against Mexico had not met such an ethical standard. Lt. George Meade, for instance, believed it had been "brought on by our injustice to a neighbor." Ulysses S. Grant later attributed this "unjust" conflict to "a conspiracy to acquire territory out of which slave states might be formed for the American Union."[2]

President Polk's hands-on approach to the war reflected his resolute faith in the volunteer citizen-soldier, populist disdain for military professionals, and intense partisanship. He did, however, recognize that state militias were an unreliable source of manpower for an offensive war of choice. Secretary of War Joel Poinsett's disastrous attempt to reform the militia eight years earlier under President Martin Van Buren had been a frightening deterrent to substantive discussion of the matter, and by 1846 eight states had done away with even the fiction of compulsory militia training. The day before sending his war message to Congress, President Polk thus met with senior members of the House Military Affairs Committee, who offered up a hastily written bill authorizing him to raise as many as 50,000 volunteers for twelve-month enlistments. With minor changes, Congress approved the statute, under which recruits would provide their own clothing, and officers would be appointed by the states. The president also signed a long-stalled measure that increased the number of privates in regular units to an even hundred, to be reduced to sixty-four when the emergency had ended.[3]

Two regular army bills came up for vote during the week following the declaration of war. The House of Representatives, overcoming vocal opposition from Ohio Joshua Giddings—the self-educated Whig whose denunciations of slavery were matched in vigor only by his opposition to a standing army—approved an earlier proposal to organize a new engineer company. It also passed the dormant Senate bill to create a Regiment of Mounted Riflemen, but only after amending it to require that all officers for the new unit come from the regular army. This latter provision sparked a partisan firestorm in the Senate, where Whigs argued that such was necessary to check the president's "arbitrary, absolute, and unregulated" authority. Not so, responded Democrats, with Texas senator Sam Houston—a war hero for his victory over Santa Anna at the Battle of San Jacinto—reasoning that doing so would unnecessarily limit the candidate pool. "There was less science than was generally imagined necessary to make a good officer," Houston assured his colleagues. In a straight party-line vote in the Senate, twenty-two Whigs voted in favor of the House's amendment, with an equal number of Democrats opposed. Joining his fellow Democrats, Vice President George M. Dallas, acting in his capacity as president of the upper chamber, broke the tie, thereby opening commissioned slots in the Riflemen to civilians. Collectively, these moves increased the regular army to 15,540 men.[4]

Initially summoning 20,000 volunteers, Polk soon judged that the army's senior officers failed to grasp the urgency of his war. Whereas the president assumed that the aristocratic Winfield Scott would immediately go to Texas, the general believed that operations along the Rio Grande could not

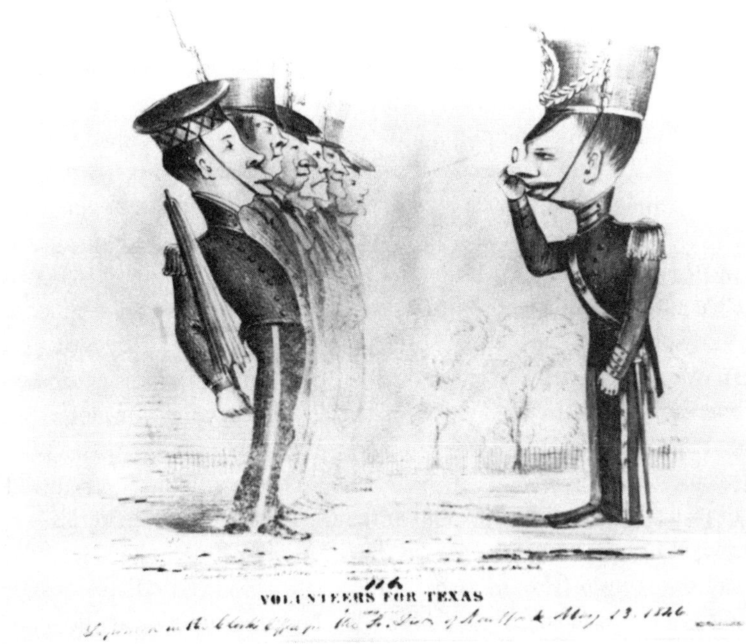

"Volunteers for Texas." Many criticized the quality of troops who turned out for Polk's first call for volunteers. The only man wearing a uniform carries a parasol rather than a musket, and their chinless officer sports a monocle. Library of Congress, USZ62-1272.

commence until after the sickly summer season. Ignoring the desires of his impatient commander in chief, Scott remained in Washington overseeing efforts to equip, clothe, feed, and train the new volunteers. Any chance that the two might form a workable alliance ended on May 21, when Polk was shown a letter in which Scott had predicted that the administration would not commission any Easterners, Whigs, or military academy graduates into new units. Later that evening, Secretary of War William M. Marcy delivered an even more imprudent missive in which Scott expressed his fear that he might be placed "in the most perilous of all positions—*a fire upon my rear from Washington, and a fire in front from the Mexicans.*" In a fury, the president ordered Scott to remain in Washington.[5]

Besieged by applicants for commissions in the new volunteer regiments and the Mounted Rifles, Polk instructed Col. Stephen W. Kearny (who he would soon promote to brigadier general) to seize New Mexico and California. But the president found little comfort as he looked elsewhere to find initiative from senior military officers. Second in lineal rank was Brig. Gen. Edmund P. Gaines, an outspoken critic of "the *quiet* and *almost exclusively sedentary mode of living*" found at West Point. Gaines's contempt for professional soldiers like Scott (those "who have acquired distinction only in the mazes of French books . . . better adapted to the Quackery of Charlatans, than the common sense science of war") would seem to have been a good match with Polk. Unfortunately, Gaines's extravagant schemes had isolated him from official army circles, and the general's plan to capture Mexico City with 125,000 unauthorized volunteer call-ups eliminated him from presidential favor. Others in Washington, most notably Brig. Gen. John E. Wool and Inspector General Roger Jones, were, in Polk's view, "whigs & violent partisans . . . not having the success of my administration at heart [and] . . . disposed to throw every obstacle in the way of my prosecuting the Mexican War successfully." He would later excoriate Quartermaster General Thomas S. Jesup and his chief assistant, Col. Henry Stanton, for acting with "extravagance & stupidity" in making contracts. In a bid to offset Whig influence and to energize an army that he believed was still mired in the dull habits of peacetime routine, Polk appointed thirteen volunteer generals—all of them loyal Democrats.[6]

News from the war front in Texas rendered moot the immediate question of field command. Zachary Taylor's regulars, boasting superior artillery and benefiting from the intensive drills they had undergone during their rendezvous at Corpus Christi, had on May 8 and 9 won a pair of victories at Palo Alto and Resaca de la Palma. "A more efficient army for its number and armament, I do not believe ever fought a battle," Grant wrote later. "You don't know," Lt. Napoleon Jackson Tecumseh Dana told his wife, "how much we rejoiced that all this has happened before the volunteers arrived. The country will see that it is the regulars which can do their business." Added the recently promoted Capt. William S. Henry: "We all feel proud that these conquests have been effected by the *army proper*." Polk rewarded Taylor with a brevet promotion to major general, and the military success and rising popularity of "Old Rough and Ready" meant that he would continue to lead the principal United States field army as it advanced into northern Mexico. Reinforced by twelve-month volunteers, Taylor won another hard-fought victory at Monterrey during September 21–24. However, Taylor—stung by the loss of a tenth of his 6,220-man army, short on ammunition, and out of ideas—agreed to an armistice that allowed Mexican troops to retain their personal arms but gave the Americans control of the city.[7]

Polk fumed at the resulting delays. Clearly, the original mobilization was insufficient to win the war, with most of the volunteers declaring their intention to go home when their required service had ended. It was equally apparent that Taylor was stuck in northern Mexico. Polk had long harbored doubts about Taylor, guilty by association with other regulars, presumed to be a Whig, and a critic of the administration's wartime strategy. Seeking a decisive solution that might also scuttle the possibility of Taylor's future presidential candidacy, Polk, his cabinet, and Senator Thomas Hart Benton determined on an invasion through Veracruz into central Mexico. The president reluctantly concluded that Scott, because of his rank, must lead this campaign. To secure the necessary manpower, Polk issued a second call for volunteers that required enlistment for the war's duration, and in December 1846 he requested ten additional regular regiments for wartime service. To soften such a move against populist criticism, Secretary Marcy reasoned that "it is no disparagement to them [volunteers] to say that a regular force is to be preferred in a war to be prosecuted in a foreign country."[8]

In a last-ditch bid to replace Scott and outflank Taylor, Polk also proposed creating a new post of lieutenant general, enabling him to appoint someone who would outrank both Whigs. But the lieutenant general bill—widely understood to have been promised to Senator Benton—went nowhere. On January 9, 1847, the House rejected it by a 120–90 margin. In the Senate, North Carolina's George E. Badger, a Whig, denounced the measure as "but the first step for perpetuating . . . the powers of the Chief Magistrate." The administration mounted no effective countermeasure, and three southern Democrats—the South Carolinians John Calhoun and Andrew P. Butler and Florida's David Yulee—joined every Whig in tabling the proposal by a 28–21 count. Seven Democrats did not vote.[9]

The ten-regiment bill also met stiff opposition from a Congress already embroiled in animated debates regarding the fate of slavery in territories that might be acquired from Mexico. Administration supporters insisted that the new measure was needed to bring the war to a speedy conclusion. They also pointed out that Polk had appointed several Whigs, including the son of Senator John J. Crittenden (KY), to the Mounted Riflemen. Such assurances did little to pacify the opposition, which condemned regulars as "mere machines." Critics also pounced on a clause authorizing the president, in light of the looming end of the current congressional session, to make recess appointments to the new units. Georgia congressman Robert Toombs (W) insisted that any new recruits be volunteers with the power to elect their own officers, dismissed the generals appointed by Polk as "political adventurers whom the soldiers would not elect," and lambasted the administration's handling of the war. Joining the fray, New York's antislavery House Democrat George Rathbun argued that no self-respecting patriot would submit himself to "the difficulties, trials, degradation, and tyranny which exist in the regular army."[10]

In mid-January 1847, Democrats loyal to the administration muscled the ten-regiment bill through the House of Representatives. A month later, however, the Senate voted 22–18 against a compromise that would have restricted presidential recess appointments to company-grade officers. Democrats

Butler, Calhoun, and Yulee again sided with the Whigs. An enraged Polk gave Butler a presidential dressing-down, apparently convincing him to relent. The president's unofficial organ, Thomas Ritchie's *Washington Union*, upped the pressure by depicting the Senate's failure to pass the measure as "ANOTHER MEXICAN VICTORY." After minor tweaking to the bill, the Senate finally conceded on February 10.[11]

Most soldiers raised from the wartime legislation never made it to Mexico, and Polk's preference for commissioning officers from civilian life galled the regulars. In all, 40 percent of the sixty-three volunteer colonels were elected by their soldiers. Of the colonels whose political affiliation can be surmised, 38 were Democrats and 18 were Whigs. Another 1,016 officers and 35,009 enlisted men joined the additional regular regiments. West Pointers returning to the army included Henry Clay, Jr., Albert Sidney Johnston, and Jubal Early. Capt. Robert Allen, a West Point graduate and ten-year veteran, took his case directly to Polk, pointing out that his father-in-law, Judge William P. Preble of Maine, was "one of your *first* and firmest friends" and had "contributed, largely, to your election." Allen snared a position on the quartermaster staff for his troubles. Only five active-duty officers, however, won promotions in the new regular-line units, whereas more than five dozen men who had dropped out of West Point managed to wrangle commissions. "What is the use of graduating from West Point and studying one's profession if we are to be rated thus by the executive?" grumbled one lieutenant. Decrying "the decided hostility evidenced by President Polk to the Army," Capt. Robert Anderson, a twenty-two-year veteran, complained that the only prerequisite for officers in the new units was "that they or their friends have proved faithful in their worship of the President's party."[12]

As the United States struggled to raise, equip, and train more soldiers for the invasion of central Mexico, volunteers proved their worth in operations south of Monterrey, in New Mexico, and in California. In late February 1847, with virtually all regulars—save several artillery batteries and dragoon squadrons—diverted to the Veracruz Expedition, Taylor's outnumbered army of about five thousand men narrowly turned back a determined Mexican assault at Buena Vista. The previous June, Kearny had headed west from Fort Leavenworth leading three hundred First Dragoons and Col. Alexander Doniphan's 1,300 Missouri Volunteers. With the loyalties of *Nuevomexicanos* and *Californios* toward Mexico City strained by years of neglect, Kearny's Army of the West, in New Mexico, occupied Santa Fe without firing a shot. He then pushed west toward California with a hundred-man escort. Upon the arrival of another regiment of volunteers to hold Santa Fe, Doniphan's Missourians then undertook a seven-week campaign against the Navajos before marching south across the border into Chihuahua, where on February 28, 1847, they decisively defeated three thousand Mexican troops at the Battle of the Sacramento River. In their triumphant return to New Orleans, Doniphan's men were justly celebrated as "the lions of the town" and discharged following their twelve months' service.[13]

Upon arriving in California, Kearny had found a chaotic situation in which American filibusters (rogue nonstate actors trying to take over territories through privately financed expeditions), U.S. naval forces in the area, and Mexican loyalists competed for supremacy. The most notable filibuster was Lt. John C. Frémont, who had been ordered to survey the Arkansas and Red Rivers and "the geography of localities within reasonable distance to Bents Fort." Frémont instead headed to California, claiming to have had "private instructions . . . if needed, to foil England carrying the war now imminent with Mexico into its territory of California." In June 1846, the Bear Flag Rebellion broke out in Northern California; Frémont organized the California Battalion and allied with U.S. naval forces led by Commodore John D. Sloat and then the more bombastic Commodore Robert F. Stockton as they seized Sutter's Fort, Monterey, San Diego, and Los Angeles. At San Pascual on December 6, Mexican troops nearly wiped out Kearny's bedraggled little command, which was only saved thanks to a relief force dispatched from San Diego.[14]

Commodore Stockton then engaged Kearny in an escalating feud for control. Although Kearny bore explicit orders to command operations and establish a civil government, Frémont pledged his support to Stockton, who repaid the favor by appointing the opportunistic explorer as governor of California. Only with the arrival of Commodore W. Branford Shubrick (the senior military officer on the Pacific Coast) and Col. Richard B. Mason (who carried new instructions further defining the army's responsibilities in California) did Kearny secure authority. An army court-martial later found Frémont guilty of mutiny, disobeying a legal command, and conduct unbecoming an officer, sentencing him to dismissal from the service but recommending leniency. After discussing the matter with his cabinet at least seven times, Polk approved only the findings regarding disobedience and misconduct and ordered the explorer back to duty. Believing that the president's failure to completely vindicate him had besmirched his honor, Frémont angrily resigned.[15]

As Americans scrambled to consolidate their hold over California, Scott organized the expeditionary force against Veracruz. Shortages in transports and supplies, combined with the withdrawal of the twelve-month volunteers in the middle of his campaign, meant that he usually operated with less than 11,000 men. In the nation's first major amphibious operation into foreign soil, Scott landed at Veracruz on March 9, 1847, with the city surrendering twenty days later. Moving inland to avoid yellow fever, Scott routed Santa Anna's army at Cerro Gordo in mid-April, then cut loose from his supply lines and marched west against Mexico City. Victories at Contreras and Churubusco, Molina del Rey, and Chapultepec opened the capital to Scott's forces on September 13. Mexico then turned to guerrilla warfare, forcing the American commander to deploy a quarter of his command to protect his tenuous line of communications and marking a period of escalating army violence against Mexican citizens and suspected insurgents. On February 2, 1848, a treaty was agreed to at Guadalupe-Hidalgo.[16]

Occupying the new domains posed a major challenge. New Mexico, where the army had been tasked with forming a temporary civilian government for the largely Hispanic population, presented special complications. On the eve of the U.S. invasion of New Mexico, Secretary Marcy had issued broad instructions to Kearny: "It is the wish and design of the United States to provide for them a free government . . . similar to that which exists in our Territories," he explained. "They will then be called on to exercise the rights of freemen in electing their own representatives to the territorial legislature." Acknowledging that doing so would "be a difficult and unpleasant part of your duty," Marcy left much to Kearny's discretion.[17]

Having been an officer since 1812 in an army that had long dealt with matters of nation-building, Kearny boasted considerable familiarity with civilian affairs; American military officers had frequently ruled during periods of martial law. Such experiences had not extended to actual governing, however, that Kearny and others (Scott, for example, appointed several military governors in occupied Mexico) were now expected to undertake. Upon taking Santa Fe, Kearny had declared residents of New Mexico to be United States citizens, reminding his soldiers that "humanity as well as policy requires that we should conciliate the inhabitants by kind and courteous treatment." Until the organization of a permanent civilian government was in place, Kearny appointed Anglo merchants from the so-called American Party to most positions of authority, with the New Mexico resident Charles Bent acting as provisional governor. In a nod toward the majority population, Kearny named Hispanics as territorial secretary and chief justice. Finally, Kearny designated Colonel Doniphan, a well-known Whig lawyer in civilian life, to head a team to write a territorial constitution and body of laws, leaving the latter in command as he embarked for California.[18]

For the time being, civilian rule in New Mexico was dependent on Doniphan's judgment and the army. Including volunteers Pvt. William Hall and Capt. David Waldo, Governor Bent, and the new U.S. territorial attorney, Frank Blair, Jr., Doniphan's team cranked out a lengthy organic law, printed in both English and Spanish, featuring a territorial constitution and bill of rights, election procedures, and duties of officeholders. The Kearny Code, as it is known to history, reflected classic small *r* republican principles: guarantees of trial by jury and rights of habeas corpus, freedom of speech

Winfield Scott. Pilloried in the popular press, the argumentative and imperious Winfield Scott (1786–1866) led an outnumbered army in a successful campaign through enemy territory to capture Mexico City. Library of Congress, USZ62-110151.

and religion, separation of church and state, a bicameral legislature, and a superior court. Along with sweeping changes to old laws regarding land titles and taxation, it encouraged public education. Carefully avoiding any mention of slavery, the new organic law granted "all free male citizens" the right to vote.[19]

But hopes for a smooth transition to United States–style democracy were soon shattered by the realities of racism, competing economic interests, and localized resistance to a new order imposed by outsiders. Polk, Marcy, and Congress agreed that the Kearny Code had gone too far in recognizing existing land titles, and the president temporarily rescinded the pledge of automatic U.S. citizenship for New Mexico residents. As soldiers under Kearny and Doniphan departed to California or to fight Indians, the newer volunteers who replaced them made no effort to conceal their contempt for Hispanics. American troops in Santa Fe, wrote one English traveler, were "the dirtiest, rowdiest crew I have ever seen together. Crowds of drunken volunteers filled the streets brawling and boasting but never fighting." Resentful of the boisterous newcomers, traditional ruling families of Santa Fe and Taos, resident Indians, and angry Hispanics rose in revolt, assassinating Bent and several of his pro-American allies. Volunteers commanded by Brig. Gen. Sterling Price crushed the short-lived insurrection and restored military rule.[20]

The status of government in New Mexico then became entangled in two very different disputes. At a local level, some *Nuevomexicanos* hoped to free themselves from the control of the army and federal officials through immediate statehood; others, seeking the benefits of federal subsidies, favored territorial status. Politically, the fate of New Mexico was embroiled in fierce debates over slavery and Texas's expansive claims to all lands east of the Rio Grande. Subsequent military chiefs of the Ninth Military Department (New Mexico)—Col. John McRae Washington, Maj. Benjamin "Old Brilliant" Beall, and Col. John Munroe—all beseeched federal officials to remove them from the burden of overseeing the messy situation, but amid the jousting they determined above all else to maintain public order. When Texas dispatched Robert S. Neighbors to make its claim to eastern New Mexico in early 1850, General Scott instructed Munroe to "repel force, by force." If Texans tried to occupy New Mexico, Senator William L. Dayton (W-NJ) warned that the regular army would stand as "a lion in her path." Only with the death of President Taylor and passage of the Compromise of 1850 did New Mexico secure territorial status and the return of civilian government.[21]

Following the clash between Kearny, Stockton, and Frémont regarding authority in California, Col. Richard B. Mason had assumed command of the Tenth Military Department. A veteran of three decades, Mason, who had his hands full trying to keep Indians and non-Indians from killing each other, joined his comrades in New Mexico in wanting no part of the myriad responsibilities of military government. The discovery of gold at Sutter's Mill in spring 1848 made the task even more difficult. "We are all going . . . gold mad here," exclaimed Lt. E. O. C. Ord, Third Artillery. Desertion, a perpetual concern in the nineteenth-century army, exceeded 40 percent annually in California, where a soldier could easily earn two months' regular pay in one day working the mines. Officers joined the scramble to get rich, demanding immediate pay raises and speculating in a host of real estate and mercantile ventures. The mania spread to Oregon; before the discovery of gold, noted the recent West Point graduate Lt. John P. Hatch, residents had been "industrious and intelligent," but the huge infusion of new capital "has run them completely crazy."[22]

Disgusted by the disorder and pressed by locals to relinquish control, Colonel Mason in November 1848 concluded that "unless a civil government is specially organized, anarchy and confusion will arise, and murder, robbery, and all sorts of crime will be committed with impunity." He also requested a transfer. With regulars in California barely able to prevent mob rule, Mason's replacement, Lt. Col. Bennett Riley, agreed with Col. Persifor F. Smith, newly arrived commander of the Pacific Division (California and Oregon), that the formation of civilian government must proceed with all haste. Accordingly, in August 1849 Riley called for elections to a special convention at Monterey, where delegates would discuss measures "for forming a State constitution or a plan for territorial government." Among those elected to the convention were Lieutenants Cave J. Couts and Henry W. Halleck (who had acted as Mason's secretary of state). Most Californians concluded that the plan represented "the only remedy for the present deplorable situation." After some debate, the Monterey Convention determined to seek immediate statehood and recommended that Governor Riley and Secretary Halleck receive stipends of $10,000 and $6,000, respectively, as thanks for their efforts to bring about civilian rule. When California voters overwhelmingly approved the state constitution, Riley gladly resigned his governorship. Congress finally authorized statehood as part of the Compromise of 1850. John C. Frémont, now amassing a fortune in private life, was selected to be one of the state's first senators.[23]

The victory against Mexico had cost the United States an estimated $100 million in treasure and nearly 14,000 dead, but even former critics of the conflict now celebrated the enormous territorial gains. As Ralph Waldo Emerson later put it: "Most of the great results of history are brought about by discreditable means." Unrecognized in the surge of public adulation of the citizen-soldier, regulars had borne the brunt of the fighting. Of the troops who took part in the final campaigns against Mexico City, for instance, 6,446 were in old regular regiments, joined by 271 Marines, 2,365 men in new regular units, and 1,569 volunteers. Battle-related casualties among volunteers for the entire war totaled less than two thousand, with another 415 soldiers in the temporary regular units also falling casualty. The old regular regiments, by contrast, suffered 2,592 killed and wounded. Disease and illness claimed the majority of American deaths, especially among the volunteers and newly raised regular regiments. "You know the effect of discipline on the health of troops," explained Lt. Col. Joseph E. Johnston to his brother-in-law, Robert McLane, recently resigned from the Topographical Engineers to become a Democratic congressman from Maryland.[24]

Despite its battle record, the regular army received little public gratitude for its actions during the war against Mexico. James K. Polk's steely determination had overcome numerous hurdles, especially during the early mobilization, and few Americans dared challenge the victorious president's well-known aversion to the regulars. Even as the nation had grown from 1.79 to 2.94 million square miles, Polk saw no reason to expand the army and brushed aside entreaties from Senators Jefferson Davis (MS) and Sam Houston (TX), both fellow Democrats, that he consider augmenting the regular force. The president also rejected suggestions from the House to increase the number of privates per company, complaining that supporters of a larger army "favor, as a party, large expenditures, high tariffs, & Banks." As such, by 1851 regulars represented less than a quarter of total federal employees.[25]

Volunteers had done much to help win the war. Under the capable leadership of West Point graduate Davis, the red-shirted First Mississippi Rifles, carrying Model 1841 percussion lock rifles, performed superbly at Monterrey and did much to save Taylor's army at Buena Vista. Texas volunteer units, particularly those mustered early in the war, also provided invaluable service in reconnaissance and, with many wielding five-shot Colt Paterson revolvers, boasted fearsome firepower in close combat. "Texas ahead like devils," marveled one West Point graduate after observing their successful charge against prepared Mexican positions at Monterrey. Having won the Battle of Buena Vista, volunteers also provided the manpower to occupy New Mexico and northern Mexico and gave Scott enough men to hold Mexico City against guerrilla incursions.[26]

Wartime atrocities, most of which were committed by volunteers, tarnished the nation's reputation but failed to shake the public's confidence in its citizen-soldiers. Lieutenant Grant reported to his fiancée that "some of the volunteers and about all of the Texans seem to think it perfectly right . . . to murder them where the act can be covered by the dark. . . . I would not pretend to guess the number of murders that have been committed upon the persons of poor Mexicans . . . but the number would startle you." Texas Rangers were particularly brutal, with Taylor complaining that they "have scarcely made one expedition without unwarrantedly killing a Mexican." Scott agreed, reasoning that his small army could not afford to provoke a general uprising that such repeated atrocities might cause. "The people must be conciliated, soothed, or well treated by every officer and man of this army," Scott had instructed his soldiers as they prepared for the campaign to Mexico City. He also beseeched his men "to pay to the Catholic religion and to its ceremonies every decent mark of respect and deference." Despite such entreaties, he could never master his volunteers, who used whatever means necessary to quell the irregular resistance.[27]

As the occupation dragged on, even regulars bristled at perceived challenges to their authority from the Mexican people. Pressured by Polk to force Mexico to pay for some of the war's costs and under Scott's guidance, the army extracted about $4 million of assessments, seizures, and levies, but the amount was less than one-sixth of what the general had hoped. Seeking to reduce the simmering violence, Scott repeatedly declared martial law in areas occupied by U.S. troops, threatening his own soldiers and Mexican civilians alike with trial by military courts. Although blaming most of their problems on the misbehavior of the volunteers, regulars found their patience exhausted in the face of stubborn local resistance. By December 1847, an exasperated Brig. Gen. John E. Wool, commanding the Army of Occupation at Monterrey, issued General Order 11. U.S. occupation policy had been fair and reasonable, Wool asserted, only to find that "our citizens and soldiers have been murdered, and their bodies mutilated, mutilated in cold blood, by hands of savages and cowardly guerrillas." In future, anyone who assisted the insurgents "will be severely punished, and heavy contribution levied upon the inhabitants of all cities, towns, villages, and haciendas, who either harbor them or furnish them with supplies or who do not give information of their haunts or places of abode."[28]

West Pointers had dominated the ranks of junior officers in the regular units, and, as their former superintendent Sylvanius Thayer proclaimed, "covered themselves with glory." Sharp criticisms from Polk, Taylor, and Scott notwithstanding, the staff bureaus, dominated by West Point graduates, had a credible job of organizing, equipping, transporting, and supplying the armies in Mexico—the largest projection of U.S. military power to date. In presenting several flagstaffs captured during his Mexico City campaign, Scott asserted, with only slight exaggeration, that "it was mainly to the Military Academy that the United States became indebted for these brilliant achievements." Grant, Robert E. Lee, George G. Meade, P. G. T. Beauregard, Braxton Bragg, Joseph E. Johnston, Thomas J. Jackson, and countless other future Civil War generals demonstrated courageous leadership. Graduates had "vindicated that institution," concluded the *Arkansas Intelligencer*. "No one, we think, can now fail to perceive the good results of it [West Point]," added the *Georgia Telegraph*, reprinting an editorial first published in the *New Orleans Times and Mercury*. Legislation passed in 1843 formalizing a congressionally apportioned system of appointments had also done much to ease suspicions that some regions benefited more than others. In Washington, Representative Robert C. Schenck (W-OH) remembered that in past times it had "become the fashion to abuse the Military Academy at West Point, as an institution where young lordlings were educated and prepared to oppress with iron heel the people of the country." The war, he now asserted, showed that it had "furnished to the country capable and accomplished officers—men who were the most efficient in service, and, consequently, came again into such repute that we have only occasional whispers of disapprobation, faint and few, and far between."[29]

West Point's enhanced reputation, however, did not end suspicions about maintaining a professional army. Volunteers chafed under the efforts by regulars to instill military discipline, with Brig. Gen. John E. Wool—a rigid disciplinarian who had frequently clashed with populists in the Cherokee removal and along the Canadian border—winning their special enmity. A disgruntled contractor described him as "petulant and whimsical—decidedly old-womanish." As one Indiana volunteer recalled: "General Wool's reputation was that of a martinet, prim, formal, and stern to an offensive degree." Stationed with him at Saltillo in northern Mexico, one Illinois volunteer complained that "Old Granny Wooll will not allow us to impose on them [the Mexican people] in the least." Wool had the temerity to dismiss two volunteers for merely "taking blankets from the Mexicans." A third man, the volunteer explained in disbelief, was drummed out of the service "for shooting at a Mexican dog and did not kill him either." Wool gave as good as he got. Singling out Texans as "the greatest rascals I have had anything [to] do with," he extended his condemnations to "the insubordinate volunteers, who are full of the devil and always ready for blood and murder."[30]

Displaying a typical tin ear for public relations, General Scott's actions increased the antiregular sentiment. While still stationed in Washington, in May 1846, he grumbled that his duties left him time only for "a hasty plate of soup" for dinner. For years to come, Democratic satirists would use the phrase to bedevil him and the army. In late 1847, the egocentric Scott compounded the problem by arresting Maj. Gen. (Volunteers) Gideon J. Pillow, Col. William J. Worth, and Capt. James Duncan on suspicious that they had penned anonymous letters crediting themselves for victories at his expense. As Pillow was a personal friend and political ally, Polk exploded. Deeming Scott's charges "highly prejudicial to the public service" and attributing them to his rival's "vanity and tyrannical temper," the president directed the release of the three officers, relieved Scott from command while his army still occupied Mexico City, and appointed a court-martial (later downgraded to a court of inquiry). Cases involving Worth and Duncan were dropped, but Pillow, confident in Polk's support and in the friendly composition of the court, demanded his hearing. After several weeks of testimony, the court judged Pillow's performance to have been "highly meritorious."[31]

The near-monopoly of West Point over the regular army's officer corps also ran counter to egalitarian rhetoric. By 1860, three-fourths of all officers

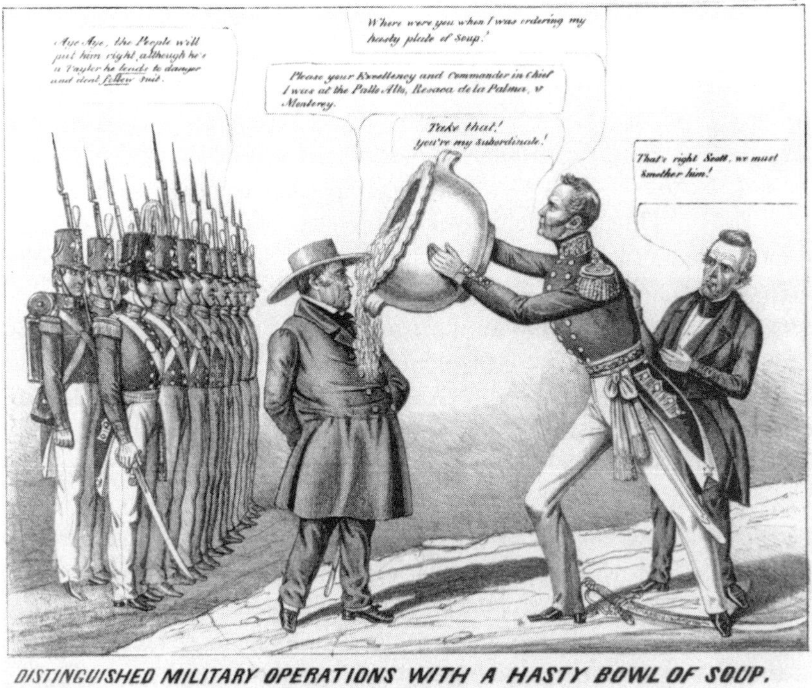

"Distinguished Military Operations with a Hasty Bowl of Soup." Scott's "hasty plate of soup" comment brought forth a torrent of criticism. In this lithograph, Scott, wearing a formal uniform, is pouring soup over the more casually dressed Zachary Taylor. "Take that! You're my subordinate!" proclaims Scott, who is portrayed as hoping the liquid might douse his rival's victory-fueled popularity. Library of Congress, USZ62-62676.

were United States Military Academy graduates. Particularly irksome was the rarity of promotions from the ranks. As one army surgeon put it: A "sharp line of demarcation" divided officers and men. Enlisted appointees had been fairly common in the early republic, but between 1821 and 1838 no soldier had received such a commission. Secretary of War Joel Poinsett had selected seven men from the ranks during the 1838 expansion, but the door was again shut until 1847, when Congress declared that one noncommissioned officer per company could receive the supernumerary rank of brevet second lieutenant. Even so, only twenty-nine such promotions were granted. One aggrieved sergeant (who later received such a promotion) complained to his wife: "Although I should, unaided and alone surround the whole Mexican Army and take them all prisoners of war, Santa Anna included, it would not be deemed a deed worthy of remark, being done as it would be, by a man not a graduate of West Point."[32]

At the insistence of Congress, the War Department in 1854 established special procedures, featuring four-officer regimental screening boards and an annual examination, through which an enlisted man might obtain a brevet second lieutenancy. Despite such prodding, regulars still resisted granting commissions to enlisted personnel, with only eleven soldiers receiving such an honor before the Civil War. The case of Cpl. William Henry Hubbs, Company H, Ninth Infantry, illuminates the problem. Hubbs began his quest for a commission in 1857, securing the support of Indiana's entire Democratic congressional delegation. But the army stalled. "It appears to me that it is more difficult for one to advance themselves in a military life from a low position, in this republican government, than in any other," complained Hubbs two years later. With the Adjutant General's office acknowledging that "an indisposition to carry out the law regarding promotion of [noncommissioned] officers, has in some cases prevented the recommendations from being made," only after a direct War Department order did the board examine now-Sergeant Hubbs. Convening in October 1860, it found that he met the necessary physical standards but lacked the competence in geography, U.S. history, math, and astronomy required of an officer.[33]

Public unwillingness to reconsider the status of the regular army was also attributable to the grim realities of mid–nineteenth century military life, which held little appeal to a middle-class man on the make. In peacetime, most recruits applied because they needed a job. The historian Edward Coffman has shown that, in purely economic terms, enlisted men probably fared at least as well as farmhands or common laborers. Moreover, they enjoyed much better job security. Though monotonous—bread, salt pork or boiled beef, and cabbage or potatoes during good times, which many garrisons supplemented with post gardens—the rations were large. But no one was going to get rich by joining the army, and a soldier faced degrading punishments that most Americans would have considered intolerable. As Representative George Rathbun (D-NY) declared in early 1847, no self-respecting patriot would submit himself to "the difficulties, trials, degradation, and tyranny which exist in the regular army."[34]

Convinced that their commissions set them apart from the lowly enlisted folk, some officers used brutal techniques to maintain order. Although technically guided by the Articles of War (1819), military justice at far-flung garrisons depended heavily on the whims of the post commander and garrison court. Deserters could be executed, branded, or whipped (between 1833 and 1861) by up to fifty lashes. Whereas the Fourth Infantry's Maj. Robert C. Buchanan observed that such punishment was ineffective and "opposed to the enlightened spirit of the age," fellow West Pointer Capt. Samuel P. Heintzelman opined that flogging two men had quelled "that spirit of insubordination. . . . Several men fainted, but not a whisper was heard. I think we have the upper hand of them now." Other corporal punishments included tying the accused's hands to his ankles, binding him to a stick placed between his arms and legs, mounting him aboard a punishment horse, or forcing him to carry weights while marching in a circle. Attempting to justify such practices, one army inspector explained that many soldiers were "of a description of persons dead to everything like moral feelings and whom nothing can degrade or humiliate."[35]

On occasion, enlisted men took matters into their own hands. On Christmas Day 1829, two dozen armed men occupied the parade ground while three of their comrades attacked the much-disliked officer of the day "with evident intention to take his life." Only the intervention of fellow officers prevented a fragging. At Green Bay two and a half years later, "a drunk soldier" murdered Lt. Amos Foster. Under what seem to have been similar circumstances, deserters in California killed Capt. Louis S. Craig, twice brevetted for distinguished service in the Mexican–American War. In 1855, drunken First Dragoons mutinied against their major, who responded by "challenging the company to fight him, man by man." Four privates were sentenced to three years' hard labor, with the entire company disbanded and the men distributed to other companies in the regiment. Company G, Eighth Infantry, was also broken up at Fort Davis in 1860 after they broke into the guardhouse and lynched a civilian whiskey trader suspected of killing one of their comrades.[36]

Many believed that the regular army was becoming too un-American. Lt. George McClellan, who had graduated second in his West Point class of 1846, denounced the "wretched Dutch and Irish immigrants" in the ranks. Most enlistments still came from big recruiting stations in Atlantic coastal cities in the North. Married men were discouraged and African Americans were entirely excluded; eligible recruits had to be between 18 and 35 years old, at least five feet, four inches tall, and "effective, able-bodied, sober, free from disease, and who have a competent knowledge of the English language." Of the 16,064 men who attempted to join the army in 1852, 83 percent failed examination, with age and language requirements counting for nearly half of all dismissals. As immigration to the United States increased (from 10,837 in 1826 to 114,371 in 1845), so did the number of immigrant enlistees (5.5 percent to 50.6 percent). By 1852, more than three-fourths of recruits were foreign-born. As Assistant Surgeon Richard Coolidge explained: "A large proportion of the immigrants who are landed at our seaport cities, where the army is principally recruited, are extremely destitute; and to those not finding immediate employment, the army . . . offers a temporary resource, of which many avail themselves." Amid growing nativist influence, the increased number of foreign-born soldiers gave many civilians added reason to be suspicious of the regulars.[37]

Class and ethnic divisions extended to the women who accompanied the army. Recognizing years of tradition, Congress in March 1802 had authorized one daily ration "to the women who may be allowed to any particular corps not exceeding the proportion of four to a company." The oblique reference was to laundresses, who did their washing at rates set by the post council of officers and held their positions at the whim of the post commander. Often married to enlisted men, they lived in separate housing and were, like their husbands, overwhelmingly foreign-born. Officers' wives, by contrast, generally shared the middle-class backgrounds of their husbands; indeed, one-fifth of officers' marriages were to relatives of other regulars. Their spouses made sure that strict army hierarchy applied to post society. "I had 'gone for a soldier,' and a soldier I determined to be," wrote one wife. As partners in the effort to conquer and civilize a continent, the wives of officers used domestic rituals, leisure activities, and a feminized military ranking structure to ensure their own authority, identity, and status, creating a world very different from the one fancied by Jacksonian rhetoric.[38]

Continued reservations about the regulars, however, did little to damage the popularity of one war hero. Whereas the imperious Winfield Scott seemed best characterized by the sobriquet "Old Fuss and Feathers," the more politically attractive Zachary Taylor, fondly dubbed "Old Rough and Ready," became a national icon. Deeming an electoral triumph more important than the clear delineation of a party platform in the 1848 election, a divided Whig Party convention nominated Taylor on its fourth ballot. Seeking to counterbalance Taylor, Democrats paired their candidate, Senator Lewis Cass, with Maj. Gen. William O. Butler (Volunteers), a Polk appointee who had been Taylor's second in command. Horace Greeley, the liberal journalist who contemplated the formation of a new party based on the principles of land and labor reform and the "abolition of the army and navy," warned that a Taylor victory would increase the army's role in matters of patronage. Supporters countered by arguing that Taylor, "a true follower of General Washington," would maintain his political independence, an image the candidate himself assiduously attempted to foster. Regulars largely formed ranks behind one of their own. "The studious neglect & odious discrimination against the army practiced in the adm. of Mr. Polk should make us willing for any change," grumbled one officer, "especially one which brings Genl Taylor to the chair of state."[39]

In results complicated by the strong showing of the Free Soil Party, Taylor carried the day, winning half of the states and 47 percent of the popular vote. After Georgia's Robert Toombs turned down the secretary of war position, the president-elect picked George W. Crawford, a Georgia lawyer and former governor. In his only annual address, Taylor backed river and harbor improvements, pensions for disabled officers, an asylum for aged and infirm former enlisted personnel, and "some addition" to the regular forces. Secretary Crawford fleshed out the administration's platform, calling for small bounties to attract veterans who reenlisted at frontier stations, an increase in the number of privates in companies stationed in the West from 42 (dragoon companies had 50, and the Mounted Rifles 64) to 74, and the authority to mount some regular infantrymen. Reflecting widely held army sentiments, Lieutenant Colonel Johnston advised his brother-in-law, Representative McLane, that considerably more troops were needed to enforce provisions in the Treaty of Guadalupe-Hidalgo obligating the United States to guard the borderlands. "We Democrats ought to provide for the fulfillment of our treaty," reasoned Johnston.[40]

But army legislation was engulfed by sectional conflicts over slavery and threats of secession, which drew the scrutiny of many regulars. North Carolina's Capt. Braxton Bragg left no doubt about his sympathies. "Every day renders it more certain," he proclaimed in 1848, "that the south must take a stand and maintain it." Bragg resigned eight years later. Most soldiers, however, feared the disorder that would accompany secession, which Quartermaster General Jesup described as "the doctrine of cowardice." Vermont's Capt. Benjamin Alvord advised one South Carolinian that his state must remain "calm and temperate in her actions." Although the government should show "forbearance" to hardline Southerners, Connecticut's Col. Joseph G. Totten feared "that these madmen are leading their section of the country into a position whence there can be no return."[41]

Complicated by the ferocious debates regarding the Compromise of 1850, Congress in May took up Crawford's proposal to augment the regular force. Jefferson Davis, Democratic chair of the Senate Military Affairs Committee, shepherded the increase through the upper body, but the House turned rancorous. Representative Volney E. Howard (D-TX) instead wanted two regiments of rangers, claiming that "Americans, or western men, will not . . . enlist for five years in the regular army in the time of peace." W. R. W. Cobb (D-AL) charged that too many soldiers were already "idle and unemployed" in the Ordnance Department. Even though he was "no political friend" of Crawford, House Military Affairs Committee chairman Armistead Burt (D-SC) defended the administration against Cobb's attack, speculating that his fellow Democrat did not even know what the Ordnance Department did. In the end, 35 Democrats and two Free Soilers joined 72 Whigs in supporting the bill, with 44 Democrats, four Whigs, and five Free Soilers opposed. The measure increased the army's maximum strength by some 2,500 men, to about 11,000.[42]

Still, the nation expected much from an army whose growth had not matched that of the country it served, with matters complicated by the resignation of Secretary Crawford following the Galphin Affair, in which he had accepted nearly $100,000 in settlement fees. Excluding the war against Mexico, federal spending (excluding service on the national debt) on the army and veterans had fallen from 49.1 percent of the annual budget in 1833 to 29.6 percent in 1851. The number of soldiers per thousand square miles also decreased from 7 to 3.7. Moreover, moving troops to and supplying the far-flung garrisons in Texas, New Mexico, and California stretched the Quartermaster's and Subsistence Departments to the breaking point. In 1844, army transportation costs totaled less than $120,000; in 1850, that figure had ballooned to $1.9 million. For a similar period, Subsistence expenditures rose from $347,389 to $1,235,632. Costs for forage, fuel, mounts, and barracks also skyrocketed. Cognizant of the resulting outcry, recently appointed Secretary of War Charles M. Conrad demanded in January 1851 that all military contracts exceeding $2,000 secure his personal approval.[43]

The financial shortfalls did not mean the end of army contributions to national development. Although President Polk had opposed a system of federally sponsored internal improvements, army engineers still assisted specific lighthouses, surveys of the coasts and the Great Lakes, and studies to alleviate flooding in the Mississippi River Delta, along with construction of the New Orleans customhouse, marine hospitals, and bridges and streets in the District of Columbia. With surveys and roads needed to secure the nation's new Western empire, the Engineers and Topographical Engineers began examining Texas, New Mexico, Oregon, and California. In 1849, Congress authorized $50,000 to locate the best routes from the Mississippi River to the Pacific Ocean. Other tasks followed, and over the next decade army engineers spearheaded efforts to determine the feasibility of artesian wells in West Texas and to direct road construction in California, Minnesota, and the territories of Kansas, Nebraska, New Mexico, Oregon, Utah, and Washington.[44]

The possibility of war with Britain in 1846–1847, along with the shooting war against Mexico, had also rekindled interest in funding coastal defenses. Fortification and associated armament appropriations had fallen from more than $4.3 million from 1838 through 1841 to less than half of that amount during the next four years. Between 1846 and 1851, by contrast, Congress increased these monies to more than $5 million, with Whig Party stalwarts defending such moves against jealous Western Democrats. Firm in their advocacy of national defense and confident in their technical expertise, army engineers eagerly made their cases before the court of public opinion. "Engineers can render great service to the cause of their country by diffusing light through the newspapers," now–Chief of Engineers Joseph Totten opined to a subordinate. "I would say all that could be proper to urge such action upon you and all our confreres."[45]

Institutional changes stemming from the territorial acquisitions also impacted the regulars. In March 1849, Congress had created the Department of the Interior, which incorporated functions of the General Land Office, the Patent Office, Bureau of Indian Affairs, and various pension offices (formerly housed in the Treasury, State, War, and Navy Departments). Supported by the unlikely alliance of Senators Davis and Daniel Webster (W-MA), the new department expanded the federal bureaucracy to meet the needs of a sprawling Western empire. But the restructuring also meant that soldiers would now operate under civilian authority when dealing with Indian reservations and negotiating with tribal leaders. Resenting such constraints, army officers for the next five decades would almost universally condemn the decision to remove Indian Affairs from the War Department—an unanticipated consequence of manifest destiny.[46]

Chapter Nine
New Challenges for the Old Army

The 1850s represented a new era for the United States Army. So long as regular forces remained small, only a tiny minority of Americans, devoid of real political power, now called for its outright elimination. The tepid criticism against the formation of the Aztec Club by officers in the closing stages of the war against Mexico, for example, contrasted sharply with the widespread denunciations of the Society of the Cincinnati half a century earlier. Other than in the District of Columbia, the War Department's direct engagement with public works would, with a few temporary exceptions, be more limited than it had been in the 1820s and 1830s. Yet in a time of growing sectional rivalries, the federal government still turned to the army to promote a transcontinental railroad, referee the bitter rivalries over the expansion of slavery, and encourage the non-Indian occupation of the vast lands acquired during the previous decade. To do the latter, the regulars were called on to overawe Mormons in Utah and to pacify Native Americans very different from those encountered east of the Mississippi River, posing a major challenge for the conventional arms of the United States. Whereas regulars recorded 122 engagements with Indians between 1790 and 1849, they listed 121 combat actions during the 1850s alone.[1]

Soldiers and War Department officials routinely blamed Indian conflicts on shady contractors and the Indian Bureau, whose civilian agents now oversaw the distribution of treaty allotments and also conducted diplomacy. Typical was the 1855 complaint by an officer at Fort Ridgeley (in present-day Minnesota) that the pork delivered to the Dakotas was "entirely rotten" and the flour "as hard as a similar lump of mortar dried." Lamenting what he believed to be the poor quality and uncooperative attitudes of most Indian agents, Winfield Scott asserted that "we might begin to hope for a general peace—but we cannot get it, unless we are at peace with the Indian Department." From Texas, Col. Persifor F. Smith claimed that the decision by the San Antonio–based agent to encourage Lipan Apaches back to South and Central Texas had only sparked more violence. Speaking for many, Smith concluded: "The military can be of no avail if the Indians, instead of remaining where they were driven at so much expense & trouble by the troops, are brought back into the settlements by the civil agents of another branch of government over whom we have no control."[2]

Regular officers were often as contemptuous of the white and Hispanic borderlands residents they were tasked to protect as they were of the Indians. The people of Corpus Christi, Texas, reported Capt. Randolph B. Marcy, "are about as lawless a set of scamps as can be found. There are not probably more than half a dozen families that are fit to associate with." Regulars charged that civilians invariably exaggerated the numbers of those killed by Indian attacks. "Half the murders that are committed on the plains, and laid to the Indians," contended West Point–educated Maj. John Sedgwick, "are committed by white men." Virtually all regulars nevertheless viewed the struggle as one in which civilization must ultimately triumph over savagery. "The Indian in the end has to 'move on' or do worse," wrote Capt. Rufus Ingalls, First Dragoons. After graduating from West Point in 1832, Capt. Erasmus D. Keyes spent considerable time observing Indians on reservations, concluding that they are "everywhere the same degraded, debased, unworthy creature. . . . Without prudence, without self-denial, without wisdom, to avail himself of his capacities for any enduring object, he pursues the way to destruction which has been manifestly marked out by the finger of an overruling Providence." After visiting a Kiowa encampment along the Canadian River, another officer wrote: "I never had more reason for thanking God that I was born civilized."[3]

As violent encounters with Indians escalated, Zachary Taylor's sudden death in July 1850 led to Millard Fillmore's accession to the presidency. Seeking to heal wounds in the divided Whig Party through his cabinet appointments, Fillmore selected Representative Charles M. Conrad (W-LA), an early Taylor ally who had voted in favor of the recent army increase, to head the War Department. Conrad inherited a difficult job. In Texas, the enormous distances, the state's ownership of its public lands, and a surging non-Indian population with a seemingly insatiable desire for expansion and a tradition of ethnic cleansing confounded the army's efforts to bring peace to a violent frontier. With only three Indian agents and four interpreters assigned there, achieving a lasting settlement seemed impractical. "Every mail brings us news of some fresh murder or depredation," proclaimed Democratic congressman Volney H. Howard. Between 1848 and 1852, the army constructed twenty forts throughout the Lone Star State, but the 1,600 regulars stationed there—less than half of whom were mounted—could not enforce order. "The Indians disperse themselves over this country in small bands, prowl around the settlements, awaiting a favorable moment to murder and rob," explained Capt. William J. Hardee, a cavalryman since his graduation with the West Point class of 1838. "It is difficult, nay, impossible, to overtake and punish any of the parties. . . . If in danger of being overtaken, they scatter, and, each pursuing a different route to some remote point, they effectually baffle the skill of the most experienced trailers."[4]

Denouncing the federal government as unsympathetic to their needs, Texans demanded more mounted troops. "The government had as well place its soldiery on crutches and command them to capture the wild antelope, as to send them, on foot, in the war path of the well-mounted warriors of the plains," complained a typical editorial. Ideally, mounted forces would come in the form of Texas Rangers, whose reputation within the state had already reached mythic proportions. Largely unstated was the importance of payments to and supplies for such volunteers, which brought considerable federal dollars into the cash-strapped frontiers. Seeking to limit costs and dubious about the extent of actual Indian attacks, officials in Washington usually balked at the incessant calls for rangers. But to pacify the hue and cry in 1851, Col. George Mercer Brooke, commanding what later became the Department of Texas, received authority to raise three companies of mounted troops. The volunteers did not bring about peace, but they did bring in $317,674 (more than $7.9 million at time of publication) to the Texas economy.[5]

To the west, in April 1851, Lt. Col. Edwin V. "Bull" Sumner assumed command of the Ninth Military Department (roughly present-day New Mexico and Arizona). Every inch the fighting cavalryman, Sumner erected several new posts and launched an offensive against the Navajos, but he disparaged Hispanics and butted heads with local authorities and Indian Bureau officials. After a little more than a year on the scene, Sumner angrily concluded: "The New Mexicans are thoroughly debased and totally incapable of self-government, and there is no latent quality about them that can ever make them respectable citizens." In other words, Washington should arm the territory's residents to defend themselves and withdraw the army to better protect more valuable regions. In a desperate gambit designed to highlight the need for new funding, Secretary Conrad sought to use Sumner's proposal as a means of convincing Congress that it must increase military spending rather than abandon newly acquired lands. If it were really interested in saving money, Conrad contended, Congress could buy out the property of everyone (as high as four times actual value, he calculated) and induce them to move elsewhere. Predictably, the secretary's scheme went nowhere.[6]

The precarious state of army-sponsored order was nowhere better evidenced than in 1851 efforts to sign a treaty with the most influential Northern Plains tribes. Thirty-five miles southeast of Fort Laramie (Wyoming), a grand council of Lakotas, Cheyennes, Arapahos, Crows, Assiniboines, Gros Ventres, Mandans, and Arikaras met with Superintendent of Indian Affairs David D. Mitchell and the longtime Agent Thomas Fitzpatrick. After much discussion and negotiation, individuals from the tribes signed a vague treaty in which they promised to remain at peace, allow whites unmolested passage and the right to establish military posts, and accept assigned tribal boundaries in perpetuity. In return, the federal government agreed to pay damages caused by emigrants and an annual annuity of $50,000 for fifty years. The treaty looked impressive on paper, but the presence of 270 regular soldiers failed to convince the ten thousand Indians in attendance of the government's power. "If there was any disposition on the part of the Sioux, Cheyennes and Arapahos to destroy us they could have done so in an hour," acknowledged one enlisted man.[7]

As the army struggled to impose federal authority in the borderlands, President Fillmore turned to a traditional Whig theme as he implored Congress to renew appropriations for internal improvements. Stuffing the bill with enough goodies (more than a hundred line items for river surveys and obstruction removals, harbor landfills, pier repairs, breakwater construction, and the U.S. Lake Survey) to attract the backing of many "Young America" Democrats, supporters of the 1852 Harbor and River Act appropriated $2 million dollars, to be administered by the War Department. Congress also approved $50,000 to continue surveys of the Mississippi River Delta, and subsequent legislation mandated military involvement in the Coast Survey and lighthouse inspections. In work on customhouses and other Treasury Department buildings, army engineers were detailed "from the conviction that the great interests of the country . . . would be best served." Astonished by the scope of the new task, Secretary Conrad assigned the Corps of Engineers responsibility for projects along the Atlantic and Gulf Coasts and tasked the Topographical Engineers with jobs on the western rivers and the Great Lakes.[8]

Fillmore also charged regulars with improving the quality of life in the District of Columbia. The combination of civilian mismanagement, a disastrous 1851 fire that destroyed much of the Library of Congress, and behind-the-scenes lobbying by Chief Engineer Joseph Totten convinced the president to give the Corps of Engineers greater oversight of improvements in the city's water supply. Assigned to the duty, Lt. Montgomery C. Meigs threw himself behind ambitious plans to construct an aqueduct from the Great Falls of the Potomac River to the capital. In late February 1853, Meigs and Mayor John Walker Maury convinced Congress to appropriate $150,000 for the project.[9]

In a similar vein, the military complemented economic modernization. Ordnance Bureau standards for testing ferrous materials, first initiated in 1841, set nationwide criteria for private manufacturers. Especially in New England, the bureau's quest for technological innovation, and its insistence that civilian contractors share knowledge, had begun to revolutionize the light machine tool industry through new specialized jigs, milling machines, lathes, and die-forging technologies. Though labor costs remained high, quality and interchangeability improved, and American exhibits at London's

Aqueduct Bridge, Georgetown, District of Columbia. Tasked with supplying the nation's capital with water, Capt. Montgomery C. Meigs oversaw construction of the tubular Aqueduct Bridge in Georgetown. Library of Congress, DIG-ppmsca-08302.

Crystal Palace Exhibition in 1851 led the British engineer and machinist Joseph Whitworth to praise what he dubbed the "American System of Manufactures." Regulars also applied habits learned at the United States Military Academy to management and accounting, as recording, classifying, and interpreting data to make good business decisions seemed a natural progression from their daily West Point recitations. Private enterprise—especially railroads, where complex operations required a precision not typically evident in the premarket economy—found in army officers an excellent pool of business leaders. Academy graduates Herman Haupt, George W. Whistler, William G. McNeill, and George E. McClellan resigned to take positions with railroad companies; of the 1,058 graduates of West Point between 1802 and 1866, 35 became corporate presidents, 41 superintendents and general managers, and 56 chief engineers or treasurers.[10]

Planning for a transcontinental railroad suggested the army's potential to remain an agent for national unity. Consensus held that such a project required federal support and that only one line was feasible, setting off a fierce competition for Washington's assistance. Congress had for years engaged in fruitless debate over the proper location for a railroad to the Pacific. With every route defeated by a combination of other aspirants for the prize, Congress in 1853 turned to the Topographical Engineers. Sponsored by Pennsylvania senator Richard Brodhead (D) as "the only practicable mode" to resolve the impasse, the measure allotted the Topographers $150,000 "to ascertain the most practicable and economical route for a railroad from the Mississippi River to the Pacific Ocean."[11]

Implementation of the railroad reconnaissance fell to newly elected President Franklin Pierce (1853–1857), a Democrat and former volunteer general during the Mexican War. Divided and dispirited because the soaring US economy rendered their calls for government intervention less attractive, Whigs had turned to Winfield Scott in a desperate effort to mobilize voters for the 1852 presidential election. Not surprisingly, Scott (who had routinely used his military office as a clearinghouse for his political correspondence) could not deliver in the court of public opinion, and Pierce carried all states save four. Explaining his opposition, the Texan Guy M. Bryan pointed to Scott's support for stricter naturalization laws, hostility to slavery, and lack of experience outside the army. The general "knows nothing else," proclaimed Bryan, and was "*purely a military man.*" Pierce appointed Jefferson Davis, a West Point graduate and Mississippi senator, as his war secretary. Like Pierce, Davis advocated state rights and usually opposed federal involvement in internal improvements, but the secretary envisioned a well-planned system of railroads and canals as essential to national defense. Despite only tepid support from Pierce, Davis eagerly mobilized the topographical surveys.[12]

The Topographers welcomed the task. "It [the Transcontinental Railroad] fills the imagination," bureau chief Col. John J. Abert had written in the influential *DeBow's Review*, "and unless I am much mistaken, it would also fill the pockets of our people." Confident that the results would confirm the superiority of a southern route from El Paso to California, the War Department organized five teams to reconnoiter alternatives. Accompanied by military escorts and swarms of civilian scientists, engineers, artists, and adventurers, the surveys revealed the West to be far more valuable than previously believed. Fired by a sense of national mission, personal ambition, and optimism in man's ability to conquer nature, the Topographers waxed poetic about the benefits of several routes. Buoyed by the acquisition of southernmost New Mexico and Arizona in the Gadsden Purchase, Secretary Davis continued to champion the southernmost road, although supporters of rival lines could rightfully claim that the surveys had justified their particular favorite. The collections, catalogues, and observations produced by the Pacific Railroad Surveys were eventually printed in thirteen massive volumes but failed to break the sectional impasse.[13]

Working from a cramped office under a stairway in the War Department, Secretary Davis threw himself into every arena of army activity. Less than three weeks after taking office, President Pierce transferred efforts to expand the United States Capitol Building and relocate the Patent Office from the Interior to the War Department. Newly promoted Captain Meigs, who was

Jefferson Davis. Having graduated from West Point in 1828, Jefferson Davis (1808–1889) resigned from the regular army seven years later, but he was a distinguished leader of volunteer troops during the war against Mexico. Keenly interested in military affairs during his subsequent time in the Senate, he ranked among the ablest war secretaries during the antebellum period. The photograph is by Mathew Brady. Library of Congress, DIG-ppmsca-23852.

already directing work on the aqueduct, received a promotion (to captain) and oversight of these tasks as well. Under the watchful eye of Secretary Davis, who protected his War Department turf against rivals in the Interior Department and the House Committee on Public Buildings, Meigs resolved to showcase the nation's glory through smooth-running public works and architectural majesty. Eventually cultivating productive relations with his largely Democratic labor crews, his efficiency—if not his artistic taste—won grudging respect as his portfolio expanded to include construction of a new Capitol Dome. "The whole District is under deep obligation" to Meigs, concluded the editor of the Washington *Evening Star*, "who has defended himself and his plans against combinations and demagogues on the one hand, and speculators on the other, which would have ground almost any other man to powder."[14]

Davis also pushed to restore coastal defense funding, which had been eliminated in 1852 and 1853. Responsible for national security and protective of their own work, the Engineers mobilized well-orchestrated lobbying campaigns. "Engineer Officers can render great service to their cause & to their country by diffusing light through the Newspapers," explained Chief Engineer Totten. Despite significant House opposition, funding was restored in 1854. Increasing fears over the diplomatic effects of the Ostend Manifesto (on Cuba), disputes over the implementation of the Clayton-Bulwer Treaty (on Central America) with Great Britain, and the success of Russia's seaboard fortifications during the Crimean War (1853–1856) convinced Congress to increase appropriations to nearly $8.4 million (roughly $190 million at time of publication) between fiscal years 1855 and 1858.[15]

Not confining his interests to the Transcontinental Railroad, the District of Columbia, and coastal defense, Secretary Davis organized a three-man team of officers to study European military practices, imported camels as an experimental means of traversing the arid Southwest, supported technical improvements resulting in the .58-caliber Model 1855 U.S. Rifle and U.S. Rifled Muskets, and backed a new manual for infantry tactics. The tireless Davis also helped to institute a fifth year of study at the United States Military Academy, badgered Texas into creating two Indian reservations, and helped secure pay raises for officers and men. Costs of constructing new barracks, and vocal demands for a local military presence, however, blunted his attempt to concentrate scattered borderlands garrisons to larger, more accessible posts, a move he hoped would improve morale and reduce expenses.[16]

Despite his accomplishments, the self-righteous Davis clashed with many regulars. "I have not seen an officer who has not condemned the course & conduct" of the secretary, complained one veteran. Jealous of the perks of the "set of loafers" in the staff bureaus, line officers had long demanded a system of rotation, a process Davis supported. But the attempt largely failed, and staff officers held him accountable for threatening their security. The secretary also engaged in childish public feuds with the equally sanctimonious Brig. Gen. John E. Wool—once over the location of Wool's Department of the Pacific headquarters, and again when Davis did not forward a ceremonial sword as quickly as Wool had expected. Davis also engaged in an unprofessional war of words with the contentious Winfield Scott over the latter's emoluments and attempts to keep his headquarters in New York rather than in Washington. Their clash highlighted continuing struggles between war secretaries and commanding generals that would carry through most of the nineteenth century. Holding constitutional authority over the army, civilian secretaries commonly corresponded directly with military personnel without going through the office of the commanding general, a practice the latter greatly resented. This particular situation devolved into a childlike correspondence in which the general accused Davis of being "an enraged imbecile" and the secretary characterized Scott's career as having "been marked by querulousness, insubordination, greed of lucre, and want of truth." When printed by Congress, their letters and supporting documents totaled a whopping 254 pages.[17]

Scott and Davis did agree on one thing: the army, which mustered just two regiments of dragoons and one of Mounted Riflemen, needed more mounted men. Some infantrymen temporarily received horses, but as one officer conceded: "Footmen, in the saddle, represent a mongrel force—inefficient, with great excess in the wear & tear of horses and equipments." The Fillmore administration's previous bid to add two new mounted units had failed in 1850, and a Senate effort to raise three regiments of mounted volunteers to protect communications between the Missouri River and the Pacific Coast also miscarried. Predictably, tensions heightened along the central Overland Trail to California and Oregon, where tens of thousands of emigrants trekked through lands claimed by Lakotas and Northern Cheyennes, threatening the fragile economies, sense of sovereignty, and military reputations of the aggrieved tribes. On August 18, 1854, Brevet Lt. John L. Grattan, later remembered as "impetuous, bold, and daring . . . unchecked by age or experience," led twenty-nine soldiers with two cannons into a large Brulé and Oglala camp outside Fort Laramie, demanding that the alleged thief of a lame cow be turned over. Following forty-five minutes of verbal posturing, Grattan ordered his men to open fire. He thereby started the First Sioux War, and the Indians responded by annihilating his entire command.[18]

The nation demanded revenge for what one newspaper inaccurately described as "a treacherous slaughter." Embarrassed by suggestions that the Grattan defeat reflected "the total inefficiency of United States troops in Indian warfare," President Pierce insisted that two additional infantry and two new cavalry regiments—which would increase the army to slightly more than 18,000 officers and men—were required to mete out the requisite punishment. In the ensuing congressional debates, Secretary Davis emphasized that territorial expansion had far exceeded the pace of army growth, in addition pointing out that volunteers cost three times more than regulars. The Whiggish *Daily National Intelligencer* argued that an army increase enjoyed "almost universal concurrence," and Philadelphia's *North American and United States Gazette* lamented the earlier failure to add more regulars as "deplorably fatal." Two-thirds of both Whigs and Democrats in the House supported the increase; the growing tendency of Western legislators to support a larger regular army was also evident, with twenty-two of twenty-six borderlands representatives backing the measure. The Senate concurred by a 32–7 margin.[19]

Regulars joined more than 1,500 civilians (431 from New York state alone) in a frenzied scramble for commissions in the new regiments. Capt. Samuel P. Heintzelman, Second Infantry, determined that he "must go to Washington & see that no one below me gets above," scoring a promotion to major in the First Infantry in the process. Less successful was New York's Lt. John P. Hatch, who had pinned his hopes on a recommendation from his state's Horatio Seymour (a Democrat who had recently lost a gubernatorial reelection bid). Davis and Pierce allotted all sixteen field-grade ranks in the four new units to regulars, but altogether about half (116) of their appointments in 1855–1856 were civilians, of whom fifty (the overwhelming majority being Democrats) had no military experience. Speaking for many, Lt. William P. Craighill, a recent graduate of West Point, thought that "the President made some very strange appointments or rather promotions in the new regiments."[20]

In the meantime, the campaign to avenge the disastrous Grattan episode slowly materialized. The army cobbled together nine companies of infantry, dragoons, and artillery from five different regiments at Fort Kearny (Nebraska Territory), and Col. William S. Harney was recalled from a furlough in Paris to lead the offensive. Emotional and profane, at six feet, four inches tall Harney towered above his comrades as the Sioux Expedition finally departed in August 1855. Many of the foot soldiers wielded newly improved shoulder arms with rifled barrels and Minié balls, which significantly improved accuracy and range; moreover, they had recently undertaken considerably more tactical drill and target practice than was the norm. On the morning of September 3, a battalion of infantrymen advanced toward Little Thunder's camp at Blue Water Creek, their fire driving the Brulé and Oglala into dismounted dragoons and infantrymen positioned to prevent their escape. At a cost of four killed, seven wounded, and one missing, Harney's regulars killed more than eighty Sioux and captured seventy others. "It was all on our side," wrote one infantryman, "the Indians not dreaming that we could reach them at that distance." Many of the casualties were women and children, however, earning Harney the epithet of "Squaw Killer." The soldiers then destroyed the Indian camp, effectively ending the First Sioux War.[21]

Conflicts between Native Americans and newcomers also increased in California and Oregon, where for most Anglos the lure of agricultural and mineral riches trumped any notions of honoring Indian land rights and respecting reservations. "Our people will go to the mines and they must have protection," insisted Oregon's delegate to Congress. Attempts by fragmented Pacific Coast tribes to fight back against better-armed regulars often resulted in near-extermination. Along the Russian River in 1850, for example, Second Infantry Capt. Nathaniel Lyon's mixed command of infantry, dragoons, and a mountain howitzer turned Indian defenses of island strongholds into "a perfect slaughter pen"; they killed 135 Indians (undoubtedly including many noncombatants) while only two soldiers were wounded.[22]

In 1855, affairs in the Pacific Northwest exploded after tit-for-tat massacres of Rogue River Indians and white civilians left fifty dead. Farther north, a Yakima assault on the town of Seattle (Washington Territory) was turned aside only by a combination of volunteers and the sailors, Marines, and sixteen guns of the USS *Decatur* anchored offshore. Commanding the Department of the Pacific, the pugnacious Wool dubbed Washington territorial governor Isaac Stevens "a drunken sot." The general blamed the conflicts on "a reckless population who regard the treasury of the United States as a legitimate subject of plunder, and, if for no other reason than the expenditure of large sums of money among them, would strive to plunge the government into a war with those Indians." Although Wool might have been correct—the Washington and Oregon territories secured nearly $2.5 million in federal compensation for expenses incurred during the conflicts—Stevens, himself a former topographical engineer, fired back in kind, accusing the general of "utter and signal incapacity." Oregon's territorial legislature demanded that the president sack Wool; using rhetoric sure to appeal to the antiregular tradition, the delegate Joseph Lane described the general as nothing more than "a tactician after the fashion of the military fogies of Europe."[23]

Battling to regain the initiative from volunteers bent on vengeance, regulars by 1856 were involved in wars against Rogue River and Yakima Indians that spread to encompass much of the Pacific Northwest. Oregon volunteers bent on killing any Indians unfortunate enough to be in their path, later reinforced by smaller regular columns under Maj. Robert C. Buchanan, bested the Rogue River tribes at the Battle of Big Meadows. Col. George Wright's new Ninth Infantry Regiment spearheaded a march into the heart of Yakima country, establishing Forts Simcoe and Walla Walla that summer. An uneasy peace was shattered in May 1858, when parties of Spokanes, Coeur d'Alenes,

John Ellis Wool. Pugnacious, tenacious, and experienced, as commander of the military Department of the Pacific John Ellis Wool (1784–1869), here photographed in his brevet uniform of major general by Mathew Brady, engaged in epic wars of words with Secretary Davis and Governor Isaac Stevens. Library of Congress, USZ62-110101.

Palouses, and other Northern tribes defeated Maj. Edward J. Steptoe's column at the Battle of Pine Creek. In response, Wright was ordered to make "vigorous war" against all Indians who did not accept the government's terms. Carrying new Model 1855 rifles and assisted by "our eagle-eyed Allies, the Nez Percés," the bluecoats routed several hundred Coeur d'Alenes, Palouses, and Spokanes at the Battles of Four Lakes and Spokane Plains. As Wright reported: "Our long-range rifles can reach the enemy where he cannot reach us." Ruthlessly pursuing his advantage, the colonel ordered his troops to slaughter nearly seven hundred Indian horses and used public hangings of captured leaders to demonstrate the government's power. By early fall 1858, the northern Pacific tribes had accepted reservations.[24]

Violence in New Mexico also spiked. On March 30, 1854, Chacón's Jicarilla Apache and Ute warriors ambushed Lt. John W. Davidson's company of dragoons at the Battle of Cieneguilla. Seeking revenge, dragoon columns under Lt. Col. Philip St. George Cooke and Capt. James H. Carleton combed the area around Taos, destroying much Jicarilla property and forcing most of the tribe to accept an unofficial peace. A big Ute raid against Pueblos that Christmas, however, sparked another round of fighting. Counterattacks by dragoons led by Col. Thomas T. Fauntleroy and territorial forces under Ceran St. Vrain secured a truce in northern New Mexico. To the south, after several army incursions into the Guadalupe, Capitan, and Manzanos Mountains, the establishment of Fort Stanton in April 1855 finally brought about an uneasy cease-fire with the Mescaleros.[25]

Following the close of the Second Seminole War, the few hundred Seminole and Miksukis remaining in Florida had fallen back to their reservation in the southern peninsula. Under increasing pressure to move, the Indians retreated to increasingly remote locations, striking back in December 1855 by ambushing a small army patrol and killing four soldiers. Imagined and real tales of Seminole attacks and slave revolts (a dozen warriors freed several slaves from the state senate president's home in Sarasota) terrorized south-central Florida. Volunteers, militia, and more than two regiments of regulars, now commanded by Colonel Harney (the Democratic Party's favored frontier troubleshooter), began the slow, laborious task of rounding up small groups of well-concealed Seminole. Guerrilla operations—described by one officer as being "by far the most wearisome toil I had ever undertaken"—continued until March 1858, when all but a handful of Seminole agreed to move west.[26]

Events in Kansas further tested the army's ability to enforce federal order. In a region already fraught with bitter competition over land and the expansion of slavery, the involvement of Maj. William R. Montgomery in speculative property deals at Fort Riley (a court-martial found him guilty of abusing his authority) dampened hopes that the regulars would be considered impartial arbiters. As the situation deteriorated, territorial governor Wilson Shannon in late 1855 requested that five hundred soldiers be dispatched to enforce a peace between free soilers and proslavery Kansas militiamen, reasoning that "they [the regulars] can be controlled, the others cannot."[27]

In late January 1856, President Pierce threw his support behind the fraudulently elected proslavery territorial legislature at Shawnee Mission (later relocated to Lecompton). At the governor's request, Lieutenant Colonel Cooke (the new commander at Fort Riley) and Colonel Sumner (commanding Fort Leavenworth) were authorized to suppress "insurrectionary combinations or armed resistance to the law." Whig Party attempts to dispatch General Scott to Kansas went nowhere as Governor Shannon instead ordered Sumner to disperse a rival free-state legislature scheduled to convene at Topeka, "peacefully if you can, forcibly if necessary." Assembling four cavalry companies and a section of artillery at noon on Independence Day, "Bull" Sumner, cousin of the abolitionist Charles Sumner, strode into the hall where the rump convention was meeting and, after proclaiming this to be "the most painful duty of my life," dispersed the free soilers.[28]

Several Northern newspapers equated Pierce's use of the military with that of Oliver Cromwell and deemed the dispersal of the Topeka assembly a "coup d'etat." Frederick Douglass lamented that when free soilers had been under threat by Border Ruffians, "Fort Leavenworth was silent." But "as soon as one Border Ruffian is shot down, troops leap forth . . . at the call of the President." Furious antislavery House members refused to pass that year's army bill unless it included a rider forbidding the use of regulars in support of the proslavery legislature at Lecompton. When the Democratic Senate rejected the House proposal, Pierce had to call a special session, during which a divided House agreed to the Senate funding bill by a 101–98 margin. Seeking to salvage the situation in time to prevent the Democratic Party's defeat that fall, Pierce dispatched Col. Persifor F. Smith to handle army affairs in Kansas and picked John W. Geary to replace Shannon as governor. Pennsylvania Democrats who recognized the moral and political need to check the escalating conflict, Smith and Geary released free soilers from arrest and reorganized the territorial militia. Orders to transfer the First Dragoons from Kansas were rescinded. Lieutenant Colonel Cooke's troopers intercepted a Free Soil mob led by James H. Lane before it could get to Lecompton, then disbanded 2,500 Missouri Ruffians before they could close in on the free-state headquarters at Lawrence. "Take it all in all," the free-state activist Charles L. Robinson later concluded, "the conduct of the army during the Kansas conflict . . . is worthy of praise. . . . No branch of the Government is so free from partisan or personal influence, and no officials are governed by a sense of honor as are army officers."[29]

The Pierce administration also reflected its pro-South bent in its hands-off approach to filibusters and the zealous prosecution of the Fugitive Slave Act. Under Presidents Taylor and Fillmore, regulars had twice arrested José M. J. Carvajal, who on several occasions raised volunteers (often including former Texas Rangers and U.S. Army deserters) in a plot to carve out an independent fiefdom in northern Mexico. Col. Ethan A. Hitchcock, commanding the Division of the Pacific, had cracked down hard on William A. Walker's efforts to organize an expedition to Latin America. Pierce, however, sometimes turned a blind eye toward filibusters, whose actions might make it easier for the United States to expand into Cuba, Mexico, and Central America. Davis sharply reprimanded Hitchcock's successor on the Pacific Coast, Brig. Gen. John E. Wool, for what the administration believed to be his overly harsh treatment of suspected filibusters there. In a similarly pro-South move designed to ease enforcement of the Fugitive Slave Act, Attorney General Caleb Cushing determined that, upon the request of a federal marshal, regulars could be used as a *posse comitatus* against domestic disturbances (the so-called Cushing Doctrine). Pierce used the ruling to justify employing federal troops to guard attempts to execute the return of fugitive slaves, most notably Anthony Burns, whose case had become a cause célèbre for abolitionists.[30]

Left to their own devices, most regulars wanted no part in peacekeeping operations in Kansas, had little patience with filibusters, and resented efforts to scapegoat the army. "There are a great many rascals on both sides," wrote Lt. John P. Hatch, "who only make these troubles an excuse for plundering the timid of both sides." Though supportive of expansion, most regulars insisted that it occur in accord with appropriate government actors. "All good men shd. disapprove of it, as illegal or contrary to the spirit of our treaties or laws," advised one veteran upon learning of Narciso López's scheme to seize Cuba. Officers also saw themselves as devoted to the maintenance of order in rough-and-tumble San Francisco, torn by vigilance committees, rivalries within the dominant Democratic Party, and frequent filibustering excitement. Constitutional protections of civil liberties and individual freedoms were to most regulars less important than defending order and property.[31]

There were, of course, exceptions to this general sympathy for order among officers, especially when it came to filibustering. Although claiming to despise "filibusterism," Maj. William H. Emory, a native of Maryland, admitted to conspiring with those seeking U.S. annexation of the Mexican state of Chihuahua. Alleged promises of a $3 million bounty were enough to at least attract the interest of Brevet Maj. Gen. William J. Worth to command Cuban exiles seeking to free the island from Spanish rule. North Carolina's Charles C. Hornsby, a captain in one of the temporary regular regiments during the war against Mexico, fought with William Walker's army in Nicaragua; cashiered for showing up drunk to a court-martial, former captain

Philip R. Thompson was to serve as Walker's adjutant general, but he died in June 1857. Mansfield Lovell and Gustavus W. Smith, classmates at West Point, both resigned from the army on December 18, 1854, to join John A. Quitman's proposed expedition to Cuba, and Lt. Cadmus M. Wilcox, another academy graduate, took a seventy-day leave with the intention of scouting the island in advance of Quitman's planned strike.[32]

In less spectacular, but more substantive, action in the East, Democrats returned civilian superintendents to the Springfield and Harpers Ferry arsenals. Whereas supporters of continued army control lauded the better quality, lower costs, and depoliticization of the system, the House Committee on Military Affairs in 1852 charged that military supervision of the armorers had placed "the free and independent mechanics of this nation" under "restrictions that would be revolting to a slave." For skilled artisans and mechanics of western Virginia and New England, a way of life seemed endangered by the army's incessant demand for efficiency. Representing Virginia's Shenandoah Valley (which included the Harpers Ferry arsenal), Charles J. Faulkner (D) coordinated efforts to replace the army superintendents. A congressionally mandated commission produced a tangled dissertation that included individual reports or opinions from every member. The two regulars on the committee voted to retain the existing system, but all four civilians wanted to end army oversight. "I, in common with most Americans," wrote committee member John Hardy Steele, the former Democratic governor of New Hampshire, "feel a dread . . . of tyranny or oppression, and believe it to be my duty to resist every attempt to degrade any class of our fellow-citizens, by placing them under men who cannot, or will not, recognize them as men entitled to the respect due from man to man."[33]

In spring 1854, spurred by the investigation, petitions against military supervision of any civilian projects poured into congressional offices. Judging from the outburst of public dissatisfaction—2,765 signatures from Massachusetts, 669 from Connecticut, 78 from South Carolina, 295 from Rhode Island, 63 from Kentucky, 245 from Ohio, more than a hundred from Missouri, 1,377 from the Baltimore–Washington–Alexandria district, plus another 506 from elsewhere in Maryland and Virginia—participatory democracy was alive and well. The petition from Pittsfield, Massachusetts, denounced "the increase of the Standing Army . . . [as] repugnant to the genius of republican institutions, and dangerous to civil liberty." Placing "*those hot bed plants of the aristocratic, national, military, charity school*" over civilians was a "usurpation of the rights and privileges of civilians and mechanics," complained Baltimore and Maryland petitioners. The protests worked: in August, that year's army bill removed the military supervisors in favor of civilians appointed by the president.[34]

The decade also revealed increasing controversies regarding the desirability of a federal military presence. The possibility of securing a national armory or foundry still attracted petitions and memorials in many regions. In 1854, for example, the Evansville, Indiana, city council bragged that the "unparalleled facilities" for transportation and the "peculiarly advantageous" proximity of mineral resources made it an ideal location for a western armory. Four years later, the Alabama state legislature highlighted the availability of coal, the healthy climate, and abundant water power in its quest for the prize, reminding Congress that the region "has not received as much attention from the government as we think it deserves." Citing the need for protection against Indian attacks, more than seven hundred largely Hispanic residents in southern New Mexico signed an 1860 petition supporting the continuation of the garrison at Fort Craig. Thousands of residents of St. Louis, which in contrast was more settled, petitioned that year for the transfer of that city's arsenal, whose arms and ammunition stores posed a "dangerous evil, and no longer necessary obstruction," to nearby Jefferson Barracks. Similarly, talk of a new cavalry depot at Harrodsburg, Kentucky, led 257 residents to sign petitions protesting such action, which would threaten the region's two existing female academies and a proposed new college. The petitioners cautioned against the "establishment of this depot with four or five hundred soldiers gathered as they generally are from the alleys and sewers of our great cities, bringing with them all that vice and dissipation and debauchery which follow in the wake of such soldiery."[35]

Soldiers and former soldiers nonetheless remained frequent presidential candidates. Taylor, of course, had won in 1848; even as the Whigs nominated Winfield Scott four years later, General Wool lobbied hard—and unsuccessfully—to win the Democratic Party's bid. In 1856, the newly formed Republican Party picked former topographical engineer John C. Frémont as its standard-bearer. Estranged from the army, Frémont campaigned as a dashing explorer and committed opponent of the expansion of slavery rather than as a veteran soldier. Desiring order, and critical of those they believed to be extremists on both sides, most regulars sympathized with his dough-faced Democratic opponent, James Buchanan. Even as he lambasted "the fanatic portion" of the South, Pennsylvania-born Lt. Edward L. Hartz denounced "the accursed fanatical interference in slavery and their support of such an unprincipled scoundrel as John C. Frémont." Similarly, Wool asserted that "the whole army" had supported Buchanan. Still, it seems striking that regulars or former regulars had been presidential candidates in three successive elections. In this era of delicate political balance, allegations of military aristocracy and criticisms of a standing army continued to be tempered by admiration for feats of martial glory, especially those earned by leaders perceived as being citizen-soldiers.[36]

Having been rejected by his first three choices as secretary of war, Buchanan finally convinced former Virginia governor John B. Floyd to take the job. The two shared a firm commitment to state rights, but both were devoid of military or managerial experience. In 1857, the president precipitated a crisis with the Church of Latter Day Saints by naming Alfred Cumming, an overweight, semialcoholic former Indian Affairs superintendent, to supersede Brigham Young as Utah's territorial governor. Envisioning the regulars as a *posse comitatus,* the president determined that Cumming needed a sizeable escort for installation into his new office. Polygamy among many church officials fueled Buchanan's decision to employ the army, as did the hope that such a campaign might divert attention from divisions over slavery and serve as a lucrative plum for Democratic contractors.[37]

Quartermasters hustled to assemble the supplies and transportation necessary for the army's largest operation since the war against Mexico. Although both Scott and Harney advised that winter weather and logistical difficulties would prevent the occupation of Salt Lake City until the following spring, the campaign seemed to take on a life of its own. In July, lead elements marched out of Fort Leavenworth. Other units, eventually totaling four regiments and a reinforced battery of artillery, slowly followed. Col. Albert Sidney Johnston assumed command of the scattered strike force when events in Kansas prevented Harney's departure. In November, badly in need of supplies and reorganization in the wake of devastating Mormon raids on their supply trains, Johnston's command limped into winter quarters near old Fort Bridger, which the Mormons had recently burned.[38]

With Young threatening guerrilla warfare, Buchanan asked Congress to raise four new regular regiments. Defeated by what the *New York Herald* described as "an unholy alliance" of abolitionists and antiadministration Democrats, the president settled for a measure authorizing him to raise two volunteer regiments for the Utah campaign in exchange for a provision allowing him to call up a regiment of mounted volunteers for Texas. A new set of presidential envoys to Utah, along with the renewed offensive by Johnston that spring—now featuring all or parts of eight of the army's nineteen regiments—led to a negotiated settlement, so Buchanan decided not to raise any volunteers. In late June, Johnston entered Salt Lake City and established Camp Floyd. Cumming became governor, but Young and the Saints established a shadow government that still dominated most of the territory. Ironically, the brisk army trade with residents, in combination with the subsequent sale of federal property at steeply discounted rates, provided badly needed infusions into Utah's fledgling economy.[39]

Predisposed to dislike the Mormons and having endured a hard winter at Fort Bridger, most regulars were disappointed by the failure to crush

Young's followers. News of the dreadful affair at Mountain Meadows, in which members of the Mormon Nauvoo Legion murdered more than a hundred emigrants, further inflamed emotions. "The people are all like fanatics," complained Capt. Jesse A. Gove to his family. Only through firm military authority could the "polygamous immorality, cloaked beneath the garb of fanaticism and tempered by the lust of the harem!" be stamped out. "A more miserable set of wretches I never beheld," observed Lt. George D. Bayard.[40]

The administration's muscular policies extended to the Indian borderlands. Ignoring peace agreements between Agent Thomas Twiss and forty-two Cheyenne chiefs and leaders, Secretary Floyd in April 1857 authorized a punitive expedition against the Cheyennes in the Platte Road area. Commanding the strike force, Colonel Sumner learned in late July of a big encampment near the Solomon River. "I don't know how many warriors the Cheyennes can bring against us," boomed Sumner, "but . . . we can whip the whole tribe." Leaving their infantry escorts behind, just after one o'clock on July 29, three hundred cavalrymen began a slow trot toward their enemy. Confident that waters from a holy lake would shield them from the white man's bullets, a roughly equivalent number of Indians rode ahead in their brilliant military finery to meet the intruders. About one hundred yards from the enemy Sumner suddenly roared in quick succession: "Sling—carbine!" "Draw—saber!" "Gallup—march!" and finally, "CHARGE!" The Cheyennes were even more stunned by the order to draw swords than Sumner's cavalrymen were, and their medicine promised no protection against the cold steel of army sabers. The Indians scattered with the soldiers in hot pursuit; the troops killed nine and wounded many others before a bugler sounded recall about three o'clock. Two days later, the soldiers destroyed the hastily abandoned remnants of a big Cheyenne village. In 1858, Agent Robert C. Miller reported "a wondrous change" among the Cheyennes, Comanches, Kiowas, and Arapahos. "They said they had learned a lesson last summer in their fight with Colonel Sumner; that it was useless to contend against the white man."[41]

Offensive operations also continued in Texas. The new Brazos and Clear Fork reservations, created through the influence of Secretary Davis and Agent Robert Neighbors, proved but a temporary counterbalance to the historic enmity between Texans and the Southern Plains tribes. In May 1858, state-funded Texas Rangers led by Capt. John S. "Rip" Ford, enjoying the assistance of auxiliaries from the Brazos Reservation (an assemblage of long-time rivals of the Comanches), surprised and destroyed a large Comanche camp near Antelope Hills. Four months later, Capt. Earl Van Dorn's four regular companies, also aided by Brazos auxiliaries, dealt a devastating blow to Buffalo Hump's village at Rush Creek, killing 56 warriors, burning 120 lodges, and capturing three hundred horses. Tragically, Van Dorn had mistakenly attacked Comanches who had been attempting to make peace thirty miles away at Fort Arbuckle. That December, Van Dorn himself urged that the Comanches be allowed a larger reservation in Texas: "It cannot reasonably be expected that they, as wild and as free by nature as the eagle, would voluntarily shut themselves up in such a coop, or that they would be driven there without a violent struggle. Who would?"[42]

But no matter in the ferocious contest for North Texas. In May 1859, reinforced by two more companies of Second Cavalrymen and guided by fifty-eight auxiliaries from the Brazos Reservation, Van Dorn hit another large camp near Crooked Creek, claiming to have killed forty-one men and eight women and captured thirty-six others. Two of his invaluable Indian auxiliaries were also wounded even as the Texas reservations were being closed and their former residents escorted north of the Red River, victims of a determined push by brigands like John R. Baylor to cleanse the Lone Star State of all Indians. In summer 1860, four army columns totaling twenty-two mounted companies from North Texas and Forts Riley, Cobb, and Union conducted massive—and largely unsuccessful—sweeps through Kiowa and Comanche lands.[43]

In New Mexico Territory, the murder by Mogollon Apaches (Bidanku or Nde) of Navajo Agent Henry L. Dodge, eldest son of a U.S. senator and brother to another, gave federal authorities the necessary excuse to go to war. In late spring 1857, Col. Benjamin Bonneville dispatched columns totaling nearly a thousand men against suspected Apache haunts. Anticipating trouble, the Mogollon fled south across the border into Mexico, but regulars surprised bands of Mimbre and Coyotero (White Mountain) Apaches, killing or executing more than two dozen of the former. The strikes against Indians who had up to this point focused their raids against more lucrative targets in Mexico led many Apaches to vow revenge against Americans. In the winter of 1860–1861, miners at Pinos Altos administered a public whipping to Mangas Coloradas, who had advocated good relations with Americans; at Apache Pass, Lt. George N. Bascom bungled an attempt to take hostage Mangas's son-in-law, Cochise. A quarter of a century of savage conflict with the Chiricahuas resulted, with Apache attacks soon closing the road between Mesilla and Tucson.[44]

Agent Dodge's death also eliminated a voice of moderation in U.S.-Navajo relations. For nearly a decade, Fort Defiance had served as a base for periodic expeditions into Navajo lands. Just before dawn on April 30, 1860, hundreds of Navajos assaulted the fort's three-company garrison. Like most posts in the West, Defiance had no outer walls, just a collection of sod and adobe buildings surrounding a parade ground. Although the attack failed with minimal casualties, it represented an enormous symbolic threat to U.S. authority. That fall, with instructions "to seize and destroy the crops of the Navajoes, and to surprise them while in their planting grounds," Maj. Edward R. S. Canby led six hundred regulars, supplemented with sizeable numbers of Ute auxiliaries and locally raised scouts, into Diné bikéyah, the Navajo homelands. The Navajos avoided pitched battles but lost a thousand horses and seven thousand sheep in a tortuous campaign through drought-stricken terrain; in February 1861, with Canby's men continuing to patrol their lands and pillage their crops, the two sides agreed to an armistice.[45]

In what he hoped would be a cornerstone of his administration, Buchanan's hawkish foreign policy had reflected his commitment to rekindling a distinctly Southern brand of Manifest Destiny. Distracted by the Panic of 1857 and growing sectional turmoil, Congress, as did the rest of the nation, ignored his calls to send U.S. troops into Chihuahua and Sonora against "lawless Mexicans" and "large bands of hostile and predatory Indians." Buchanan's expansionist dreams, however, did not extend to the Pacific Northwest. Recently promoted Brig. Gen. William S. Harney, the temperamental commander of the new Department of Oregon and Democratic Party darling, had in summer 1859 nearly precipitated a conflict by ordering the occupation of the disputed San Juan Islands. Bewildered by Harney's actions, the administration dispatched Winfield Scott to the Pacific Northwest to arrange an understanding with the British.[46]

With sectional tensions on the rise, the Buchanan administration also acted prudently in response to turmoil in South Texas. In July 1859, thirty-five-year old Juan N. Cortina sparked a rebellion in the Matamoros-Brownsville region against Anglos, local officials, and land lawyers who had formed "a secret conclave . . . for the sole purpose of despoiling the Mexicans of their lands and usurp them afterwards." Secretary Floyd dispatched three companies under Maj. Samuel P. Heintzelman to "attack and disperse" Cortina's supporters. Clashes between Texas Rangers, Heintzelman's regulars, and *Cortinistas* on both sides of the Lower Rio Grande led Governor Sam Houston to threaten open conflict with Mexico. To restore order, the Third Infantry reoccupied Fort Brown, Ringgold Barracks, and Fort Clark. Regulars twice crossed the Rio Grande in search of Cortina as Lt. Col. Robert E. Lee, commander of the Department of Texas, hastened to the scene. Lee's presence calmed uneasy residents; as one lieutenant put it, "his smooth easy way has acted like oil in troubled waters, and a quietness and feeling of security are now to a great extent restored." With Mexican authorities now hot on Cortina's trail, the crisis petered out, soon to be forgotten amid the calamity of secession.[47]

Chapter Ten

Army Regulars and the Crisis of Union

As the Pulitzer Prize–winning historian James McPherson has observed, the Civil War was one "of peoples rather than of professional armies." The regular army of the United States was quickly dwarfed by volunteer forces, which at peak strength numbered more than a million men. Still, antebellum regular officers played an outsized role in the Civil War, and both the Union and Confederate armies used the conventional organization and tactics of the old army. Beyond the battlefields, West Point graduates dominated the Union's Quartermaster's, Subsistence, and Ordnance Departments, which handled most of the $3 billion spent by the federal government fighting the war.[1] Overseeing this expansion brought regulars into extensive contact with contractors and workers in war-related industries, profoundly increasing their significance to the everyday lives of Northern civilians.

The Civil War also saw another reexamination of the role of the United States Military Academy in American society. By 1860, three-fourths of regular officers boasted West Point educations, and the public saw their attitudes toward slavery and secession as reflecting those of the entire army. Abolitionists—who had long associated regulars with the continuation of human bondage—were especially incensed by the decision by nearly a quarter of the officers to resign their commissions for Confederate service. The poor performances of several prominent West Pointers in battle added to the sense of unease, reawakening longstanding suspicions about the appropriateness of a national military academy. And if West Point were unnecessary, or antithetical to republican government, was there need for a regular army?

* * * * *

Army officers craved order, and during the 1850s their politics leaned strongly Democratic, largely from the fear that the increasingly antislavery Whig and Republican Parties would aggravate sectional tensions. But the corruption and mismanagement that had marked the Buchanan administration—and particularly John B. Floyd's War Department—caused regulars to join a critical public in censuring what a Milwaukee newspaper dubbed "the army plunder contracts." Groaned one staff officer: "Every thing is now governed and controlled by politicians." Many suspected that the expedition into Utah had been a ploy designed to help the administration's friends with lucrative government contracts. In several instances—the sale of Fort Snelling, Minnesota; the purchase of land for a fort at Willett's Point, New York; the acquisition of a tract at Lime Point, California, for a similar purpose—Floyd engineered deals that rewarded fellow Democrats at the government's expense. "It is d——d hard if the army is to be made a tool to advance a political hack like Floyd," complained an officer from faraway Fort Yuma, Arizona. From the Washington headquarters of the Topographical Engineers, Capt. George G. Meade decried "the intrigues & machinations for the advancement of personal interests, the selfishness & cold-hardedness that is there daily & hourly exhibited." Secretary Floyd had also butted heads with Capt. Montgomery C. Meigs, whose oversight of District of Columbia projects promised enormous opportunities for political patronage. "I am surrounded by speculators & villains," complained Meigs. Hoping to open new contacts for his Democratic allies, Floyd in early November 1859 banished the troublesome Meigs to duty at Fort Jefferson, accessible only by boat, sixty miles from Key West, Florida.[2]

In spring 1860, a House Select Committee chaired by John Covode (R-PA) began investigating the Buchanan administration, eventually issuing a scathing 838-page report denouncing the president's use of patronage. It was also revealed that Secretary Floyd had engaged in a series of unethical attempts to keep the giant Russell, Majors & Waddell freighting and staging partnership afloat. Capitalizing on the opportunity to distance itself from such endemic corruption, the Republican Party nominated for president a clean-cut Illinois lawyer and former congressman named Abraham Lincoln. Mustering his own powerful allies, the formidable Captain Meigs also won his revenge. The government appropriations bill for 1860–1861, which included $500,000 ($11.9 million at time of publication) for the Washington Aqueduct, specified that the monies "be expended according to the plans and estimates of Captain Meigs, and under his superintendence."[3]

In November 1860, Lincoln's victory brought with it more serious talk of secession. Many regulars still hoped that the Union could be saved. According to Capt. Richard Ewell, a Virginian boasting a quarter-century of military service, "officers generally are very much averse to anything like civil war. . . . The truth is in the army there are no sectional feelings and many from extreme ends of the Union are the most intimate friends." "Secession is no remedy," declared the Tennessee-born Lt. Moses Hanibal Wright on November 21. Critical of Lincoln's election "on the 'Nigger' question," Wright nonetheless insisted that he had been "elected according to the Constitution, which must be held inviolate." Ominously, however, twelve days later Wright added: "I know one thing—I go with Tennessee." From West Point, "all Southerners . . . say too that if their own state secedes they will join her," reported the Massachusetts native Lt. Cyrus B. Comstock.[4]

Scattered across the country, regulars thirsted for news and pondered their prospects as South Carolina, Mississippi, Florida, Alabama, Georgia, Louisiana, and Texas seceded in the winter of 1860–1861. From Texas, Lt. Edward L. Hartz, though unwavering in his support for the Union, blamed the crisis on "Black Republicans" who would sacrifice the Union "for the emancipation of so many miserable negroes." With his typical restraint, Lt. Col. Robert E. Lee opined: "God alone can save us from our folly, selfishness & short sightedness." Based at Albuquerque, Capt. John P. Hatch queried his father on February 3. "Is the Union gone? . . . Our latest dates are to Jan. 11th, at which time things looked very bad indeed." Even so, Hatch added that "I cannot still help hoping." From Colorado Territory, Lt. Edward G. Bush succinctly captured the mood of most officers: "I do think they have all gone clean mad."[5]

Others had fewer misgivings about their proper course. "Secession is treason," concluded Col. Edwin V. Sumner. "Hurrah for Lincoln!" proclaimed Connecticut's Maj. John Sedgwick. Repugnant to slavery, Meigs blamed the crisis on "the mad men of the South." Denouncing the Buchanan administration's inaction, Lt. James H. Wilson, a native of Illinois, vowed that officers stationed at Fort Vancouver, Washington Territory, "are for 'the Union, now and forever.'" Though disappointed that "the nigger question" had caused so much acrimony, Brig. Gen. John E. Wool criticized the "imbecility and timidity, if not treason in high places." But South Carolina's Henry C. Farley, then a cadet at West Point, resigned four weeks before his state's secession convention. In late January, Capt. James J. Archer, a decorated Mexican War veteran who had received his commission as part of the army expansion of 1855, declared his intention to quit the service as soon as his native Maryland left the Union. In mid-May, with Maryland still having failed to act, Archer resigned and made the long journey back east from Fort Colville, Washington Territory, accepting a colonelcy in a newly forming Confederate regiment.[6]

In sharp contrast to his willingness to use force in Utah, President Buchanan did little to check the dissolution of the Union. In one of his last acts as war secretary before resigning in December 1860, Floyd attempted to authorize the transfer of 125 cannons from Pittsburgh to Mississippi and Texas, and General Scott accused him of having "shifted" 115,000 rifles and muskets to the South during the past year and a half. Especially egregious was the unilateral decision by the commander of the Department of Texas, Brig. Gen. David E. Twiggs, to surrender all federal posts in the Lone Star State. After considerable equivocation, Buchanan finally opted to maintain garrisons at Fort Sumter (Charleston, South Carolina) and Fort Pickens (Pensacola, Florida). Amid rumors of secessionist plots to seize the capital, officials mobilized six hundred troops to maintain order in the District of

Edwin Vose Sumner. Longtime dragoon, veteran of fighting against Mexicans and Indians, frustrated arbiter of disputes in Kansas, and a confirmed Unionist, Edwin V. "Bull" Sumner (1797–1863) appointed himself as one of President-elect Lincoln's security detail in early 1861. He commanded Second Corps, Army of the Potomac, for much of the bitter fighting in 1862, but he died in March 1863 while awaiting a transfer. Library of Congress, DIG-ppmsca-32294.

Columbia. Four regulars—Sumner, Maj. David Hunter, Capt. John Pope, and Capt. George W. Hazzard—took it upon themselves to act as an ad hoc security detail for the president-elect. They accompanied his inaugural train from Indiana to Harrisburg, Pennsylvania, where fears of a possible assassination attempt led Lincoln and a civilian bodyguard to debark in favor of a less-public carriage ride into Washington.[7]

Many regulars, like the seventy-seven-year old Wool, still hoped that a last-minute deal might avert a terrible war. Although he had proclaimed secession to be "treasonable" and made known that any soldier under his command who admitted even "the possibility of disunion" would be court-martialed, the conservative Democrat accepted the New York state legislature's invitation to attend the so-called Virginia Peace Convention, assembled at Washington in February 1861. But the Confederate bombardment of Fort Sumter, followed by the secession of Virginia, Arkansas, North Carolina, and Tennessee, soon forced wavering soldiers to make harsh choices. Between Lincoln's election in November 1860 and the summer of 1861, 269 regular officers (24.7 percent of the officer corps) resigned to take up Confederate service. Kinship, community ties, state loyalties, and an identification with the white South's racial order were especially significant factors in their decision-making; and though envisioning "no greater calamity" than secession, Virginia's Lieutenant Colonel Lee concluded that "if the Union is dissolved, and the Government disrupted, I shall return to my native State and share the miseries of my people." By contrast, only about 3.3 percent (508) of enlisted personnel went South, even when offered considerable Confederate inducements.[8]

Three days after Fort Sumter, Lincoln directed the states to provide 75,000 militiamen to restore federal authority. By law, their terms were limited to three months. With the War Department overwhelmed by the task, Treasury Secretary Salmon P. Chase formed an advisory board composed of Adjutant General Lorenzo Thomas (who apparently never attended), Capt. Irvin McDowell, and Capt. William B. Franklin to determine the force structures needed to defeat the rebellion. The board recommended increasing the regular army by ten regiments and advised that new volunteers enlist for three years. On May 3, using his powers to protect the constitution from "insurrectionary combinations," the president unveiled plans to raise the new regular regiments in addition to 42,000 volunteers.[9]

As the crisis unfolded, nowhere were the actions of regulars on the ground more obvious in keeping federal control than Missouri. The largest lead-mining state in the Union, the state also controlled strategic access to the Missouri and Mississippi Rivers. Governor Claiborne Fox Jackson was a proslavery Democrat, as was Sterling Price, who commanded the state's militia. In the presidential election of 1860 there, Stephen A. Douglas (D) had narrowly bested John Bell (Constitutional Union), with Abraham Lincoln having limped in fourth, having received just over half as many votes as John C. Breckinridge (Southern Democrat). From his headquarters in St. Louis, the Tennessee native Brig. Gen. William S. Harney commanded the Department of the West. Even with recent reinforcements, only about 360 regulars garrisoned strategic St. Louis. But Capt. Nathaniel Lyon and Lt. John M. Schofield had no question about their determination to preserve the Union and, with the backing of the powerful Blair family, ensured that friendly Home Guards joined the federal garrison to secure the St. Louis Arsenal (which housed as many as 75,000 weapons) and disarmed secessionists attempting to organize just outside the city. After some hesitation, Harney on May 30 was replaced by Lyon, thus sealing the state, for the short term at least, for the Union.[10]

In contrast to such decisive action by relatively junior officers, Maj. Gen. Winfield Scott, seventy-four years old and in failing health, lacked both the vigor and the imagination needed to meet the crisis. Unable to ride a horse, Scott's suggestion that Lincoln evacuate Forts Sumter and Pickens as a conciliatory gesture to the South was ignored as politically impracticable. His so-called Anaconda Plan—a naval blockade, slow buildup of military forces, and eventual offensive (spearheaded by regular troops) down the Mississippi River against New Orleans to force the Confederacy to accept a political settlement—seemed too cautious for a war that many assumed would soon come to a glorious end. Scott's lessened influence hurt the cause of the regular army, and the outpouring of volunteers seemed to justify public faith in citizen-soldiers. In a July 1 letter to the president, Secretary of War Simon Cameron thus criticized "a cumbrous and dangerous standing army" and decried the "startling defection" of regular officers.[11]

When Congress reconvened in early July, Lincoln asked it to authorize 400,000 men and appropriate $400 million to defeat the Confederacy. In consultation with Henry Wilson (R-MA), chair of the Senate Military Affairs Committee, bills to flesh out the details of Lincoln's earlier emergency actions (the number of regular regiments was increased to eleven) were hastily prepared for congressional action. Swayed by the Ohio Copperhead Clement Vallandigham (D), the House of Representatives initially voted to convert the new regular regiments to volunteers. Only in exchange for a provision reducing the permanent force to 25,000 men once the war ended did a conference committee restore the new regulars. Congress also added four major generals and six brigadier generals to the regular establishment, authorized the president to accept as many as 500,000 volunteers, and set enlistments at three years. Early August saw passage of measures expanding War Department staff and engineers, allowing female nurses, creating a retired list for

Henry Wilson. Massachusetts senator from 1855 to 1873 and later eighteenth vice president of the United States, as head of the Senate Committee on Military Affairs Henry Wilson (1812–1875) worked hard to fund and protect the army. Library of Congress, DIG-cwpbh-00671.

officers, increasing rations, abolishing flogging, returning control of national armories to Ordnance officers, and raising pay for privates.[12]

Several contemporaries speculated on the decision to maintain separate regular and volunteer establishments. In memoirs published after war's end, Generals George B. McClellan, Ulysses S. Grant, and John M. Schofield all concluded that it would have been preferable to either disband the regular army entirely or find some way of dispersing regular officers among the volunteers. More contemporaneous had been Captain Franklin's suggestion that the volunteers simply "be considered a part of the Regular Army." Secretary Cameron had also proposed consolidating the two forces. But Scott and army staff would have none of that, instead demanding that most officers who wanted to accept volunteer commissions resign their regular commissions, in the process potentially losing their tenure in a postwar army. This meant that officers who had resigned before the war, but then volunteered for service after the firing began, were better positioned to accept higher ranks in volunteer units compared to their active-duty counterparts. Thus, while McClellan (who had left the army in 1857) was rising to become army commander and Ulysses S. Grant (1854) was forcing the surrender of Forts Henry and Donelson, Phil Sheridan remained a captain in the regular army until May 1862, when he belatedly received permission to take the colonelcy of the Second Michigan Cavalry.[13]

In retrospect, Lincoln's biggest mistake had been his choice of Cameron as secretary of war, which had followed the long tradition of using the office as a means of distributing partisan favors. A Pennsylvanian skilled in the arts of political cronyism, Cameron possessed neither the managerial skills nor the strength of character to mobilize the Union for war. Almost immediately, tales of corruption dogged Cameron's department; a House Select Committee headed by Charles H. Van Wyck (R-NY) revealed that the secretary's decision to bypass regular army procurement bureaus had resulted in "personal favoritism at the public expense, the corruption of public morals, and a ruinous profligacy in the expenditure of public treasure." In a letter to the president, a New Yorker put it more directly: "It is universally believed that Cameron is a thief."[14]

In January 1862, Lincoln forced Cameron's resignation, but the immediate trigger seems to have been something other than his financial shenanigans. In a draft of his annual report for the previous year, Cameron had argued that the government had the right "to arm slaves . . . and employ their service against the rebels." Several newspapers immediately printed the leaked draft. Lincoln had already revoked an August emancipation proclamation by his commander of the Western Division, Maj. Gen. John C. Frémont, and feared that freeing the slaves might drive the border slave states of Missouri, Kentucky, and Maryland into the welcoming arms of the Confederacy. The president thus saw to it that the final Cameron report was shorn of any such references, and the secretary left shortly thereafter.[15]

It was ironic that the regular army or the War Department would be in the vanguard of efforts to end slavery, given trends of the previous seventy years. Individual officers had on occasion expressed concerns about slavery. Capt. Samuel P. Heintzelman sympathized with the Free Soil Party; Capt. Henry C. Symonds was "a fiery republican"; Capt. George W. Hazzard denounced

Indiana's state Democratic Party in three personal letters to Lincoln. Tasked with obeying the policies of their civilian masters, however, regulars shared the beliefs of a nation that had countenanced human bondage since its inception. They were more sympathetic with the need for order than the ideals of liberty. Since the mid-1840s, fourth-year cadets at West Point had read a widely used ethics textbook written by Francis Wayland, but its chapter criticizing slavery had been expunged so that "this exciting & dangerous subject shall not be placed under the eyes of the Cadets thereby leading to discussions amongst themselves." In years prior to the war, regulars had in the Anthony Burns case been deployed to enforce the Fugitive Slave Act and dispersed the Free Soil convention at Topeka in 1856. Moreover, Lieutenant Colonel Lee and Lt. J. E. B. Stuart had crushed John Brown's raid on Harpers Ferry.[16]

As army regulations provided allowances for officers to have one or more servants, more than a few commissioned personnel received compensation for a slave or had grown up in households where slaves were present. The parents of George Pickett and P. G. T. Beauregard were large slaveowners, and upon resigning from regular duty, Braxton Bragg purchased a sugar plantation and eventually owned 109 slaves. Robert E. Lee's mother had bequeathed him several slaves, and in 1857 he became executor for his father-in-law's estate, which included at least 150 bondsmen. Lieutenant Stuart and his wife owned two slaves. Dred Scott's attempts to secure his freedom, denied by the Supreme Court in 1857, had in part been based on his having accompanied his owner, Assistant Surgeon John Emerson, to Forts Armstrong (Illinois) and Snelling (Minnesota Territory), where slavery had been forbidden. While at Fort Wayne (Indiana) in 1844, Lt. Richard S. Ewell purchased a teenager "to cook and take care of my horses." Ewell later bought an Apache lad named Friday, who accompanied him to Virginia during the Civil War. Yet the direct association between army officers and slavery must not be overstated; in the most comprehensive analysis of the issue to date, the historian Ty Smith has calculated that less than 10 percent of commissioned personnel in Texas during the census years of 1850 and 1860 owned slaves.[17]

Antislavery groups had nonetheless long viewed regulars as willing tools of the slave-power alliance. In 1845, sixty-two residents from the abolitionist stronghold of Mount Pleasant, Ohio, petitioned to dissolve West Point, which "tends to perpetuate slavery, as it is mainly in defence of that accursed system that those who have been thus educated by Government have been called to fight." Charles Sumner denounced the military academy as "one of the martial cancers of our country"; following passage of the Fugitive Slave Act, editors of the *Christian Secretary* attributed the rumored transfer of twelve companies of regulars to Boston to "the purpose of awing *our own citizens* into obedience to the powers that be." Efforts to increase the army in

1858 had floundered in part because critics charged that it "did nothing" to protect free soilers in Kansas.[18]

The departure of hundreds of regular officers following secession, along with the presence of conservative, West Point–educated Democrats like Major Generals (Volunteers) McClellan and Don Carlos Buell in command positions, stoked further criticism. Representative Martin F. Conway (R-KS) doubted that "there is more than one sincere abolitionist or emancipationist among the military authorities." Joseph Medill, editor of the *Chicago Tribune*, claimed that the army contained "scores of luke warm, half secession officers in command who can not bear to strike a vigorous blow lest it hurt their rebel friends or jeopardize the precious practice of slavery." In his letter to Lincoln widely republished as the "Prayer of Twenty Millions," Horace Greeley, now editor of the *New-York Tribune*, complained "that a large proportion of our regular Army officers . . . evince far more solicitude to uphold slavery than to put down the rebellion."[19]

Subsequent measures authorizing the president to raise additional volunteers and directing the states to enforce conscription thereby ensured that regulars never dominated the Union ranks. Secure in this triumph, congressional opponents of the regular establishment trained their sights on the United States Military Academy. Of the 978 graduates between 1833 and 1861 who were still alive when the war began, 259 (26.5 percent, including 32 from Northern states) joined the Confederate Army. Another 80 (8.4 percent) did not serve. Critics argued that the large number of resignations vindicated their assertions that the aristocratic and monopolistic institution on the Hudson was a corrupt drain on federal coffers. Animosity boiled over during July 1861 congressional debates, when Senator Wilson attempted to push through a measure to fill vacancies created when cadets resigned to join the Confederacy. "I do not believe that in the history of the world you can find as many men who have proved themselves utterly faithless to their oaths," roared Senator Benjamin Wade (R-OH), "guilty of treason and a deliberate intention to overthrow that Government which has educated them and given them its support, as have emanated from this institution." Wilson dropped the matter.[20]

Setbacks on the battlefield fed the frustrations of those dissatisfied with the war effort, with West Point a frequent target. At the First Battle of Bull Run, Confederate West Pointers like Beauregard, Joseph E. Johnston, and Thomas J. "Stonewall" Jackson had outperformed their Union counterparts, most notably Brig. Gen. Irvin McDowell and Col. Dixon S. Miles. George McClellan's ascendency to command infused a new spirit into the Army of the Potomac, but the cautious West Pointer refused to bend to popular demands for faster action. Following the humiliating defeat at Ball's Bluff of Union forces led by Brig. Gen. Charles P. Stone, also a West Point graduate and a political conservative, angry Republicans established the Joint Committee on the Conduct of the War, which would bedevil Democratic generals for the rest of the war.[21]

In late December 1861, attempts to increase the number of appointments to the military academy provided another opening for critics. Senate debate opened two days before Christmas and extended into the first week of January 1862, with opponents focusing on the need to save money, the sympathy many West Point graduates seemed to have for the rebels, the deficiencies of regular officers, and the desire to decentralize military education. Some even hinted that the army—its senior ranks dominated by Democrats—might stage a coup and make terms with the Confederacy. New Hampshire's John P. Hale (R) described regulars as "utterly worthless" and "leeches upon the Treasury"; Michigan's Zachariah Chandler (R) declared that the academy "has produced more traitors within the last fifty years than all the institutions of learning and education that have existed since Judas Iscariot's time." Even Ohio's John Sherman (R), brother of William T. Sherman (class of 1840), joined the dissenters. "The ordeal and the mode of education at West Point rather tend to make men martinets than soldiers and officers," asserted Senator Sherman, who later suggested "that the military knowledge acquired by the country at West Point could be gained better and more cheaply by encouraging the study of military science at State institutions."[22]

West Point was not without its defenders. Iowa Republican James Grimes pointed out that the percentage of graduates who had turned against their country was half that of officers appointed from civilian life. "If you are going to abolish West Point because officers who graduate there turn traitors," added Oregon Democrat James Nesmith, "you had better abolish the Senate, because you had some traitors in it." James Pearce (D-MD) also supported an army led by educated officers. "Great military genius," reasoned Pearce, was, "like all great abilities, the gift of Heaven. But I had supposed that proficiency in the profession of arms was to be acquired by study as in any other art." In the end, the attempt to add cadets was defeated 25–12. Twenty Republicans, four Democrats, and one Unionist formed the majority, whereas five Republicans, five Democrats, and two Unionists supported the increase.[23]

Military education again became a topic of public interest in summer 1862, when Representative Justin S. Morrill (R-VT) secured passage of a bill granting public lands for each state to use in establishing at least one agricultural and mechanical college. President Buchanan had vetoed a similar measure in 1859, but this more recent effort also included a requirement that the curriculum at the land grant colleges include military tactics. "The national school at West Point may suffice for the regular Army in ordinary years of peace, but it is wholly inadequate when a larger army is to be suddenly put into service," reasoned Morrill. "Nurseries in every State" would ensure that men with at least a modicum of military training would be ready to lead citizen-soldiers in future emergencies.[24]

In the coming months, Lincoln's Emancipation Proclamation unleashed a huge new source of manpower for the Union armies, but the disastrous attack at Fredericksburg and subsequent "mud march" by Maj. Gen. (Volunteers) Ambrose Burnside—West Point graduate of 1847—sparked another round of assaults on an institution accused of privileging a fortunate few. "A man can no more be made a first-class general than a first-class painter, or a great poet, by professors and text-books," reasoned the editors of *Harper's Weekly*. "The prevailing spirit in West Point was and is rather monarchical and altogether Pro-Slavery," growled a Polish émigré. Senate Radicals and Midwestern Republicans pounced on the January 1863 appropriations bill for the academy. Should the government fall, James H. Lane (R-KS) suggested that its epitaph should be "'died of West Point pro-slaveryism.'" Leading the Radical attack, Senator Wade identified the military academy as "the hotbed in which rebellion was hatched, and from thense emanated your principal traitors and conspirators." Buttressing his argument with heavy doses of Jacksonian populism and Republican free-labor ideology, Wade contended that the government had no business supporting such a "close, aristocratical corporation," a monopoly whose graduates "are invested with special privileges which we do not bestow upon anybody else."[25]

But the steam had gone out of the latest challenge. The long supportive *New York Times* praised "the high integrity of the West Point graduates." Acknowledging that its alumni too often affected "an assumed superiority," Senator Wilson denied that it had been a "nursery of treason" and noted that nine of the seventeen general officers killed in battle thus far had been West Pointers. A military education, added Senator Nesmith, "and a knowledge of the sciences connected with it, in order to render men useful in the scientific corps, are a practical and absolute necessity." Secessionists were hardly limited to graduates of West Point, reasoned Lafayette Foster (R-CT), who wondered if Yale, Williams College, and Harvard should also be abolished because some of their graduates had joined the rebellion. In the subsequent count, nine Republicans and one Democrat voted to eliminate funding, whereas twenty-one Republicans, six Democrats, and two Unionists supported continuation of the military academy.[26]

Outside the halls of Congress, mobilizing the Northern economy to arm, equip, and supply Union soldiers presented a staggering challenge. Over the course of the conflict, the War Department provided troops with a billion small arms cartridges, nearly 3.5 million small arms, 7,892 cannons, and more than 6 million artillery projectiles. Union soldiers had access to

6 million woolen blankets and 10 million pairs of trousers. Nearly a million horses and mules supported military operations. One hundred million pounds of coffee, 128 million pounds of hay, 1.5 million barrels of pork, 504 million pounds of corn meal, 43 million pounds of soap, and countless other materials sustained man and beast through four years of conflict. As a regular assigned to the Quartermaster's Department put it: "It would be difficult to convey in words an adequate idea . . . of the description of property and material with which our immense volunteer army had encumbered itself." Initially flummoxed by the limitations of antebellum public financing, the government printed Greenbacks, passed an income tax, reformed tariffs, and created something approaching a national banking system.[27]

With demand exceeding the capacities of army production facilities, the government let out most work to private contractors. Initially, individual states and Secretary Cameron's specially appointed procurement agents tried to oversee the gargantuan task. In light of the urgency of expanding a peacetime army of 16,000 regulars to more than 700,000 volunteers by early 1862, this decentralized system invited mischief. As one frustrated congressman put it: "We have opened the doors to all the thieves on the earth to plunder this Government." Although boasting distinguished careers, many bureau heads were too old and too set in the more deliberate ways of the peacetime army to handle the bigger challenges of the nation's bloodiest war. Adjutant General Samuel Cooper, a forty-year veteran, resigned in March 1861 to join Confederate service. Seventy years old and in bad health, Chief of Ordnance Henry K. Craig was relieved a month later. Surgeon General Thomas Lawson, aged seventy-one, died that May. Inspector General Sylvester Churchill, born in 1783, was retired in September, as was seventy-three-year old Chief of Topographical Engineers John J. Abert. That same month, Commissary General of Subsistence George C. Gibson died at the age of eighty-seven.[28]

In June 1861, President Lincoln took an important step in appointing (over Cameron's objection) Montgomery C. Meigs to lead the Quartermaster's Department, which was responsible for securing and transporting most of the army's needs other than food and arms. Honest, every inch the West Pointer, and confident in the abilities of his department to do what it had been doing for two decades (albeit on a scale forty to fifty times greater), Meigs sought to make procurements more transparent and to entrust the process to his own bureau staff. As the difficulties of mass purchases and the uncertainty of federal compensation for their expenses overwhelmed the states, Washington incrementally moved to take over the contracting. Meigs asserted his authority even to the president. In December 1861, when Lincoln suggested appointing a particular inspector for the crucial Eastern District of New York, the Quartermaster General stood firm: "I never interfere

Montgomery C. Meigs. Temporarily banned from the nation's capital after clashing with President James Buchanan, Meigs (1816–1892) made a triumphant return to oversee public building projects in the District of Columbia before the Civil War, then served as Abraham Lincoln's handpicked Quartermaster General. Library of Congress, DIG-cwpb-07055.

between the [local] Quartermaster and those whom he hires, and I trust that the President will not permit the recommendations of any person's friends to induce him to interfere."[29]

In early 1862, Lincoln named Edwin M. Stanton, an antislavery Pennsylvania Democrat who had served as Attorney General in the fleeting days of the Buchanan administration, to head the War Department. Intelligent and energetic, Stanton dismissed several clerks suspected of colluding in shady contracts and developed an excellent relationship with the president. With Stanton's protection from overbearing partisan interference, the Quartermaster's Department dominated what the historian Mark R. Wilson has identified as the "biggest government spending project of the century." In August 1861, regular officers in the department had been nearly doubled to sixty-four; by May 1862, more than 150 volunteer assistant quartermasters (ranked as captains) supplemented the regulars. Most had to learn on the job; as one confessed, he had come "entirely inexperienced" and was "only guided by my own sense of right." Fortunately, they could work according to the established rules of a highly regulated bureaucracy. The 1861 Army Regulations, for example, featured hundreds of pages of instructions and forms (nine for each quartermaster every month, along with thirty-seven others compiled in a quarterly report) for supply officers. By 1865, 130,000 of the 160,000 civilians employed by the military bureaus worked for the Quartermaster's Department, which oversaw more than a third of the federal budget. The seven officers responsible for the largest contracts were all regulars and West Point graduates, three of whom—David H. Vinton (New York City), George H. Crosman (Philadelphia), and Robert Allen (Louisville and St. Louis)—each dispersed more than $100 million over the course of the war.[30]

Depot-level quartermasters enjoyed considerable latitude as to the best means of securing the public good. Sometimes this meant keeping open state-run plants for the sake of their workers. Upon his arrival in St. Louis as a quartermaster in early 1862, Capt. Samuel E. Meigs, younger brother of the Quartermaster General, found that two of the city's big clothing halls had been shut down, presumably for reasons of efficiency. "It is a terrible sight to see so many women, most of them appear to have seen much better days, almost crying for work, with starvation staring them in the face," Samuel advised his brother. "I cannot but think that a disposition should [be made] on the part of Uncle Sam, to pity the poor here." His superior, Major Allen, agreed, noting that "starving women" would suffer. In response, the War Department transferred more textile orders to St. Louis, with 450 persons on army payrolls by 1864. Similarly, in January 1865 the Quartermaster's office directed "that it is believed to be good policy to encourage the manufacture of clothing by the wives and relatives of soldiers in Cincinnati."[31]

The enormous demand for goods—along with the government's chronically late payments, which could be devastating to a struggling start-up—meant that the majority of Quartermaster, Ordnance, and Commissary purchases came from large companies. Based in New York and Connecticut, the Union India Rubber Company supplied two-thirds of all rubber blankets and ponchos; Henry Burden & Company of Troy, New York, the nation's biggest antebellum producer of horseshoes and mule shoes, enjoyed "a practical monopoly" over such materials during the war. Most gunpowder contracts went to established firms such as the famous Delaware company E. I. DuPont de Nemours. In dollar terms, the largest orders were supplied by mercantile clothing and textile wholesalers that already boasted purchasing, production, and distribution networks in Boston, Philadelphia, and New York City.[32]

Meigs recognized the jealousies inspired by the enormous contracts that seemed to shut out small operators. "The evil of dealing too much with large contractors I have attempted to mitigate by establishing as many depots for contracting for supplies as possible," he explained to Senator Wilson. Meigs also stressed the importance of public advertisements, even in the face of quartermasters' protests that such practices gave away information that allowed colluding contractors to charge more money. "If it costs more to advertise, the law of the land has indicated the choice of the people," he reasoned. "They prefer equal chance to all to compete." The army did allow purchasers of grain and hay and, beginning in 1864, purchasers of horses and mules to skirt statutory requirements for contracting and preliminary bidding. By using such open-market purchases, the army believed it saved money and engaged more small suppliers.[33]

The system was hardly perfect, and the popular stereotypes of army bureaucrats working in league with big contractors did nothing to change perceptions of a faceless military that seemed disinterested in the fortunes of average Americans. And even the voluminous regulations could not check human incompetence and avarice. From Washington, one regular assigned to the Quartermaster's Department acknowledged that many volunteer quartermasters joined only for "the wholesale plunder of the public." Even long-serving regular officers were occasionally found guilty of either outright corruption or of acting against the public interests. In 1863, Maj. Justus McKinstry (West Point class of 1838) was dismissed for mismanagement after fifteen years of service in the department. Capt. John H. Dickerson, another West Pointer, resigned in early 1864 amid charges that he was insufficiently loyal to the Republican Party and had used his brother-in-law as a contracting agent. Col. James Belger, who had risen from the enlisted ranks to secure his commission in 1838, was dismissed in November 1863 for failing to sufficiently advertise for coal and transports.[34]

Through its quartermasters, the army was crucial to the lives of many working-class women. Established in 1800, Philadelphia's Schuylkill Arsenal had long been the primary supplier of uniforms, employing about five hundred people in peacetime. Ten times that number worked there by the middle of the Civil War. Col. George H. Crosman, a West Point graduate of 1823 whom a delegation of women workers once described as "a warm and steadfast friend," oversaw operations there. Following five days of draft riots in New York City in 1863, Colonel Crosman, acting on information supplied by Representative William D. Kelley (R-PA), announced that seamstresses must provide either written evidence of their loyalty or a direct relationship with a soldier. Within days, 143 discharged workers petitioned Secretary Stanton for the return of their jobs. A "large and enthusiastic" group met and drew up resolutions demanding Crosman's removal and an end to the "oppressive and prejudicial" loyalty policy, which would "deprive many of family of that little sustenance which alone they have been in the habit of receiving, and for want of which they will be brought to want and beggary."[35]

Buffeted by inflation and stagnant wages, organized opposition to the private contractors spread to New York City, which saw the formation of the Working Women's Union. Philadelphia women spoke the loudest, holding meetings in which they condemned profiteering by "soulless subcontractors" and urged the army to require private contractors to match wages found in the public arsenals. In early June 1864, "twenty thousand Working Women of Philadelphia" appealed to Stanton for "IMMEDIATE AID" in the form of increased wages and a quadrupling of the arsenal workforce. The beleaguered Crosman supported the pay hike, as did depot chiefs in Cincinnati, St. Louis, and New York City. But nothing was done until a delegation of seamstresses traveled to Washington and met with Stanton and the president. On August 18, the war secretary issued a written promise to do all he could to "secure a fair rate of compensation to the operatives, without an unauthorized exercise of power over Government contractors." More substantively, he agreed to raise wages of clothing workers at Schuylkill Arsenal by 20 percent and to add another two thousand "soldiers' and sailors' widows, wives, widowed mothers, and orphaned daughters" to the payroll.[36]

Such ad hoc concessions, however, failed to address the more systematic problems with the mixed military economy. Radical reforms—which would have eliminated private contractors or established government-imposed wages for their workers—were anathema to Republican free-labor ideology and the essential conservatism of army quartermasters. Protests from Philadelphia, New York, and Cincinnati thus continued. "We want arsenal work, and that we will have, or die in the attempt to get it," bellowed one worker to the applause of a large crowd at Jefferson Hall, Philadelphia. A four-woman committee, joined by former secretary of war Cameron, Representative Charles O'Neill (R-PA), and several journalists, secured another meeting with the president in late January 1865. Although sympathetic, Lincoln made no additional promises.[37]

In fighting the war, leaders on both sides espoused a conventional view of armies organized by nation-states, clad in traditional uniforms, and holding to Western ethical conventions. Such concepts fit comfortably with army habits, and regulars and former regulars dominated the highest ranks.

Despite criticisms of "the clique of West Pointers" by nonacademy men like Major Generals (Volunteers) John A. McClernand, John A. Logan, and John M. Palmer, West Point graduates comprised eighty of the 131 major generals in the Union Army, and antebellum regulars commanded seventeen of the Confederacy's twenty-two corps when Lee surrendered at Appomattox. The regulars made countless blunders; inexperienced in leading armies tens of thousands strong, many failed to grasp the lethality of new rifled weapons or to understand the nature of a people's war. But their tactical manuals and specialized knowledge about training, organizing, disciplining, supplying, and moving military forces gave them enormous advantages over most volunteers.[38]

In contrast to the impact of regular officers in shaping the Northern wartime economy and commanding conventional forces, old army regiments made less impression on Civil War battlefields. To most potential soldiers, volunteer units—often recruited and led by men from their own communities—seemed a far more attractive option compared to the stodgy regular army, with its well-deserved reputation for tough discipline. The states also resented any competition that threatened their ability to fill manpower quotas. Thus, the regular regiments (old and new alike) never came close to meeting authorized limits. Of the more than two million men who served in the Union Army during the Civil War, only about 67,000 were regulars.[39]

In the East, regulars played an outsized role in the First Battle of Bull Run, where eight infantry companies, seven mounted companies, and eight artillery batteries formed the core of a rear guard that covered the withdrawal of the demoralized Union Army. Following the defeat, McClellan assumed command and built the Army of the Potomac, using regulars to help maintain order in Washington, D.C., and to train volunteers. By March 1862, McClellan had collected his regular infantry—six regiments of the old army and four of the newly forming regiments—into what was designated the Infantry Reserve. "The advantage of such a body of troops at a critical moment . . . has been frequently illustrated in military history," he explained. "I have always found them to be relied on. Whenever they have been brought under fire they have shown the utmost gallantry and tenacity." McClellan seems to have had similar intentions for his regular cavalrymen, concentrating them as part of a Cavalry Reserve.[40]

Supplemented by a brigade of volunteers and regular artillery batteries, the Infantry Reserve (sometimes referred to as the Regular Division) defended the Union right flank at Gaines' Mill (the first of the 1862 Seven Days Battles) until driven back by superior numbers. "My regulars were superb," proclaimed McClellan in defeat. In the Second Battle of Bull Run, they helped to hold strategic Henry House Hill against Confederate assaults. "They saved the army," General McDowell reportedly exclaimed after the battle. "God bless the Regulars!" At Gettysburg, the Regular Division fell back with heavy losses near the base of Little Round Top. In August 1863, the War Department dispatched two brigades of regulars to New York City in the wake of the previous month's draft riots. The following spring, what was left of the regular infantry regiments in the East, joined by four regiments of volunteers, formed a brigade in the 1st Division of V Corps. Outflanked at the Battle of the Wilderness, the brigade was shattered, suffering 302 casualties among the 2,000-plus men engaged. "I had regulars . . . before I went into the battle of Gettysburg. I left one-half of them there, and buried the rest in the Wilderness," testified their latest commander, Brig. Gen. Romeyn B. Ayers. The decimated unit nonetheless remained in the lines through the fighting at Spotsylvania Court House, after which the remnants of the regular infantry regiments in the East guarded various headquarters and fortifications.[41]

At the war's outset, most regulars stationed in the West had been rushed eastward, but the Fifth Infantry remained in New Mexico and the Ninth Infantry continued to garrison the Pacific Coast. Elsewhere, Brigadier General Twiggs's surrender of his entire Department of Texas even before that state's citizens had ratified the ordinances of secession resulted in the capture of 1,300 regulars and numerous arms and materials by Texas authorities. On July 27, 1861, another seven companies of the Seventh Infantry surrendered at San Augustine Spring, New Mexico. Partially restoring their reputation, about a thousand regulars fought at Wilson's Creek, Missouri, with the Second Artillery playing a key role in covering the retreating Union forces. Among the most notable casualties was former regular (and now Brigadier General of Volunteers) Nathaniel Lyon, the first Union general killed in the Civil War. At the Battle of Valverde, New Mexico, however, elements of several regular regiments retreated in the face of a frenzied Texan attack. "We turned their tactics upside down, and gave the regulars hell," bragged one Confederate.[42]

By early 1862, companies from several new regular infantry regiments were brigaded together in the Army of the Ohio (and later in the Army of the Cumberland). They did well in the second day's fighting at Shiloh but lost a third of their number at Stones River. "I was compelled to sacrifice my regulars to save the rest of the army," Maj. Gen. William S. Rosecrans reportedly admitted. At Chickamauga, the brigade was again in the thick of the fighting. On the first day, nearly an entire battalion was surprised and captured, but on the second day the remainder of the brigade helped to form a rear guard that protected the retreat of the shattered Army of the Cumberland. A small "demi-brigade" of regulars, now part of XIV Corps, participated in Sherman's Atlanta Campaign.[43]

The withdrawal of most regular units had a significant impact throughout the western borderlands. Despite the war, thousands of non-Indians headed westward, lured by new mineral discoveries, the admission of Kansas and Nevada as states, and the formation of the territories of Colorado, Dakota, Arizona, and Montana. Regular soldiers had long acted as the most visible agents of federal order in this ever-changing political and demographic environment. While by no means accepting American Indians as equals, regulars had traditionally represented a mediating presence. The wartime mobilization of volunteers gave Western states and territories access to significantly more soldiers; by late 1862, more than 18,000 soldiers served in those regions alone—more than the entire regular army before the war.[44]

The extra troops allowed for larger military operations. Thus, while Col. William S. Harney's 1855 campaigns against the Brulés and Oglalas had numbered about six hundred regulars, Brig. Gen. Henry Hastings Sibley and Col. Alfred Sully led more than four thousand volunteers in their 1863 offensives against the Dakotas, Lakotas, and Yanktonais. Temporarily gone were the days of limited government spending, and the enormous costs of fighting the Confederacy made it easier to accept bigger expenses incurred in Indian warfare. Meigs estimated that the Quartermaster Department's extra costs (excluding salaries, purchases of animals, and ordnance) of supplying the 22,000 men of Brig. Gen. John Pope's summer 1865 operations on the Great Plains at $10 million—a figure that equaled 60 percent of the entire War Department budget for 1860.[45]

Indian campaigns undertaken by largely volunteer armies were especially savage. Here, the volunteers were sometimes commanded by regular officers, most notably Sully (victor at the fierce fight at Whitestone Hill), Pope (Department of the Northwest and later the Division of the Missouri), Col. George H. Wright (Department of the Pacific), and Brig. Gen. James H. Carleton (Department of New Mexico). They often acted with a startling ferocity. If Mescalero Apaches tried to make peace, for instance, Carleton instructed to a subordinate to "tell them fairly and frankly . . . that we believe if we kill some of their men in fair open war they will be apt to remember that it will be better for them to remain at peace than to be at war."[46]

Volunteer officers could be even crueler. On January 29, 1863, Col. Edward Connor attacked a Shoshoni village at Bear River, Idaho Territory, killing 224 people, destroying more than seventy lodges, and abandoning 170 women and children in the numbing cold with only "a small quantity of wheat." One sergeant admitted that "their was no quarters given that day." Even more infamous was the November 29, 1864, massacre of more than 150 Cheyennes and Arapahos at Sand Creek, Colorado, by Colorado volunteers and militia commanded by Col. John P. Chivington. Described as a "crazy preacher who thinks he is Napoleon Bonaparte," Chivington told a council of officers the evening before his attack "that he believed it to be right or honorable to use any means under God's heaven to kill Indians that would kill women and children." After slaughtering the Indians—mostly women and children—some of Chivington's volunteers systematically mutilated the corpses. Formal condemnations by two military committees, as well as the Joint Committee on the Conduct of the War, could not begin to erase the terrible stain left by Chivington's butchery.[47]

* * * * *

To most Northerners, the savagery of the wars against the Indians seemed little more than an unfortunate footnote to the feats of the volunteer armies of the Civil War. Two million citizen-soldiers had restored the Union through force of arms, and the Union Army emerged as a symbol of American nationalism. By equating the end of slavery with the end of the Confederacy, volunteer soldiers had also accelerated the process of emancipation. Upon learning of the Emancipation Proclamation, then–Capt. Robert Gould Shaw (later to be killed in battle as colonel of the all-black 54th Massachusetts Volunteer Infantry Regiment), pointed out the reality of the emancipation process: "Wherever our army has been, there remain no slaves, and the Proclamation will not free them where we don't go."[48]

Little of the public acclaim accorded the volunteers during the Civil War carried over to the regular army itself. Regular regiments, which represented only a fraction of Union forces, understandably received scant notice. Similarly, behind-the-scenes achievements of regulars in the Quartermaster's, Ordnance, and Subsistence Departments were rarely recognized. However, efforts to abolish West Point had again been defeated; criticisms resulting from the defection of regular officers to the Confederacy, the slow reaction by Winfield Scott and army bureaucrats to the crisis, and the sluggish performances of West Pointers like McClellan and Buell were eventually offset by victories of graduates such as Ulysses Grant, William Sherman, and Phil Sheridan. Such hard-earned triumphs restored to the regulars a degree of public credibility. But whether that trust would translate to acceptance of a larger regular army remained very much in question.

Chapter Eleven
An Elusive Peace

At nine o'clock on the glorious late spring morning of May 23, 1865, veterans of Maj. Gen. George G. Meade's Army of the Potomac began marching from the Capitol Building down Pennsylvania Avenue, past the Executive Mansion. Red, white, and blue bunting and scores of national flags replaced the mourning black memorializing Abraham Lincoln's death five weeks earlier. More than fifty thousand visitors had flocked to Washington to watch this grandest of reviews. The next day was reserved for Maj. Gen. William T. Sherman's western commands. Though imperfect—no African American regiments had been present (neither Meade's nor Sherman's armies had any United States Colored Troops)—the Grand Review symbolized the centrality of citizen-soldiers to the restoration of the Union and the end of slavery. "In a war beset by deep divisions in the loyal states," observes the modern historian Gary Gallagher, "the army stood as a powerful national symbol and the largest and most important unifying institution, one that brought together men from all parts of the nation and both major political parties."[1]

Contemporary newspapers reflected the public adulation of the volunteers who had won the war. "There is the American people looking reverently, admiringly, affectionately on this march of their brothers through their capital," proclaimed the *New-York Tribune*. "The gallant conquerors of many a hard fought field are going home to share the blessings they have won for the nation," added the rival *New York Herald*. The *Baltimore American and Commercial Advisor* emphasized that these were hardly the men of standing armies: "The soldier of yesterday is the citizen of to-day."[2] Indeed, while praising the West Point–trained generals who had led those troops to victory (Grant, Sherman, and Meade had all graduated from the military academy), the public failed to convey that admiration to the regular army.

Unfortunately, peace was not at hand. French troops propping up Emperor Maximilian in Mexico posed a threat, and the nation remained at war on two other fronts. In the South, states adopted a series of black codes that attempted to reestablish slavery in everything but name, endangering emancipation and the Thirteenth Amendment. In response, Washington undertook a revolutionary new step: the military occupation of the former Confederate states. To the west, the Plains were also aflame, fired by the Dakota Rebellion of 1862 and the Sand Creek Massacre by Chivington's volunteers

The Grand Review. On May 23 and 24, the armies of Ulysses S. Grant and William T. Sherman marched down Pennsylvania Avenue (note the Capitol Building in the background) through Washington, D.C. Library of Congress, USZ62-107052 (b&w film copy neg. of half stereo, left side).

in late 1864. These conflicts jeopardized the federal government's effort to spur the more rapid occupation of the continent through the Homestead Act of 1862 (which allowed farmers to claim 160 acres of the public domain for only a small title fee) and the Pacific Railway Acts of 1862 and 1864 (which, along with subsequent grants to other railroads, transferred 131,230,358 acres to stimulate construction). The army was essential to both projects. So even as volunteers returned to civilian life, regulars remained on a war footing, tasked with consolidating the federal government's hold over the former Confederacy as well as the American West, a linked process that the historian Richard White has called "Greater Reconstruction."[3]

* * * * *

General Grant identified the situation in Mexico as posing the most immediate challenge. Concerned that French troops might make that scarred nation a haven for unrepentant former Confederates, he dispatched Maj. Gen. Philip H. Sheridan, a middling student at West Point who had become a favorite during the late war, to take command of 50,000 Union soldiers assembling in Texas. Seeking the same goal by a different means, Matías Romero, head of Benito Juarez's legation in Washington, had long hoped that a U.S. incursion might drive out Maximilian. Such a force needed a respected American commander, so on Grant's recommendation Romero solicited the services of Maj. Gen. (Volunteers) John M. Schofield, victor of the Battle of Franklin, Tennessee. A West Point graduate, Schofield was promised a $100,000 bounty and a major general's commission in the Mexican Army (neither of which he ever received) for his services. Hoping to promote national reconciliation, Grant and Schofield planned to include both Union and Confederate veterans in this strike force.[4]

Sheridan joined Secretary of State William Seward in fearing a disaster. Logistics, funding, and basic operational details remained fuzzy, and Seward resented the army's interference in matters more appropriate to his department's portfolio. In early August, the secretary convinced Schofield to deliver a personal warning to Napoleon III rather than lead a hastily organized army into a foreign country whose citizens would hardly welcome a Yankee invasion. After the general arrived in Europe, American diplomats did not know quite what to do with their military visitor, but they arranged for him to make a toast at the annual Thanksgiving dinner in Paris as well as meet with several Imperial staffers and the emperor's cousin, Prince Napoleon. Following a conciliatory speech in which Napoleon III implied that French troops would soon be withdrawn from Mexico, Schofield returned to Washington in early June 1866, his diplomatic mission a striking example of the army's multipurpose role in American life.[5]

Potential alliances with Mexican-sponsored filibusters and the use of one of its own as a reminder of American strategic interests were not the army's only tools for defying the French presence in Mexico. Heading the Division of the Gulf (Texas, Florida, and Louisiana), Sheridan executed Grant's orders to "place a strong force on the Rio Grande." Sheridan allowed passage of arms and ammunition bound for anti-Imperialist forces in Mexico, chipping in with 30,000 muskets from the Baton Rouge Arsenal. In January 1867, Napoleon III sealed Maximilian's fate by ordering the withdrawal of French troops. "I doubt very much whether such results could have been achieved without the presence of an American army on the Rio Grande," Sheridan later recalled with justifiable pride.[6]

Considerably more challenging was the disposition of the former Confederate states. Union troops had long occupied some areas, most notably the lower Mississippi River Valley, with West Point graduate Brig. Gen. (Volunteers) Thomas Williams assuming duties "not only as a military commander,

John M. Schofield. The prematurely balding John Schofield (1831–1906) is pictured during or shortly after the Civil War wearing his uniform as a major general of volunteers. Believed to be a favorite of Grant, he was involved in complex negotiations regarding France's intervention in Mexico and between President Andrew Johnson and the War Department. From 1888 to 1895, he served as commanding general of the United States Army. Library of Congress, LC-DIG-cwpbh-01147.

but necessarily an administrator of civil affairs, judge, court and jury in more cases than I would wish to be." But hundreds of thousands of slaves lived in lands yet reclaimed by Yankee soldiers. Following a tour of South Carolina, Carl Schurz, an antislavery advocate recently retired from the Union Army, divided residents into two camps: "Those who . . . have come into direct contact with our forces," and "those who have not." In Arkansas, "practical freedom has been experienced by that part of the colored population only, which is within the lines of permanent military occupation," opined Lt. Col. (Volunteers) Charles Bentzoni. From Texas, as provisional governor Andrew Jackson Hamilton acknowledged, "there are some sections of the State remote from any Military force where I am informed the late Slave owners stoutly deny the power of the Gov't to free the Negros and who still claim and control them as property." Even when bondsmen had been freed, they were often compelled to work for little or no pay.[7]

To grapple with the human problems posed by the Reconstruction, Congress had in March 1865 created the Bureau of Refugees, Freedmen, and Abandoned Lands. West Point–educated Maj. Gen. (Volunteers) Oliver O. Howard was appointed commissioner. Housed in the War Department, the Freedmen's Bureau functioned with a military hierarchy of command, and agents followed army accounting procedures and filed mountains of paperwork. In addition to their normal responsibilities, men in uniform often held dual appointments with the bureau. As Howard advised Col. Alvan C. Gillem, the agency's assistant commissioner in Mississippi: "The army cannot be a political machine; yet Congress has given the work of reconstruction into its hands and the law, like every other, must be executed by the Army with energy and good faith." At its height in fiscal year 1867, the Freedmen's Bureau dealt with nearly three hundred thousand acres of unclaimed land, arranged transportation allowing more than seventeen thousand refugees and freedpersons to return to their homes or find employment, provided medical care to 8,853 refugees and 135,296 freedpeople, distributed more than four million rations, and maintained 1,839 schools attended by 111,442 pupils.[8]

In accord with contemporary assumptions that an army of occupation possessed the legitimate authority to ensure order, firmly held beliefs that slavery must end, and their own rough sense of justice, soldiers fanned out across the South. By September 1865, 146,482 Union troops held 324 posts throughout the former Confederacy (excluding Texas). Stationed at Petersburg, Virginia, Maj. Gen. (Volunteers) John Gibbon explained his position: "I am . . . trying to reconcile civil and military law in the same place, very difficult by the way, but I hope it will all come out straight in the end. . . . With moderation and no disposition to be a *despot* I hope to have no trouble." Although critical of what they believed to be the corruption of many agents, soldiers did yeoman work associated with the Freedman's Bureau, serving as temporary agents and field officers and preventing enforcement of many state-level black codes. In doing so the army enjoyed the support of Congress, which was wary of President Andrew Johnson's willingness to accept former Confederates into local governments and unwillingness to protect freedpeople or Unionists.[9]

Army notions of justice, however, were limited. Arbitrary use of military power seemed dangerously akin to tyranny, and most doubted the wisdom of using troops to enforce social change and of extending the franchise to black males. As members of a hierarchical institution, officers were inclined to emphasize the need for order rather than implementing equality. Blacks, alleged Gibbon, "are lazy and disinclined to work, and the mischief of it is that the negro question is a delicate one to handle without burning one's fingers in these ticklish times." Maj. Gen. (Volunteers) Gordon Granger maintained that accounts of atrocities against blacks were wildly exaggerated. Sympathetic with the volunteers' desire to go home and in no mood to undertake a long military occupation, Grant initially believed that the army could soon withdraw from the South. As his ally Schofield put it, the former Confederate states should undergo military government only "until the people should come to their senses."[10]

Jolted by the government's cash crisis stemming from the onset of an economic recession in late spring 1865 and confident that regulars best fit the nation's security needs, Grant and Sherman understood the urgency of demobilizing volunteers. This also meant limiting combat operations against Indians. Commanding the newly created Division of the Missouri, Maj. Gen. (Volunteers) John Pope hoped that a big offensive into the Great Plains that summer might "finish off this Indian war this season so that it will stay finished." Anxious to save money, Grant implored Pope to "cut down the expeditions all you can." Despite the admonition, Pope organized nearly five thousand volunteer cavalrymen—numbers unheard of in the regular army's long wars against the Indians—in a three-pronged offensive through Nebraska, Wyoming, Montana, and the Dakotas. The campaign, which encountered few Indians but cost some $20 million ($324 million at time of publication), only increased the need to rein in spending.[11]

Grant's willingness to limit military strikes stemmed in part from his belief that the nation could avoid many of its Indian wars. Construction of a Pacific railroad would stimulate the economic development that would encourage whites to occupy the West and overwhelm the tribes; replacing ill-disciplined volunteers with regulars and transferring control of Indian affairs back to the War Department would further reduce conflict. "As soon as the Indians see that we have Regular Cavalry among them," Sherman predicted, "they will realize that we are in condition to punish them for any murders or robberies." Consistent with such notions, commissioners in October 1865 joined Cheyenne, Arapaho, Kiowa-Apache, Comanche, and Kiowa delegations in agreeing to a "perpetual peace" in the Little Arkansas River treaties. To the north, they hammered out treaties at Fort Sully with nine Lakota and Dakota Sioux tribes, also featuring mutual promises to restore peace, respect reservation boundaries, and provide annual annuities.

Ominously, however, the Cheyenne Dog Soldiers did not participate in the Little Arkansas River agreements, and few influential Indian leaders signed the Fort Sully compacts.[12]

As peace initiatives proceeded in the West, authorities approached the herculean task of demobilizing Union armies with a vengeance. All but 11,043 of the 1,034,064 volunteers on the rolls on May 1, 1865, were mustered out within the year. Between May 1 and August 2, 1865, the Quartermaster's Department sold more than two hundred thousand horses and mules. By November, $4 million in clothing contracts had been cancelled, nearly six hundred ships on western lakes and rivers were decommissioned or had their contracts negated, seventeen hundred miles of military railroads were returned to civilian owners, and 283 locomotives and more than three thousand cars were sold. In fiscal year 1866, the department sold 4,395 barracks, hospitals, storehouses, sheds, stables, corrals, wharves, and docks; 15,891 wagons; 3,495 ambulances and carts; 820 forges; and harnesses for 112,607 animals.[13]

Demobilization most directly impacted the South, where efforts by former slaves to assert their freedom often depended on a military presence. Short on manpower (especially cavalry), the army abandoned more and more of the backcountry, leaving freedpeople and Union sympathizers to their own devices against armed vigilantes. By December 1865, troop strengths in the former Confederacy (excluding Texas) had fallen to 88,246; army posts were down to 208. Attacks on blacks in Texas, wrote Col. (Volunteers) Edgar M. Gregory, "increase just in proportion to their distance from United States authorities." Even a racist such as Maj. Gen. (Volunteers) George A. Custer decried the "rebellious spirit" among whites. "The traffic in human flesh is continued," he declared. From Kentucky, a Freedmen's Bureau superintendent judged that "freedmen cannot receive their just rights without a considerable military force." More ominously, Meade warned "that the withdrawal of all military force would very likely be followed by a war of races" in Virginia and the Carolinas.[14]

With former Confederate states determined on restoring the old regime and President Johnson's racism and strict constructionism becoming increasingly evident, Congress and Grant reversed course. On January 8, 1866, by a wide margin the House resolved to stop withdrawing occupation forces. Four days later, Grant issued General Orders No. 3, which instructed commanders throughout the former rebel states to protect soldiers, loyal citizens, and African Americans from unfair prosecution by state and local courts. On January 13, he advised the president against removing the remaining federal troops. Similarly, Congress turned to the one institution that could enforce its will: the regular army. As Senator Lyman Trumbull (R-IL) declared: "The war powers of the Government do not cease with the dispersion of the rebel armies. They are to be continued and exercised until the civil authority of the Government can be established firmly and upon a sure foundation not again to be disturbed or interfered with." In February, Senate Republicans explicitly authorized the War Department to use soldiers as Freedmen's Bureau agents and to provide food, clothing, fuel, medical supplies, shelter, and schools to freedpersons and refugees. Denouncing the measure "as a war upon the liberties of the people," Senator Thomas A. Hendricks (D-IN) asserted that "military law no longer governs." Republican senator Henry Wilson (MA), longtime chair of the Committee on Military Affairs, fired back: "Sir, we want these freedmen protected; we mean to have them protected." The House approved the Senate bill by an overwhelming majority. But the President vetoed it, reasoning that civil authorities must do such work.[15]

That spring's debates over a civil rights bill also involved the army. In addition to providing that all citizens had basic legal rights, the proposal authorized the president to employ soldiers to enforce it. First-term senator James Guthrie (D-KY) declared that the legislation, along with the earlier attempt to expand the Freedmen's Bureau, amounted to "military despotism." Again rising in defense, Senator Wilson censured the black codes and insisted that white Southerners "must learn, if they are compelled to learn by the bayonets of the Army of the United States, that the civil rights of the freedmen must and shall be protected." On March 27, Johnson vetoed the bill; less than a week later, he proclaimed the insurrection to be over and ordered the return of civilian government to all former Confederate states except Texas. "Standing armies, military occupation, martial law, military tribunals, and the suspension of the writ of habeas corpus are in time of peace dangerous to public liberty," the president asserted. Congress quickly overrode his veto of the Civil Rights Act and began reformulating efforts to protect the Freedmen's Bureau.[16]

Congressional activism reflected the belief that the nation remained at war—and that Congress had to direct that war. On May 1, three days of rioting broke out in Memphis after a policeman pistol-whipped a recently mustered black veteran, leaving three whites and forty-six blacks dead, dozens of others wounded, several black women raped, and more than a hundred churches, schools, and houses torched. In response, Grant determined that troops must occupy the South for an extended period. Only the "strong hand" of the Freedmen's Bureau in North Carolina, concluded one officer, offered blacks protection and opportunities for advancement. Former slaves had little chance in Arkansas, wrote Assistant Surgeon Henry Lilly from Little Rock, "except such hope for them as lies in the strong arm of the general government," without which they would "be *practically* slaves." In June, Congress passed the Fourteenth Amendment. New Orleans race riots on June 30, which claimed the lives of thirty-four blacks and four whites,

"The Freedmen's Bureau." Published in *Harper's Weekly*, this classic Alfred R. Waud drawing depicts a soldier representing the Freedmen's Bureau interposed between a group of angry armed whites and African Americans, many of whom seem to have been former soldiers. Library of Congress, USZ62-105555.

reaffirmed the need for action. Congress quickly overrode another veto, extended the Freedmen's Bureau for two years, and required the president to "extend military protection and . . . military jurisdiction over all cases and questions" regarding racial discrimination wherever "the ordinary course of judicial proceedings has been interrupted by the rebellion." Grant issued General Orders No. 44, directing soldiers in these areas to confine persons charged with crimes against government agents.[17]

Enforcing federal justice in the South depended on the regular army, whose size had yet to be determined. Back in April 1865, calculating that the six years of reductions following the War of 1812 had left one soldier per every 963 civilians, President Lincoln suggested using a similar proportion following the Civil War, which would have resulted in a 35,000-strong regular force. By October, Grant, in consideration "of future local disturbances arising from ill feeling left by the war or the unsettled questions between the black and white races at the south," instead recommended a regular army of 80,000, with the president authorized to raise 20,000 additional African American troops.[18]

In early 1866, Grant joined Republicans Robert C. Schenck (OH) (chair of the House Military Affairs Committee) and Wilson (still heading the Senate Military Affairs Committee) in cobbling together an army bill. If it were to pass, their wide-ranging measure would have to satisfy the demands of widely competing constituencies: West Point graduates; volunteers seeking to remain in the service; advocates of an African American presence in the armed forces; racists who wanted to eliminate all black troops; War Department staff; Westerners insisting on a stronger military presence in the borderlands; small government conservatives; and those hoping to use a Veteran Reserve Corps to employ wounded Union soldiers. Early in the House debates, Andrew J. Rogers (D-NJ) challenged the force envisioned by Grant, reminding his colleagues "that large standing armies in time of peace were not only dangerous to liberty, but they involved the country in heavy and enormous expenses." With the general's reputation riding high, the House rejected Rogers's amendment by a resounding 79–16 count. Still, in early May, following nearly three weeks of debate, dissatisfied elements of the rival interest groups combined to reject the bill.[19]

On July 27—the final day of the session—a House-Senate conference committee rammed through an act that established ten cavalry, five artillery, and forty-five infantry regiments. Two cavalry and four infantry regiments were reserved for black enlisted personnel, and four infantry regiments filled a Veteran Reserve Corps (limited to disabled veterans). Appointments of volunteer officers to this force would be distributed among the states and territories in proportion to the number of soldiers they had furnished the Union during the Civil War. In all, the legislation provided for 54,641 officers and men (nearly three times that allowed in 1860); the president could also raise one thousand Indian scouts and increase the number of enlisted personnel in infantry and artillery companies, thus allowing for a possible aggregate of 80,258.[20]

Even with this larger force, competing demands for troops from Western states and territories sharply limited the army's reach in the South. As one officer observed: "If it be the intention of the Government to enforce the laws of Congress, they must find more troops. . . . Wherever there are bayonets *there* the people respect the laws, but nowhere else." In January 1866, 61,835 soldiers had been stationed in 191 posts in the former Confederacy (excluding Texas), which constituted slightly more than half a million square miles. By September, those numbers had fallen to 25,235 soldiers and 101 posts. Shortages of cavalry (by October 1866, only 48 of 120 cavalry companies were in the South) exacerbated the difficulties in occupying lands roughly equal to the size of Western Europe.[21]

A defiant President Johnson upped the ante on August 20, declaring the insurrection at an end and civil authority restored. As officers in the field struggled to determine their legal roles, Grant concluded that the executive proclamation nullified General Orders 3 and 44, which had empowered soldiers to arrest civilians as part of their efforts to protect freedmen and bureau officials. Grant's headquarters thus advised officers to "exercise a wise discretion acting whenever possible in concert with the civil authorities." Some local governments promptly used the president's declaration against their army antagonists. In Brenham, Texas, for example, a grand jury investigating the murder of two soldiers no-billed the accused assassins, instead indicting Capt. George W. Smith, whose men had broken into a house while making the arrests. Only the presence of soldiers, asserted another officer, saved the life of Lt. Alfred S. Newlin from a vengeful West Virginia mob after a grand jury refused to indict him for an alleged offense against a local resident.[22]

By fall 1866, the situation was grim. The United States Supreme Court's *ex parte Milligan* ruling stripped the army of a powerful tool by sharply restricting the use of military commissions during wartime. Even as he decried Mississippi's discriminatory laws, district commander Col. Thomas J. Wood reduced the number of garrisons from ten to six and charged former slaves with being "restless, unquiet, and indisposed to make arrangements for continuous labor." Governor Benjamin G. Humphreys, a Democrat and former Confederate army officer, had in most cases "heartily co-operated," but a lieutenant serving with the Freedman's Bureau had been murdered. Following elections in Kentucky, Col. Jeff C. Davis (no relation to the former Confederate president) reported that victorious pro-rebels perpetrated a wave of violence against blacks and Unionists. Florida was calm, according to Sheridan, because the people had concluded "that their best interest was to take off their coats and go to work to repair the disaster of the rebellion." In Texas, by contrast, "the trial of a white man for the murder of a freedman . . . would be a farce."[23]

Even as most white Southerners resented the regulars in their midst, Westerners relentlessly lobbied for a larger military presence. Kansas governor Samuel J. Crawford complained that "the Indians are murdering robbing and driving the settlers from their homes." From Texas, Governor James Throckmorton demanded that soldiers be moved from their Reconstruction duties to the Indian frontiers. Thomas Meagher, governor of Montana Territory, peppered anyone he thought might listen with calls for troops, denouncing "the savagery of the Indians" as well as "a band of desperadoes—outlaws from neighboring territories and states." Attacks by Indians "whose hands are yet red with the blood of their slaughtered victims" threatened whites in Dakota Territory, claimed its governor. Without a garrison, a petition signed by twenty-seven residents of Sioux Falls warned, "it will not be safe for us to remain one hour."[24]

Like their civilian counterparts, few regulars recognized Indians as equal to white Americans, and nearly all tended to discount military successes against Indians as a legitimate means of professional advancement.

According to Senator John Sherman (R-OH), Indian war "is an inglorious contest—one in which our Army certainly does not desire to take part. They can gain no reputation by fighting with these Indians." Warfare against Indians was "a miserable affair, & no credit can be gained from it: national, or individual," agreed Lt. Col. Luther P. Bradley, Twenty-Seventh Infantry. Soldiers routinely acknowledged the injustice of U.S. policy. Stationed on the Bozeman Trail, Capt. Edward L. Hartz pointed to "the just complaint of the Sioux." But most believed that only hard blows would convince the tribes to accept the government's oversight and begin the passage to civilization. "They won't respect us 'til they are whipped," reasoned one colonel. Characteristically blunt, Sheridan described Indians as "a fading-out people" who must be dealt with by force rather than "moral suasion."[25]

Regulars continued to assert that Westerners exaggerated the Indian threat to serve their own purposes. "The difficulty here [Nevada], as it is everywhere else," concluded Brig. Gen. Irvin McDowell, "is with the whites more than the Indians. . . . A few of the settlers . . . believe in shooting every Indian on sight." Sherman asserted that "every little drunken quarrel or horse-thieving is exaggerated into a big bug-bear." And most suspected that Westerners would do almost anything to secure the economic benefits of an army garrison. White emigrants to the Little Blue River Valley in Nebraska, observed Capt. Lewis Thompson, were "delighted at the presence of the troops—and have good reason to be, for the company probably spent more money there in two days of our encampment, than was in the whole settlement before." Inspector General Nelson H. Davis added that the townspeople near Fort Benton, Montana Territory, wanted troops "for the purpose of putting a few dollars in their own pockets."[26]

Arizona and New Mexico posed special dilemmas. "The Apaches and cognate tribes in Arizona and northern Sonora are the natural and hereditary enemies of the whites," Maj. Gen. Henry Halleck, commanding the Division of the Pacific, wrote in 1867. "They probably resemble the African Bedouins more than any other people. . . . With them, there is no alternative but active and vigorous war till they are completely destroyed, or forced to surrender as prisoners of war." Two years later, Brig. Gen. Edward O. C. Ord, chief of the Department of California (which then included Nevada and Arizona), used a similar theme, describing Apaches as the "Arabs of Arizona . . . whose hands have always been bloody, their favorite pursuit killing and plundering, their favorite ornaments the finger and toe nails, the teeth, hair, and small bones of their victims." Such "wolves" must be hunted "as they would wild animals." In 1870, the War Department carved out a separate military Department of Arizona in hopes of improving security.[27]

Soldiers had little better to say about the region's non-Indian inhabitants and the environment. Pennsylvania's Capt. Charles McClure described

New Mexico as a "godforsaken country" filled with "hell hounds who prowl around its kennel of injustice." In October 1868, Capt. S. B. M. Young, Eighth Cavalry, lambasted the "low-lived-drunken, cowardly villains" who had massacred some Mojave Indians near La Paz, Arizona Territory. The following year, General Ord denounced the "vicious renegade population of Texan Union haters, who help to keep up Indian wars by occasional murders of stray Indians" in southern Arizona. "They will keep up a hue and cry for more troops as long as Uncle Sam will spend a dollar that they can get and will shoot a Union officer without regret if they can make a dollar." The only way to quiet Arizona, according to Ord, was to herd Indians into reservations, build and secure roads to the few places capable of supporting white settlement, and abandon the rest. In early 1874, Sherman went even further: "If you, gentlemen, will get Mexico to take Arizona back," he told the House Military Affairs Committee, "I will agree to knock two regiments of cavalry from our estimates."[28]

The army "cannot be in force everywhere," complained Sherman. "To suppress riots in the South, Indians in [the West] . . . where whites and Indians both require watching, and the thousand and one duties that devolve on us" were impossible tasks with existing forces. Buffeted by competing demands, army brass hoped to delay a major Indian war and instead protect lines of communication. Construction of the Pacific railroads received top priority, and new forts would guard the Platte Road from Omaha and the recently opened Bozeman Trail to Virginia City. The army was also establishing posts along the Smoky Hill Trail and the Arkansas River Road, which formed the southern boundary of what Sherman hoped would become an Indian-free "middle belt." But war with the Paiutes had already broken out in Oregon and Idaho, where Lt. Col. George Crook assumed command of the Military District of the Boise in December 1866 and initiated a series of grueling campaigns that would continue for nearly two years. That same month, skirmishing along the Bozeman Trail also erupted into a full-scale war when Lakota warriors wiped out Capt. William Fetterman's eighty-one-man detachment just outside Fort Phil Kearny. A week later, Sherman wired Grant: "We must act with vindictive earnestness against the Sioux, even to their extermination, men, women & children."[29]

To Sherman's consternation, regulars assumed ever-greater responsibilities in the South. Frustrated by the refusal of former Confederate states to accept the Fourteenth Amendment, as well as Johnson's decision to forbid military commissions and bureau courts—often the only legal entities that offered a modicum of justice to freedpersons—Grant was, as an aide put it, "getting more & more radical." That fall, he began distancing himself from the president, vowing not to allow the army to "be made a party machine." When elections returned a veto-proof Republican majority in Congress, the

Ulysses S. Grant. Once described as wearing "an expression as if he had determined to drive his head through a brick wall, and was about to do it," the unassuming Grant (1822–1885) here poses outside his Virginia headquarters in 1864 or 1865. Library of Congress, DIG-cwpb-04407.

general blocked Johnson's attempt to dispatch him on a mission to Mexico. Attempting to circumvent Grant, Johnson sounded out Sherman on becoming secretary of war, but the latter refused out of loyalty to Grant and his belief that the army must "keep out of quasi-political offices." Reasserting the use of General Order No. 44 to enforce the Civil Rights Act, Grant slowly reaffirmed his control over the army, through which he could frame Reconstruction. Acknowledging that "military rule is always odious," editors of the *Army and Navy Journal* urged that "measures must be taken to arrest that lawlessness of the South."[30]

In a whirlwind of frenetic debate, improvisation, and political maneuvering, a lame-duck Congress in late February 1867 patched together legislation designed to ensure that soldiers could enforce the Republican vision of Reconstruction. First was the Tenure of Office Act, which forbade the president from removing an array of long-serving federal officials without Senate approval. Next came the First Reconstruction Act, which divided ten former Confederate states (Tennessee had already been restored to the Union) into five military districts. Appointed by the president, district commanders gained sweeping powers to preserve order. Only after securing congressional approval of new constitutions and endorsing the Fourteenth Amendment could these rebel states reenter the Union. A third measure retroactively validated the military commissions, thereby freeing officers from a torrent of civil suits in Southern courts. Finally, the annual Army Appropriations Act disbanded militias in the unreconstructed states and strengthened Grant's influence, specifying that military orders emanating from the executive branch had to be issued through the general's headquarters and requiring Senate approval for his reassignment or removal.[31]

Debate had been tumultuous. "The Army will pave the way," proclaimed Representative Giles W. Hotchkiss (R-NY). "We want the Army, the military power, there [in the South], and then civil authority can go there in safety." In agreement, James A. Garfield (R-OH) insisted "the time has come when we must lay the heavy hand of military authority upon these rebel communities, and hold them in its grasp till their madness is past." Opponents decried the limits on executive powers and the costly "military despotism," but Congress overrode several presidential vetoes. As the historian Harold Hyman notes, the broad responsibilities accorded the regulars suggested "that Americans still trusted their soldiers."[32]

By contrast, Congress displayed considerably less confidence in the army when it came to Indian affairs. A bill to return the Indian Bureau to the War Department, which supporters contended would harmonize relations with Indians and reduce fraud and corruption, slipped through the House by a 76–73 vote but met stiff Senate opposition. James R. Doolittle (R-WI), whose investigation condemning the Sand Creek Massacre afforded him considerable credibility, came out strongly against it. Smarting from repeated defeats on Reconstruction, Thomas A. Hendricks (D-IN) wryly noted that many of his colleagues who had voted to divide jurisdiction in the South between military and civil authorities were now seeking to consolidate such powers when it came to Indian affairs. "I voted for the military bill as a necessity to keep order in the South," countered William M. Stewart (R-NV). "I vote now for turning the charge of Indian affairs over to the military, for the purpose of keeping order and peace in the Territories." Rejecting such arguments, senators defeated the transfer bill by a 24–13 count. Thirteen Republicans who had voted to override the president's veto of military government in the South now refused to return the Indian Bureau to the War Department.[33]

"We are pressed for men at all points," Sherman complained. "Outrages on negroes and Union men appear to increase. . . . If our army has to do all the dirty police work of the south, you can see it will all be absorbed there, giving us but a small share of the army for the real public enemy—the Indian." Rather than increasing the regular army, Interior Secretary Orville H. Browning in February 1867 convinced the president to negotiate with the Northern tribes. Until these peace talks could come to fruition, Secretary of War Stanton promised not to undertake offensive operations on the northern Plains. Meanwhile, reinforcements and new breechloading Springfield rifles helped small detachments hold off Indian attacks along the Bozeman Trail outside Fort C. F. Smith (the Hayfield Fight) and Fort Phil Kearny (the Wagon Box Fight).[34]

Nothing limited activities in the Department of the Missouri, where Maj. Gen. Winfield S. Hancock declared that "a war with the Cheyennes would answer our purposes." In April 1867, leading a column that eventually swelled to 1,400 men, Hancock marched out from Fort Riley. "No insolence will be tolerated from any bands of Indians whom we may encounter," the expedition orders proclaimed. Following perfunctory talks, Hancock burned several villages near Pawnee Fork and dispatched Lt. Col. George A. Custer on a vain chase after Lakotas and Cheyennes. Hancock's enterprise was a "disaster," observed Agents J. H. Leavenworth and G. W. Wynkoop, who predicted that the operations would merely provoke open warfare.[35]

Continued failures of Indian policy led John B. Henderson (R-MO), chair of the Senate Committee on Indian Affairs, to sponsor the creation of a new Peace Commission in July. Henderson joined Sherman in wanting to move Indians to reservations north of the Platte River and south of the Arkansas River, but he contended that the new Bozeman Trail garrisons violated earlier treaties. "Civilization ought to be civil," the senator reasoned. To appease Westerners always keen on federal dollars, an additional provision allowed the president to raise four thousand volunteers if the commission failed to secure a settlement. The act named Senator Henderson and three others, most notably Samuel F. Tappan, as the Peace Commission's civilian members. President Johnson selected Sherman, Brig. Gen. William S. Harney (retired), and Brig. Gen. Alfred H. Terry, a lawyer-turned-soldier who commanded the Department of Dakota, as its military delegation. In October 1867, commissioners (with Col. Christopher Augur standing in for Sherman, who had been summoned to Washington) struck a settlement with Southern Plains tribes at Medicine Lodge Creek. An accord with the Lakotas and Northern Cheyennes came only after the government agreed to abandon Forts Phil Kearny and C. F. Smith.[36]

Agreements on the Great Plains masked reality: the United States was still at war. Crook's patrols were still hard on the trail in Oregon, dealing calamitous losses to the Paiutes. In Arizona, Apache warriors raided at will. The ten unreconstructed states, declared the *Army and Navy Journal*, remained in "the same state of war which prevailed at Lee's surrender." From Arkansas, an officer asserted, "force alone is respected." Using wartime powers granted in the Reconstruction Acts, soldiers throughout the South registered voters, suppressed the conservative press, educated freedpersons, removed (and, more commonly, suspended or threatened to remove) civil officials, regulated liquor sales, built roads and infrastructure, arrested and jailed criminals, revised laws, settled labor disputes, established military commissions and justice systems, issued rations to the indigent, reorganized police departments, and integrated streetcars.[37]

Following Grant's advice, Johnson's choices to the commands created by the 1867 Reconstruction Acts boasted considerable familiarity with occupation duties. Least experienced in such matters was Brig. Gen. John Pope, transferred from the Plains to take over the Third District (Georgia, Florida, and Alabama). Commanding the First District (Virginia), Brig. Gen. John Schofield had overseen occupying forces in Missouri and North Carolina during the war. Col. Dan Sickles, considered a radical when it came to enforcing federal law in the South, remained in the Carolinas, administering the Second Military District. Mississippi and Arkansas made up the Fourth District, headed by Brig. Gen. E. O. C. Ord (the most conservative of the lot). Major General Sheridan retained Texas and Louisiana (Fifth Military District). All save Sickles (trained as a lawyer) were West Point graduates.[38]

With too few troops to be everywhere, Reconstruction commanders struggled to interpret the new laws and restore order. In Mobile, Alabama, shots were fired when Representative William Kelley (R-PA) tried to speak in favor of black rights; when city police failed to respond effectively, the entire force was suspended. On March 27, Sheridan sacked the Louisiana state attorney general, the mayor of New Orleans, and a district court judge, all of whom he believed had been involved in the previous year's riots. Nine weeks later, he dismissed the unpredictable Governor James Madison Wells, "a political trickster" whose "conduct has been as sinuous as the mark left in the dust by the movement of a snake." Gideon Welles, the conservative secretary of the navy, described Sheridan's action as "arbitrary, tyrannical, and despotic." Hectored by Johnson, U.S. Attorney General Henry Stanbery issued legal opinions designed to reduce the powers of military officers to remove civil officials, interfere with courts, and establish military commissions. In so doing, Stanbery identified Sheridan and Sickles as having been especially egregious offenders.[39]

Undeterred, Congress and Grant flexed their political muscle. Irritated by Commissioner of Public Buildings Benjamin F. French's support for the president, Congress abolished his office and reassigned oversight of capital construction projects to the army engineers, who Senator George F. Edmunds (R-VT) praised as being able to master "questions of practical science and engineering, or architecture, of science, of taste." The chief engineer, countered the conservative Hendricks, "has enough to do without seeing to putting down the carpet in the President's House and without looking after the President's stables." Grant assured district commanders that, because the Attorney General's restrictions had not been distributed through official military channels, they should use their own judgment. Fearing Election Day riots, the general ordered Maj. Gen. George Thomas, heading the Department of the Cumberland, to Memphis, where he was to "let it be felt that where the military is law must prevail and guilty be punished. Do not wait for a riot to take place but use the military vigorously to prevent one commencing."[40]

In July 1867, an emboldened Congress passed—again over Johnson's veto—the Third Reconstruction Act, which strengthened the authority of military chiefs in the ten unreconstructed states. Collectively, argued Representative William Mungen (D-OH), the legislation showed that Republicans "are intent upon, not only the amalgamation of races, but the utter destruction of our system of government and the erection of a vast consolidated empire to be administered upon the maxims of military despotism." Soon thereafter, Sheridan removed Governor Throckmorton in Texas (with whom he had long quarreled about the advisability of shifting troops from Reconstruction duties to the frontier), twenty-two New Orleans city councilmen, and a bevy of other Louisiana officials.[41]

Significantly, however, the Senate refused to go along with House language that would have taken away the president's power to replace district commanders. When Congress recessed for the summer, Johnson struck back. On August 11, he suspended (but did not remove) Stanton and convinced Grant to become interim secretary of war. "He [Grant] has allowed himself to be imposed upon and placed in a false position," complained one

Republican. Others came to the general's defense. "He was actuated by good motives," wrote one after meeting with him. "I have no doubt that Grant's object was to prevent a *general sweep of the Military Reconstruction District Commanders*, and the substitution of *obstructionists*." Whatever Grant's rationale, his strenuous objections did not prevent Johnson from removing Sheridan, whose handling of Reconstruction had been, in the president's words, "absolute tyranny, without reference to the principles of our government or the nature of our free institutions." Further alienating Grant, Johnson named the conservative Hancock as Sheridan's replacement. On August 26, the hammer also fell on the troublesome Sickles.[42]

Amid the sparring, the army's Southern duties continued. Officers hated such work; as one grumbled from Florida, "anything is better than this Reconstruction business." Lt. Col. Samuel D. Sturgis complained that his official responsibilities went "entirely outside the duty of my profession." Most nevertheless tried to do their best. Sickles's replacement in the Second District, Brig. Gen. E. R. S. Canby, continued to remove civil officers in accord with Grant's instructions, leading North Carolina governor Jonathan Worth to observe that the change had been "a devil for a witch." Complained Maj. Samuel H. Starr, Freedmen's Bureau subcommissioner at Mount Pleasant, Texas: "The darkies take up a great deal of my time and some times exhaust my patience." Still, even Starr protested the ongoing racial violence. "They [white Texans] think no more of killing a negro here than they do a dog in the north." In his district, Pope sacked the sheriff and deputy sheriff of Bartow County, Georgia, and removed virtually all city officials of Mobile, Alabama. As assistant commissioner for the Freedmen's Bureau in North Carolina, Col. Nelson A. Miles investigated widespread disputes regarding contracts, nonpayments of debt, and voter fraud. Ominously, even as he praised the bureau's efforts to help blacks and Unionists, Miles observed that animosity among former rebels was on the rise.[43]

The army's tenuous grip on the South seemed to be slipping as Democrats enjoyed a resurgence in the fall 1867 elections and white supremacy groups like the Ku Klux Klan and the Knights of the White Camellia gained influence. From Texas, Hancock pleased conservatives by ordering that when "the civil authorities are ready and willing to perform their duties, the military power should cease to lead, and the civil administration resume its natural and rightful dominion." Military-led Reconstruction, barked Johnson in his annual message to Congress, meant that white Southerners were bound "hand in foot in slavery." The president also removed Pope from command over Alabama, Georgia, and Florida. As he departed, Pope cautioned his successor, Major General Meade, that "the Rebellion is as active & so far as the people of this Dist. are concerned, nearly as powerful as during the War." A Virginia district judge accused local conservatives of persecuting anything resembling a Republican. "Can Congress save us from annihilation?" he wondered.[44]

With less than 19,000 regulars in the former Confederate states (excluding the western borderlands of Texas), district commanders oversaw constitutional conventions that met between November 1867 and June 1868. Thanks largely to army protection against terrorist threats, more than 600,000 black men registered to vote. Cumulatively, a quarter of delegates to the conventions were black, and in South Carolina, African Americans commanded a solid majority. In Georgia, Meade removed Governor Charles J. Jenkins for refusing to use state funds to pay the expenses of the convention, replacing him with Col. Thomas Ruger; in Florida, he dispatched troops to prevent a split between Radical and moderate Republicans that threatened to tear apart that state's meeting. The situation was less certain in Virginia. Schofield, who opposed universal male suffrage and worked hard to limit Radical influence, delayed a vote to ratify the so-called Underwood Constitution (which he dubbed "one big elephant"), fearing that its disfranchisement of former Confederates would stoke a political backlash. In the interim, Schofield stepped up efforts to install "competent" Republicans in civil offices and removed the conservative city government in Petersburg. At the behest of Republicans, he also replaced Governor Francis H. Pierpont with Henry Horatio Wells, a former Union officer from Michigan. By the end of the summer, only Virginia (delayed by Schofield), Mississippi (where voters rejected the proposed constitution), and Texas (whose convention would not adjourn until February 1869) had yet to reenter the Union.[45]

As Southerners debated their fates, on January 13, 1868, the Senate rejected the president's suspension of Secretary Stanton, citing the Tenure of Office Act. The following morning, Grant surrendered the keys to War Department offices so that Stanton could resume his duties. Infuriated by what he deemed to have been Grant's breach of faith, Johnson rebuked the general in a cabinet meeting, signaling the final collapse of their brittle relationship. Seeking an alternative to Stanton in the War Department, Johnson again courted Sherman, sweetening the proposition with promises of a nomination to the brevet rank of full general and command of a new Division of the Atlantic. Sherman once again refused to betray his old comrade, citing his desire to be free of the "intrigue, gossip, & slander" of the nation's capital. George Thomas also rejected the offer of a specially created division command.[46]

In a desperate bid to end the imbroglio, Johnson fired Stanton on February 21 and appointed Adjutant General Lorenzo Thomas as interim secretary. A sixty-three-year old bureaucrat who had distinguished himself by recruiting former slaves for the army during the Civil War, Thomas promptly embarked on a drunken binge that shocked even the most hardened Washington

THE SITUATION.

"The Situation." Published in *Harper's Weekly* in March 1868, this wood engraving shows General Grant, an unknown officer, and Secretary Stanton readying to fire a cannon named "Congress" at Adjutant General Lorenzo Thomas and President Andrew Johnson. Library of Congress, USZ62-127515.

observers. To a Congress that had been considering the president's impeachment for a year and a half, Johnson's direct challenge to the Tenure of Office Act seemed to be the last straw. Three days after Stanton's removal, the House of Representatives impeached the president. Anticipating a constitutional crisis, Schofield tried to reassure his subordinates in Virginia. "As long as the army is united and right," he asserted, "the country is safe from all ordinary dangers."[47]

On March 4, the Senate took up the case. Republicans could convict if they voted as a block, but the dubious constitutionality of the Tenure of Office Act and the prospect that the blustering president pro tempore, Benjamin Wade (R-OH), would become president gave cause for concern. Both sides thus began exploring a compromise, and on April 21, William M. Evarts, counsel for the president, met with Schofield, believed to be a close Grant ally, at Washington's Willard Hotel. Evarts's plan enjoyed the support of several moderate senators: in return for Johnson's acquittal, the president would nominate Schofield as secretary of war. After initially blessing the deal, Grant changed his mind, but Schofield had already gone forward. "The generally accepted theory is that the President in nominating General Schofield holds out the olive branch to the Conservative Republicans," speculated the Washington *Evening Star*, "as an assurance that if acquitted on the Impeachment trial he will endeavor to get along amicably with the party."[48]

By a single vote on May 16, the Senate declined to convict Johnson. Five days later, the Republican Party nominated for president Ulysses S. Grant, West Point graduate and steadfast supporter of the most aggressive use of armed forces to affect social and political change in U.S. history. On May 31, the Senate approved Schofield's nomination as secretary of war, reaffirming congressional faith in the regular army, at least when it came to Reconstruction.[49]

Chapter Twelve
Continued Challenges South and West

As the army waited for the Indian Peace Commission of 1867 to do its work, the newly promoted Brig. Gen. Christopher Augur counseled William T. Sherman to remain patient. A clash of arms was inevitable, predicted Augur, so the mandated truce would give the regulars time to prepare. Augur's prognostication proved correct, for the government remained chronically slow in supplying Indian annuities, and white Westerners expected the regulars to crush any Indian resistance. Twitchy Republicans worried that delays in opening an increasingly romanticized American West would prevent free laborers from securing their economic liberties and deprive the nation of the only remaining area where, as the historian Heather Cox Richardson puts it, "northerners and southerners met on common ground." Blaming the army's inactivity on Reconstruction, Washington's *Daily National Intelligencer* asserted that "the people in the remote States and Territories are paying in blood for Radicalism."[1]

In mid-August 1868, resentful of the never-ending encroachments on their resources, Cheyenne Dog Soldiers swept through white settlements on the Saline, Solomon, and Republican Rivers. Though many Southern Cheyennes and Arapahos tried to distance themselves from these incidents, the army believed that all deserved a good thrashing. "These Indians require to be soundly whipped," wrote Sheridan, "& the ringleaders in the present trouble hung, their ponies killed, & such destruction of their property as will make them very poor." To rally support, Sherman brought the matter before the Peace Commission in early October. Senator John B. Henderson's absence deprived the peace faction of its most powerful proponent, so the soldiers on the commission rammed through recommendations to transfer the Bureau of Indian Affairs to the War Department and to initiate military operations.[2]

Not since the days of Anthony Wayne's Legion had the army developed anything resembling official doctrine for Indian warfare, but astute observers had identified several common features of Plains conflicts. "Indians have some practical sense," acknowledged Ohio's Capt. Caleb H. Carlton. "They will not attack unless there is a good deal to gain and but little risk to run." Eschewing pitched battles against prepared foes, warriors usually opted to scatter in hopes of creating other situations that might offer more favorable circumstances. Each warrior typically enjoyed the use of several horses, and their grass-fed ponies could outpace the army's bigger, grain-fed mounts in warm weather. The problem was forcing the Indians to fight, which soldiers believed could best be done by threatening their villages. Now, Sherman also urged that the campaigns continue until "winter strains their ponies."[3]

Following the Peace Commission's adjournment, Sherman and Sheridan put the finishing touches on their 1868 Southern Plains campaign. Indians who left their reservations or did not turn themselves in at Fort Cobb, Indian Territory (in present-day Oklahoma), would be treated as hostile. Large scouting parties already in the field were but precursors to the real blow: "As soon as the failure of the grass and the cold weather forces the scattered bands to come together to winter in the milder latitudes south of the Arkansas," explained Sheridan, "a movement of troops will then take place . . . which I hope will be successful in gaining a permanent peace." In November and early December, columns led by Maj. Andrew W. Evans (Fort Bascom, New Mexico Territory), Lt. Col. George A. Custer (Camp Supply, Indian Territory) and Maj. Eugene A. Carr (Fort Lyon, Colorado Territory) took the field. Carr and Evans, Sheridan later explained, "were really beaters in," meant to ensure that Comanches, Kiowas, Southern Cheyennes, and Arapahos could not elude Custer.[4]

The plan worked—at least to Sheridan's satisfaction. Just after dawn on November 27, Custer's bluecoats galloped into an Indian camp along the Washita River, firing wildly into the tipis as men, women, and children frantically scrambled for safety. The regulars burned all the possessions left behind and slaughtered the nine hundred ponies and mules that had served as the lifeblood of the community's economy and culture. Threatened by oncoming warriors from nearby villages, Custer and his main body then retreated; only later was it learned that Maj. Joel Elliott and a scratch force of seventeen troopers trying to chase down escaping villagers had been killed to a man. On Christmas Day, Major Evans destroyed the winter stores of a Nakoni Comanche village at Soldier Spring. The final military blow came on July 11, 1869, when Major Carr whipped the Dog Soldiers at Summit Springs, Colorado Territory. Sheridan declared victory: "Punishment was inflicted; property destroyed; the Indians disabused of the idea that winter would bring security; and all the tribes south of the Platte forced on to the reservations set apart for them by the government." But it was not so simple, for Custer had destroyed the village of Black Kettle (previously the target of Chivington's brutal assault of 1864), who had been attempting to secure terms for his followers. Samuel F. Tappan, a Peace Commission member, censured "the stupid and criminal blundering of military officers" who struck "a small detached camp of men, women, and children, who were evidently moving south to avoid contact with the troops—an attack that notifies the Indians of a determination on the part of the army to exterminate them." As a result, whatever credit the regulars might have claimed for a successful campaign was negated in the court of public opinion.[5]

As war raged on the Southern Plains, about 18,000 regulars remained on Reconstruction duties. Although all states except Virginia, Mississippi, and Texas had been readmitted into the Union, conflicts over civil rights and federal authority still wracked the South. In Georgia, the legislature expelled its twenty-eight black members, and at least a dozen African Americans were killed during Mitchell County's Camilla Massacre. The Ku Klux Klan was terrorizing Tennessee, and "considerable lawlessness" plagued Kentucky. Loyalists and freedpeople in Scott County, Mississippi, were threatened by "rampant, half-horse, half-alligator, walking arsenals." Less than half of registered voters had gone to the polls to ratify Alabama's new constitution. Louisiana was "in terrible condition." In Texas, where Indians had killed twenty-six residents during the first nine months of 1869, there had been 384 murders. To stem the carnage, U.S. Attorney General William Evarts ruled that the army could assist local federal agents during emergencies. Accordingly, Secretary of War John Schofield encouraged officers to preempt violence by stationing troops at potential trouble spots.[6]

Doing so prevented greater horrors, for even small garrisons could carve out zones of relative safety for Unionists and blacks against former Confederates and white supremacists. From Kentucky, the district chief of the Freedmen's Bureau noted that detachments of one company at Lexington and thirty men each at Maysville and Covington "caused a marked change for the better . . . and gave confidence to the many good men (white people) who accept the present condition of affairs, and are willing when assured of protection, by the United States authorities, to aid by their influence and action." In North Carolina, Col. Nelson A. Miles and Governor William W. Holden agreed to disperse troops widely to overawe rebel sympathizers and suppress terrorists. Maj. Gen. George G. Meade increased the number of posts in the Carolinas, Georgia, Florida, and Alabama from fifteen to forty. Responding to Ku Klux Klan outrages, six companies of infantry were dispatched to Tennessee, and the governor of Arkansas was authorized to declare martial law in several counties. Conservatives denounced such moves. "In a time of profound peace a large standing army is kept quartered in our midst to protect carpet-bag governments in their oppressive and irresponsible rule," declared editors of the *Daily Arkansas Gazette*.[7]

Hesitant to directly challenge Secretary Schofield, President Johnson nonetheless exerted considerable influence through his power to appoint military commanders. In his most dramatic move, in July 1868, the president selected Brig. Gen. Lovell Rousseau to head the Department of Louisiana. A Civil War veteran and congressman who had voted not to extend the

Freedmen's Bureau, Rousseau had only recently returned to the army. With fall elections nearing, as department commander he did everything he could to avoid intervening against whites bent on restoring conservative control. "All is quiet here now and likely to be. . . . A fair vote will give the state to the democrats," he assured Johnson. Ignoring orders to "take all legitimate steps necessary and proper to prevent breaches of the peace of hostile collisions between citizens," Rousseau's inaction meant that the Republican Party suffered major losses in Louisiana's election.[8]

As regulars remained embroiled in Reconstruction, former Civil War volunteers jealous of West Point domination of the army's highest ranks allied themselves with attempts to reduce the military. In 1868, hoping to stave off even bigger cutbacks, James A. Garfield (R-OH), chair of the House Military Affairs Committee, suggested eliminating nineteen of the army's sixty regiments. Convinced that a cabal of West Pointers had stymied his Civil War career, Representative Benjamin Butler (R-MA) insisted that Garfield's measure did not go far enough. "I am very anxious there should be a reduction of this Army," roared Butler, "and I wish to begin with the generals." Denouncing the "aristocracy" of officers, fellow congressman John A. Logan (R-IL), still smarting from Sherman's 1864 decision not to award him command of the Army of the Tennessee, chided regulars for assuming that they had "an inalienable right" to their commissions. Those favoring a reduction won a smashing House victory, producing a bill that would have eliminated half of the staff and seven of the fifteen major and brigadier generals.[9]

Alarmed by the House's actions, Senate Military Affairs Committee chair Henry A. Wilson introduced a measure resembling Garfield's original proposal. A last-minute amendment to distribute surplus federal weapons to newly forming Southern militias complicated Wilson's task, as several senators saw the move as a thinly veiled attempt to empower black–Republican–Unionist coalitions against conservative whites. Blaming the army for the continued Indian wars, Senator James R. Doolittle (R-WI) instead proposed cutting the number of regiments to twenty. In a feat of mental gymnastics, Doolittle also insisted that this diminished regular force oversee upcoming elections in the former Confederate states. Army supporters seized on the incongruity of Doolittle's position to defeat his amendments and pass their own measure in the Senate, but the session ended before the two chambers could reach an accord.[10]

As Congress debated the army's role in American life, Republicans had nominated General of the Army Ulysses S. Grant for president. Only their party could win the ongoing struggle over Reconstruction, they reasoned, and only Grant—a political outsider and military hero—could guarantee a meaningful peace. Regulars lined up behind Grant's candidacy. "Surely it will give us four years and I hope eight years of calm, quiet, firm administration,"

John A. Logan. One of the ablest political generals of the Civil War, John A. Logan (1826–1886) while in Congress proved to be a fierce critic of the regular army, motivated at least in part by his belief that his military career had been stymied by a West Point clique. Library of Congress, DIG-cwpbh-00598.

wrote Sherman, "during which all these ugly questions left by the war may be adjusted." Fueled by the ballots of newly enfranchised African Americans, Grant captured 53 percent of the popular vote and twenty-six of thirty-four states. Democratic warnings that his election would lead to a military dictatorship gained little traction, for this unassuming soldier seemed to offer a pathway to peace: an end to partisan bickering and a way forward for repentant Southerners eager for reunion. "He was a great soldier," Henry Adams later observed, "and the soldier always represented order."[11]

But Grant's triumph failed to save the regulars from "the wrath of the demagogues" in Congress. Privately, Secretary Schofield beseeched competing army factions to discuss the matter "*among themselves*, differences compromised, & plans of organization & administration harmonized, so that we may stand before Congress & the country a unit." To assuage critics, military authorities slowed recruiting, cashiered unqualified officers, and recommended dissolving the four Veterans Reserve Corps regiments and consolidating black infantry regiments. Seeking to avoid deeper cuts, Garfield's House Committee on Military Affairs in February 1869 rolled out proposals to merge several staff bureaus, eliminate most regimental bands and fifteen infantry regiments, and transfer the Indian Bureau to the War Department. "We are looking to you now," Brig. Gen. Irvin McDowell told Garfield, "and trusting to you."[12]

Garfield's plan met stiff resistance from an informal coalition of factions jealous of West Point, determined to limit federal spending, resentful about the army's role in Reconstruction, and opposed to transferring the Indian Bureau. "If there is one thing upon which the people of all political parties in this country are united in opinion it is that there ought to be a reduction in the expenditures for the Army and for the Navy," opined William Lawrence (R-OH). Benjamin Boyer (D-PA) insisted that occupation troops in the South were unnecessary. "It is the reconstruction policy of Congress which has necessitated the continuance of this vast Army at this enormous cost of the nation," he charged. By a 111–65 margin, the House sliced the regular establishment to thirty regiments. The Senate refused to go that far, and the resulting compromise cut the number of generals from seventeen to fifteen and reduced infantry regiments from forty-five to twenty-five, in the process eliminating the Veteran Reserve Corps and consolidating the four black infantry regiments into two.[13]

Although the regular army had temporarily escaped even bigger cutbacks, relations between Sherman and Grant fractured almost immediately with the latter's ascension to the presidency. The root of the issue—which pitted the president's constitutional power to command the armed forces (and, by implication, his authority to appoint a secretary of war as his designated deputy) against the ranking military officer's ability to lead the army—had long bedeviled soldiers and politicians alike. A decade and a half before, the dispute had been partially responsible for Winfield Scott's decision to move his headquarters from Washington to New York. In 1864, President Abraham Lincoln had given Grant extraordinary powers, but when the war ended, Secretary of War Edwin Stanton had reasserted his office's authority.[14]

Cognizant of the problem, Grant seemed poised to make good his pledge to rectify the situation. His initial slate of cabinet officers did not include a new war secretary, thus allowing Schofield to remain in office long enough to publish instructions requiring staff officers to report to commanding general Sherman and proclaiming that "all orders from the President or Secretary of War to any portion of the army, line or staff, will be transmitted through

African American soldier, 25th Infantry, Co. A. The photograph of this unidentified regular is believed to have been taken during the late 1880s by the noted western photographer O. S. Goff. Library of Congress, DIG-ppmsca-11346.

the General of the Army." Yet Grant had promised the war office to his former chief of staff John A. Rawlins, who had for the previous eight years stood with his general through every crisis. Terminally ill with tuberculosis, Rawlins had no intention of serving under the restrictions outlined by Schofield's edict. Staff officers—whose long tenures and Washington offices enabled them to make powerful allies—also revolted against the bullheaded Sherman's pronouncement that they would report to him through the Adjutant General. In effect, this meant they would have to surrender their independence to one of their own. Loyal to Rawlins, Grant rescinded Schofield's order, paving the way for his old aide to take office and the bureaus to maintain their independence. Grant "went back on me," protested Sherman, who never really forgave his old superior and former friend.[15]

President Grant also dismayed his old comrades by initiating what has come to be known as his "Peace Policy," through which church-sponsored Indian agents would administer annuity shipments and encourage reservation peoples to adopt "the comforts and benefits of a Christian civilization." A sincere effort to reduce violence in the western borderlands, the Peace Policy nevertheless suffered from several fatal flaws: its assumption that a government characterized by partisanship and patronage could deliver annuities efficiently; its presumption that religious organizations could provide enough qualified people to staff the agencies; and, most significant, its failure to incorporate Indian traditions, cultures, and beliefs into the "civilization" it demanded they accept. Even under this regime, the army would continue to implement Indian policy. Although few soldiers wanted a Native American extermination, most were willing to engage in ethnic cleansing and cultural genocide to help the United States achieve what they presumed to be its manifest destiny.[16]

Conditions were ripe for tragedy. Responding to complaints about raids by Piegan Indians in Montana, Sheridan, now commanding the massive Division of the Missouri, authorized Maj. Eugene Baker, who had fought with him in the Shenandoah Valley in 1864, to attack Mountain Chief's band. "Tell Baker to strike them *hard*," insisted Sheridan. On January 19, 1870, Baker attacked a Piegan village along the Marias River—but it was that of Heavy Runner, who possessed a safe conduct pass from the Indian Bureau. Surprising a community already ravished by smallpox, the regulars swept through the village with a vengeance; a hurried count totaled 173 dead Indians (Baker acknowledged that the toll included 53 women and children) and 140 prisoners. Mountain Chief's followers fled to Canada, but Sheridan characterized the expedition as a "complete success."[17]

Such was hardly the case, for the public reacted in horror to news of Baker's savage assault. "Shame should mantle the cheek of the officer who ordered this bloody deed," proclaimed a correspondent to the *Pittsburgh Daily Post*.

The *New York Times*, which had defended Custer's attack at the Washita two years earlier, described the Piegan affair as "a sickening slaughter." Eager to pounce on army misbehavior, the staunchly conservative Louisville *Courier-Journal* insisted "that Col. Baker cut the throats of the Indians simply to quench his own individual thirst for aboriginal blood." Responding to such criticism, Sheridan's intemperate denunciations of humanitarian critics and salacious recitations of cumulative barbarities attributed to Indians weakened the army's public relations counteroffensive; the repercussions were starkly evident in that year's appropriation act. A vocal critic of the Grant administration, Representative Daniel Vorhees (D-IN) promised that he "shall not vote for one dollar of an appropriation that upholds such a system of warfare as the indiscriminate massacre of all ages and both sexes." Any hope of transferring the Indian Bureau to the War Department during that session vanished, and the Baker affair provided an excuse for Congress to forbid army officers from holding civil offices, thereby opening to congressional patronage scores of Indian agency positions normally assigned to soldiers.[18]

Now chair of the House Military Affairs Committee, John A. Logan seized the opportunity to further reduce the regulars. The current structure, he quipped, allowed for "a brigadier general of bean soup." Warming to the task, he later condemned Sherman's criticism of his proposals as "military despotism" and an affront to the volunteers who had won the Civil War. Senator Willard Warner (R-AL), a former Union general of volunteers who had migrated southward after the war, vainly rose in opposition: "I beg of you not to reduce the Army. . . . The presence of United States troops everywhere in the South is to preserve peace." A conference committee reduced the number of enlisted men to 30,000, mustered out (with a year's pay) 353 officers who had been awaiting regimental appointments, and curtailed future promotions to brigadier and major general. Whereas the War Department budget had represented 40.9 percent of total federal appropriations in 1869, it had dwindled by nearly half of that by 1871. Soldiers recoiled from the ferocity of the attacks. Maj. Gen. George Thomas declared that "it exhibits more heartlessness than I supposed our congress could be guilty of"; Maj. Samuel H. Starr deemed it "ungenerous and ungrateful."[19]

Although by October 1870 less than 14 percent of all regulars were stationed in the South (including Kentucky but not Texas), the army's association with Reconstruction generated much of the hostility. Texas, Mississippi, and Virginia were readmitted to the Union that year, but Georgia's failure to ratify the Fifteenth Amendment led Congress to again bar the state's delegation. In response, Brig. Gen. Alfred H. Terry increased the number of military posts there from six to twenty-three, purged former Confederates from public offices, and restored Republicans to power. The show of force worked, at least temporarily, and Congress readmitted Georgia. Convinced that strong measures had been necessary, the usually even-tempered Terry nevertheless complained about having "to be always a sort of wet-nurse to the negroes."[20]

Even after creating the United States Department of Justice in 1870, Congress relied on soldiers to protect voting rights in the former Confederacy. Three Enforcement Acts (1870–1871) and the Ku Klux Klan Act (1871) empowered the army to supervise elections and prevent voter intimidation. Grant also returned two regiments to the South, and in fall 1871 regulars conducted more than two hundred patrols against suspected wrongdoers in South Carolina, Mississippi, Tennessee, and Kentucky. The following year, threats of army intervention helped to restore Republicans to power in Alabama. As a federal official in Mississippi later put it: "'A little '*Color-line*' of *blue* had a wonderful influence upon these people." From North Carolina, even a skeptical Capt. George B. Rodney admitted that "we are doing some little good" in that state. Blacks and Unionists—the heart of the Republican Party in the South—voted in large numbers in counties with a military garrison. But a growing cadre of Liberal Republicans now focused on reducing federal spending and taxation, and the involvement of soldiers in politics such as Brig. Gen. Adelbert Ames (a Mississippi senator and governor) and Col. Joseph J. Reynolds (a West Point graduate who made little effort to conceal his attempts to become a senator from Texas) ran counter to deeply held fears of military rule, especially when that force was used to protect the liberties of African Americans. As the historian Andrew Lang notes, Reconstruction forced a choice "between faith in democratic majority rule and self-determination at the ballot box . . . over the idealism of racial equality."[21]

Elsewhere, regulars continued to assume duties for which no other federal agency existed. During the winter of 1874–1875, for instance, soldiers distributed shoes, clothing, and more than a million rations to civilians in Kansas and Nebraska ravaged by a plague of grasshoppers and drought. And as head of the District of Columbia Office of Public Buildings and Grounds, Maj. Nathaniel N. Michler oversaw a sprawling portfolio that included maintenance of federal buildings, landscaping the associated grounds, grading city roads, building sewers, disbursing care for the indigent, and planting the first of 64,920 trees. In 1870, the War Department initiated a new weather observation program; according to the resolution's sponsor, Representative Halbert E. Paine (R-WI), "military discipline would probably secure the greatest promptness, regularity, and accuracy." In accord with this move, the U.S. Army Signal Corps provided soldier-observers with basic meteorological training, established a storm-warning system along the Atlantic Coast, and began compiling weather summaries and predictions that it telegraphed daily throughout the country. By 1880, the Signal Corps boasted a chief signal officer, several detached commissioned personnel and civilians, 450 enlisted men, and 110 regular stations.[22]

When the Great Chicago Fire of 1871 killed upward of three hundred people and left a third of city residents homeless, the army immediately intervened. Phil Sheridan, with his Division of the Missouri headquarters in ashes, organized volunteers, called in regulars, and at the request of Mayor Roswell B. Mason assumed responsibility for "the preservation of the good order and peace of the city." Distributing blankets, clothing, and food, soldiers also tamped down widespread looting. William Bross, publisher of the *Chicago Tribune*, credited Sheridan's "prompt, bold, and patriotic action" for saving the remnants of the city. On October 28, the Chicago Relief and Aid Society requested that Sheridan keep four companies of regulars in Chicago to deter "evil-disposed persons from organizing a breach of the peace & reassure the public mind." The Grant administration approved such a step three days later.[23]

As the immediate crisis in Chicago ended, however, Illinois governor John M. Palmer (R) insisted that the regulars depart. A former major general of volunteers, Palmer had never forgiven his treatment by West Pointers during the Civil War; Sheridan in particular was "a humbug." In a nod to the ongoing disputes regarding the army's role in Reconstruction, he insisted that the state take over the recovery tasks. The Democratic *Illinois State Register* cautioned that "a tinseled military satrap in the pay of the Federal government" was afoot. The Illinois Supreme Court upheld Palmer's claim that Sheridan's actions had been unconstitutional, but the governor's attempt to prosecute Sheridan, his brother Michael (a longtime military aide), and Mayor Mason for the murder of a man killed by one of the volunteers went nowhere.[24]

With only a tiny bureaucracy available to the federal government, the War Department also assumed responsibility for the national effort to memorialize Union soldiers killed during the Civil War. Spurred by Clara Barton, Capt. Edmund B. Whitman, and Quartermaster General Meigs, Congress passed legislation in 1867 accepting federal responsibility for locating, identifying, and reburying the fallen. "Every civilized man desires to have his friend's name marked on his monument," reasoned Meigs. In 1871, as the gargantuan task neared completion, he reported that, at a cost of slightly more than $4 million, 303,536 bodies (54 percent of whom had been identified) had been interred in seventy-four national cemeteries.[25]

As they had since their inception, regulars continued to promote national expansion. Following the purchase of Alaska in 1867, Washington deployed regulars to assert its authority. Four years later, it dispatched Maj. Gen. John Schofield, commanding the Division of the Pacific, to investigate the commercial and military prospects of Hawaii. He found the islands ripe for U.S. takeover, reckoning that their inhabitants "are now better qualified for self government than the colored people of our Southern States." Pearl Harbor, "easily defensible" by shore batteries, could be developed into a fine protected anchorage. Following his return to the mainland, Schofield lobbied for the acquisition of Hawaii, warning that if the United States failed to take it, then another foreign power surely would. To Representative Gilbert C. Walker (D-VA), the general argued that "control of those Islands in time of war would be indispensably necessary to command of the Pacific Ocean and the security of our commerce."[26]

Regulars also supported efforts by the Northern Pacific Railroad to locate a route through Yellowstone Valley. In 1871, seven infantry companies escorted the company's surveying party westward out of Fort Rice (in what is now North Dakota). The following year, regulars protected teams from Forts Rice and Ellis (Montana), but Sitting Bull's attack drove back another army column before it reached its planned rendezvous at the Powder River. "Our force was wholly inadequate to pass down the Yellowstone Valley," observed one correspondent. Determined to make a better showing, Col. David S. Stanley, 1,300 regulars, two artillery pieces, and 353 civilians (among them the president's son Fred and a swarm of reporters) rumbled out of Fort Rice in mid-June 1873. Leading the mounted contingent, Lt. Col. George A. Custer won two sharp fights that allowed the expedition to push all the way to Pompeys Pillar in Montana. "WHOOP!" celebrated the *Bismarck Tribune*. "THE INDIANS ARE MOST WOEFULLY THRASHED. THE HATCHET BURIED—WHERE IT WILL DO MOST GOOD."[27]

Far to the south, Arizona also remained a chronic sore. On April 30, 1871, a posse of Papago Indians, Hispanics, and Americans slaughtered 125 Aravaipa Indians who had been promised safety near Camp Grant. The massacre led Grant to dispatch Vincent Colyer, an artist and acclaimed humanitarian, to broker a peace. Brig. Gen. Oliver O. Howard, former commissioner of the Freedmen's Bureau, followed on a similar mission the next year. Grant also ordered Lt. Col. George Crook, who had forced the Pauites to accept reservations in Oregon, to take command of the Department of Arizona. In several meetings with the peace emissaries, Crook insisted that the Indians needed a sound drubbing before they would accept peace, and the army documented fifty-four Indian raids in the department between September 1871 and October 1872. With permission from Commissioner of Indian Affairs Francis A. Walker, newly appointed to the position, Crook's forces, assisted by Indian auxiliaries and the ubiquitous pack mules that became features of his operations, began moving out on November 15 from Camps Verde, McDowell, Grant, and Apache. Converging on Tonto Basin, the soldiers claimed to have killed 194 Indians (including scores of women and children in the hellish nightmare of Skeleton Cave) and captured another seventy-six in eighteen combat operations that winter. More than six thousand Apaches and Yavapais enrolled at army camps, and the first message to pass over the newly installed military telegraph to Fort Whipple brought word of Crook's promotion from lieutenant colonel to brigadier general.[28]

Crook's force of will and the government's overwhelming superiority in resources masked several army weaknesses. Target practice was almost unheard of, and the physical conditioning of the regulars paled in comparison to that of their Apache foes. Formal West Point education did little to prepare cadets for borderlands realities, and too many officers succumbed to the bottle in their frontier stations. Crook's assessment of his subordinate officers was stark. Only two officers under his command "really grasped the situation." A half-dozen others "could carry out orders understandingly"; though brave, the rest were useless when it came to field operations.[29]

Such problems became all too evident among the lava beds and lakes of Northern California, where from December 1872 to May 1873 five dozen Modoc fighters held off hundreds of regulars. The roots of the conflict lay in the Indian Bureau's insistence on removing the Modocs to the Klamath Reservation, but the army neglected to assemble the force necessary to prevent the Indians from escaping to the natural defenses of what came to be known as the "Stronghold." Attempts to storm the Modoc position failed miserably (one assault resulted in thirty-seven army casualties without a single Indian being hit); as the siege continued, on April 11 the Modocs assassinated Brig. Gen. Edward R. S. Canby and another commissioner while negotiating. Subsequent attacks fared no better. "We seem to be acting somewhat in the dark," muttered Schofield from his Division of the Pacific headquarters. In the end, internal divisions among the Modocs, rather than the skill of the besiegers, led to their withdrawal from the Stronghold and ultimate surrender. As one soldier admitted: "Those men don't know how to fight Indians."[30]

Regulars took matters into their own hands along the Rio Grande, where Indians saw no reason that a boundary drawn by faraway governments should stop the raids into Texas, Coahuila, and Chihuahua that were essential to their economies and cultures. In early 1873, President Grant transferred Col. Ranald B. Mackenzie and his Fourth Cavalry to Fort Clark, Texas. In meetings with Mackenzie, Secretary of War William Belknap, and General Augur (now commanding the Department of Texas), Sheridan seems to have assured the colonel that the president would support whatever steps he took to end the cross-border raids. On May 17, Mackenzie, six companies of Fourth Cavalrymen, a handful of civilian scouts, and twenty black Seminole auxiliaries splashed across the Rio Grande. About seven o'clock the next morning, they surprised a cluster of villages at Remolino, forty-five miles west of Piedras Negras. Most of the warriors were away, so resistance was light, and Mackenzie's troopers claimed to have killed nineteen Indians, taken another forty captives, and destroyed at least 150 lodges. "We just about exterminated what we did not bring back," one scout remembered. After a brief rest, the exhausted command raced back to Texas before Mexico could respond. Fearing the raid might encourage Mexico to launch its own strike into Arizona, Sherman was dubious: Mackenzie "will of course be sustained, but for the sake of history I would like to have him report clearly the facts that induced him to know that the Indians he attacked & captured were of the identical Indians then engaged in raiding Texas." Somewhat chastened, Sheridan advised Augur and Mackenzie not to cross the border again without clear provocation.[31]

As violence in the western borderlands increased and Republican support for Reconstruction waned, by October 1873 only 3,265 soldiers were in Kentucky and the former Confederate states (excluding Texas). Clearly, the army's reach was now painfully short. Little concerned with racism but always devoted to order, Sherman seemed almost despondent. "We are simply powerless, and the Rebels whom we defeated in war will beat us by politics," he complained. Sheridan's threats to execute Democrats in Louisiana following the tumultuous 1872 elections heightened the sense that military occupation must end as conservatives and budget-minded Republicans redoubled efforts to reduce the army. "We call on the Army for our stump orators, we call on them to preside at the polls," complained Representative Henry W. Slocum (D-NY). "If we desire to negotiate for the purchase of an island in the sea, the negotiations must be carried on by a brigadier general. . . . We can hardly pass a bill through Congress without the aid at least of a field officer." Substantive manpower cuts were avoided in 1872 and 1873 only by streamlining arsenals and armories and slowing work on coastal fortifications and public buildings in the District of Columbia.[32]

In late 1873, the collapse of Jay Cooke and Company, one of the nation's leading investment houses, sparked an economic panic that would last for half a decade. Frantically seeking retrenchment in government spending, Congress trained its sights on the army, which was still three-quarters larger than it had been before the Civil War. "Many honest men & conscientious legislators are puzzled by this fact," Sherman acknowledged, but such well-meaning men must be made to understand "that the actual frontier has increased four & five-fold since then." Cutbacks, it was contended, should come from the staff rather than infantry or cavalry regiments. To mobilize political support, he encouraged Sheridan "to use your influence with any [member of Congress]." From the Division of the Pacific, Schofield reached out to Senator Aaron A. Sargent (R-CA), reasoning that "our little army" was converting the West "into a populous and wealthy empire."[33]

House debates centered on an Appropriations Committee proposal to cut the number of enlisted men from 30,000 to 25,000 and to trim emoluments, coastal fortifications, other construction, and lower-grade staff positions. With an eye to winning Liberal Republican support, committee chair William A. Wheeler (D-NY) explained: "Economy in public expenditure is now the profession of every lip; its practice is the universal, imperative demand of the hour." This could be done by eliminating expenditures such as the Northern Pacific Railroad surveys, which merely protected "adventurous men who push out beyond the bounds of civilization, often for the very purpose of inciting Indian outrages, in order that they may invoke the military arm of the Government, and then profit by the attendant pecuniary expenditures." Even James Garfield, a Civil War veteran and normally a reliable army ally, insisted on retrenchment. Representative John Coburn (R-IN), chair of the Military Affairs Committee, wanted to disband seven regiments. Anticipating the howls from western legislators who depended on the regulars to push Indians aside, Coburn reasoned that garrisons in the Great Lakes, along the Atlantic and Pacific Seaboards, and throughout the South could be transferred westward. After all, militia remained the bulwark of national defense, and "disturbances in the South have in a large degree ceased." William E. Niblack (D-IN) agreed: "I say, take your Army from the South . . . and put it to its legitimate purposes—for the defense of the lives of our citizens, and not for the crushing of the liberties of our people."[34]

Perhaps the most influential critic of the regulars, John A. Logan (by now a senator) urged the upper chamber to slash the number of regiments from forty to twenty-five. Logan's harsher Senate proposal failed by a 27–18 count; still, War Department appropriations for the fiscal year ending June 30, 1875, were reduced by 12 percent. The regular army was now half the size it had been in 1866. "We have almost reached the point where the main question will be how to shelter and supply an army too small and scattered to do any efficient service," sighed Schofield as he sized up the latest carnage. "Local interests everywhere on the frontier require protection. Posts established for that purpose can not be abandoned without the most strenuous opposition from citizens in the vicinity, through the State or Territorial government, and their representatives in Congress."[35]

Sherman's decision to move his headquarters from Washington to St. Louis further lessened the army's political influence. Following Secretary Rawlins's death in 1869, among the men Sherman had recommended for the war office was William W. Belknap, formerly a brigade commander in his Army of the Tennessee. Belknap got the job, but he invariably supported the bureau chiefs against line officers. Disenchanted by his old subordinate's grasp for power, Sherman began floating the idea of a move. "Now my sphere is more advisory than real," he complained in 1871. Humiliated by the failure of either his old friend Grant or his former subordinate Belknap to rectify

William T. Sherman. After succeeding Grant as commanding general of the army, Sherman (1820–1891) attempted—often with only mixed success—to defend what he believed to be the interests of the regular army from 1869 to 1883. Library of Congress, USZ62-72801.

the situation, Sherman had made up his mind by May 1874. "I hope you won't do it," pleaded longtime aide Maj. Cyrus B. Comstock. "Aside from your direct influence & control of questions [in] relation to the army, you will very largely lose indirect influence. In Washington, every member of Congress sees you—knows you—knows what you have done," added Comstock. "I will do it," retorted Sherman, even if it were to "result in the abolition of my office." The regulars thus lost their most powerful voice in the capital.[36]

Sherman scored his revenge two years later, when the corruption that marred the Grant administration was revealed to have extended to Secretary Belknap. In February 1876, the *New York Herald* ran a long exposé into the nefarious activities involving the post trader at Fort Sill, Indian Territory. Seeking to embarrass the Grant administration, the House Committee on Expenditures in the Department of War, chaired by Hiester Clymer (D-PA), summoned several witnesses to testify. Most notable was Lieutenant Colonel Custer, who implicated the president's worthless brother, Orvil. The committee also discovered that Belknap and his wife had pocketed at least $20,000 from kickbacks in sales of post sutlerships, forcing the secretary's resignation. After much coaxing and assurances that military orders would go through his office, Sherman returned to Washington to assist the interim secretary, Alfonso Taft.[37]

Scandals also tainted the army itself. Most spectacular was that involving Col. Orville Babcock, a personal secretary and longtime aide to Grant, who had been appointed Superintendent of Public Buildings and aqueduct superintendent. A West Point graduate, Babcock pushed through District of Columbia appropriations requests that improved public life. Unfortunately, he was also a member of the notorious St. Louis "Whiskey Ring," which defrauded the federal government of millions of dollars. Although President Grant's favorable deposition helped to acquit Babcock, the verdict of history has been severe.[38]

As the improprieties mounted, Sheridan's Division of the Missouri again braced for war. Reservation life for Comanches, Southern Cheyennes, and Kiowas was difficult, as whiskey peddlers, shoddy government annuities, ineffective agents, and buffalo hunters imperiled their economic and cultural existence. In 1871, Sherman had nearly been killed during an inspection tour near Fort Richardson, Texas, when a Kiowa raiding party determined that an approaching wagon train would yield better booty than the general's small escort. By summer 1874, increasing numbers of Indian strikes into Kansas and Texas led one officer to declare that the Indians "seem determined to have war." The Interior Department, pressed by Sherman, on July 18 gave the army permission to enter the reservations and inflict collective punishment, thereby beginning the Red River War. Rather than wait for winter, Sheridan opted to attack before Interior Department officials changed their minds. By late August, five columns were converging on the Texas Panhandle and the western reaches of Indian Territory. In accord with normal procedure, each command enjoyed considerable latitude, as long as they hit the enemy when the opportunity arose. Amid confused efforts to enroll friendly Indians at the Anadarko and Darlington Agencies, about five thousand (including some 1,200 fighting men) Cheyennes, Comanches, and Kiowas assembled into a formidable enemy.[39]

This would be a war of endurance, with army contractors often failing to meet deadlines and Indians desperately endeavoring to protect their families and winter stores from the incessant columns of bluecoats. The soldiers boasted two singular advantages: their women and children were safe, and they could eventually restock their supplies. On August 30, Col. Nelson A. Miles, delighted to be freed from his Reconstruction duties, hit Kiowa and Comanche encampments at Tule Canyon; four weeks later, Colonel Mackenzie surprised the inhabitants of several hundred Kiowa, Cheyenne, and Comanche lodges at nearby Palo Duro Canyon and slaughtered nearly a thousand Indian ponies—a blow of devastating consequences to the horse people of the Plains. As Miles observed on November 12: "It is now a question of who gives up first as the Indians are in wretched condition." As northers pounded the region, the trickle of Indian defectors, decimated by the loss of winter stores and demoralized by the constant fear of attack, became a flood. The last Comanche holdouts finally surrendered on June 2, 1875. The campaign, Sheridan concluded, had been "wonderfully successful."[40]

The army was also continuing its contested operations in the Yellowstone River country. By 1874, its official goal was to locate a site for a military post; unofficially, it was to follow up rumors that gold had been found in the Black Hills. "The time has now come when the entire army could not, much longer, keep the country from being over run by the invincible white man—by the hardy pioneer," announced the *Bismarck Tribune*. In July, Lieutenant Colonel Custer set out from Fort Abraham Lincoln (in present-day North Dakota) ahead of nearly a thousand regulars and Indian scouts, four scientists, three newspaper correspondents, a photographer, and two "practical miners." Custer's initial reports about gold were fairly restrained, but in a widely reprinted interview with a *Tribune* correspondent he declared that "the prospects are even better than represented."[41]

As the *New-York Tribune* observed: "If there is gold in the Black Hills, no army on earth can keep the adventurous men of the West out of them." On May 25, 1875, leading 452 soldiers and scouts, 71 wagons carrying three months' worth of provisions, a herd of 134 cattle, and swarms of scientists, correspondents, and assorted civilians, Lt. Col. Richard I. Dodge marched north from Fort Laramie. Three weeks later, Dodge's report—"gold has been found in paying quantities"—set off an incoming stampede of miners. Facing public demand that the Black Hills be officially opened to the thousands of trespassers already there, the Grant administration in late January 1876 determined to wage war against the Lakotas and Northern Cheyennes. But late winter operations located few Indians and shattered the health of many soldiers. "These winter campaigns in this latitude should be prohibited," complained Col. Joseph J. Reynolds, recently transferred from the warmer climes of Texas.[42]

Girding for additional strikes, Sheridan brushed aside Sherman's suggestion that he enlarge George Crook's Department of the Platte (where he had assumed command in May 1875) to include all of the Sioux country, thus placing the various columns under a single head. Residents of Saint Paul, headquarters of the Department of Dakota, could not afford to lose valuable federal patronage, Sheridan noted. He also reckoned that each column could take care of itself, as "hostile Indians, in any great numbers, cannot keep the field as a body for a week or at most ten days." By late May, three expeditions were poised to strike. Col. John Gibbon, with nearly five hundred soldiers and Crow auxiliaries, would prevent the enemy from moving north of the Yellowstone River. Crook would march east from Fort Fetterman with a thousand soldiers and two hundred allied Crows and Shoshonis. From Fort Abraham Lincoln, Brig. Gen. Alfred H. Terry would push west with nine hundred men, three Gatling guns, and three dozen Arikara scouts. As usual, commanders enjoyed considerable discretion other than the expectation that they bring the enemy to battle.[43]

This time the situation was different, because a coalition of Lakotas and Cheyennes had gathered under the spiritual leadership of Sitting Bull. "He was strong in religion—the Indian religion," recalled one Cheyenne. "We supposed that the combined camps would frighten off the soldiers. We hoped thus to be freed from their annoyances. Then we could separate again into the tribal bands and resume our quiet wandering and hunting." On June 17, Indians bested Crook at the Battle of the Rosebud. "I am a loss what to do," confessed the rattled general as he retreated. The triumph inspired still more Indians to join Sitting Bull, doubling the camp's size to 1,800 fighting men. Eight days later, leading a mounted detachment from Terry's main column, Lieutenant Colonel Custer discovered signs of a village along the Little Bighorn River in southeastern Montana Territory. Keen to deliver the critical blow, Custer divided his forces in hopes of surprising and preventing the flight of the villagers. But these Indians, buoyed by their large numbers and recent success at the Rosebud, were in no mood to run. They annihilated the five companies with Custer to a man; the remainder of the Seventh Cavalry, now led by Maj. Marcos A. Reno and Capt. Frederick W. Benteen, barely managed to hold out until relieved by Terry. Army casualties totaled 263 killed, with another fifty-nine wounded. Indian losses probably numbered less than fifty. Paralyzed by the calamity, Crook, Gibbon, and Terry fell back.[44]

The stunning defeat came amid continuing talk of further army reductions. The Democratic Party had regained a House majority for the first time since 1859 and had been poised to reduce the regular force, producing rhetorical flourishes not seen in decades. Representative Fernando Wood (D-NY) contended that the War Department should be eliminated as a threat to civilian government. "The idea of a large standing Army is un-American and anti-republican," proclaimed the Tennessee Democrat J. D. C. Atkins, a former lieutenant colonel in the Confederate Army. On June 1, the House voted 123–82 to eliminate five infantry and two cavalry regiments. The Republican-dominated Senate rejected the measure, but some cutbacks seemed inevitable.[45]

On July 6, however, newspapers across the country blared news of the Indian triumph at the Little Bighorn. "MASSACRE OF OUR TROOPS," proclaimed the *New York Times.* "HORRIBLE! THE AMERICAN INDIAN EXALTS HIS REPUTATION FOR SATANIC FEROCITY," shrieked the *Chicago Tribune*. Calls for revenge soon drowned out demands for army reductions. Legislation moved slowly as many congressmen were away on summer recess, but $200,000 was appropriated for new military posts in the Yellowstone River country. In August, Congress increased cavalry companies to a hundred men each (thereby reinforcing the army by 2,500 soldiers) until the close of hostilities. Still, a sense of unease permeated the dispirited regulars even as reinforcements began to reach the Departments of the Platte and Dakota, with the newly arrived Colonel Miles characterizing Terry's command as "entirely stampeded." Crook (now with two thousand men) and Terry (1,700) blundered into one another in the Rosebud Valley on August 10, the size of their combined forces overstretching all support trains as chronic diarrhea broke out among enlisted personnel. After the commands separated, Crook's men nearly starved in the infamous "Mud March."[46]

Despite the near disasters, the government's superiority in manpower and logistical resources was decisive. Deftly balanced during normal times, fragile Indian economies were strained to the breaking point by the relentless campaigns. Their coalition dissolved as game and grassland grew scarcer. Establishing an advanced base at Cedar Creek (Montana Territory) on October 21–22, Miles and about five hundred infantrymen engaged in a running battle with Sitting Bull. "They are in great want of food, their stock is nearly worn down and they cannot have a large amount of ammunition," reported the colonel. Five weeks later, Mackenzie and 1,100 cavalrymen destroyed Dull Knife's Cheyenne village on the Powder River (Wyoming Territory). Determined not to be outdone despite the subzero temperatures, Miles kept up the pressure, throwing back Crazy Horse's attack on January 8, 1877, at Wolf Mountains (Montana Territory). In a final battle that May, Miles defeated Lame Deer's Miniconjous at Muddy Creek (Montana Territory). By this time, Sitting Bull had fled to Canada and virtually all of the remaining Lakotas and Cheyennes had turned themselves in. The Great Sioux War was over.[47]

* * * * *

Embroiled in the Sioux campaigns and with the politics of Reconstruction turning increasingly against the Republican Party, Sherman believed that the United States Army's involvement in the South must come to an end. As he put it in 1875: "Outside help sooner or later must cease, for our army is ridiculously small, in case of actual collision. It is only the memory of our war power that operates on the Rebel Element now. They have the votes, the will, and will in the End prevail." The San Francisco *Daily Evening Bulletin* decried "GOVERNMENT BY BAYONET" in the South. Confident that the Grant administration had neither the resources nor the will to use force everywhere, the *Augusta* (Georgia) *Constitutionalist* proclaimed the "bayonet program" to be "a mere scarecrow, a scheme of bombast, full of sound and fury."[48]

By 1876, nearly a third of the three thousand regulars in the South (excluding Texas) were stationed in Louisiana and South Carolina, where Republicans required assistance if they hoped to stay in power. "It is perfectly clear to me," wrote Horace Redfield, an observer for the *Cincinnati Commercial*, "that without the presence of troops the whites would overbear and override the blacks to such an extent that no fair election could be held." Although sensitive of the need to pacify Liberal Republicans by withdrawing from the South, Grant instructed the regulars to protect the voting process. By November, Augur had scattered his men at sixty-two points throughout the Department of the Gulf. That year's hard-fought contest between New York governor Samuel J. Tilden (D-) and Rutherford B. Hayes (R), governor of Ohio, had in the meantime attracted the highest rate of voter participation in the history of American presidential elections. Wounded five times as a volunteer during the Civil War, Hayes's personal bravery—along with the potential betrayal of 400,000 dead Union soldiers if former Confederates gained control of the federal government—helped to explain the enormous Republican appeal in the North. By contrast, the use of regular troops to implement Reconstruction mobilized Southerners. All sides conceded that the Electoral College tabulation would be tight. "A DOUBTFUL ELECTION," explained the *New York Times* the morning after the vote.[49]

Chapter Thirteen

The Army of the Gilded Age

Early returns from the 1876 presidential election put the Democrat Samuel J. Tilden ahead of the Republican Rutherford B. Hayes but a single vote shy of the necessary majority in the Electoral College, with twenty disputed electors from Oregon, Florida, Louisiana, and South Carolina. As results trickled in, commanding general William T. Sherman predicted that a Tilden victory would mean the army must "expect no favors." Three days after ballots had been cast, reports of violence in the South led President Ulysses S. Grant to order the army to intervene. General Philip Sheridan was dispatched to New Orleans to observe the counting process and to use the twenty-six companies at his disposal to prevent violence. Commanders in Florida and Louisiana were instructed "to preserve peace & good order and to see that the proper & legal boards of Canvassers are unmolested in the performance of their duties." Fearing that "these Politicians may again embroil us in Civil War," Sherman reinforced garrisons in and around the District of Columbia.[1]

Regulars saw their role as preventing anarchy while politicians sorted things out. "We must sustain the president who is declared to have been elected," wrote Sherman. He advised Sheridan, whose command was still embroiled in the Great Sioux War, to concentrate as many men as he could at points "convenient for moving." Sherman speculated that, if the Senate chose Hayes and the House backed Tilden, new elections would be necessary. Maj. Gen. Winfield Scott Hancock, who had placed third in that year's Democratic National Convention, echoed his party's line, arguing that the House of Representatives (where Democrats enjoyed a healthy majority) should determine the election; Maj. Gen. John M. Schofield proposed that regulars act in accord with "what the public conscience shall believe just." In the end, both Sherman and Schofield applauded the formation of an Electoral Commission to adjudicate the disputes.[2]

Only in the wee hours of the morning of March 2, 1877, did Congress recognize the Electoral Commission's decision to award all disputed electors to Hayes. Having anticipated that such would be the case, Grant had determined that Brig. Gen. Christopher C. Augur, whose Department of the Gulf remained the scene of many disputes, must now "limit his orders to the mere preservation of peace in case of riot." Republican governors of Louisiana and

South Carolina would have to "work out their own precedence for Executive recognition in the same manner as any Northern states would have to do under the circumstances." A relieved Schofield predicted that the army's "unpleasant" duties in the South would soon come to an end.[3]

Jousting over the presidency and Reconstruction directly impacted army appropriations. For months, a joint commission including Sherman, Don Cameron, newly appointed secretary of war, and Henry B. Banning (D-OH), chair of the House Military Affairs Committee, had attempted to strike a deal, but floor discussion of army matters had been postponed until the fate of the presidency was determined. That afternoon, Senator Thomas F. Bayard (D-DE) immediately castigated the use of the army for "purposes dangerous to the liberties of the country." Denouncing a large standing army as "un-American and antirepublican," Tennessee Democrat congressman J. D. C. Atkins demanded cuts to officers' salaries, a reduction of enlisted personnel to 17,000, and a ban against troops supporting state governments. The Senate refused to go along, and when conference committee attempts to craft a compromise failed, Congress adjourned on March 3 without passing any army appropriations. At the end of the fiscal year (June 30), soldiers would go without pay. "Our enemy is not now the Indians but Congress," complained Sherman.[4]

On May 14, still smarting from the failure of the appropriations bill, Sherman reminded attendees at a New York Chamber of Commerce banquet of the military's multiple roles in American society. As well as providing security against foreign invasion, regulars served as "the great High Sheriffs of the nation, necessary and essential parts of every organized court or government, especially such as ours." Sherman's words were prophetic, for in July strikes and riots paralyzed freight rail traffic east of the Mississippi River, spread to the coal-mining regions of Pennsylvania, and destroyed millions of dollars in property. Police and state militias seemed powerless, so the governors of West Virginia, Maryland, and Pennsylvania called for federal assistance. President Hayes generally complied with these as well as local requests from Indiana, Illinois, and Missouri, reasoning that the army could aid federal marshals in deterring domestic violence and guarding federal property as a *posse comitatus*. Sheridan deployed the equivalent of nearly two full regiments in Chicago. In Hancock's Division of the Atlantic, detachments of Marines joined three thousand regulars in mobilizing to preserve order. Although some militiamen opened fire on the angry crowds, the regulars did not.[5]

The major media outlets regarded the protests as an existential threat. As regulars streamed into Chicago, a grateful *Daily Tribune* declared "The Fight with the Communists is at an End." Many asserted that the inability of state militias to deal with the strikes had demonstrated the need for a larger army. The *New York Times* concluded that only regulars could check "dangerous social elements." The *Philadelphia Inquirer* suggested that 40,000 men—an increase of more than 50 percent from current levels—seemed reasonable. The *Southwestern Christian Advocate* added another 10,000. Meanwhile, several states resolved to transform their feeble militias into better-prepared National Guards.[6]

Amid these debates regarding the use of federal force to quell domestic turbulence, warfare against Indians also continued. In mid-June 1877, angered by a litany of broken promises, unanswered grievances, and fresh demands that they move to a reservation, nontreaty Nez Perce warriors launched a series of raids in the Salmon River region of Idaho Territory. The rout of a mixed force of regulars and volunteers at White Bird Canyon (June 17), followed by an army assault on Looking Glass's camp (July 1), convinced more Nez Perce people to join the struggle, bringing the number of children, women, and men to more than seven hundred. Fending off the soldiers, the Nez Perces headed east through the Bitterroot Mountains toward the plains of Montana, then turned north toward Canada. Leading another column from Fort Keogh, Col. Nelson A. Miles caught them short of the border at the Bear Paw Mountains, where about four hundred Indians surrendered. The others escaped into Canada, having eluded the army for 1,700 miles. In June 1878, Bannocks and Paiutes broke from scattered reservations in Nevada and Oregon, leading army pursuers on a twisting chase that finally culminated three months later with their surrender. The following year, less than three dozen Sheepeater fighters (generally regarded as Bannocks and Shoshonis) eluded the regulars for three months in the foreboding Salmon River Mountains. That year also saw the first of four thousand soldiers take the field in support of the Indian Bureau's attempts to transform the Utes into sedentary farmers, an effort that lasted nearly two years before they were forced from Colorado to new reservations in Utah.[7]

In addition, activities in Brig. Gen. Edward O. C. Ord's Department of Texas continued to roil international relations. Col. Ranald B. Mackenzie's earlier incursion had not ended violence attributed to Indians or Mexican bandits, with one spectacular raid reaching more than one hundred miles from the border to Corpus Christi. Ord demanded authority to send troops into Mexico. "It is hardly fair to expect me to keep even a tolerably safe frontier when the only means of making it safe are not allowed," he contended. Claiming to enjoy Sheridan's backing, Ord instructed subordinates to cross the river if "on a fresh trail." On three occasions in the summer of 1876, regulars entered Mexico, and the following year three more army incursions came in the wake of President Hayes's so-called Ord Order. Such belligerence made Ord a hero in the Lone Star State, with Representative Gustav Schleicher (D) proclaiming him to be among "the most popular and requested men in Texas." In 1878, Texans again cheered when Mackenzie led more than a thousand soldiers into Mexico.[8]

The regulars had needed every friend they could muster as President Hayes called on the new Forty-fifth Congress to convene and pass an army appropriations bill. "The present trouble with the Army is that it is separated from the knowledge and affections of the people who pay the taxes, and is only seen from year to year in the form of heavy appropriations," complained editors of the *Army and Navy Journal.* With Republicans controlling the Senate and Democrats the House, the key to any compromise was the Texas delegation, which opposed the continued garrisons in South Carolina and Louisiana but wanted regulars along their own state's southern and western borderlands. In the end, amid rancorous debate, five Texas Democrats opposed army cutbacks, Schleicher complaining that the Appropriations Committee had not "made the slightest inquiry" into frontier needs. On November 17, three other Democrats joined the Texans in defying their party leadership in a 134–129 vote to keep enlisted personnel at 25,000. "Army people are all much obliged to you especially and the Texas Delegation generally for your successful efforts in our favor," a grateful Ord told Schleicher. Sherman concurred, predicting that, without Texas support, the regulars would be "slaughtered" in the next session.[9]

Sherman's fears seemed validated in early 1878, when House Military Affairs Committee chair Banning rolled out a new army bill. In conjunction with amendments from Representative Abram S. Hewitt (D-NY), Banning's proposal would decrease enlisted personnel to 20,000, consolidate the Quartermaster's and Subsistence Departments, limit promotions to general, and cut officers' pay and construction monies. Any failure to pass an appropriations bill would automatically trigger the abolition of the entire army. Although appreciative that it would rotate staff positions and (as amended) transfer the Indian Bureau to the War Department, Sherman judged the proposition "disorganizing and unjust." He also saw to it that friends of the regulars gained access to unflattering personal information about Banning's chief lieutenant, Representative Edward S. Bragg (D-WI).[10]

As debates continued, Lt. Col. Richard I. Dodge observed that the "people of the country are not hostile to the army, but deceived by the arts & lies of demagogues," who "regard us as a lazy set of loafers." Opponents denounced the army's role in Reconstruction and in quelling the recent strikes. High taxes needed to keep a regular force, reasoned Hewitt, fanned the flames of communism by taking money from workers. Militias must serve as the bulwark of freedom, insisted fellow Democrat William Kimmel (MD). "A standing army should never be a police force in the land," added Missouri's Thomas T. Crittenden (D). In June, a conference committee compromise cut the Gordian knot. At the Senate's behest, enlisted personnel remained at

"The Lightning Speed of Honesty." This wood engraving by Thomas Nast decries the snail-like speed of the 45th Congress in passing military pay bills. Here Uncle Sam, carrying the "Army Navy Payroll," rides the congressional snail. Library of Congress, USZ62-79081.

25,000 and the transfer of the Indian Bureau was rejected; the House secured significant decreases in officers' allowances and restrictions against employing regulars as a *posse comitatus.*[11]

To craft a long-term compromise, a new committee was formed, chaired by Senator Ambrose Burnside (R-RI), a West Point graduate and former general of volunteers. To set the stage for much-needed reform, essays by the retired general and presidential candidate George McClellan and Representative Garfield had appeared in *Harper's New Monthly Magazine* and the *North American Review*. Sherman furnished copies of Lt. Col. Emory Upton's recent *Armies of Asia and Europe*, the product of the author's seventeen-month-long observations abroad. Released in December 1878, the resulting Burnside Report featured 724 sections (including one containing 146 Articles of War) of revised army regulations and weighed in at 519 pages. While maintaining the 25,000-man enlisted force, it proposed trimming the number of generals from eleven to six, infantry regiments from twenty-five to eighteen, cavalry regiments from ten to eight, and officers by three hundred. The report also called for a disabled list for officers, provided for the rotation of staff and line positions, defined the powers of the secretary of war and the commanding general, consolidated the Adjutant General's and Inspector General's Departments, and specified that future ordnance "shall not be fabricated by the government." Pointedly, it did not forbid using regulars as a *posse comitatus.*[12]

Burnside's proposals enjoyed the strong support of Sherman and Schofield, but the *Army and Navy Journal* joined Sheridan in offering only tepid backing. In February 1879, Sherman made matters worse by opting to go on a tour of Civil War battlefields rather than defending the reforms before Congress. Moreover, as he had predicted, "all the staff . . . oppose the bill tooth & nail." Having no desire to leave the nation's capital and return to a line position, one staffer described the Burnside measure as "monstrous." Friends of reform, complained Col. William B. Hazen, were isolated "in the remote and frozen Territories . . . Even if they [line officers] could be heard, the gentlemen of the staff by long acquaintance, contact and friendship can impress their views and wishes both upon Congress and the press with a facility and power which the Army cannot hope to do." Astonished by the criticism, Burnside complained "that some of these [staff] officers have gone beyond the line of duty."[13]

Inserting a clause that forbade stationing troops near polling places, the House agreed to a trimmed-down version of Burnside's proposals as part of the 1879 army appropriations bill. Yet as the historian David J. Fitzpatrick has pointed out, Republican senators—usually sympathetic to the army—now blocked even this measure. Consistent with civil-service reforms of the period, Burnside had sought to constrain the president's power to appoint staff officers, reasoning that the chief executive must not be able to use such spoils "at the solicitation of friends outside of the Army, and friends who know nothing about the subject." Fearing the loss of even more patronage, the "Stalwart" faction of Republicans such as Senator Roscoe Conkling (NY) opposed the reforms, and the New York state senate denounced its restrictions against government weapons production. By a 45–18 margin (with 30 of 34 Republicans joining the majority), the Senate voted down the Burnside proposals. In a party line vote of 34–30, Republicans then rejected a House provision forbidding the use of troops at elections. The third session of the Forty-fifth Congress thus ended on March 3, again without an army appropriations bill.[14]

President Hayes immediately summoned the Forty-sixth Congress into session. Now controlling both houses, Democrats jammed through a bill that barred military forces from voting locations. On April 29, and again on May 12, Hayes vetoed measures containing such restrictions. "The army is now ground between the upper and nether mill-stones of Democratic and Republican struggles for power," complained the *Army and Navy Journal*. In the end, Democrats satisfied themselves with a clause that disallowed spending that might allow regulars "to be used as a police force to keep the peace at the polls at any election held within any State." On June 23, the president signed off, ending the last titanic legislative struggle over the army before the onset of the Spanish–American War.[15]

Paradoxically, the same Forty-fifth Congress that had failed to pass appropriations for the regulars had agreed on a massive expansion of pension benefits for disabled veterans and dependents of those killed or wounded during the Civil War. Congress had offered limited assistance to Union veterans as early as 1861, but complex laws and a notoriously unhelpful bureaucracy had discouraged applications. With tens of thousands of ailing and indigent veterans needing a dose of common decency, the Arrears Act of 1879 allowed former soldiers and dependents who now declared their war-related disabilities to receive a payment equal to all monies they would have received since the war. The lump-sum pensions meant serious money, averaging two and a half times the annual income of a nonfarm employee. Supported by Republicans, Northern Democrats, veterans' groups, and pension attorneys, its passage reflected not only the desire to reward volunteers who had won the war but also the power of patronage and distributive politics. By the late 1880s, these allowances cost nearly twice as much as the remaining War Department budget.[16]

Supplemented by the Dependent Pension Act of 1890, pension-related legislation revealed stark differences in attitudes about regulars and volunteers, a perspective reinforced by contemporary observers. In his 1883 classic titled *Social Problems*, Henry George maintained that "science and invention" could better defend America than the regulars, who posed "a danger to popular liberties." The most notable congressional critic of West Point's domination of the regular army, John A. Logan, published his celebratory *The Volunteer Soldier in America* in 1887. Thomas A. Bland, a former volunteer surgeon and outspoken defender of American Indian rights, dubbed the regulars a "barbarous fungi" whose officers had "become as aristocratic and arrogant as were the slave drivers of the cotton states." Building on the work of Professor William Graham Sumner of Yale, business pacifists such as Andrew Carnegie asserted that "a nation with a large standing army and navy is bound to make wars."[17]

Infuriated by continuing suspicions of his army such as these, Sherman delighted in denouncing Gilded Age politicians. Many of his comrades adopted the same view, reflecting a basic continuity of army thinking since the 1830s. They acknowledged their subordination to these civilians, but they resented it enormously. "I'll leave politics to you civilians," proclaimed Cadet Tasker Bliss. "Members of Congress are most ignorant," asserted Lt. Col. August V. Kautz, "and in their legislation in regards to the army, the lack of knowledge on their part affects us most severely." Col. Emory Upton, later hailed as one of the army's most influential thinkers of the period, dismissed Congress as a body that "make[s] a merit of neglecting the national defense." Of a former volunteer soldier's decision to enter politics, Brig. Gen. Alfred Terry let loose this fusillade: "The politics of this country are a dirty puddle & unless a man can make up his mind to have his name and character dragged through mire & filth he had better let them alone." Rejecting a nomination to the highly politicized Soldiers and Sailors Convention of 1866, Lt. Col. Stewart Van Vliet declared: "An officer should have nothing to do with politics—tis not his province. He belongs to the country, the whole country, & to no party."[18]

At the opposite extreme, a few regulars eagerly entered the political arena. Before his death at the Little Bighorn, Custer had been the darling of many Democrats. Capt. Almon Rockwell helped to prepare for publication James A. Garfield's speeches following his election as the Republican candidate to the presidency in 1880, receiving the plum appointment as Superintendent of Public Buildings for his troubles. That same year, Grant had engaged in an unseemly bid to secure a third term as president, and Maj. Gen. Winfield Scott Hancock accepted the Democratic Party's nomination while still commanding the Division of the Atlantic. Colonels seeking appointments to scarce brigadier generalships (which did not always follow strict seniority) took pains to arrange political support for their candidacies. In 1897, for example, Col. John R. Brooke lined up both senators and the governor of his native Pennsylvania behind his successful bid to secure a star.[19]

Although popular attitudes toward the army remained lukewarm, numerous regulars attempted to capitalize on the public's fascination with the Civil War. In 1884, nearly bankrupted by terrible investments, Grant agreed to write a book for Samuel L. Clemens's newly formed Webster and Company. Grant died just days after completing his memoir, but the nearly half a million dollars in royalties from the sale of 350,000 copies of the two-volume set supported his surviving family in fine style. More acerbic and contentious than his old comrade, Sherman had published the first edition of his own memoir a decade earlier, but this and a second edition (1886) generated more modest sales.[20] A pantheon of others—including Sheridan, Schofield, Meade, Howard, and McClellan—joined in the scramble to influence historical memory (and to make some money) by writing memoirs themselves. Nelson A. Miles put out two full-length autobiographies. John Pope wrote twenty-nine installments of his wartime experiences for the Washington *National Tribune*. Others contributed essays to the multivolume *Battles and Leaders of the Civil War*, as well as widely read periodicals like *Century Illustrated Magazine*, *Harper's Magazine*, and the *North American Review*.

The postwar era also saw the proliferation of published accounts of military life in the American West. The newspapermen De B. Randolph Keim (*Sheridan's Troopers on the Borders*, 1870; reprinted at least five times before the turn of the century) and John F. Finerty (*War-Path and Bivouac*, 1890) penned volumes about their campaign experiences. The former sergeant H. H. McConnell wrote *Five Years a Cavalryman* (1889). Custer and his wife, Libbie, turned this genre into a cottage industry; many of his *Galaxy* magazine essays were collected in *My Life on the Plains* (1874). Using the pseudonym "Nomad," he also contributed fifteen letters to the New York–based *Turf, Field, and Farm*. Libbie later added a trio of her own books: *Boots and Saddles* (1885), *Tenting on the Plains* (1887), and *Following the Guidon* (1890).[21] Other authors among officers' wives included Margaret Irvin Carrington (*Ab-Sa-Ra-Ka, Home of the Crows*, 1868), Lydia Lane (*I Married a Soldier*, 1893), and Mrs. Orsemus Bronson Boyd (*Cavalry Life in Tent and Field*, 1894).

Seizing on the interest in things military, Frederick Whittaker whipped out a sympathetic biography of Custer only months after his death, thereby burnishing the slain officer's growing legend. A dime novelist, Whittaker also penned *The Cadet Button: A Novel of American Army Life* (1878), which one review praised for the "fine and just picture which it presents of the *esprit de corps* of the American regular army; of the strict honor, simple bravery, patience under poverty and exile, and somewhat scornful superiority to sordid conditions which have characterized its officers as a class." Most prolific was the West Point graduate Charles King. More than half of King's sixty-two books and two hundred–plus periodical articles dealt with army life in the borderlands. "King has perhaps done more than any other man in this country to acquaint the public with life in the army through the medium of fiction," observed a writer for *Current Literature*.[22]

In the post–Civil War decades, the rugged masculinity of Frederic Remington's art often focused on regular soldiers. In illustrations for *Collier's*, *Harper's Magazine*, and *Outing: An Illustrated Monthly Magazine of Recreation*, as well as paintings such as *The Advance Guard, or the Military Sacrifice (The Ambush)* (1890), *Colored Troopers to the Rescue* (ca. 1890), *A Cavalryman's Breakfast on the Plains* (1892), and *Through the Smoke Sprang the Daring Soldier* (1897), Remington's heroic images helped to shape popular conceptions of warfare in the West. Charles Schreyvogel's painting *My Bunkie* (1899), which depicted a mounted cavalryman scrambling to lift a comrade to his horse during a clash with unseen Indians, won critical acclaim from New York's National Academy of Design in 1900. Schreyvogel's subsequent paintings, most notably *On the Skirmish Line* (1900), *A Sharp Encounter* (1901), *Breaking Through the Line* (1903), *Custer's Demand* (1903), and *Defending the Stockade* (1905), also portrayed regulars as the leading edge of civilization's triumph over savagery.[23]

Officers' wives joined their husbands in what they believed to be a righteous struggle to establish bastions of culture throughout the American West. As the historian Verity McInnis explains, they "acted as imperial ambassadors" who "held a duty to design, and officiate at, social occasions and . . . ceremonial performances to symbolize and maintain the authority and prestige of empire." As did their husbands, these ladies reaffirmed the rigid class boundaries that distinguished them from enlisted men and laundresses. Officers' wives thus maintained tight control over post society through domestic rituals, the maintenance of traditional dress codes, the subordination of domestic workers, segregated housing, and informal influence with their commissioned husbands. "The ladies do not only manipulate the social affairs of the army," charged one critic, "but they are the power behind the throne which directs the administration of much of the official business." Their attempts to impose a distinctly Victorian culture were reinforced by military authorities, who authorized boardwalks, cupola-topped bandstands, picket fences, village greens, and ornamental gardens in hopes of re-creating islands of middle-class eastern architecture at western garrisons.[24]

As the army attempted to transplant eastern culture to its western posts, its senior leaders attempted to promote serious discussion of military science. In 1878, Generals Sherman and Hancock founded the Military Service Institution of the United States. Its bimonthly *Journal of the Military Service Institution*, joined a year later by *United Service Magazine*, became essential reading for professionally minded officers. Building on that success were

Officer holding a woman's horse. The subjects of this mid-1880s photograph at Camp Verde, Arizona, are not known, but they share a sense of humor, as each is wearing the other's hat. Library of Congress, USZ62-55841.

Officers' quarters, Fort Wingate, New Mexico. Taken about 1873, this photograph by Timothy O'Sullivan shows two sets of officers' quarters at Fort Wingate. Note the picket fence and newly planted trees in front; two junior officers, or a more senior officer (with their families), would have occupied each building. Library of Congress, DIG-ppmsca-15918.

more specialized options: the *Journal of the United States Cavalry Association* (which began publication in 1888), the *Journal of the United States Artillery* (1892), and the *Infantry Journal* (1904). As a former president of what came to be Louisiana State University, Sherman also championed the revival of the Artillery School at Fortress Monroe (1868) and formation of the School of Application for Infantry and Cavalry at Fort Leavenworth (1881), to which one lieutenant from every infantry and cavalry regiment would be assigned every two years. Although Leavenworth was initially derided as "'The Army English High School'" and "Kindergarten," by the late 1880s commandant Col. Alexander McCook and longtime instructor Lt. Arthur Wagner were nurturing a growing cadre of educated officers. In the following decade, commanding general John M. Schofield ordered every garrison to establish an "officers' lyceum" to encourage self-development.[25]

Ironically, the greater emphasis on their own group identity resulting from such efforts further isolated officers from civilian society. In 1885, the Military Service Institution's prize-winning essay, which advocated better relations between regulars and the people, warned that unrestricted immigration would cause "ignorant suffrage" and "a reign of unbridled license and rampant communism." Moreover, the road to military professionalism remained incomplete, with Lt. Col. Edwin V. Sumner, Jr., exemplifying conservative skepticism of the bookish education emphasized at Leavenworth and the divide between Civil War veterans and fresh West Point graduates. The "artificial military intelligence" gained by reading military science tracts, claimed Sumner, meant nothing without combat experience. Further, the abuse of alcohol remained a chronic problem. With one observer calculating that it would take a quarter-century for a second lieutenant to rise to the rank of major, long stretches of garrison duty remained stultifying; as Sumner put it, the "dry rot of frontier posts" often took its toll.[26]

As progressives and conservatives battled over the army's soul, officers from all branches became for the first time eligible for the superintendency of the United States Military Academy, which returned to supplying most new officers. Technical engineering had lost some of its dominance in the curriculum, and as the historian Russell Weigley has noted, "with these changes the Academy lost its eminence among American engineering schools without commensurate gain in the quality of its military instruction." Sensing a growing malaise and seeking a means to allow a trusted subordinate to revise army regulations, Sherman in 1876 had convinced Major General Schofield to "add new luster to the old academy" by becoming superintendent (a position traditionally held by a colonel). As an alumnus and former instructor, Schofield hoped to modernize its curriculum, improve the quality of instruction, and end hazing.[27]

On April 6, 1880, any hope that Schofield might enact his ambitious agenda vanished. That morning, Johnson C. Whittaker, the only African American cadet, was found in his room, bound and bloodied from cuts to his ears. Following a superficial investigation, Schofield—who a year earlier had intervened to keep Whittaker in school despite deficiencies on his midterm exams—concluded that the cadet had staged the incident to generate sympathy. Denying the charge, Whittaker demanded a court of inquiry, which devolved into an embarrassing media circus for the army. Mishandling the crisis, Schofield asserted that blacks were not ready to attend the academy. In December, at the insistence of the outgoing President Hayes, Schofield was reassigned from West Point to a cobbled-together (and short-lived) Division of the Gulf, which included Arkansas, Indian Territory, Louisiana, and Texas.[28]

In addition to stalling efforts to reenergize West Point, the Whittaker debacle revealed the army's inability to escape the racial divisions that plagued the segregated society from which it came. Custer had refused to serve in a black regiment, and his rival Frederick W. Benteen had taken a captain's bars in the Seventh Cavalry rather than becoming a major in the all-black Ninth. The *Army and Navy Journal* carried advertisements promising "liberal inducements" or "a reasonable bonus" for officers who might exchange service from white to black regiments. The first African American graduate of West Point, Lt. Henry Flipper, was dismissed by a court-martial board in 1881. Yet as the historians William A. Dobak and Thomas D. Phillips have shown, the segregated army did not engage in systematic efforts to provide black troops with inferior weapons, horses, equipment, food, or housing. And black soldiers joined African American civilians in considering military service to be a respectable career choice, deserting less frequently and reenlisting more often than their white counterparts.[29]

* * * * *

What editors of the *Army and Navy Journal* called the army's "collateral" duties continued to consume enormous time and resources. Ongoing demands for retrenchment, however, temporarily allowed the War Department to end its oversight of Alaska. In 1872, the discovery of gold in British Columbia had convinced authorities to reactivate Fort Wrangell, but efforts by the tiny garrisons there and at Sitka to police the fur trade and prevent liquor smuggling had been problematic. Drunkenness and sexually transmitted diseases ravaged the isolated commands, and the courts had challenged the army's authority to extend military rule to the Great Land. The Treasury Department seemed happy to take charge, and a February 1877 fire that destroyed much of officers' row at Sitka gave the War Department the excuse to withdraw in favor of patrols by naval or revenue cutters. The move, observed the *New-York Tribune*, was "not only a measure of wise economy, but one of great humanity to the soldiers." Protests from merchants at Wrangell went unheeded.[30]

Undeterred by these experiences, and upon taking command of the Department of the Columbia in 1881, Brig. Gen. Nelson A. Miles (who had earlier lobbied for permission to cross the border and fight Sitting Bull) looked north to continue U.S. expansion. "I think it too soon to occupy the Boundary line now, [but] when we are ready for that the North Pole may be the boundary," he once observed. Exploiting his prerogatives as department commander, Miles sponsored exploring teams in 1883, 1884, and 1885 that logged more than four thousand miles in the rugged Alaska interior. Prompted by New England mining interests who wanted an army presence, as well as competition with the navy over the fruits of exploration, the War Department lobbied Congress in 1890 for a $100,000 appropriation for further surveys, but was denied.[31]

Elsewhere, regular soldiers continued their scientific activities. In addition to two well-received books about George Crook's campaigns in the Southwest, the West Point graduate John G. Bourke compiled several ethnological studies of Native Americans. Surgeon Washington Matthews wrote widely on Indian skulls, the Navajos, and the Hidatsas, and Capt. William Philo Clark's posthumous *The Indian Sign Language* (1885) became a classic. Assistant Surgeon Elliott Coues penned the seminal *Key to North American Birds* (1872) and coauthored several analyses of mammals. In addition to assisting U.S. Geological and Geographical Surveys, the War Department organized expeditions by the civilian Clarence King (the U.S. Geological Expedition of the Fortieth Parallel) and Lt. George M. Wheeler (the U.S. Geographical Surveys West of the One Hundredth Meridian). Examining hundreds of terminal springs, mining districts, mountain ranges, passes, and peaks, Wheeler delivered 61,659 specimens of birds, reptiles, fishes, and insects to the Smithsonian Institution. Per an 1867 order, several surgeons engaged in the barbaric task of decapitating the bodies of dead Indians to ship crania to Washington. The West Point–trained Capt. George W. Goethals (who as a civilian would later oversee completion of the Panama Canal) supervised final stages of work on the long-delayed Muscle Shoals Canal, streamlined the management of the Florence District of the Tennessee River, and integrated new electric power plants into seacoast defenses.[32]

The army also preserved the national parks. Since its establishment in 1872, Yellowstone National Park had been endangered by hunters, tourists, and vandals, for the Interior Department lacked the resources to patrol its vast wilderness. Prompted by a request from the Wyoming territorial governor to make "an intelligent appeal to the nation's legislators," Sheridan in

1882 organized a large hunting expedition into Yellowstone, where he was stunned to learn that a company had secured rights to 4,400 acres of choice parklands for an annual lease of two dollars per acre. Bemoaning the slaughter of big game and the looming exploitation by private interests, Sheridan pledged to use regular soldiers to protect an expanded park. Needing friends to save Yellowstone, he appealed "to all sportsmen of this country, and to the different sportsmen's clubs, to assist in getting Congress to make the extension I describe, thus securing a refuge for our wild game." George Bird Grinnell, editor of *Forest and Stream*, promptly labelled the scheme to grant monopoly rights in Yellowstone a "bare-faced plot to rob the people." Sheridan also wooed President Chester A. Arthur (who took office in September 1881 following Garfield's death), George G. Vest (D-MO), who was chair of the Senate Committee on Territories, and other dignitaries during another monthlong excursion into Yellowstone. In 1886, amid continuing scandals associated with the Interior Department's administration of the park, regulars assumed control.[33]

In 1893, impressed by the army's work, the dendrologist Charles S. Sargent proposed that the Interior Department cede responsibilities for the national forests to the regulars and that the West Point curriculum incorporate forestry instruction. "A handful of soldiers is worth a hundred civilians for such work, for the presence of the uniform inspires a respect which is felt far beyond the limits of the region actually patrolled," he reasoned. The famed conservationist John Muir had no doubts about the army, under whose care the national parks were "flourishing. . . . In pleasing contrast to the noisy, ever changing management, or mismanagement, of blundering, plundering, money-making vote-sellers who receive their places from boss politicians as purchased goods, the soldiers do their duty so quietly that the traveler is scarce aware of their presence." Theodore Roosevelt also saw promise in the idea, but most agreed with Frederick Law Olmstead, who observed that "a military man ought not to be a Jack-of-all-trades." Sargent's proposal thus went nowhere.[34]

Regulars also enforced the law, a key element in what the historian Richard Maxwell Brown calls "the Western Civil War of Incorporation." Hampered by shortages of local courts and unprepared militias, western governors often sought loopholes in the 1878 *posse comitatus* restrictions through which they could call in regulars, who almost invariably sided with those (usually elites) claiming to seek order. Col. Nathan A. M. Dudley and thirty-five enlisted men, accompanied by a Gatling gun and a mountain howitzer, intervened in New Mexico Territory's Lincoln County War. In 1885, regulars deployed to protect Chinese laborers against white rioters in Seattle and Rock Springs, Wyoming; seven years later, soldiers from Fort McKinney earned the enmity of many residents by rescuing a posse of thugs hired by the Wyoming Stock

Fort Yellowstone Cavalry. In 1886, the army began stationing troops in Yellowstone National Park and would continue to administer the park for thirty-two years. Library of Congress, USZ62-52425.

Growers' Association from an angry mob. The army also attempted to keep intruders out of Indian Territory. When President Grover Cleveland (first elected in 1884 and again in 1892) opened additional sections of Indian Territory in 1889 to non-Indians, for example, more than two regiments were deployed in a largely futile attempt to forestall complete pandemonium.[35]

Army engineers remained a major force for national development. From 1867 to 1879, the Board of Engineers for Fortifications expanded its role to study an eclectic array of issues ranging from the hydrology of San Francisco Bay to a pedestal for "the proposed colossal Statue of Liberty." A new board, the Board of Engineers for Fortifications and River and Harbor Improvements, assumed a similarly broad agenda. In addition to underwater mines and coastal fortifications, in 1881 and 1882, for example, the board's letters dealt with a railroad right of way through Richmond County, New York, harbor improvements in eight states, and dikes at Coney Island.[36]

As the historian Albert E. Cowdrey has put it, the Corps of Engineers "touched every body of navigable water in the nation." In 1866, federal outlays for rivers and lakes had been roughly $3.5 million (more than $49 million at time of publication) for 49 projects and 26 surveys; by 1882, spending on 371 projects and 135 surveys had ballooned to nearly $19 million. In 1873, army engineers finally broke through the raft that had blocked navigation on the Red River; after numerous false starts, Congress in 1877 approved a Corps of Engineers plan for moveable dams to accommodate shipping on the Ohio River. Two years later, the Mississippi River Commission (whose seven members included three officers from the Corps of Engineers and one from the Coast and Geodetic Survey) began a comprehensive (and ultimately unsuccessful) attempt to build levees to control flooding and aid navigation. Tragically, failed attempts to improve the Kentucky River led one engineer to take his own life in 1883.[37]

The Corps of Engineers also remained active in the District of Columbia. In 1878, scandals, mounting debts, and Reconstruction politics had led Congress to create a three-man Board of Commissioners to administer the city. The House would select one member, the Senate another, and the president a final commissioner from the army engineers. The latter designee, explained Representative Joseph C. S. Blackburn (D-KY), would serve as "an umpire." Only the Corps of Engineers, he reasoned, could provide the necessary expertise without becoming "burdened with politics." From attempting to rid the president's house of rats to completing the long-delayed Washington Monument (1884), military engineers had a hand in virtually all segments of life in the nation's capital. Through the Washington Engineer District, Lt. Col. Peter C. Hains oversaw reclamation of the Potomac Flats (thought to be the area's chief source of malaria) and recovered 621 acres now boasting the Lincoln and Jefferson Memorials. After considerable trial and error, they also improved sewerage and introduced asphalt in order to smooth city streets.[38]

Clumsy attempts to meet the District's continuing demands for water, however, cost the engineers much of their prestige. Maj. Garret Lydecker, appointed district engineer commissioner in 1882, badly underestimated the time and cost of building a tunnel to solve the problem. Spearheading the opposition was Crosby Noyes, editor of the Washington *Evening Star*, who dubbed Lydecker a "miserable humbug" and demanded an investigation of a suspected "Tunnel Ring." Washingtonians were incredulous when Lydecker received only a slap on the wrist. The project lurched to completion in 1902, seventeen years late and millions of dollars over budget. As the historian Alan Lessoff has correctly pointed out, the problem wasn't one of corruption or competence—the tunnel seems to have been the best technical solution available—but rather the haughtiness and lack of accountability of uniformed officers. Lydecker's successor, Col. William Ludlow, "runs the machine like a barrack and sneers at the taxpayers like common cattle," scoffed one editor. Increasing criticism from Congress, municipal engineers, public health specialists, and consultants further eroded the reputation of the Corps of Engineers.[39]

Army engineers also resumed their efforts to improve coastal defenses, as the Civil War had demonstrated that modern artillery had rendered the antebellum masonry fortifications largely obsolete. Congress initially frowned upon implementing a new system, but in 1881 it began approving substantial increases for improving ordnance. Pleas from Presidents Cleveland and Arthur—reinforced by essays in the *North American Review* and *Harper's New Monthly Magazine*—convinced Congress to authorize a special fortifications board in 1885. The resulting Endicott Board (named for its head, Secretary of War William C. Endicott) represented a new approach to the politics of coastal defenses by including two naval officers, two ordnance officers, and three civilians in addition to two army engineers. Its 393-page report called for modernized defenses at twenty-seven cities, featuring a sophisticated system of artillery, armor-plated fortifications, mines, searchlights, torpedo boats, and floating batteries estimated to cost more than $126 million (slightly more than $3.1 billion at time of publication). An initial appropriation of $21.5 million would kick-start the effort, of which $8 million was intended "to induce responsible steel manufacturers to erect and complete the plants to produce the steel for the guns needed for national defense."[40]

Partisanship and cost concerns immediately engulfed the Endicott Report. As House Appropriations Committee chair William Forney (D-NY) put it, because the nation was "at peace with all the world . . . it is not necessary for us to enter at this time upon the immense work which the Board recommend." The Democratic House and Republican Senate could not agree on an amount, so Congress failed to appropriate any money for such projects in 1886 and 1887. The impasse sparked another round of anguished essays from soldiers and sailors, a flood of state petitions, a resolution by the New York City Chamber of Commerce, and formation of the Coast Defense Association by several Southern cities. Funding returned in 1888, with $3.47 million for fortifications and another $6.5 million for private ordnance contracts. Although never meeting levels sought by coastal defense hawks, appropriations over the next decade spawned an American industrial complex capable of producing heavy ordnance.[41]

Since the late 1870s, the army's shooting wars had been confined to the Apaches. Frustrated by rivalries between civilian agents and regular soldiers, demands that they locate themselves at ever-changing reservations, and threats to their traditional raiding culture, Victorio (Bi-du-ya) and his Chihenne followers went to war against the United States in August 1879.

From southwestern New Mexico into far western Texas and Chihuahua, Victorio eluded the Ninth and Tenth Cavalry Regiments before being killed by Chihuahuan state troops at Tres Castillos, Mexico. Raiding nevertheless continued, and on August 30, 1881, Apache scouts attached to Col. Eugene A. Carr's command mutinied at Cibecue Creek, Arizona, killing or wounding ten troopers. Sensationalized accounts of the defeat—which mistakenly reported that Carr's entire force of 117 officers and men had been massacred—attracted national attention. "I want this annual Apache stampede to end right now," demanded Sherman, "and to effect that result will send every available man in the Army if necessary."[42]

With war threatening the booming Arizona economy (between 1880 and 1882, the territorial population doubled to 80,000), pressure on the regulars multiplied. Crook was transferred back to head the Department of Arizona, where his chief nemesis was Geronimo, war leader of elements of the Chiricahuas. Armed with Mexico's explicit permission to cross the border, Crook in May 1883 led 45 regular cavalrymen, 193 (mostly Apache) scouts, and 350 pack mules into Geronimo's Sierra Madre base. Stunned by the appearance of Crook's command, Geronimo agreed to return to the San Carlos Reservation. In mid-May 1885, forty-two men and ninety-two women and children again fled. Two army columns—each featuring a small detachment of regulars buttressed by much larger numbers of Indian auxiliaries—moved back into Chihuahua but failed to convince the escapees to give themselves up. Phil Sheridan, who had in February 1884 become commanding general of the army following Sherman's retirement, grew disenchanted with Crook's methods as pressure from Washington escalated. "I go to bed tonight very much dejected," wrote President Cleveland on December 22, 1885, "and wondering if something cannot be done to better protect our citizens on the frontier and put a stop to these dreadful murders."[43]

In March 1886, Crook again ventured into Mexico, but when Geronimo and a few followers failed to carry through with their agreement to surrender, the general requested a transfer, which was immediately granted. Replacing Crook was Brigadier General Miles, bearing orders to make "active and prominent use of the Regular troops of your command." Eager to please his superiors, Miles outfitted an elite force of fifty-five soldiers and twenty Apache scouts that marched deep into Mexico. Although logging more than two thousand miles, they managed only a single fleeting glimpse of Geronimo's party. Removal of the remaining Chiricahuas and Warm Springs Apaches from their Arizona reservations to Florida proved more effective in leading to a deal, and on September 4 Geronimo surrendered for the last time.[44]

With Sheridan's sudden death on August 5, 1888, Maj. Gen. John M. Schofield was named the army's commanding general. More cerebral than

"Peace—Insecure and Secure." Funding and systematizing coastal defenses remained a controversial political issue for much of the nineteenth century. Following the Civil War, Thomas Nast attempted to call attention to the matter, and *Harper's Weekly* published these sketches in its February 13, 1875 edition. Library of Congress, USZ62-129686. Library of Congress, USZ62-129685.

PEACE SECURE—SAFE AND PROTECTED.—[See Page 138.]

his fiery predecessor, Schofield took a pragmatic approach to the thorny dilemmas relating to the army's role in politics and the powers of his office. In an 1892 address to West Point graduates, Schofield urged his junior officers to "abstain from active participation in party politics," but he also insisted that they "keep in touch with the people of the country, and [be] thoroughly familiar with all the great political questions that concern your fellow citizens. The American soldier should never cease to be in heart and soul in fully sympathy with the citizens of the country. He is no less a citizen because he has become a soldier." Whereas Secretaries of War Robert Todd Lincoln (1881–1885) and William C. Endicott (1885–1889) had slapped down Sheridan's attempts to rein in the independent bureau chiefs, Schofield concluded that the commanding general could "be at most only a 'chief of staff'" who served at the president's pleasure. Only by cultivating a working relationship with the war secretary could the commanding general exert genuine influence. In spring 1889, Schofield thus invited his new boss, Vermont Republican Redfield Proctor (appointed by President Benjamin Harrison in 1889), to his private club on Pelee Island, Lake Erie. Several days of fishing, cigar-smoking, card-playing, and free-flowing alcohol cemented their personal and professional rapport. Parlaying the relationship to his advantage, Schofield secured Proctor's promise to consult with him before issuing any order "affecting the discipline and military control of the Army."[45]

Until Proctor's resignation in November 1891 to become a United States senator, the partnership brought a zeal for reform to the War Department not seen since the 1850s. Together they continued to reduce the number of scattered garrisons in favor of larger posts situated on railroads, causing considerable consternation among local civilians at decommissioned sites but improving training and morale. They also promoted a program to set aside one company in most regiments for Indian enlisted personnel. By providing "employment, in useful and legitimate channels, to a considerable number of Indians of the warlike tribes," the plan won President Harrison's endorsement and was consistent with efforts to assimilate American Indians into white society.[46]

Schofield and Proctor also made a concerted effort to improve the quality of life for enlisted men. Since 1867, the toxic combination of fatigue details, harsh discipline, capricious justice, unappealing rations, abuse of alcohol, soldiers' "alliance with a loose population," low pay, and the difficulty of tracking down AWOLs had resulted in *annual* desertion rates of nearly 15 percent. Whereas new enlistees were largely recruited from large cities and were disproportionately foreign-born, genteel observers insisted that "American born and country bred" men became the best soldiers. Criticizing the "foreign paupers, former criminals, adventurers, and loafers in the large cities" among the regulars, the New York *Sun* reminded readers: "The regular army in all times, ancient and modern, has been the instrument by which republics have been overthrown." In 1887, the author of the prize-winning essay for the *Journal of the Military Service Institution* decried the tradition of locating recruiting offices "in those parts of the great cities where not only the floating population is the greatest, but where the lower haunts of dissipation abound." The following year, Inspector General Roger Jones (son of the former Adjutant General by the same name) declared the number of foreign-born enlisted men (which had in reality fallen from a high of two-thirds during the 1850s to about one-third) to be a "mortifying spectacle."[47]

Tougher recruiting standards (in 1897, for example, the army rejected 83 percent of applicants), increased vegetable rations, speedier summary courts for minor offenses, post canteens (replacements for military sutlers), more comfortable uniforms, and a program allowing enlisted men to purchase their early release from military service reduced annual desertion rates by more than two-thirds, to about 5 percent. Echoing the public's increasing distaste for unrestricted immigration, an 1894 law required that recruits be able to read, write, and speak English and be either citizens or have declared their intent to become so. By 1897, foreign-born recruits and reenlistees made up less than a quarter of all enlisted personnel, a rate undoubtedly skewed by the ongoing economic depression, which made native-born males more likely to enlist.[48]

Tragically, the reforms did not extend to Indian affairs, especially the 20,000 people living on the Pine Ridge, Rosebud, Lower Brule, Crow Creek, Cheyenne River, and Standing Rock Reservations of the northern Plains. Buffeted by drought, loss of their lands (collectively, the reservations represented less than a quarter of the territory promised in the 1851 Treaty of Fort Laramie), inadequate government annuities, weak agents, and government dissembling, Lakotas and Northern Cheyennes began to find hope in the *wanagi wacipi* (Ghost Dance), a spiritual quest for an Indian millennium in which they might rid themselves of white domination. As the Ghost Dance ceremonies spread, fearful non-Indians cried out for more regulars, and the assemblage of bluecoats eventually totaled more than five thousand officers and men, commanded by Major General Miles. On three occasions, Miles warned subordinates against intermingling small detachments of their troops with Indians as they broke up the Ghost Dancers. Sitting Bull, the venerable Hunkpapa leader who had come to symbolize the quest to return to the old ways, was killed on December 15, 1890, by Indian police during a bungled arrest attempt at Standing Rock. In the following panic, Col. James W. "Tony" Forsyth's Seventh Cavalry blocked the flight of Big Foot's 370 Miniconjous at Wounded Knee Creek, South Dakota, and demanded that they turn over their weapons.[49]

On December 29, things went horribly wrong. As two companies of

Seventh Cavalrymen struggled to disarm warriors, a shot rang out, followed by the Indians' frantic firing into the regulars. The soldiers' initial defensive response then turned into an indiscriminate slaughter. Army casualties numbered sixty-six, with another scout, an interpreter, and a Catholic priest also falling. Lakota dead numbered at least two hundred, many of whom were women or children. Fighting at White Clay Creek the following day led to eight additional soldier casualties, but the overwhelming army presence rendered further resistance futile. Miles attempted to pin the disaster on Forsyth, describing the latter's troop dispositions as "incomprehensible and inexcusable." Other Seventh Cavalry officers came to Forsyth's defense in the resulting court of inquiry; to avoid additional scrutiny of the army or the administration, Schofield and Secretary Proctor restored Forsyth to command and terminated the investigations. "The interests of the military service do not . . . demand any further proceedings," concluded Schofield.[50]

American society soon turned to matters other than the slaughter at Wounded Knee, and the Schofield/Proctor reforms seem to have had no discernable impact on civilian perceptions of the regulars. Furthermore, by the 1890s the army went beyond merely enforcing the law, in the process losing any pretense of neutrality among working-class circles. Angry about the army's role in ending the Coeur d'Alene mining strike in 1892, one union journal complained that "the capitalist and the scab are on top, and the armies of the Union, with shotted guns, stand guard to see that they remain on top." Fearing the rise of the Populist Party and the impact of the Panic of 1893, elites (and most army officers) frequently lumped protesters, strikers, unemployed workers, union members, immigrants, socialists, and anarchists into a single "other." By order of President Cleveland, soldiers in spring 1894 arrested hundreds of protesters and deployed to protect the Northern Pacific Railroad. That June, soldiers began evicting striking coal miners and their families from Indian Territory, and troops were put on alert in response to the supposed threat of Jacob Coxey's "army" of unemployed protesters to the nation's capital. But commanding general Schofield rejected calls to prevent Coxeyites from using the rails, insisting that such persons "have the same right as other citizens to go West or come East."[51]

More widespread was that year's Pullman railroad strike, which impacted twenty-seven states. Particularly in the West, militia and National Guard units either sympathized with the strikers or lacked the power to reopen the railroads. Under the pretext of protecting the mails and interstate commerce, Cleveland summoned the regulars. The biggest confrontation came in Chicago, where department commander Miles concluded that foreign-born strikers threatened the very soul of America. "Shall I give the order for troops to fire on mob obstructing trains?" he asked on July 5. As rioting and destruction spread, one reporter proclaimed that the protesters "seemed to take it as a personal insult that the soldiers were there." Two days later, Illinois National Guardsmen fired into a crowd, killing or wounding twenty persons. Although 3,500 police, five thousand federal marshals and deputies, four thousand Illinois guardsmen, and nearly two thousand federal troops assembled in Chicago, Miles warned that "rioters or anarchists have 6000 Winchester rifles and bushels of dynamite bombs."[52]

On July 18, federal troops began withdrawing, and city police and Illinois National Guardsmen eventually dispersed the mobs. But in its determination to guard the private property of the railroads, the army had gone beyond simply protecting the mails and federal buildings—a reality not lost to Americans resentful of growing corporate power. On three occasions—only once under orders—regular soldiers opened fire on civilians. Top army brass had long solicited (and accepted) railroad passes and complimentary berths on luxurious company railcars, a cozy practice that junior officers, most of whom came from middle or upper-class backgrounds, undoubtedly internalized. Although Congress had in 1878 and again in 1892 attempted to make it easier for enlisted personnel to secure commissions, in 1895 only 109 men (out of more than two thousand officers) from the ranks had been appointed. In part, the infrequency of such commissions stemmed from demographics: because the huge number of relatively young officers from the immediate post–Civil War period had not reached mandatory retirement age, there were few available vacancies. Even then, most officers had little desire to democratize their ranks; as the editor of the *Army and Navy Journal* put it: "There are social objections . . . to the appointment of non-commissioned officers which cannot be overcome until the whole character of our service is changed, and appointees from the ranks must necessarily contend against a powerful prejudice."[53]

Essays published by officers denouncing those engaging in domestic disturbances highlighted the growing divide between the military and working-class Americans. The army was "now a gendarmerie—a national police," declared Lt. William Wallace. "There is a large class—the lowest class of laborers and foreigners principally—who are tinctured with anarchy, and secretly and openly advocate any measures that are riotous and incendiary." Miles was even more direct: "Men must take sides either for anarchy, secret enclaves, unwritten law, mob violence, and universal chaos under the red or white flag of socialism on the one hand . . . or on the side of established government, the supremacy of the law, the maintenance of good order, universal liberty, all under the shadow and folds of 'Old Glory,' on the other."[54]

Even as regulars aligned themselves more openly with interests of the elites, they found little new support in Congress. For four straight years (1891–1894), Harrison and Cleveland used their annual messages to endorse Schofield's recommendation that the army adopt a three-battalion system for infantry regiments, a logical organizational improvement that would have increased enlisted personnel by about 3,000. In 1894, soldiers published supporting essays in the *North American Review* and *United Service*. Press reaction, however, was lukewarm; the Republican *New-York Tribune* insisted that the army had "become an indispensable instrument for the suppression of mobs," while the Democratic New York *World* denounced Schofield's call for more regulars as "the professional soldier's hobby." The *Washington Times* condemned all talk about giving anyone the authority to levee more troops as "disturbing." Although Senator Joseph R. Hawley (R-CT) stressed that the legislation had been "very laboriously and carefully considered," Congress took no action, and Presidents Cleveland and William McKinley never again mentioned army increases in their annual messages prior to the Spanish–American War.[55]

Epilogue: Old Army, New Empire

In March 1899, an essayist for *Forum* magazine titled his piece "Is Our Army Degenerate?" The author, Alexander S. Bacon, was a United States Military Academy graduate who had resigned from regular service in 1878 and become a well-known New York lawyer. Writing for a respected journal, Bacon acknowledged that the army's performance in the recent war against Spain had been significantly less impressive than that of the navy. After thirteen pages of agonized analysis, Bacon concluded that the "army as a whole is not degenerate," but he maintained that the failure to promote "scientific" men—that is, West Point graduates—to its highest commands represented a signal failure of national policy. Much as had been the case before the Civil War, at the beginning of the Spanish–American War only one of the regular army's nine major generals and brigadier generals was a West Pointer, and Bacon contended that President William McKinley's wartime appointments merely exacerbated the problem. "Why does the Government expend so much money on it [West Point] each year, if its graduates are not utilized, if one may become a great soldier by merely possessing the friendship of a Senator?" wondered Bacon.[1]

In a broader sense, Bacon's essay—and his use of the word "degenerate" as a possible descriptor of the army's performance—reflected a keen awareness of the public's continuing ambivalence about the regulars. Congress had come to acknowledge that a standing army, once seen as a threat to republican government, was needed to maintain the new American empire—which had grown to encompass Puerto Rico, Cuba, Alaska, Hawaii, Guam, American Samoa, and the Philippines—so long as that army remained small. Similarly, West Point, although suspected as being overly aristocratic and elitist, had since the 1830s earned a reputation for furnishing officers who could instill discipline and expertise to an institution that could be depended on to act in accord with the United States Constitution and the wishes of the duly elected civilian authority. Even so, the notion that citizen-soldiers (and citizen-generals) could meet the nation's military needs still held considerable appeal, as evidenced by the wartime appointments so criticized by Bacon and the transformation of the old militia system into the National Guard.[2]

* * * * *

In 1895, the Commanding General of the United States Army, Lt. Gen. John M. Schofield, reached the mandatory retirement age of sixty-four. As had become customary, President Grover Cleveland tabbed the army's senior officer, Maj. Gen. Nelson A. Miles, as the new commanding general. Lacking a formal military education, Miles personified the patriotic citizen-soldier, having borrowed money to raise a company of volunteers from Boston soon after the outbreak of the Civil War. In the Army of the Potomac, he was wounded three times and rose to the rank of brevet major general of volunteers. Appointed a colonel in the postbellum army, he proved a tenacious campaigner against Indians, winning laurels for his leadership in the Red River War and the Great Sioux War. Chief Joseph of the Nez Perces and Geronimo of the Apaches had surrendered to troops under his command. It was a matter of faith that political connections assisted in the quest for promotion, but Miles ranked first among equals when it came to self-aggrandizement. Believing that the lack of influential friends had cost him a more advanced volunteer commission in 1861, he subsequently mounted a dizzying array of campaigns on his own behalf as he rose to become the army's ranking officer.[3]

As commanding general, Miles championed more vigorous physical training programs, reorganizing infantry regiments into three battalions, equipping more troops with bicycles to improve mobility, and making it easier for enlisted men to secure commissions. He also published an autobiography, secured "slight changes" in his official uniform (featuring more gold embroidery and a Russian leather belt piped with gold bullion), and took an extended tour of Europe (followed by another book about his experiences). Following the discovery of gold in the Klondike in 1897–1898, Miles oversaw the return of the army to Alaska. Attempting to bring order to the chaos and to rescue thousands of miners rumored to be starving, regulars established posts at St. Michael, Skagway, and Dyea and organized an exotic relief expedition that featured 538 reindeer, 418 sleds, and 113 herders imported from Norway and Sweden. By 1900, the army had added a dozen new garrisons and created a separate Department of Alaska.[4]

Miles and the old army faced bigger challenges in dealing with Spanish-held Cuba, where open insurrection had begun in 1895. Although the recently retired General Schofield argued that it was the nation's "duty" to halt human rights violations there, most officers probably shared the views of Capt. Thomas Cruse, who recalled that, even though he and fellow officers at Key West sympathized with the Cuban rebels, actual "intervention or involvement of any kind was the furthest thing from our minds." Similarly, Brig. Gen. John R. Brooke (then commanding the Department of Missouri) hoped "that our people in Washington will go slow as regards Cuba." The Military Information Division (formally organized in 1889) had drawn up maps and estimates of Spanish military strength in the Caribbean as part of its normal duties, but army planning for a war against Spain paled in comparison to that of the Naval War College, which had by mid-1897 prepared at least five distinct reports. Details varied considerably, but the navy envisioned blockades of Puerto Rico, Cuba, and Manila, the capture of Havana and Puerto Rico, and naval raids into Spanish waters.[5]

On February 15, 1898, the explosion of the USS *Maine* in Havana Harbor killed 266 American sailors. Beyond the desire for revenge for this tragedy, economic interests, Protestant humanitarian sentiment, and the belief that a conflict would provide a much-needed dose of masculinity to what many perceived as a faltering American culture fanned increasingly bellicose talk. To improve coastal defenses, Congress authorized two new artillery regiments on March 8. A day later, President McKinley secured $50 million "for the national defense." Whereas the War Department spent the bulk of its money to prepare against a possible Spanish invasion, the navy used it to improve readiness for quick offensive action. On March 17, Senator Joseph R. Hawley (R-CT) and Representative John A. T. Hull (R-IA) submitted to their respective chambers a bill to expand the regular army "in time of war" from 27,000 to 104,000 men. By creating a third battalion for each infantry regiment and increasing the number of enlisted men per company, this force was designed to meet all needs in case of a war against Spain. Sponsored by longtime chairs of the Military Affairs Committees of both chambers, the bill enjoyed the administration's support, and the *Army and Navy Journal* predicted that it would "probably pass both Houses at an early date."[6]

But Hull's bill went nowhere, doomed in two days of contentious House debate (April 6–7) by National Guard lobbying, acclaim for the abilities of America's citizen-soldiers, and criticism of regulars. "In all of our wars, we have depended upon the citizen-soldiery of the country to defend the flag," proclaimed Benjamin F. Marsh (R-IL), inspiring applause from the gallery. "And, Mr. Speaker, the country has never depended upon them in vain." If the nation must enter into war, continued Marsh—again to the cheers of listeners—"we want it to be a popular war; and you can never popularize a war in this country by means of the Regular Army." Voicing a common sentiment, Edward E. Robbins (R-PA) asserted "that under this law there will not be a single member of the National Guard of a citizen in civil life in their States who could get a commission in the regular service." Avowed David G. Colson (R-KY): "The people of this country are opposed to a large standing army. They know that standing armies may become corrupt, may become partisans of would-be despots." By a resounding 155–61 margin, a stripped-down version of the bill was sent back to committee, where it died a quiet death.[7]

On April 19, Congress authorized intervention in Cuba, and three days later it approved a measure to mobilize troops that enjoyed the blessing of state National Guards. To supplement the regulars, Congress created the Volunteer Army, which whenever possible would be drawn from existing militia units. Governors would appoint company- and field-grade officers to their states' forces, and at-large United States Volunteers were limited to three thousand men. The next day, McKinley startled military officials by asking for 125,000 volunteers (two and a half times more than they expected), thus ensuring that there would be room for all National Guardsmen who wished to join. On March 25, 1898, Congress declared war on Spain; the following day brought legislation authorizing the wartime expansion of regular forces to more than 61,000. On May 11, Congress approved another 3,500 men for a volunteer engineer brigade, plus an additional 10,000 troops "possessing immunity from diseases incident to tropical climates." Two weeks later, McKinley's call for 75,000 additional volunteers again caught the army flat-footed.[8]

By the end of June, 160,524 officers and men had been mustered into the Volunteer Army; regulars numbered 51,711. Unfortunately, the preparedness of militia and National Guard units—more than a third of whose members either refused to serve or failed their physical examinations—fell woefully short of prewar expectations. Feeding, housing, equipping, and training such numbers would have strained even the most efficient bureaucracy, and the War Department's admission that "the government machinery was altogether inadequate to immediately meet the emergency" was a monumental understatement. The recently created Chickamauga National Military Park (temporarily renamed Camp George H. Thomas) and Camp Alger (outside Washington, D.C.) served as temporary assembly points before embarkation for overseas service, but the abominable conditions led to sensational reports of unpreparedness, mismanagement, and incompetence. From Tampa, Theodore Roosevelt, newly commissioned as a lieutenant colonel in the First U.S. Volunteer Cavalry, condemned "the confusion and lack of system and general mismanagement of affairs." Added one journalist: "It is the most awful picnic that ever happened." Conditions at Chickamauga, wrote another officer, were "enough to make a martyr's flesh to creep and writhe in anguish. There is a sanitary condition existing which would cause a microbe to rub its hands in anticipation of a feast of Moloch."[9]

McKinley's changing war goals and predilection for announcing policy before consulting his advisers further complicated the work of military and civilian bureaucrats. Hoping until the very end for a diplomatic resolution of the Cuban crisis, the president seems to have had as much difficulty coming to grips with the possibility of a shooting war as did senior army officers. Once conflict seemed inevitable, however, he understood that the American people expected swift action; like Polk half a century earlier, McKinley showed no hesitation in using military might to secure his imperial goals. He also concluded that neither Secretary of War Russell A. Alger (described by one official as "a small man in a big place") nor General Miles could immediately resolve the complex demands of an overseas war. In late March, the president therefore brought on the retired Schofield as an unofficial adviser, but the latter seemed no more cognizant of domestic political realities than did Alger or Miles. The army's emphasis on protecting against a Spanish attack, calls for a careful mobilization, warnings that tropical disease would cripple a summer expedition to Cuba, and inability to organize a strike force to bring about a quick end to hostilities led McKinley—again like Polk—to take charge of military planning. "We shall end the war before the General [Miles] would have us begin operations," a confidante remembered McKinley muttering. "He little understands me, no more does he know the temper of our people. I deplore the war, but it must be short and quick to the finish."[10]

Turning to Adjutant General Henry C. Corbin to implement his wishes, McKinley transformed offices located on the second floor of the White House into a war room, replete with maps, twenty telegraph wires, fifteen telephone lines, and a graphophone (an early version of a Dictaphone). On May 1, the annihilation of Spain's obsolete Pacific fleet by Commodore George Dewey's Asiatic Squadron presented the president with even grander opportunities. Operating under "the general principle of holding on to what we get," McKinley ordered the formation of a new Philippines expeditionary force, the lead elements of which sailed from San Francisco on May 25. After several false starts, Maj. Gen. (Volunteers) William Shafter's Fifth Corps began landing at Daiquiri and Siboney, Cuba, on June 22; eleven days later, the navy's Flying Squadron destroyed Spain's Atlantic Squadron off Santiago de Cuba. Following several sharp fights, Spanish troops at Santiago capitulated on July 16. Invasion forces under Miles also occupied Puerto Rico. In the Philippines, the Spanish garrison at Manila allowed Maj. Gen. Wesley Merritt's Eighth Corps to occupy the city before insurgents could secure control.[11]

For the army, it had hardly been the "splendid little war" described by John Hay, the future secretary of state. Individual units generally performed well in overcoming shortages in artillery and supplies, but the army's collective efforts suffered when compared to the navy's spectacular triumphs. Unfortunately, Shafter had inspired little confidence. Once a courageous, colorful cavalryman who had compiled a good record fighting Confederates and Indians, at sixty-three years old "Pecos Bill" now weighed north of three hundred pounds and suffered from varicose veins and gout. Malaria, dysentery, and yellow fever threatened to decimate his Fifth Corps; by late July, more than four thousand men—better than a quarter of his command—were

Temporary war room. Frustrated by his inability to get the War Department to move more swiftly at the outset of the Spanish-American War, President McKinley set up his own war room in the White House. Library of Congress, Z62-105703.

reported as sick. "Until the yellow fever broke out the army never took a step toward sanitary precautions at Siboney," claimed one nurse from the scene. In early August, Shafter began withdrawing Fifth Corps from Cuba as "immunes" became available. Unfortunately, the army's debarkation site at Camp Wikoff, New York, was initially ill-prepared to handle the 20,000-plus soldiers who would pass through, inspiring another round of blistering newspaper criticism. In all, the army's combat-related deaths totaled only 345, but disease claimed another 2,565 soldiers, three-fourths of whom had been volunteers in assembly camps in the United States.[12]

Commanding general Miles did nothing to improve the army's image. His Puerto Rico campaign, wrote the correspondent Richard Harding Davis, "was one which should make all Americans pleased with themselves and with their army." But it had received scant newspaper coverage. More important, Miles's criticisms of the army's Krag-Jorgensen rifles, opposition to the Cuba expedition, refusal to inspect several army camps, and general lack of cooperation had alienated Secretary Alger and the president. Any possibility that Miles might patch relations with his civilian superiors vanished on August 23, when in a sensational interview with the *Kansas City Star* he accused the War Department of leaking his original landing site on

"Modern Military Tactics—Our Major-General and His Staff." Brave and effective in the field, the ambitious Nelson A. Miles (1839–1925) was nonetheless widely disliked, especially by his civilian superiors. In this print for *Puck*, artist Udo J. Keppler depicts the general in a full-dress uniform, holding a book titled *How to Become President*, speaking with a bevy of reporters eager for a sensational story. In the background, cobwebs cover the telephone "To the Administration." Library of Congress. DIG-ppmsca-28580.

Puerto Rico to the press. Responding to these and other criticisms, McKinley named the retired Maj. Gen. (Volunteers) Grenville M. Dodge to lead an investigation. When called to testify that December, Miles added even more dramatic charges: the canned beef supplied to troops in the Caribbean had been unpalatable, and a mysterious chemical process had "embalmed" 337 tons of refrigerated beef. Defending his department, Commissary General Charles P. Eagan exploded: Miles "lies in his throat, he lies in his heart, he lies in every hair of his head and every pore of his body. . . . I wish to force the lie back into his throat, covered with the contents of a camp latrine."[13]

Eagan was relieved of command, but the astonishing public airing of the army's dirty laundry reinforced perceptions that it badly needed a shake-up. To replace the ineffectual Alger, McKinley selected Elihu Root, a hard-charging corporate lawyer, as secretary of war. Unfazed, Miles compounded the problem by continuing to air his grievances to the press. In February 1899, the Dodge Commission concluded that, while the tropical heat could change the appearance of canned beef "as to become repulsive," it found no evidence of chemical tampering. At Miles's request, an army court of inquiry reinvestigated the beef matter, but this gambit backfired when that body instead censured his failure to air his concerns through official channels.[14]

Miles still enjoyed some political support, as evidenced by his promotion to lieutenant general the following year. But this elevation was misleading, as his advancement had been tied to a deal making Adjutant General Corbin, the president's favorite, a major general. In September 1901, things went from bad to worse for Miles with President McKinley's assassination. Whereas McKinley had found it easier to ignore Miles than to fire him, the new president, Theodore Roosevelt, had developed a special animus for the general, who had the temerity to suggest that Roosevelt had not led the famous charge up San Juan Hill. Secretary Root had already clashed with the cantankerous Miles over the prerogatives of their respective offices, so when the general publicly disparaged a naval court of inquiry's criticisms of Commodore Winfield Schley, the administration issued a blistering reprimand.[15]

In 1902, Miles further infuriated Roosevelt by complaining that fighting in the Philippines "has been conducted with marked severity" and by opposing Secretary Root's attempts to create an army general staff. The latter, Miles told the Senate Military Affairs Committee, would "Germanize and Russianize the small army of the United States" and throw "the door wide open for a future autocrat or a military despot." Miles kept his job only through the intervention of several senators, who convinced the president that, because Miles would soon reach the mandatory retirement age, it would be more prudent to "let him scold and plot and make mischief to his heart's content" than risk a political fight.[16]

Fears that the resulting controversy might endanger Root's ongoing efforts to increase the regular army and secure long overdue structural reforms added to Roosevelt's hesitancy to get rid of Miles. State troops had provided the manpower for campaigns in Puerto Rico and the Philippines, but thoughtful observers agreed that the continuing Filipino insurrection and the needs of administering an overseas empire demanded major changes. As a stopgap measure, Congress had established a temporary limit of 65,000 enlisted regulars, supplemented by 35,000 U.S. Volunteers. In February 1901, following considerable debate and two conference committee reports, Congress increased the regular army by ten regiments, authorized three new engineer battalions, and allowed the president to expand the number of enlisted men per company. The latest legislation, which set the army's maximum strength at 3,820 officers and 84,799 enlisted personnel, also provided for the mandatory rotation of staff officers to the line and created the permanent female Nurse Corps, professionalizing what had been a mix of volunteers and contract nurses.[17]

Army progressives had long championed better cooperation with the militia as a means of improving relations with the public. To do so, Secretary

Root cultivated the support of the National Guard Association, goading Congress to increase annual federal appropriations for state militias from $400,000 to $1 million and collaborating with Guard leaders to develop politically acceptable plans for reform. Representative Charles W. F. Dick (R), an Ohio Guardsman, Spanish–American War veteran, and chair of the House Military Affairs Committee, took the legislative lead. The resulting Militia Act of 1903 established the modern National Guard by creating a statutory relationship between the War Department and the states and linking federal funding to stricter standards of training, organization, and equipment.[18]

Enjoying Roosevelt's support, Root believed that a general staff would eliminate the interdepartmental rivalries that had slowed mobilization for the Spanish war, resolve the century-long disagreements between commanding general and secretary of war, and encourage more rational planning for future conflicts. Favorable testimony from the retired generals Schofield and Wesley Merritt initially failed to sway traditionalists—most notably Miles and the staff bureau chiefs—but Root redoubled his efforts, deeming it "the most important thing to be done now for the Regular Army." Shepherding a general staff bill through the House, Representative Hull assured his colleagues that it "recognizes in law what is recognized by the Constitution—that there is no commanding general of the Army except the President of the United States." By a 154–52 margin (30 of 81 Democrats broke with party leaders and supported the measure), the House in early January 1903 passed a somewhat watered-down bill. After demanding an amendment that delayed its implementation until a week after Miles's scheduled retirement, the Senate agreed. Approved on February 14, the "act to increase the efficiency of the Army" created the General Staff Corps (a Chief of Staff plus forty-four officers appointed by the president) tasked with preparing plans for national defense and mobilization, overseeing army efficiency, and rendering "professional aid and assistance to the Secretary of War and to general officers and other superior commanders." Effectively abolishing the position of commanding general, it gave the chief of staff "supervision of all troops." On August 8, 1903—Miles's sixty-fourth birthday—he left the army; the Roosevelt administration released only a curt statement with nary a word of praise for the general's forty-two years of service.[19]

The composition and distribution of the regular army had also changed. In 1895, the regular force had consisted of 27,172 officers and men distributed in eighty-two posts ranging from Fort Preble, Maine, to Alcatraz Island, California. That year's enlistments totaled 1,869, of whom about 70 percent were native-born. West Point graduates dominated the officer corps below the rank of general. By 1903, the regular army had grown to 59,181 officers and men on duty. Alaska and the Hawaiian Islands hosted 563 and 197 soldiers, respectively. More than two hundred troops joined a 546-strong

"Root's Portfolio." *Puck* magazine, an influential weekly featuring colorful cartoons and satire, celebrated the close of the year 1903 with this Udo J. Keppler cartoon. Uncle Sam carries a briefcase, "Root's Portfolio," which includes files of critical army interests labeled "General Staff," "Modernized Military," "Coast Defense," "Insular Policy," and "Army War College," and waves his hat to the soon-departing Secretary of War Elihu Root (1845–1937). Library of Congress, DIG-ppmsca-25808.

Porto Rico Regiment in garrisoning that island, and another 719 occupied Cuba. Four officers and 147 enlisted men remained with U.S. expeditionary forces in China (which had participated in the international coalition that put down the Boxer Rebellion). In the Philippines, more than 15,000 regulars, supplemented by nearly five thousand Philippine Scouts and 2,807 hospital corpsmen, garrisoned more than six hundred towns and villages. New enlistments that fiscal year numbered 11,385, with another 6,906 soldiers having reenlisted. Eighty-five percent of enlistees were native-born. As of late 1902, 1,818 of the 2,900 officers had secured their commissions after the beginning of the war with Spain. Of the former, 276 were from West Point, 414 from the ranks, 512 from civilian life, and 616 from the volunteers.[20]

Military expenditures and the army's role in administering government reflected its considerable responsibilities in managing the new empire. Between 1895 and 1903, federal outlays (excluding debt service) had increased from $325 million to $488 million (roughly $14.4 billion in 2018 terms), during which time spending on the army had increased from 15.9 to 24.3 percent of total government disbursements. McKinley's instructions to Shafter on July 15, 1898—four weeks before the armistice that ended the fighting, and five months before the Treaty of Paris that ended the war—reflected the president's determination to bring about a "new order of things" in Cuba. Through means "as free from severity as possible," the army was to assert its "absolute and supreme" power in protecting property and imposing American-style justice. Taxes and duties collected there would help to defray the occupation costs, with all public life conducted "under the supervision of the American commander in chief." As military governor of Cuba, Brig. Gen. (Volunteers) Leonard Wood, a former surgeon and Roosevelt's colonel in the volunteer Rough Riders, became the public face of the U.S. takeover until the May 1902 proclamation of the semiautonomous Republic of Cuba. Merely a captain in the regular army but a skillful self-promoter, Wood sparred with senior military officers resentful of his new power as he strove to modernize the island according to North American standards. Of the $45 million collected during the occupation, roughly half was devoted to charities and hospitals, public education, public works, and sanitation. Ambitious, energetic, and convinced that Cubans were incapable of chartering their own fate, he worked hard—with only mixed success—to instill a conservative, pro-American regime and to Americanize life in Cuba.[21]

Roosevelt followed McKinley's lead in using the military to promote American overseas interests. The army had been and would remain, Roosevelt exclaimed in his first annual message, "a great constructive force, the most potent implement for the upbuilding of a peaceful civilization." Yet things had not gone smoothly for the Yankee occupiers in the Philippines, where soldiers were expected to ensure "the establishment of a new political power." In February 1899, open warfare broke out between Emilio Aguinaldo's Army of Liberation and U.S. forces, now commanded by Maj. Gen. Elwell S. Otis. A Civil War volunteer and veteran Indian campaigner, Otis invested considerable resources to establishing health clinics, schools, sanitation projects, and marketplaces designed to win the hearts and minds of Filipinos, and soldiers assumed key civil functions ranging from provincial governors to police chiefs and sanitation inspectors. Moody and overly optimistic, Otis nonetheless managed to disperse Aguinaldo's conventional forces in late November 1899.[22]

The daunting task of stamping out continued guerrilla resistance fell to Otis's successor as military governor, Maj. Gen. Arthur MacArthur, Jr. As Rudyard Kipling had predicted in his poem "The White Man's Burden," conflict in the Philippines devolved into "the savage wars of peace." A volunteer who had joined the regular army after the Civil War, MacArthur believed that military operations were key to overcoming the resistance, therefore he was less interested in the civil projects touted by his predecessor. This change in emphasis, however, did not slow construction of roads and telegraph lines, communications improvements critical to the army's efforts to occupy and control the country. In the Department of Northern Luzon alone, more than a thousand miles of roads had been improved or built by August 1900; by the end of the war, the army had strung ten thousand miles of telegraph lines. As pacification operations turned increasingly punitive, human rights abuses became more widespread (especially in Batangas and Samar), a sharp contrast to the "benevolent assimilation" once advocated by William McKinley. As military governor, MacArthur clashed with William Howard Taft, head of the Philippines Commission, and in July 1901 was replaced by Maj. Gen. Adna R. Chaffee. Taft became civilian governor; although he and Chaffee disliked one another, the latter was more politically adroit compared to his egotistical predecessor.[23]

In July 1902, Secretary of War Elihu Root declared the insurgency to be at an end and terminated the office of military governor. Most soldiers in the Philippines had worked earnestly to help the locals, but their own paternalism convinced them that those same people lacked the ability to make intelligent decisions on their own behalf. As Hugh Lenox Scott, who had for three years served as governor in the Sulu Archipelago, later explained upon accepting a transfer to West Point: "I felt sorry to leave the Moros, with whom many strong ties of mutual regard had been knit. I felt as does one who leads a child by the hand through the woods, then suddenly pulls his hand away, leaving the child to wander alone. . . . I was not a missionary but a soldier who must follow his career wherever it took him."[24]

* * * * *

So it was for the institutionalized army. Overcoming traditional fears that a standing army posed an inherent threat to republican government, its involvement in territorial expansion, economic development, civil government, and development projects was hardly new. During the early republic period, regulars had seized the Northwest Territory by force of arms and administered the nascent Louisiana Territory. In the antebellum years, it expropriated huge swaths of land from American Indians, organized local governments following the war against Mexico, intervened in Bleeding Kansas, and served as an agent of federal authority and order in protecting slavery. Following the Civil War, the army temporarily propped up Republican governments and provided a modicum of protection for African Americans in the South during Reconstruction even as it completed the military defeat of Native Americans.

Throughout the first 125 years of the American experiment, ordnance projects had spawned crucial technical and managerial changes, and the presence of an army garrison could be an economic boon to a community or region. Moreover, the civil works projects undertaken by the army in Cuba and the Philippines bore a striking resemblance to the roads, scientific surveys, and disaster relief efforts that it had sponsored throughout the nineteenth century on American soil. When measured by the number of regular soldiers per capita, the size of the 1903 army (.81 per 1,000) was almost precisely that of 1794 (.85 per 1,000), when Anthony Wayne's Legion had laid claim to much of the Old Northwest in the Battle of Fallen Timbers.[25] Often unrecognized and unappreciated by the public, in fulfilling their duties regulars had spearheaded the nation's claims to empire through force of arms in the continental borderlands as well as Mexico, Cuba, Puerto Rico, and the Philippines. Most significant, they had served as the federal government's only reliable means of ensuring that new lands acquired through blood and treasure remained under Washington's control.

Notes

Abbreviations Used in Notes

AG	Adjutant General
Annals	Annals of Congress
ANJ	*Army and Navy Journal*
ASP	American State Papers
ASPIA	American State Papers, Indian Affairs
ASPMA	American State Papers, Military Affairs
CGlobe	*Congressional Globe*
CULR	Confidential and Unofficial Letters Received by the Secretary of War, 1832–1846
CULS	Confidential and Unofficial Letters Sent by the Secretary of War
CRec	*Congressional Record*
DHRCDE	Documentary History of the Ratification of the Constitution Digital Edition
FC	Kurland and Lerner, eds., *Founder's Constitution*
Heitman	Heitman, *Historical Register and Dictionary of the United States Army*
HD	House Document
HED	House Executive Document
HMD	House Miscellaneous Document
HR	House Report
HSP	Historical Society of Pennsylvania
JCC	Ford, ed., *Journals of the Continental Congress*
LC	Library of Congress
LDC	Smith, ed., *Letters of Delegates to Congress*
LR	Letters Received
LRSW	Letters Received by the Secretary of War, Registered Series
LROAG	Letters Received by the Office of the Adjutant General, Main Series, 1822–1860
LS	Letters Sent
LSSW	Letters Sent by the Secretary of War
MdHS	Maryland Historical Society
MPP	Richardson, *Messages and Papers of the Presidents*
NARA	National Archives and Records Administration
NYSL	New York State Library
New ASPMA	New American State Papers, Military Affairs

OR	*War of the Rebellion: A Compilation of the Official Records of the Union and Confederate Armies*
PAH	Syrett, ed., *Papers of Alexander Hamilton*
PTJ	Papers of Thomas Jefferson
PWD	Papers of the War Department, 1784–1800
PUSG	Simon, ed., *Papers of Ulysses S. Grant*
RDebates	*Registers of Debates*
RG	Record Group
SD	Senate Document
SED	Senate Executive Document
SMD	Senate Miscellaneous Document
SR	Senate Report
Statutes	U.S. *Statutes at Large*
SW	Secretary of War
TP	Carter, ed., *Territorial Papers of the United States*
USAMHI	United States Army Military History Institute
USMA	United States Military Academy Library
WDAR	Department of War, Annual Report
WGW	Fitzpatrick, ed., *Writings of George Washington*

Introduction

1. Terry M. Neal, "Bush Backs Into Nation-Building," *Washington Post*, February 26, 2003.

2. Francis Paul Prucha, *Broadax and Bayonet: The Role of the United States Army in the Development of the Northwest, 1815–1860* (1953; rpt. Lincoln: University of Nebraska Press, 1967); Forest G. Hill, *Roads, Rails & Waterways: The Army Engineers and Early Transportation* (Norman: University of Oklahoma Press, 1957); William H. Goetzmann, *Army Exploration in the American West, 1803–1863* (New Haven: Yale University Press, 1959).

3. Marcus Cunliffe, *Soldiers & Civilians: The Martial Spirit in America, 1775–1865* (Boston: Little, Brown, 1968); Michael L. Tate, *The Frontier Army in the Settlement of the West* (Norman: University of Oklahoma Press, 1999).

4. Richard H. Kohn, *Eagle and Sword: The Federalists and the Creation of the Military Establishment in America, 1782–1802* (New York: Free Press, 1975); Theodore J. Crackel, *Mr. Jefferson's Army: Political and Social Reform of the Military Establishment, 1801–1809* (New York: New York University Press, 1987); Andrew R. L. Cayton, "'Separate Interests' and the Nation-State: The Washington Administration and the Origins of Regionalism in the Trans-Appalachian West," *Journal of American History* 79 (June 1992): 39–67.

5. Thomas T. Smith, *The U.S. Army and the Texas Frontier Economy, 1845–1900* (College Station: Texas A&M University Press, 1999); Mark Wilson, *The Business of Civil War: Military Mobilization and the State, 1861–1865* (Baltimore: Johns Hopkins University Press, 2006); Paul A. C. Koistinen, *Beating Plowshares into Swords: The Political Economy of American Warfare, 1607–1865* (Lawrence: University Press

of Kansas, 1996), and *Mobilizing for War: The Political Economy of American Warfare, 1865–1919* (Lawrence: University Press of Kansas, 1997); Merritt Roe Smith, *Harpers Ferry Armory and the New Technology: The Challenge of Change* (Ithaca, NY: Cornell University Press, 1977); William D. Adler and Andrew J. Polsky, "Building the New American Nation: Economic Development, Public Goods, and the Early U.S. Army," *Political Science Quarterly* 125 (March 2010): 87–110. For an excellent overview of American Political Development, see Richard R. John, "The State *Is Back* In: What Now?" *Journal of the Early Republic* 38 (Spring 2018): 105–118. The current work depends only peripherally on more specialized political science analyses of "civil-military relations."

6. Brian McAllister Linn, *The Echo of Battle: The Army's Way of War* (Cambridge: Harvard University Press, 2007), 3–8; J. P. Clark, *Preparing for War: The Emergence of the Modern U.S. Army, 1815–1917* (Cambridge: Harvard University Press, 2017), Chapter One.

7. Henry David Thoreau, "Resistance to Civil Government," *Aesthetic Papers*, ed. Elizabeth P. Peabody (Putnam, 1849), ¶ 4, http://commons.digitalthoreau.org/civil/resistance-to-civil-government/rcg-1-14.

8. Samuel J. Watson, *Jackson's Sword: The Army Officer Corps on the American Frontier, 1810–1821* (Lawrence: University Press of Kansas, 2012), and *Peacekeepers and Conquerors: The Army Officer Corps on the American Frontier, 1821–1846* (Lawrence: University Press of Kansas, 2013); William Blair, "The Use of Military Force to Protect the Gains of Reconstruction," *Civil War History* 51 (December 2005): 388–402; Gregory P. Downs, *After Appomattox: Military Occupation and the Ends of War* (Cambridge: Harvard University Press, 2015); Andrew F. Lang, *In the Wake of War: Military Occupation, Emancipation, and Civil War America* (Baton Rouge: Louisiana State University Press, 2017); Donald B. Connelly, *John M. Schofield and the Politics of Generalship* (Chapel Hill: University of North Carolina Press, 2006), 11, 340.

9. Brian Balogh, *Government Out of Sight: The Mystery of National Authority in Nineteenth-Century America* (Cambridge: Cambridge University Press, 2009); *Historical Statistics of the United States: Earliest Times to the Present*, Millennial Edition, 5 vols. (Cambridge: Cambridge University Press, 2006), 5:127, 353–358; *The Statistical History of the United States: From Colonial Times to the Present* (New York: Basic Books, 1976), 8, 1114–1115; Max Edling, *Hercules in the Cradle: War, Money, and the American States, 1783–1867* (Chicago: University of Chicago Press, 2014), 237.

10. Daniel Walker Howe, *What Hath God Wrought: The Transformation of America, 1815–1848* (New York: Oxford University Press, 2007), 7 (quotation); Samuel J. Watson, "How the Army Became Accepted: West Point Socialization, Military Accountability, and the Nation-State During the Jacksonian Era," *American Nineteenth Century History* 7 (June 2006): 219–251; Charles Sellers, *The Market Revolution: Jacksonian America, 1815–1846* (New York: Oxford University Press, 1991); Robert J. Wettemann, Jr., *Privilege vs. Equality: Civil-Military Relations in the Jacksonian Era, 1815–1845* (Santa Barbara: Greenwood Press, 2009).

11. Merritt Roe Smith, ed., *Military Enterprise and Technological Change: Perspectives on the American Experience* (Cambridge: MIT Press, 1985); David A. Hounshell,

From the American System to Mass Production, 1800–1932: The Development of Manufacturing Technology in the United States (Baltimore: Johns Hopkins University Press, 1984); David R. Meyer, *Roots of American Industrialization* (Baltimore: Johns Hopkins University Press, 2003).

12. Theda Skocpol, *Protecting Soldiers and Mothers: The Political Origins of Social Policy in the United States* (Cambridge: Belknap Press of Harvard University Press, 1995); Laura Jensen, *Patriots, Settlers, and the Origins of American Social Policy* (Cambridge: Cambridge University Press, 2003); John Resch, *Suffering Soldiers: Revolutionary War Veterans, Moral Sentiment, and Political Culture in the Early Republic* (Amherst: University of Massachusetts Press, 2000).

13. Ira Katznelson, "Flexible Capacity: The Military and Early American Statebuilding," in *Shaped by War and Trade: International Influences on American Political Development*, ed. Ira Katznelson and Martin Shefter (Princeton: Princeton University Press, 2002), 58–71; Stephen Skowronek, *Building a New American State: The Expansion of National Administrative Capacities, 1877–1920* (Cambridge: Cambridge University Press, 1982).

14. Harvey Meyerson, *Nature's Army: When Soldiers Fought for Yosemite* (Lawrence: University Press of Kansas, 2001), outlines the army's early experiences with the parks; for management and accounting, see Keith W. Hoskin and Richard H. Macve, "The Genesis of Accountability: The West Point Connections," *Accounting, Organizations, and Society* 13 (1988): 37–73; Charles F. O'Donnell, "United States Army and the Origins of Modern Management, 1818–1860," (Ph.D. diss., Ohio State University, 1982). Alan Lessoff, *The Nation and Its City: Politics, "Corruption," and Progress in Washington, D.C., 1861–1902* (Baltimore: Johns Hopkins University Press, 1994), offers a nuanced analysis of the growth of Washington.

15. Francis Paul Prucha, *The Sword of the Republic: The United States Army on the Frontier, 1783–1846* (London: Macmillan Co., 1969) (first quotation); Robert Wooster, *The Military and United States Indian Policy, 1865–1903* (New Haven: Yale University Press, 1988); Kevin Adams, *Class and Race in the Frontier Army: Military Life in the West, 1870–1890* (Norman: University of Oklahoma Press, 2009); Verity McInnis, *Women of Empire: Nineteenth-Century Officers' Wives in India and the U.S. West* (Norman: University of Oklahoma Press, 2017); John F. Marszalek, *Sherman: A Soldier's Passion for Order* (New York: Free Press, 1993), 453 (second quotation).

16. Downs, *After Appomattox*, 249 (first quotation); Robert M. Citino, "Military Histories Old and New: A Reintroduction," *American Historical Review* 112 (October 2007): 1070 (second quotation).

1. A Standing Army, the Role of National Government, and the Constitution

1. William C. Banks and Stephen Dycus, *Soldiers on the Home Front: The Domestic Role of the American Military* (Cambridge: Harvard University Press, 2016), 18–19; Jason W. Warren, "Liberty Paradox: The Failure of the Military System in Mid Seventeenth-Century New England," in *Drawdown: The American Way of Postwar*, ed. Jason W. Warren (New York: New York University Press, 2016), 54–57; Richard H. Kohn, ed., *Anglo-American Antimilitary Tracts, 1697–1830* (New York: Arno Press, 1979), Trenchard (1698), 1 (first quotation); Trenchard (1697), 28 (second quotation).

2. English Bill of Rights, Vol. 3, Article 1, Section 8, Clause 12, Document 1, *FC*, http://press-pubs.uchicago.edu/founders/documents/a1_8_12s1.html.

3. John A. Shy, *A People Numerous and Armed: Reflections on the Military Struggle for American Independence* (New York: Oxford University Press, 1976), 24–31. Colonials thus found Britain's return of Louisbourg to France in the subsequent Treaty of Aix-la-Chapelle (in exchange for the trading post at Madras, India) especially galling.

4. Shy, *People Numerous and Armed*, 30–33; James Kirby Martin and Mark Edward Lender, *A Respectable Army: The Military Origins of the Republic, 1763–1789* (Arlington Heights, IL: Harlan Davidson, 1982), 19 (quotations).

5. Martin and Lender, *Respectable Army*, 15–16, 20–25 (first and second quotations); Kohn, ed., *Anglo-American Antimilitary Tracts*, Lovell, 5 (third quotation). For the original, see *Blackstone's Commentaries on the Laws of England*, The Avalon Project: Documents in Law, History, and Diplomacy (Yale Law School), book 1, Chapter 13, 395, 400.

6. Martin and Lender, *Respectable Army*, 27; Adams Diary, March 5, 1773, Founders Online, Correspondence and Other Writings of Six Major Shapers of the United States, NARA, http://founders.archives.gov/documents/Adams/01-02-02-0003-0002-0002 (first quotation); Pennsylvania Constitution of 1776, Declaration of Rights, Article 13, *FC*, http://press-pubs.uchicago.edu/founders/documents/amendIIs5.html (second quotation); Barbara Oberg and J. Jefferson Looney, eds., *The Papers of Jefferson, Digital Edition* (Charlottesville: University of Virginia Press, Rotunda, 2008), Main Series 1:353 (third quotation).

7. Mercy Otis Warren, *The Blockheads: or, The Affrighted Officers. A Farce* (Boston: n.p., 1776), 13.

8. Charles Royster, *A Revolutionary People at War: The Continental Army and American Character, 1775–1783* (1979; rpt. New York: W. W. Norton, 1981), 67; Russell F. Weigley, *History of the United States Army*, Enlarged Edition (Bloomington: Indiana University Press, 1984), 29; *LDC* 4:640–642; 5:191–192; *JCC* 2:90–91; *WGW* 6:380 (first quotation), 112 (fourth quotation), 110 (fifth and sixth quotations); Richard K. Showman, ed., *The Papers of Nathanael Greene*, 13 vols. (Chapel Hill: University of North Carolina Press, 1976–2005), 1:300–301 (second and third quotations). Trust of military men, even in Washington, was still limited. John Adams described Washington as "modest and virtuous . . . generous and brave" but nonetheless worried that Congress had given him too much power. *LDC* 1:497–498 (quotation), 652, 667.

9. Matthew H. Spring, *With Zeal and Bayonets Only: The British Army on Campaign in North America, 1775–1783* (Norman: University of Oklahoma Press, 2008), 209; *PAH* 2:420–421 (first quotation); *WGW* 20:49–50 (second quotation).

10. Gregory T. Knouff, *The Soldiers' Revolution: Pennsylvanians in Arms and the Forging of Early American Identity* (University Park: Pennsylvania State University Press, 2004), xiii-xiv (quotation), 2, 48–49, 77–78.

11. Jackson Turner Main, *Political Parties Before the Constitution* (Chapel Hill: University of North Carolina Press, 1973), 385–387; *JCC* 2:100–101; *WGW* 21:374–377; Weigley, *History of the United States Army*, 30; Richard H. Kohn, *Eagle and Sword: The Federalists and the Creation of the Military Establishment in America, 1782–1802* (New York: Free Press, 1975), 10–13; *LDC* 16:131–132 (quotations).

12. David Ramsay, *The History of the American Revolution in Two Volumes,* vol. 2 (Indianapolis: Liberty Fund, 1990) http://oll.libertyfund.org/titles/547#Ramsay_0015-02_297 (first quotation); Publius, The Federalist 25, Commentaries, DHRCDE 15:364 (second quotation).

13. John Ferling, *Almost a Miracle: The American Victory in the War of Independence* (New York: Oxford University Press, 2007), 195–197, 339–342; Martin and Lender, *Respectable Army*, 107 (quotation); John Resch and Walter Sargent, "Changing Meanings of the American Revolution: An Overview, 1789–2006," in *War & Society in the American Revolution: Mobilizing and Home Fronts,* eds. John Resch and Walter Sargent (DeKalb: Northern Illinois Press, 2007), 291–299.

14. E. Wayne Carp, *To Starve the Army at Pleasure: Continental Army Administration and American Political Culture, 1775–1783* (Chapel Hill: University of North Carolina Press, 1984), 77, 87, 135, 217, 220; Adams to his wife, May 22, 1777, Lester J. Cappon, ed., *The Adams-Jefferson Letters: The Complete Correspondence between Thomas Jefferson and Abigail and John Adams* (Chapel Hill: University of North Carolina Press, 1959), (quotations); Royster, *Revolutionary People at War*, 326–334.

15. *JCC* 24:291–293; Royster, *Revolutionary People at War*, 337 (first quotation); *LDC* 19:639 (second quotation); *PAH* 3:253–254 (third and fourth quotations).

16. *JCC* 24:295–299 (first, second, and third quotations); Ferling, *Almost a Miracle*, 555–556 (fourth quotation); Josiah Quincy, *The Journals of Major Samuel Shaw, the First American Consul at Canton* (Boston: W. Crosby and H. P. Nichols, 1847), 101–105; William T. Hutchinson, et al., eds., *The Papers of James Madison: Congressional Series*, 17 vols. (Chicago and Charlottesville: University of Chicago Press and University Press of Virginia, 1962–1991), 6:348–356 (fifth quotation); *WGW* 22:222–229, 291–295; *PAH* 3:315–316 (sixth quotation), 317–321. For conflicting interpretations of the Newburgh Conspiracy, see C. Edward Skeen and Richard H. Kohn, "The Newburgh Conspiracy Reconsidered," *William and Mary Quarterly* 31 (April 1974): 273–298; and Richard H. Kohn, "Inside History of the Newburgh Conspiracy: America and the Coup d'Etat," *William and Mary Quarterly* 27 (April 1970): 187–220.

17. Mary A. Y. Gallagher, "Reinterpreting the 'Very Trifling Mutiny' at Philadelphia in June 1783," *Pennsylvania Magazine of History and Biography* 119 (1995): 3–35; Martin and Lender, *Respectable Army*, 134 (quotations).

18. Paul A. C. Koistinen, *Beating Plowshares into Swords: The Political Economy of American Warfare, 1607–1865* (Lawrence: University Press of Kansas, 1996), 10, 29–30, 33–34; *Articles of Confederation and Perpetual Union*, The Avalon Project, Yale Law School, http://avalon.law.yale.edu/18th_century/contcong_07-12-76.asp (first and second quotations); *LDC* 20:260–261 (third quotation).

19. Max Farrand, ed., *The Records of the Federal Convention of 1787*, 4 vols. (New Haven: Yale University Press, 1966), 3:88; *LDC* 22:652 (first quotation), 618 (second quotation); Kohn, ed., *Anglo-American Antimilitary Tracts,* quoted from Burke, 8 (third quotation).

20. Max M. Edling, *A Revolution in Favor of Government: Origins of the U.S. Constitution and the Making of the American State* (New York: Oxford University Press, 2003), 76; Hutchinson, ed., *Papers of Madison: Congressional Series* 7:161 n. 10; *PAH*

3:322 (first quotation), 378–397; *WGW* 26:274–298 (second and third quotations); Karl-Friedrich Walling, *Republican Empire: Alexander Hamilton on War and Free Government* (Lawrence: University Press of Kansas, 1999), 67–70; *JCC* 25:722–745.

21. *LDC* 21:817; 22:36–37; Lee to Monroe, January 5, 1784, Vol. 3, Article 1, Section 8, Clause 12, Document 8, *FC,* http://press-pubs.uchicago.edu/founders/documents/a1_8_12s8.html (quotations); Charles Royster, "Founding a Nation in Blood: Military Conflict and American Nationality," in *Arms and Independence: The Military Character of the American Revolution*, ed. Ronald Hoffman and Peter J. Albert (Charlottesville: University Press of Virginia, 1984), 28.

22. R. Lamb, *An Original and Authentic Journal of Occurrences During the Late American War* (Dublin: Wilkinson & Courtney, 1809), 291–292 (first quotation); *WGW* 6:435 (second quotation); John Grenier, *The First Way of War: American War Making on the Frontier, 1607–1814* (Cambridge: Cambridge University Press, 2005), 152, 166 (third quotation); Colin G. Calloway, *The American Revolution in Indian Country: Crisis and Diversity in Native American Communities* (Cambridge: Cambridge University Press, 1995).

23. Frederick Cook and George S. Conover, eds., *Journals of the Military Expedition of Major General John Sullivan Against the Six Nations of Indians in 1779* (Auburn, NY: Knapp, Peck, & Thompson, 1887), 101; Calloway, *American Revolution in Indian Country*, 20 (first, second, and third quotations), 272, 278–229; Gregory Evans Dowd, *A Spirited Resistance: The North American Indian Struggle for Unity, 1745–1816* (Baltimore: Johns Hopkins University Press, 1992), 93; Knouff, *Soldiers' Revolution,* passim; Wayne to Martin, March 26, 1782, Wayne Papers, LC (fourth quotation).

24. Dowd, *Spirited Resistance*, 88–89; Speech of the United Indian Nations, November 28, December 18, 1786, Berthrong Collection, University of Oklahoma Libraries, *PWD* (first quotation); Martin to Thompson, January 5, 1787, roll 69, M247, Papers of the Continental Congress, RG 360, NARA (second quotation); Butler to Knox, March 20, 1787, ibid., roll 164 (third quotation).

25. Brodhead to Irvine, December 4, 1780, Brodhead Letterbook, HSP (first quotation); Brodhead to Washington, February 18, 1781, ibid. (second quotation); Edward C. Burnett, ed., *Letters of Members of Congress*, 8 vols. (Washington, D.C.: Carnegie Institution of Washington, 1921–1936), 7:365–367, 546–547; *JCC* 25:806–807; 27:379–382; *LDC* 21:504–505.

26. Weigley, *History of the United States Army*, 83; *A Journal of the Honourable House of Representatives at a General Court of the Commonwealth of Massachusetts . . . October 13–October 14, 1784* (Boston, 1784), 174; *LDC* 21:556–557, 618, 639–642 (first and second quotations), 644, 668–669; *PTJ* 7:280, 300; *JCC* 27:407, 428–432, 433–434 (third quotation), 499, 512–524, 530 (fourth quotation).

27. Burnett, ed., *Letters of Members* 7:587–858 (first and second quotations; Gerry's emphasis), 605–605 (third quotation), 546–547, 594 (fourth quotation); *LDC* 21:712–713.

28. William B. Skelton, "The Confederation's Regulars: A Social Profile of Enlisted Service in America's First Standing Army," *William and Mary Quarterly* 46 (October 1989); 773–776, 782–783, and "Social Roots of the American Military

Profession: The Officer Corps of America's First Peacetime Army, 1784–1789," *Journal of Military History* 54 (October 1990): 438–450.

29. *JCC* 28:375–381; Harmar to Dickinson, February 8, 1785, roll 68, Harmar Papers, Draper Collection, PWD (first and second quotations); Harmar to Doughty, October 3, 1785, ibid.; Kohn, *Eagle and Sword*, 67; Harmar to Knox, June 1, 1785, Goodman Papers, Western Reserve Historical Society History Library, PWD; William Henry Smith, *The St. Clair Papers: The Life and Public Service of Arthur St. Clair*, 2 vols. (Cincinnati: Robert Clarke, 1882), 2:10 (third quotation).

30. "A Citizen," *Maryland Journal*, January 30, 1787 (first quotation); Harmar to Knox, May 7, 1786, Goodman Papers, Western Reserve Historical Society History Library, *PWD* (second and quotation); John Ferling, *A Leap in the Dark: The Struggle to Create the American Republic* (New York: Oxford University Press, 2003), 265–266; *JCC* 31:891–893 (third and fourth quotations).

31. *WGW* 29:50–52 (first and second quotations); Edling, *Revolution in Favor of Government*, 4, 8 (third quotation); Richard H. Kohn, "The Constitution and National Security: The Intent of the Framers," in *The United States Military Under the Constitution of the United States, 1789–1989*, ed. Richard H. Kohn (New York: New York University Press, 1991), 64; Don Higginbotham, "War and State Formation in Revolutionary America," in *Empire and Nation: The American Revolution in the Atlantic World*, ed. Elija T. Gould and Peter S. Onuf (Baltimore: Johns Hopkins University Press, 2005), 70–71; Farrand, ed., *Records of the Federal Convention* 1:25 (fourth quotation), 3:598; *Columbian Herald*, July 26, 1787 (fifth and sixth quotations).

32. Farrand, ed., *Records of the Federal Convention* 2:617 (first quotation); Max M. Edling, *A Hercules in the Cradle: War, Money, and the American States, 1783–1867* (Chicago: University of Chicago Press, 2014), 31; Hutchinson, ed., *Papers of Madison: Congressional Series* 10:86–87 (second and third quotations).

33. J. C. A. Stagg, *Mr. Madison's War: Politics, Diplomacy, and Warfare in the Early American Republic, 1783–1830* (Princeton: Princeton University Press, 1983), 123; Banks and Dycus, *Soldiers on the Home Front*, 7, 31–34 (first quotation); William C. Banks, "Providing 'Supplemental Security': The Insurrection Act and the Military Role in Responding to Domestic Crises," *Journal of National Security Law & Policy*, 3 (no. 1, 2009): 49–53; Kohn, *Eagle and Sword*, 74–78; Farrand, ed., *Records of the Federal Convention* 1:246 (second quotation), 2:317–330 (third quotation), 334, 616–617 (fourth quotation), 509 (fifth quotation), 632–633. Remaining quotations are from the Constitution.

34. Parsons to Cushing, January 11, 1788, Ratification by the States, DHRCDE 3:569 (quotation); William A. Benton, "Pennsylvania Revolutionary Officers and the Federal Constitution," *Pennsylvania History* 31 (1964): 419–435; Edwin G. Burrows, "Military Experience and the Origins of Federalism and Anti-Federalism," in *Aspects of Early American Society and Politics*, ed. Jacob Jubb and Irwin Polishook (Tarrytown, NY: Sleepy Hollow Restorations, 1924), 84; Forrest McDonald, *We the People: The Economic Origins of the Constitution* (Chicago: University of Chicago Press, 1958), 263 n. 11.

35. Kohn, "Constitution and National Security," 80–81; Luther Martin, Genuine Information IX, January 29, 1788, Commentaries, DHRCDE 15:484; Saul Cornell, *The Other Founders: Anti-Federalism and the Dissenting Tradition in America, 1788–1828* (Chapel Hill: University of North Carolina Press, 1990), 30–31; Brutus, *New York Journal*, January 24, 1788 (first quotation); George Mason, Debate in Virginia Ratifying Convention, June 14, 1788, Vol. 3, Article 1, Section 8, Clause 12, Document 27, *FC*, http://press-pubs.uchicago.edu/founders/documents/a1_8_12s27.html (second quotation); *Independent Gazetteer*, October 5, 24, 1787, Commentaries, DHRCDE 14:162, 465 (third quotation); *Virginia Independent Chronicle*, February 27, 1788, 8:422, ibid. (fourth quotation).

36. *Pennsylvania Packet*, December 18, 1788, Commentaries, DHRCDE 15:32 (first quotation); *Philadelphia Freeman's Journal*, December 12, 1788, ibid., 14:420 (second quotation); Jonathan Elliott, ed., *Debates in the Several State Conventions on the Adoption of the Federal Constitution*, 5 vols. (Washington, D.C.: n.p., 1836), 3:169 (third and fourth quotations); *New York Journal*, January 10, 1788, Ratification by the States, DHRCDE 20:593–594 (fifth quotation).

37. Edling, *Hercules in the Cradle*, 37–38; Edling, *Revolution in Favor of Government*, 76, 88; Stagg, *Mr. Madison's War*, 120; Nicholas, Virginia Ratification Debates, DHRCDE 9:1129–1130; Wilson, Pennsylvania Ratifying Convention, December 11, 1787, Vol. 3, Article 1, Section 8, Clause 12, Document 13, *FC*, http://press-pubs.uchicago.edu/founders/documents/a1_8_12s13.html (first and second quotations); Federalist Number 4 (third quotation) 24, 25, 28.

38. Publius, Federalist 25, Commentaries, DHRCDE 15:364 (first quotation); Hutchinson, ed., *Papers of Madison: Congressional Series* 10:392–395 (second, third, fourth, fifth, and sixth quotations); Publius, Federalist 46, Commentaries, DHRCDE 15:492 (last quotation).

39. Burrows, "Military Experience," 91; Hutchinson, ed., *Papers of Madison: Congressional Series* 10:156 n. 1; "Plain Truth," *Independent Gazetteer*, November 10, 1787, Ratification, DHRCDE 2:220 (first quotation); Publius, Federalist 26, Commentaries, ibid., 15:68 (second quotation); Publius, Federalist 28, ibid., 15:102–106; Aristides, "Remarks on the Proposal Plan," January 31, 1788, ibid., 15:532; Edling, *Revolution in Favor of Government*, 117.

40. Edling, *Revolution in Favor of Government*, 89–91; Cornell, *Other Founders*, 31; Richard Henry Lee's proposed amendments, September 27, 1787, Constitutional Documents, DHRCDE 1:337–338 (quotation); New York Ratification Convention, July 3, 1788, Ratification, ibid., 22:2088; Jefferson to Donald, February 7, 1788, ibid., 8:354; Oberg and Looney, eds., *Papers of Jefferson, Digital Edition* 13:490.

41. David C. Hendrickson, *Peace Pact: The Lost World of the American Founding* (Lawrence: University Press of Kansas, 2003), 40, 59; Hutchinson, ed., *Papers of Madison: Congressional Series* 11:159 (quotations); Elliott, ed., *Debates in the Several State Conventions*, 3:90–97, 249–252, 381–383; Debate in Virginia Ratifying Convention, June 16, 1788, Vol. 5, Amendment 3, Document 8, *FC*, http://press-pubs.uchicago.edu/founders/documents/amendIIIs8.html; Publius, Federalist 41, Commentaries, DHRCDE 15:463.

2. The Army and Muscular Nationalism: Nation-building and the Federalists

1. *JCC* 33:602–605 (quotation); Andrew R. L. Cayton, "'Separate Interests' and the Nation-State: The Washington Administration and the Origins of Regionalism in the Trans-Appalachian West," *Journal of American History* 79 (June 1992): 39–67.

2. *ASPMA* 1:5–7 (quotations); Correspondence—First Session, *Documentary History of the First Federal Congress of the United States of America, March 4, 1789–March 3, 1791*, 17 vols. (Baltimore: Johns Hopkins University Press, 1972–2004), 16:988–990; *Senate Journal*, 1st Cong., 1st sess., 71; Gerry, August 17, 1789, Vol. 5, Amendment II, Document 6, *FC*, http://press-pubs.uchicago.edu/founders/documents/amendIIs6.html.

3. Publius, Federalist 24, Commentaries, DHRCDE (first and second quotations); Knox to Harmar, May 12, 1786, Goodman Papers, Western Reserve Historical Society Library, PWD; Knox to Butler, March 13, 1787, New York Public Library, PWD; *ASPIA* 1:53 (third and fourth quotations), 60; *JCC* 32:327–328.

4. Pendleton to Knox, November 1, 1790, Knox Papers, Pierpont Morgan Library, PWD (first and second quotations); Richard H. Kohn, *Eagle and Sword: The Federalists and the Creation of the Military Establishment in America, 1782–1803* (New York: Free Press, 1975), 69; Martin to Thompson, January 5, 1787, roll 69, M247, Papers of the Continental Congress, NARA (third and fourth quotations); *JCC* 28:381–386; John Grenier, *The First Way of War: American War Making on the Frontier, 1607–1814* (Cambridge: Cambridge University Press, 2005), 172–175, 180–181; Kevin T. Barksdale, *The Lost State of Franklin: America's First Secession* (Lexington: University Press of Kentucky, 2009), 177; *ASPIA* 1:38, 48.

5. Knox to Willett, July 3, 1790, Knox Papers, Chicago Historical Society, PWD; Butler to Knox, March 20, 1787, roll 164, M247, Papers of the Continental Congress, NARA; Grenier, *First Way of War*, 193; Wayne to Knox, December 25, 1789, March 20, 1790 (first quotation), Knox Papers, Pierpont Morgan Library, PWD; Knox to Wayne, April 10, 1790, ibid.; Wayne to Knox, May 12, 1790, ibid.; Harmar to Knox, May 14, 1787, Goodman Papers, Western Reserve Historical Society Library, PWD; Knox to Harmar, November 14, 1787, ibid.; Harmar to Knox, December 15, 1788, ibid.; William T. Hutchinson, et al., ed., *The Papers of James Madison: Congressional Series*, 17 vols. (Chicago and Charlottesville: University of Chicago Press and University Press of Virginia, 1962–1991), 12:442–446; 13:186–187, 337–339 (second quotation); *PTJ* 19:469, editorial note.

6. *The Papers of George Washington: Presidential Series*, 21 vols. (Charlottesville: University of Virginia Press, 1987–2020), 3:585–588 (first quotation); *ASPIA* 1:115–116; *TP* 2:26–27, 31–35 (second quotation); Andrew R. L. Cayton, *The Frontier Republic: Ideology and Politics in the Ohio Country, 1780–1825* (Kent, OH: Kent State University Press, 1986), 19–21; Cayton, "'Separate Interests' and the Nation-State," 47–52. As Washington explained, using Revolutionary War veterans to colonize the west "would connect our Governments with the frontiers, extend our Settlements progressively, and plant a brave, a hardy and respectable Race of People, as our advanced Post." *WGW* 17:16–18 (quotation).

7. Eric Hinderaker, *Elusive Empires: Constructing Colonialism in the Ohio Valley,*

1673–1800 (Cambridge: Cambridge University Press, 1997), 236–237; *TP* 2:339; Putnam to Knox, January 4, 1788, Dawes Memorial Library, PWD (first quotation); Harmar to Knox, May 26, (second quotation), July 15, 1788, Goodman Papers, Western Reserve Historical Society Library, PWD; Knox to Hutchins, December 15, 1788, HSP, PWD (third quotation).

8. *TP* 2:119–120, 151–152, 196; Harmar to Knox, December 15, 1788, Goodman Papers, Western Reserve Historical Society Library, PWD; Hamtramck to Harmar, April 11, 1789, vol. 10, Harmar Papers, Clements Library; *ASPIA* 1:59–64; *Documentary History of the First Federal Congress* 5:1293–1298; Edgar S. Maclay, ed., *Journal of William Maclay, United States Senator from Pennsylvania, 1789–1791* (New York: D. A. Appleton and Co., 1890), 239–240, 244–245 (first quotation); John Adams Diary 46, August 6, 1787–September 10, 1796, "Adams Family Papers: An Electronic Archive," Massachusetts Historical Society, www.masshist.org/digitaladams/archive/popup?id=D46&page=D46_8 (second quotation; accessed December 5, 2019); *Statutes* 1:119–121; Saul Cornell, *The Other Founders: Anti-Federalism and the Dissenting Tradition in America, 1788–1828* (Chapel Hill: University of North Carolina Press, 1999), 164.

On efforts to reform the militia, see Knox to Lincoln, January 31, 1790, Robert G. Harper Papers, South Caroliniana Collection, PWD; Lincoln to Knox, February 12, 1790, Henry Knox Papers, Pierpont Morgan Library, PWD; Jackson to Knox, February 21, 1790, ibid.; Vanderkemp to Knox, March 12, 1790, ibid.

9. Wiley Sword, *President Washington's Indian War: The Struggle for the Old Northwest, 1790–1795* (Norman: University of Oklahoma Press, 1985), 82, 89–96; Mary Ellen Rowe, *Bulwark of the Republic: The American Militia in the Antebellum West* (Westport, CT: Praeger, 2003), 10; Knox to Harmar, September 3, 1790, Henry Knox Papers, LC, PWD (quotation); *New ASPMA* 8:23–30, 77–87; Denny to Knox, January 1, 1791, Goodman Papers, Western Reserve Historical Society Library, PWD. Washington pinned the blame squarely on Harmar: "I expected *little* from the moment I heard he was a *drunkard.* I expected less as soon as I heard that on *this account* no confidence was reposed in him by the people of the Western Country. And I gave up *all hope* of Success, as soon as I heard that there were disputes with *him* about command" (Washington's emphasis throughout). After an embarrassing congressional investigation, Harmar was allowed to retire. *WGW* 31:156.

10. Kohn, *Eagle and Sword*, 108–110; *ASPIA* 1:121–122 (first quotation), 108–113 (second, fourth and fifth quotations); *PTJ* 19:521 (third quotation), 22:416 editorial note); Paul D. Nelson, "General Charles Scott, the Kentucky Mounted Volunteers, and the Northwest Indian Wars, 1784–1794," *Journal of the Early Republic* 6 (Fall 1986): 226–227; Jackson to Knox, February 20, 1791, Knox Papers, Pierpont Morgan Library, PWD; Maclay, ed., *Journal*, 384–385; *Statutes* 1:222–224; *Senate Journal*, 1st Cong., 3rd sess., 1:267–268, 275; *Annals* 1st Cong., 3rd sess., 1804. Linked to the military effort was a promise of a renewed diplomatic push to secure Spain's agreement on navigation rights to the Mississippi. *PTJ* 19:517 editorial note.

11. Maclay, ed., *Journal*, 383, 388–390, 396 (first and second quotations); *PTJ* 20:236; *PAH* 8:124 (third quotation).

12. Knox to Washington, March 19, 1791, M 367, Northwest Territory Collection,

Indiana Historical Society Library, PWD (first, second, and third quotations); Kirkland to Knox, April 22, 1791, Kirkland Papers, Buffalo and Erie County Historical Society, PWD; *ASPIA* 1:171–174 (fourth and fifth quotations); White to Gentlemen, April 26, 1791, roll 116, Shepherd Papers, Draper Manuscripts, LC.

13. Nelson, "General Charles Scott," 219–220, 234 (first quotation); "Extract of a Letter from an Officer . . . 31st August 1791," *American Mercury*, October 6, 1794; "Winthrop Sargent's Diary while with General Arthur St. Clair's Expedition Against the Indians," *Ohio Archaeological and Historical Society Publications* 33 (1924): 242 (second quotation); Newman Diary, August 20, 1791, roll 62, Frontier Wars Papers, Draper Manuscripts, LC; *PTJ* 22:175–177, 442 editorial note (third quotation), 447–448, 462–466, 469, 514, 517; Sword, *Washington's Indian War*, 148–149; Knox to Duer, January 27, 1791, Knox Papers, Pierpont Morgan Library, PWD; William H. Bergmann, *The American National State and the Early West* (Cambridge: Cambridge University Press, 2012), 53–54. Formerly Hamilton's assistant secretary of the treasury, Duer sparked a speculative bubble that, when burst, set off a financial panic in spring 1792. He wound up in jail. Gordon S. Wood, *Empire of Liberty: A History of the Early Republic, 1789–1815* (New York: Oxford University Press, 2009), 152–153.

14. *ASPIA* 1:122, 131–132; William Henry Smith, ed., *The St. Clair Papers: The Life and Public Service of Arthur St. Clair*, 2 vols. (Cincinnati: Robert Clarke, 1882), 2:233–239, 245–246, 262–267 (second quotation); *ASPMA* 1:36–39; Robert S. Allen, *His Majesty's Indian Allies: British Indian Policy in the Defence of Canada, 1774–1815* (Toronto: Dundurn Press, 1992), 74–77 (first quotation); "Winthrop Sargent's Diary," 244–248.

15. Knox to Wilkinson, February 11, March 10, 1791, Wilkinson Papers, Chicago Historical Society, PWD; *ASPIA* 1:197–201 (first quotation); *WGW* 31:450–451 (remaining quotations); *PTJ* 19:517 editorial note; *PAH* 11:108.

16. *Annals* 2nd Cong., 1st sess., 327–329, 337–355 (first quotation); Kohn, *Eagle and Sword*, 122 (second quotation), 126. Anthony Wayne, newly elected representative from Georgia, was listed as one of the speakers opposed to the bill, yet he supported it when the actual vote came. One might presume that this future leader of the new army might have been the object of administration lobbying. Paul David Nelson, *Anthony Wayne: Soldier of the Early Republic* (Bloomington: Indiana University Press, 1985), 222–223.

17. McClure to Knox, September 3, 1792, Knox Papers, Pierpont Morgan Library, PWD; *Annals* 2nd Cong., 1st sess., 80, 84; *Papers of Washington: Presidential Series* 9:554–557; Kohn, *Eagle and Sword*, 122–123; Wayne to Wilkinson, August 5, 1792, Wayne Manuscripts, HSP; *Statutes* 1:241–243, 279–281; *PAH* 12:185–187.

18. *Statutes* 1:271–274; Russell F. Weigley, *History of the United States Army*, Enlarged Edition (Bloomington: Indiana University Press, 1984), 89–90, 93–94; Michael D. Doubler, *Civilian in Peace: Soldier in War: The Army National Guard, 1636–2000* (Lawrence: University Press of Kansas, 2003), 66–69 (quotation).

19. *PTJ* 23:240–242 (quotation); Orders of the Legion, July 21, 24, August 12, 16, 1792, Legion of the United States Papers, USAMHI; Wayne to Knox, August 17, 1792, Wayne Letterbooks, Clements Library, PWD; Knox to Carrington, July

24, 1792, Knox Papers, Virginia Historical Society, PWD; R. C. Knopf, ed., *Campaign into the Wilderness: The Wayne-Knox-Pickering-McHenry Correspondence*, 5 vols. (Columbus: Anthony Wayne Parkway Board, Ohio State Museum, 1955), 1:49, 62–68, 90; Knox to Shelby, July 12, 1792, Wilkinson Papers, Chicago Historical Society, PWD (quotation).

For the origins of legionary formations in the United States, see Knox, "Plan for the General Arrangement of the Militia of the United States," March 18, 1786, Lehrman Collection, Pierpont Morgan Library, PWD; Hutchinson, ed., *Papers of Madison: Congressional Series* 12:220–221; Knox to Wayne, August 9, 1789, Wayne Manuscripts, HSP, PWD; and Andrew J. Birtle, "The Origins of the Legion of the United States," *Journal of Military History* 67 (October 2003): 1249–1262.

20. Thomas P. Slaughter, *The Whiskey Rebellion: Frontier Epilogue to the American Revolution* (New York: Oxford University Press, 1986), 71, 105, 212; *PAH* 12:312 (first quotation), 330–331, 340, 344–347, 390 (second and third quotations). Republicans hoped the success of volunteers and militia in handling the crisis would "be a stumbling block to the advocates for a standing Army." Hutchinson, ed., *Papers of Madison: Congressional Series* 15:386 (quotation), 406.

21. Telfair to Knox, May 8, 1791, Independence Hall Autograph Collection, LC, PWD; *TP* 4:258; Knox to Shelby, July 12, 1791, Wayne Manuscripts, HSP, PWD; *PAH* 14:494–495; *ASPIA* 1:364; *Annals* 2nd Cong., 2nd sess., 750, 762–768, 773–802 (first and second quotations); *Federal Gazette*, January 15, 1793 (third quotation); Wilkinson to Shelby, December 4, 1792, box 2, Shelby Family Papers, LC; Kohn, *Eagle and Sword*, 148. The test vote came just before the vote on the actual bill, which lost by a 36–20 count. Madison joined Steele in the test vote but abstained from voting on the resulting bill.

22. Kohn, *Eagle and Sword*, 148 (first quotation); *North Carolina Journal*, February 20, 1793 (second quotation); Seth Ames, ed., *Works of Fisher Ames, with a Selection from his Speeches and Correspondence* (Boston: Little, Brown and Co., 1854), 126–127 (third quotation); Wayne to Knox, January 24, 1793, Wayne Manuscripts, HSP, PWD (fourth quotation).

23. Gregory Evans Dowd, *A Spirited Resistance: The North American Indian Struggle for Unity, 1745–1816* (Baltimore: Johns Hopkins University Press, 1992), 105–112; House and House to Knox, August 21, 1794, Wayne Letterbooks, Clements Library, PWD; Knopf, ed., *Campaign into the Wilderness* 2:127–135 (quotations).

24. *PTJ* 28:84; *ASPIA* 1:480; Ogden to Knox, May 27, 1794, Knox Papers, Pierpont Morgan Library, PWD; Chapin to Knox, June 7, 1794, O'Reilly Collection, New York Historical Society, PWD; Knox to Chapin, June 12, 1794, U.S. War Department Papers, New York State Library, PWD; *Annals* 3rd Cong., 1st sess., 556–557, 561; *Statutes* 1:345–347, 350–352, 366–367; Knopf, ed., *Campaign into the Wilderness* 3:36–42 (quotations); Slaughter, *Whiskey Rebellion*, 194–195.

For this and subsequent estimates of costs at time of publication of historical spending or investments, see Officer and Williamson, "Explaining the Measures of Worth," and "Seven Ways to Compute the Relative Value of a U.S. Dollar Amount," in www.measuringworth.com/index.php.

25. *PAH* 16:134; Brown to Shelby, March 12, 1794, box 3, Shelby Family Papers,

LC; *PTJ* 28:38 (first quotation), 41 (second quotation), 71–72, 84–86 (third quotation); Hutchinson, ed., *Papers of Madison: Congressional Series* 15:379, 405–407; *MPP* 1:154–155; *Annals* 3rd Cong., 1st sess., 111, 709, 735–740, 773–779; Peter S. Onuf, *Jefferson's Empire: The Language of American Nationhood* (Charlottesville: University Press of Virginia, 2000), 42. See also "A Calm Observer," May 12, 1795, *The Argus, & Greenleaf's New Daily Advertiser.*

26. Knopf, ed., *Campaign into the Wilderness* 3:63–68 (first quotation); *ASPIA* 1:490 (second quotation); Orders of the Legion, August 23, 1794, 136–137, Legion of the United States Papers, USAMHI; O'Hara to Hodgdon, September 9, 1794, Post-Revolutionary War Papers, RG 94, NARA, PWD (third quotation). For the roots of Wilkinson's discontent with Wayne, see Brown to Innes, April 13, 1792, box 1, Innes Papers, LC.

27. *ASPIA* 1:318 (first quotation), 364; *ASPMA* 1:67; Brown to Shelby, July 14, 1793, box 2, Shelby Family Papers, LC; *PTJ* 27:630; Telfair to Knox, May 8, 1793, Independence Hall Autograph Collection, LC, PWD (second and third quotations); *PAH* 14:494–495; Gunn to Knox, June 10, 1793, Knox Papers, Pierpont Morgan Library, PWD; Knox to Gaither, July 17, 1793, Independence Hall Autograph Collection, LC, PWD; Knox to Telfair, September 5, 1793, 3rd Cong., House, Sec. of War Confidential Report, RG 233, NARA, PWD; Colin G. Calloway, *The American Revolution in Indian Country: Crisis and Diversity in Native American Communities* (Cambridge: Cambridge University Press, 1995), 284; E. Merton Coulter, *Georgia: A Short History* (Chapel Hill: University of North Carolina Press, 1947), 183–184.

28. *The Papers of Andrew Jackson*, 10 vols. to date (Knoxville: University of Tennessee Press, 1980-), 1:49 (quotation); *TP* 4:336–338, 355–357, 361–362, 364–370; *ASPMA* 1:67, 75; *ASPIA* 1:531, 539; Grenier, *First Way of War*, 178–181.

29. *ASPMA* 1:68 (first quotation); HD 353, 54th Cong., 2nd sess., serial 3550, 1:967–971, 1007–1009, 1033, 1037, 1041, 1056–1057 (second quotation); *PTJ* 28:9–10; Knox to Wayne, March 31, 1794, Wayne Letterbooks, Clements Library, PWD (third quotation); *PAH* 16:136–137, 140 n. 5 (fourth quotation).

30. *ASP: Foreign Relations* 1:456–457; *TP* 4:337–338; Wood, *Empire of Liberty*, 197–198; George C. Herring, *From Colony to Superpower: U.S. Foreign Relations since 1776* (New York: Oxford University Press, 2008), 79–81.

31. Cayton, "'Separate Interests' and the Nation-State," 53–54; Estimate of the expense . . . for the defensive protection of the frontier . . . during 1790 and 1791, PWD; Henley, General Estimate of Expenses for the defence of the Southwestern Territory for 1793, Post-Revolutionary War Manuscripts, NARA, PWD; O'Hara, Estimate of Quartermaster Stores wanted for the year 1794 for the use of the Western Army, March 5, 1794, Coxe and Irvine Papers, RG 92, NARA, PWD; Estimate for expenditures in the Quartermaster's Dept. at the post of Pittsburgh . . . during the second quarter of the year 1796, April 15, 1796, Craig Papers, Carnegie Library, PWD; Amount of payments made by the Accountant of the War Department in pursuance of warrants issued by the Secretary of War in the years 1794–96 for Militia services performed in the defensive protection of the frontiers of the United States, June 17, 1797, Post-Revolutionary War Manuscripts, RG 94, NARA, PWD; Richard C. Wade, *The Urban Frontier: The Rise of Western Cities, 1790–1830* (Cambridge:

Harvard University Press, 1959), 45, 79; Bergmann, *American National State and the Early West*, 62–64, 70–72, 128–129.

32. "Political Observations, 20 April 1795," Founders Online, NARA https://founders.archives.gov/documents/Madison/01-15-02-0423 (first and second quotations); *ASPIA* 1:543–544 (third and fourth quotations), 525–526; Kohn, *Eagle and Sword*, 176; *Annals* 3rd Cong., 2nd sess., 1122–1126, 1163–1172, 1220–1222 (fifth quotation); Ames, ed., *Works of Ames* 1:166; Hutchinson, ed., *Papers of Madison: Congressional Series* 15:474, 518, 521 (sixth quotation).

33. Kohn, *Eagle and Sword*, 178–183; Ron Chernow, *Washington: A Life* (New York: Penguin Books, 2010), 720–728; *WGW* 34:265; Knox to Wilkinson, December 4, 5, 1795, box 8, Innes Papers, LC; Wilkinson to Innes, December 9, 1794, box 1, ibid.; Wilkinson to Innes, April 16, 1796, box 1, ibid.; Wilkinson to Knox, January 1, 2, 1795, box 8, ibid.; *Annals* 4th Cong., 1st sess., 151–154; "Statement of the present military force of the United States," December 12, 1795, 4th Cong., Senate, SW Reports, RG 46, NARA, PWD; *ASPMA* 1:112–113 (quotation); Pickering to Washington, January 30, 1796, series 4, Washington Papers, LC.

At Wilkinson's bidding, Harry Innes described Wayne "as a man of very moderate abilities, vain, capricious, jealous in the extreme and a Dupe to a few who flatter him." *PTJ* 27:630. See also Wilkinson to Innes, October 23, 1793, July 6, October 13, November 10, 1794, box 1, Innes Papers, LC. In response to Wilkinson's charges, Wayne labeled his rival the "'worst of all bad men.'" Nelson, *Wayne*, 291–295.

34. *Annals* 4th Cong., 1st sess., 906–913 (quotations), 1417–1424, 1462; *ASPMA* 1:114; McHenry to Washington, February 25, 1797, series 4, Washington Papers, LC; *House Journal* 4th Cong., 1st sess., 568–569, 572–573; J. C. A. Stagg, *Mr. Madison's War: Politics, Diplomacy, and Warfare in the Early American Republic, 1783–1830* (Princeton: Princeton University Press, 1983), 128.

35. Kohn, *Eagle and Sword*, 185 (first quotation); *ASPMA* 1:114 (second quotation); Lawrence Cress, *Citizens in Arms: The Army and the Militia in American Society to the War of 1812* (Chapel Hill: University of North Carolina Press, 1982), 132.

36. *Statutes* 1:137–138, 469–473 (quotation); *Annals* 1st Cong., 2nd sess., 1575; Francis Paul Prucha, *American Indian Policy in the Formative Years: The Indian Trade and Intercourse Acts, 1790–1834* (1962; Lincoln: University of Nebraska Press, 1970), 51–52, 60–61.

37. *PAH* 24:40 n. 1; *Statutes* 1:483–486; Washington to McHenry, July 1, 1796, Chase Collection, Dartmouth College Library, PWD; Birtle, "Origins of the Legion," 1260.

3. The Army and the Rise of the Jeffersonians

1. *MPP* 1:323 (quotations); *Annals* 9th Cong., 2nd sess., 332–333; *ASPMA* 1:227–228. For the concept of a multipurpose army, see Michael L. Tate, *The Frontier Army and the Settlement of the West* (Norman: University of Oklahoma Press, 1999).

2. *Annals* 4th Cong., 2nd sess., 1963, 1947, 1951–1962, 1966–1969, 1971, 1982, 2066–2070, 2094, 2328–2332; McHenry to Sir, February 25, 1797, McHenry Papers, Clements Library, PWD; Draft, "Gentlemen of the House of Representatives,"

February 28, 1797, ibid.; *MPP* 1:211–212. An exception to the more moderate trend was Virginia's Robert Rutherford, who denounced a large army as "an evil in any country. . . . Where, said he, are the great characters of 1776? . . . How would Warren and Mercer, with a long train of heroes, now no more, blush for their degraded sons, were they now to behold them in their cry for a Standing Army!" It was a last gasp for the lame-duck Rutherford, who had been defeated in his reelection attempt the previous fall. *Annals* 4th Cong., 2nd sess., 2066, 2086.

3. Richard H. Kohn, *Eagle and Sword: The Federalists and the Creation of the Military Establishment in America, 1782–1802* (New York: Free Press, 1975), xii-xiii; Samuel J. Watson, "The Army Secures the Mississippi Valley: Officers, Filibusters, and Spain, 1793–1798," *Southern Studies: An Interdisciplinary Journal* 20 (Winter 2013–14): 33–63; Hamtramck to McHenry, January 21, 1799, Hamilton Papers, LC, PWD (first quotation); *PAH* 20:509, 545 (second quotation), 21:99, 24:14–15; Aaron N. Coleman, "'A Second Bounaparty?': A Reexamination of Alexander Hamilton during the Franco-American Crisis, 1796–1801," *Journal of the Early Republic* 28 (Summer 2008): 183–214; McHenry to Hamilton, March 14, 1797, McHenry Papers, LC; McHenry, "Copy of a paper delivered to the President this 8th of April 1797," McHenry Papers, LC; "Propositions for Defence, given to Wm. Smith," May 24, 1797, McHenry Papers, Clements Library, PWD; "Sec of War's ideas on defense 1797 commucd. to Mr. Smith," William Loughton Smith Papers, LC; *Annals* 5th Cong., 1st sess., 240; *MPP* 1:228 (third quotation).

For the army's activities in the borderlands between 1796 and 1798, see especially "Evidence of foreign interference to excite Indian Hostility," McHenry Papers, Clements Library, PWD; and *New ASPMA* 4:1–6. In case of war with France, McHenry called for a new regiment of regular artillery, a new regiment of regular infantry, two additional companies of light dragoons, and 10,000 provisional troops. Should France make an alliance with Spain, the nation needed two new regiments of artillerists, two of infantry, six companies of dragoons, and 15,000 contingent troops. Hamilton had initially proposed a provisional force of 25,000.

4. *Annals* 5th Cong., 1st sess., 17–25, 327–328, 343 (first and second quotations), 346–348; Tazewell to unknown, January 20, 1796, Tazewell Papers, LC; Tazewell to Cocke, June 7, 1797, ibid. (third quotation); *Statutes* 1:522; *PTJ* 29:421, 423, 433; Kohn, *Eagle and Sword*, 222–223.

5. *WGW* 35:490–492; Ron Chernow, *Alexander Hamilton* (New York: Penguin Books, 2010), 546; McHenry to Forrest, November 26, 1797, McHenry Papers, Clements Library, PWD; McHenry to Craig, January 5, 1798, ibid.; McHenry to Adams, February 15, 1798, Adams Papers, Massachusetts Historical Society, PWD (quotation). Before responding to Adams, McHenry had queried Hamilton, who advised 20,000 regulars and 30,000 provisional troops.

6. Adams to Smith, January 10, 1798, July 18, 1798 (first quotation), William L. Smith Papers, LC; McHenry to Smith, April 2, 1798, ibid.; Hindman to McHenry, August 12, 1798, McHenry Family Papers, MdHS, PWD (second and third quotations); *PAH* 22:163–164, 452–453, 23:122–123, 24:32; Lawrence Cress, *Citizens in Arms: The Army and the Militia in American Society to the War of 1812* (Chapel Hill: University of North Carolina Press, 1982), 143; McHenry to Smith, October

20, 1798, William L. Smith Papers, LC; *Annals* 5th Cong., 2nd sess., 1988–1989, 2092–2093; Gordon S. Wood, *Empire of Liberty: A History of the Early Republic, 1789–1815* (New York: Oxford University Press, 2009), 246–267; Kohn, *Eagle and Sword*, 214–219; Coleman, "'Second Bounaparty,'" 187–195; *Statutes* 1:552–554 (quotation), 604–605.

Republican Senator Henry Tazewell lamented the high degree of absenteeism among his House colleagues. "The shameful dereliction of their stations by many of the republican members has rendered any attempt to prevent war measures quite useless. From our State [Virginia] Nicholas, Giles, Cabell, Clay, Mackie, and Parker are absent. Many more from other states." Tazewell to Page, June 17, 1798, Tazewell Papers, LC. Of these men, only John Nicholas and Josiah Parker voted on the New Army, with Parker in favor and Nicholas opposed.

7. McHenry to Adams, June 29, 1799, Adams Papers, Massachusetts Historical Society, PWD (quotations); *PAH* 22:4–17, 24.

8. *PAH* 22:37–38, 56–59, 62–65; *WGW* 36:441–443 (quotation); Adams to McHenry, July 6, 1798, McHenry Papers, Huntington Library, PWD; *WGW* 36:323–327, 329–335, 356–360, 447–448, 453–462; John Ferling, *John Adams: A Life* (Knoxville: University of Tennessee Press, 1992), 357–361, 368–369.

9. McHenry to Adams, August 4, 1798, Stephen Raphel Papers, MdHS, PWD; *WGW* 36:333–334 (first quotation), 411–412, 488–493; McHenry to Washington, May 2, 1799, McHenry Collection, MdHS, PWD; McHenry to Sir, April 10, 1798, McHenry Papers, Clements Library; Gilman to McHenry, May 22, 1799, ibid.; W. W. Abbott, ed., *The Papers of George Washington: Retirement Series*, 4 vols. (Charlottesville: University Press of Virginia, 1998–1999), 3:35, 59 (second and third quotations), 128–129, 134–135; McHenry to Dayton, November 19, 1798, HSP, PWD; McHenry to Smith, November 30, 1798, William L. Smith Papers, LC; *PAH* 22:355–356, 466–467 (fourth quotation); Robert Gough, "Officering the American Army, 1798," *William and Mary Quarterly* 43 (July 1986): 465; Kohn, *Eagle and Sword*, 244.

10. Chernow, *Hamilton*, 562–568; Coleman, "'Second Bounaparty,'" 203–207; *PAH* 22:374–375, 381–382, 409, 422–425, 433–434, 441, 469–471; 23:25, 46–47, 186–187, 227, 323–324, 377–393, 402–407, 417–420, 515–522, 534–537, 549–550, 599–604; 24:81–82; Wolcott to Smith, November 29, 1798, William L. Smith Papers, LC; McHenry to Smith, November 30, 1798, ibid.; *Annals* 5th Cong., 3rd sess., 2224, 2237, 2926, 3022–3044; *Statutes* 1:725–726 (quotations); Noble E. Cunningham, ed., *Circular Letters of Congressmen to Their Constituents, 1789–1829*, 3 vols. (Chapel Hill: University of North Carolina Press, 1978), 1:166; Kohn, *Eagle and Sword*, 252.

11. Barbara Oberg and J. Jefferson Looney, eds., *The Papers of Jefferson, Digital Edition* (Charlottesville: University of Virginia Press, Rotunda, 2008), 30:434; Tazewell to Cocke, March 17, 24, 1798, Tazewell Papers, LC; Tazewell to Page, April 6, 1798, ibid.; Tazewell to Ambler, May 20, 1798, ibid.; *Annals* 5th Cong., 2nd sess., 1632–1634 (first quotation), 1638–1641 (second quotation), 1760 (third quotation), 1651–1653 (fourth quotation), 1648 (fifth quotation), 1746; Tazewell to Ambler, May 9, 1798, Tazewell Papers, LC (sixth quotation); *Centinel of Freedom*, October 1, 1799; *New London Bee*, August 28, 1799 (seventh quotation); *Aurora General Advertiser*,

April 2, 1798 (eighth and ninth quotations). For the best assessment of Republican thought during the period, see Cress, *Citizens in Arms*, 137–143.

12. McHenry to Adams, March 16, 1799, Adams Papers, Massachusetts Historical Society, PWD; Adams to McHenry, April 5, 1799, ibid.; McHenry to MacPherson, March 21, 1799, 6th Cong., Senate, Executive Messages, RG 46, NARA, PWD; Theodore J. Crackel, *Mr. Jefferson's Army: Political and Social Reform of the Military Establishment, 1801–1809* (New York: New York University Press, 1987), 21–25 (quotation); *PAH* 22:539–541, 552–553, 23:280–281.

13. Heitman, 2:563–567; Kohn, *Eagle and Sword*, 248–249; *WGW* 37:157–164; *PAH* 22:469–471, 23:1, 325–327, 371–372; 24:552–565; Ferling, *Adams*, 355 (first quotation); McHenry to Adams, October 22, 1797, November 25, 1798, Adams Papers, Massachusetts Historical Society, PWD; *MPP* 1:250–254; Charles Francis Adams, ed., *The Works of John Adams, Second President of the United States*, 10 vols. (Boston: Little, Brown, 1850–1856), 9:290; Wood, *Empire of Liberty*, 264 (second quotation), 272–274; Abigail to John Adams, January 12, 1799, Adams Family Papers; McHenry to Adams, July 12, 1799, McHenry Papers, LC; Lester J. Cappon, ed., *The Adams-Jefferson Letters: The Complete Correspondence between Thomas Jefferson and Abigail and John Adams* (Chapel Hill: University of North Carolina Press, 1959), 583.

14. Adams, ed., *Works of John Adams* 9:290; Hodgdon to Craig, January 24, 1799, Robertson Papers, Tennessee State Library and Archives, PWD; *New London Bee*, May 8, 1799 (first quotation); Charles T. Cullen and Leslie Tobias, eds., *The Papers of John Marshall*, vol. 4: *Correspondence and Papers, January 1799–October 1800* (Chapel Hill: University of North Carolina Press, 2015), 76; *Annals* 6th Cong., 1st sess., 247–370 (second and third quotations 298), 425; *PAH* 24:219–220, 236–237; *Statutes* 2:85–86; Cunningham, ed., *Circular Letters* 1:158–226; Kohn, *Eagle and Sword*, 266–267; William T. Hutchinson, et al., eds., *The Papers of James Madison: Congressional Series*, 17 vols. (Chicago and Charlottesville: University of Chicago Press and University Press of Virginia, 1962–1991), 17:382; Wood, *Empire of Liberty*, 267–268; Amendment I, Vol. 5, Document 21, *FC*, http://press-pubs.uchicago.edu/founders/print_documents/amendI_speechs21.html.

In December 1800, the Federalist lame-duck Congress blocked an attempt to reduce one of the artillery regiments from four to three battalions. *Annals* 6th Cong., 2nd sess., 825–826.

15. "Draft Constitution for Virginia 1776," Avalon Project, Yale Law School, http://avalon.law.yale.edu/18th_century/jeffcons.asp (first quotation); Jefferson to Madison, December 20, 1787, Series 1, Jefferson Papers, LC; Heitman, 2:568; Crackel, *Mr. Jefferson's Army*, 34–35; Jefferson to Lewis, February 23, 1801, Series 1, Jefferson Papers, LC (second quotation); Donald Jackson, "Jefferson, Meriwether Lewis, and the Reduction of the United States Army," *Proceedings of the American Philosophical Society* 124 (June 1980): 91–96.

16. Samuel J. Watson, "Surprisingly Professional: Trajectories in Army Officer Corps Drawdowns, 1783–1848," in *Drawdown: The American Way of Postwar*, ed. Jason W. Warren (New York: New York University Press, 2016): 73–106; Jefferson to Macon, May 14, 1801, Series 1, Jefferson Papers, LC (quotation); *PAH* 24:185–192;

Simmons to McHenry, March 20, April 25, 1800, Letterbook, War Dept. Accountant, RG 217, NARA, PWD; "About the Papers of the War Department: Project Overview," PWD; *PTJ* 33:5–6, 34:96; Peter Onuf, *The Mind of Thomas Jefferson* (Charlottesville: University of Virginia Press, 2007), 127, 133; Edward M. Coffman, *The Old Army: A Portrait of the American Army in Peacetime, 1784–1898* (New York: Oxford University Press, 1986), 8; *New ASPMA* 8:2; Bissell to Bissell, July 9, 1801, box 2, Kingsbury Papers, LC; Dearborn to Perkin and Ames, June 2, 1801, roll 1, M 370, Miscellaneous LS by the SW, NARA; Dearborn to Ames, December 17, 1801, ibid.; Dearborn to Hobby, December 1, 1801, ibid.; Dearborn to Heath, et al, March 26, April 30, 1801, ibid.; SED 196, 47th Cong., 1st sess., serial 1992, 591, 603.

17. Jefferson to Duane, July 24, 1803, Series 1, Jefferson Papers, LC (quotation); Theodore J. Crackel, "The Military Academy in the Context of Jeffersonian Reform," in *Thomas Jefferson's Military Academy: Founding West Point*, ed. Robert M. S. McDonald (Charlottesville: University of Virginia Press, 2004), 108–111; Crackel, *Mr. Jefferson's Army*, 39, 49–50; *MPP* 1:329; *ASPMA* 1:133, 139, 155–157.

18. Heitman, 2:568–569; *Annals* 7th Cong., 1st sess., 196, 417, 426–431; J. C. A. Stagg, *Mr. Madison's War: Politics, Diplomacy, and Warfare in the Early American Republic, 1783–1830* (Princeton: Princeton University Press, 1983), 130–131; *Statutes* 2:86, 137 (quotation); *ASPMA* 1:155, 177; Samuel J. Watson, "Trusting to 'the Chapter of Accidents': Contingency, Necessity, and Self-Constraint in Jeffersonian National Security Policy," *Journal of Military History* 76 (October 2012): 978–980; Coffman, *Old Army*, 8; Cunningham, ed., *Circular Letters* 1:276, 305; *The Statistical History of the United States: From Colonial Times to the Present* (New York: Basic Books, 1976), 8, 1114–1115. Crackel, *Mr. Jefferson's Army*, 44–46, suggests fewer spending reductions. Actually, the army had only about four thousand men in service.

19. Crackel, *Mr. Jefferson's Army*, 42, 44, 49–50, 193 n. 3; Watson, "Surprisingly Professional;" *PTJ* 34:629–630 (quotations); Peter S. Onuf and Jeffrey L. Hantman, "Introduction," in *Across the Continent: Jefferson, Lewis and Clark, and the Making of America*, ed. Douglas Seefeldt, Jeffrey L. Hantman, and Peter S. Onuf (Charlottesville: University of Virginia Press, 2005), 11–12; William B. Skelton, *An American Profession of Arms: The Army Officer Corps, 1784–1861* (Lawrence: University Press of Kansas, 1992), 25, 73–74, argues that the Republicanization of the officer corps did not come until the army expansion of 1808.

20. *PTJ* 34:21–23; Crackel, *Mr. Jefferson's Army*, 42 (first quotation), 48–53 (second and third quotations), 74; Jackson, "Jefferson, Meriwether Lewis," 96.

21. Preble to Stoddard, September 6, 1801, vol. 4, Preble Papers, LC; Crackel, *Mr. Jefferson's Army*, 47–50 (quotation); Coffman, *Old Army*, 10; "From the Washington Federalist," *Republican or, Anti-Democrat*, April 3, 1802. On the eve of the reductions in force, Dearborn claimed that "merit alone" would determine the fate of the army's commissioned personnel. Dearborn to Wilkinson, February 22, 1802, roll 1, M15, LS by the SW Relating to Indian Affairs, RG 75, NARA. See also Watson, "Surprisingly Professional."

22. Dearborn to Eustis, 2 May 1808, roll 1, Eustis Papers, LC; Bruff to Nicholson, March 29, 1806, box 3, Nicholson Papers, LC (quotation); *PTJ* 27:428, 453–454;

Crackel, *Mr. Jefferson's Army*, 55–57; Onuf, *Mind of Jefferson*, 171, 175; David N. Mayer, "'Necessary and Proper': West Point and Thomas Jefferson's Constitutionalism," in *Thomas Jefferson's Military Academy: Founding West Point*, ed. Robert M. S. McDonald (Charlottesville: University of Virginia Press, 2004), 63–64, 69–70; Jennings L. Wagoner Jr., and Christine Coalwell McDonald, "Mr. Jefferson's Academy," ibid., 118–130; Ian Hope, *A Scientific Way of War: Antebellum Military Science, West Point, and the Origins of American Military Thought* (Lincoln: University of Nebraska Press, 2015), 35. Reginald C. Stuart, *Civil-Military Relations During the War of 1812* (Santa Barbara, CA: Praeger, 2009), 40–41, points out that Jefferson drew heavily on the ideas of Joseph Priestly.

For earlier Federalist proposals regarding a military academy, see *JCC* 5:838, 6:860; *LDC* 4:116, 5:261; Knox to Wilkinson, July 17, 1792, Wayne Manuscripts, HSP; *MPP* 1:140, 212; *PAH* 22:28–29, 521; 23:417–420, 591–598; 24:69–71, 236–237; *ASPMA* 1:133–139, 142–144; *New ASPMA* 16:271–273; McHenry to Otis, February 11, 1800, McHenry Papers, Clements Library; Dexter to Adams, July 16, August 4, 1800, Adams Papers, Massachusetts Historical Society, PWD; Adams to Dexter, August 13, 1800, ibid.

23. Hope, *Scientific Way of War*, 34–36; Crackel, *Mr. Jefferson's Army*, 56–57; Wagoner and McDonald, "Mr. Jefferson's Academy," 134–135; *PAH* 23:205, 259–260; Jefferson to Williams, July 3, 1796, Series 1, Jefferson Papers, LC; Williams to Jefferson, March 7, 1801, ibid.

24. Wagoner and McDonald, "Mr. Jefferson's Academy," 135–141; Sidney Foreman, "The United States Military Philosophical Society, 1802–1813," *William and Mary Quarterly* 2 (July 1945): 273–285; "Constitution of the United States Military Philosophical Society," November 12, 1802, Series 1, Jefferson Papers, LC (first quotation); Williams to Jefferson, December 12, 1802 (second and third quotations), June 18, 1805, February 3, May 28, August [n.d.], November 15, 1806, June 12, 1807, January 18, September 20, October 24, 31, 1808, ibid.; Jefferson to Williams, December 23, 1802, July 14, 1805, February 23, 1806, January 3, 21, October 28, November 23, 1808, February 23, 1809, ibid.; *MPP* 1:379, 409–410, 445; Peter Michael Molloy, "Technical Education and the Young Republic: West Point, America's Ecole Polytechnique, 1802–1833" (Ph.D. diss., Brown University, 1975), 310–311; *PTJ* 33:275–276, 280–281. Jefferson remained a dues-paying member of the society throughout his presidency. Williams to Jefferson, June 28, 1805, Series 1, Jefferson Papers, LC.

25. Peter S. Onuf, *Jefferson's Empire: The Language of American Nationhood* (Charlottesville: University Press of Virginia, 2000), 70; Onuf, *Mind of Jefferson*, 112–116, 124–126; James E. Lewis, "A Tornado on the Horizon: The Jefferson Administration, the Retrocession Crisis, and the Louisiana Purchase," in *Empires of the Imagination: Transatlantic Histories of the Louisiana Purchase*, ed. Peter J. Kasor and François Weil (Charlottesville: University of Virginia Press, 2009), 118 (first quotation); *PTJ* 33:5–6; *MPP* 1:326, 352–354 (second quotation); Robert Wooster, *The American Military Frontiers: The United States Army in the West, 1783–1900* (Albuquerque: University of New Mexico Press, 2009), 28–30; Dearborn to Meigs,

October 23, 1801, roll 1, M 370, Miscellaneous LS by the SW, RG 107, NARA; Dearborn to Harrison, December 22, 1801, roll 1, M 15, LS by the SW Relating to Indian Affairs, RG 75, NARA; *MPP* 1:352–354 (third quotation).

26. *ASPMA* 1:176–177; Mary A. Hackett, et al., eds., *The Papers of James Madison: Secretary of State Series*, vol. 8 (Charlottesville: University of Virginia Press, 2007), 279 (first and quotations); *TP* 9:499–504 (third and fourth quotations); Tommy R. Young II, "The United States Army and the Institution of Slavery in Louisiana," *Louisiana Studies* 13 (Fall 1974): 201–222.

27. Stoddard to Preble, August 25, 1801, vol. 4, Preble Papers, LC (first quotation); Skelton, *American Profession of Arms*, 78; Prucha, *Sword of the Republic*, 70–73 (second quotation); *TP* 13:5 (third quotation), 267–268; Crackel, *Mr. Jefferson's Army*, 102–104, 109–110; Jefferson to Smith, May 4, 1806, Series I, Jefferson Papers, LC.

28. Crackel, *Mr. Jefferson's Army*, 127–132, 153–160; Skelton, *American Profession of Arms*, 80–81; Burwell Diary, 39, LC; Macon to Nicholson, January 6, 1807, box 3, Nicholson Papers, LC; *New York Herald*, January 14, 1807; *People's Friend and Daily Advertiser*, January 15, 1807; *American Citizen*, January 16, 1807; Dearborn to Jefferson, March 23, 1807, Series 1, Jefferson Papers, LC; Jefferson to Dearborn, March 29, 1807, ibid. (quotations). Skelton identifies those with the closest association to the Burr conspiracy as Capt. William L. Cooper, Capt. Daniel Bissell, Lt. Josiah Taylor, and Ensign William C. Meade. Crackel singles out Ensign William C. Meade and Lt. George Washington Sevier. For the most authoritative account, see James E. Lewis, *The Burr Conspiracy: Uncovering the Story of an Early American Crisis* (Princeton: Princeton University Press, 2017).

29. William C. Banks and Stephen Dycus, *Soldiers on the Home Front: The Domestic Role of the American Military* (Cambridge: Harvard University Press, 2016), 53; *Statutes* 2:443 (first quotation): *Annals* 9th Cong., 1st sess., 1120–1121, 2nd sess., 332–333; *MPP* 1:384–385, 405–406, 410; Everett S. Brown, ed., *William Plumer's Memorandum of Proceedings in the United States Senate, 1803–1807* (New York: Macmillan Co., 1923), 153 (second quotation). For Federalist opposition, see Cunningham, ed., *Circular Letters* 1:467.

30. *Annals* 9th Cong., 2nd sess., 31, 36, 342–359 (first, second, and third quotations), 362–374 (fourth quotation), 616, 68; *New ASPMA* 4:10, 12. The only Federalist to enter the verbal deliberations was Connecticut's Benjamin Tallmadge, a Continental Army veteran who described the militia as "a broken reed, which could not be depended on." *Annals* 9th Cong., 2nd sess., 362–374.

31. Crackel, *Mr. Jefferson's Army*, 161; Henry Adams, ed., *The Writings of Albert Gallatin*, 3 vols. (Philadelphia: J. B. Lippincott, 1879), 1:340–353; Dearborn to Jefferson, August 7, 1807, Series 1, Jefferson Papers, LC; *Aurora General Advertiser*, November 2, 1807 (quotation); *MPP* 1:429 (first quotation); Jefferson to Smith, July 30, 1807, Series 1, Jefferson Papers, LC; Jefferson to Taylor, August 1, 1807, ibid.; Jefferson to Dearborn, August 9, 1807, ibid.; Skelton, *American Profession of Arms*, 82; Robert W. Coakley, *The Role of Federal Military Forces in Domestic Disorders, 1789–1878* (Washington, D.C.: Center of Military History, 1988), 84–90; Dearborn to Governors, August 3, 1807, roll 3, M 370, Miscellaneous LS by the SW, RG 109,

NARA; Randolph to Nicholson, June 28, 1807, box 3, Nicholson Papers, LC (second quotation); *Statutes* 2:451; *Annals* 10th Cong., 1st sess., 1224–1228, 1395–1396, 1398–1399 (third and fourth quotations), 1522–1523.

32. Jefferson to Cabinet, February 18, 1808, Series 1, Jefferson Papers, LC; *MPP* 1:428–429; *ASPMA* 1:227–228; *Annals* 10th Cong., 1st sess., 1691–1692, 2062, 2849; Macon to Nicholson, March 28, April 4, 6, 8, 11 (quotations) 1808, box 4, Nicholson Papers, LC.

33. Cunningham, ed., *Circular Letters* 2:545 (first quotation), 561–562 (second quotation), 596 (third, fourth, and fifth quotations), 569 (sixth quotation), 537 (seventh quotation), 575.

34. Skelton, *American Profession of Arms*, 29; Dearborn to Eustis, May 2, 14 (first quotation), 1808, roll 1, Eustis Papers, LC; Dearborn to Varnum, May 10 (second and seventh quotations), June 12, 1810, Dearborn Papers, LC; *Commercial Gazette*, July 14, 1808 (third quotation); *Memoirs of Lieut.-General Scott: Written by Himself* (New York: Sheldon and Co., 1864), 1:35–36 (fourth, fifth, and sixth quotations); Heitman, 1:375.

35. Skelton, *American Profession of Arms*, 86; Orderly Book, February 19, 1801, Wilkinson Papers, LC (first quotation); General Orders, September 26, 1804, roll 3, M 654, Gen. James Wilkinson's Order Book, RG 94, NARA (second quotation); Crackel, *Mr. Jefferson's Army*, 172–177 (fourth and fifth quotations); Jefferson to Wilkinson, August 30, 1808, Series 1, Jefferson Papers, LC; Duane to Jefferson, February 28, 1809, ibid. (third quotation); Hanson to Harper, February 7, 1809, March 3, 1810, Harper Papers, LC.

36. Watson, "Trusting to 'the Chapter of Accidents,'" 978–1000; Patterson to Nicholas, May 21, 1808, box 2, Nicholas Papers, LC; SD 209, 57th Cong., 2nd sess., serial 4430, 51–53; *Statutes* 2:510, 528; *Statistical History*, 8, 1114–1115.

4. President Madison's Army

1. Max Farrand, ed., *The Records of the Federal Convention of 1787*, 4 vols. (New Haven: Yale University Press, 1966), 1:464–465 (first and second quotations); "Political Observations, 20 April 1795," Founders Online, Correspondence and Other Writings of Six Major Shapers of the United States, NARA (third and fourth quotations) https://founders.archives.gov/documents/Madison/01-15-02-0423; "Political Reflections," *Philadelphia Aurora*, February 23, 1799 (fifth quotation); Barbara Oberg and J. Jefferson Looney, eds., *The Papers of Jefferson Digital Edition, Main Series* (Charlottesville: University of Virginia Press, Rotunda, 2008), 36:19, note; J. C. A. Stagg, *Mr. Madison's War: Politics, Diplomacy, and Warfare in the Early American Republic, 1783–1830* (Princeton: Princeton University Press, 1983), 126; Andrew Burstein and Nancy Isenberg, *Madison and Jefferson* (New York: Random House, 2010), 468; *MPP* 1:468 (sixth quotation).

2. *ASPMA* 1:252–253; *MPP* 1:486–487 (quotation).

3. *ASPMA* 1:268–295 (first quotation 269); Robert A. Rutland, et al., eds., *The Papers of James Madison: Presidential Series*, 10 vols. (Charlottesville: University of Virginia Press, 1984–2020), 2:189 (second quotation); John Maass, "'Humanity

Mourns over Such a Site': The Army's Disaster at Terre aux Boeufs, 1809," *Army History* 85 (Fall 2012): 6–23; Samuel J. Watson, "Developing 'Republican Machines': West Point and the Struggle to Render the Officer Corps Safe for America, 1802–1833," in *Thomas Jefferson's Military Academy: Founding West Point*, ed. Robert M. S. McDonald (Charlottesville: University of Virginia Press, 2004), 160; *ASP: Foreign Affairs* 3:397–398; James G. Cusick, *The Other War of 1812: The Patriot War and the American Invasion of Spanish East Florida* (Gainesville: University Press of Florida, 2003), 33–35; J. S. A. Stagg, "James Madison and George Mathews: The East Florida Revolution of 1812 Reconsidered," *Diplomatic History* 30 (January 2006): 23–55; Samuel J. Watson, *Jackson's Sword: The Officer Corps on the American Frontier, 1810–1821* (Lawrence: University Press of Kansas, 2012), 64–66 (third and fourth quotations); *Statutes* 3:472.

4. Watson, *Jackson's Sword*, 42–58.

5. *ASPMA* 1:256–257; Stagg, *Mr. Madison's War*, 140, 142–143; Theodore J. Crackel, *Mr. Jefferson's Army: Political and Social Reform of the Military Establishment, 1801–1809* (New York: New York University Press, 1987),182; Watson, "Developing 'Republican Machines,'" 159–160; "A Militia-Man," *Balance and State Journal*, December 28, 1810.

6. *MPP* 1:470 (first quotation), 476 (second quotation), 478–479.

7. Harry L. Coles, "From Peaceable Coercion to Balanced Forces, 1807–1815," in *Against All Enemies: Interpretations of American Military History from Colonial Times to the Present*, ed. Kenneth J. Hagan and William R. Roberts (Westport, CT: Greenwood Press, 1986), 79; *Annals* 11th Cong., 2nd sess., Appendix, 2185–2190; 2nd sess., 1863 (first quotation), 1879, 1883; Noble E. Cunningham, ed., *Circular Letters of Congressmen to Their Constituents, 1789–1829* (Chapel Hill: University of North Carolina Press, 1978), 2:700, 704, 739–741 (second and third quotations); C. Edward Skeen, *Citizen Soldiers in the War of 1812* (Lexington: University Press of Kentucky, 1999), 11; Stagg, *Mr. Madison's War*, 142–143; *ASPMA* 1:256 (fourth quotation). The measure calling for army reductions passed by an 81–31 count; a similar bill recommending naval reductions passed by a smaller 65–46 margin. For other calls for militia reform, see Logan Esarey, ed., *Governors Messages and Letters: Messages and Letters of William Henry Harrison*, 2 vols. (Indianapolis: Indiana Historical Commission, 1922), 1:407–417.

8. Stagg, *Mr. Madison's War*, 143; William H. Bergmann, *The American National State and the Early West* (Cambridge: Cambridge University Press, 2012), 222–226, 234–236; Esarey, ed., *Messages and Letters of Harrison* 1:224, 417, 433–434, 571, 614–615 (quotation); Gregory Evans Dowd, *A Spirited Resistance: The North American Indian Struggle for Unity, 1745–1816* (Baltimore: Johns Hopkins University Press, 1992), 143–146; Muster Rolls and Payrolls of Militia and Regular Army Organizations in the Battle of Tippecanoe, November 1811, T1085, RG 94, NARA; *ASPIA* 1:776–779.

9. *ASPMA* 1:776; *MPP* 1:494 (first and second quotations); *Annals* 12th Cong., 1st sess., 15–17, 30, 35, 39–41 (third quotation), 52, 54–60 (fourth quotation), 68 (fifth quotation), 83–85, 691. Four days after the House vote, Randolph, who had opposed the additional forces, put forth a measure to employ the troops on public

works projects. "Let not gentleman deceive themselves—the army of the present day is not the army of the Revolution. General Wilkinson is not General Washington. A more corrupt military body never existed than this Praetorian band." His colleagues rejected the proposal by a 15–102 margin. *Annals* 12th Cong., 1st sess., 726–728.

10. *Annals* 12th Cong., 1st sess., 108–112 (first quotation), 1069, 1376 (third and fourth quotations); *Statutes* 1:676, 696–697, 732–733; Donald R. Hickey, *The War of 1812: A Forgotten Conflict* (Urbana: University of Illinois Press, 1989), 33; Madison to Jefferson, February 7, 1812, Series 1, Madison Papers, LC (second quotation); Rutland, ed., *Papers of Madison: Presidential Series* 4:308, 332, 391–392.

11. *Annals* 12th Cong., 1st sess., 731 (first quotation); M. L. Weems and P[eter] Horry, *The Life of Gen. Francis Marion, a Celebrated Partisan Officer in the Revolutionary War* (1809?; rpt. Philadelphia: Joseph Allen, 1833), 245 (second quotation); Esarey, ed., *Messages and Letters of Harrison* 1:402–403 (third quotation); *ASPMA* 1:239, 298, 331, 264–265 (fourth quotation); Timothy Crabshaw, [pseud.], "The Militia Muster: In a Letter to a Friend," *The Port Folio* (November 1817): 395–399.

12. *New ASPMA* 5:6; *ASPMA* 1:320; "Washington City," *National Intelligencer*, March 19, 1812; Stagg, *Mr. Madison's War*, 164–165, 170–176; Izard to Adj. Gen., May 15, 1812, M566, LR Office of the Adjutant General, 1805–1821, RG 94, NARA; Madison to Jefferson, August 17, 1812, Madison Papers, LC; Lewis to Madison, August 21, 1812, ibid.; *The Papers of Andrew Jackson*, 10 vols. to date (Knoxville: University of Tennessee Press, 1980-), 2:283.

13. Stagg, *Mr. Madison's War*, 165–166 (first quotation); Rutland, ed., *Papers of Madison: Presidential Series* 4:440–441 (second and third quotations), 4:258 (fourth quotation), 4:262–263 (fifth quotation), 4:273–274 (sixth quotation).

14. Hickey, *War of 1812*, 46; Madison to Nicholas, April 2, 1813, Madison Papers, LC; Hull to Eustis, August 4, 1812, H-336, roll 45, M221, LRSW, RG 107, NARA; Hull to Eustis, August 8, 1812, H-329, ibid.; Hull to Eustis, August 26, 1812, H-361, ibid.; William C. Wood, ed., *Select British Documents of the Canadian War of 1812*, 3 vols. (1920–1928; rpt. New York: Greenwood Press, 1968), 1:461–463; Van Rensselaer to Dearborn, October 14, 1812, D-209, roll 43, M221, LRSW, RG 107, NARA; Rutland, ed., *Papers of Madison: Presidential Series* 5:158, 331 (quotation), 6:664–665; Stagg, *Mr. Madison's War*, 259; *ASPMA* 1:322–326.

15. [Thomas O'Connor], *Impartial and Correct History of the War between the United States of America and Great Britain* (New York: John Low, 1815), 34 (first quotation); "Washington City," *Daily National Intelligencer*, December 22, 1812 (second and third quotations); Untitled, *Daily National Intelligencer*, January 28, 1813; Gallatin to Jefferson, December 18, 1812, Jefferson Papers, LC (fourth quotation).

16. Stagg, *Mr. Madison's War*, 272–273, 283; *The Papers of Henry Clay*, 10 vols. (Lexington: University of Kentucky Press, 1959–1991), 1:750 (first quotation); *The Papers of John C. Calhoun*, 28 vols. (Columbia: University of South Carolina Press, 1959–2003), 1:146–147; Lowndes to Dear Sir, December 23, 1812, Lowndes Papers, LC; Rutland, ed., *Papers of Madison: Presidential Series* 5:557–558; Skeen, *Citizen Soldiers*, 21; *Annals* 12th Cong., 2nd sess., 537–539 (second and third quotations).

17. Lowndes to Dear Sir, January 16, 1813, Lowndes Papers, LC; Gallatin to Madison, March 5, 1813, Madison Papers, LC; *Annals* 13th Cong., 1st sess., 540–544

(quotations); Hickey, *War of 1812*, lists 30,000 men in uniform in spring 1813, whereas Russell F. Weigley, *History of the United States Army*, Enlarged Edition (Bloomington: Indiana University Press, 1984), 120, estimates about 20,000 at the end of that year.

18. Harrison to Armstrong, October 9, 1813, roll 8, M222, LR by the SW, Unregistered Series, RG 107, NARA; Esarey, ed., *Messages and Letters of Harrison* 2:442–447, 651–653; "Militia Patriotism and Bravery," *Daily National Intelligencer*, October 28, 1813 (first quotation); *ASPMA* 1:487–488 (second and third quotations). "Our army is full of men, fresh from lawyers shops & counting rooms, who know little of the physical force of man—of the proper means of sustaining & improving it—or even the mode of its application," complained Porter. "With them, the whole of the military art consists in knowing how to maneuver a regiment—how to form & deploy a column, and the scientific shape in which their troops are to be represented, to meet a give movement or position of the enemy," he continued. "With these requirements they are sent out in quest of adventures, without object or design; without knowing where they are to go—what to do—or when return. The result is obvious. They break their heads against wind mills." Porter to Armstrong, July 27, 1813, roll 9, M222, LR by the SW, Unregistered Series, RG 107, NARA.

19. Armstrong to Madison, December 5, 1813, Madison Papers, LC; Stagg, *Mr. Madison's War*, 366–368, 374; *MPP* 1:538; "An Officer of the Army," *Columbian Patriot*, December 15, 1813, reprinting an article from the *Albany Argus*; "A Militia Soldier," *Albany Register*, December 17, 1813; "Events of the War," *Niles' Weekly Register*, December 18, 1813; Monroe to Madison, December 27, 1813, Madison Papers, LC (quotation); "Militia Patriotism and Bravery," *Daily National Intelligencer*, October 28, 1813.

20. Robert S. Quimby, *U.S. Army in the War of 1812: An Operational and Command Study* (East Lansing: Michigan State University Press, 1997), 498; Brown to Williams, December 13, 1813, Brown Papers, Clements Library (first and second quotations); Scott to Brown, May 23, 1814, ibid. (third quotation); Scott to Irvine, May 27, 1814, Scott Papers, Clements Library; Brown to Armstrong, July 7, August 7, 1814, Brown Papers, LC.

21. *Memoirs of Lieut.-Gen. Scott, Written by Himself* (New York: Sheldon and Co., 1864), 1:118–121 (first three quotations); Quimby, *U.S. Army in the War of 1812*, 497–545 (fourth quotation 526); Timothy D. Johnson, *Winfield Scott: The Quest for Military Glory* (Lawrence: University Press of Kansas, 1998), 47–61; "Battle of Chippewa," *Niles' Weekly Register*, August 6, 1814, 6:399–401. For Scott's excesses in describing the camp of instruction, see Quimby, *U.S. Army in the War of 1812*, 581–582 n. 70. My special thanks to Samuel J. Watson for his wise insistence that the Niagara campaigns merited greater attention than I had originally given them.

22. Beatty to Kingsbury, September 16, 1814, vol. 3, Kingsbury Papers, LC (fifth quotation). Madison attempted to define his relationship with the War Department in "For the Department of War," August 13, 1814, Series III, roll 27, Madison Papers, LC.

23. Stagg, *Mr. Madison's War*, 457–458; *ASPMA* 1:514–517; *Annals* 13th Cong., 3rd sess., 538 (first and second quotations), 817 (third quotation); Desha to Shelby,

December 9, 1814, box 5, Desha Papers, LC; "From the Political Examiner," *Daily National Intelligencer*, October 27, 1814. For Armstrong's defense of his own actions and criticisms of Monroe, see Armstrong to Madison, September 4, 1814, Madison Papers, LC; Armstrong to Desha, 16 January, March 6, 1815, box 1, Desha Papers, LC. For one governor's efforts to mobilize state resources, see Journal, December 14, 1815, Williams Papers, LC; Williams to Madison, January 8, 1815, ibid.; Williams to Monroe, January 11, 1815, ibid.

24. Jefferson to Monroe, October 16, 1814, Jefferson Papers, LC (first and second quotations); C. H. Van Tyne, ed., *The Letters of Daniel Webster, From Documents Owned Principally by the New Hampshire Historical Society* (New York: McClure, Phillips & Co., 1920), 62 (third quotation); Skeen, *Citizen Soldiers*, 35–37.

25. Stagg, *Mr. Madison's War*, 325–326; Shelby to Desha, November 28, 1814, box 1, Desha Papers, LC; "From the Southwestern Frontier: Tennessee in Arms," *Independent Chronicle*, November 1, 1813 (first quotation); HD 146, 20th Cong., 1st sess., serial 172, 8–14 (second quotation); General Order, March 14, 1814, roll 62, Jackson Papers, LC.

26. *Papers of Jackson* 3:49, 52–55 (quotation).

27. Robert V. Remini, *The Battle of New Orleans* (New York: Viking, 1999); *Papers of Jackson* 3:258 (quotations); Joseph E. Stoltz, *A Bloodless Victory: The Battle of New Orleans in History and Memory* (Baltimore: Johns Hopkins University Press, 2017, Kindle edition), Chapter One.

28. Stoltz, *Bloodless Victory,* Chapter Two (first and second quotations); *Daily National Intelligencer*, February 16, 1815, reprinting excerpts from the *Philadelphia Aurora* (third quotation) and the *Boston Yankee* (sixth and seventh quotations); Jefferson to Crawford, February 11, postscript February 26, 1815, Jefferson Papers, LC (fourth quotation); M[ichael] Smith, *A Complete History of the Late American War with Britain and Her Allies*, 6th ed. (Lexington, KY: F. Bradford, 1816), 211 (fifth quotation); Skeen, *Citizen Soldiers*, 172; *Papers of Jackson* 3:252.

29. Stagg, *Mr. Madison's War*, 505; Skeen, *Citizen Soldiers*, 172; Stoltz, *Bloodless Victory,* Chapter Two; *Papers of Jackson* 3:240 (first quotation), 3:255 (second quotation). Although even Henry Clay acknowledged the failure of the Kentucky militiamen on the right bank of the Mississippi, Jackson's criticisms would later be used against him on the campaign trail. *Papers of Clay* 2:11; Skeen, *Citizen Soldiers*, 170–171.

30. *MPP* 1:553 (quotations); Stanislaus M. Hamilton, ed., *The Writings of James Monroe*, 7 vols. (New York: G. P. Putnam's Sons, 1898–1903), 5:321–327; Monroe to Madison, February 22, 1815, Madison Papers, LC.

31. "The Army," *Daily National Intelligencer*, February 24, 1815 (first quotation); "To the Army," ibid., February 28, 1815, (second quotation); "The Army," ibid., March 3, 1815; "The Army," ibid., April 1, 1815, reprinting excerpt from the *Albany Argus*; "From the Correspondent of the Commercial Advertiser," *Albany Argus*, March 7, 1815; *TP* 10:535–537, 573–575; *ASPMA* 1:664 (third and fourth quotations); William Theobald Wolfe Tone, *Essay on the Necessity of Improving our National Forces* (New York: Kirk and Mercein, 1819), vii (fifth quotation). For an insightful analysis of the administration's thinking, see Michael S. Fitzgerald,

"'Nature Unsubdued': Diplomacy, Expansion and the American Military Buildup of 1815–1816," *Mid-America* 77 (Winter 1995): 5–32.

32. *Annals* 13th Cong., 3rd sess., 1200–1201 (first quotation), 1220, 1223, 1233 (second quotation), 1225 (third quotation), 1251–1252.

33. *Annals* 13th Cong., 2nd sess., 286–287, 291–292, 297–298, 1251–1252, 1265–1267, 1271–1273 (quotation); Fitzgerald, "'Nature Unsubdued,'" 10–11.

34. Leavenworth to McNeil, March 19, 1815, Benham-McNeil Family Papers, LC (first quotation); "To the Disbanded Officers of the Late Army," *Daily National Intelligencer*, June 28, 1815 (second and third quotations); "Disbanded Officers," *Niles' Weekly Register*, July 1, 1815; "Washington," *Richmond Enquirer*, February 27, March 4, 1815; Monroe to Scott, February 21, 1815, roll 1, CULS (fourth quotation); Madison to Dallas, April 14, 1815, Madison Papers, LC; *Statutes* 3:224–225 (fifth quotation); George M. Dallas, ed., *Life and Writings of Alexander James Dallas* (Philadelphia: J. B. Lippincott, 1871), 367–374; Heitman, 2:570–571, 578–579.

35. Watson, "Surprisingly Professional," 85–110; Dallas to Brown, May 17, 1815, Brown Papers, LC (first quotation); Monroe to Dearborn, January 31, 1815, ibid.; Monroe to King, February 5, 1815, ibid.; Dallas to Brown, Macomb, and Scott, 8 (second quotation), April 17, 1815, roll 1, CULS; Dallas, ed., *Life and Writings of Dallas*, 423, 411 (third quotation), 417.

36. Max M. Edling, *A Hercules in the Cradle: War, Money, and the American States, 1783–1867* (Chicago: University of Chicago Press, 2014), 119; Mark A. Smith, *Engineering Security: The Corps of Engineers and Third System of Defense Policy, 1815–1861* (Tuscaloosa: University of Alabama Press, 2009), 5–6, 12, 31–42; *MPP* 2:45, 79 (quotation); Robert Browning, *Two if by Sea: The Development of American Coastal Defense Policy* (Westport, CT: Greenwood Press, 1983), 33–53.

37. Paul A. C. Koistinen, *Beating Plowshares into Swords: The Political Economy of American Warfare, 1607–1865* (Lawrence: University Press of Kansas, 1996), 29–30, 53; Andrew R. L. Cayton, "'Separate Interests' and the Nation-State: The Washington Administration and the Origins of Regionalism in the Trans-Appalachian West," *Journal of American History* 79 (June 1992): 39–67; Bergmann, *American National State and the Early West*, 242–245; Norman W. Caldwell, "The Frontier Army Officer, 1794–1814," *Mid-America* 37 (April 1955): 114–116; Johnson to Partridge, January 4, 1818, Johnson Papers, LC.

38. Koistinen, *Beating Plowshares into Swords*, 64; Paul Wilhelm, *Travels in North America, 1822–1824*, ed. Savoie Lottinville (Norman: University of Oklahoma Press, 1973), 327 (first quotation); *ASPMA* 1:623; Wool to SW, December 24, 1818, box 18, Wool Papers, NYSL (second quotation); Wool to Parker, December 1, 1817, box 48, Wool Papers, NYSL (third quotation); Cunningham, ed., *Circular Letters* 3:1343 (fourth quotation); Hickey, *War of 1812*, 227–230; "Patriotism of Kentucky," *Boston Patriot*, November 10, 1813 (fifth and sixth quotations).

39. Dallas, ed., *Life and Writings of Dallas*, 373–375 (first quotation), 413; *MPP* 1:564 (second quotation); *ASPMA* 1:636 (third quotation); *Annals* 14th Cong., 1st sess., 1234–1240, 1249–1250, 1410–1411; *Statutes* 3:224–225, 297–299; Ian C. Hope, *A Scientific Way of War: Antebellum Military Science, West Point, and the Origins of American Military Thought* (Lincoln: University of Nebraska Press, 2015), 174–175.

40. *MPP* 1:564; *Statutes* 3:321, 330; C. Edward Skeen, *1816: America Rising* (Lexington: University Press of Kentucky, 2003), 138–146; *Annals* 14th Cong., 1st sess., 989–991, 1038–1041 (quotations); Laura Jensen, *Patriots, Settlers, and the Origins of American Social Policy* (Cambridge: Cambridge University Press, 2003), 161–162.

41. *Historical Statistics of the United States, Earliest Time to the Present*, Millennial Edition, 5 vols. (Cambridge: Cambridge University Press, 2006), 5:127, 353–358; *MPP* 1:567–568 (quotation); Daniel Walker Howe, *What Hath God Wrought: The Transformation of America, 1815–1848* (New York: Oxford University Press, 2007), 80–85; Smith, *Engineering Security*, 202–203.

5. The Army and the New Nationalism

1. Daniel Walker Howe, *What Hath God Wrought: The Transformation of America, 1815–1848* (New York: Oxford University Press, 2007), 91–92; *MPP* 2:8, 10 (first quotation); Samuel J. Watson, "James Monroe and American Military Policy: A Lifetime of Connection and Advocacy for a Standing Army," *Virginia Magazine of History and Biography* 128 (March 2020): 2–43. "President's Visit," "Era of Good Feelings," *Columbian Centinel*, July 12, 1817 (second quotation).

2. Howe, *What Hath God Wrought*, 92 (first quotation); *The Papers of John C. Calhoun*, 28 vols. (Columbia: University of South Carolina Press, 1959–2003), 2:22 (second and third quotations); John Niven, *John C. Calhoun and the Price of Union: A Biography* (Baton Rouge: Louisiana State University Press, 1993), 60–61. Henry Clay, William Lowndes, and Isaac Shelby had declined Monroe's offer of the War Department.

3. Nevin, *Calhoun and the Price of Union*, 63–66; Jesup to Calhoun, March 18, 1818, Jesup Papers, USAMHI; Brown to Calhoun, October 16, 1818, Brown Papers, LC; *ASPMA* 2:450; *Papers of Calhoun* 2: lxi-lxix, 121, 132, 147; Paul C. Koistinen, *Beating Plowshares into Swords: The Political Economy of American Warfare, 1607–1865* (Lawrence: University Press of Kansas, 1966), 53–55; William B. Skelton, *An American Profession of Arms: The Army Officer Corps, 1784–1861* (Lawrence: University Press of Kansas, 1992), 120; Robert P. Wettemann Jr., *Privilege vs. Equality: Civil-Military Relations in the Jacksonian Era, 1815–1845* (Santa Barbara: Greenwood Press, 2009), 23–24; *MPP* 2:190; "Military Service of the U.S. for 1824," *Niles' Weekly Register*, March 27, 1824 (quotation).

4. *MPP* 2:298, 311–314; *Historical Statistics of the United States, Earliest Times to the Present*, Millennial Edition, 5 vols. (Cambridge: Cambridge University Press, 2006), 5:127.

5. Francis Paul Prucha, *Broadax and Bayonet: The Role of the United States Army in the Development of the Northwest, 1815–1860* (1953; rpt. Lincoln: University of Nebraska Press, 1967), 220–221.

6. John Resch, *Suffering Soldiers: Revolutionary War Veterans, Moral Sentiment, and Political Culture in the Early Republic* (Amherst: University of Massachusetts Press, 2000), 71–78 (first quotation); "Criticism—For the Port Folio," *The Port Folio*, New Series 8, no. 6 (December 1812): 551–552; "Unpublished Letter of General Washington," *The Port Folio*, New Series 2, no. 6 (December 1812): 604–609; *MPP*

2:19; McLane to Kitty, January 29, 1818, box 1, McLane Papers, LC (second quotation); *Annals* 15th Cong., 1st sess., 144 (third quotation). Previous assistance had come in the form of land bounties, buyouts for commissioned personnel, and cash payments to widows and those having incurred wartime disabilities.

7. *Statutes* 3:410–411 (first quotation); Laura Jensen, *Patriots, Settlers, and the Origins of American Social Policy* (Cambridge: Cambridge University Press, 2003), 3 (second quotation).

8. *The Statistical History of the United States: From Colonial Times to the Present* (New York: Basic Books, 1976), 8, 114–1115; Koistinen, *Beating Plowshares into Swords*, 63–64; William D. Adler and Andrew J. Polsky, "Building the New American Nation: Economic Development, Public Goods, and the Early U.S. Army," *Political Science Quarterly* 125 (March 2010): 87–110.

9. Merritt Roe Smith, *Harpers Ferry Armory and the New Technology: The Challenge of Change* (Ithaca, NY: Cornell University Press, 1977); David A. Hounshell, *From the American System to Mass Production, 1800–1932: The Development of Manufacturing Technology in the United States* (Baltimore: Johns Hopkins University Press, 1984), 25–27, 45; David R. Meyer, *Networked Machinists: High-Technology Industries in Antebellum America* (Baltimore: Johns Hopkins University Press, 2006), 73–75; Nathan Rosenberg, "Technological Change in the Machine Tool Industry," *Journal of Economic History* 23 (December 1963): 414–443; Merritt Roe Smith, "Introduction," in *Military Enterprise and Technological Change: Perspectives on the American Experience*, ed. Merritt Roe Smith (Cambridge: MIT Press, 1985), 7, 11 (quotation), 20–21; Koistinen, *Beating Plowshares into Swords*, 79. Donald R. Hoke, *Ingenious Yankees: The Rise of the American System of Manufactures in the Private Sector* (New York: Columbia University Press, 1990), challenges the significance of the armories in manufacturing development.

10. *Statutes* 3:203–205 (first quotation); Merritt Roe Smith, "Army Ordnance and the 'American System' of Manufacturing, 1815–1861," in *Military Enterprise and Technological Change: Perspectives on the American Experience*, ed. Merritt Roe Smith (Cambridge: MIT Press, 1985), 40–41, 48–54, 61–69, 76–77; *ASPMA* 2:553–554 (second quotation); Meyer, *Networked Machinists*, 75–79, 92–96; Brian Balogh, *Government Out of Sight: The Mystery of National Authority in Nineteenth-Century America* (Cambridge: Cambridge University Press, 2009), 213; Keith W. Hoskin and Richard H. Macve, "Reappraising the Genesis of Managerialism: A Re-examination of the Role of Accounting in the Springfield Armory, 1815–1845," *Accounting, Auditing & Accountability Journal* 7, no. 2 (1994): 6, 9; Smith, "Introduction," 1–2, 5, 11.

11. Francis Paul Prucha, *The Great Father: The United States Government and the American Indians*, Abridged Edition (Lincoln: University of Nebraska Press, 1986), 21, 31–34; Francis Paul Prucha, *American Indian Policy in the Formative Years: The Indian Trade and Intercourse Acts, 1790–1834* (1962; rpt. Lincoln: University of Nebraska Press, 1970), 54–57; William S. Belko, "John C. Calhoun and the Creation of the Bureau of Indian Affairs: An Essay on Political Rivalry, Ideology, and Policymaking in the Early Republic," *South Carolina Historical Magazine* 105 ((July 2004): 174; Whistler to Stickney, November 15, 16 (quotation), 1816, S-10, roll 76, M221, LRSW (quotation).

12. *MPP* 2:16–17; Brown to Dallas, August 14, 1815, Brown Papers, LC; Brown to Crawford, November 30, 1815, ibid.; *ASPIA* 2:13–14, 161 (first and second quotations); J. Franklin Jameson, ed., *Correspondence of John C. Calhoun,* American Historical Association, *Annual Report,* 1899 (Washington, D.C.: Government Printing Office, 1900), 145–147, 159; *ASPIA* 2:201, 275–287, 542–544 (third quotation); *Papers of Calhoun* 8:574–575; Belko, "Calhoun and the Creation of the Bureau of Indian Affairs," 193–197.

13. Francis Paul Prucha, *The Sword of the Republic: The United States Army on the Frontier, 1783–1846* (London: Macmillan, 1969), 251–253; *TP* 19:462–463, 570–571, 602, 634; *ASPMA* 1:816–820; *Papers of Calhoun* 2:194–195 (first quotation), 3:64, 214–216, 633–634 (second quotation).

14. *St. Louis Enquirer*, September 4, 1818, as quoted in *Niles' Register*, October 17, 1818 (first quotation); *MPP* 2:47 (second quotation); *ASPMA* 2:69 (third quotation).

15. Prucha, *Sword of the Republic*, 144–147, 162–163; *Annals* 16th Cong., 1st sess., 545–547, 1633–1634; *Papers of Calhoun* 3:395–396, 422–424, 436–438, 639–640 (first quotation); 4:31–33, 388–389, 573–574, 612, 684; 5:19–21. Although Long returned with important information regarding the Great Plains, his published report, which judged the region to be "almost wholly unfit for cultivation, and of course uninhabitable by people depending upon agriculture for their subsistence," was hardly the stuff to excite the popular imagination. Edwin James, comp., *Account of an Expedition from Pittsburgh to the Rocky Mountains, Performed in the Years 1819, 1820*, 3 vols. (London: Longman, Hurst, Rees, Orme, and Brown, 1823), 2:361.

16. Prucha, *Sword of the Republic*, 129–133; Extract of a confidential report, Jesup to Jackson, June 25, 1816, Jesup Papers, USAMHI; Jesup to Jackson, August 18, 21, 1816, box 2, Jesup Papers, LC; Jesup to Claiborne, August 24, 1816, box 17, ibid.; Jesup to Monroe, September 3, 8, 1816, box 2, ibid.; Jesup to Monroe, August 21, 1816, Jesup Papers, Clements Library; Clinch to Butler, August 2, 1816, L-158, 1819, roll 82, M221, LRSW; John Spencer Bassett, ed., *Correspondence of Andrew Jackson*, 7 vols. (1926–1933; rpt. New York, Kraus Reprint, 1969), 2:374–375 (quotation); Samuel J. Watson, *Jackson's Sword: The Army Officer Corps on the American Frontier, 1810–1821* (Lawrence: University Press of Kansas, 2012), 123–187.

17. *ASPMA* 1:689 (quotation); Niven, *Calhoun and the Price of Union*, 69; Charles Francis Adams, ed., *Memoirs of John Q. Adams*, 12 vols. (Philadelphia: J. B. Lippincott, 1874–1877), 4:189–201; David S. Heidler and Jeanne T. Heidler, *Old Hickory's War: Andrew Jackson and the Quest for Empire* (Baton Rouge: Louisiana State University Press, 2003), 183.

18. Wettemann, *Privilege vs. Equality*, 24–26; *Papers of Jackson* 4:9–11 (first quotation); Ethan Allen Hitchcock, *Fifty Years in Camp and Field*, ed. W. A. Croffut (New York: G. P. Putnam's Sons, 1909), 47; Brown to Dallas, November 20, 1815, Brown Papers, LC; Hamilton to Jesup, June 13, 1817, box 2, Jesup Papers, LC; "From the Southern Army," *Philadelphia Magazine and Weekly Repertory*, June 13, 1818; Gaines to Jesup, July 2, 1817, box 2, Jesup Papers, LC; Mitchell to Jesup, July 28, 1817, Jesup Papers, USAMHI; Randall to Bache, March 4, 1818, Randall-Bache Collection, USAMHI; Calhoun to Scott, March 5, 11, 1819, roll 1, CULS; Adams, ed., *Adams Memoirs* 5:510–511; Timothy D. Johnson, *Winfield Scott: The Quest for*

Military Glory (Lawrence: University Press of Kansas, 1998), 97; Brown to Scott, August 10, 1815, Brown Papers, Clements Library; Scott to Brown, August 21, 1816, ibid. (second quotation).

19. Abert to Partridge, March 5, 1814, box 1, Partridge Papers, LC (quotation); handwritten copy of petition to Partridge, November 24, 1816, ibid.; Pleasanton to Partridge, March 25, 1817, ibid.; Samuel J. Watson, "Developing 'Republican Machines': West Point and the Struggle to Render the Officer Corps Safe for America, 1802–1833," in *Thomas Jefferson's Military Academy: Founding West Point*, ed. Robert M. S. McDonald (Charlottesville: University of Virginia Press, 2004), 162–166; Skelton, *American Profession of Arms*, 122–123; Marcus Cunliffe, *Soldiers & Civilians: The Martial Spirit in America, 1775–1865* (Boston: Little, Brown, 1968), 257–263; Partridge to Worthington, September 26, 1817, roll 11, Worthington Papers, LC; Mansfield, Elliott, Beraw, Douglass, and Crozet to President, undated, HR 16A-D14.1, RG 233, NARA.

20. Mansfield to Worthington, January 23, 1819, roll 12, Worthington Papers, LC; Partridge to Monroe, November 20, 1820, box 1, Partridge Papers, LC; Charges of Partridge against Thayer, December 5, 1817, HR 16A-D14.1, RG 233, NARA; Memorial of Loring, Ragland, Vining, Holmes, and Fairfax, December 20, 1819, ibid. (quotation); "Expose of Facts, Concerning Recent Transactions, relative to the Corps of Cadets of the United States Military Academy," ibid.; Report of the Military Committee, April 11, 1820, ibid.; Calhoun to Smyth, February 1, 1820, ibid.

21. Charles M. Wiltse, *Calhoun: Nationalist, 1782–1828* (Indianapolis: Bobbs-Merrill, 1944), 166–168, 182–188, 203–205; "Regarding John C. Calhoun's record as Secretary of War, and endorsing him for President in the Presidential Campaign of 1824" file, box 5, Van Deventer Papers, Clements Library; HD 148, 15th Cong., 2nd sess., serial 24, 12–13, 29; *The Papers of Henry Clay*, 10 vols. (Lexington: University of Kentucky Press, 1959–1991), 2:598–599; Johnson to Smith, March 29, 30, April 16, June 9, July 5, 1819, Richard M. Johnson Papers, LC; Johnson to Cheves, October 17, 1819, ibid.; Calhoun to Johnson, 20 September 1819, roll 1, CULS (quotation); *Papers of Calhoun* 4:284–285.

22. Noble E. Cunningham, ed., *Circular Letters of Congressmen to Their Constituents, 1789–1829*, 3 vols. (Chapel Hill: University of North Carolina Press, 1978), 2:1004, 1008; *Annals* 14th Cong., 2nd sess., 123–130, 152–164; "Washington," *Daily National Intelligencer*, March 11, 1817; Scott to Brown, July 29, 1818, Brown Papers, Clements Library; Adams, ed., *Memoirs of Adams* 4:324; *ASPMA* 2:779 (first quotation); *Annals* 15th Cong., 2nd sess., 630, 634, 742 (second quotation), 799, 853, 908–909, 1071–1072; Robert V. Remini, *Andrew Jackson and the Course of American Empire, 1767–1821* (New York: Harper and Row, 1977), 371–374; McLane to Kitty, January 18, 20, 23, February 9, 1819, box 1, McLane Papers, LC. Condemning the army's opponents in the House, one officer decried "the House of Misrepresentatives." Randall to Bache, February 21, 1817, Randall-Bache Collection, USAMHI.

23. Adams, ed., *Memoirs of Adams* 4:512, 5:237–238, 514–515; *Annals* 15th Cong., 2nd sess., 390 (first quotation); Cunningham, ed., *Circular Letters* 3:1049–1050, 1057–1058, 1061, 1070, 1090–1091, 1155–1166; Charles Sellers, *The Market Revolution: Jacksonian America, 1815–1846* (New York: Oxford University Press, 1991),

103, 125; Heidler and Heidler, *Old Hickory's War*, 229; *Papers of Jackson* 5:192–195; Resch, *Suffering Soldiers*, 142–143; Crawford to Daniel, May 2, 1821, Crawford Papers, LC; *Papers of Calhoun* 4:249 (second quotation).

24. "Army of the United States," *Niles' Weekly Register*, February 5, 1820; Resch, *Suffering Soldiers*, 146; Michael S. Fitzgerald, "Rejecting Calhoun's Expansible Army Plan: The Army Reduction Act of 1821," *War in History* 3 (April 1996): 172; *Annals* 16th Cong., 1st sess., 1607 (first quotation), 1602 (second and third quotations), 2143–2145, 2232–2234.

25. *Papers of Calhoun* 4:748 (first quotation), 5:293–296, 317–319, 377–380, 436–438; Adams, ed., *Memoirs of Adams* 5:128; Calhoun to Brown, July 31, 1820, roll 1, CULS; Macomb to Calhoun, November 9, 1819, roll 90, LRSW; Scott to Calhoun, August 20, 1820, S-37, roll 91, ibid. (second quotation); Atkinson to Calhoun, October 18, 1820, A-29, roll 88, ibid.; Macomb to Calhoun, September 30, 1820, M-122, roll 90, ibid.; *ASPMA* 2:188–198.

26. *Papers of Calhoun* 5:406–407, 496; Fitzgerald, "Rejecting Calhoun's Expansible Army," 174–176; *Annals* 16th Cong., 2nd sess., 715–734 (first and second quotations), 928, 895 (third and fourth quotations), 788 (fifth quotation), 813–817; Robert Wooster, *The American Military Frontiers: The United States Army in the West, 1783–1900* (Albuquerque: University of New Mexico Press, 2009), 62–63.

27. *MPP* 2:86–87; Mark A. Smith, *Engineering Security: The Corps of Engineers and Third System Defense Policy, 1815–1861* (Tuscaloosa: University of Alabama Press, 2009), 3, 42–43, 51–57; *ASPMA* 2:304–313; *Annals* 16th Cong., 2nd sess., Appendix, 1615, 1723–1742 (quotation); *Annals* 18th Cong., 1st sess., 331–332. The case concerned the merits of establishing fortifications at Mobile as well as across the bay at Dauphin Island, Alabama. See HR 103, 17th Cong., 2nd sess., serial 87, and *MPP* 2:119–126. Smith, 57, acknowledges that the new "itemized appropriations instituted in 1821 gave Congress a powerful oversight of the Third System," but insists that the Corps "retained firm control over the formation of policy."

28. *Annals* 16th Cong., 2nd sess., 367–375, 937; Fitzgerald, "Rejecting Calhoun's Expansible Army," 176–185; Estimate of army expenses under the House and Senate bills, February 1821, SEN 15A-D8, RG 46, NARA; Abert to Van Deventer, January 25, 1821, box 4, Van Deventer Papers, Clements Library (quotations); Roberdeau to Fay, February 13, 1821, Entry 306, Correspondence of Topographical Engineer Stationed in Washington, RG 77, NARA; *Statutes* 3:615–616; Heitman 2:578–581; Skeen, *1816*, 149; *Historical Statistics, Millennial Edition* 5:127, 353–358.

29. *Papers of Jackson* 5:10 (first quotation), 5 (second quotation); "The Army," *Louisville Public Advertiser*, September 8, 1821 (third quotation); "A," ibid., February 7, 1821; Roberdeau to Fay, February 13, 1821, Entry 306, Correspondence of the Topographical Officer Stationed in Washington, RG 77, NARA; Skelton, *American Profession of Arms*, 288–289; Wiltse, *Calhoun: Nationalist*, 230; *Papers of Calhoun* 5:669–670, 7: xi-xx; Samuel J. Watson, "How the Army Became Accepted: West Point Socialization, Military Accountability, and the Nation-State During the Jacksonian Era," *American Nineteenth Century History* 7 (June 2006): 222; Samuel J. Watson, "Surprisingly Professional: Trajectories in Army Officer Corps Drawdowns,

1783–1848," in *Drawdown: The American Way of Postwar*, ed. Jason W. Warren (New York: New York University Press, 2016), (fourth quotation).

30. Charles F. O'Connell Jr., "Corps of Engineers and the Rise of Modern Management, 1827–1856," in *Military Enterprise and Technological Change: Perspectives on the American Experience*, ed. Merritt Roe Smith (Cambridge: MIT Press, 1985), 89–100 (quotation); Hoskin and Macve, "Reappraising the Genesis of Managerialism," 5–9; Darwin L. King, Kathleen M. Premo, and Carl J. Case, "Historical Influences on Modern Cost Accounting Practices," *Academy of Accounting and Financial Studies Journal* 13 (September 2009): 22–27. For a challenge to the significance of West Point, see Richard K. Fleischman and Thomas N. Tyson, "Developing Expertise: Two Episodes in Early Nineteenth Century U.S. Management Accounting History," *Business and Economic History* 26 (Winter 1997): 371–377.

31. Adams, ed., *Memoirs of Adams* 5:237–238 (first quotation), 326–327, 496; Remini, *Jackson and the Course of American Empire*, 197, 211; *MPP* 2:129–136; *Annals* 17th Cong., 1st sess., 921, 948, 1198–1202, 1310, 1455–5148, 1565–1586, 1591–1594, 1616; "Army of the United States," *Niles' Weekly Register*, June 9, 1821 (second and third quotations).

32. *TP* 19:95–96, 413, 462–463, 472–473, 570–571, 602–603, 680, 685–686; *Papers of Calhoun* 7:534–536, 8:102–107 (first quotation); HR 42, 19th Cong., 1st sess., serial 141, 15; *ASPIA* 2:318–320; *TP* 11:65–69, 374; Prucha, *Sword of the Republic*, 149–151; Brown to Calhoun, May 12, 1823, Brown Papers, LC; Jameson, ed., *Correspondence of Calhoun*, 208 (second quotation).

33. Prucha, *American Indian Policy in the Formative Years*, 88–93; Belko, "Calhoun and the Creation of the Bureau of Indian Affairs," 170; *New ASPMA* 8:321 (first quotation), 15:66; *ASPIA* 2:451–453; "Letters relating to the Auricarse war," *St. Louis Enquirer*, October 18, 1823 (second quotation); *ASPIA* 2:448–449, 452–456, 595–609, 656–657; *ASPMA* 2:623–624; *Annals* 18th Cong., 1st sess., 443–445, 449–461, 505–507, 752–753; Barbour to Benton, July 20, 1825, vol. 12, LSSW; Jameson, ed., *Correspondence of Calhoun*, 217–218; *Papers of Calhoun* 9:54; *MPP* 2:261–262.

34. HD 17, 15th Cong., 2nd sess., serial 17; *ASPMA* 1:713; SD 18, 17th Cong., 2nd sess., serial 74; *MPP* 2:198; HD 55, 18th Cong., 2nd sess., serial 115 (first quotation); Nazum, Ashcraft et al to Moore, August 25, 1818, HR 19A-D12.1, RG 233, NARA; Shepperd to Verner, December 20, 1825, ibid.; "Resolution Respecting the Western Armory," Petition of Citizens of Pendleton County, ibid.; HD 88, 19th Cong., 1st sess., serial 135, 5 (second quotation); HD 136, 19th Cong., 1st sess., serial 138, 3–8 (third quotation); HD 214, 20th Cong., 1st sess., serial 173.

35. Skelton, *American Profession of Arms*, 138; Sellers, *Market Revolution*, 76–79, 83–89; Calhoun to Brown, July 31, 1820, roll 1, CULS (first quotation); Wettemann, *Privilege vs. Equality*, 55; Watson, "Developing 'Republican Machines,'" 167–173; Macomb to Roberdeau, November 11, 1821, Entry 306, Correspondence of Topographical Officer Stationed in Washington, RG 77, NARA; Report of the Board of Internal Improvement, February 3, 1825, vol. 2, Entry 250, Reports on Internal Improvements, 1823–1839, RG 77, NARA; Hope, *Scientific Way of War*, 65, 125–127; Ticknor, *Life, Letters and Journals*, 375 (second quotation).

36. John Lauritz Larson, *Internal Improvement: National Public Works and the Promise of Popular Government in the Early United States* (Chapel Hill: University of North Carolina Press, 2001), 31, 36, 58, 63–67; *Papers of Jackson* 3:396; *MPP* 2:8, 17–18; *New ASPMA* 15:12–13 (first quotation); *ASP: Miscellaneous* 2:533–537; Porter to Calhoun, August 21, 1819, Brown Papers, Clements Library; *Papers of Calhoun* 4:342 (second quotation), 5:539–540, 578; HR 48, 21st Cong., 2nd sess., serial 207; Prucha, *Sword of the Republic*, 188–192; *ASPMA* 4:626–627, 815, 849–850; Barbour to Brown, March 21, 1827, vol. 12, LSSW; *TP* 12:431; HR 42, 19th Cong., 1st sess., serial 141, 6–18 (third quotation).

37. Larson, *Internal Improvement*, 117–128; *Papers of Calhoun* 2:229, 3:425–426 (quotation); *Annals* 15th Cong., 1st sess., Appendix 1318–1339; HD 11, 15th Cong., 1st sess., serial 6, 1–11; *ASP: Miscellaneous* 2:533–537; *Annals* 17th Cong., 1st sess., 1684–1685 (first quotation); *ASP: Miscellaneous* 2:934–937; *MPP* 2:144–1485 (second quotation 173); Sellers, *Market Revolution*, 149–150; Forest G. Hill, *Roads, Rails, and Waterways: The Army Engineers and Early Transportation* (Norman: University of Oklahoma Press, 1957), 44–45.

38. Frank N. Schubert, ed., *The Nation-Builders: A Sesquicentennial History of the Corps of Topographical Engineers* (Washington, D.C.: Government Printing Office, 1989), 6; Hill, *Roads, Rails, and Waterways*, 24–33; Totten and Bernard to Macomb, November 5, 1823, vol. 2, Entry 250, Reports on Internal Improvements, 1823–1839, RG 77, NARA (first and second quotations); Roberdeau to Cocke, April 1, 1822, Entry 306, Correspondence of Topographical Officer Stationed in Washington, RG 77, NARA (third quotation); Long to Roberdeau, April 16, 1822, ibid. (fourth quotation).

39. *Annals* 17th Cong., 2nd sess., 605–606 (first quotation), 18th Cong., 1st sess., 990–996, 1037–1039 (fourth quotation); Sellers, *Market Revolution*, 151; *MPP* 2:216 (second and third quotations); *Statutes* 4:22–23, 32–33; Shallat, "Structures in the Stream," 8; Larson, *Internal Improvement*, 146.

40. Macomb to Bernard, Totten, and Sullivan, May 31, October 2 (first quotation), 1824, roll 1, M65, LS by the Office of the Chief of Engineers Relating to Internal Improvements, RG 77, NARA; Hill, *Roads, Rails, and Waterways*, 52–55, 78, 163; SD 32, 18th Cong., 2nd sess., serial 109, 68–69; Niven, *Calhoun and the Price of Union*, 105–106; Schubert, ed., *Nation-Builders*, 15; *MPP* 2:255; *Papers of Calhoun* 9:307–308; Macomb to Abert, September 18, 1824, ibid.; Larson, *Internal Improvement*, 165; *MPP* 2:255–256 (second and third quotations).

41. *MPP* 2:300–309; Ian C. Hope, *A Scientific Way of War: Antebellum Military Science, West Point, and the Origins of American Military Thought* (Lincoln: University of Nebraska Press, 2015), 115; *ASPMA* 5:715 (first quotation); Kearny to Roberdeau, October 8, 1821, Entry 306, Correspondence of Topographical Officer Stationed in Washington, RG 77, NARA (second quotation); Long to Roberdeau, March 16, 1825, ibid.; Roberdeau to Barbour, July 18, 1825, ibid.; *ASPMA* 4:12–17; "Army of the United States," *Niles' Weekly Register*, August 9, 1828; Larson, *Internal Improvement*, 149–150, 165–166; HD 261, 20th Cong., 1st sess., serial 174, 3–6; Barbour to Thomas, June 25, 1827, roll 2, M65, LS by the Office of the Chief of Engineers Relating to Internal Improvements, RG 77, NARA (third quotation); Hill,

Roads, Rails, and Waterways, 100–101; O'Connell, "Corps of Engineers and Modern Management," 99–104; Francis Wayland, *Report to the Corporation of Brown University on Changes in the System of Collegiate Education* (Providence: George H. Whitney, 1850), 18.

42. Charles D. Lowery, *James Barbour: A Jeffersonian Republican* (University: University of Alabama Press, 1984), 89, 102, 145; *ASPIA* 2:646–649 (first quotation); *ASPMA* 3:330–331, 342, 617–618; *Papers of Calhoun* 7:534–536; Brown to Calhoun, May 12, 1823, Brown Papers, LC (second quotation); Adams, ed., *Memoirs of Adams* 7:79; *TP* 11:1093–1095, 1102–1103, 1109–1110; HED 2, 20th Cong., 1st sess., serial 169, 146–158; Barbour to Cass, August 16, 1827, vol. 12, LSSW; Barbour to Edwards, September 10, 1827, ibid.; HD 277, 20th Cong., 1st sess., serial 175, 5–19; SD 169, 20th Cong., 1st sess., serial 166, 26.

43. Adams, ed., *Memoirs of Adams* 7:252–253, 456, 504–505, 507, 513, 525, 528, 538–539, 546, 8:4–5, 10–14; Scott to Barbour, January 19, 1826, Scott Papers, Clement Library; Barbour to Gaines and Scott, April 2, 1827, vol. 12, LSSW. Col. Zachary Taylor wrote that the action "astonished me not a little," adding: "I sincerely hope the days of the present dynasty are numbered, & that the 4th of March '29 will bring about a complete change." Taylor to Lawson, August 28, 1828, Series 2, roll 1, Taylor Papers, LC.

44. Samuel J. Watson, *Peacekeepers and Conquerors: The Army Officer Corps on the American Frontier, 1821–1846* (Lawrence: University Press of Kansas, 2013), 89–102; "Army of the United States," *North American Review* 23 (October 1826): 265–275 (first, second, and third quotations); *MPP* 2:305–306; *ASPMA* 4:2 (fourth quotation); HD 174, 20th Cong., 1st sess., serial 174, 4–5; "Internal Improvements," *North American Review* 24 (January 1827): 15.

45. Larson, *Internal Improvement*, 149–150; *RDebates* 19th Cong., 2nd sess., 571–572, 1267–1268; 20th Cong., 1st sess., 1661–1662 (first quotation), 2608, 2626–2627 (second quotation); *Annals* 18th Cong., 1st sess., 1308 (third and fourth quotations).

46. Larson, *Internal Improvement*, 149–150, 171–174; *Papers of Calhoun* 10:401, 404, 418 (first quotation); *RDebates*, 20th Cong., 1st sess., 604–608, 632 (second quotation), 787, 1648, 1653–1654; *Statutes* 4:275–276 (second quotation); SD 129, 61st Cong., 1st sess., serial 5568, 271–272; Wettemann, *Privilege vs. Equality*.

6. Mr. Jackson's Army

1. John Lauritz Larson, *Internal Improvement: National Public Works and the Promise of Popular Government in the Early United States* (Chapel Hill: University of North Carolina Press, 2001), 149–150, 171; *MPP* 2:436–437 (quotations). Federal spending figures include costs of the army and veteran pensions and exclude debt service. *The Statistical History of the United States: From Colonial Times to the Present* (New York: Basic Books, 1976), 8, 1114–1115.

2. Heitman 2:586–589; John C. Niven, *Martin Van Buren: The Romantic Age of American Politics* (New York: Oxford University Press, 1983), 164, 259–260.

3. "A Brief Account of the Execution of the Six Militia Men," Portfolio 193, Folder 11, Printed Ephemera: Three Centuries of Broadsides and Other Printed

Ephemera, LC, www.loc.gov/resource/rbpe.19301100; *Daily National Journal*, October 3, 1828 (quotations); *Daily National Intelligencer*, October 14, 1828.

4. *ASPMA* 4:154–155, 558–559, 587; *TP* 12:294; Eaton to Macomb, March 24, 1830, vol. 12, LSSW; John W. Hall, *Uncommon Defense: Indian Allies in the Black Hawk War* (Cambridge: Harvard University Press, 2009), 103–104; [Lewis Cass], "Removal of the Indians," *North American Review* 30 (January 1830): 99 (first quotation), 121 (second quotation); *ASPMA* 4:714–716, 5:22, 26 (third quotation), 169–171, 631–632; Cass to Everett, February 10, 1836, roll 2, M7, CULS.

5. *Statutes* 4:411–412. In 1830–1831, the War Department attempted to use volunteer cavalry to intimidate the Choctaws into moving, as well as private contractors to provide supplies during their subsequent emigration. Political embarrassment resulting from the exorbitant costs and evident confusion in these operations soon led the administration to summon the regulars. Samuel J. Watson, *Peacekeepers and Conquerors: The Army Officer Corps on the American Frontier, 1821–1846* (Lawrence: University Press of Kansas, 2013), 123, 128–135.

6. Watson, *Peacekeepers and Conquerors*, 107–117, 132; Wool to Cass, Sept. 10, 1836, W-233, roll 134, M567, LROAG (first quotation); HR 98, 19th Cong., 2nd sess., serial 161, 172–173; Wool to Warren, Nov. 1, 1836, Wool Papers, LC; Wool to Miss Warren, Jan. 27, 1837, box 4, Wool Papers, NYSL; Wool to Poinsett, April 20, 1837 [misfiled], roll 19, LRSW; Churchill Journals, July 3, 8, 1836, LC; HD 59, 19th Cong., 2nd sess., serial 151, 373 (second quotation).

7. Wool to Cass, July 1, 1836, W-148, roll 134, M567, LRAGO; Wool to Cass, July 1, 1836, W-148, ibid.; Wool to AG, Aug. 16, 1836, W-205, ibid.; Wool to Jones, attached to Nov. 9, 1835, W-307, ibid.; Watson, *Peacekeepers and Conquerors*, 132–140; Ronald N. Satz, *American Indian Policy in the Jacksonian Era* (Lincoln: University of Nebraska Press, 1976), 82–83; Monte Ross Lewis, "Chickasaw Removal: Betrayal of the Beloved Warriors, 1794–1844" (Ph.D. diss., North Texas State University, 1981).

8. Eaton to Macomb, April 5, 1830, vol. 12, LSSW; Gaines to Marcy, May 10, 1832, vol. 6, Part 1, Entry 5568, LS, Western Division and Department, RG 393, NARA; Watson, *Peacekeepers and Conquerors*, 56; Hall, *Uncommon Defense*, 115–116; Francis Paul Prucha, *The Sword of the Republic: The United States Army on the Frontier, 1783–1846* (London: Macmillan, 1969), 211–231; *ASPMA* 5:23–24, 29–31.

9. *New ASPMA* 8:183–185; Philip St. George Cooke, *Scenes and Adventures in the Army; or, Romance of Military Life* (1857; rpt. New York: Arno Press, 1973), 158 (quotation); *ASPMA* 5:18; Anderson to Brother, August 5, 1832, box 1, Anderson Papers, LC.

10. Patrick J. Jung, *The Black Hawk War of 1832* (Norman: University of Oklahoma Press, 2007), 185; *New ASPMA* 8:179–180; Taylor to Jesup, December 4, 1832, box 17, Jesup Papers, LC (first and second quotations); Wool to Brown, Nov. 9, 1823, Wool Papers, NYSL (third quotation); Eustis to Poinsett, December 30, 1837, box 9, Poinsett Papers, HSP (fourth, fifth, and sixth quotations).

11. Brown to Calhoun, July 20, 1818, Brown Papers, LC; *New ASPMA* 12:185–188; *ASPMA* 3:108, 194–199, 274–277; "Gen. Jackson's Address to the Army," *Niles' Weekly Register*, September 22, 1831; Edward M. Coffman, *The Old Army: A Portrait of the American Army in Peacetime, 1784–1898* (New York: Oxford University

Press, 1986), 151, 193, 196–197; *The Papers of John C. Calhoun*, 28 vols. (Columbia: University of South Carolina Press, 1959–2003), 2:435–436 (first quotation); Taylor to Jesup, September 18, 1820, box 17, Jesup Papers, LC; "New Army Regulation," *National Register*, September 19, 1818; Phillips to Johnson, December 8, 1835, House 24A-D 13.2, RG 233, NARA (second quotation); "Communications: Desertions from the Army," *Army and Navy Chronicle*, April 25, 1838; Ernest H. Cherrington, *The Evolution of Prohibition in the United States of America* (Watersville, OH: American Issue Press, 1920), 93; "Non-Commissioned Officers of the Army," *Military and Naval Magazine of the United States* 2 (October 1833): 65–72; "Temperance in the Army," ibid., 4 (January 1835): 350–353; "Temperance Department," *Christian Advocate and Journal and Zion's Herald*, December 28, 1832; Diary, July 17, 1830, Warfield Papers, MdHS (quotation); Taylor to Jesup, December 15, 1829, roll 1, Taylor Papers, LC; *TP* 12:517, 27:1101; Murray, *Travels in North America* 2:67–68; *ASPMA* 5:20; "Intemperance and Crime in the United States Army," *New York Evangelist*, April 30, 1831; "War Department," *Christian Watchman*, December 23, 1831; *Statutes* 4:647–648. The annual rate of desertion from 1820 to 1860 was 14.8 percent.

12. *ASPMA* 3:615–616, 828–829, 4:2, 5–6, 154, 219, 277–280, 371, 585, 716; *RDebates* 20th Cong., 1st sess., 2054; *RDebates* 21st Cong., 1st sess., 272–273; Cooke, *Scenes and Adventures*, 59 (quotations); SD 90, 22nd Cong., 1st sess., serial 213.

13. *RDebates* 22nd Cong., 1st sess., 1067–1088 (quotations); Eaton to Miller, July 29, 1829, vol. 12, LSSW; *ASPMA* 4:277–280; *Statutes* 4:533.

14. *ASPMA* 3:828–829, 5:19, 31, 126; *New ASPMA* 8:197–198, 336–338; *The Papers of Andrew Jackson*, 10 vols. to date (Knoxville: University of Tennessee Press, 1980–), 7:356; Henry L. Ellsworth, *Washington Irving on the Prairie: or, A Narrative of a Tour of the Southwest in the Year 1832* (New York: American Book Co., 1937), 24–25 (first and second quotations); *RDebates* 22nd Cong., 2nd sess., 1728, 1756; *Statutes* 4:652 (third quotation).

15. *Papers of Jackson*, 6:168 (first quotation); James Hildreth, *Dragoon Campaigns to the Rocky Mountains, by a Dragoon* (1836; rpt. New York: Arno Press, 1973), 14, 42–43 (second quotation); William B. Skelton, *An American Profession of Arms: The Army Officer Corps, 1784–1861* (Lawrence: University Press of Kansas, 1992), 143; Dodge to Jones, August 28, 1833, D-81, LROAG (third quotation); *Senate Executive Journal* 4:283–284, 354–355, 4:554–555.

16. Richard N. Grippaldi, "The Politics of Appointment in the Jacksonian Army: The (Non)Transfer of Ethan Allen Hitchcock to the Regiment of Dragoons, 1833," *Army History* 70 (Winter 2009): 27–36; "United States Dragoons," *Military and Naval Magazine of the United States* 1 (April 1833): 118–122 (first quotation); Hitchcock to Garland, May 12, 1833, box 1, Hitchcock Papers, LC (second quotation); Hitchcock to Brother, March 31, 1834, ibid.; Ripley to Anderson, December 26, 1834, box 1, Anderson Papers, LC (third quotation). For earlier criticisms of the administration's use of patronage, compare Alfred Mordecai's letters of February 11 and May 26, 1829, Mordecai Papers, LC.

17. James E. Wright, *The Galena Lead District: Federal Policy and Practice, 1824–1847* (Madison: State Historical Society of Wisconsin, 1966), 12–19; *RDebates*, 19th

Cong., 2nd sess., 52–54; *ASPMA* 6, 926; Christopher McGrory Klyza, "The United States Army, Natural Resources, and Political Development in the Nineteenth Century," *Polity* 35 (Fall 2002): 4–7; HD 7, 19th Cong., 2nd sess., serial 149.

18. *TP* 12:93–98 (first and second quotations); Klyza, "U.S. Army, Natural Resources, and Political Development," 4–7 (second quotation); Wright, *Galena Lead District*, 34–36, 41–46. Legate resigned from the army, effective December 31, 1836. Heitman 1:626.

Lieutenant Thomas, who seemed to have been enjoying a promising military career, was dismissed in early 1831 for failing to appear at a court of inquiry investigating charges that he had mishandled public funds. Some suspected that he was responsible for the violent turn of a dispute between his friend Representative Spencer D. Pettis (a Jacksonian Democrat from Missouri) and Maj. Thomas Biddle (brother to Bank of the United States president Nicholas Biddle). In their August 1831 duel, both Pettis and Biddle were mortally wounded. Fifteen years later, the now-former lieutenant Thomas successfully sued for monies owed him by the government for what a congressional committee dubbed his "prompt and energetic" services in Missouri. Adjutant General's Department, *Subject Index of the General Orders of the War Department, from January 1, 1809, to December 31, 1860* (Washington, D.C.: Government Printing Office, 1886), 61; Bomford to Eaton, Nov. 8, 1830, T-128, roll 56, M567, LRAGO; Endorsements, ibid.; Nicholas B. Wainwright, "The Life and Death of Major Thomas Biddle," *Pennsylvania Magazine of History and Biography* 104 (July 1980): 326–344; HR 576, 29th Cong, 1st sess., serial 490 (quotation).

19. *Papers of Jackson* 7:357, 464 (first quotation); *ASP: MA* 4:626–627; Cullum to Heidekoper, August 1833, Cullum Papers, LC; Mordecai to Ellen, December 31, 1828, box 7, Mordecai Papers, LC; Satz, *American Indian Policy*, 73 (second quotation); SR 283, 36th Cong., 1st sess., serial 1040, 7; Lewis, "Chickasaw Removal," 134–150; SD 512, pt. 1, 23rd Cong., 1st sess., serial 244, especially 949–1177.

20. HR 349, 23rd Cong., 1st sess., serial 262, 9; Bomford to Cass, January 18, 1836, Bomford to Benton, February 18, 1836, box 19, Senate 24A-D10, RG 46, NARA; HD 154, 23rd Cong., 2nd sess., serial 274; SD 182, 24th Cong., 1st sess., serial 281; Senate 25A-G11, box 107, RG 46, NARA; SD 231, 25th Cong., 2nd sess., serial 316; SD 310, 25th Cong., 2nd sess., serial 317; HD 47, 25th Cong., 3rd sess., serial 346; Docket Volume, Committee on Military Affairs, 23–27 Congress, 23A-D12.3, RG 233, NARA; Citizens of Beaver County to Congress, December 15, 1837, House 25A-G11.2, RG 233, NARA (first and second quotations); House 26A-G11.3, RG 233, NARA; Hinde and Lesher to Congress, December 22, 1837, House 25A-G11.2, RG 233, NARA (third quotation).

21. Robert W. Coakley, *The Role of Federal Military Forces in Domestic Disorders, 1789–1878* (Washington, D.C.: Center of Military History, 1988), 93–106; Gaines to Jones, November 3, 1831, vol. 6, pt. 1, Entry 5568, LS, Western Division and Department, RG 393, NARA (first quotation); Gaines to Clinch, December 2, 1831, ibid.; Ritner to Anderson, September 16, 1831, box 1, Anderson Papers, LC; *ASPMA* 5:156–161; Cass to Twiggs, December 14, 1832, roll 1, M7, CULS; Cass

to Lumpkin, ibid.; Twiggs to Cass, December 24, 1832, T-1, CULR; *Memoirs of Lieut.-General Scott, Written by Himself* (New York: Sheldon and Co., 1864), 1:234–254; Scott to Jones, November 27, 1832, S-2, ibid.; Scott to Jones, December 6, 1832, S-5, ibid.; Scott to Jones, December 15, 1832, S-17, ibid.; *Telegraph*, April 5, 1833 (second quotation); Skelton, *American Profession of Arms*, 351; Richard B. Morris, "Andrew Jackson, Strikebreaker," *American Historical Review* 55 (June 1949): 54–68; *New ASPMA* 10:109–111.

White Southerners saw slave patrols and state militia as their first lines of defense against slave insurrections, but occasionally called upon regulars to supplement their strength and viewed them "as essential to their safety." Tommy R. Young, "The United States Army in the South" (Ph.D. diss., Louisiana State University, 1973), 444–522 (quotation p. 520).

22. Cass to McKean, January 6, 1834, vol. 15, LSSW (first and second quotations); Watson, *Peacekeepers and Conquerors*, 350–351; *ASPMA* 5:170, 358, 373–382, 627, 6:130–144; Hildreth, *Dragoon Campaigns*, 101–183; William Salter, ed., "Letters of Henry Dodge to General George W. Jones," *Annals of Iowa*, 3rd series, 3 (October 1897): 222 (third quotation); HD 181, 24th Cong., 1st sess., serial 289, 9, 32–33, 36–37 (fourth and fifth quotations); Worth to Jesup, May 20, 1834, box 5, Jesup Papers, LC.

23. Cass to Kearny, October 15, 1835, vol. 15, LSSW; Brown to Clinch, January 4, 1827, Brown Papers, LC (first quotation); Eaton to Macomb, March 24, 1830, vol. 12, LSSW; Brady to Eaton, June 12, 1830, roll 1, M1635, LR by the Headquarters of the Army, RG 108, NARA; Brady to Macomb, July 18, 1830, ibid.; McCall to Wickliffe, September 22, 1832, vol. 6, pt. 1, Entry 5568, LS, Western Division and Department, RG 393, NARA; McCall to Wickliffe, September 22, 1832, ibid.; Gaines to Atkinson, 25 January 1832, ibid. (second and third quotations).

24. Kearny to Atkinson, May 19, 1837, A-178, roll 948, M234, Wisconsin Superintendency, LR by the Office of Indian Affairs, RG 75, NARA; Cooke, *Scenes and Adventures*, 160–161; Francis Paul Prucha, ed., *Army Life on the Western Frontier: Selections from the Official Reports Made Between 1826 and 1845 by Colonel George Croghan* (Norman: University of Oklahoma Press, 1958), 165–166; *ASPMA* 5:506–510, 7:970; *TP* 12:525, 20:784–785, 21:710–712, 907–908; *New ASPMA* 8:356 (first quotation); *ASPIA* 2:661; Gaines to Jones, February 12, 1832, vol. 1, pt. 1, Entry 5568, LS, Western Division and Department, RG 393, NARA; *ASPMA* 5:506–510; Manning to Cass, October 20, 1833, LROAG (second quotation); Francis Paul Prucha, *Broadax and Bayonet: The Role of the United States Army in the Development of the Northwest, 1815–1860* (1953; rpt. Lincoln: University of Nebraska Press, 1967), 67; *ASPMA* 7:532–572.

25. *ASPMA* 4:3 (first quotation), 6:814; *New ASPMA* 8:332; Whistler to Stickney, November 18, 1816, S-10, roll 76, LRSW; Morgan to SW, October, 12, 1817, M120 [1818], Records of the Tenth Military Department, RG 393, NARA; Francis Paul Prucha, *American Indian Policy in the Formative Years: The Indian Trade and Intercourse Acts, 1790–1834* (1962; rpt. Lincoln: University of Nebraska Press, 1970), 252–273; *Statutes* 4:729–738; HR 474, 23rd Cong., 1st sess., serial 263, 14–18, 34–37,

100–102; *RDebates* 23rd Cong., 1st sess., 4763–4779. For comments on subsequent attempts to create legally recognized self-government for Indians, see Hitchcock to Poinsett, December 1, 1838, box 11, Poinsett Papers, HSP; *TP* 28:301.

26. *ASPMA* 5:729–731, 6:13–15 (quotation), 149–153; *Statutes* 5:6; Kearny to Poinsett, March 18, 1838, Poinsett Papers, HSP. For the genesis of the Cass proposals, see HR 474, 23rd Cong., 1st sess., serial 263; *TP* 27:621–624.

27. Ian C. Hope, *A Scientific Way of War: Antebellum Military Science, West Point, and the Origins of American Military Thought* (Lincoln: University of Nebraska Press, 2015), 12, 75 (first quotation); John Spencer Bassett, ed., *Correspondence of Jackson*, 7 vols. (1926–1933; rpt. New York: Kraus Reprint, 1969), 3:190–191 (second quotation); *MPP* 2:456 (third quotation); Robert P. Wettemann Jr., *Privilege vs. Equality: Civil-Military Relations in the Jacksonian Era, 1815–1845* (Santa Barbara: Greenwood Press, 2009), 67–68; Calhoun to Poinsett, March 9, 1837, Poinsett Papers, HSP; *Correspondence of James K. Polk*, 13 vols. to date (Knoxville: University of Tennessee Press, 1969-), 2:373–374, 3:189–190. Although Jackson had lobbied President Monroe on his behalf, Lyncoya never attended.

28. Hope, *Scientific Way of War*, 65; *RDebates* 20th Cong., 1st sess., 634–643 (first quotation), 21st Cong., 1st sess., 522–526 (third quotation), 583 (fourth quotation), 756–757, 774–795, 807–818; Wettemann, *Privilege vs. Equality*, 55–58 (second quotation), 166–169; Samuel J. Watson, "How the Army Became Accepted: West Point Socialization, Military Accountability, and the Nation-State During the Jacksonian Era," *American Nineteenth Century History* 7 (June 2006): 226; *ASPMA* 4:683–686, 5:307; HD 2, 24th Cong., 2nd sess., serial 301, 314; *ASPMA* 5:347–355; Gaines to Poinsett, July 27, 1834, box 8, Poinsett Papers, HSP; "Notes on the Army of the United States," *Military and Naval Magazine of the United States* 1 (April 1833): 97; *RDebates* 23rd Cong., 1st sess., 2550, 4497; *House Journal*, 23rd Cong., 1st sess., 465–466. Under the pseudonym "Americanus," the Partridge tract may be found in Richard H. Kohn, ed., *Anglo-American Antimilitary Tracts, 1697–1830* (New York: Arno Press, 1979).

29. *ASPMA* 4:676–679; Ethan Allen Hitchcock, *Fifty Years in Camp and Field*, ed. W. A. Croffut (New York: G. P. Putnam's Sons, 1909), 65–66; Marcus Cunliffe, *Soldiers & Civilians: The Martial Spirit in America, 1775–1865* (Boston: Little, Brown, 1968), 261–262; Thayer to Swift, February 29, 1832, vol. 5, Thayer Papers, United States Military Academy Library (first quotation); Thayer to Gratiot, July 29, 1832, ibid.; Thayer to Cass, November 26, 1832, ibid.; Cass to Thayer, December 27, 1832, ibid.; Cass to Thayer, December 28, 1832; Thayer to Gratiot, January 1833, ibid.; Wettemann, *Privilege vs. Equality*, 57; Gratiot to Poinsett, July 27, 1837, box 8, Poinsett Papers, HSP (second and third quotations); *MPP* 3:169–170. For the best overview of the controversy, see William Kershner, "Sylvanus Thayer: A Biography" (Ph.D. diss., West Virginia University, 1976).

30. Charles Sellers, *The Market Revolution: Jacksonian America, 1815–1846* (New York: Oxford University Press, 1991), 381 (first quotation) Robert V. Remini, *Andrew Jackson and the Course of American Freedom, 1822–1832* (New York: Harper and Row, 1981), 252–254; *MPP* 2:487–490 (second and third quotations); *Papers of*

Jackson 7:656, 8:566–567; Bassett, ed., *Correspondence of Jackson* 5:165–166 (fourth quotation); Wettemann, *Privilege vs. Equality*, 16, 87–90.

31. Larson, *Internal Improvement*, 150, 171; Robert P. Wettemann Jr., "A Part or Apart: The Alleged Isolation of Antebellum U.S. Army Officers," *American Nineteenth Century History* 7 (June 2006): 198, 202; Todd Arkin Shallat, "Structures in the Stream: A History of Water, Science, and the Civil Activities of the U.S. Army Corps of Engineers, 1700–1861" (Ph.D. diss., Carnegie-Mellon University, 1986), 275; Todd Shallat, *Structures in the Stream: Water, Science, and the Rise of the U.S. Army Corps of Engineers* (Austin: University of Texas Press, 1994), 140–153; *ASPMA* 4:631, 710–716, 766–768, 5:19–20, 219, 358–359, 425, 711–716; 6:795–797; *MPP* 3:113, 168–169; Forest G. Hill, *Roads, Rails, and Waterways: The Army Engineers and Early Transportation* (Norman: University of Oklahoma Press, 1957), 60–61; Mordecai to Ellen, December 31, 1828, box 7, Mordecai Papers, LC; Abert to Roberdeau, undated, filed in Entry 306, "Topographical Engineers, Letters Sent & Returned, Jan.–Dec. 1825" folder, RG 77, NARA; Abert to Butler, January 1837, roll 2, M66, LS by the Topographical Bureau, RG 77, NARA; Abert to Porter, February 12, 1829, roll 1, ibid.; Cullum to Heidekoper, April 11, 1827, Cullum Papers, LC (quotation).

32. Bernard to Poussin, February 19, 1829, vol. 3, Entry 250, Reports on Internal Improvements, RG 77, NARA (quotation); Thomas Hart Benton, *Thirty Years' View: or, a History of the Working of the American Government for Thirty Years, from 1820 to 1850*, 2 vols. (New York: D. Appleton and Co., 1858), 1:26; Hill, *Roads, Rails, and Waterways*, 75–76, 81–82, 111; Larson, *Internal Improvement*, 149–150, 165–166, 183.

The Chesapeake and Ohio Canal was arguably the engineers' greatest fiasco. Insisting upon the best, in 1826, they estimated the cost of the entire sixty-foot-wide structure, which would have run 341 miles and featured 398 locks, at $22.4 million. The Erie Canal, which ran 362 miles, had cost a third of that amount. Only half of the C&O was completed, and the project never generated the tolls needed to repay the investment. HD 10, 19th Cong., 2nd sess., serial 149; HD 192, 20th Cong., 1st sess., serial 173; Shallat, *Structures in the Stream*, 129–140.

33. *New ASPMA* 15:292–309; Wettemann, "A Part or Apart," 200–206; Cass to Trowbridge, November 17, 1835, roll 2, LSSW; Mahan to Poinsett, December 27, 1837, box 9, Poinsett Papers, HSP (first quotation); *MPP* 2:256, 3:113, 168–169; Headquarters of the Army, 18 May 1833, part III, paragraph 7, roll 3, M1094, General Orders and Circulars of the War Department and Headquarters of the Army, RG 108, NARA (second and third quotations); Abert to Butler, January 1837, 240–252, roll 2, LS by the Topographical Bureau, M66, RG 77, NARA; "Engineers and Topographical Engineers," *Army and Navy Chronicle*, January 22, 1835. For protests, presumably from officers, see *New Orleans Commercial Bulletin*, July 13, 1833, and *United States Telegraph*, July 20, 1833.

34. *ASPMA:* 6:417; Bassett, ed., *Correspondence of Jackson* 5:423–424; *TP* 21:1154–1156, 1211, 1230–1231, 1236–1237; *New ASPMA* 6:5–6, 10–11; Watson, *Peacekeepers and Conquerors*, 331–340, 547n. 24; Gaines to Cass, March 29, 1836,

G-99, LRAOG; Houston to Many, August 11, 13, 1836, roll 8, M1302, Records of Headquarters, Army of the Southwestern Frontier, RG 393, NARA; Gaines to Arbuckle, August 10, 1836, roll 2, ibid.; Poinsett to General, March 20, 1837, vol. 17, LSSW. As a second classman at West Point, Virginia's Jubal Early had unsuccessfully petitioned his father for permission to leave the academy and join the Texas Revolution. Early to Father, November 8, 1835, box 1, Early Papers, LC.

35. Clinch to Jones, January 18, 22, 1835, Clinch Papers, LC; Cass to Scott, June 24, 1835, vol. 6, Jesup Papers, LC; *ASPMA* 5:627; Frank Laumer, *Dade's Last Command* (Gainesville: University Press of Florida, 1993); *Correspondence of Polk* 3:467; Buchanan to Anderson, January 13, 1836, box 1, Anderson Papers, LC; Atkinson to Anderson, March 28, 1836, box 2, ibid.; "Political Economy—The Army," *Army and Navy Chronicle*, February 25, 1836; Jackson to Poinsett, October 1, 1837, box 9, Poinsett Papers, HSP; Jackson to Blair, February 28, 1840, vol. 7, Jesup Papers, LC; Prucha, *Sword of the Republic*, 274–281; *ASPMA* 7:820–821 (quotations).

36. Cullum to Heidekoper, December 13, 1834, Cullum Papers, LC; (first quotation); *CGlobe* 23rd Cong., 1st sess., 199–200 (second quotation); *RDebates* 23rd Cong., 1st sess., 4594 (third quotation); Mark A. Smith, *Engineering Security: The Corps of Engineers and Third System Defense Policy, 1815–1861* (Tuscaloosa: University of Alabama Press, 2009), 67–69, 80, 90; *ASPMA* 6:366–396.

37. *RDebates* 24th Cong., 1st sess., 2211–2212 (first quotation), 3371, 4569–4572; Shallat, "Structures in the Stream," 306 (second quotation); Pearce to Cass, March 24, 1835, P-514, box 72, part 1, Entry 18, LR, RG 77, NARA; Pearce to Gratiot, May 28, 1835, P-530, ibid.; Totten to Pearce, June 30, 1836, vol. 4, Part 1, Entry 146, Letters and Reports of Joseph G. Totten, RG 77, NARA; Eldredge to President, February 5, 1836, E-1, CULR (third quotation); Haywood to Jackson, March 30, 1836, H-5, ibid. (fourth quotation). For other correspondence regarding the political implications of appointments to internal improvements projects, see Bennett to Cass, September 16, 1832, B-3, and November 8, 1832, B-6, ibid.

38. *ASPMA* 6:158–169; "Political Economy—The Army, no. II," *Army and Navy Chronicle*, March 24, 1836; "Appointments in the Army," ibid., January 24, 1839; *House Journal*, 24th Cong., 1st sess., 847–848; *Senate Journal*, 24th Cong., 1st sess., 371–372; *RDebates* 24th Cong., 1st sess., 1745–1758, 1851–1852; *Statutes* 5:32–33; *Senate Executive Journal* 4:554–555; www.govtrack.us/congress/votes/24-1/h179. Rhode Island's Dutee J. Pearce, disappointed that no one from his state had been appointed, claimed to have received "assurances some time since, from the President and Secretary of War, that in the event of a vacancy in the dragoon corps . . . [that] anyone I might nominated [sic] would be appointed." Pearce to Harris, August 3, 1836, P-103, LROAG.

39. *Papers of Jackson* 7:188–189, 592 (first quotation), 8:469; Cullum to Heidekoper, August 20, 1836, Cullum Papers, LC; Journal, June 13, 1836, Churchill Papers, LC; Conover, "Kentuckian in King Andrew's Court," 191–192, 197–198; Wettemann, "A Part or Apart," 204–205; Wettemann, *Privilege vs. Equality*, 56, 65–67, 193 n. 53 (second quotation); "Pay of the Army," *Army and Navy Chronicle*, May 19, 1835; "The Army," ibid., May 19, 1836; "Officer's Friend," ibid., September 1, 1836; "The Army," ibid., October 12, 1837. For an officer's reflections upon the

resignations, see Humphreys to Andrew, July 20, 1836, box 1, and undated [1846] draft letter to Haralson, box 2, both in Humphreys Papers, HSP.

In 1835–1836, a pay raise for naval officers led 252 commissioned personnel (from an army officer corps of slightly more than six hundred) to seek "a moderate increase of our compensation" in a petition to the Senate. Filed in Senate 24A-G9, box 85, RG 46, NARA. See also a petition from officers at Fort Gibson, October 14, 1835, Senate 24A-D10, box 19, ibid.

40. Wall to Anderson, August 19, 1836, box 2, Anderson Papers, LC (first quotation); Buchanan to Anderson, March 18, 1836, ibid.; Journals, July 3, 8, Churchill Journals, LC; Watson, *Peacekeepers and Conquerors*, 138–140, 144–160; Ross et al to Wool, Sept. 30, 1836, box 52, Wool Papers, NYSL; Wool to Harris, Oct. 5, 1836, ibid.; Wool to Butler, November 20, 1837, ibid.; Wool to Poinsett, April 20, 1837 (misfiled), roll 19, M 222, LRSW, Unregistered Series, NARA (second quotation); *ASPMA* 7:551–553, 557 (third quotation), 565 (fourth quotation), 545, 540; Wool to Warren, November 21, 1837, Wool Papers, LC; Gary Anderson, *Ethnic Cleansing and the Indian: The Crime That Should Haunt America* (Norman: University of Oklahoma Press, 2014), 164–166. For a less favorable assessment of Wool, see Lawrence M. Hauptman, "General John E. Wool in Cherokee Country, 1836–1837: A Reinterpretation," *Georgia Historical Quarterly* 85 (Spring 2001): 1–26.

41. Watson, *Peacekeepers and Conquerors*, 160–176; Anderson, *Ethnic Cleansing*, 166–170; Russell Thornton, "Cherokee Population Losses during the Trail of Tears: A New Perspective and a New Estimate," *Ethnohistory* 31 (Fall 1984): 289–300, and *American Indian Holocaust and Survival: A Population History since 1492* (Norman: University of Oklahoma Press, 1987).

42. Gibson to Butler, January 12, 1837, House 24A-G11.1, RG 233, NARA; *ASPMA* 6:806–807, 822–824; Robert V. Remini, *Andrew Jackson and the Course of American Democracy, 1833–1845* (New York: Harper and Row, 1984), 304, 311 (first quotation); *United States Telegraph*, June 24, 1836; Wettemann, "A Part or Apart," 203; Gadsden to Poinsett, August 24, 1837, box 9, Poinsett Papers, HSP (second quotation); McLane to Mrs. Louis McLane, December 24, 1837, box 2, McLane Papers, LC; McLane to Father, January 6, 1837 [should be 1838], ibid.; Heiskell to King, February 6, 13, 1838, King Papers, LC; Tripler to King, February 10, 1838, ibid.; Taylor to Jesup, November 26, December 31, 1837, roll 1, Taylor Papers, LC; Jesup to Jones, February 7, 1837, J-19, roll 166, LROAG (third and fourth quotations); Jesup to Butler, February 17, 1837, J-27, ibid.; Poinsett to Jesup, July 25, 1837, roll 17, LSSW; *ASPMA* 7:588, 593; Jackson to Poinsett, December 13, 1837, box 9, Poinsett Papers, HSP; Jesup to Poinsett, January 5, 1838, roll 167, LROAG; Poinsett to Jesup, March 1, 1838, roll 18, LSSW; Jesup to Poinsett, March 14, 1838, J-743, roll 167, LROAG.

43. John K. Mahon, *History of the Second Seminole War* (Gainesville: University of Florida Press, 1967), 219, 225–229; Matthew T. Pearcy, ed., "Andrew Atkinson Humphreys' Seminole War Field Journal," *Florida Historical Quarterly* 85 (Fall 2006): 214 (first quotation); Nauman to Nauman, July 6, 1838, Nauman Family Papers, HSP (second quotation); Grandin to Heintzelman, November 11, 1839, box 6, Heintzelman Papers, LC. For the Taylor controversy, see *ASPMA* 7:987–988; SD

356, 25th Cong., 2nd sess., serial 317; *CGlobe* 25th Cong., 2nd sess., 182–183, 193; Taylor to Hitchcock, July 28, 1841, roll 1, Taylor Papers, LC; Resolution, Missouri Senate and House, February 13, 1839, B-69, roll 202, LROAG.

44. Worth to Poinsett, January 3, February 17, 1838, box 9, Poinsett Papers, HSP; Poinsett to Scott, January 12, 1839, ibid.; Wool to Macomb, February 26, 1838, roll 6, M1635, LR by the Headquarters of the Army, RG 108, NARA; *MPP* 3:403–404 (first and second quotations); C. P. Stacey, ed., "A Private Report of General Winfield Scott on the Border Situation in 1839," *Canadian Historical Review* 21 (December 1940): 411–414 (third, fourth, and fifth quotations); "From the Frontier," *New York Spectator,* Feb. 19, 1838; "Invasion of Lower Canada," *Albany Evening Journal*, March 5, 1838; "From the Globe," *New York Spectator*, March 15, 1838; Samuel J. Watson, "United States Army Officers Fight the 'Patriot War': Responses to Filibustering on the Canadian Border, 1837–1839," *Journal of the Early Republic* 18 (Fall 1998): 492–497; Heiskell to King, January 31, 1838, King Papers, LC; Scott to Poinsett, February 22, 1838, box 10, Poinsett Papers, HSP.

45. "Increase of the Army," *The New Yorker*, June 23, 1838 (first and second quotations); Underwood to Jesup, September 19, 1837, vol. 6, Jesup Papers, LC; HR 297, 24th Cong., 1st sess., serial 293, 2 (third quotation); Gratiot to Poinsett, October 30, 1837, December 27, 1837, January 4, 1838 (fourth quotation), vol. 1, Entry 8, part 1, Letters, Reports, and Statements Sent to the SW and Congress, RG 77, NARA; *RDebates* 24th Cong., 1st sess., 4569–4572; "The Army, Military Academy, Etc.," *Army and Navy Chronicle*, October 19, 1837; "Prospects of the Army," ibid., January 4, 1838; Abert to Butler, January 1837, 240–252, roll 2, M66, LS by the Topographical Bureau, RG 77, NARA; Jesup to Hunt, August 4, 1837, roll 22, M745, LS by the Office of the Quartermaster General, RG 92, NARA; Van Antwerp to Van Buren, November 20, 1837, box 9, Poinsett Papers, HSP (fifth and sixth quotations).

46. *CGlobe* 25th Cong., 2nd sess., 136, 482–489, 496; Thomas to Polk, February 3, 1838, roll 14, Polk Papers, LC; Gadsden to Poinsett, December 15, 1837, box 9, Poinsett Papers, HSP; Benton to Poinsett, "Friday morning," folder 16, box 9, ibid.; Poinsett to Scott, February 5, 1838, box 10, ibid.; Mahan to Poinsett, March 1, 1838, ibid.; Towson to King, August 18, 1837, King Papers, LC; Heiskell to King, January 31, 1838, ibid.; Tripton to King, February 16, 1838, ibid.; Abert to Poinsett, March 17, 1837, roll 2, M66, LS by the Topographical Bureau, RG 77, NARA; *Correspondence of Polk* 4:341–342; "Prospects of the Army," *Army and Navy Chronicle*, January 4, 1838; "One Way of Being Preserved from Large Standing Armies," ibid., March 1, 1838; "The Army—The Militia—and the Public Interest," ibid., March 8, 1836; *New ASPMA* 13:134–136; Underwood to Jesup, March 20, 1838, Jesup Papers, USAMHI; Johnson to Young, June 4, 1838, Young Papers, LC; *House Journal* 25th Cong., 2nd sess., 1191–1192, 1247–1248; Rutledge to Poinsett, August 8, 1838, Poinsett Papers, HSP; Humphreys to Humphreys, April 8, 1838, vol. 1, Humphreys Papers, HSP; Alvord to Hammond, August 20, 1838, box 4, Hammond Papers, LC; *Statutes* 5:256–260 (quotation). Correspondence regarding costs of volunteers is reprinted in WDAR, 1857, 85–87.

For changes in the bill, see S. 138, "Senate Bills and Resolutions," 25th Cong.,

2nd sess., "Bills and Resolutions," A Century of Lawmaking for a New Nation, LC https://memory.loc.gov/ammem/amlaw/lwsblink.html; Kemble to Poinsett, June 26, 1838, box 10, Poinsett Papers, HSP. For army dissatisfaction with McKay, see Poinsett to Hunter, December 28, 1839, box 14, Poinsett Papers, HSP; Eustis to Anderson, January 21, 1840, box 3, Anderson Papers, LC.

7. An Uncertain Future

1. "Mr. Van Buren's Reply," July 31, 1840, *Extra Globe*, August 12, 1840, 139 (first quotation); *MPP* 3:535; Robert P. Wettemann Jr., *Privilege vs. Equality: Civil-Military Relations in the Jacksonian Era, 1815–1845* (Santa Barbara: Greenwood Press, 2009), 93. *MPP* 4:48–49 (second and third quotations), 268; *Correspondence of James K. Polk*, 13 vols. to date (Knoxville: University of Tennessee Press, 1969-), 5:387 (fourth quotation).

2. William H. Goetzmann, *Army Exploration in the American West, 1803–1863* (New Haven: Yale University Press, 1959), 17 (first quotation); Samuel J. Watson, *Peacekeepers and Conquerors: The Army Officer Corps on the American Frontier, 1821–1846* (Lawrence: University Press of Kansas, 2013), 379–383; William B. Skelton, *An American Profession of Arms: The Army Officer Corps, 1784–1861* (Lawrence: University Press of Kansas, 1992), 338–342; Jesup to Croghan, December 5, 1819, box 3, Jesup Papers, LC; Schureman to Mary, April 10, 1844, Schureman Papers, LC (second and third quotations); Meade to Wife, August 15, 1845, box 2, Meade Papers, HSP; Worth to Lawson, November 1, 1845, Lawson Papers, LC; Anderson to Scott, July 3, 1846, box 5, Anderson Papers, LC; Vose to Arbuckle, October 12, 1838, roll 2, M1302, Records of Headquarters, Army of the Southwestern Frontier, RG 393, NARA (fourth quotation).

3. Skelton, *American Profession of Arms*, 182–183, 285, 359; Wettemann, *Privilege vs. Equality*, 45–52, 134–135; Watson, *Peacekeepers and Conquerors*; "Subordination of the Military," *Niles' Weekly Register*, November 7, 1818; Justice, "Politics and Officers," *Army and Navy Chronicle*, May 19, 1836 (first quotation); Alvord to Hammond, December 1, 1841, roll 5, Hammond Papers, LC (second quotation). For a different perspective, see Alcibiades, "Politics and Officers," *Army and Navy Chronicle*, January 7, 1836.

4. Jennings to Early, September 20, 1839, box 1, Early Papers (first quotation); Woods to Early, November 13, 1838, ibid.; Hatch to sister, July 17, 1857, Hatch Papers, LC; Hatch to Father, July 27, August 31, 1857, ibid.; Archer to Mother, December 23, 1855, box 2, Archer Collection, MdHS; Hartz to Jenny, October 30, 1859, box 1, Hartz Papers, LC (second quotation); Hartz to Father, January 1, 1858, ibid. (third quotation); Comstock to McPherson, August 13, 1859, McPherson Papers, LC; Cullum to Heidekoper, September 22, 1833, Cullum Papers, LC (fourth quotation). Jennings died a month after writing his letter. Hatch remained in the army for forty-six years; Hartz died, still a soldier, in 1868; Comstock and Cullum each served forty-four years. All graduated from West Point. For their records, see Heitman.

5. Watson, *Peacekeepers and Conquerors*, 399 (first quotation); J. P. Clark, *Preparing*

for War: The Emergence of the Modern U.S. Army, 1815–1917 (Cambridge: Harvard University Press, 2017), 3 (second quotation); Charles Augustus Murray, *Travels in North America during the Years 1834, 1835, & 1836*, 2 vols. (New York: Harper and Brothers, 1839), 2:67–68 (third quotation). For Croghan, see Croghan to Jesup, February 7, 1826, box 20, Jesup Papers; John Croghan to Jesup, May 26, 1829, ibid.; William Croghan to Jesup, August 1, 1826, box 4, ibid.; Lindsey to Jesup, August 11, 1828, ibid.; Ann Jesup to Husband, February 7, 1839, box 7, ibid. (fourth quotation); Jesup to John Croghan, April 10, 1839, September 13, 1840, box 7, ibid.; Wool to Poinsett, July 26, 1839, box 13, Poinsett Papers, LC. For the Lane-Ewing incident, see Order Book, 1834–35, Fort King, Clinch Papers, LC (fifth and sixth quotations).

6. Skelton, *American Profession of Arms*, 293–295; Skelton, "Officers and Politicians: The Origins of Army Politics in the United States before the Civil War," *Armed Forces and Society* 6 (Fall 1979): 22–48; Wool to Sarah, July 24, 28, 1850, box 1, Wool Papers, NYSL; Wool to Stewart, May 28, 1852, January 6, 1855, box 5, ibid.; Wool to Townsend, May 30, 1856, box 5, ibid. Wool chalked up his 1852 defeat to the "demagogues and political traders" who had dominated the convention. Wool to Stewart, June 8, 1852, box 5, ibid. For Scott's political activities during the late 1830s and early 1840s, see *National Gazette and Literary Register*, November 21, 1839; "Additional Symptoms," *New York Spectator*, June 17, 1839; "General Scott," ibid., November 21, 1839; "The National Convention," ibid., December 12, 1839; Towson to Towson, August 19, 1842, Towson Correspondence, MdHS. For political correspondence in Scott's files, see roll 15, M 1635, LR by the Headquarters of the Army, RG 108, NARA. On Wool, see Durwood Ball, *Army Regulars on the Western Frontier, 1848–1861* (Norman: University of Oklahoma Press, 2001), 97, 106; Harwood Perry Hinton, "The Military Career of John Ellis Wool" (Ph.D. diss., University of Wisconsin, 1963), 65, 233; "Democratic Candidates for the Presidency," 316; *The Papers of Jefferson Davis*, 14 vols. (Baton Rouge: Louisiana State University Press, 1971–2015), 5:87–89. Among his thirty-four potential presidential candidates for the 1860 nomination, one prognosticator included three men who had served in the regular army: John Frémont, Wool, and Jefferson Davis. Not included was Abraham Lincoln. John Savage, *Our Living Representative Men. From Official and Original Sources* (Philadelphia: Childs & Peterson, 1860).

7. Cullum to Heidekoper, May 19, 1838, Cullum Papers, LC; Mordecai to Ellen, January 26, 1830, box 7, Mordecai Papers, LC; Meigs to Meigs, May 4, 1840, roll 4, Addition 1, Meigs Papers, LC; Alvord to Hammond, March 11, 1842, roll 5, Hammond Papers, LC; Schureman to Mary, October 19, 1840, Schureman Papers, LC; Martin to Poinsett, August 21, 1840, M-2, CULR; Poinsett to Martin, September 28, 1840, ibid.; McClellan to Brother, February 3, 1852, roll 2, McClellan Papers, LC; Mary to Tompkins, October 10, 1848, box 78, Marcy Papers, LC; Mary to Jesup, November 14, 1848, ibid.; Gaines to Smith, et al., January 15, 1838, *Army and Navy Chronicle*, February 15, 1838 (first and second quotations); Schureman to Mary, December 15, 1841, Schureman Papers, LC; [Braxton Bragg], "Notes on Our Army," *Southern Literary Messenger* 10 (February 1844): 86 (third quotation); *Correspondence of Polk*, 4:342 (fourth quotation); Jesup to Heintzelman, October 9, 1840, Poinsett Papers, HSP; Sherburne to Jesup, August 16, 1842, box 8, Jesup Papers, LC; Jesup

to Edge, September 24, 1842, ibid.; Cantis to Jesup, January 20, 1843, ibid.; Jesup to Cantis, March 22, 1843, ibid.; M. A. DeWolfe Howe, ed., *Home Letters of General Sherman* (New York: Charles Scribner's Sons, 1909), 26–28. For more documents related to the Buckshot War, see *New ASPMA* 10:26–34 (quotation); HD 28, 25th Cong, 3rd sess., serial 345, 4–16. The commander at Frankford Arsenal, Capt. George D. Ramsey, was reprimanded for having issued supplies and ammunition to Pennsylvania authorities.

8. Skelton, *American Profession of Arms*, 144; Poinsett to Mason, July 15, 1837, vol. 17, LSSW; *ASPMA* 7:578; *Niles' National Register*, May 15, 1841, 164–165; David F. Ericson, "The United States Military, State Development, and Slavery in the Early Republic," *Studies in American Political Development* 31 (April 2017): 140. Notably, only six of the thirty-three officers assigned to the new Eighth Infantry Regiment, specifically designed for service along the volatile Canadian frontier, came directly from civilian life. Watson, *Peacekeepers and Conquerors*, 280–281.

9. John Niven, *Martin Van Buren: The Romantic Age of American Politics* (New York: Oxford University Press, 1983), 466; *CGlobe* 25th Cong., 3rd sess., Appendix, 266–267 (first and second quotations); Jackson to Poinsett, December 13, 1837, box 9, Poinsett Papers, HSP (third quotation); Buchanan to Poinsett, April 5, 1839, box 12, ibid.; Morgan to Brother, July 13, 1840, Morgan Papers, LC; John Campbell, "The Seminoles, the 'Bloodhound War' and Abolitionism, 1796–1865," *Journal of Southern History* 72 (May 2006): 259–302; Francis Paul Prucha, *The Sword of the Republic: The United States on the Frontier, 1783–1846* (London: Macmillan Co., 1969), 294–295; E. W. S., "The Bloodhound War," *Liberator*, January 24, 1840; "The Bloodhound War," *Albany Evening Journal*, January 28, 1840. For the administration's attempts to disassociate itself from the bloodhounds, see S-21, CULR; and HR 26A-G 11.2, RG 233, NARA, which contains eight folders of materials.

10. Watson, *Peacekeepers and Conquerors*, 185–187; John K. Mahon, *History of the Second Seminole War* (Gainesville: University of Florida Press, 1967), 309–327; October 16, 1838, Churchill Journals, LC; Woods to Early, April 23, 1839, box 1, Early Papers, LC; Pegram to Anderson, December 1, 1840, January 18, 1841, box 3, Anderson Papers, LC; Kearny to Anderson, January 10, 1841, ibid.; Hitchcock to "Dear Sir" (marked "not sent"), December 5, 1840, box 1, Hitchcock Papers, LC; Hitchcock to Bell, January 11, 1841, ibid.; Taylor to Hitchcock, July 28, 1841, roll 1, Taylor Papers, LC; Birdsall to King, July 19, 1841, King Papers, LC (first quotation); Steptoe to Early, February 25, 1840, box 1, Early Papers, LC (second quotation); Matthew T. Pearcy, ed., "Andrew Humphreys' Seminole War Field Journal," *Florida Historical Quarterly* 85 (Fall 2006): 214 (third quotation); *TP* 26:436–440 (fourth quotation), 538, 548–550 (fifth quotation), 551–553.

For officers retiring or seeking leaves or transfers from Florida, see Humphreys to Abert, August 7, 1838, vol. 1, Humphreys Papers, HSP; Randall to Alexander, January 1, 1843, box 5, Philpot-Randall Family Papers, MdHS; Hitchcock to Bliss, March 11, 1841, box 1, Hitchcock Papers, LC; Poinsett to Gregory, February 19, 1838, box 10, Poinsett Papers, HSP.

11. Johnston to Young, June 4, 1838, Young Papers, LC (first quotation); Meigs to Meigs, May 4, 1840, roll 4, Addition I, Meigs Papers, LC; Cullum to Heidekoper,

January 9, 1835, August 20, 1836 (second and third quotations), Cullum Papers, LC; "Appointments in the Army," *Army and Navy Chronicle*, January 24, 1839; "Civilian Appointments to the Army," ibid., February 21, 1839; Morgan to Buchanan, October 6, 1840, box 1, Buchanan Papers, MdHS; Towson to Towson, May 2, 1838, Towson Correspondence, MdHS; Morgan to Buchanan, October 1840, box 1, Buchanan Papers, MdHS; Larned to Buchanan, August [20], 1841, ibid.; Eustis to Anderson, June 5, 1840, October 2, 1840, box 3, Anderson Papers, LC; Scott to Clinch, October 22, December 4, 1842, box 4, ibid.

12. Niven, *Van Buren*, 406–407; Robert V. Remini, *Andrew Jackson and the Course of American Democracy, 1833–1845* (New York: Harper and Row, 1984), 243–249; Cardozo to Poinsett, March 7, 1837, box 8, Poinsett Papers, HSP; Bernard to Poinsett, April 23, 1838, box 10, ibid.; Rutledge to Poinsett, April 8, 1838, ibid.; *ASPMA* 7:573–580, 589. For the development of Poinsett's recommendations, see Kemble to Poinsett, July 19, August 16, 1837, box 9, Poinsett Papers, HSP; Eustis to Poinsett, July 28, 1837, box 8, ibid.; Poinsett to [Kemble], July 31, 1837, box 9, ibid.; Poinsett to Jackson, August 19, 1837, ibid.; Jackson to Poinsett, October 1, 1837, ibid.; Totten to Poinsett, November 7, 1837, ibid.; *MPP* 3:389–390.

In refusing to accept the War Department portfolio in 1841, John McLean explained, "It is connected with an extensive patronage but not that kind of patronage, which makes a deep impression upon the country. It affords little or no opportunity to the incumbent to give an elevated tone to the action of the government, and to increase its moral power. . . . The duties of the War Department are generally matters of routine, and can be as well discharged by a chief clerk as any other person." Harold D. Moser, ed., *The Papers of Daniel Webster: Correspondence*, vol. 5 (Lebanan, NH: Dartmouth College Press, 1982), 157.

13. Skelton, *American Profession of Arms*, 240; James L. Morrison, *"Best School in the World": West Point, the Pre-Civil War Years, 1833–1866* (Kent, OH: Kent State University Press, 1986), 29; WDAR, 1839, 49 (first quotation); WDAR, 1840, 29; Mark A. Smith, "The Politics of Military Professionalism: The Engineer Company and the Political Activities of the Antebellum U.S. Army Corps of Engineers," *Journal of Military History* 80 (April 2016): 385; Poinsett to Cass, December 30, 1839, roll 21, LSSW; Poinsett to Beall, Hardee, and Newton, November 26, 1840, roll 23, ibid.; SED 229, 26th Cong., 2nd sess., serial 378; Poinsett to Cummings, Armstrong, and Street, July 22, 1837, roll 17, LSSW; Poinsett to Cummings, October 2, 1837, roll 18, ibid.; J. Fred Rippy, *Joel R. Poinsett: Versatile American* (Durham: Duke University Press, 1935), 171–172; Pegram to Anderson, January 18, 1841, box 3, Anderson Papers, LC (second quotation). For Poinsett's efforts to return Thayer, see Mahan to Poinsett, May 17, June 23, 30, July 16, August 16, 1837, box 8, Poinsett Papers, HSP; Kemble to Poinsett, August 16, November 4, 20, 1837, box 9, ibid.; Thayer to Kemble, October 29 [1837], ibid.

14. *ASPMA* 5:605, 606, 779–781, 7:575; 777–778 (quotation), 784–785; Poinsett to Linn, January 11, 1839, roll 20, LSSW; WDAR, 1838, 1–2, 99–100; SD 379, 26th Cong., 1st sess., serial 359, 6–8; HD 278, 25th Cong., 2nd sess., serial 328; WDAR, 1839, 47, 113; *MPP* 3:497; Yell to Poinsett, June 30, 1838, box 10, Poinsett Papers,

HSP; Kemble to Poinsett, April 14, 1840, box 14, ibid.; Docket Volume, Committee on Military Affairs, 25th Cong., 3rd sess., 23A-D12.3, RG 233, NARA.

15. Gaines to Poinsett, May 22, 1837, roll 5, M857, LS by the Headquarters of the Army, RG 108, NARA; HD 311, 25th Cong., 2nd sess., serial 329; *Niles' National Register*, January 23, 1841, 59:322. While he was at it, Gaines offered up a seven-step plan for the occupation of Mexico City. After newly appointed Secretary of War John Bell expressed an interest (probably as a courtesy), Gaines acknowledged that some called his scheme "a Don Quixotish project." Gaines to Bell, April 21, 1841, vol. 127, LRSW (quotation); Gaines to Bell, June 28, 1841, vol. 129, ibid. See also his earlier "Military Importance of Railroads," *American Magazine of Useful and Entertaining Knowledge* 2 (March 1836): 283–284.

16. Scott Kaufman and John A. Soares Jr., "'Sagacious Beyond Praise?' Winfield Scott and Anglo American-Canadian Border Diplomacy, 1837–1860," *Diplomatic History* 30 (January 2006): 66–68; *Statutes* 5:351–352, 355–356.

17. Croghan to Poinsett, March 8, 1839, C-4 (first quotation); Gibson to Poinsett, March 9, 1839, G-10; Gratiot to Poinsett, March 9, 1839, G-10; Jesup to Poinsett, March 21, 1839, J-5 (second quotation); Abert to Poinsett, March 11, 1839, A-2 (third quotation); Jones to Poinsett, March 11, 1839, J-6 (fourth quotation); Bomford to Poinsett, 11 March 1839, B-18; Towson to Poinsett, March 11, 1839, T-3; all in CULR. Gaines to Macomb, July 6, 1833, vol. 1, Part 1, Entry 5568, LS, Western Division and Department, RG 393, NARA; Gaines to Poinsett, March 18, 1839, G-84, box 83, Part 1, Entry 18, LR, RG 77, NARA (fifth quotation); Gaines to Poinsett, March 20, 1839, G-67 ibid., (sixth quotation); Gaines to Poinsett, March 22, 23, 1839, G-9, CULR; Gaines to Poinsett, May 6, 1839, G-101, roll 187, LROAG. For evidence of later strategic discussion, see Poinsett to Abert, April 17, 1840, vol. 22, LSSW, 126; and SD 85, 28th Cong., 2nd sess., serial 451.

A subsequent board, headed by Totten, estimated the need for nine thousand cannons and $32 million for additional fortifications, along with $1.47 million for arsenals and depots, a national foundry, and a western armory. HD 206, 26th Cong., 1st sess., serial 368, 69–117. Gaines later concocted a scheme to establish several floating batteries for every inlet to a United States seaport, with each to be 200–300 feet long and 90–150 feet wide, capable of mounting 120–200 cannons. He estimated the cost at $11 million per annum for six years. HD 206, 26th Cong., 1st sess., serial 368, 118–143.

18. Poinsett to Totten and Thayer, October 18, 1838, roll 2, CULS; Scott to Poinsett, February 4, 1839, box 11, Poinsett Papers, HSP; Kemble to Poinsett, June 7, 1839, ibid.; Niven, *Van Buren*, 441–443; Scott to Clinch, December 4, 1842, box 4, ibid.; Anderson to Kemble, January 12, 1839, box 2, Anderson Papers, LC; Scott to Anderson, April 15, 1839, ibid. (first and second quotations); Scott, Confidential Circular, April 15, 1839, S-39, CULR; Heiskell to King, January 31, 1838, King Papers, LC; Churchill Journals, July 26, 1838, LC (third quotation); Mansen to Wool, February 21, 1838, box 47, Wool Papers, NYSL (fourth and fifth quotations); Bromley to Wool, April 17, 1838, ibid.; Kaufman and Soares, "'Sagacious Beyond Praise,'" 66–71; *Memoirs of Lieut.-Gen. Scott, Written by Himself* (New York: Sheldon and Co.,

1864), 2:334–347; Scott to Poinsett, March 7, 1838, S-25, January 20, 1839, S-26, CULR; Scott to Harvey, March 25, 1839, S-30, ibid.; Scott to Arthur, November 9, 1839, S-32, ibid.; John S. D. Eisenhower, *Agent of Destiny: The Life and Times of General Winfield Scott* (1997; rpt. Norman: University of Oklahoma Press, 1999), 200.

19. Major T. Wilson, *The Presidency of Martin Van Buren* (Lawrence: University Press of Kansas, 1984), 188; Williams to Monroe, December 22, 1815, January 12, 1816, Williams Papers, LC; Williams to Gaines, October 19, 1815, ibid.; William H. Sumner, *An Inquiry into the Importance of the Militia to a Free Commonwealth . . .* (Boston: Cummings and Hilliard, 1823); Bennett to Poinsett, July 27, 1840, B-10, CULR (first quotation); Joseph Story, *Commentaries on the Constitution of the United States . . .* (Boston: Hilliard, Gray and Co., 1833), 3:1890; "Notes on the Army of the United States," *Military and Naval Magazine of the United States* (April 1833), (second quotation); *ASPMA* 1:642–644, 3:418, 451–452, 4:134, 712; 5:630–631; WDAR, 1839, 43–44; HD 153, 26th Cong., 1st sess., serial 366. For the efforts of J. C. Bennett, the quartermaster general of Illinois, to secure militia reform while the Democrats retained control of the state legislature, see Bennett to Poinsett, July 27, 1840, B-10; November 20, 1840, B-15; November 25, 1840, B-16, all in CULR.

20. *Raleigh Register and North Carolina Gazette*, February 4, 1840 (first quotation); *Ohio Statesman*, April 1, 1840; *Fayetteville Observer*, May 27, 1840; *Natchez Daily Courier*, June 11, 1840 (second quotation); *Correspondence of Polk* 5:364, 390, 441, 456, 474–475 (third and fourth quotations), 488; Read to Poinsett, April 26, 1840, box 14, Poinsett Papers, HSP; Benton to Poinsett, May 27, 1840, ibid.; Richie to Poinsett, May 29, 1840, ibid. (fifth quotation); Wallace to Van Buren, June 13, 1840, ibid.; "The Great Whig Humbug about a Standing Army, Exploded," *The Crisis: Devoted to the Support of Democratic Principles*, March 28, 1840; Niven, *Van Buren*, 463–644. A draft of Poinsett's response may be found in box 14, Poinsett Papers, HSP.

21. "Politics of the Day: The Standing Army of 200,000 Men!" *Niles' National Register*, September 5, 1840; *Virginia Free Press*, September 10, 1840 (first quotation); *Cleveland Daily Herald*, September 5, 1840 (second and third quotations); Niven, *Van Buren*, 463–465; Brown to Poinsett, September 23, 1840, box 14, Poinsett Papers, HSP (fourth quotation); *Correspondence of Polk* 5:593; "The 'Standing Army'—the President," *Extra Globe*, August 12, 1840, 129; Wilson, *Presidency of Van Buren*, 189; "The Army Bill," *Log Cabin*, October 24, 1840 (fifth quotation). For Van Buren's tortured attempts to explain his position, see "Mr. Van Buren's Reply," July 31, 1840, *Extra Globe*, August 12, 1840, 137–140.

22. Skelton, *American Profession of Arms*, 282.

23. Robert W. Coakley, *The Role of Federal Military Forces in Domestic Disorders, 1789–1878* (Washington, D.C.: Center of Military History, 1988), 119–127; HD 225, 28th Cong., 1st sess., serial 443, 48 (third quotation); HR 546, 28th Cong., 1st sess., serial 447; *Luther* v. *Borden*, 48 U.S. 1 (1849); Erik J. Chaput, *The People's Martyr: Thomas Wilson Dorr and His 1842 Rhode Island Rebellion* (Lawrence: University Press of Kansas, 2013). From New York City, Capt. Robert Anderson proclaimed: "An attempt on the part of the Genl Govt to put down the revolutionists in R. Island

by U.S. troops, would produce bad feelings and end in blood shedding." Anderson to Clinch, April 17, 1842, Anderson Papers, LC.

24. Norma Louis Peterson, *The Presidencies of William Henry Harrison and John Tyler* (Lawrence: University Press of Kansas, 1989), 156–158; Edward P. Crapol, *John Tyler: The Accidental President* (Chapel Hill: University of North Carolina Press, 2006), 23, 56, 74–75, 95, 173; *Correspondence of Polk* 6:250.

25. *Historical Statistics of the United States, Earliest Times to the Present*, Millennial Edition, 5 vols. (Cambridge: Cambridge University Press, 2006), 5:127, 353–358; WDAR, 1840, 48; "Non-Commissioned Officers of the Army," *Military and Naval Magazine of the United States* (October 1833): 65; Cynthia Allen Miller, "The U.S. Army Logistics Complex: A Case Study of the Northern Frontier" (Ph.D. diss., Syracuse University, 1991), 69; Jesup to Whiting, December 18, 1837, J-53 1838, roll 167, LROAG; Coffman, *Old Army*, 139, 210; Robert Wooster, *The American Military Frontiers: The United States Army in the West, 1783–1900* (Albuquerque: University of New Mexico Press, 2009), 65–68; Charles Francis Adams, ed., *Memoirs of John Q. Adams*, 12 vols., (Philadelphia: J. B. Lippincott, 1874–1877), 7:29; Larned to Buchanan, August [20], 1841, box 1, Buchanan Papers, MdHS (first quotation); "Day Police—alias Standing Army," *Subterranean, United with the Workingman's Advocate*, November 2, 1844 (second and third quotations); "Reduction of the Army and Navy," *The Huntress*, June 11, 1842 (fourth quotation); *C Globe* 27th Cong., 2nd sess., 659, 683–684, 691, 698, 825, 838–839, 845, 848; *House Journal* 27th Cong., 2nd sess., 921–927; *Statutes* 5:512–513; *MPP* 4:198–199 (fifth quotation). Fearing that critics would attack West Point as elitist, War Department officials had instructed the superintendent to ascertain, "in a quiet and unofficial way," the backgrounds of cadets. Totten to Delafield, January 19, 28, 1842, Entry 146, vol. 6, Letters and Reports of Totten, RG 77, NARA.

26. "Mr. Tyler's Acceptance," *Niles' National Register*, June 8, 1844, 234 (first quotation); *New ASPMA* 4:80–82; SD 231, 26th Cong., 1st sess., serial 358; WDAR, 1841, 62; WDAR, 1842, 179–180, 188–189, 199–200; WDAR, 1844, 126; *MPP* 4:87; Spencer to Linn, March 23, 1842, vol. 24, LSSW; Watson, *Peacekeepers and Conquerors*, 357–365; William E. Connelley, ed., "Journal of the Santa Fe Trail," *Mississippi Valley Historical Review* 12 (June 1925): 228–230 (second and third quotations); Prucha, *Sword of the Republic*, 377–379; "Gen. Gaines and the Santa Fe Traders," *Niles' National Register*, August 19, 1843, 386.

27. *MPP* 4:268; *Daily National Intelligencer*, August 17, 1842; WDAR, 1843, 52, 64; HR 77, 28th Cong., 1st sess., serial 445, 5–6 (first quotation); "Memorial, to the Honorable Senate and House of Representatives," 28A-G 13.5, RG 233, NARA (second quotation); Military Notebook, January 1843, Halleck Papers, LC; Jesup to Spencer, March 30, 1842, box 8, Jesup Papers, LC; Jesup to Wilkins, April 4, 1844, box 9, ibid.; *Correspondence of Polk* 7:98; *CGlobe* 28th Cong., 1st sess., 347, 415 (third quotation), 442; *Statutes* 5:654.

28. WDAR, 1844, 130 (first quotation); Clifton Wharton, "The Expedition of Major Clifton Wharton in 1844," *Collections of the Kansas State Historical Society* 16 (1925): 272–273, 295, 305; *New ASPMA* 8:371–372; Jacob Van der Zee, ed.,

"Captain Edwin V. Sumner's Dragoon Expedition in the Territory of Iowa in the Summer of 1845," *Iowa Journal of History and Politics* 11 (April 1913): 259–261 (second and third quotations); WDAR, 1845, 196–197, 208–212, 217–220.

29. *The Statistical History of the United States: From Colonial Times to the Present* (New York: Basic Books, 1976), 8, 1114–1115; James J. Farley, *Making Arms in the Machine Age: Philadelphia's Frankford Arsenal, 1816–1870* (University Park: Pennsylvania State University Press, 1994), 11–37; Richard C. Wade, *The Urban Frontier: The Rise of Western Cities, 1790–1830* (Cambridge: Harvard University Press, 1959), 25–26, 63–64; Paul A. C. Koistinen, *Beating Plowshares into Swords: The Political Economy of American Warfare, 1607–1865* (Lawrence: University Press of Kansas, 1996), 52–98; Mark A. Smith, *Engineering Security: The Corps of Engineers and Third System Defense Policy, 1815–1861* (Tuscaloosa: University of Alabama Press, 2009), 156–178.

30. WDAR, 1839, 633–640; William D. Adler, "State Capacity and Bureaucratic Autonomy in the Early United States: The Case of the Army Corps of Topographical Engineers," *Studies in American Political Development* 26 (October 2012): 107–124; Frank N. Schubert, ed., *The Nation-Builders: A Sesquicentennial History of the Corps of Topographical Engineers* (Washington, D.C.: Government Printing Office, 1989), 23–56; *New ASPMA* 15:94–95; Volpe, "Origins of the Frémont Expeditions," 244–262; Goetzmann, *Army Exploration*, 74–108; H. A. S. Dearborn, *Letters on the Internal Improvements and Commerce of the West* (Boston: H. P. Lewis, 1839), 58; Andrew Menard, "Striking a Line through the Great American Desert," *Journal of American Studies* 45 (May 2011): 267–280; Watson, *Peacekeepers and Conquerors*, 29–32. Frémont's reports are in SD 243, 27th Cong., 3rd sess., serial 416; and HD 166, 28th Cong., 2nd sess., serial 467.

31. W. Turrentine Jackson, *Wagon Roads West: A Study of Federal Road Surveys and Construction in the Trans-Mississippi West, 1846–1869* (New Haven: Yale University Press, 1963), 11; Davis to Poinsett, May 23, 1838, box 10, Poinsett Papers, HSP; Ed Bearss and Arrell M. Gibson, *Fort Smith: Little Gibraltar on the Arkansas* (Norman: University of Oklahoma Press, 1969), 137–154, 167–170, 188; *TP* 21:803–805, 896–899, 916–918; Cross to Thomas, May 24, 1838, roll 13, M745, LS by the Office of Quartermaster General, RG 92, NARA; Jesup to McKay, March 23, 1844, vol. 9, Jesup Papers, LC; Francis Paul Prucha, ed., *Army Life on the Western Frontier: Selections from the Official Reports Made Between 1826 and 1845 by Colonel George Croghan* (Norman: University of Oklahoma Press, 1958), 31–32; Petition from Citizens of Platte County, Missouri, HR 27A-G 12.3, RG 233, NARA (quotation); *CGlobe* 25th Cong., 3rd sess., Appendix, 266–269; HR 27A-G 12.2, RG 233, NARA.

Large military reservations sometimes limited the space available for private development. The big post at Fort Snelling, for example, meant that the little community of nearby Mendota was, according to an observer in the early 1850s, "a less rapidly progressive place than is usual in these parts, having suffered from those obstructive tendencies which characterize war-departments generally, and in consequence of which the large military reserve attached to Fort Snelling, upon which it is situated, has only recently been available for practical purposes." Laurence Oliphant, *Minnesota and the Far West* (Edinburgh: William Blackwood and Sons, 1855), 248–249.

32. *MPP* 3:391 (first quotation), 497; SD 231, 25th Cong., 2nd sess., serial 316; SD 304, 25th Cong., 2nd sess., serial 317; SD 465, 25th Cong., 2nd sess., serial 318; HD 268, 25th Cong., 2nd sess., serial 328; HD 312, 25th Cong., 2nd sess., serial 329; SD 260, 25th Cong., 3rd sess., serial 341; HR 168, 25th Cong., 3rd sess., serial 351; HD 140, 26th Cong., 1st sess., serial 365; HD 177, 26th Cong., 1st sess., serial 366; HD 8, 27th Cong., 1st sess., serial 392; various materials in Senate 25A-G 11, RG 46, NARA; Petition from Danville, Pennsylvania, HR 27A-G 12.3, RG 233, NARA; Memorial from Memphis, September 28, 1841, HR 27A-G 12.3 (second quotation); HD 23, 28th Cong., 1st sess., serial 441; SD 231, 25th Cong., 2nd sess., serial 316, 2–3 (third and fourth quotations). For a protest lodged by a private manufacturer, see HR 168, 25th Cong., 3rd sess., serial 351, 59.

33. HD 36, 27th Cong., 2nd sess., serial 402; various materials in HR 28A-G 13.3, RG 233, NARA (first quotation); HD 149, 27th Cong., 2nd sess., serial 403; SD 206, 28th Cong., 1st sess., serial 434; HD 33, 28th Cong., 1st sess., serial 441; HD 119, 28th Cong., 1st sess., serial 442; "To the Hon. the Senate & House of Representatives . . . ," December 1845, HR29A-G10.1, RD 233, NARA; General Orders 63, October 15, 1841, roll 4, M1094, General Orders and Circulars of the War Department and Headquarters of the Army, RG 94, NARA; HD 133, 27th Cong., 3rd sess., serial 421; HR 441, 28th Cong., 1st sess., serial 446 (second quotation); HR 27, 28th Cong., 2nd sess., serial 468; HR 451, 29th Cong., 1st sess., serial 489.

34. Merritt Roe Smith, *Harpers Ferry Armory and the New Technology: The Challenge of Change* (Ithaca, NY: Cornell University Press, 1977), 64–66, 80–82, 101, 148–149, 175, 177–181, 252–256, 328; *ASPMA* 2:541–543; David R. Meyer, *Networked Machinists: High Technology Industries in Antebellum America* (Baltimore: Johns Hopkins University Press, 2006), 80–82; Merritt Roe Smith, "Army Ordnance and the 'American System' of Manufacturing, 1815–1861," in *Military Enterprise and Technological Change: Perspectives on the American Experience*, ed. Merritt Roe Smith (Cambridge: MIT Press, 1985), 81; Merritt Roe Smith, "Industry, Technology, and the 'Labor Question' in 19th Century America: Seeking Synthesis," *Technology and Culture* 32 (July 1991): 558–563.

35. Smith, "Army Ordnance," 61–64, 80–81; Brian A. Balogh, *A Government out of Sight: The Mystery of National Authority in Nineteenth-Century America* (Cambridge: Cambridge University Press, 2009), 212; Keith W. Hoskin and Richard H. Macve, "Reappraising the Genesis of Managerialism: A Re-examination of the Role of Accounting in the Springfield Armory, 1815–1845," *Accounting, Auditing & Accountability Journal* 7, no. 2 (1994): 4–5; Meyer, *Networked Machinists*, 7–9, 94–95, 236–238; David A. Hounshell, *From the American System to Mass Production, 1800–1932: The Development of Manufacturing Technology in the United States* (Baltimore: Johns Hopkins University Press, 1984), 39–40; Smith, *Harpers Ferry*, 184, 219–222; Koistinen, *Beating Plowshares into Swords*, 79–80.

36. Smith, "Army Ordnance," 82–85; Meyer, *Networked Machinists*, 278–279; *MPP* 4:12; HD 76, 33th Cong., 1st sess., serial 741, 78; Memorial of July 31, 1841, HR 27A-G12.3, RG 233, NARA; Memorial of March 29 and 30, 1842, ibid. (first and second quotations); HD 207, 27th Cong., 2nd sess., serial 404, 2–8 (third and fourth quotations); WDAR, 1841, 67.

37. *CGlobe* 27th Cong., 2nd sess., 683–685, 691–692, 845, 862, 868, 902; *Statutes* 5:512; [Charles Stearns], *The National Armories: A Review of the System of Superintendency, Civil and Military, Particularly with Reference to Economy, and General Management, of the Springfield Armory*, 2nd ed. (Springfield: G. W. Wilson's Steam Power Presses, 1852), 4–7. Fifteen Whigs (including both senators from Massachusetts) and eight Democrats had supported the proposal to restore civilian control, with nine Whigs and five Democrats in opposition. The subsequent reversal, by a 21–13 margin, was not included as a roll-call vote, although in debate two Democrats said that they had changed their minds.

38. "1844 Democratic Party Platform," American Presidency Project, www.presidency.ucsb.edu/ws/?pid=29573 (first quotation); *Correspondence of Polk* 9:135, 140, 225; *MPP* 4:413 (second quotation).

39. Skelton, *American Profession of Arms*, 338 (first and second quotations); Atkinson to Anderson, May 1, 1839, box 2, Anderson Papers, LC (third quotation); Jesup to Wilkins, May 22, 1844, vol. 9, Jesup Papers, LC; Havt to Father, March 24, 1855, box 1; Hartz Papers, LC; Howe, *Home Letters of Sherman*, 26 (fourth and fifth quotations); Watson, *Peacekeepers and Conquerors*, 379–403.

40. K. Jack Bauer, *The Mexican War, 1846–1848* (New York: Macmillan, 1974), 18, 20, 33, 40; SD 337, 29th Cong., 1st sess., serial 476, 74–76 (first quotation), 78, 82–83, 90–92, 98–100, 106–107; Hatch to Eliza, October 14 (second quotation), 28, November 22, 1845, Hatch Papers, LC (second quotation); Crapol, *Tyler*, 198, 203; Paul H. Bergeron, *The Presidency of James K. Polk* (Lawrence: University Press of Kansas, 1987), 62–64, 69–71. Texans were delighted with the prospect of U.S. occupation, their constitutional convention having on July 7, 1845—just three days after the meeting began—adopted a resolution calling upon the president "to occupy and establish posts without delay." *Journal of the Convention Assembled at the City of Austin on the 4th of July 1845 for the Purpose of Framing a Constitution for the State of Texas* (1845; rpt. Austin: Shoal Creek Publishers, 1974), 20. My thanks to Dr. William J. Chriss for calling this to my attention.

41. Bergeron, *Presidency of Polk*, 114–130; *MPP* 4:396 (first quotation); WDAR, 1845, 195–197; *CGlobe* 29th Cong., 1st sess., 153, 162, 542 (second quotation), 534–535 (third quotation), 543–544, 552, 655, 658–659.

42. John C. Pinheiro, *Manifest Ambition: James K. Polk and Civil-Military Relations during the Mexican War* (Westport, CT: Praeger Security International, 2007), 37–45; Bauer, *Mexican War*, 48, 67, 397; *MPP* 4:442 (quotation); Milo M. Quaife, ed., *The Diary of James K. Polk During His Presidency, 1845–1849*, 4 vols. (1910; rpt. New York: Kraus, 1970), 1:384–385, 390–394.

8. Manifest Destiny and the Regular Army

1. *MPP* 4:631–633.

2. Samuel J. Watson, *Peacekeepers and Conquerors: The Army Officer Corps on the American Frontier, 1821–1846* (Lawrence: University Press of Kansas, 2012), 388–398; Edward M. Coffman, *The Old Army: A Portrait of the American Army in Peacetime, 1784–1898* (New York: Oxford University Press, 1986), 79–80; Worth to

Lawson, November 1, 1845, Lawson Papers, LC (first quotation); Philip St. George Cooke, *Scenes and Adventures in the Army; or, Romance of Military Life* (1857; rpt. New York: Arno Press, 1973), 175–176 (second quotation); *PUSG* 1:154; *An Artillery Officer in the Mexican War, 1846–7: Letters of Robert Anderson* (New York: Knickerbocker Press, 1911), 19, 181, 270 (third quotation); George Gordon Meade, ed., The *Life and Letters of George Gordon Meade, Major-General United States Army*, 2 vols. (New York: Charles Scribner's Sons, 1913), 1:48, 154 (fourth quotation); Ulysses S. Grant, *Memoirs and Selected Letters* (New York: Library of America, 1990), 41 (fifth and sixth quotations); M. A. DeWolfe Howe, ed., *Home Letters of General Sherman* (New York: Charles Scribner's Sons, 1909), 26; [Edward B. Hunt], "Army Attack and National Defense," *American Whig Review* 4 (August 1846): 146–147.

William B. Skelton, *An American Profession of Arms: The Army Officer Corps, 1784–1861* (Lawrence: University Press of Kansas, 1992), 294, 330–332, finds a more aggressive expansionism among officers, who "greeted the outbreak of fighting in 1846 with an enthusiasm bordering on mania." Racist overtones are emphasized in James M. McCaffrey, *Army of Manifest Destiny: The American Soldier in the Mexican War, 1846–1848* (New York: New York University Press, 1992); Reginald Horsman, *Race and Manifest Destiny: The Origins of American Racial Anglo-Saxonism* (Cambridge: Harvard University Press, 1981); and Paul Foos, *A Short, Offhand, Killing Affair: Soldiers and Social Conflict during the Mexican-American War* (Chapel Hill: University of North Carolina Press, 2002).

3. Paul A. C. Koistinen, *Beating Plowshares into Swords: The Political Economy of American Warfare, 1607–1865* (Lawrence: University Press of Kansas, 1996), 90–91; K. Jack Bauer, *The Mexican War, 1846–1848* (New York: Macmillan, 1974), 394; *MPP* 4:413; Milo M. Quaife, ed., *The Diary of James K. Polk During His Presidency, 1845–1849*, 4 vols. (1910; rpt. New York: Kraus, 1970), 1:388–389; *Statutes* 9:9–11. For continuing memories of the Poinsett debacle, see Stanton to Chase, July 17, 1849, roll 1, Stanton Papers, LC.

4. *CGlobe* 29th Cong., 1st sess., 94, 101, 113, 804–805, 826–827 (quotations), Appendix, 641–645; Julian to Julian, January 25, 1850, box 1, Giddings and Julian Papers, LC; Mark A. Smith, "The Politics of Military Professionalism: The Engineer Company and the Political Activities of the Antebellum U.S. Army Corps of Engineers," *Journal of Military History* 80 (April 2016): 361–370; *Statutes* 9:12–13; John C. Pinheiro, *Manifest Ambition: James K. Polk and Civil-Military Relations during the Mexican War* (Westport, CT: Praeger Security International, 2007), 41–43.

5. Quaife, ed., *Diary of Polk* 1:391, 395–396, 400–401, 407–408, 414–415 (first quotation), 420–421, 424; Scott to Archer, February 6, 1846, series 2, roll 44, Polk Papers, LC; HED 60, 30th Cong., 1st sess., serial 520, 446; SD 378, 29th Cong., 1 sess., serial 477, 5–12; Scott to Clinch, July 10, 1846, box 5, Anderson Papers, LC; Bauer, *Mexican War*, 73–74; John S. D. Eisenhower, *Agent of Destiny: The Life and Times of General Winfield Scott* (1997; rpt. Norman: University of Oklahoma Press, 1999), 224–225; *CGlobe*, 29th Cong., 1st sess., Appendix, 650 (second quotation).

6. HED 92, 37th Cong., 2nd sess., serial 1135, 180 (first quotation); Ian C. Hope, *A Scientific Way of War: Antebellum Military Science, West Point, and the Origins of American Military Thought* (Lincoln: University of Nebraska Press, 2015), 135–136;

Gaines to Poinsett, 6 May 1839, G 101, 103/1839, roll 187, LROAG (second quotation); Quaife, ed., *Diary of Polk* 1:405, 412–413, 418 (third quotation), 431, 438–439, 443, 493; 2:117–119, 128, 132–134, 430–431 (fourth quotation); Bauer, *Mexican War*, 20; SD 378, 29th Cong., 1st sess., serial 477, 23–31, 50–55, 59–61; SD 402, 29th Cong., 1st sess., serial 477, 1–3; Richard Bruce Winders, *Mr. Polk's Army: The American Military Experience in the Mexican War* (College Station: Texas A&M University Press, 1997), 37. Jesup complained bitterly about the president's appointees to his office, and his wife's death during the war made his job all the more difficult. See Jesup to Stanton, November 27, 1846, box 11, Jesup Papers, LC; Jesup to Daughter, January 20, 1847, box 13, ibid.; Jesup to Marcy, February 16, 1847, ibid.; Jesup to Mary, February 21, 1847, box 14, ibid.

7. Douglas A. Murphy, *Two Armies on the Rio Grande: The First Campaign of the US-Mexican War* (College Station: Texas A&M University Press, 2015), 34, 45, 207; Quaife, ed., *Diary of Polk* 1:428–429, 2:119; Grant, *Memoirs and Selected Letters*, 50 (first quotation); Robert H. Ferrell, ed., *Monterrey Is Ours! The Mexican War Letters of Lieutenant Dana, 1845–1847* (Lexington: University Press of Kentucky, 1990), 69–70 (second and third quotations); Scott to Clinch, July 10, 1846, box 5, Anderson Papers, LC; W. S. Henry, *Campaign Sketches of the War with Mexico* (New York: Harper & Brothers, 1847), 112 (fourth quotation); Bauer, *Mexican War*, 90–100.

8. Winders, *Mr. Polk's Army*, 70; Quaife, ed., *Diary of Polk* 2:119, 221–225, 229, 239–245, 270–277, 282–283, 286, 293–295, 297, 301–304, 307, 355; "Letter from General Taylor," *Niles' National Register*, January 30, 1847, 342; Pinheiro, *Manifest Ambition*, 64–67; Bauer, *Mexican War*, 361; Paul H. Bergeron, *The Presidency of James K. Polk* (Lawrence: University Press of Kansas, 1987), 94; WDAR, 1846, 54 (quotation); *MPP* 4:508.

9. *CGlobe* 29th Cong., 2nd sess., 160, 184–187 (quotation); *Senate Journal* 29th Cong., 2nd sess., 104. By Polk's admission, of the eleven congressmen consulted on the lieutenant general bill, only Senators Ambrose Sevier (D-AR) and John M. Niles (D-CT), had supported the proposal. Quaife, ed., *Diary of Polk* 2:173, 275–276, 282–283, 293. The text of the Senate proposal (29th Cong., 2nd sess., Senate Bill 80) to create a lieutenant general may be found at http://memory.loc.gov/cgi-bin/ampage?collId=llsb&fileName=029/llsb029.db&recNum=331.

10. Quaife, ed., *Diary of Polk* 1:412, 416, 2:334; Treadway to Early, December 9, 1846, box 2, Early Papers, LC; Skelton, *American Profession of Arms*, 145; *CGlobe* 29th Cong., 2nd sess., 95, 154, 221 (first quotation) 279, 140 (second quotation), 127 (third quotation), 301.

11. Quaife, ed., *Diary of Polk* 3:371–372; *CGlobe* 29th Cong., 2nd sess., 346–349, 366, 375–377; Bergeron, *Presidency of Polk*, 175–179 (second quotation); *Statutes* 9:123–126. Accusing Ritchie of libel and arguing that he and Polk were trying to destroy the separation of powers by forcing Congress to approve executive wishes, the Senate expelled all *Union* reporters from its chambers.

12. Winders, *Mr. Polk's War*, 70–74, 77; [Hunt], "Army Attack and National Defense," 146–148; Bauer, *Mexican War*, 397; Skelton, *American Profession of Arms*, 145–146; "Mr. Polk and the Army," *Cleveland Herald*, August 16, 1845; Joseph G. Dawson III, "Leaders for Manifest Destiny: American Volunteer Colonels Serving

in the U.S.-Mexican War," *American Nineteenth Century History* 7 (June 2006): 253–280; Allen to Polk, January 22, 1846, Entry 225, Quartermasters Consolidated File, box 27, RG 92, NARA (first and second quotations); Hannigan and Bright to Jesup, January 30, 1846, ibid.; Smith to Scott, April 10, 1846, ibid.; [John James Peck], *Sign of the Eagle: A View of Mexico—1830 to 1850* (San Diego: Copley Press, 1970), 79 (third quotation); *Artillery Officer in the Mexican War*, 83, 108 (fourth quotation); Meade, *Life and Letters*, 102. Polk issued a furious presidential dressing-down to at least one disappointed cadet in a private interview. Eugene C. Tidball, "A Subaltern's First Experiences in the Old Army," *Civil War History* 45 (September 1999): 201–203.

13. Joseph G. Dawson III, *Doniphan's Epic March: The First Missouri Volunteers in the Mexican War* (Lawrence: University Press of Kansas, 1999); WDAR, 1847, 497–502; HED 60, 30th Cong., 1st sess., serial 520, 1128–1130; "Col. Doniphan's Command," *Daily Picayune*, June 17, 1847 (quotation). In letters to his brother, Taylor lambasted "Marcy, Scott & all their creatures" and complained about "the outrageous manner" in which he had been stripped of most of his regulars. Taylor to Brother, April 25, 1847, March 27, 1847, roll 1, Series 2, Taylor Papers, LC.

14. Donald Jackson and Mary Lee Spence, eds., *The Expeditions of Frémont*, 3 vols. (Urbana: University of Illinois Press, 1970), 1:395–397 (first quotation), 407–408; John Charles Frémont, "The Conquest of California," *Century Illustrated Magazine* 6 (April 1891): 919 (second quotation); Bauer, *Mexican War*, 164–189.

15. Bauer, *Mexican War*, 129, 189–196, 367–368; Durwood Ball, "Stephen W. Kearny," in *Soldiers West: Biographies from the Military Frontier*, 2nd ed., ed. Paul Andrew Hutton and Durwood Ball (Norman: University of Oklahoma Press, 2009), 59–61; Quaife, ed., *Diary of Polk* 1:443, 2:493, 3:11, 120–123, 176–177, 197–199, 204–207, 324, 327–328, 335–339; HED 60, 30th Cong., 1st sess., serial 520, 153–155; Kearny to Hardie, March 17, 1847, Hardie Papers, LC; Kearny to Marcy, April 28, 1847, roll 1, Records of the Tenth Military Department, M-210, RG 393, NARA; SED 33, 30th Cong., 1st sess., serial 507, 6, 190; SED 31, 30th Cong., 2nd sess., serial 531, 28–29; HED 17, 31st cong., 1st sess., serial 573, 283–284.

For the proceedings of the Frémont court-martial, see SED 33, 30th Cong., 1st sess., serial 507. Defending his son-in-law to the bitter end, Benton later excoriated Kearny in a thirteen-day address before the Senate. *CGlobe* 30th Cong., 1st sess., Appendix, 977–1040.

16. HED 60, 30th Cong., 1st sess., serial 520, 1273; Irving W. Levinson, *War within War: Mexican Guerrillas, Domestic Elites, and the United States of America, 1846–1848* (Fort Worth: Texas Christian University Press, 2005), 18, and "New Paradigm for an Old Conflict: The Mexico-United States War," *Journal of Military History* 73 (April 2009): 393–416, points out that the vast social gulf between the Mexican government and the peasantry did much to preclude a general revolt.

17. HD 19, 29th Cong., 2nd Sess., serial 499, 6 (quotations); Dawson, *Doniphan's Epic March*, 80–102.

18. Joseph G. Dawson III, "American Civil-Military Relations and Military Government: The Service of Colonel Alexander Doniphan in the Mexican War," *Armed Forces and Society* 22 (Summer 1996): 555–558; Orders No. 13, Army of the West,

August 17, 1846, K-209, roll 309, LROAG; HED 60, 30th Cong., 1st sess., serial 520, 168, 170–171; Howard Lamar, *The Far Southwest, 1846–1912: A Territorial History* (New Haven: Yale University Press, 1966), 52, 64–65.

19. Dawson, *Doniphan's Epic March*; HED 60, 30th Cong., 1st sess., serial 520, 28–76 (quotation 30); Ralph Emerson Twitchell, *The History of the Military Occupation of the Territory of New Mexico from 1846 to 1861 by the Government of the United States* (Denver: Smith-Brooks Co., 1909).

20. *MPP* 4:506–507; Quaife, ed., *Diary of Polk* 2:281–282; HED 70, 30th Cong., 1st sess., serial 521, 11–14; Dawson, *Doniphan's Epic March*, 88–96; George F. Ruxton, *Adventures in Mexico and the Rocky Mountains* (London: John Murray, 1847), 189 (quotation); Lamar, *Far Southwest*, 67–70.

21. Durwood Ball, *Army Regulars on the Western Frontier, 1848–1861* (Norman: University of Oklahoma Press, 2001), 3–8; Lamar, *Far Southwest*, 70–82; HED 66, 31st Cong., 1st sess., serial 577, 2; *CGlobe* 31st Cong., 1st sess., Appendix, 871, 1013 (second quotation), 1714; Thomas W. Cutrer, "'Lion in Her Path': Texas, New Mexico, and the United States Army, 1850," *Military History of the West* 34 (2004): 75–80; Annie Abel, ed., *The Official Correspondence of James S. Calhoun* (Washington, D.C.: Government Printing Office, 1915), 164–165 (second quotation). Taylor backed Munroe's stance, privately vowing to go to New Mexico to prevent a takeover by slave states, muttering that "the whole business is infamous, and must be put down." Thurlow Weed Barnes, *Memoir of Thurlow Weed*, 2 vols. (Boston: Houghton, Mifflin and Co., 1884), 2:180.

22. Durwood Ball, "By Right of Conquest: Military Government in New Mexico and California," *Journal of the West* 41 (Summer 2002): 11–12; HED 17, 31st Cong., 1st sess., serial 573, 657–658; William Tecumseh Sherman, *Memoirs* (New York: Library of America, 1990), 54; Mason to Jones, June 18, 1847, roll 1, M210, Records of the Tenth Military Department, RG 393, NARA; Mason to Anderson, July 21, 1847, ibid.; Sherman to Hunter, August 1, 1847, ibid.; Sherman to Stevenson, May 8, 31, 1848, ibid.; Riley to Sherman, April 16, 1849, ibid.; WDAR, 1848, 51–64; Ord to Ord, June 29, 1848, box 1, part 2, Ord Family Papers, Georgetown University (first quotation); *CGlobe* 31st Cong., 1st sess., Appendix, 10; Hatch to Mother, January 7, 1849, Hatch Papers, LC; Hatch to Father, October 21 (second and third quotations), December 5, 18, 1849, ibid.; Williamson to Brother, April 10, September 11, November 21, 1850, Williamson Papers, LC.

23. "Military Despotism," *Californian*, June 5, 1847; Mason to Jones, November 24, 1848, roll 1, M 210, Records of the Tenth Military Department, RG 393, NARA; "The Interview Between Com. Jones and Gov. Mason—Civil Organization," *California Star and Californian*, November 25, 1848; "Address of the Legislative Assembly of the District of San Francisco to the people of California," *Alta California*, June 14, 1849; "A Revolution—Its Progress," ibid.; HED 17, 31st Cong., 1st sess., serial 573, 276, 279–280, 648–649 (first quotation), 708, 712, 736–737, 777–780 (second quotation); Theodore Grivas, *Military Governments in California, 1846–1850* (Glendale, CA: Arthur H. Clark, 1963), 193–218; Ball, *Army Regulars*, 8–9; "Shall We Have a Government?" *Placer Times*, June 23, 1849; J. Ross Browne, *Report of the Debates of the Convention of California, on the Formation of the State Constitution*

(Washington, D.C.: John T. Towers, 1850), 476–477; SED 52, 3st Cong., 1st sess., serial 561, 40.

24. Ralph Waldo Emerson, *Essays & Lectures* (New York: Library of America, 1983), 1085 (first quotation); Henry L. Scott, *Military Dictionary: Comprising Technical Definitions; Information on Raising and Keep Troops; Actual Service, Including Makeshifts and Improved Matériel; and Law, Government, Regulation, and Administration Relating to Land Forces* (New York: D. Van Nostrand, 1861), 644–651; Winders, *Mr. Polk's Army*, 239 n. 2, 244 n. 28; Johnston to McLane, January 30, 1848, box 3, McLane Correspondence, LC (second quotation).

25. Quaife, ed., *Diary of Polk* 3:494–498, 4:48 (quotation); Thompson to Early, February 16, 1848, box 3, Early Papers, LC; *Historical Statistics of the United States, Earliest Times to the Present*, Millennial Edition, 5 vols. (Cambridge: Cambridge University Press, 2006), 5:127, 353–358.

26. Jochen S. Arndt, "The Highly Effective First Mississippi Volunteer Regiment in the Mexican War, 1846–1848," *Journal of Mississippi History* 69 (2007): 63–78; Ferrell, ed., *Monterrey is Ours!*, 132, 135 (quotation); Nathan A. Jennings, "Texas Ranger Auxiliaries: Double-Edged Sword of the Campaign for Northern Mexico, 1846–1848," *Small Wars & Insurgencies* 26, no. 2 (2015): 313–326.

27. *PUSG* 1:102–103 (first quotation); HED 60, 30th Cong., 1st sess., serial 520, 1178 (second quotation); T[homas] B[angs], Thorpe, *Our Army at Monterey . . .* (Philadelphia: Carey and Hart, 1847), 120–121; Wool to Jones, December 7, 1847, W-996, roll 367, LRAGO, NARA; Max M. Edling, *A Hercules in the Cradle: War, Money, and the American States, 1783–1867* (Chicago: University of Chicago Press, 2014), 157; General Order No. 128, April 30, 1847, reprinted in *Niles' Weekly Register*, May 29, 1847, 198 (third quotation); Irving W. Levinson, "Occupation and Stability Dilemmas of the Mexican War: Origins and Solutions," in *Armed Diplomacy: Two Centuries of American Campaigning* (Fort Leavenworth, KS: Combat Studies Institute Press, 2003), 3 (fourth quotation); HED 8, 30th Cong., 1st sess., serial 515, 386–389.

28. General Order 20, August 28, 1846, box 28, Wool Papers, NYSL; Wool to Sarah, February 1, 1847, box 1, ibid.; *Memoirs of Lieut-Gen. Scott, Written by Himself* (New York: Sheldon and Co., 1864), 2:540–546; Timothy D. Johnson, *Winfield Scott: The Quest for Military Glory* (Lawrence: University Press of Kansas, 1998), 165–166; Thomas M. Davies Jr., "Assessments During the Mexican War: An Exercise in Futility," *New Mexico Historical Review* 41 (Summer 1996): 197–216; General Orders 11 (quotations), 143, December 17, 1847, box 28, Wool Papers, NYSL.

29. Thayer to Chadbourne, June 28, 1846, vol. 8, Thayer Papers, United States Military Academy Library (first quotation); Hope, *Scientific Way of War*, 172–175; Scott to Brewerton, September 14, 1848, *Niles' National Register*, November 8, 1848, 291 (second quotation); "West Point Graduates," *Arkansas Intelligencer*, May 1, 1847 (third quotation); "West Point," *Georgia Telegraph*, May 4, 1847 (fourth quotation); Samuel J. Watson, " Developing 'Republican Machines': West Point and the Struggle to Render the Officer Corps Safe for America, 1802–1833," in *Thomas Jefferson's Military Academy: Founding West Point*, ed. Robert M. S. McDonald (Charlottesville: University of Virginia Press, 2004), 171; "Naval Appropriation

Bill," *Daily Globe*, September 21, 1850, 3 (fifth and sixth quotations). For other favorable newspaper comments, see "West Point Graduates, Commanding Volunteer Regiments," *North Carolina Standard*, April 14, 1847; "West Point Academy," *The Constitution*, May 12, 1847; "Our Military Academy," *New York Herald*, October 24, 1847; WDAR, 1848, p. 283.

30. Maurice Garland Fulton, ed., *Diary and Letters of Josiah Gregg*, 2 vols. (Norman: University of Oklahoma Press, 1941), 1:259–260 (first quotation); "A Volunteer, Correspondence *St. Louis Republican*," December 26, 1846, *Niles' Register*, 264; Lew Wallace, *Autobiography*, 2 vols. (New York: Harper and Brothers, 1906), 1:163 (second quotation); Alfred J. Henderson and J. B. Duncan, "A Morgan County Volunteer in the Mexican War," *Journal of the Illinois State Historical Society* 41 (December 1948): 394 (third, fourth, and fifth quotations); Wool to Sarah, September 5, 1847, Wool Papers, box 1, NYSL (sixth and seventh quotations).

31. SD 378, 29th Cong., 1st sess., serial 477, 12 (first quotation); "Increase of the Army," *Daily Ohio Statesman*, January 3, 1850; Johnson, *Scott: Quest*, 210–212; Eisenhower, *Agent of Destiny*, 310–320; Quaife, ed., *Diary of Polk* 3:266 (second and third quotations), 272–273, 278, 281–282, 292; SED 65, 30th Cong., 1st sess., serial 510, 335 (fourth quotation).

32. Skelton, *American Profession of Arms*, 138–139, 147–148 (second quotation), 396n.49; R[odney] Glisan, *Journal of Army Life* (San Francisco: A. L. Bancroft and Co., 1874), 453 (first quotation); *Statutes* 9:186; Robert M. Utley, *Frontiersmen in Blue: The United States Army and the Indian, 1848–1865* (1967; rpt. Lincoln: University of Nebraska Press, 1981), 34 n .60.

33. *Statutes* 11:574–575; Skelton, *American Profession of Arms*, 148–149. The Hubbs case may be found in H-301 (1860), roll 642, LROAG, with quotations from Hubbs to Father, May 8, 1859, and endorsement of Townsend, June 29, 1859.

34. Coffman, *Old Army*, 144–155, 196–198; *CGlobe* 29th Cong., 2nd sess., 127 (quotation).

35. James M. McCaffrey, *The Army in Transformation, 1789–1860* (Westport, CT: Greenwood Press, 2006), 114–126; *ASPMA* 2:268–274; Coffman, *Old Army*, 196–200; Mark A. Vargas, "The Military Justice System and the Use of Illegal Punishments as Causes of Desertion in the U.S. Army, 1821–1835," *Journal of Military History* 55 (January 1991): 1–19; Order No. 59, October 18, 1853, "Special Orders File, 1848–1857," box 4, Starr Papers, Missouri Historical Society; Buchanan to Scott, December 31, 1857, box 3, Buchanan Papers, MdHS (first quotation); Journal, June 24, 1849, box 4, Heintzelman Papers, LC (second and third quotations); Francis Paul Prucha, ed., *Army Life on the Western Frontier: Selections from the Official Reports Made Between 1826 and 1845 by Colonel George Croghan* (Norman: University of Oklahoma Press, 1958), 132–133 (fourth quotation).

36. Journal, March 2, 1830, April 3, 1832 (first quotation), box 2, Heintzelman Papers, LC; Heintzelman to Townsend, June 12, 1852, roll 12, ibid.; General Orders 12, August 9, 1855, 2C432, Chapman Papers, Briscoe Center for American History (second quotation); Heitman, 1:431, 333; Robert Wooster, "'The Whole Company Have Done It': The U.S. Army and the Fort Davis Murder of 1860," *Journal of the West* 32 (April 1993): 19–28.

Enlisted men of the First Dragoons had probably rebelled against Brevet Maj. Philip Thompson, who had himself suffered long bouts of alcoholism. A West Point graduate who had won his brevet during the war against Mexico, Thompson was drummed out of the service for his heavy drinking in 1855. He then served on the staff of the filibuster William Walker. Will Gorenfeld and John Gorenfeld, *Kearny's Dragoons Out West: The Birth of the U.S. Cavalry* (Norman: University of Oklahoma Press, 2016), 357, 405 n. 20; Robert E. May, *Manifest Destiny's Underworld: Filibustering in Antebellum America*, Kindle edition (Chapel Hill: University of North Carolina Press, 2002), 102.

37. Watson, *Peacekeepers and Conquerors*, 396 (first quotation); WDAR, 1849, 90; SED 96, 34th Cong., 1st sess., serial 827 (second and third quotations), 631–632; *The Statistical History of the United States: From Colonial Times to the Present* (New York: Basic Books, 1976), 106; Dale Richard Steinhauer, "'Sogers': Enlisted Men in the U.S. Army, 1815–1860" (Ph.D. diss., University of North Carolina, 1992), 81; WDAR, 1857, 12; Coffman, *Old Army*, 139–141.

38. *Statutes* 2:134 (first quotation); Coffman, *Old Army*, 104–136; Skelton, *American Profession of Arms*, 209; Caleb Atwater, *Remarks made on a Tour to Prairie du Chien; thence to Washington City, in 1829* (Columbus, OH: Isaac H. Whiting, 1831),178; Anni P. Baker, "Daughters of Mars: Army Officers' Wives and Military Culture on the American Frontier," *Historian* 67 (Spring 2005): 22, 41; Theresa Griffin Viele, *Following the Drum: A Glimpse of Frontier Life* (1858; rpt. Lincoln: University of Nebraska Press, 1984), 13; Lydia Lane, *I Married a Soldier; or, Old Days in the Old Army* (1893 rpt. Albuquerque: Horn and Wallace, 1964), 22 (second quotation); Verity McInnis, *Women of Empire: Nineteenth-Century Army Officers and the U.S. West* (Norman: University of Oklahoma Press, 2017). Of the ten laundresses listed in the U.S. Censuses of 1850 and 1860 for Fort Duncan, Texas, all were foreign-born, as were six of the nine at Forts Lincoln and Martin Scott, Texas, in 1850. U.S. Manuscript Census, 1850, Fort Duncan (Bexar County), Fort Lincoln (Medina County), Fort Martin Scott (Gillespie County), Texas, M432, RG 29, NARA; U.S. Manuscript Census, 1860, Fort Duncan (Maverick County), Texas, M653, RG 29, NARA.

39. *The Mammoth*, November 15, 1848 (first and second quotations), K. Jack Bauer, *Zachary Taylor: Soldier, Planter, Statesman of the Old Southwest* (Baton Rouge: Louisiana State University Press, 1985), 220–237; Michael F. Holt, *The Rise and Fall of the American Whig Party: Jacksonian Politics and the Onset of the Civil War* (New York: Oxford University Press, 1999), 271; Beman Brockway, *Fifty Years in Journalism: Embracing Recollections and Personal Experiences with an Autobiography* (Waterton, NY: Daily Times Printing and Publishing House, 1891), 116 (third quotation); "Politics of Gen. Taylor," *Sun*, April 10, 1847 (fourth quotation); Alvord to Hammond, January 13, March 20 (fifth and sixth quotations), 1849, roll 8, Hammond Papers, LC. George Julian, an acerbic Free Soiler, found nothing to like in Taylor, who he described as "an old, outrageously ugly, uncultivated, uninformed man, & sure enough a <u>mere</u> military chieftain. He can't converse in decent language, mispronouncing words, stuttering, stammering, & frequently making a break-down in the middle of a sentence." Julian to Julian, January 25, 1850, box 1, Giddings and Julian Papers, LC.

40. *MPP* 5:21 (first quotation); *CGlobe* 31st Cong., 1st sess., Appendix, 10–11; Johnston to McLane, December 15, 1849, box 3, McLane Correspondence, LC (third quotation).

41. Bragg to Hammond, August 15, (first and second quotations), October 20, 1848, roll 8, Hammond Papers, LC; Diary, September 14, 1851, box 22, Jesup Papers, LC (third quotation); Alvord to Hammond, January 13, 1849, roll 8, Hammond Papers, LC (fourth quotation); Totten to Scott, August 23, 1851, entry 146, vol. 7, Letters and Reports of Totten, RG 77, NARA (fifth and sixth quotations); Randall to Alexr., December 21, 1850, box 5, Philpot-Randall Papers, MdHS.

42. *CGlobe* 31st Cong., 1st sess., 359, 884, 1047–1061 (quotations); *Statutes* 9:438–439; *New ASPMA* 4:105–106. Representative McLane, target of Johnston's lobbying, did not vote on the House bill. The Senate had initially shorn the measure of the mounted infantrymen, with Texan Thomas Rusk lambasting the effectiveness of such troops. Davis, noting that the House amendment was "not . . . quite so bad" as Rusk suggested, called on the Senate to agree, winning a 24–18 vote in favor of the amended measure. *CGlobe* 31st Cong., 1st sess., 1179–1181.

43. Russell F. Weigley, *History of the United States Army*, Enlarged Edition (Bloomington: Indiana University Press, 1984), 596–599; *Statistical History*, 8, 1114–1115; Crawford to Bayly, May 7, 1850, D24.7, RG 233, NARA; WDAR, 1850, 8–9; Gibson to Conrad, November 1, 1850, Entry 49, Reports on Annual Expenditures of the War Department Bureaus on Special Matters, RG 107, NARA; Jesup to Conrad, November 4, 11, 1850, ibid.; Gibson to Conrad, November 21, 1850, ibid.; WDAR, 1851, 109–111, 216–225; Heintzelman to Canby, August 14, 1850, roll 12, Heintzelman Papers, LC; Conrad to Quartermaster General, Commissary General, and Col. of Ordnance, January 29, 1851, roll 31, LSSW. Conrad denounced the "reckless extravagance" in army spending on transportation and barracks but concluded that conditions in the newly acquired regions made such increases impossible to avoid. Conrad to Adj. Gen., February 25, 1851, ibid.

44. *MPP* 4:610–626; WDAR, 1848, 161, 327; Abert to Conrad, November 6, 1850, Entry 49: Reports on Annual Expenditures of the War Department Bureaus on Special Matters, RG 107, NARA; Forest G. Hill, *Roads, Rails and Waterways: The Army Engineers and Early Transportation* (Norman: University of Oklahoma Press, 1957), 222; "Additions proposed to the rough draft of instructions for the joint board on the Pacific Coast," [ca. November 1848], vol. 7, Entry 146: Letters and Reports of Totten, RG 77, NARA; *Statutes* 9:372; Davis to Pope, January 5, 1855, vol. 36, LSSW; Floyd to Pope, May 5, 1857, vol. 39, ibid.; WDAR, 1855, 12; WDAR, 1856, 17; WDAR, 1858, 562–563.

45. Mark A. Smith, *Engineering Security: The Corps of Engineers and Third System Defense Policy, 1815–1861* (Tuscaloosa: University of Alabama Press, 2009), 80–92, 112–119, 202; Totten to Davis, December 19, 1850, Entry 146, vol. 8, Letters and Reports of Totten, RG 77, NARA; Totten to Gilmer, December 22, 1851, ibid. (quotations).

46. Holt, *Rise and Fall of the American Whig Party*, 527–528; HED 7, 30th Cong., 2nd sess., serial 538, 35–37; Henry Barrett Learned, "Establishment of the Secretaryship of the Interior," *American Historical Review* 16 (July 1911): 751–773; Robert

M. Utley and Mackintosh, *The Department of Everything Else: Highlights of Interior Department History* (Washington, D.C.: Government Printing Office, 1988).

9. New Challenges for the Old Army

1. Robert P. Wettemann Jr., *Privilege vs Equality: Civil-Military Relations in the Jacksonian Era, 1815–1845* (Santa Barbara: Greenwood Press, 2009), 17–18; Adjutant General's Office, *Chronological Lists of Actions &c., with Indians, from January 15, 1837 to January 1891* (1891; rpt. The Old Army Press, 1979), 10–22.

2. Day to AAG, January 26, 1855, H-88, roll 517, LROAG (first and second quotations); *New ASPMA* 8:452–453; 10:365 (third quotation); Smith to Thomas, April 8, 1854, A-54, roll 532, LROAG (fourth quotation). For an outstanding analysis of the fraud practiced by Indian depredations claimants, army contractors, and local boosters, see Gregory F. Michno, *Depredation and Deceit: The Making of the Jicarilla and Ute Wars in New Mexico* (Norman: University of Oklahoma Press, 2017).

3. Marcy to Nelly, August 2, 1855, roll 44, McClellan Papers, LC (first quotation); *Correspondence of John Sedgwick, Major-General*, 2 vols. (Printed for Carl and Ellen Battelle Stoeckel, 1902–1903), 2:24 (second and third quotations); WDAR, 1855, 163 (fourth quotation); Keyes to Townsend, August 15, 1855, box 73, Wool Papers, NYSL (fifth quotation); Stanley Diary, September 9, 1853, Briscoe Center for American History (sixth quotation). For examples of officer sympathy for Indians, see Heintzelman to Canby, October 20, 1850, roll 12, Heintzelman Papers, LC; Day to AAG, July 8, 1856, H-88, roll 517, LROAG; R[odney] Glisan, *Journal of Army Life* (San Francisco: A. L. Bancroft and Co., 1874), 259.

4. *CGlobe* 31st Cong., 1st sess., 1050 (first quotation) WDAR, 1850, 58–59 (second and third quotations); WDAR, 1849, 182; WDAR, 1851, 200; WDAR, 1852, 58; Gary Clayton Anderson, *The Conquest of Texas: Ethnic Cleansing in the Promised Land, 1820–1875* (Norman: University of Oklahoma Press, 2005).

5. *Texas Democrat*, July 14, 1849; *Texas State Gazette*, July 1, 1854, quoting the *American Flag; Telegraph and Texas Register*, August 7, 1850; *South-Western American*, December 1, 1852; Conrad to Rusk, January 24, 1852, roll 32, LSSW; Starr to Eliza, February 22, 1852, box 1, Starr Papers, Missouri State Historical Society; Crawford to Brooke, June 4, 1849, vol. 29, LSSW; Conrad to Brooke, March 8, 1851, vol. 31, ibid.; *Statutes* 9:573; 10:17. Among those allegedly killed by Indians was Lt. George B. McClellan, who later commanded the Union Army of the Potomac. McClellan to John, September 3, 1852, roll 2, McClellan Papers, LC; McClellan to Mother, September 26, 1852, ibid.

6. Conrad to Sumner, April 1, 1851, vol. 31, LSSW; Sumner to Conrad, October 29, 1852, vol. 48, LRSW; Lane to Sumner, October 22, 1852, ibid.; Sumner to Cooper, October 25, 1852, ibid.; WDAR, 1852, 5, 23–25 (quotation); Conrad to Sumner, December 23, 1852, vol. 34, LSSW; Conrad to Lane, January 21, 1853, ibid.

7. Robert A. Trennert, *Alternative to Extinction: Federal Indian Policy and the Beginnings of the Reservation System, 1846–51* (Philadelphia: Temple University Press, 1975), 178–192; Percival Green Lowe, *Five Years a Dragoon ('49 to '54) and other Adventures on the Great Plains* (Norman: University of Oklahoma Press, 1965), 68 (first

quotation); Catherine Price, "Lakotas and Euroamericans: Contrasted Concepts of 'Chieftainship' and Decision-Making Authority," *Ethnohistory* 41 (Summer 1994): 447–463; "Letter from the Editor," *Daily Missouri Republican*, November 9, 1851.

8. *MPP* 5:90–91, 130; Yonatan Eyal, "Young America and the Transformation of the Democratic Party," *Civil War History* 51 (September 2005): 245–268; Conrad to Abert, November 18, 1852, roll 33, LSSW; *Daily Globe*, September 14, 1852; *Statutes* 10:56–60; Abert to Totten, September 21, 1852, roll 15, M66, LS by the Topographical Bureau, RG 77, NARA; General Order, September 16, 1852, Entry 459, Correspondence, Reports, Orders, and Regulations, 1851–53, Entry 53, Board on River and Harbor Improvements, RG 77, NARA; Totten to DeRussy, December 1, 1852, ibid.; Totten to Davis, April 6, 1854, Entry 146, vol. 8, Letters and Reports of Totten, RG 77, NARA (quotation).

9. Albert E. Cowdrey, *A City for the Nation: The Army Engineers and the Building of Washington, D.C., 1790–1976* (Washington, D.C.: Historical Division, Office of the Chief of Engineers, 1979), 13–21; Pamela Scott, *Capital Engineers: The U.S. Army Corps of Engineers in the Development of Washington, D.C., 1790–2004* (Alexandria, VA: U.S. Army Corps of Engineers, Office of History, 2005), 30–32, 39–40, 46, 51–52; Alan Lessoff, *The Nation and Its City: Politics, "Corruption," and Progress in Washington, D.C., 1861–1902* (Baltimore: Johns Hopkins University Press, 1994), 38–39, 166–167; *MPP* 4:162; Totten to Ingersoll, March 3, 1853, entry 146, vol. 8, Letters and Reports of Totten, RG 77, NARA; Meigs to Hunter, February 26, 1853, Addition I, roll 11, Meigs Papers, LC; Meigs to Hale, ibid.; Meigs to Cass, ibid.; Meigs to Maury, ibid.; Meigs to Pearce, ibid.; Diary, February 28, 1853, roll 1, ibid.; Meigs to Cass, March 1, 1853, Addition 1, roll 11, ibid.

Completed a decade later, the Washington Aqueduct supplied the District with 35 million gallons of water per day. Another West Point graduate, Capt. Alexander H. Bowman, joined with architect Ammi B. Young in constructing dozens of new federal buildings in the District.

10. Merritt Roe Smith, "Introduction," in *Military Enterprise and Technological Change: Perspectives on the American Experience*, ed. Merritt Roe Smith (Cambridge: MIT Press, 1985), 8, 11 (quotation), 18–19, 36–37; Merritt Roe Smith, "Army Ordnance and the 'American System' of Manufacturing, 1815–1861," ibid., 77–78; Charles F. O'Connell Jr., "The Corps of Engineers and the Rise of Modern Management, 1827–1856," ibid., 110–116; Nathan Rosenberg, "Technological Change in the Machine Tool Industry, 1840–1910," *Journal of Economic History* 23 (December 1963): 417–423, 426–428; David R. Meyer, *Networked Machinists: High-Technology Industries in Antebellum America* (Baltimore: Johns Hopkins University Press, 2006), 2–4, 232–239; Merritt Roe Smith, *Harpers Ferry Armory and the New Technology: The Challenge of Change* (Ithaca, NY: Cornell University Press, 1977), 17–19; David A. Hounshell, *From the American System to Mass Production, 1800–1932: The Development of Manufacturing Technology in the United States* (Baltimore: Johns Hopkins University Press, 1984), 49; Darwin L. King, Kathleen M. Premo, and Carl J. Case, "Historical Influences on Modern Cost Accounting Practices," *Academy of Accounting and Financial Studies Journal* 13 (September 2009): 29; Forest G. Hill, *Roads, Rails, and Waterways: The Army Engineers and Early Transportation*

(Norman: University of Oklahoma Press, 1957), 138–149 n. 40; WDAR, 1848, 295; WDAR, 1857, 205.

11. William H. Goetzmann, *Army Exploration in the American West, 1803–1863* (New Haven: Yale University Press, 1959), 262–274; Scurry et al to Conrad, May 17, 1852, roll 64, LR by the Topographical Bureau, M506, NARA; *CGlobe* 32nd Cong., 2nd sess., 471, 715, 756, 799 (first quotation); *Statutes* 10:219 (second quotation). For the railroad bill's intricate route to passage, see *Senate Journal*, 32nd Cong., 2nd sess., 210–211, 233–236.

12. Michael F. Holt, *The Rise and Fall of the American Whig Party: Jacksonian Politics and the Onset of the Civil War* (New York: Oxford University Press, 1999), 682–687; Bryan to Bryan, November 1, 1852, box 2Q453, Bryan Papers, Briscoe Center for American History (first and second quotations); William Davis, *Jefferson Davis: The Man and His Hour* (New York: HarperCollins, 1991), 224; William J. Cooper, *Jefferson Davis: American* (New York: Alfred A. Knopf, 2000), 257; *MPP* 5:221; WDAR, 1855, 16; Davis to Sandridge, January 29, 1856, vol. 37, LSSW; WDAR, 1856, 19–22; *MPP* 5:221. Thanks to Dr. Ariel (Allie) Kelley for bringing the Bryan letter to my attention. Scott's political correspondence is in roll 15, M 1635, LR by the Headquarters of the Army, RG 108, NARA.

13. Abert to Markoe, May 18, 1849, roll 11, M66, LS by the Topographical Bureau, RG 77, NARA; Abert, "Internal Improvements by Government," 402–406 (quotations); Goetzmann, *Army Exploration*, 274–313; Vincent Ponko Jr., "The Military Explorers of the American West, 1838–1860," in *North American Exploration*, ed. John Logan Allen (Lincoln: University of Nebraska Press, 1997), 410; WDAR, 1855, 13–17; Pope to Hart, et al., February 19, 1854, roll 503, LROAG; *New ASPMA* 15:284–286, 365–390.

14. Cooper, *Davis: American*, 247; Totten to Bache, July 20, 1850, Entry 146, vol. 8, Letters and Reports of Totten, RG 77, NARA; Totten to Ingersoll, March 1853, 8, ibid.; *MPP* 5:204–205; *National Era*, April 14, 1853; Davis, *Jefferson Davis*, 236, Davis to Meigs, April 4, 1853, roll 34, LSSW; Meigs to Father, August 12, 1853, roll 4, Addition I, Meigs Papers, LC; Journal, December 22, 1853, March 4, 1855, roll 13, ibid.; *New ASPMA* 15:42–44, 16:62–116; Scott, *Capital Engineers*, 45, 51–52; French to Houston, March 23, 1853, McFarlan Papers, LC; McFarlan to Abert, April 1853, ibid.; Meigs to McFarlan and Jones, July 21, 1853, ibid.; Meigs to McFarlan, September 7, 1854, ibid.; Davis to Meigs, April 4, 1856, roll 36, LSSW; WDAR, 1854, 24; "Local News," *Daily Globe*, December 16, 1853; *Evening Star* clipping, March 5, Journal, roll 13, Meigs Papers, LC (quotations). For criticisms of Meigs' choice of interior art, see "American Art and the Capitol," *National Era*, May 27, 1858, and "Washington Gossip," *New York Times*, June 25, 1858.

15. Mark A. Smith, *Engineering Security: The Corps of Engineers and Third System Defense Policy, 1815–1861* (Tuscaloosa: University of Alabama Press, 2009), 122–126 (quotation 122), 202–203; WDAR, 1854, 19, 93–94; WDAR, 1856, 272; WDAR, 1857, 17. The Panic of 1857 forced cutbacks in coastal defense appropriations to slightly more than $2 million between fiscal years 1859 and 1861.

16. Davis, *Jefferson Davis*, 224–238; *The Papers of Jefferson Davis*, 14 vols. (Baton Rouge: Louisiana State University Press, 1971–2015), 1: lx; Cooper, *Davis: American*,

247–250; Robert Wooster, *The American Military Frontiers: The United States Army in the West, 1783–1900* (Albuquerque: University of New Mexico Press, 2009), 134–135; Edward M. Coffman, *The Old Army: A Portrait of the American Army in Peacetime, 1784–1898* (New York: Oxford University Press, 1986), 59–60, 152–153; Davis to Bell, September 19, 1853, vol. 34, LSSW; *MPP* 5:287–288; WDAR, 1856, 8. See also Matthew Moten, *The Delafield Commission and the American Military Profession* (College Station: Texas A&M University Press, 2000).

17. Davis, *Jefferson Davis*, 226–227, 230, 238; Taylor to Hitchcock, May 19, 1841, roll 1, Taylor Papers, LC; round-robin memorials and petitions in Sen25A-G11.1, box 107, and Sen26A-G10.1, box 93, both in RG 46, NARA; Ord to Anderson, August 22, 1860, box 8, Anderson Papers, LC; Wool to Hardie, May 4, 1857, Hardie Papers, LC (first quotation); Wool to Cobb, February 1, 1856, box 73, Wool Papers, NYSL; Bragg to Hammond, October 20, 1848, roll 8, Hammond Papers, LC (second quotation); [Braxton Bragg], "Notes on Our Army," *Southern Literary Messenger* 10 (February 1844): 86–88; Meade to Macomb, August 4, 1857, box 1, Entry 153, Papers of Col. John H. Macomb, Office of the Chief Engineer, RG 77, NARA; Journal, January 31, 1855, box 4, Heintzelman Papers, LC. SED 34, 34th Cong., 3rd sess., serial 880, includes some of the Davis-Scott correspondence, with quotations from 252 and 240. See also *New ASPMA* 12:409–491. Trying to separate himself from that year's presidential campaign and to be closer to his wife's family home, Scott had moved his headquarters to New York in July 1848. John S. D. Eisenhower, *Agent of Destiny: The Life and Times of General Winfield Scott* (1997; rpt. Norman: University of Oklahoma Press, 1999), 321–323.

In late 1857, the Wool-Davis feud again became public. Whereas the general accused Davis of having "falsely and covertly slandered me through the newspapers and in his official correspondence," Davis dismissed Wool's publications as "a remedy not recognized among gentlemen, and one to the enjoyment of which I now dismiss him." "A Personal Controversy: General Wool and Jefferson Davis," *New York Times*, December 8, 1857; "Jefferson Davis in Reply to General Wool," December 23, ibid.; "Gen. Wool's Reply to Jefferson Davis," December 26, ibid.

18. Johnson and Sebastian to Scott, February 23, 1851, unregistered letters, roll 15, LR by the Headquarters of the Army, M1635, NARA; Johnston to McLane, January 26, 1850, box 3, McLane Papers, LC; Conrad to McDougal, April 30, 1851, vol. 31, LSSW; Davis to McClelland, August 11, 1854, roll 36, ibid.; Conrad to Mallory, August 2, 1853, vol. 33, ibid.; *New ASPMA* 4:101 (first quotation), 108–109; WDAR, 1850, 4; WDAR, 1854, 30, 34; Brooks to unknown, June 29, 1854, Brooks Papers, USAMHI; *MPP* 5:87; SED 91, 34th Cong., 1st sess., serial 823, 12 (second quotation).

19. "Treacherous Slaughter of U. States Troops a Fort Laramie," *Daily Missouri Republican*, September 10, 1854 (first quotation); "Indian Difficulties," *Ohio State Journal*, September 20, 1854 (second quotation); WDAR, 1853, 11–12; WDAR, 1854, 5; *MPP* 5:286–287, 298–299; *CGlobe*, 33rd Cong., 2nd sess., 460–463, 520, 525, 1011–1013, 1064; Sherman to Hardie, February 1, 1855, Hardie Papers, LC; *Daily National Intelligencer*, January 4, 1855 (third quotation); "The Increase of the Army," *North American and United States Gazette*, January 20, 1855 (fourth quotation); *Statutes* 10:639–640; Heitman, 2:597 note h. Borderlands states were

Arkansas, California, Florida, Iowa, Missouri, Texas, and Wisconsin. A year earlier, President Pierce had supported the "augmentation" of the regular army, which he "regarded . . . as a nucleus around which the volunteer forces of the nation gather in the hour of danger." *MPP* 5:215.

20. Williams to Scott, October 30, 1851, frame 435, roll 15, LR by the Headquarters of the Army, M1635, NARA; Hazzard to John W. Houston, February 21, 1851, H-64, roll 447, LROAG; Bayard to Father, January 2, 1857, Bayard Papers, Missouri State Historical Society; Journal, February 3, 1855, box 4, Heintzelman Papers, LC (first quotation); Hatch to Father, January 11, 1854, Hatch Papers, LC; William B. Skelton, *An American Profession of Arms: The Army Officer Corps, 1784–1861* (Lawrence: University Press of Kansas, 1992), 146; Robert M. Utley, *Frontiersmen in Blue: The United States Army and the Indian, 1848–1865* (1967: rpt. Lincoln: University of Nebraska Press, 1981), 34 n. 60; Bonneville, to Wool, January 29, 1855, box 15, Wool Papers, NYSL; Craighill to McPherson, April 4, 1855, McPherson Papers, LC (second quotation). Entry 253, Registers of Applications for Commissions or Promotions in the Regular Army, RG 107, NARA, includes a state-by-state list of applications. As a clerk later advised one candidate: "You have enough of army recommendations, you don't have political ones." Garesche to Hardie, July 24, 1857, Hardie Papers, LC.

21. R. Eli Paul, *Blue Water Creek and the First Sioux War, 1854–1856* (Norman: University of Oklahoma Press, 2004), 35 (first quotation), 51–53, 88–108 (second quotation 98); *New ASPMA* 8:444–554; Todd to Sumner, September 6, 1855, Sumner Family Papers, LC (third and fourth quotations); Durwood Ball, *Army Regulars on the Western Frontier, 1848–1861* (Norman: University of Oklahoma Press, 2001), 46–47; Eugene Bandel, *Frontier Life in the Army, 1854–1861*, ed. Ralph P. Bieber (Glendale, CA: Arthur H. Clark Co., 1932), 84–88; WDAR, 1855, 49–51; Theo F. Rodenbough, *From Everglade to Canyon with the Second United States Cavalry* (1875; rpt. Norman: University of Oklahoma Press, 2000), 181–184; SED 76, 34th Cong., 1st sess., serial 822, 19.

22. Ethan Allen Hitchcock, *Fifty Years in Camp and Field*, ed. W. A. Croffut (New York: G. P. Putnam's Sons, 1909), 390–391; WDAR, 1851, 141–143, 146 (first quotation); WDAR, 1852, 30; WDAR, 1853, 41–42; Lyons to Canby, May 22, 1850, L-105, roll 430, LROAG (second quotation).

23. Utley, *Frontiersmen in Blue*, 181–189, 194, 200–210; Wool to Cobb, February 1, 1856, box 73, Wool Papers, NYSL; Wool to Wright, April 24, 1856, box 69, ibid.; Wool to Thomas, May 4, 1856, ibid.; Wool to Sage, January 3, 1857, ibid.; HED 93, 34th Cong., 1st sess., serial 858, 87 (first quotation); Wool to Townsend, May 30, June 18, 1856, box 5, Wool Papers, NYSL (second quotation); SED 66, 34th Cong., 1st sess., serial 822, 8 (third quotation), 23–27; WDAR, 1855, 73–76, 81–89; Stevens to Wool, December 23, 1855, box 73, Wool Papers, NYSL; "The Indian War in Oregon," *New York Herald*, May 3, 1856; "Letter from an Oregonian," *Alta California*, January 28, 1856; *Oregon Statesman*, February 12, 1856; *Cong. Globe*, 34th Cong., 1st sess., 1144–1145 (fourth quotation).

24. Utley, *Frontiersmen in Blue*, 194–209; HED 45, 35th Cong., 1st sess., serial 955; WDAR, 1856, 180–182, 194; *CGlobe* 34th Cong., 1st sess., 1788–1789; Buchanan to

Jones, April 23, 1856, box 2, Buchanan Papers, MdHS; *Personal Memoirs of P. H. Sheridan, General United States Army*, 2 vols. (New York: Charles L. Webster & Co., 1888), 1:54, 68; WDAR, 1858, 363–365 (first quotation), 383–404 (second quotation 385; third quotation 388); E. D. Keyes, *Fifty Years' Observations of Men and Events, Civil and Military* (New York: Charles Scribner's Sons, 1884), 265–288; Donald L. Cutler, *"Hang Them All": George Wright and the Plateau Indian War* (Norman: University of Oklahoma Press, 2016), 234.

25. Utley, *Frontiersmen in Blue*, 143–152; WDAR, 1854, 33–36; WDAR, 1855, 52–71.

26. WDAR, 1856, 5; Daniel P. Whiting, *A Soldier's Life: Memoirs of a Veteran of 30 Years of Soldiering, Seminole Warfare in Florida, the Mexican War, Mormon Territory, and the West*, ed. Murphy Givens (Corpus Christi, TX: Nueces Press, 2011), 178–179; Marcy to McClellan, April 24, 187, roll 5, McClellan Papers, LC; WDAR, 1858, 21, 236–242; John Missall and Mary Lou Missall, *The Seminole Wars: America's Longest Indian Conflict* (Gainesville: University Press of Florida, 2004), 209–221 (quotation 219).

27. Tony R. Mullis, *Peacekeeping on the Plains: Army Operations in Bleeding Kansas* (Columbia: University of Missouri Press, 2004), 119–165; Shannon to Sumner, December 1, 1855, K-164, roll 520, LROAG (quotation); Shannon to Sumner, December 4, 1855, K-165, ibid.

28. Mullis, *Peacekeeping on the Plains*, 166–193; SED 97, 34th Cong., 1st sess., serial 823, 2 (first quotation); *CGlobe* 34th Cong., 1st sess., 1381–1395; SED 17, 35th Cong., 1st sess., serial 923, 25–26 (second quotation); Ball, *Army Regulars*, 172–177; "Interesting from Kansas," *New York Herald*, July 17, 1856 (third quotation). Nine days before the sack of Lawrence (May 21, 1856), Sumner had advised Shannon to place "a large and commanding force" between Lecompton and Lawrence to prevent any disturbances. Sumner to Shannon, May 12, 1856, S-244, roll 548, LROAG.

29. "The New Kansas Bill of Mr. Toombs Passed Kansas to be a Slave State," *New York Herald*, July 4, 1856; "Stirring News from Kansas! Pierce Rivalling Cromwell!!" *Milwaukee Daily Sentinel*, July 10, 1856; "The Fourth of July at Topeka," ibid., July 17, 1856; "Important From Kansas," *New York Daily Tribune*, July 14, 1856 (first quotation); John W. Blassingame, ed., *Frederick Douglass Papers*, Series I, vol. 3, *1855–63* (New Haven: Yale University Press, 1985), 125 (second and third quotations); "The President, the Army, and the Territories," *National Era*, July 31, 1856; petitions from Monroe, Lansing, Marshall, and Ypsilanti, 1856, HR34A-H1.1, RG 233, NARA; Ball, *Army Regulars*, 177–180; Mullis, *Peacekeeping on the Plains*, 193–233; WDAR, 1856, 35–146; *CGlobe*, 34th Cong., 1st sess., 1790–1794, 2239–2240; *CGlobe*, 34th Cong., 2nd sess., 5–6, 83; Charles Robinson, *The Kansas Conflict* (New York: Harper & Brothers, 1892), 337 (fourth and fifth quotations).

30. *MPP* 5:7–8, 111–112; Ball, *Army Regulars*, 90–103, 127–131; HED 88, 35th Cong., 1st sess., serial 956, especially 122–128; Wool to Bell, December 15, 1854, Bell Collection, LC; Robert W. Coakley, *The Role of Federal Military Forces in Domestic Disorders, 1789–1878* (Washington, D.C.: Center of Military History, 1988), 129–137.

31. Hatch to Father, September 1, 21 (first and second quotations), 1856, Hatch

Papers, LC; Bayard to Sister, December 7, 1856, Bayard Papers, Missouri State Historical Society; Bayard to Father, January 2, 1857, ibid.; Randall to Alex., May 15, 1850, vol. 5, Philpot-Randall Papers, MdHS (third quotation); Wool to Hardie, May 4, June 17, 1857, Hardie Papers, LC; Ball, *Army Regulars*, 106 (fourth quotation).

32. Robert E. May, *Manifest Destiny's Underworld: Filibustering in Antebellum America*, Kindle Edition (Chapel Hill: University of North Carolina Press, 2002), 19–20 (quotation), 24, 82, 83–84, 102, 198; Heitman, 1:644, 898, 957, 1034. Lovell, Smith, and Wilcox all became major generals in the Confederate Army.

33. HR 169, 32nd Congress, 1st sess., serial 656, 3 (first and second quotations); Smith, *Harpers Ferry*, 298–301; *Statutes* 10:217; HMD 76, 33rd Cong., 1st sess., serial 741, 24, 35–36, 218–222 (third and fourth quotations).

34. HMD 76, 33rd Cong., 1st sess., serial 741; HR 191, 33rd Cong., 1st sess., serial 743, 20; *Statutes* 10:578; Stephen B. Benet, *A Collection of Annual Reports and other Important Papers, Relating to the Ordnance Department*, 3 vols. (Washington, D.C.: Government Printing Office, 1880), 2:532–538. The original petitions are in HR 33-A files G12.3 and G27.5, RG 233, NARA. Quotations are from the March 1854 petition from Pittsfield, Massachusetts, and three printed petitions from Baltimore and Washington, all in file G27.5. A counter-petition (file G12.1), bearing several hundred signatures and signed by those claiming to be "inhabitants, and legal voters of Springfield," praised the "new life, vigor, and economy" under military supervision.

35. For Evansville, see HMD 3, 31st Cong., 2nd sess., serial 605; SMD 27, 33rd Cong., 1st sess., serial 705 (first two quotations). For Alabama, see SMD 141, 35th Cong., 1st sess., serial 935 (third quotation); and HMD 52, 35th Cong., 1st sess., serial 961. For Fort Craig, see Petition Referred to House Military Affairs Committee, June 18, 1860, HR 36A-G11.2, RG 233, NARA. For St. Louis and Harrodsburg, see materials in HR 36A-G11.2, RG 233, NARA (fourth quotation). At least one Harrodsburg resident claimed that those opposing the depot were "outsiders or strangers from the Lord knows where." King to Sir, April 6, 1860, HR 36A-G11.2, RG 233, NARA.

36. "Subscriptions to Mr. Scott's Text," *New York Times*, May 31, 1852; Wool to Stewart, May 28, June 8, 1852, box 5, Wool Papers, NYSL; Tom Chaffin, *Pathfinder: John Charles Frémont and the Course of American Empire* (Norman: University of Oklahoma Press, 2002), 433–448; Peters to Father, August 16, 1856, Peters Papers, Bancroft Library; Hartz to Father, February 10, 1857 (first quotation), December 9, 1856 (second quotation), Hartz Papers, LC; Wool to Jones, January 4, 1857, box 69, Wool Papers, NYSL (third quotation); Marcy to Nellie, November 15, 1856, roll 45, McClellan Papers, LC; Goodard to Scott, January 10, 1851, roll 15, M1635, LR by the Headquarters of the Army, RG 108, NARA. Skelton, *American Profession of Arms*, 353, calculates that of those officers with known political affiliations from 1856–1860, 29 (72.5 percent) were Democrats, 8 (20 percent) Republicans, and 3 (7.5 percent) Constitutional Union. That Skelton could judge the political affiliations of only forty officers suggests that norms against writing about partisan allegiances had become increasingly strong among the regulars.

37. John M. Belohlavek, "The Politics of Scandal: A Reassessment of John B.

Floyd as Secretary of War, 1857–1861," *West Virginia History* 32 (April 1970): 147 n. 9; William P. MacKinnon, "Prelude to Armageddon: James Buchanan, Brigham Young, and a President's Initiation to Bloodshed," in *James Buchanan and the Coming of the Civil War*, ed. John W. Quist and Michael J. Birkner (Gainesville: University Press of Florida, 2013), 46–68; *New ASPMA* 10:329–333; Jean H. Baker, *James Buchanan* (New York: Henry Holt, 2004), 91–93, 110; *MPP* 5:456; *Memoirs of Lieut.-General Scott, Written by Himself* (New York: Sheldon and Co., 1864), 2:604.

38. William P. MacKinnon, ed., *At Sword's Point*, Part I: *A Documentary History of the Utah War to 1858* (Norman, OK: Arthur H. Clark Co., 2008), 130–132, 154–156, 428–432; Jesup to Thomas, June 21, 1857, roll 33, LS by the Quartermaster General, M745, RG 92, NARA; Ball, *Army Regulars*, 160–163; David T. Bigler and Will Bagley, *The Mormon Rebellion: America's First Civil War, 1857–1858* (Norman: University of Oklahoma Press, 2011), 244. Estimates varied on the necessary strength. Scott suggested 2,500 men; Harney eventually settled on 8,000–10,000; Persifor Smith called for 15,000.

39. WDAR, 1857, 48; *MPP* 5:458, 487; "The Defeat of the Army Bill," *New York Herald*, March 4, 1858 (quotation); *The Mississippian*, March 16, 1858; *Statutes* 11:262–263; William P. MacKinnon, "Hammering Utah, Squeezing Mexico, and Coveting Cuba: James Buchanan's White House Intrigues," *Utah Historical Quarterly* 80 (no. 2, 2012): 132–151. Sam Houston, a self-described "Democrat of the true Jackson American stamp" who believed the standing army and navy would "ruin the country," theorized that Buchanan never really wanted the army increase. Madge Thornall Roberts, ed., *The Personal Correspondence of Sam Houston*, 4 vols. (Denton: University of North Texas Press, 1996–2001), 4:296–297.

40. Rich to Marcy, October 18, 1857, roll 45, McClellan Papers, LC; Porter to McClellan, February 28, 1858, roll 5, ibid.; Hatch to Father, January 20, 1858, Hatch Papers, LC; Otis G. Hammond, ed., *The Utah Expedition, 1857–1858: Letters of Capt. Jesse A. Gove, 10th Inf., U.S. A., of Concord, N.H., to Mrs. Gove, and Special Correspondence of the New York Herald* (Concord: New Hampshire Historical Society, 1928), 59, 66, 68, 179 (first quotation), 247–248 (second quotation); Bayard to Ettie, June 28, 1858, Bayard Papers, Missouri State Historical Society (third quotation).

41. William Y. Chalfant, *Cheyennes and Horse Soldiers: The 1857 Expedition and Battle of Solomon's Fork* (Norman: University of Oklahoma Press, 1989); Ball, *Army Regulars*, 39–43; Robert Morris Peck, "Recollections of Early Times in Kansas Territory, from the Standpoint of a Regular Cavalryman," *Transactions of the Kansas State Historical Society* 8 (1903–4): 495, 497 (first, second, and third quotations); SED 1, 35th Cong., 2nd sess., serial 974, 450 (fourth and fifth quotations).

42. Utley, *Frontier Regulars*, 127–135; Stephen Oates, ed., *Rip Ford's Texas* (Austin: University of Texas Press, 1963), 223–236; Anderson, *Conquest of Texas*, 259–326; Floyd to Runnels, August 28, 1858, vol. 40, LSSW; WDAR, 1858, 267–276; Twiggs to Thomas, November 20, 1858, T-216, roll 592, LROAG; WDAR, 1859, 357 (quotation); WDAR, 1860, 13–25, 56–60.

43. WDAR, 1859, 356–357, 368–371.

44. William S. Kiser, *Dragoons in Apacheland: Conquest and Resistance in Southern New Mexico, 1846–1861* (Norman: University of Oklahoma Press, 2012), 202–231;

WDAR, 1857, 135–140; Hatch to Father, March 2, 1857, Hatch Papers, LC; Hatch to Sister, July 17, 1857, ibid.; Frank D. Reeve, ed., "Puritan and Apache: A Diary," *New Mexico Historical Review* 23 (October 1948): 288; SED 11, pt. 1, 35th Cong., 1st sess., serial 911, 63–64; Paul Andrew Hutton, *The Apache Wars: The Hunt for Geronimo, the Apache Kid, and the Captive Boy Who Started the Longest War in American History* (New York: Crown, 2016), 30–33, 42–58.

45. WDAR, 1859, 258–259, 264–268, 273, 325–327, 332–333, 345–354; WDAR, 1860, 52–56, 60–68 (quotation); Utley, *Frontier Regulars*, 167–173.

46. Baker, *Buchanan*, 110; John M. Belohlavek, "In Defense of Doughface Diplomacy: A Reevaluation of the Foreign Policy of James Buchanan," in *James Buchanan and the Coming of the Civil War*, ed. John W. Quist and Michael J. Birkner (Gainesville: University Press of Florida, 2013), 114, 118–119; *MPP* 5:514 (quotations), 568; Ball, *Army Regulars*, 139–149; HED 65, 36th Cong., 1st sess., serial 1051; HED 77, 36th Cong., 1st sess., serial 1056; HED 98, 36th Cong., 1st sess., serial 1057.

47. Ball, *Army Regulars*, 132–138; Jerry Thompson, *Cortina: Defending the Mexican Name in Texas* (College Station: Texas A&M University Press, 2007), 1–95; HED 52, 36th Cong., 1st sess., serial 1050, 36, 41, 54–56 (second quotation), 70–72 (first quotation); Hartz to Father, May 2, 1860, box 1, Hartz Papers, LC (third quotation).

10. Army Regulars and the Crisis of Union

1. James M. McPherson, *Battle Cry of Freedom: The Civil War Era* (New York: Oxford University Press, 1988), 332 (quotation); Wayne Wei-siang Hsieh, *West Pointers and the Civil War: The Old Army in War and Peace* (Chapel Hill: University of North Carolina Press, 2009), 1–2; Clayton R. Newell and Charles R. Shrader, *Of Duty Well and Faithfully Done: A History of the Regular Army in the Civil War* (Lincoln: University of Nebraska Press, 2011), 42; Mark Wilson, *The Business of Civil War: Military Mobilization and the State, 1861–1865* (Baltimore: Johns Hopkins University Press, 2006), 38.

2. Wool to Hardie, April 5, 1857, Hardie Papers, LC; Bayard to Ettie, March 10, 1857, Bayard Papers, Missouri State Historical Society; "Army Supplies," *New York Herald*, February 4, 1858; "The Army Plunder Contracts," *Milwaukee Daily Sentinel*, September 15, 1858 (first quotation); Mark W. Summers, *The Plundering Generation: Corruption and the Crisis of the Union, 1849–1861* (New York: Oxford University Press, 1987), 243–246; Jesup to Thomas, December 22, 1858, vol. 16, Entry 999, LS Relating Clothing and Equipage, RG 92, NARA (second quotation); Tyler to McPherson, March 28, 1858, McPherson Papers, LC (third quotation); Meade to Macomb, March 12, 1858, Entry 153, Papers of Col. John N. Macomb, box 1, RG 77, NARA (fourth quotation); Scott to McDowell, April 11, 1857, Scott Papers, Clements Library; Hartz to Father, July 1, 1858, box 1, Hartz Papers, LC; Hunter to Lincoln, November 1, 1860, Lincoln Papers, LC; Custis Lee to McPherson, November 19, 1860, McPherson Papers, LC; HD 439, 57th Cong., 2nd sess., serial 4534, III: 1667; Pamela Scott, *Capital Engineers: The U.S. Army Corps of Engineers in the Development of Washington, D.C., 1790–2004* (Alexandria, VA: U.S. Army Corps of Engineers, Office of History, 2005), 62; Totten to Meigs, April 25, 1857,

November 15, 1859, vol. 8, Entry 146: Letters and Reports of Joseph G. Totten, RG 77, NARA; Diary, October 18, 1857, roll 1, Meigs Papers, LC; Meigs to Meigs, August 21 (fifth quotation), September 17, November 5, 15, 1858, Addition I, roll 4, Meigs Papers, LC; Meigs to Father, January 13, 1860, Addition I, roll 5, ibid.; Meigs to Holt, January 28, 1861, Addition I, roll 12, ibid.

3. HR 648, 36th Cong., 1st sess., serial 1071; Meigs to Father, January 13, 1860, Addition I, roll 5, Meigs Papers, LC; Totten to Scott, January 22, 1861, Entry 146, vol. 8, Letters and Reports of Totten, RG 77, NARA; Meigs to Holt, January 28, 1861, Addition I, roll 12, Meigs Papers, LC; Totten to Meigs, February 21, 27, 1861, ibid.; *Statutes* 12:106 (quotation). President Buchanan signed the bill but protested that, as commander in chief, "my perfect right still remains, notwithstanding the clause, to send him away from Washington to any part of the Union . . . on any other appropriate duty." *MPP* 5:597–599.

4. Scott Memorandum, October 29, 1860, Series I, Lincoln Papers, LC; Percy Gatling Hamlin, ed., *The Making of a Soldier: Letters of General R. S. Ewell* (Richmond: Whitter & Shepperson, 1935), 97 (first quotation); Talbot to Sister, October 22, 1860, box 2, Talbot Papers, LC; Wright to Carlton, November 21, 1860 (second and third quotations), December 3, 1860 (fourth quotation), box 2, Carlton Papers, LC; Comstock to McPherson, November 11, 1860, McPherson Papers, LC (fifth quotation).

5. Hartz to Father, December 15, 1860, February 25, March 11, 1861 (first and second quotations), box 1, Hartz Papers, LC; Francis R. Adams, "An Annotated Edition of the Personal Letters of Robert E. Lee, April 1855–April 1861" (Ph.D. diss., University of Maryland, 1955), 717 (third quotation); Burbank to Carlton, January 7, 1861, box 2, Carlton Papers, LC; Hatch to Father, February 3, 1861, Hatch Papers, LC (fourth and fifth quotations); Bush to Carlton, May 15, 1861, box 2, Carlton Papers, LC (sixth quotation).

6. Sumner to Lincoln, December 17, 1860, Series I, Lincoln Papers, LC (first quotation); *Correspondence of John Sedgwick, Major-General*, 2 vols. (Printed for Carl and Ellen Battelle Stoeckel, 1902–1903), 2:26–28 (second quotation); Meigs to Father, December 13, 1860, Addition 1, roll 5, Meigs Papers, LC (third quotation); James L. Morrison, *"Best School in the World": West Point, the Pre-Civil War Years, 1833–1866* (Kent, OH: Kent State University Press, 1986), 126; James Tyrus Seidule, "'Treason is Treason': Civil War Memory at West Point, 1861–1902," *Journal of Military History* 76 (April 2012): 430; Wilson to Logan, January 1, 1861, Logan Family Papers, LC (fourth quotation); Wool to Combs, November 23, 1860, box 5, Wool Papers, NYSL (fifth quotation); Wool to Vail, December 17, 1860, ibid. (sixth quotation); Archer to Mother, October 1, 1860, box 2, Archer Collection, MdHS; Archer to Archer, January 27, 1861, box 3, ibid.; Archer to Mother, March 17, May 1, 1861, ibid.

7. *MPP* 5:656; Scott to Lincoln, January 4, [1861], Series I, Lincoln Papers, LC (first quotation); Wool to Lincoln, January 11, 1861, ibid.; McPherson, *Battle Cry of Freedom*, 226, 264–266; *OR* 51, pt. 1:314–316; Sumner to Lincoln, December 17, 1860, Series I, Lincoln Papers, LC; Hunter to Lincoln, December 18, 1860, ibid.; Sumner to Nicolay, January 7, 1861, ibid.; Hazzard to Lincoln [January] 1861,

ibid.; Washburne to Lincoln, February 3, 1861, ibid.; Durwood Ball, "The Regulars Return: The U.S. Army's Protection of Lincoln's Journey in February 1861," paper presented at the Society for Military History Conference in April 2018, copy in author's possession.

8. Wool to Olin, December 10, 1860, *New York Times*, January 16, 1861 (first quotation); "The Way the Army Feels," *Burlington Free Press*, January 4, 1861; *New York Senate Journal, 1861*, 142, 144; Wool to Sarah, February 16, 23, 26, 27, March 1, 1861, box 2, Wool Papers, NYSL; William B. Skelton, *An American Profession of Arms: The Army Officer Corps, 1784–1861* (Lawrence: University Press of Kansas, 1992), 355–356; Hardee to Mordecai, March 4, 1861, box 3, Mordecai Papers, LC; Mordecai to Hardee, March 10, 1861, ibid.; Comstock to McPherson, June 13, 1861, McPherson Papers, LC; Gary Gallagher, "A Question of Loyalty," *Civil War Times* 52 (October 2013); 30–37; Adams, "Personal Letters of Lee," 721–722 (second and third quotations); Mark W. Johnson, "Emory Upton's Twenty-Six: Desertion and Divided Loyalty of U.S. Army Soldiers, 1860–1861, " *Journal of Military History* 81 (July 2017): 747–774; Richard B. McCaslin, "United States Regulars in Gray: Edward Ingraham and Company A, 1st Regular Confederate Cavalry," *Southwestern Historical Quarterly* 118 (July 2014): 25–27.

9. *MPP* 5:13, 15–16 (quotation); Shrader and Newell, *Of Duty Well and Faithfully Done*, 41; Emory Upton, *The Military Policy of the United States* (Washington, D.C.: Government Printing Office, 1904), 233–235.

10. *OR* 1:669–672, 3:369–370, 376, 381; Donald B. Connelly, *John M. Schofield and the Politics of Generalship* (Chapel Hill: University of North Carolina Press, 2006), 26–29, 349–350 n. 3.

11. Timothy D. Johnson, *Winfield Scott: The Quest for Military Glory* (Lawrence: University Press of Kansas, 1998), 226–228; *OR* 51, pt. 1:369–370, 386–387; William Howard Russell, *My Diary North and South* (Boston: T. O. H. P. Burnham, 1863), 390; *Diary of Gideon Welles, Secretary of the Navy Under Lincoln and Johnson*, 3 vols. (Boston: Houghton & Mifflin, 1911), 1:12–14, 242; *OR* Series III, 1:305–309 (quotations).

12. *MPP* 5:26 (quotation); "For the Prosecution of the War," *New York Times*, July 1, 1861; *CGlobe* 37th Cong., 1st sess., 21, 27, 50, 123–127, 205, 220, 228, 274, 279; *Statutes* 12:274, 279–281, 287–291, 317, 318, 326; Russell, *My Diary*, 390.

13. Newell and Shrader, *Of Duty Well and Faithfully Done*, 39–40, 53; George B. McClellan, *McClellan's Own Story: The War for the Union, the Soldiers Who Fought It, the Civilians Who Directed It, and His Relations to It and to Them* (New York: Charles L. Webster & Co., 1887), 97; Ulysses S. Grant, *Memoirs and Selected Letters* (New York: Library of America, 1990), 187–188; John M. Schofield, *Forty-six Years in the Army* (1897; rpt. Norman: University of Oklahoma Press, 1998), 423; Upton, *Military Policy*, 234 (quotation); *OR* Series III, 1:704; *CGlobe* 37th Cong., 1st sess., 123; Paul Andrew Hutton, *Phil Sheridan and His Army* (Lincoln: University of Nebraska Press, 1985), 11–12. Schofield believed that noncommissioned personnel from the regulars should also be distributed among the volunteers.

14. David Donald, *Lincoln* (New York: Simon & Schuster, 1995), 249–250, 266–267, 281, 325–326; Fred Nicklason, "The Civil War Contracts Committee," *Civil*

War History 17 (September 1971), 234, 237–238; HR 2, pt. 1, 37th Cong., 2nd sess., serial 1142, 68 (first quotation); HR 2, pt. 2, 37th Cong., 2nd sess., serial 1143, 885–886; Wilson, *Business of Civil War*, 151–158, 163; Crawford to Lincoln, August 10, 1861, Series 2, Lincoln Papers, LC (second quotation).

15. Donald, *Lincoln*, 325–326. Copies of sections of the original draft, as well as the final version of those sections, may be found at "Draft and Final Versions of a Passage in the Secretary of War's Annual Report," Freedmen & Southern Society Project, www.freedmen.umd.edu/cameron.htm (quotation).

16. Skelton, *American Profession of Arms*, 170–171, 332; Comstock to McPherson, February 18, 1860, McPherson Papers, LC (first quotation); Hazzard to Lincoln, July 11, 31, August 5, 1860, Series I, Lincoln Papers, LC; Totten to Delafield, February 28, 1843, vol. 6, Entry 146, Letters and Reports of Totten, RG 77, NARA (second quotation); Edward M. Coffman, *The Old Army: A Portrait of the American Army in Peacetime, 1784–1898* (New York: Oxford University Press, 1986), 94; Journal, August 23, 1848, box 4, Heintzelman Papers, LC; William C. Banks and Stephen Dycus, *Soldiers on the Home Front: The Domestic Role of the American Military* (Cambridge: Harvard University Press, 2016), 63; David F. Ericson, "The United States Military, State Development, and Slavery in the Early Republic," *Studies in American Political Development* 31 (April 2017), 132; Adams, "Personal Letters of Lee," 245.

17. Lesley J. Gordon, *General George E. Pickett in Life and Legend* (Chapel Hill: University of North Carolina Press, 2002), 6–7, 184 n. 4; T. Harry Williams, *P. G. T. Beauregard: Napoleon in Gray* (Baton Rouge: Louisiana State University Press, 1955), 2–3; Grady McWhiney, *Braxton Bragg and Confederate Defeat* (New York: Columbia University Press, 1969), 142–144; Jeffry D. Wert, *Cavalryman of the Lost Cause: A Biography of J. E. B. Stuart* (New York: Simon & Schuster, 2008), 30–31, 47; Thomas Ty Smith, "Slave-Owning U.S. Army Officers in Texas, 1850, 1860," August 24, 2020 (unpublished copy in author's possession); Emory M. Thomas, *Robert E. Lee: A Biography* (New York: W. W. Norton, 1997), 72, 174, 175; Paul D. Casdorph, *Confederate General R. S. Ewell: Robert E. Lee's Hesitant Commander* (Lexington: University Press of Kentucky, 2015), 27 (quotation), 141, 206. In late 1862, Lee, commanding the Army of Northern Virginia, fulfilled his obligations as executor by manumitting the estate's slaves. For assertions that Lee whipped his slaves, see "Some Facts that Should Come to Light," *New-York Tribune*, June 24, 1859; John W. Blassingame, ed.; *Slave Testimony: Two Centuries of Letters, Speeches, Interviews, and Autobiographies* (Baton Rouge: Louisiana State University Press, 1977), 467–468.

18. "Immediate Abolition of the Army and Navy," *The Liberator*, June 30, 1843; Petition from Mount Pleasant, Ohio, HR 28-G13.1, RG 233, NARA (first quotation); Sumner to Giddings, July 11, 1849, box 1, Giddings/Julian Papers, LC (second quotation); "West Point Military Academy," *Advocate of Peace*, October 1, 1852; "The Standing Army," *Christian Secretary* 29 (November 8, 1850): 2 (third quotation) "The Proposed Increase of the Standing Army," *Bangor Daily Whig & Courier*, February 8, 1858 (fourth quotation); "The Army Bill—Policy of the Administration," *National Era*, February 4, 1858; "Standing Army," ibid., February 18, 1858.

19. T. Harry Williams, "The Attack Upon West Point During the Civil War," *Mississippi Valley Historical Review* 25 (March 1939): 496; *CGlobe* 37th Cong., 2nd sess., 83 (first quotation); Medill to Stanton, January 21, 1862, roll 1, Stanton Papers, LC (second quotation); 'The Prayer of Twenty Millions," *New-York Tribune*, August 20, 1862 (third quotation).

20. *MPP* 6:115–116, 120; *Statutes* 12:597–600, 731–737; Morrison, *"Best School in the World,"* 133–134; *OR* Series III, 1:309; *CGlobe* 37th Cong., 1st sess., 85, 89 (quotations), 178–180. At 28.8 percent, the percentage of defecting regular officers who were not academy graduates was slightly higher than that of graduates. Either figure compares favorably with the 48 percent of U.S. senators who either withdrew or were expelled from the upper chamber. "The Civil War Senate Reacts to Secession," www.senate.gov/artandhistory/history/common/expulsion_cases/Civil War_Expulsion.htm.

21. Lori Lisowski, "The Future of West Point: Senate Debate on the Military Academy During the Civil War," *Civil War History* 34 (March 1988): 7; "The Appeals for Action," *New-York Tribune*, December 13, 1861; Williams, "Attack Upon West Point," 492–494.

22. Adam Gurowski, *Diary* (Boston: Lee and Shepard, 1862), 1:127; WDAR, 1861, 8; Lisowski, "Future of West Point," 7–13; *MPP* 5:48; Editorial, *New-York Tribune*, December 14, 1861; Medill to Stanton, January 21, 1862, roll 1, Stanton Papers, LC; Williams, "Attack Upon West Point," 493–495; *CGlobe* 37th Cong., 2nd sess., 162–164, 202, 204 (quotations).

23. *CGlobe* 37th Cong., 2nd sess., 200–203 (quotations).

24. *Statutes* 12:504; *CGlobe* 37th Cong., 2nd sess., Appendix, 256 (quotations).

25. "Have We a General Among Us?" *Harper's Weekly* 6 (January 17, 1863): 34 (first quotation); Gurowski, *Diary* 2:90–92 (second quotation); Lisowski, "Future of West Point," 16–21; *CGlobe* 37th Cong., 3rd sess., 324–330 (remaining quotations).

26. "Loyalty of the West Point Graduates," *New York Times*, January 23, 1863 (first quotation); *CGlobe* 37th Cong., 3rd sess., 324–327 (remaining quotations); Williams, "Attack Upon West Point," 504 n. 60; Lisowski, "Future of West Point," 16–21. Ralph Waldo Emerson, member of the Board of Visitors in 1863, came away impressed. "'West Point a hotbed of aristocracy' is the word of some political hack." Linda Allart and David W. Hill, eds., *The Journals and Miscellaneous Notebooks of Ralph Waldo Emerson*, vol. 15 (Cambridge: Belknap Press of Harvard University Press, 1982), 215.

27. Wilson, *Business of Civil War*, 1; WDAR, 1866, 656; WDAR, 1867, 586–587; Report of Hartz, August 31, 1863, box 3, Entry 1127, Copies of Annual Reports of Quartermaster Officers, 1863, RG 92, NARA (quotation); Jane Flaherty, "'The Exhausted Condition of the Treasury' on the Eve of the Civil War," *Civil War History* 55 (June 2009): 274–277.

28. Wilson, *Business of Civil War*, 5–33; Weasner to Pendleton, July 19, 1861, S-906, box 6, Entry 22, LR from the SW, RG 92, NARA; Pendleton to Cameron, July 29, 1861, ibid.; "Corruption in Government Contracts," *Newark Advocate*, August 23, 1861; Report attached to Scott to Seward, February 9, 1862, roll 2, Stanton

Papers, LC; Davis to Cameron, October 13, 1861, roll 9, Cameron Papers, LC; Meigs to Meigs, January 5, 1862, Addition I, roll 12, Meigs Papers, LC; *CGlobe* 37th Cong., 2nd sess., 565 (quotation); *OR* Series III, 1:964.

29. Erna Risch, *Quartermaster Support of the Army: A History of the Corps, 1775–1939* (Washington, D.C.: Center of Military History, 1989), 335–336; Blair to Cameron, June 2, 1861, Addition I, roll 12, Meigs Papers, LC; Lincoln to Scott, June 5, 1861, Series 1, Lincoln Papers, LC; Scott to Lincoln, June 5, 1861, ibid.; Wilson, *Business of Civil War*, 37; Meigs to McClellan, June 20, 1861, roll 35, M 745, LS by the Office of the Quartermaster General, RG 92, NARA; Meigs to Rollins, July 16, 1861, roll 36, ibid.; Meigs to Mrs. Lincoln, October 4, 1861, roll 36, ibid.; Meigs to Eddy, December 16, 1861, ibid.; Meigs to Myers, November 13, 1861, ibid.; Meigs to Father, June 22, 1861, Addition I, roll 5, Meigs Papers, LC; Meigs to Cameron, August 27, September 3, 1861, Addition I, roll 12, ibid.; Campbell to Cameron, October 11, 1861, roll 8, Cameron Papers, LC; Morton to Cameron, October 11, 1861, roll 9, ibid.; *Journal of the Constitutional Convention of the State of Illinois, Convened at Springfield, January 7, 1862* (Springfield: Charles H. Lanphier, 1862), 678, 681; *OR* Series III, 1:748; Meigs to Lincoln, December 21, 1861, Series 1, Lincoln Papers, LC (quotation).

30. Wilson, *Business of Civil War*, 66–70 (first quotation), 78, 38; Allen Nevins and Martin Hosley Thomas, eds., *The Diary of George Templeton Strong*, 4 vols. (New York: Macmillan, 1952), 3:187, 276; Report of Wilson, September 30, 1863, box 5, Entry 1127, Copies of Annual Reports of Quartermaster Officers, RG 92, NARA (second and third quotations); Darwin L. King, Kathleen M. Premo, and Carl J. Case, "Historical Influences on Modern Cost Accounting Practices," *Academy of Accounting and Financial Studies Journal* 13 (September 2009), 24–25. Close auditing of wartime accounts of individual quartermasters continued after the war. In June 1868, for example, Lt. Col. Osborn Cross, a West Point graduate responsible for nearly $7 million in wartime accounts, was found to have $107,000 "suspended against him, and awaiting his explanation." Miller, Report on the Money Accounts of Lt. Col. O. Cross, June 15, 1868, Entry 225, box 439, Quartermasters Consolidated File, RG 92, NARA.

31. Blair to Lincoln, September 14, 1861, Series 1, Lincoln Papers, LC; Meigs to Meigs, January 5, 1862, Addition I, roll 12, Meigs Papers, LC (first and second quotations); Allen to Meigs, February 3, 1862, vol. 1, Entry 381, General William Myers, LS, RG 92, NARA (third quotation); report attached to Scott to Stanton, February 9, 1862, roll 2, Stanton Papers, LC; Wilson, *Business of Civil War*, 86–89; Perry to McKim, January 4, 1865, vol. 24, Entry 9999, LS Relating to Clothing and Equipage, RG 92, NARA (fourth quotation); Crossman to Flagg, September 26, 1864, ibid.; Myers to Meigs, October 6, 1864, ibid. Another directive ordered that the Philadelphia depot furnish materials for producing 17,000 pairs of uniform trousers to Madison, Wisconsin, to support "the wives, widows, and other female relatives of Wisconsin soldiers." Perry to Van Slyke, January 4, 1865, ibid.

32. Meigs to Vinton, September 9, December 2, 1861, vol. 18, Entry 9999, LS Relating to Clothing and Equipage, RG 92, NARA; Allen to Coleman, October 14, 1861, vol. 1, Entry 381, General William Myers, LS, RG 92, NARA; Meigs to

Stanton, June 7, 1865, W-682, box 3, Entry 27, LR from the War Department, RG 92, NARA (quotation); Wilson, *Business of Civil War*, 102–104, 116–125.

33. Wilson, *Business of Civil War*, 138–146; Meigs to Wilson, February 20, 1864, roll 45, M745, LS by the Office of the Quartermaster General, RG 92, NARA (first quotation); Crossman to Cameron, March 18, 1863, roll 9, Cameron Papers, LC; Meigs to Crosman, April 17, 1863, vol. 21, Entry 9999, LR Relating to Clothing and Equipage, RG 92, NARA (second and third quotations); Brown to Thomas, December 23, 1861, B-674, box 126, Entry 20, LR, RG 92, NARA; Boyd to Meigs, December 22, 1863, B-574, box 126, ibid.; Meigs to Brown, March 4, 1864, QMG 119, roll 51, M494, LR by the SW from the President, Executive Departments, and War Department Bureaus, NARA; Brown to Meigs, October 22, 1864, B-318, box 136, Entry 20, LR, RG 92, NARA.

34. Philip Shaw Paludan, *A People's Contest: The Union and Civil War, 1861–1865* (New York: Harper and Row, 1988), 98, 112–113; Report of Jenkins, September 18, 1863, box 3, Entry 1127, Copies of Annual Reports of Quartermaster Officers, RG 92, NARA; Report of Parsons, October 6, 1863, box 4, ibid.; Report of Swords, October 6, 1863, ibid.; Report of Wilson, September 30, 1863, box 5, ibid.; Report of Hartz, August 31, 1863, box 3, ibid. (quotation); Paul A. C. Koistinen, *Beating Plowshares into Swords: The Political Economy of American Warfare, 1607–1865* (Lawrence: University Press of Kansas, 1996), 6–7; Wilson, *Business of Civil War*, 162–174. In 1871, Belger was restored to his rank. HED 72, 41st Cong., 2nd sess., serial 1417.

Captain Meigs claimed that $20 million passed through his office during the war and that he personally repaid the $130 shortage in his accounts when he left the army. Personal Recollections of S. Emlen Meigs, addition I, roll 11, Meigs Papers, LC.

35. Wilson, *Business of Civil War*, 75; "City Affairs: A Meeting of Female Operatives in the Arsenal," *North American and United States Gazette*, September 4, 1861 (first quotation); "City Affairs: Commendable Movement," ibid., July 27, 1863; Judith Giesberg, *Army at Home: Women and the Civil War on the Northern Home Front* (Chapel Hill: University of North Carolina Press, 2009), 137–139; "Meeting of Oppressed Workwomen," *Philadelphia Daily Age*, August 5, 1863 (second, third, and fourth quotations).

36. "The Working Women's Union," *New York Times*, November 19, 1863; "The Sewing Women of New York," *Daily Age*, March 3, 1864; "City Affairs: The Sewing Women Again," *North American and United States Gazette*, May 19, 1864; "Another Meeting of the Sewing Women," *Philadelphia Inquirer*, April 27, 1864; "City Intelligence: Meeting of Sewing Women," *Philadelphia Inquirer*, May 5, 1864; "City Intelligence: The Wrongs of the Working Women," *Daily Age*, May 7, 1864; Wilson, *Business of Civil War*, 96–99 (first quotation); "City Affairs: The Working Women," *North American and United States Gazette*, August 4, 1864; Roy P. Basler, *Collected Works of Abraham Lincoln*, 9 vols. (New Brunswick: Rutgers University Press, 1951–1955), 7:467 (second and third quotations); Giesberg, *Army at Home*, 140–141; "The Wages of Sewing Women," *New York Times*, August 26, 1864 (fourth and fifth quotations).

37. Wilson, *Business of Civil War*, 99–100; Giesberg, *Army at Home*, 140–141; "City Intelligence: Tremendous and Enthusiastic Meeting of Working Women,"

Daily Age, January 20, 1865 (quotation); "Interview of the Committee of Sewing Women with the President," *Public Ledger*, January 28, 1865.

38. Hsieh, *West Pointers and the Civil War*, 3–4, 5–9, 94, 111; *OR* Series I, 17, pt. 2, 566–567 (quotation); Logan to Wife, August 6, 1862, July 14 [1864], box 33, Logan Family Papers, LC; U.S. War Department, Military Secretary's Office, *Memorandum Relative to the General Officers in the Armies of the United States During the Civil War, 1861–1865* (Washington, D.C.: Government Printing Office, 1906), 4–8; John H. Eicher and David J. Eicher, *Civil War High Commands* (Palo Alto: Stanford University Press, 2002), 855–864. The percentage of former regular officers among Confederate generals of all grades (36.7 percent) was slightly less than that in the Union Army (43.9 percent). Hsieh, *West Pointers and the Civil War*, 200 n. 4. Herman Hattaway and Archer Jones point out that West Point training, in conjunction with Mexican War service, held the real keys to high advancement: *How the North Won: A Military History of the Civil War* (Urbana: University of Illinois Press, 1983), 503.

39. Newell and Shrader, *Of Duty Well and Faithfully Done*, 39–48; Mark W. Johnson, *That Body of Brave Men: The U.S. Regular Infantry and the Civil War in the West* (New York: Da Capo Press, 2003), 23.

40. Newell and Shrader, *Of Duty Well and Faithfully Done*, 205–210, 229–234, 248; *OR* Series I, 5:14 (quotations); Stephen W. Sears, ed., *The Civil War Papers of George B. McClellan: Selected Correspondence, 1860–1865* (New York: Ticknor and Fields, 1989), 101.

41. *OR* Series I, 11, pt. 1:61 (first quotation); ibid., 12, pt. 2:482–483; Rufus Fairchild Zogbaum, "The Regulars in the Civil War," *North American Review* 167 (July 1898): 20–23 (second and third quotations p. 21); John Pope, "The Second Battle of Bull Run," *Battles and Leaders of the Civil War* 2 (1884–1887): 489; *OR* Series I, 27, pt. 1:634–635, 645; Fox, *Regimental Losses*, 523; Newell and Shrader, *Of Duty Well and Faithfully Done*, 235–236; *OR* Series I, 36, pt. 1:123, pt. 2:821; *Supplement to the Official Records of the Union and Confederate Armies,* 100 vols. (Wilmington, NC: Broadfoot Publishing, 1994–2001), Part I, 8:254 (fourth quotation).

42. Newell and Shrader, *Of Duty Well and Faithfully Done*, 217–221, 247–251; *OR* Series I, 3:72–79; Donald S. Frazier, *Blood and Treasure: Confederate Empire in the Southwest* (College Station: Texas A&M University Press, 1995), 157–178 (quotation 157). For an exhaustive account of war in the Trans-Mississippi, see Thomas W. Cutrer, *Theater of a Separate War: The Civil War West of the Mississippi River, 1861–1865* (Chapel Hill: University of North Carolina Press, 2017).

43. Newell and Shrader, *Of Duty Well and Faithfully Done*, 239–242; Lewis M. Hosea, "The Regular Brigade of the Army of the Cumberland," in *Sketches of War History, 1861–1865: Papers Prepared for the Commandery of the State of Ohio, Military Order of the Loyal Legion of the United States*, ed. W. H. Chamberlin, A. M. Van Dyke, and George A. Thayer, vol. 5 (Cincinnati: Robert Clarke Co., 1903), 330–343 (quotation 343).

44. *OR* Series I, 25, pt. 1:720. For troop strengths, see WDAR, 1860, 214–229; *OR* Series III, 2:957; and Robert M. Utley, *Frontiersmen in Blue: The United States Army and the Indian, 1848–1865* (1967; rpt. Lincoln: University of Nebraska Press, 1981), 216.

45. Robert Wooster, *The American Military Frontiers: The United States Army and the West, 1783–1900* (Albuquerque: University of New Mexico Press, 2009), 136, 181; *OR* Series I, 48, pt. 2:1167, 1178, 1197–1198.

46. *OR* Series I, 15:579–580.

47. *OR* Series I, 50:185–187 (first quotation); Harold Schindler, "The Bear River Massacre: New Historical Evidence," *Utah Historical Quarterly* 67 (Fall 1999), 307 (second quotation); Alvin M. Josephy Jr., *The Civil War in the American West* (New York: Alfred A. Knopf, 1991), 305–310 (third quotation 305); SED 26, 39th Cong., 2nd sess., serial 1277, 47 (fourth quotation); SR 156, pt. 3, 39th Cong., 2nd sess., serial 1279.

48. Gary Gallagher, *The Union War* (Cambridge: Harvard University Press, 2011), 140–147; Russell Duncan, ed., *Blue-Eyed Child of Fortune: The Civil War Letters of Colonel Robert Gould Shaw* (Athens: University of Georgia Press, 1999), 245 (quotation).

11. An Elusive Peace

1. Gary Gallagher, *The Union War* (Cambridge: Harvard University Press, 2011), 7–32, 120–121 (quotation). Stuart McConnell, *Glorious Contentment: The Grand Army of the Republic, 1865–1900* (Chapel Hill: University of North Carolina Press, 1992), 1–17, presents a darker vision of the Grand Review.

2. "The Grand Review," *New-York Tribune*, May 25, 1865 (first quotation); "The Grandest Military Display in the World," *New York Herald*, May 24, 1865 (second quotation); Gallagher, *Union War*, 28 (third quotation).

3. Gregory P. Downs, *After Appomattox: Military Occupation and the Ends of War* (Cambridge: Harvard University Press, 2015), 7, 104; Richard White, *The Republic for Which It Stands: The United States during Reconstruction and the Gilded Age, 1865–1896* (New York: Oxford University Press, 2017), 109 (quotation), 117–124. Subsequent legislation, most notably the Timber Culture Act (1873), the Desert Land Act (1877), and the Timber and Stone Act (1878), also used federal land grants to spur non-Indian development of the West.

4. Gregory P. Downs, "Three Faces of Sovereignty: Governing Confederate, Mexican, and Indian Texas in the Civil War Era," in *Civil War Wests: Testing the Limits of the United States*, ed. Adam Arenson and Andrew R. Graybill (Berkeley: University of California Press, 2015), 119–125; *The Papers of Andrew Johnson*, 16 vols. (Knoxville: University of Tennessee Press, 1967–2000), 8:257; *Personal Memoirs of P. H. Sheridan, General United States Army*, 2 vols. (New York: Charles L. Webster & Co., 1888), 2:208–211, 217–218; John M. Schofield, *Forty-six Years in the Army* (1897; rpt. Norman: University of Oklahoma Press, 1998), 378–385; Thomas D. Schoonover, ed. and trans., *Mexican Lobby: Matías Romero in Washington, 1861–1867* (Lexington: University Press of Kentucky, 1986), 31, 50–51, 64–66, 72–74, 81, 84–85; Mariscal to Schofield, June 6, 12, 15, 1865, box 77, Schofield Papers, LC; "The following proposition is made by the Government of the Republic of Mexico & Maj. Genl. U.S.A.," undated, "Important Correspondence/Confidential" File, box 77, ibid.; Romero to Schofield, July 2, 12, 21, 1865, ibid.; Romero to Santacilia,

June 13, 1865, exped. 1281, fs. 1–2 of 2 fojas, Archivo Benito Juárez. Thanks to Dr. Patrick J. Carroll for bringing my attention to the last document.

5. *Personal Memoirs of Sheridan* 2:208–214; Schoonover, ed., *Mexican Lobby*, 90–91, 103; Schofield, *Forty-six Years*, 385–392; Schofield to Seward, August 4, 1865, roll 90, Seward Papers; Sheridan to Grant, November 5, 1865, roll 2, Sheridan Papers, LC; "Needless Alarm," *New York Times*, December 19, 1865; "Gen. Schofield's Visit," ibid., December 28, 1865; John Bigelow, *Retrospectives of an Active Life*, 5 vols. (New York: Baker Taylor & Co., 1909–1913), 3:265–267; Bigelow to Seward, December 8, 1865, roll 92, Seward Papers. Henry Adams, who was the son of Charles Francis Adams (minister to England), and John Bigelow (minister to France) both concluded that Seward had concocted the European venture to "get him [Schofield] of the way." J. C. Levenson, et al., eds., *The Letters of Henry Adams*, 6 vols. (Cambridge: Belknap Press of Harvard University, 1982–1988), 6:308.

6. *Personal Memoirs of Sheridan* 2:208 (first quotation), 224–228 (second quotation); Sheridan to Getty, April 25, May 25, 1866, box 1, Gibson-Getty-McClure Family Papers, LC.

7. G. Mott Williams, ed., "Letters of General Thomas Williams, 1862," *American Historical Review* 14 (January 1909): 321 (first quotation); Downs, *After Appomattox*, 5, 42, 44, 49; *MPP* 6:308; Journal, April 27, 1865, roll 7, Heintzelman Journal, LC; Brooks D. Simpson, LeRoy P. Graf, and John Muldowny, eds., *Advice After Appomattox: Letters to Andrew Johnson, 1865–1866* (Knoxville: University of Tennessee Press, 1987), 78–79 (second and third quotations); *OR* I: 47, pt. 3, 627; Bentzoni to Sir, July 7, 1865, B-230, roll 13, M752, Registers and LR by the Commissioner, RG 105, NARA (fourth quotation); *Papers of Johnson* 9:262–263 (fifth quotation); Miles to Senator, September 13, 1865, Miles Collection, USAMHI.

8. John Cox and LaWanda Cox, "General O. O. Howard and the 'Misrepresented Bureau,'" *Journal of Southern History* 19 (November 1953): 427–456 (quotation 443); WDAR, 1867, 620–657. Most officers were skeptical of the Bureau, but Col. (Volunteers) Samuel C. Armstrong resigned from the army in favor of a Freedmen's Bureau position. Armstrong to Howard, June 18, 1865, A-106, roll 13, M752, Registers and LR by the Commissioner, RG 105, NARA.

9. Downs, *After Appomattox*, 7, 12–14, 47, 81–87, 258–259; George H. Gordon, *A War Diary of Events in the War of the Great Rebellion: 1863–1865* (Boston: James R. Osgood and Co., 1882), 418; *OR* I, 47, pt. 3:411–412, 619; "Suppression of a Disloyal Paper," *Philadelphia Inquirer*, August 1, 1865; Clayton R. Newell and Charles R. Shrader, "The U.S. Army's Transition to Peace, 1865–66," *Journal of Military History* 77 (July 2013): 885–886; Gibbon to Latrobe, September 7, 1865, Gibbon Papers, MdHS (quotation); "The Military Departments," *ANJ* 3 (January 6, 1866): 311; *CGlobe* 39th Cong., 1st sess., 603.

10. Gibbon to Latrobe, September 7, 1865, Gibbon Papers, MdHS (first quotation); *Papers of Johnson* 11:127–128; Sherman to Schofield, May 28, 1865, box 28, Barney Collection, Huntington Library; *OR* III: 5, 212; *PUSG* 16:259; Downs, *After Appomattox*, 104, 258–259; Andrew F. Lang, *In the Wake of War: Military Occupation, Emancipation, and Civil War America* (Baton Rouge: Louisiana State University Press, 2017), 67; *OR* I: 47, pt. 3:461–463 (second quotation).

11. "The Financial Crisis," April 2, 1865, *New York Times;* Downs, *After Appomattox*, 92–93; *OR* I: 48, pt. 2, 933 (quotations); *PUSG* 15:306–307.

12. *PUSG* 15:377, 16:116–117, 221; Sherman to Grant, November 6, 1865, roll 10, Sherman Papers, LC (first and second quotations); Howard Lamar, *Dakota Territory: A Study of Frontier Politics, 1861–1889* (New Haven: Yale University Press, 1956), 100, 104–106; HED 23, 39th Cong., 2 sess., serial 1288, 16; Sherman to Grant, August 29, 1866, series 5, roll 24, Grant Papers, LC; *Statutes* 14:703–706 (third and fourth quotations), 708–749; Elliott West, *Contested Plains: Indians, Goldseekers, and the Rush to Colorado* (Lawrence: University Press of Kansas, 1998), 308; Pekka Hämäläinen, *The Comanche Empire* (New Haven: Yale University Press, 2008), 314; Robert M. Utley, *Frontiersmen in Blue: The United States Army and the Indian, 1848–1865* (1967; rpt. Lincoln: University of Nebraska Press, 1981), 337–338.

13. Gallagher, *Union War*, 125; Newell and Shrader, "Transition to Peace," 877–879.

14. Downs, *After Appomattox*, 48–51 96, 104, 106–108, 258–259; Lang, *In the Wake of War*, 218; SED 27, 39th Cong., 1st sess., serial 1238, 78 (first quotation); Custer to Chandler, January 8 (second quotation), 14 (third quotation), 1866, roll 2, Chandler Papers, LC; HED 70, 39th Cong., 1st sess., serial 1256, 237 (fourth quotation); *PUSG* 15:399–400 (fifth quotation).

15. *PUSG* 16:7–8, 52–54, 69, 114, 459; Brooks D. Simpson, *Let Us Have Peace: Ulysses S. Grant and the Politics of War and Reconstruction, 1861–1868* (Chapel Hill: University of North Carolina Press, 1991), 128; Simpson, et al., *Advice After Appomattox*, 222; "Military Occupation of the South," *ANJ* 3 (February 3, 1866): 380; Karen Orren and Stephen Skowronek, *The Search for American Political Development* (Cambridge: Cambridge University Press, 2004), 138; "General Grant on the Withdrawal of Troops," *Hartford Daily Courant*, January 16, 1866; *CGlobe* 39th Cong., 1st sess., 137, 320 (first quotation), 316–317 (second and third quotations), 340–341 (fourth quotation), 688; *MPP* 6:398–405. A copy of the original measure, Senate Bill 60, is at http://memory.loc.gov/cgi-bin/ampage?collId=llsb&fileName=039/llsb039.db&recNum=304. The Senate's 30–18 vote to override the veto failed to meet the necessary two-thirds requirement. *CGlobe* 39th Cong., 1st sess., 421, 943.

16. *Statutes* 14:27–30; *CGlobe* 39th Cong., 1st sess., 478–480, 597–601 (first and second quotations), 1115–1119; *MPP* 6:405–413, 429–432 (third quotation).

17. Downs, *After Appomattox*, 7, 129–131; Stephen V. Ash, *A Massacre in Memphis: The Race Riot that Shook the Nation One Year after the Civil War* (New York: Hill and Wang, 2013), 93–94, 103, 162–163, 193; *PUSG* 16:228, 233–236, 258–259; Miles to Howard, August 24, 1866, Howard Papers, Bowdoin College (first quotation); Lilly to Horner, April 11, 1866, HR 39A-F2.16, RG 233, NARA (second and third quotations); Ira Berlin, ed., *Freedom: A Documentary History of Emancipation, 1861–1867*, Series II, *The Black Military Experience*, 759–761; HR 30, 39th Cong., 1st sess., serial 1273; Joseph G. Dawson III, *Army Generals and Reconstruction Louisiana, 1862–1877* (Baton Rouge: Louisiana State University Press, 1982), 39–41; *CGlobe*, 39th Cong., 1 sess., 2776–2780, 3409–3413, 3839–3842; *Statutes* 14:173–177 (fourth and fifth quotations).

18. Harold Holzer and Sara Vaughn Gabbard, eds., *1865: America Makes War*

and Peace in Lincoln's Final Year (Carbondale: Southern Illinois University Press, 2015), 171; Roy P. Basler, ed., *The Collected Works of Abraham Lincoln*, 9 vols. (New Brunswick: Rutgers University Press, 1953–1955), 8:408–409; *PUSG* 15:358 (quotation); 16:10–18.

19. Senate debates are in *CGlobe*, 39th Cong., 1 sess., 1379–1386. Convoluted House debates are in ibid., April 13–May 2, with the vote on the Rogers amendment on 1977 and the defeat of the initial House measure on 2352. See also Brincklé to Sister, January 25, 1866, Brincklé Papers, LC; Hazen to Wilson, May 20, 1866, Wilson Papers, LC; "Is there any prospect . . . ," *ANJ* 3 (June 16, 1866): 684–685.

20. *CGlobe*, 39th Cong., 1 sess., 3162–3163, 3270–3276, 3329–3332, 3650, 4228, 4230, 4246; *PUSG* 16:199–200; Heitman, 2:597 (note i), 602–605.

21. "The following is an extract . . . ," *ANJ* 3 (July 14, 1866): 743 (quotation); Downs, *After Appomattox*, 142–143, 262–263; WDAR, 1866, 4–5; *PUSG* 16:393; Mark Bradley, *The Army and Reconstruction, 1865–1877* (Washington, D.C.: Center of Military History, 2015), 34.

22. *MPP* 6:434–438; Downs, *After Appomattox*, 151; *PUSG* 16:390–391, 401 (quotation); WDAR, 1866, 48; Bates to Schofield, November 20, 1866, box 2, Schofield Papers, LC. Although West Virginia had become a state in 1863, state officials saw federal garrisons there as a means of ensuring their dominance over former Confederates. Randall Scott Gooden, "The Completion of a Revolution: West Virginia from Statehood through Reconstruction" (Ph.D. diss., West Virginia University, 1995), 64.

23. WDAR, 1866, 51–56 (first and second quotations), 58, 48–49 (third and fourth quotations); Downs, *After Appomattox*, 156.

24. *PUSG* 16:24; Stanton to Grant, October 11, 1866, series 1, roll 24, Andrew Johnson Papers, LC; WDAR, 1866, p. 48; Crawford to Stanton, July 28, 1866, series 5, roll 24, Grant Papers, LC (first quotation); Meagher to Wheaton, October 20, 1865, roll 1, M356, State Department Territorial Papers: Montana, RG 59, NARA (second and third quotations); Meagher to Seward, December 11, 1865, February 20, 1866, ibid.; Meagher to the Legislature, March 6, 1866, ibid.; Spink to Burleigh, July 16, 1866, D-28, box 1, Entry 371: LR, Department of the Platte, RG 393, NARA; Spink to Sherman, July 11, 1866, D-26, ibid. (fourth quotation); Petition to SW, July 10, 1866, D-28, ibid. (fifth quotation).

25. *CGlobe* 40th Cong., 1st sess., 680 (first quotation); Bradley to Nichols, July 12, 1867, box 3, Bradley Papers, USAMHI (second quotation); Hartz to Father, January 11, 1868, box 1, Hartz Papers, LC (third quotation); Bradley to Ione, [May 25, 1867?], box 2, Bradley Papers, USAMHI (fourth quotation); WDAR, 1869, 37–38; HR 384, 43rd Cong., 1st sess., serial 1624, 221 (fifth and sixth quotations).

26. WDAR, 1866, 21, 31–33 (first and second quotations); Sheridan to Grant, April 5, 1867, Series 1, roll 26, Andrew Johnson Papers, LC; HED 23, 39th Cong., 2 sess., serial 1288, 16 (third quotation); Sherman to Grant, August 29, 1866, series 5, roll 24, Grant Papers; Thompson to Litchfield, May 27, 1868, T-32 (fourth quotation), June 19, 1868, T-33, July 28, 1868, T-38, box 8, part 1, Entry 3717, LR, Department of the Platte, RG 393; WDAR, 1869, 37–38; HR 384, 43rd Cong., 1st sess., serial 1624, 161 (fifth quotation).

27. WDAR, 1867, 71–74 (first and second quotations); WDAR, 1869, 121 (third, fourth, and fifth quotations); WDAR, 1870, 8.

28. McClure to Getty, February 1, 1871, box 1, Gibson-Getty-McClure Papers, LC (first and second quotations); Young to Price, October 13, 1868, part 1, entry 517: Miscellaneous Letters and Orders Received, Department of Arizona, RG 393, NARA (third quotation); Ord to Logan, December 29, 1869, box 2, Logan Family Papers (fourth and fifth quotations); Ord to Sherman, March 30, 1870, roll 15, Sherman Papers, LC; Sherman to Belknap, January 7, 1870, roll 38, M565, LS, Adjutant General's Office, RG 94, NARA; HR 384, 43rd Cong., 1st sess., serial 1624, 5–7 (sixth and seventh quotations).

29. Rachel Sherman Thorndyke, ed., *The Sherman Letters: Correspondence between General and Senator Sherman from 1837 to 1891* (New York: Charles Scribner's Sons, 1894), 281 (first and second quotations); *PUSG* 16:116–117 (third quotation), 17:21–24, 30–31; WDAR, 1866, 20–21, 26–27; Pope to Sherman, October 25, 1866, roll 11, Sherman Papers, LC; HED 71, 39th Cong., 2nd sess., serial 1293, 11–12; Sherman to Grant, May 27, 1867, series 5, roll 24, Grant Papers, LC; Grenville M. Dodge, *Personal Recollections of President Abraham Lincoln, General Ulysses S. Grant, and General William T. Sherman* (Council Bluffs, Iowa: Monarch Printing Co., 1914), 197–198; Martin F. Schmitt, ed., *General George Crook: His Autobiography*, Revised Edition (Norman: University of Oklahoma Press, 1986), 142–145; Paul Magid, *The Gray Fox: George Crook and the Indian Wars* (Norman: University of Oklahoma Press, 2015), 3–50; SED 15, 39th Cong., 2nd sess, 2:4, serial 1277 (fourth quotation); SED 13, 40th Cong., 1st sess., serial 1308; SED 97, 49th Cong., 2nd sess., serial 2448.

30. Diary entry, March 1, 1867, Comstock Papers, LC (first quotation); "General Grant's Position," *ANJ* 4 (September 22, 1866): 71 (second quotation); Dodge, *Personal Recollections*, 197–198; Simpson, *Let Us Have Peace*, 149–171; Thorndyke, ed., *Sherman Letters*, 279–281; *PUSG* 16:338; "Views of Army Officers," *Freedom's Champion*, February 21, 1867; Charles Richard Williams, ed., *Diary and Letters of Rutherford Birchard Hayes*, 5 vols. (Columbus: Ohio State Archaeological and Historical Society, 1922), 3:38, 41; "Shall Martial Law Be Revived?" *ANJ* 4 (February 9, 1867): 396–397 (third and fourth quotations).

31. *CGlobe*, 39th Cong., 2nd sess., 1851–1852; *Statutes* 14:430–432, 428–429, 432–433, 485–487; Simpson, *Let Us Have Peace*, 172–174.

32. *CGlobe*, 39th Cong., 2nd sess., 1097–1100 (first and second quotations), 1104 (third quotation), 1353, 1355, 1468–1469 (fourth quotation), 1849, 1851–1852; Harold Hyman, "Ulysses Grant I, Emperor of America? Some Civil-Military Continuities and Strains of the Civil War and Reconstruction," in *The United States Military under the Constitution of the United States, 1789–1989*, ed. Richard H. Kohn (New York: New York University Press, 1991), 186 (fifth quotation). For convenient compilation of the legislative process, roll-call votes, and presidential vetoes, see Edward McPherson, *The Political History of the United States during Reconstruction* (Washington, D.C.: Philp & Solomons, 1871), 167–178, 192–194.

33. SED 13, 40th Cong., 1st sess., serial 1308, 49–52; SED 156, 39th Cong., 2nd sess., serial 1279, 6–7; Utley, *Frontier Regulars*, 126 n. 10; *CGlobe* 39th Cong., 2nd sess., 879–882, 895–897, 899, 1712–1714, 1624, 1681–1683, 1715–1717 (quotations).

For comparisons of the votes, see McPherson, *Political History*, 173, and *CGlobe* 39th Cong., 2nd sess., 1720.

34. Dodge, *Personal Recollections*, 197–198 (quotation); Robert W. Larson, *Red Cloud: Warrior-Statesman of the Lakota Sioux* (Norman: University of Oklahoma Press, 1997), 101–107; Augur to Sherman, May 18, 1867, LS, Department of the Platte, RG 393, NARA; James G. Randall, ed., *The Diary of Orville Hickman Browning*, 2 vols. (Springfield: Illinois State Historical Library, 1933), 2:126, 128, 135; WDAR, 1867, 32, 65–67; SED No. 13, 40th Cong., 1st sess., serial 1308, 55–56, 74; Robert M. Utley, *Frontier Regulars: The United States Army and the Indian, 1866–1891* (1973; rpt. Lincoln: University of Nebraska Press, 1981), 123–124; Hartz to Father, June 5, 1867, box 1, Hartz Papers, LC.

35. Hancock to Sherman, January 14, 1867, LS, Department of the Missouri, RG 393, NARA (first quotation); Hancock to Carleton, February 18, 1867, ibid.; Sherman to Grant, February 18, 1867, series 5, roll 24, Grant Papers, LC; SED 13, 40th Cong., 1st sess., serial 1308, 78, 81, 83–86 (second and third quotations), 113; HED 240, 41st Cong., 2nd sess., serial 1425, 99–134; WDAR, 1867, 66; HED 1, 40th Cong., 2nd sess., serial 1326, 18, 310–314; Utley, *Frontier Regulars*, 115–119.

36. *CGlobe* 40th Cong., 1st sess., 667–672 (first quotation), 680, 703–708; SED 13, 40th Cong., 1st sess., serial 1308, 1–6, 121; *Statutes* 15:17–18; *PUSG* 18:183, 187–188; "The Indians," *Evening Star*, August 9, 1867; Charles J. Kappler, ed., *Indian Affairs: Laws and Treaties*, 7 vols. (Washington, D.C.: Government Printing Office, 1903–1904), 2:977–989, 998–1007; HED 97, 40th Cong., 2nd sess., serial 1337, 5; Utley, *Frontier Regulars*, 133–136. Justin Morrill (R-VT) unsuccessfully challenged the volunteer amendment, citing the Chivington massacre. "If the military power of this Government is to be strengthened I submit that the only safe method to strengthen it is through the regular army." *CGlobe* 40th Cong., 1st sess., 708.

37. Magill, *Gray Fox*, 39–46; Paul Andrew Hutton, *The Apache Wars: The Hunt for Geronimo, the Apache Kid, and the Captive Boy Who Started the Longest War in American History* (New York: Crown, 2016), 119–124; "Mr. Stanbery's Opinion," *ANJ* 4 (June 22, 1867): 700 (first quotation); *PUSG* 17:69 (second quotation), 117–121; Simpson, *Let Us Have Peace*, 179–181; Downs, *After Appomattox*, 14, 186–188; Thomas T. Smith, et al., eds., *The Reminiscences of Major General Zenas R. Bliss, 1854–1876: From the Texas Frontier to the Civil War and Back Again* (Austin: Texas State Historical Association, 2007), 395; Dawson, *Army Generals and Reconstruction Louisiana*, 49–51.

38. Paul H. Bergeron, *Andrew Johnson's Civil War and Reconstruction* (Knoxville: University of Tennessee Press, 2011), 152; Simpson, *Let Us Have Peace*, 175–176; "In appointing generals . . . ," *ANJ* 4 (March 23, 1867): 492–493; Flournoy to Butler, June 29, 1867, box 42, Butler Papers, LC.

39. Schofield to Adjutant General, April 15, 1867, Entry 5408, LS, First Military District, RG 393, NARA; "The Mobile Riot: Report of General Swayne," *ANJ* 4 (June 1, 1867): 647; "Riot in Mobile," *New York Times*, May 15, 1867; SED 14, 40th Cong., 1st sess., serial 1308, 240; *PUSG* 17:91–92, 95–96, 98, 117–121, 186; HED 20, 40th Cong., 1st sess., serial 1311, 65 (first and second quotations); Dawson, *Army*

Generals and Reconstruction Louisiana, 53–54; Simpson, *Let Us Have Peace*, 182–183; *Diary of Gideon Welles, Secretary of the Navy Under Lincoln and Johnson*, 3 vols. (Boston: Houghton & Mifflin, 1911), 3:104 (third quotation), 105, 107, 109–115; "Reconstruction," *New York Times*, June 17, 1867.

40. Diary, January 27, February 6, 24, March 11, 12, 1867, roll 3, French Family Papers, LC; French to Harry, January 27, 1867, ibid.; *CGlobe*, 39th Cong., 2nd sess., 1983 (first and second quotations); *Statutes* 14:466; "Mr. Stanbery's Opinion," *ANJ* 4 (June 22, 1867): 700; Simpson, *Let Us Have Peace*, 183–189; *PUSG* 17:192, 196, 204, 236–237 (third quotation).

41. Downs, *After Appomattox*, 183–184; *CGlobe* 40th Cong., 1st sess., 517, 522 (quotation), 638; Dawson, *Army Generals and Reconstruction Louisiana*, 56.

42. Bergeron, *Johnson's Civil War*, 157–159; Joseph Schafer, ed. and trans., *Intimate Letters of Carl Schurz, 1841–1869* (Madison: State Historical Society of Wisconsin, 1928), 388 (first quotation); Simpson, *Let Us Have Peace*, 192–199; Cooke to Sherman, August 19, 1867, box 122, John Sherman Papers, LC (second and third quotations); John Y. Simon, ed., *The Personal Memoirs of Julia Dent Grant* (New York: G. P. Putnam's Sons, 1975), 165; *PUSG* 17:277–281 (fourth quotation), 295; *Diary of Welles* 3:182–189; Randall, ed., *Diary of Browning* 2:156, 159; "The Removal of General Sheridan," *ANJ* 5 (August 31, 1867): 31.

43. Brincklé to Sister, July 13, 1867, Brincklé Papers, LC (first quotation); HED 57, 40th Cong., 2nd sess., serial 1330, 123 (second quotation); J. G. de Roulhac Hamilton, ed., *The Correspondence of Jonathan Worth*, 2 vols. (Raleigh: Edward and Broughton, 1909), 2:1095 (third quotation), 1105–1106, 1121; Starr to Jo, September 25 (fifth quotation), October 16, November 16 (fourth quotation), 1867, box 1, Starr Papers, Missouri State Historical Society; *PUSG* 17:207; Circular No. 19, October 10, 1867, Miles Collection, USAMHI; Miles to Howard, November 1, 1867, Howard Papers, Bowdoin Library.

44. Downs, *After Appomattox*, 195, 197; Bergeron, *Johnson's Civil War*, 174–178; *PUSG* 18:178 (first quotation), 95 (third quotation); *MPP* 6:563 (second quotation); WDAR, 1868, 144–146; Underwood to Washburne, December 16, 1867, box 54, Washburne Papers, LC (fourth quotation). Hancock also attempted to remove nine New Orleans city councilmen appointed by his predecessor, but Grant rejected it and approved his request for a transfer. Dawson, *Army Generals and Reconstruction in Louisiana*, 69–75; *PUSG* 18:175–182; WDAR, 1868, 215–223.

45. Downs, *After Appomattox*, 193–194; Simpson, *Let Us Have Peace*, 237–240; *PUSG* 18:217–223 (first quotation), 226–227; Schofield to Underwood, March 13, 1868, box 86, Schofield Papers, LC; Schofield to Grant, March 21, 1868, in letterbook under "x," box 47, ibid.; Stoneman to Schofield, March 24, 1868, box 8, ibid.; Schofield to Stoneman, March 23, 1868, box 48, ibid.; *Petersburg Index*, April 18, May 11, 1868; *Richmond Daily Enquirer and Examiner*, April 18, 28, 1868; *Richmond Dispatch*, clipping, April 18, 1868, in box 88, Schofield Papers, LC; Schofield to Grant, April 18, May 8, 15, 1868, Entry 5408, LS, First Military District, RG 393, NARA; Schofield to May, May 2, 1868, box 47, Schofield Papers, LC.

46. Bergeron, *Johnson's Civil War*, 182–187; Simpson, *Let Us Have Peace*, 228–236; Randall, ed., *Diary of Browning* 2:173–175; *Diary of Welles* 3:257–261, 269–279;

John F. Marszalek, *Sherman: A Soldier's Passion for Order* (New York: Free Press, 1993), 369–374; Sherman to Johnson, January 31, February 20, 1868, roll 45, Sherman Papers, LC; Johnson to Sherman, February 19, 1868, ibid.; William Tecumseh Sherman, *Memoirs* (New York: Library of America, 1990), 911–923 (quotation 916); Edward McPherson, *Political Manual for 1868: Including a Classified Summary of the Important Executive, Legislative, and Politico-Military Facts of the Period from April 1, 1867 to July 15, 1868* (Washington, D.C.: Philp & Solomons, 1868), 346.

47. Eric L. McKitrick, *Andrew Johnson and Reconstruction* (Chicago: University of Chicago Press, 1960), 504–505; Johnson to Stanton, February 21, 1868, roll 12, Stanton Papers, LC; Stanton to Thomas, ibid.; Sumner to Stanton, ibid.; Thayer to Stanton, ibid.; Entry for February 22, 1868, Moore Diary, roll 50, Andrew Johnson Papers, LC; *PUSG* 18:138–148, 165, 173–174; William Wherry, "The foregoing [or, in this case, subsequent] paper was written by Genl. Schofield at Richmond Va in 1867–8 and has been in my custody ever since," March 16, 1880, in Virginia Constitutional Convention file, box 88, Schofield Papers, LC (quotations).

48. Evarts to Schofield, April 21, 1868, box 4, Schofield Papers, LC; "Memorandum," dated May 1868, box 82, ibid.; "The War Department," in Nomination as Sec. of War File, box 82, ibid.; Entry for April 24, May 27, 1868, Moore Diary, roll 51, Andrew Johnson Papers, LC; James Lee McDonough and William T. Alderson, eds., "Republican Politics and the Impeachment of Andrew Johnson," *Tennessee Historical Quarterly* 26 (Summer 1967): 178–183; *PUSG* 18:235; *Evening Star*, April 25, 1868 (quotations). Schofield later described the affair "as a practical compromise." Schofield to Sherman, Oct. 25, 1885, box 60, Schofield Papers, LC.

On May 12, the *Evening Star* noted: "Among the absurd rumors telegraphed from here to-day, is one to the effect that Messrs. Trumbull, Fessenden, Grimes, and Henderson [all moderate Republicans] had a private interview with the President about three weeks ago, and pledged themselves in writing to vote for his acquittal, if he would nominate Gen. Schofield as Secretary of War."

49. Moore Diary, May 27–30, 1868, roll 51, Andrew Johnson Papers, LC; *Evening Star*, May 28, 29, 1868; *Petersburg Index*, June 3, 1868; "The war office . . . ," *ANJ* 5 (May 30, 1868): 645.

12. Continued Challenges South and West

1. Augur to Sherman, June 24, 1867, Entry 3722, LS, Department of the Platte, RG 393, NARA; Heather Cox Richardson, *West from Appomattox: The Reconstruction of America after the Civil War* (New Haven: Yale University Press, 2007), 69–77, 116–118, 142 (first quotation); "Horrible Atrocities on the Frontier," *Daily National Intelligencer*, September 28, 1868 (second quotation).

2. Jerome A. Greene, *Washita: The U.S. Army and the Southern Cheyennes, 1867–1869* (Norman: University of Oklahoma Press, 2004), 48–70; WDAR, 1868, 12 (quotations); Sheridan to Bradley, September 28, 1868, Bradley Papers, USAMHI; Sherman to Augur, September 28, 1868, Augur Papers, Newberry Library; Sherman to Tappan, September 24, 1868, roll 45, Sherman Papers, LC; "The Indian Peace Commission," *New York Times*, October 7, 1868; HED No. 1, 40th Cong., 3rd sess.,

serial 1366, 831–832; WDAR, 1868, 6; Sherman to Schofield, January 17, 1869, box 28, Barney Collection, Huntington Library. Minutes of the Chicago meeting are in *Proceedings of the Great Peace Commission of 1867–1868* (Washington, D.C.: Institute for the Development of Indian Law, 1975).

3. Carlton to Wife, May 26, 1867, box 1, Carlton Papers, LC (first and second quotations); *PUSG* 17:174–178; 19:45; Sherman to Grant, July 4, 1867, series 5, roll 21, Grant Papers, LC; *OR* Ser. I, 48 pt. 1:972–973; Sherman to Sherman, September 23, 1868, roll 13, Sherman Papers, LC (third quotation). Sheridan dubbed the winter campaign "an experimental one." WDAR, 1869, 45.

4. Sherman to Hazen, September 26, 1868, roll 45, Sherman Papers, LC; SED No. 18, 40th Cong., 3rd sess., serial 1360, 4–6; WDAR, 1868, 21 (first and second quotations); Sherman to Sherman, October 14, 1868, roll 13, Sherman Papers, LC; WDAR, 1869, 44–50 (third quotation 45); Greene, *Washita*, 88, 176–177. Sheridan had hoped to supplement Custer with a regiment of Kansas volunteers, but the latter got lost and nearly starved before straggling in to Camp Supply on December 1.

5. Greene, *Washita*, 106–138; Robert M. Utley, *Frontier Regulars: The United States Army and the Indian, 1866–1891* (1973; rpt. Lincoln: University of Nebraska Press, 1984), 152–158; WDAR, 1869, 50 (first quotation); SED No. 18, 40th Cong., 3rd sess., serial 1360, 40–41; HED No. 1, 40th Cong., 3rd sess., serial 1366, 832 (second and third quotations); Elliott West, *Contested Plains: Indians, Goldseekers, and the Rush to Colorado* (Lawrence: University Press of Kansas, 1998), 312–316.

6. WDAR, 1868, xiii–xv (first quotation), xxi–xxv; Tarbell to Butler, July 13, 1868, box 45, Butler Papers, LC (second quotation); WDAR, 1869, 144–145; Chandler to Schofield, October 24, 1868, box 3, Schofield Papers, LC (third quotation); Howard to Schofield, Aug. 8, 24, 1868, box 40, ibid.; John M. Schofield, *Forty-six Years in the Army* (1897; rpt. Norman: University of Oklahoma Press, 1998), 419–420; Schofield to Buchanan, September 14, 1868, box 86, Schofield Papers, LC.

7. Ira Berlin, ed., *Freedom: A Documentary History of Emancipation, 1861–1867, Series II: The Black Military Experience* (Cambridge: Cambridge University Press, 1982), 761–762 (first quotation); Miles to Drum, September 25, October 4, 1868, LS, District of North Carolina, RG 393, NARA; Holden to North Carolina Representatives and Senators, January 20, 1869, Miles Papers, USAMHI; WDAR, 1868, xiii, 79–81; "Quiet Election," *Daily Sentinel*, November 7, 1868; Gregory P. Downs, *After Appomattox: Military Occupation and the Ends of War* (Cambridge: Harvard University Press, 2015), 206–207; WDAR, 1869, 209; Schofield to Stoneman, August 20, 1868, box 49, Schofield Papers, LC; Clayton to Schofield, November 5, 1868, box 3, ibid.; Campbell to Schofield, November 6, 1868, ibid.; Campbell to Schofield, October 22, November 9, 1868, box 39, ibid.; "The Army," *Daily Arkansas Gazette*, October 11, 1868 (second quotation).

8. *The Papers of Andrew Johnson*, 16 vols. (Knoxville: University of Tennessee Press, 1967–2000), 14:141, 15:112 (first quotation); James G. Randall, ed., *The Diary of Orville Hickman Browning*, 2 vols. (Springfield: Illinois State Historical Library, 1933), 2:204–205, 214; Joseph G. Dawson III, *Army Generals and Reconstruction in Louisiana, 1862–1877* (Baton Rouge: Louisiana State University Press, 1982), 84–92; Schofield to Buchanan, September 14, 1868, box 86, Schofield Papers, LC; WDAR,

1868, xxxiv–xxxvii (second quotation); Schofield to President, October 30, 1868, box 86, Schofield Papers, LC; Warmouth to Schofield, Oct. 15, 1868, box 9, ibid.

9. Garfield to Rockwell, July 28, 1868, box 3, Rockwell Papers, LC; *CGlobe* 40th Cong., 2nd sess., 3948–3953, 3968 (first and second quotations), 3970 (third and fourth quotations), 3973.

10. *CGlobe* 40th Cong., 2nd sess., 4238–4239, 4246, 4493; Downs, *After Appomattox*, 203; Garfield to Rockwell, July 28, 1868, box 3, Rockwell Papers, LC.

11. *PUSG* 18:295, 293 (first quotation); "North Carolina," *New York Times*, November 13, 1868; Brooks D. Simpson, *Let Us Have Peace: Ulysses S. Grant and the Politics of War and Reconstruction, 1861–1868* (Chapel Hill: University of North Carolina Press, 1991), 246; "Blair on Military Despotism," *Chicago Tribune*, August 3, 1868; "Frank Blair's Platform," *Daily Picayune*, July 11, 1868; Joan Waugh, *U. S. Grant: American Hero, American Myth* (Chapel Hill: University of North Carolina Press, 2009), 118–122; William Gillette, *Retreat from Reconstruction, 1869–1879* (Baton Rouge: Louisiana State University Press, 1979), 21–22; Henry Adams, *The Education of Henry Adams: An Autobiography* (Boston: Houghton & Mifflin Co., 1918), 249 (second and third quotations).

12. Garfield to Rockwell, July 28, 1868, box 3, Rockwell Papers, LC (first quotation); WDAR, 1868, i-x; Schofield to Sherman, November 27, 1868, box 49, Schofield Papers, LC (second quotation); *CGlobe*, 40th Cong., 3rd sess., 925–926; Hazen to Garfield, February 5, 1869, roll 15, Garfield Papers, LC; McDowell to Garfield, February 6, 1869, ibid. (third and fourth quotations).

13. *CGlobe* 40th Cong., 3rd sess., 925–926 (first quotation), 950, 1328–1329 (second quotation), 1334, 1384, 1517, 1717–1718; Appendix, 189; Heitman, 2:602–607; Garfield to Rockwell, August 30, 1869, box 3, Rockwell Papers, LC.

14. Russell F. Weigley, *History of the United States Army*, Enlarged Edition (Bloomington: Indiana University Press, 1984), 190–192, 246–250; *PUSG* 16:36–37.

15. *PUSG* 16:36–37; 17:343; 19:144–147; Sherman to Schofield, December 20, 1868, box 28, Barney Collection, Huntington Library; William Tecumseh Sherman, *Memoirs* (New York: Library of America, 1990), 931–932 (first quotation); Jean Edward Smith, *Grant* (New York: Simon & Schuster, 2001), 468–469, 477–479; John F. Marszalek, *Sherman: A Soldier's Passion for Order* (New York: Free Press, 1993), 384–385; "The War Department," in Nomination as Sec. of War file, box 82, Schofield Papers, LC; Sherman to Humphreys, April 24, 1869, roll 45, Sherman Papers, LC; *Diary of Welles, Secretary of the Navy Under Lincoln and Johnson*, 3 vols. (Boston: Houghton & Mifflin, 1911), 3:549; James Harrison Wilson, *The Life of John Rawlins: Lawyer, Assistant Adjutant-General, Chief of Staff, Major General of Volunteers, and Secretary of War* (New York: Neale Publishing Co., 1916), 354–356; Schofield to Grant, March 11, 1869, box 86, Schofield Papers, LC; Sherman to President, March 26, 1869, roll 45, Sherman Papers, LC; Rawlins to General of the Army, March 26, 1869, roll 4, M421, LS by the SW to the President and Executive Departments, RG 107, NARA; Sherman to Sheridan, April 10, 1869, roll 17, Sheridan Papers, LC (fourth quotation); Schofield to Sherman, April 2, 1869, box 49, Schofield Papers, LC; Sherman to Grant, July 27, 1870, roll 45, Sherman Papers, LC.

16. Francis Paul Prucha, *The Great Father: The United States Government and the*

American Indians, abridged edition (Lincoln: University of Nebraska Press, 1986), 152–153, 164–165; HED 1, 41st Cong., 2nd sess., serial 1414, 445–451; HED 1, 43rd Cong., 1st sess., serial 1601, iii-iv (quotation); Gary Clayton Anderson, *Ethnic Cleansing and the Indian: The Crime That Should Haunt America* (Norman: University of Oklahoma Press, 2014).

17. Paul Andrew Hutton, *Phil Sheridan and His Army* (Lincoln: University of Nebraska Press, 1985), 188–192; HED 269, 41st Cong., 2nd sess., serial 1426, 47; Sheridan to Sherman, January 29, 1870, box 53, Sheridan Papers, LC (second quotation); HED 185, 41st Cong., 2nd sess., serial 1418, and SED 49, 41st Cong., 2nd sess., serial 1406.

18. "Massacre," signed "Humanity," *Pittsburgh Daily Post*, March 23, 1870 (first quotation); "The Slaughter of the Piegans," *New York Times*, February 24, 1870 (second quotation); *Courier-Journal*, April 12, 1870 (third quotation); Hutton, *Sheridan*, 192–196; *CGlobe* 41st Cong., 2nd sess., 1576, 1577 (fourth quotation); Appendix, 150; Rockwell to Garfield, July 24, roll 18, Garfield Papers, LC; Garfield to Rockwell, August 6, 1870, box 3, Rockwell Papers, LC; *Statutes* 16:315–321. For army efforts to reshape the narrative, see Sheridan to Sherman, February 28, 1870, roll 88, Sheridan Papers, LC; Sherman to Sheridan, March 5, 7, 1870, ibid.; Sherman, endorsement of March 12, 1870, ibid.; Hardie to Butler, March 9, 1870, box 52, Butler Papers, LC; Sherman to Church, March 16, 1870, box 1, Church Papers, LC; Sherman to Sheridan, March 24, 1870, roll 38, M745, LS by the Office of the Quartermaster General, RG 92, NARA; WDAR, 1870, 29–30. Baker's belated March 23 report on the affair may be found as an enclosure to Sheridan to Sherman, March 27, 1870, box 91, Sheridan Papers, LC.

19. Sherman to Augur, June 9, 1870, Augur Papers, Newberry Library; Sherman to John Sherman, March 21, 1870, roll 15, Sherman Papers, LC; Sherman to Wilson, March 22, 1870, roll 45, ibid.; Sherman to Benham, November 17, 1873, Benham-McNeil Family Papers, LC; Sheridan to Logan, January 22, 1870, box 2, Logan Family Papers, LC; *CGlobe*, 41st Cong., 2nd sess., Appendix, 146–148 (first quotation); 2279–2280 (second quotation), 3324–3325, 3408 (third quotation); Logan to Wife, June 10, 13, 1870, box 33, Logan Family Papers, LC; Sherman to Church, June 29, 1870, box 1, Church Papers, LC; Edward M. Coffman, *The Old Army: A Portrait of the American Army in Peacetime, 1784–1898* (New York: Oxford University Press, 1986), 220; Sherman to Schofield, July 27, 1870, box 8, Schofield Papers, LC; *The Statistical History of the United States: From Colonial Times to the Present* (New York: Basic Books, 1976), 8, 1114–1115; Thomas to Sherman, March 14, 1870, roll 15, Sherman Papers, LC (fourth quotation); Starr to Jo, August 15, 1870, box 1, Starr Papers, Missouri State Historical Society (fifth quotation).

20. Bullock to Butler, July 8, 1869, box 49, Butler Papers, LC; WDAR, 1869, 66–89, 95; *MPP* 7:94; Downs, *After Appomattox*, 218–220; Gillette, *Retreat from Reconstruction*, 88; HR 22, 42nd Cong., 2nd sess., serial 1529, 311; Terry to Sherman, June 20, 1870, roll 15, Sherman Papers, LC (quotation); Sherman to Terry, June 27, July 9, 1870, roll 45, ibid.

21. Gillette, *Retreat from Reconstruction*, 25–26, 35–36 (first quotation), 71, 80, 91, 97–98, 156–159, 194–196, 231; Downs, *After Appomattox*, 224–228, 238; Larkin

to Sherman, January 15, 1870, roll 15, Sherman Papers, LC; Sherman to Sheridan, April 1, 1871, roll 45, ibid.; William Blair, "Military Force to Protect the Gains of Reconstruction," *Civil War History* 51 (December 2005), 397; "Bloodshed in Baton Rouge," *New Orleans Republican*, November 10, 1870; Rodney to Bayard, February 18, 1872, box 23, Bayard Papers, LC (second quotation); Michael F. Holt, *By One Vote: The Disputed Presidential Election of 1876* (Lawrence: University Press of Kansas, 2008), 5; Sherman to Augur, February 10, March 18, 1871, Augur Papers, Newberry Library; Richard Franklin Bensel, *Yankee Leviathan: The Origins of Central State Authority in America, 1859–1877* (Cambridge: Cambridge University Press, 1990), 382–390, 395; Andrew F. Lang, *In the Wake of War: Military Occupation, Emancipation, and Civil War America* (Baton Rouge: Louisiana State University Press, 2017), 235 (third quotation).

22. Townsend to Commander, Department of the Platte, November 7, 1874, January 6, 1875, roll 44, M565, LS, Office of the Adjutant General, RG 94, NARA; Townsend to Pope, February 4, 1875, ibid.; Olson, "Relief for Nebraska Grasshopper Victims," 140; Alan Lessoff, *The Nation and Its City: Politics, "Corruption," and Progress in Washington, D.C., 1861–1902* (Baltimore: Johns Hopkins University Press, 1994), 84–86; Pamela Scott, *Capital Engineers: The U.S. Army Corps of Engineers in the Development of Washington, D.C., 1790–2004* (Alexandria, VA: U.S. Army Corps of Engineers, Office of History, 2005), 72–74; Rebecca Robbins Raines, *Getting the Message Through: A Branch History of the U.S. Army Signal Corps* (Washington, D.C.: Center of Military History, 1996), 45–55 (quotation p. 46); *CRec* 41st Cong., 2nd sess., 177; *Statutes* 16:369; HR 384, 43rd Cong., 1st sess., serial 1624, 234–235. Paine's measure, H.R. 602, 41st Cong., may be found in the "Bills and Resolutions Section" of the *A Century of Lawmaking for a New Nation* website, http://memory.loc.gov/ammem/amlaw/lawhome.html.

Fearing that the use of regulars to provide disaster relief would lead to exaggerated claims, Sheridan urged "a good deal of caution." SED 5, 43rd Cong., 2nd sess., serial 1629, 5.

23. Hutton, *Sheridan*, 208–211; *Personal Memoirs of P. H. Sheridan, General United States Army* (New York: Charles L. Webster & Co., 1888), 2:475–476 (first quotation); Sanger to Mason, Oct. 11, 1871, roll 3, Sheridan Papers, LC; *Reminiscences of Chicago During the Great Fire* (Chicago: Lakeside Press, 1915), 90–91 (second quotation); Sherman to Sheridan, October 16, 1871, roll 17, Sheridan Papers, LC; Mason to Sheridan, October 23, 1871, roll 3, ibid.; Chicago Relief & Aid Society to Sheridan, October 28, 1871, ibid. (third quotation); Sherman to Sheridan, October 31, 1871, ibid.

24. Andrew L. Slap, "'The Strong Arm of the Military Power of the United States': The Chicago Fire, the Constitution, and Reconstruction," *Civil War History* 47 (June 2001): 148–163 (first quotation 148; second quotation 158); Hutton, *Sheridan*, 211–212; Sheridan to Belknap, November 18, 1871, roll 3, Sheridan Papers, LC; *PUSG* 22:219–222.

25. Drew Gilpin Faust, *This Republic of Suffering: Death and the American Civil War* (New York: Random House, 2008), 222–237; *Statutes* 14:399–401; *CGlobe* 42nd Cong., 2nd sess., 3220 (quotation); WDAR, 1870, 208–212; WDAR, 1871, 135–136.

26. Alexander to Humphreys, March 11, 1872, box 78, Schofield Papers, LC; Schofield to Humphreys, March 12, 1872, ibid.; Schofield to Sherman, December 24, 1872, ibid.; Sherman to Schofield, December 27, 1872, ibid.; Fish to Peirce, December 19, 25, 1872, roll 77, M77, Diplomatic Instructions of the Department of State, 1801–1906: Hawaii, RG 59, NARA; Schofield to Sherman, January 17, February 15 (first and second quotations), April 8, 1873, box 78, Schofield Papers, LC; J. M. Schofield and B. S. Alexander, "Documents: Pearl Harbor, 1873," *American Historical Review* 30 (April 1925): 560–565; Schofield to Burnside, February 25, 1875, box 49, Schofield Papers, LC; Allen to Schofield, December 18, 1875, February 16, 1876, box 2, ibid.; Allen to Schofield, January 8, 1876, box 10, ibid.; Schofield to Walker, December 2, 1875, box 49, ibid. (second quotation); Schofield to Luttrell, December 30, 1875, ibid.; Thomas W. Swails, "John McAllister Schofield: Military Diplomat" (MA thesis, University of Hawaii, 1966), 101, 108.

27. "A Brush with Indians," *New York Times*, September 30, 1872 (first quotation); M. John Lubetkin, *Jay Cooke's Gamble: The Northern Pacific Railroad, the Sioux, and the Panic of 1873* (Norman: University of Oklahoma Press, 2006), 93–267; *Bismarck Tribune*, August 27, 1873 (second and third quotations).

28. Paul Andrew Hutton, *Apache Wars: The Hunt for Geronimo, the Apache Kid, and the Captive Boy Who Started the Longest War in American History* (New York: Crown, 2016), 130–141; Utley, *Frontier Regulars*, 192–198; WDAR, 1871, 78; Schofield to Crook, November 25, 1871, February 8, 1872, box 49, Schofield Papers, LC; Martin F. Schmitt, ed., *General George Crook: His Autobiography*, Revised Edition (Norman: University of Oklahoma Press, 1986), 168; Crook to AG, September 19, 1871, Crook Papers, Hayes Library; *PUSG* 23:40–41; WDAR, 1872, 78–80; HED 1, 42nd Congress, 3rd sess., serial 1560, 394–396; Crook to Schofield, March 12, 1872, box 39, Schofield Papers, LC; John G. Bourke, *On the Border with Crook* (1891; rpt. Lincoln: University of Nebraska Press, 1971),182; Adjutant General's Office, *Chronological List of Actions, &c. with Indians, from January 15, 1837 to January 1891* (1891; rpt. The Old Army Press, 1979), 52–54.

29. Crook to Schofield, May 16, 1873, box 39, Schofield Papers, LC. For a biting assessment of the army's weaknesses in the Southwest, see Janne Lahti, *Wars for Empire: Apaches, the United States, and the Southwest Borderlands* (Norman: University of Oklahoma Press, 2017), 35–82. Nelson Miles struck a similar tone the following year while fighting the Red River War: "I find altogether too many incompetent and inefficient officers who have no interest in their duties." Miles to Wife, September 6, 1874, Sherman Miles MSS.

30. Utley, *Frontier Regulars*, 199–207; Canby to AAG, January 15, 1873, Entry 704, LS, Department of the Columbia, RG 393, NARA; Schofield to Davis, April 30, 1873, box 49, Schofield Papers, LC (first quotation); Van Vliet to Sherman, May 4, 1873, roll 19, Sherman Papers, LC (second quotation); Sheridan to Sherman, June 6, 1873, ibid.

31. WDAR, 1872, 55; Robert G. Carter, *On the Border with Mackenzie* (1935; rpt. Austin: Texas State Historical Association, 2007), 255–260, 418–455; Augur to Sherman, February 19, 1873, box 4, Augur Papers, Newberry Library; Robinson, *Bad Hand*, 127–143; Henry W. Strong, *My Frontier Days & Indian Fights on the*

Plains of Texas (N.p., N.d.) 39 (first quotation); Sheridan to Augur, May 22, 1873, box 58, Sheridan Papers, LC; Sheridan to Belknap, May 22, 1873, ibid.; Sheridan to Augur, May 27, 1873, Mackenzie Papers; Sheridan to Belknap, May 28, 1873, ibid.; Sherman to Sheridan, June 3, 1873, roll 17, Sheridan Papers, LC (third quotation); Augur to Mackenzie, June 25, 1873, box 3, Augur Papers, Newberry Library; HED 1, 43rd Congress, 2nd sess., serial 1634, 768–769.

Augur evidenced no doubts about the propriety of the raid. Other officers, however, criticized Mackenzie. From Arizona, Crook wondered what he should do in case Mexican troops crossed the border. Col. Edward Hatch believed it was part of a scheme to engineer a promotion for Mackenzie. In reminiscences published six decades later, Lt. Robert G. Carter claimed that Captains Eugene B. Beaumont and Napoleon B. McLaughlen nearly came to blows with Mackenzie when they learned that he had no written orders, asserting that the colonel had risked the lives of his command. Augur to Sheridan, June 4, 1873, and Augur to Mackenzie, June 11, 1873, box 4, Augur Papers, Newberry Library. Crook to AAG, July 7, 1873, Crook Papers, Hayes Library; Hatch to Grierson, August 13, 1873, Grierson Papers, Illinois State Historical Library; Carter, *On the Border with Mackenzie*, 255–260.

32. WDAR, 1869, 152–171; WDAR, 1873, 58–73; Downs, *After Appomattox*, 1881–1892; Blair, "Military Force to Protect the Gains of Reconstruction," 393; Holt, *By One Vote*, 21; Gillette, *Retreat from Reconstruction*, 151, 171, 248; Sherman to Augur, March 18, 1872, roll 45, Sherman Papers, LC (second quotation); "General Grant's New Departure," *New York Herald*, January 20, 1874; Belknap to Dear Sir, December 13, 1871, fifth folder, H 41A-F2.25, RG 233, NARA; *CGlobe* 42nd Cong., 2nd sess., 1875 (third and fourth quotations); Diary entries February 21, 23, 1872, January 24, February 4, 7, 10, 11, 1873, roll 1, Garfield Papers, LC.

33. HR 384, 43rd Cong., 1st sess., serial 1624, 7–15; Diary entries January 15, 29, February 3–5, 1872, roll 2, Garfield Papers, LC; Sherman to Church, January 13, 1874, box 1, Church Papers, LC (first and second quotations); Sherman to Sheridan, January 7 (third quotation), 14, 1874, roll 17, Sheridan Papers, LC; Schofield to Sargent, January 23, 1874, box 49, Schofield Papers, LC (fourth and fifth quotations); Sargent to Schofield, February 6, 1874, box 8, ibid.

34. Holt, *By One Vote*, 11–12; *CRec* 43rd Cong., 1st sess., 985 (first quotation), 986–995, 1011–1014 (second quotation), 1017–1024 (third quotation 1024), 1161–1172 (fourth quotation 1161), 1400–1402; HR 384, 43rd Cong., 1st sess., serial 1624, iii–xi; Diary entry, February 10, 12, 1874, roll 2, Garfield Papers, LC.

35. *CRec* 43rd Cong., 1st sess., 2222–2230, 2259–2276, 2303–2313; Schofield to AAG, October 30, 1874, box 49, Schofield Papers, LC (quotations). Five Democrats and thirteen Republicans had backed Logan's amendment, with eight Democrats and nineteen Republicans in opposition.

36. Sherman, *Memoirs*, 934–935; Sherman to Stanton, August 18, 1865, Belknap Papers, LC; Sherman to Grant, July 27, 1870, roll 45, Sherman Papers, LC; Sherman to Sheridan, April 1, 1871, roll 17, Sheridan Papers, LC; Sherman to Schofield, October 16, 1871, box 8, Schofield Papers, LC (first quotation); Sherman to Belknap, May 8, 1874, roll 20, Sherman Papers, LC; Comstock to Sherman, May 14, 1874, ibid. (second and third quotations); Sherman to John Sherman, May 29, 1874, ibid.;

Sheridan to Sherman, May 26, 1874, box 11, Sheridan Papers, LC; Sheridan to Ord, July 17, 1874, ibid., Sherman to Comstock, May 18, 1874, Comstock Papers, LC (fourth and fifth quotations); Sherman to Porter, February 6, 1875, box 19, Porter Papers, LC.

37. Robert M. Utley, *Cavalier in Buckskin: George Armstrong Custer and the Western Military Frontier* (Norman: University of Oklahoma Press, 1988), 158–163; Hutton, *Sheridan*, 305–315; HR 799, 49th Cong., 1st sess., serial 1715; Sherman to John Sherman, March 4, 10, 16, 1876, roll 22, Sherman Papers, LC; Moulton to Sherman, March 8, 1876, ibid.; Dayton to Sherman, March 8, 1876, ibid.; John Sherman to Sherman, March 19, 1876, ibid.; Sherman to Sheridan, April 1, 1876, ibid.; Marszalek, *Sherman*, 387–388. Blaming Custer for embarrassing his family and administration, Grant declared that he could not participate in that year's upcoming campaign against the Sioux; only the intervention of Sherman, Sheridan, and Terry freed the flamboyant cavalryman for duty. While in Washington, Custer frequently consorted with Clymer and Henry B. Banning (D-OH), chair of the House Committee on Military Affairs.

38. Timothy Rives, "Grant, Babcock, and the Whiskey Ring," *Prologue* 32 (Fall 2000): 142–153; Lessoff, *Nation and Its City*, 51, 169–172; Hutton, *Sheridan*, 309–310.

39. HR 384, 43rd Cong., 1st sess., serial 1624, 13; Utley, *Frontier Regulars*, 212–214, 219–221; Brooke to AAG, June 22, 1874, box 5, Brooke Papers, HSP (quotation); Belknap to Secretary of the Interior, July 16, 20, 1874, roll 68, LSSW; Sheridan to Pope, July 18, 24, 1874, box 56, Sheridan Papers, LC; Sheridan to Augur, July 21, 1874, ibid.; Sheridan to Pope, July 22, box 11, ibid.; Augur to Sheridan, July 28, 1874, Entry 4867, LS, Department of Texas, RG 393, NARA; Pope to Miles, July 29, August 5, 1874, Entry 2575, vol. 87, LS, Department of the Missouri, RG 393, NARA; Augur to Mackenzie, August 28, 1874, Entry 4867, LS, Department of Texas, RG 393, NARA; Sheridan to Augur, September 2, 1874, box 11, Sheridan Papers, LC.

40. Miles to AAG, November 12, 1874, I-72/3, box 42, Part I, Entry 2601 A, LR, Department of the Missouri, Headquarters Records, RG 393, NARA (first quotation); Utley, *Frontier Regulars*, 224–233; Sheridan to Coke, March 25, 1874, box 13, Sheridan Papers, LC (second quotation). For supply difficulties and internal rivalries, see Augur to Mackenzie, September 13, 1874, Entry 4867, LS, Department of Texas, RG 393, NARA; Pope to Sherman, September 16, 1874, roll 20, Sherman Papers, LC; Miles to Sherman, September 27, 1874, ibid.; Miles to Wife, October 1, 13, November 2, 1874, Sherman Miles MSS; Price to Williams, October 19, 1874, box 43, I-74/3, Part I, Entry 2601 A, LR, Department of Missouri, Headquarters Records, RG 393, NARA; Sheridan to Pope, November 18, 1874, box 56, Sheridan Papers, LC; Sheridan to Augur, December 1, 1874, ibid.; Miles to Sherman, December 27, 1874, roll 20, Sherman Papers, LC; Pope to Belknap, January 23, 1875, roll 45, Sherman Papers, LC; Sheridan to Belknap, May 19, 1875, box 13, Sheridan Papers, LC.

41. "GOLD! GOLD!!" *Bismarck Tribune*, May 27, 1874 (first and second quotations); Jackson, *Custer's Gold*, 144; "Custer Interviewed," *Bismarck Tribune*, August 26,

1874 (third quotation); "The Black Hills," *Philadelphia Inquirer*, September 10, 1874.

42. "The Spring Work of the Army," *New-York Tribune*, April 5, 1875 (first quotation); Wayne R. Kime, *Colonel Richard Irving Dodge: The Life and Times of a Career Army Officer* (Norman: University of Oklahoma Press, 2006), 190–225 (second quotation 203); HED 1, 44th Cong., 1st sess., serial 1680, 510–511; Sheridan to Terry, November 9, 1875, box 13, Sheridan Papers, LC; Chandler to Belknap, December 3, 1875, box 91, ibid.; Terry to AAG, December 28, 1875, ibid.; Sheridan to Sherman, January 3, 1876, box 14, ibid.; Smith to Chandler, January 31, 1876, box 91, ibid.; Sheridan to Terry, February 8, 1876, box 14, ibid.; Bailey, *Pacifying the Plains*, 120–127; Reynolds to Sherman, April 11, 1876, roll 22, Sherman Papers, LC (third quotation). For an outstanding analysis of Reynolds's campaign and the resulting courts-martial, see Paul L. Hedren, *Powder River: Disastrous Opening of the Great Sioux War* (Norman: University of Oklahoma Press, 2016).

43. Sherman to Sheridan, April 1, 1876, roll 22, Sherman Papers, LC; Sheridan to Sherman, April 3, 1876, ibid.; Sheridan to Terry, May 16, 1876, box 58, Sheridan Papers, LC (first quotation); Utley, *Frontier Regulars*, 258–260; Sheridan to Sherman, May 29, 1876, box 15, Sheridan Papers, LC (second quotation).

44. Robert M. Utley, *The Lance and the Shield: The Life and Times of Sitting Bull* (New York: Henry Holt, 1993), 135–164; Thomas B. Marquis, interpreter, *A Warrior Who Fought Custer* (Minneapolis: Midwest Co., 1931), 178–179 (first and second quotations); Crook to Sheridan, July 23, 1876, Crook Papers (third quotation).

45. Gillette, *Retreat from Reconstruction*, 247; Diary entry, January 28, 1876, roll 2, Garfield Papers, LC; "Army Reduction," *Galaxy: A Magazine of Entertaining Reading* 21 (February 21, 1876): 260; Sherman to Pope, April 24, 1876, roll 45, Sherman Papers, LC; *CRec* 44th Cong., 1st sess., 3780, 3839 (quotation), 3469, 4155. For proposed U.S. Military Academy budget cuts, see also unsigned, handwritten document, stamped "Feb. 1876," Committee on Appropriations investigation of investigation of the War Department, West Point Military Academy, folder 1 of 3, HR 44A-F3.18, RG 233, NARA.

46. Sherman to Sheridan, July 22 (two letters), August 8, 1876, roll 46, M565, LS by the Office of Adjutant General, RG 94, NARA; Cameron to President, August 11, 1876, roll 73, LSSW; Sherman to Sheridan, August 12, 1876, roll 45, Sherman Papers, LC; "Increasing the Army," *New York Times*, August 13, 1876; *Statutes* 19:95–96, 204; Utley, *Frontier Regulars*, 267–272; Miles to Wife, August 4, 1876, Sherman Miles MSS (third quotation); WDAR, 1876, 445–447. For a gripping account of the health problems confronting Terry and Crook, see Joan Nabseth Stevenson, *Deliverance from the Little Big Horn: Doctor Henry Porter and Custer's Seventh Cavalry* (Norman: University of Oklahoma Press, 2014).

47. Utley, *Frontier Regulars*, 272–283; Miles to Sherman, October 23, 1876, roll 23, Sherman Papers, LC; Miles to AAG, October 25, 1876, Entry 1333, LS, Yellowstone Command, RG 393, NARA (quotation).

48. Rachel Sherman Thorndyke, ed., *The Sherman Letters: Correspondence between General and Senator Sherman from 1837 to 1891* (New York: Charles Scribner's Sons, 1894), 342–344 (first quotation); "Government by Bayonet," *Daily Bulletin*,

January 15, 1875 (second quotation); Gillette, *Retreat from Reconstruction*, 310 (third quotation).

49. Gillette, *Retreat from Reconstruction*, 306, 315–320; "The Campaign in the South," *Cincinnati Commercial*, September 15, 1876 (quotations); Sherman to Sheridan, October 28, 1876, roll 17, Sheridan Papers, LC; *MPP* 7:376, 396; Holt, *By One Vote*, ix, 9, 43, 46, 150–151, 245; WDAR, 1877, 99; *PUSG* 28:18; "A Doubtful Election," *New York Times*, November 8, 1876 (quotation).

13. The Army of the Gilded Age

1. Sherman to Porter, August 29, 1876, box 19 [filed incorrectly with 1875 correspondence], Porter Papers, LC (first quotation); M. A. DeWolfe Howe, ed., *Home Letters of General Sherman* (New York: Charles Scribner's Sons, 1909), 386; Sherman to Sheridan, November 8, 1876, roll 17, Sheridan Papers, LC; Michael F. Holt, *By One Vote: The Disputed Presidential Election of 1876* (Lawrence: University Press of Kansas, 2008), ix, 167, 181; *PUSG* 28:17–20 (second quotation), 36–37; John F. Marszalek, *Sherman: A Soldier's Passion for Order* (New York: Free Press, 1993), 427 (third quotation).

2. "Desperation of the Tildenites," *New York Times*, December 14, 1876; Sherman to Sheridan, December 11 (first and second quotations), 21, 1876, January 29, 1877, roll 17, Sheridan Papers, LC; Hancock to Sherman, December 28, 1876, roll 45, Sherman Papers, LC; Schofield to Sherman, December 26 (third quotation), 28, 1876, January 1, 20, 1877, box 93, Schofield Papers, LC; Sherman to Schofield, December 28, 1876, January 10, 19, 26, 1877, ibid.; Sherman to Hancock, January 2, 1877, roll 23, Sherman Papers, LC.

3. Holt, *By One Vote*, 233–241, 247; *PUSG* 28:160, 164–165 (first and second quotations); Schofield to Sherman, March 3, 1877, Schofield Papers, USMA (third quotation). In an unwritten deal that allowed Hayes to become president, Republicans agreed that Hayes would not deploy the regular army to enforce civil rights laws in the South, thus in effect leaving freedmen to their fate. Richard White, *The Republic for Which It Stands: The United States during Reconstruction and the Gilded Age, 1865–1896* (New York: Oxford University Press, 2017), 332.

4. Robert M. Utley, *Frontier Regulars: The United States Army and the Indian, 1866–1891* (1973; rpt. Lincoln: University of Nebraska Press, 1984), 61–62; Sherman to Logan and Banning, February 5, 1877, roll 45, Sherman Papers, LC; *CRec* 44th Cong., 2nd sess., 2111–2112 (second quotation), 2114–2118, 2159 (first quotation), 2241, 2246–2249, 2251–2252; Diary entry for March 4, 1877, roll 2, Garfield Papers, LC; Sherman to Miles, June 1, 1877, box 4, Miles Papers, LC (third quotation).

5. George Wilson, comp., *Twentieth Annual Report of the Corporation of the Chamber of Commerce of the State of New York, for the Year 1877–78* (New York: Press of the Chamber of Commerce, 1878), 26–28 (quotation); Clayton D. Laurie and Ronald H. Cole, *The Role of Federal Military Forces in Domestic Disorders, 1877–1900* (Washington, D.C.: Center of Military History, 1997), 32–55; *MPP* 7:447–449; WDAR, 1877, iv, v, xii-xiii, 87–88, 91–96; *Statutes* 2:443; Getty to Wife, August 3, 1877, box

1, Gibson-Getty-McClure Family Papers, LC; Jerry Cooper, *The Army and Civil Disorder: Federal Military Intervention in Labor Disputes, 1877–1900* (Westport, CT: Greenwood Press, 1980), 46–61.

6. *Daily Tribune*, July 28, 1877 (first quotation); "The Army Must Be Increased," ibid.; "Political Aspects of the Trouble," *New York Times*, July 25, 1877 (second quotation); "The Regulars and the Riots," ibid., July 28, 1877; "Strengthening the Regular Army," *Philadelphia Inquirer*, August 1, 1877; Editorial, *Southwestern Christian Advocate*, August 2, 1877.

7. Jerome A. Greene, *Nez Perce Summer, 1877: The U.S. Army and the Nee-Mee-Poo Crisis* (Helena: Montana Historical Society Press, 2000); Utley, *Frontier Regulars*, 322–342; WDAR, 1878, 170, 235.

8. Robert M. Utley, *The Commanders: Civil War Generals Who Shaped the American West* (Norman: University of Oklahoma Press, 2018), 176; Ord to Davis, July 2, 1875, Ord Papers, Bancroft Library; Ord to Sherman, July 6, 1875, roll 21, Sherman Papers, LC; Ord to Ammen, August 17, 1875, Entry 5867, LS, Department of Texas, RG 393, NARA; Ord to AAG, November 16, 1875, ibid.; Coke to Ord, October 2, 1875, Ord Papers, Bancroft Library; Maxey to Ord, December 17, 24, 1875, ibid.; Ord to Sherman, Nov. 13, 1876, ibid. Ord to Sherman, June 27, 1876, roll 23, Sherman Papers, LC (first quotation); Sherman to Ord, Nov. 2, 1876, roll 45, ibid.; HMD 64, 45th Cong., 2nd sess., 29, 88 (second quotation); McCrary to Sherman, June 1, 1877, roll 82, LSSW; Schleicher to Sherman, April 2, 1877, roll 24, Sherman Papers, LC (third quotation); William E. Gibbs, "'Diaz' Executive Agents and United States Foreign Policy," *Journal of Interamerican Studies and World Affairs* 20 (May 1978): 165–190.

9. F[rederick] Whittaker, "The American Army," *Galaxy: A Magazine of Entertaining Reading* 24 (September 1877): 390–399; Schleicher to Sherman, April 2, 1877, roll 46, Sherman Papers, LC; "Military Reorganization," *ANJ* 15 (September 8, 1877): 72–73 (first quotation); "The President's Message," *New York Times*, October 17, 1877; "Army and Navy Deficiencies," ibid., November 1, 1877; "Work Before the Committees," ibid., November 2, 1877; "The Army Appropriation Bill," ibid., November 18, 1877; *CRec* 45th Cong., 1st sess., 288–302 (second quotation 288), 306–310, 513–514; Ord to Schleicher, November 24, 1877, Ord Papers, Bancroft Library (third quotation); Sherman to Sheridan, November 29, 1877, roll 45, Sherman Papers, LC (fourth quotation). One Texan, John Reagan [D], voted to trim the army.

10. "Reorganization of the Army" file, box 86, Schofield Papers, LC; Sherman to Cameron, January 31, 1878, roll 45, Sherman Papers, LC (first quotation); Schofield to Banning, February 10, 1878, ibid.; Sherman to Cox, February 25, 1878, roll 45, ibid.; "Gen. Sherman on the Army Bill," *New York Times*, March 1, 1878; Franklin to Randall, May 13, 1878, folder 22, HR 45A-F3.16, RG 233, NARA; Sherman to Getty, April 29, 1878, box 2, Gibson-Getty-McClure Family Papers, LC; *CRec* 45th Cong., 2nd sess., 3534–3537, 3541–3545, 3550–3551, 3555, 3838–3839, 3876–3877, 4239. For the dirt on Bragg, see Hamilton to Sherman, February 19, 1878, roll 45, Sherman Papers, LC, which he copied to Cox in his letter of February 25 (all in Sherman Papers, LC), and Hamilton to Sherman, February 25, 1877, which he provided to Garfield in a letter of May 28, 1878 (roll 128, Garfield Papers, LC).

11. Dodge to Church, March 12, 1878, box 1, Church Papers, LC (first and second quotations); *CRec* 45th Cong., 2nd sess., 3538, 3579–3586, 3615, 3631–3635, 3669–3670, 3677, 3718, 3721–3724, 3726–3727 (third quotation), 3843, 4180, 4234–4248, 4295–4307, 4685–4686; Stephen Skowronek, *Building a New American State: The Expansion of National Administrative Capacities, 1877–1920* (Cambridge: Cambridge University Press, 1982), 103–104; Sherman to Sheridan, May 26, 1878, roll 17, Sheridan Papers, LC; *Statutes* 20:145–152.

12. George B. McClellan, "The Regular Army of the United States," *Harper's New Monthly Magazine* 55 (October 1877): 774–782; James Garfield, "The Army of the United States," *North American Review* 126 (March–April 1878): 193–216, (May–June 1878): 442–465; SR 555, 45th Cong., 3rd sess., serial 1837, 54 (quotation); "The Army Bill," *St. Louis Globe Democrat*, January 6, 1879; clipping attributed to *St. Louis-Globe Democrat*, January 10, 1879, in folder 5, HR 45A-F3.16 RG 233, NARA; Utley, *Frontier Regulars*, 63–64; David J. Fitzpatrick, *Emory Upton: Misunderstood Reformer* (Norman: University of Oklahoma Press, 2017), 214–216.

13. Schofield to Sherman, July 5, 1878, Schofield Papers, USMA; Schofield to Burnside, July 11, 1878, box 89, Schofield Papers, LC; Sherman to Schofield, June 15, August 6, December 18 (first quotation), 1878, January 19, 1879, box 28, Barney Collection, Huntington Library; Sherman to Burnside, December 15, 1878, roll 45, Sherman Papers, LC; Schofield to Sherman, December 20, 24, 1878, roll 25, ibid.; "The New Army Plan," *ANJ* 16 (December 28, 1878): 356–357; Sheridan to Sherman, January 4, 1879, ibid.; Marszalek, *Sherman*, 435–436; Rockwell to Garfield, January 7, 1879 [mistakenly dated 1878], roll 128, Garfield Papers, LC (second quotation); "Burnside Army Bill," *ANJ* 16 (January 25, 1879): 438 (citing the *Cincinnati Commercial*) (third quotation); *CRec* 45th Cong., 3rd sess., 1758 (fourth quotation); Schofield to Sherman, May 29, 1879, roll 26, Sherman Papers, LC; Sherman to Schofield, June 1, 1879, box 28, Barney Collection, Huntington Library.

14. Fitzpatrick, *Upton*, 214–224; "The Army Appropriations Bill," *New York Times*, February 21, 1879; "Third Session," ibid., February 22, 1879; "The Army Appropriation Bill," ibid., February 23, 1879; State Senate of New York, January 7, 1879, HR 45A-G13.1, RG 233, NARA; *CRec* 45th Cong., 3rd sess., 299–300 (quotation), 1760; "The Record: Senate," *Chicago Tribune*, February 23, 1879.

15. "Dead-Lock on the Army Bill," *New York Times*, March 2, 1879; "The Great Contest Ended," ibid., March 4, 1879; "Congress and the Army Bill," ibid., March 15, 1879; "The Solid South in Power," ibid., April 26, 1879; *MPP* 7:520, 523–536; "Army Pay and Promotion," *ANJ* 16 (May 3, 1879): 696; *Statutes* 21:35 (second quotation).

16. Theda Skocpol, *Protecting Soldiers and Mothers: The Political Origins of Social Policy in the United States* (Cambridge: Belknap Press of Harvard University Press, 1995), 102–151; Brian Matthew Jordan, *Marching Home: Union Veterans and Their Unending Civil War* (New York: W. W. Norton, 2015), 150–169; *Statutes* 20:265; Russell L. Johnson, "'Great Injustice': Social Status and the Distribution of Military Pensions After the Civil War," *Journal of the Gilded Age and Progressive Era* 10 (April 2011): 137–160; *The Statistical History of the United States: From Colonial Times to the Present* (New York: Basic Books, 1976), 8, 1114–1115.

17. Skowronek, *Building a New American State*, 85–86, 95–96; Samuel P. Huntington, *The Soldier and the State: The Theory and Politics of Civil-Military Relations* (Cambridge: Belknap Press of Harvard University Press, 1957), 222–229; Henry George, *Social Problems* (Chicago: Belford, Clarke & Co., 1883), 226–227 (first quotation), 243; C. Robert Kemble, *Image of the Army Officer in America: Background for Current Views* (Westport, CT: Greenwood Press, 1972), 108; Thomas A. Bland, "Abolish the Army," *Council Fire* 1 (December 1878): 189 (second quotation, 2 (January 1879): 5–6 (third quotation), 2 (March 1879): 36; Charles Sumner, *Addresses on War* (Boston: Ginn & Company, 1904), 314; Andrew Carnegie, *Triumphant Democracy; or, Fifty Years' March of the Republic* (London: Sampson Low, Marston, Searle, & Rivington, 1886), 448 (fourth quotation).

18. Sherman to Draper, January 30, 1875, box 6, Draper Papers, LC; Sherman to John Sherman, October 23, 1874, roll 20, Sherman Papers, LC; Bliss to Mother, November 8, 1876, box 23, Bliss Collection, USAMHI (first quotation); Diary entry, December 31, 1873, Kautz Papers, LC (second and third quotations); Emory Upton, *The Military Policy of the United States* (Washington, D.C.: Government Printing Office, 1904), xii (fourth quotation); Terry to Pennypacker, February 2, 1872, Pennypacker Papers, HSP (fifth quotation); Van Vliet to Wilson, October 9, 1866, Wilson Papers, LC (sixth quotation); Meade to Pennie, August 3, 1872, box 2, Meade Papers, HSP.

19. Foster to Rockwell, December 12, 1880, box 4, Rockwell Papers, LC; Rockwell to Garfield, January 4, 8, 1881, box 5, ibid.; Garfield to Rockwell, January 14, 1881, ibid.; Rockwell to Garfield, February 3, 1881, ibid.; Heitman, 1:840; Robert M. Utley, *Cavalier in Buckskin: George Armstrong Custer and the Western Military Frontier* (Norman: University of Oklahoma Press, 1988), 148–164. For Brooke's political engagement, see the voluminous correspondence from 1896–1898 in vol. 35, Brooke Papers, HSP.

20. Craig E. Miller, "'Give the Book to Clemens,'" *American History* 34 (April 1999): 40–47; Hans Trefousse, "Civil Warriors in Memory and Memoir: Grant and Sherman Remember," *Georgia Historical Quarterly* 75 (Fall 1991): 542–556; James Lee McDonough, *William Tecumseh Sherman: In the Service of My Country, A Life* (New York: W. W. Norton, 2016), 708–711.

21. Paul Andrew Hutton, ed., *The Custer Reader* (Lincoln: University of Nebraska Press, 1992); Brian W. Dippie, ed., *Nomad: George A. Custer in Turf, Field and Farm* (Austin: University of Texas Press, 1980).

22. "Poganuc People, and Other Novels," *Atlantic Monthly* 42 (October 1878): 434 (first quotation); Paul L. Hedren, preface and introduction to *Campaigning with King: Charles King, Chronicler of the Old Army, by* Don Russell (Lincoln: University of Nebraska Press, 1991); Paul L. Hedren, "Charles King," in *Soldiers West: Biographies from the Military Frontier*, Second Edition, ed. Paul Andrew Hutton and Durwood Ball (Norman: University of Oklahoma Press, 2009), 358–380; "General Gossip of Authors and Writers," *Current Literature: A Magazine of Contemporary Records* 29 (August 1900): 150 (quotations).

23. Alan C. Braddock, "Shooting the Beholder: Charles Schreyvogel and the Spectacle of Gun Vision," *American Art* 20 (Spring 2006): 36–48; Gustav Kobbe, "A

Painter of the Western Frontier," *Cosmopolitan: A Monthly Illustrated Magazine* 31 (October 1901): 566; R. C. Wilson, "The Great Custer Battle of 1903," *Mankind: The Magazine of Popular History* 5 (no. 5, 1976): 52–59.

24. Verity McInnis, *Women of Empire: Nineteenth-Century Army Officers' Wives in India and the U.S. West* (Norman: University of Oklahoma Press, 2017), 81 (first and second quotations), 168–169, 209–212; "The Army and Army Society," *ANJ* 18 (October 16, 1880): 208 (third and fourth quotations, from Duane Greene, *Ladies and Officers*); Kevin Adams, *Class and Race in the Frontier Army: Military Life in the West, 1870–1890;* Alison K. Hoagland, *Army Architecture in the West: Forts Laramie, Bridger, and D. A. Russell, 1849–1912* (Norman: University of Oklahoma Press, 2004); Janne Lahti, *Cultural Construction of Empire: The U.S. Army in Arizona and New Mexico* (Lincoln: University of Nebraska Press, 2012), 150–179.

25. Skowronek, *Building a New American State*, 92–93; James B. Fry, "Origins and Progress of the Military Service Institution of the United States," *Journal of the Military Service Institution of the United States* 1 (May 1879): 27–29; Huntington, *Soldier and the State*, 243; Sherman to Getty, January 10, 1878, box 2, Gibson-Getty-McClure Papers, LC; "Leavenworth School of Application," *ANJ* 21 (October 13, 1883): 210–211 (quotations); T. R. Brereton, *Educating the U.S. Army: Arthur L. Wagner and Reform, 1875–1905* (Lincoln: University of Nebraska Press, 2000), 6–27; Thomas Cruse, *Apache Days and After* (Caldwell, ID: Caxton Printers, 1941), 243–246; J. P. Clark, *Preparing for War: The Emergence of the Modern U.S. Army, 1815–1917* (Cambridge: Harvard University Press, 2017), 133–135.

26. Huntington, *Soldier and the State*, 260–263; Charles A. Byler, *Civil-Military Relations on the Frontier and Beyond, 1865–1917* (Westport, CT: Praeger Security International, 2006), 59–60; George A. Price, *The Necessity for Closer Relations between The Army and The People and The Best Method to Accomplish The Result* (New York: G. P. Putnam's Sons, published for the Military Service Institution, 1885), 21–22 (first and second quotations); "Enforced Retirement," *ANJ* 15 (October 6, 1877): 138–139; E[dwin] V. Sumner, "American Practice and Foreign Theory," *Journal of the U.S. Cavalry Association* 3 (June 1890), 142 (third quotation), 150 (fourth quotation).

27. Russell F. Weigley, *History of the United States Army*, Enlarged Edition (Bloomington: Indiana University Press, 1984), 272 (first quotation); Sherman to Schofield, March 28, 30 (second quotation), April 8, May 4, 25, June 1, 1876, box 42, Schofield Papers, LC; Schofield to Sherman, March 29, 1876, ibid.; Sherman to Schofield, April 26, 1876, box 28, Barney Collection, Huntington; Schofield to Garfield, January 26, 1878, box 89, Schofield Papers, LC; WDAR, 1877, 150; "Suggestions for the Consideration of the Academic Board," October 9. 1879, box 89, Schofield Papers, LC; "Suggestions for the Consideration of the Academic Board," December 22, 1879, box 13, ibid.; "An Address Delivered by Maj. Gen. J. M. Schofield . . . August 11, 1879," box 91, ibid.

28. Schofield to AG, January 15, 1879, box 50, Schofield Papers, LC; Schofield to AG, April 6, 7, 1880, box 13, ibid.; John F. Marszalek, *Assault at West Point: The Court-Martial of Johnson Whittaker* (1972; rpt. New York: Collier Books, 1994); Entries of April 6, 9, 1880, Barth Diary, USMA; Proceedings of the Court of Inquiry

in the case of Johnson C. Whittaker, QQ 1858, Records of the Office of the Judge Advocate General, RG 153, NARA; Private Military Journal, April–August, 1880, box 1, Schofield Papers, LC; Editorial, *New York Daily Tribune*, April 26, December 14, 1880; WDAR, 1880, 223–230; Schofield to AG, November 12, 1880, box 50, Schofield Papers, LC; Sherman to Schofield, November 12, 27, December 13, 16, 1880, box 42, ibid.

29. William A. Dobak and Thomas D. Phillips, *The Black Regulars, 1866–1898* (Norman: University of Oklahoma Press, 2001), 30–42 (quotations 42), 112–113. Charles M. Robinson III, *Fall of a Black Army Officer: Racism and the Myth of Henry O. Flipper* (Norman: University of Oklahoma Press, 2008), makes a compelling case that Flipper merited the dismissal for having falsified reports of his accounts at Fort Davis.

30. Editorial, *ANJ* 17 (July 17, 1880): 1028 (first quotation); Jonathan M. Nielson, *Armed Forces on a Northern Frontier: The Military in Alaska's History, 1867–1987* (New York: Greenwood Press, 1988), 23–27; Bobby Dove Lain, "North of Fifty-Three: Army, Treasury Department, and Navy Administration of Alaska, 1867–1884" (Ph.D. diss., University of Texas, 1974); 175–211; "Evacuation of Alaska," *New-York Tribune*, March 30, 1877 (second quotation).

31. Miles to Sherman, Dec. 12, 1881, roll 30, Sherman Papers, LC (quotation); Nielson, *Armed Forces on a Northern Frontier*, 49–51, 65–68; Schofield, endorsement of April 13, 1889, roll 11, M857, LS by Headquarters of the Army, RG 108, NARA; Proctor to President, April 20, 1889, roll 109, LSSW; Proctor to AG July 18, 1889, ibid.; WDAR, 1890, 18–19.

32. Michael L. Tate, *The Frontier Army in the Settlement of the West* (Norman: University of Oklahoma Press, 1999), 9–19; Michael J. Brodhead, "Of Mice and Mastodons: Contributions to the Literature of Mammalogy by Officers and Men of the United States Army in the Nineteenth Century," *Archives of Natural History* 18 (no. 3, 1991): 363–374; Endicott to Secretary of the Interior, July 6, 1888, roll 106, LSSW; Rory M. McGovern, "The School of Experience: George W. Goethals and the U.S. Army, 1876–1907," *Journal of Military History* 81 (April 2017): 395–416.

33. WDAR, 1876, pt. 2, vol. 2, 605–606; Hoyt to Schurz, July 2, 1878, roll 1, M204, Interior Department Territorial Papers, Wyoming, RG 48, NARA; Hoyt to Crook, June 3, 1881, ibid.; Hoyt to Sheridan, June 20 (first quotation), 28, 1881, ibid.; Paul Andrew Hutton, *Phil Sheridan and His Army* (Lincoln: University of Nebraska Press, 1985), 354–359; P. H. Sheridan, *Report of an Exploration of Parts of Wyoming, Idaho, and Montana in August and September, 1882* (Washington, D.C.: Government Printing Office, 1882), 17–18 (second quotation); "The Park Grab," *Forest and Stream* 19 (January 4, 1883): 441 (third quotation); "The Park Monopolists Checked," *Forest and Stream* 19 (January 11, 1883): 461–464; Sheridan to Vest, December 10, 1882, roll 14, Sheridan Papers, LC; H. Duane Hampton, *How the U.S. Cavalry Saved Our National Parks* (Bloomington: Indiana University Press, 1971). Schofield, Sheridan's successor as commanding general, was less enthusiastic about saving the parks. Schofield to McMillan, October 3, 1894, box 57, Schofield Papers, LC.

34. Charles S. Sargent, "The Care of the National Forest-reservations," *Garden and Forest: A Journal of Horticulture, Landscape Art and Forestry* 6 (August 23,

1893): 351–352 (first quotation); John Muir, "Yellowstone National Park," *Atlantic Monthly* 81 (April 1898): 509–522 (second quotation 510); George S. Anderson, "A Plan to Save the Forests: Forest Preservation by Military Control," *Century Illustrated Magazine* 49 (February 1895): 626–634 (third quotation 628).

35. Richard Maxwell Brown, "Western Violence: Structure, Values, Myth," *Western Historical Quarterly* 24 (February 1993): 4 (quotation); Tate, *Frontier Army in the Settlement of the West*, 94–103; Sheridan to Pope, May 3, 1879, box 23, Sheridan Papers, LC; WDAR, 1880, 91; WDAR, 1881, 114–115; WDAR, 1883, 130; Drum to Schofield, January 20, 1885, box 16, Schofield Papers, LC; Hatch to Drum, March 11, 1885, ibid.; Drum to Schofield, August 28, November 7, 1885, box 17, ibid.; WDAR, 1889, 163–167; Murray R. Wickett, *Contested Territory: Whites, Native Americans, and African Americans in Oklahoma, 1865–1907* (Baton Rouge: Louisiana State University Press, 2000), 47–52.

36. Barnard to Humphreys, February 12, 1877, Entry 464, Letters Sent, Board of Engineers, 1869–1887, RG 77, NARA; Barnard to deStuckle, February 12, 1877, ibid. (quotation); Merrill to Morehead, May 26, 1880; letters sent from box 1 and volume 2, Entry 464, Board of Engineers for Fortification and River and Harbor Improvement, RG 77, NARA.

37. *History of the US Army Corps of Engineers* (Alexandria, VA: Office of History, Headquarters, U.S. Army Corps of Engineers, 1998), 42–49, 57–58; Albert E. Cowdrey, "Pioneering Environmental Law: The Army Corps of Engineers and the Refuse Act," *Pacific Historical Review* 44 (August 1975): 332 (quotation); Martin Reuss, "Andrew A. Humphreys and the Development of Hydraulic Engineering: Politics and Technology in the Army Corps of Engineers, 1850–1950," *Technology and Culture* 26 (January 1985): 1–33; Charles E. Parrish and Leland R. Johnson, "Engineering the Kentucky River: A Disastrous Debut," *Register of the Kentucky Historical Society* 95 (Autumn 1997): 369–394.

38. Alan Lessoff, *The Nation and Its City: Politics, "Corruption," and Progress in Washington, D.C., 1861–1902* (Baltimore: Johns Hopkins University Press, 1994), 164–165, 173–177, 192; *CRec* 45th Cong., 2nd sess., 1925 (quotations), 2345; Pamela Scott, *Capital Engineers: The U.S. Army Corps of Engineers in the Development of Washington, D.C., 1790–2004* (Alexandria, VA: U.S. Army Corps of Engineers, Office of History, 2005), 81–88, 125.

39. Lessoff, *Nation and Its City*, 184–198 (first quotation 189; third quotation 192), 236, 262; "Is There a Tunnel Ring?" *Evening Star*, September 27, 1888 (second quotation); "The Bad Tunnel Work," ibid., March 25, 1889; Editorial, *Evening Star*, May 4, 1889; "Lordly Ludlow," *Cincinnati Commercial Tribune*, August 10, 1887; *CRec* 51st Cong., 1st sess., 10419.

40. Robert Browning, *Two If By Sea: The Development of American Coastal Defense Policy* (Westport, CT: Greenwood Press, 1983), 129–182; Kenneth Earl Hamburger, "Technology, Doctrine, and Politics of U.S. Coast Defenses, 1880–1945: A Case Study in U.S. Defense Planning" (Ph.D. diss., Duke University, 1986), 12–118; *MPP* 8:137, 180–181, 211, 246, 346, 514; W. B. Franklin, "National Defense," *North American Review* 137 (November 1883): 596–604; H. A. Smalley, "A Defenseless Sea Board," *North American Review* 138 (March 1884): 233–245; Henry P. Wells,

"The Defense of Our Sea-Ports," *Harper's New Monthly Magazine* 71 (November 1885): 927–937; *Statutes* 23:434; HED 49, 49th Cong., 1st sess., serial 2395, 3–30 (quotation 27).

41. *CRec* 94th Cong., 1st sess., 7097 (quotation); Eugene Griffin, "Our Sea-Coast Defenses," *North American Review* 147 (July 1888): 64–75; W. T. Sampson, "Outline of a Scheme for the Naval Defense of the Coast," *Proceedings of the United States Naval Institute* 15 (no. 2, 1889): 169–232; F. V. Greene, "Our Defenceless Coasts," *Scribner's Magazine* 1 (January 1887): 51–66; Browning, *Two If By Sea*, 167–178; "The Country's Defense," *New York Times*, January 7, 1887; "Urging Coast Defense," ibid., January 16, 1887; Hamburger, "Technology, Doctrine, and Politics," 63–102, 134; *Statutes* 25:489–491.

42. Robert Watt, "Victorio's Military and Political Leadership of the Warm Springs Apaches," *War in History* 18 (November 2011): 464–466; Paul Andrew Hutton, *The Apache Wars: The Hunt for Geronimo, The Apache Kid, and the Captive Boy Who Started the Longest War in American History* (New York: Crown, 2016), 263–282; "Shot Down by Indians: Gen. Carr and His Command Murdered," *New York Times*, September 4, 1881; WDAR, 1881, 144 (quotations).

43. Utley, *Frontier Regulars*, 370–386; Robert Wooster, *The Military and U.S. Indian Policy, 1865–1903* (New Haven: Yale University Press, 1988), 187–188; Hutton, *Apache Wars*, 332–371; Cleveland to Endicott, December 22, 1885, series 2, roll 26, Cleveland Papers, LC (quotations).

44. WDAR, 1886, 72–73 (quotation); Utley, *Frontier Regulars*, 386–390; Hutton, *Apache Wars*, 372–387. Although neither Crook nor Miles had been totally forthcoming with Geronimo, their insistence that the Apache not be turned over to civil authorities in Arizona probably saved them from a worse fate.

45. Donald B. Connelly, *John M. Schofield and the Politics of Generalship* (Chapel Hill: University of North Carolina Press, 2006), 341 (first and second quotations); 12-page undated manuscript, "Reorganization of the Army" file, box 86, Schofield Papers, LC; John M. Schofield, *Forty-six Years in the Army* (1897; rpt. Norman: University of Oklahoma Press, 1988), 420–422 (third quotation); Proctor to Schofield, May 20, 1889, Proctor Papers, Proctor Free Library; Schofield to Proctor, March 30, 1889, box 54, Schofield Papers, LC (fourth quotation).

46. Schofield to SW, March 20, 1890, box 3, file 2425, General Correspondence of the SW, RG 107, NARA; Proctor to Governor of Wyoming Territory, Dec. 5, 1889, roll 110, LSSW; *San Antonio Daily Express*, March 27, 1891; WDAR, 1890, 172; WDAR, 1891, 14 (quotation), 57–58, 81; *MPP* 9:196; WDAR, 1892, 49; WDAR, 1893, 63–64, 168–169; WDAR, 1894, 68–69; Crook to AG, February 24, 1890, Crook Papers, Hayes Library.

47. WDAR, 1881, 149–150 (first quotation); WDAR, 1891, 9, 63–64; Edward M. Coffman, *The Old Army: A Portrait of the American Army in Peacetime, 1784–1898* (New York: Oxford University Press, 1986), 329–331; WDAR, 1892, 28 (second quotation); "Compliments to the Regular Army," *Sun*, September 26, 1877 (third and fourth quotations); A. A. Woodhull, "The Enlisted Soldier," *Journal of the Military Service Institution of the United States* 8 (March 1886): 22 (fifth quotation); WDAR, 1888, 101 (sixth quotation).

48. Coffman, *Old Army*, 225, 278–280, 331, 371–375; *Statutes* 28:215–216; *MPP* 9:115, 167–172; 196; WDAR, 1896, 82; WDAR, 1897, 16; WDAR, 1889, 8; WDAR, 1891, 9, 63–64.

49. Unless otherwise noted, this narrative is based upon Jerome A. Greene, *American Carnage: Wounded Knee, 1890* (Norman: University of Oklahoma Press, 2014). For Miles's warnings, see William to Brooke, November 18, 23, 1890, and Miles to Brooke, December 7, 1890, roll 1, M983, Reports and Correspondence Relating to the Army Investigations of the Battle of Wounded Knee and to the Sioux Campaign of 1890–91, RG 94, NARA.

50. Endorsement of Miles, January 31, 1891, Reports and Correspondence Relating to the Army Investigations, roll 1, ibid. (first quotation); Endorsement of Schofield, February 4, 1891, ibid. (second quotation).

51. "Coeur d'Alene Mine Owners and Miners," *Locomotive Fireman's Magazine* 16 (September 1892): 780 (first quotation); Laurie and Cole, *Role of Federal Military Forces*, 111–124; Schofield Memorandum, May 18, 1894, box 57, Schofield Papers, LC (second quotation).

52. Laurie and Cole, *Role of Federal Military Forces*, 124–152; Schofield to Ruger, McCook, July 1, 1894, box 57, Schofield Papers, LC; Miles to AG, July 4, 5 (first quotation), 6, 18, 1894, Chicago Riots File, box 72, Schofield Papers, LC; SED 7, 53rd Cong., 3rd sess., 365 (second quotation); Miles to Lamont, July 10, 17, 1894, Chicago Riots File, box 72, Schofield Papers, LC (third quotation).

53. Coffman, *Old Army*, 223–226, 252; Schofield to Draper, July 7, 1894, box 57, Schofield Papers, LC; WDAR, 1894, 5–7, 57–59; Laurie and Cole, *Role of Federal Military Forces*, 152–155; Hill to Lamont, July 7, 1894, box 40, Lamont Papers, LC; Miller to Lamont, July 19, 1894, ibid.; "Officering Our Army," *ANJ* 17 (August 16, 1879): 26 (quotation). For Congressional attempts to open up the system to enlisted personnel, see *Statutes* 20:150 (1878) and *Statutes* 27:336 (1892).

The refusal to acknowledge obvious class-related issues when it came to the backgrounds of its officers was exemplified in the army's 1887 annual report, when the Board of Visitors of the Military Academy claimed that the corps of cadets "is a typical representative body of the American people." Accompanying totals of parental occupations of candidates for admission from 1842 to 1887, however, showed that, whereas 8.7 percent of candidates had come from families of military officers, only 10.4 percent came from backgrounds that could be described as working-class. WDAR, 1887, 779–780.

54. William Wallace, "The Army and The Civil Power," *Journal of the Military Service Institution of the United States* 17 (March 1895): 254 (first quotation), 264 (second quotation); Nelson A. Miles, "The Lesson of the Recent Strikes," *North American Review* 159 (August 1894): 184 (third quotation).

55. *MPP* 9:196, 319–320, 535, 446; WDAR, 1894, 5–7, 57–59; Schofield to Draper, July 7, 1894, box 57, Schofield Papers, LC; George D. Ruggles, "The Proposed Increase of the Army," *North American Review* 159 (December 1894): 728–735; Oliver O. Howard, "A Plea for the Army," *Forum* 23 (August 1897): 643–652; W. A. Campbell, "The Reorganization of Our Army," *United Service* 11 (April 1894): 305–316; "Shall the U.S. Standing Army be Increased?" *Chautauquan: A Weekly*

Newsmagazine 20 (December 1894): 353 (newspaper quotations); *CRec* 53rd Cong., 3rd sess., 342 (Hawley quotation).

Epilogue: Old Army, New Empire

1. Alexander S. Bacon, "Is Our Army Degenerate?" *Forum* (March 1898): 11–24; Graham A. Cosmas, *An Army for Empire: The United States Army in the Spanish-American War* (Columbia: University of Missouri Press, 1971), 149–151, gives the administration much higher marks for its appointments.

2. *Statutes* 31:748–758; 32:775–870; Russell F. Weigley, *History of the United States Army*, Enlarged Edition (Bloomington: Indiana University Press, 1984), 317–318.

3. Robert Wooster, *Nelson A. Miles and the Twilight of the Frontier Army* (Lincoln: University of Nebraska Press, 1993).

4. "Memorandum for the AG," May 1, 1896, roll 14, M857, LS by the Headquarters of the Army, RG 108, NARA; Miles to SW, January 3, 1896, ibid.; WDAR, 1895, 69; "Bicycle" papers, box 8, Correspondence on Subjects of Concern to the Army Headquarters, Special File, RG 108, NARA; Miles to SW, May 1, 1897, box 1, Miles Papers, LC (first quotation); Edward Ranson, "Nelson A. Miles as Commanding General, 1895–1903," *Military Affairs* 39 (Winter 1966): 181 (second quotation); Nelson A. Miles, *Military Europe: A Narrative of Personal Observation and Personal Experience* (New York: Doubleday and McClure, 1898); Jonathan M. Nielson, *Armed Forces on a Northern Frontier: The Military in Alaska's History, 1867–1987* (New York: Greenwood Press, 1988), 65–68; HD 244, 55th Cong., 3rd sess., serial 3812, 3. Miles published yet another autobiography following his retirement.

5. "Gen. John M. Schofield Hits Spain," *Chicago Tribune*, January 31, 1897 (first quotation); Thomas Cruse, *Apache Days and After* (Caldwell, ID: Caxton Printers, 1941), 259–261 (second quotation); Brooke to Dorsey, December 28, 1896, vol. 35, Brooke Papers, HSP (third quotation); Cosmas, *Army for Empire*, 30–33, 70–71; David F. Trask, *The War with Spain in 1898* (New York: Macmillan, 1981), 72–80. Navy plans can be found at Naval History and Heritage Command, "Documentary Histories: Spanish-American War, Pre-War Planning," www.history.navy.mil/research/publications/documentary-histories/united-states-navy-s/pre-war-planning.html.

6. *Statutes* 30:261, 273–274 (first quotation); Cosmas, *Army for Empire*, 83, 89–97; Kristin L. Hoganson, *Fighting for American Manhood: How Gender Politics Provoked the Spanish-American and Philippine-American Wars* (New Haven: Yale University Press, 1998), 7–14; Matthew McCullough, *The Cross of War: Christian Nationalism and U.S. Expansion in the Spanish-American War* (Madison: University of Wisconsin Press, 2014); Elizabeth Samet, *Willing Obedience: Citizens, Soldiers, and the Progress of Consent in America, 1776–1898* (Palo Alto: Stanford University Press, 2003), 225; "An Army of 100,000 Men," *ANJ* 35 (March 19, 1898): 534 (second and third quotations); "Letter from Secretary Alger," ibid.; "Army on a War Footing," *New-York Tribune*, March 18, 1898; "Army Reorganization Bill," *New York Times*, April 3, 1898.

7. *CRec* 55th Cong., 2nd sess., 3624–3644 (first, second, and third quotations 3625–3626; fourth quotation 3627; fifth quotation 3629), 3667–3668, 3675–3680,

3688–3693; John Hull, "The Army Appropriation Bill," *Forum* 25 (May 1898): 396–402.

8. *Statutes* 30:361–366, 405 (quotation); Cosmas, *Army for Empire*, 100–102, 108–110, 134–135; *MPP* 10:248–249, 252; Miles to SW, Apr. 9, 1898, Miles Collection, USAMHI; Michael D. Doubler, *Civilian in Peace, Soldier in War: The Army National Guard, 1636–2000* (Lawrence: University Press of Kansas, 2003), 129.

9. WDAR, 1898, serial 3744, 260; Russell A. Alger, *The Spanish-American War* (New York: Harper and Bros., 1901), 7 (first quotation); Cosmas, *Army for Empire*, 127; Elting E. Morison, ed., *The Letters of Theodore Roosevelt*, 8 vols. (Cambridge: Harvard University Press, 1951–1954), 2:827 (second quotation); Charles Belmont Davis, ed., *Adventures and Letters of Richard Harding Davis* (New York: Charles Scribner's Sons, 1917), 245–246 (third quotation); Lucian to Mama, August 4, 1898, box 605, Breckinridge Family Papers, LC (fourth quotation).

10. Trask, *War with Spain*, 148, 168–169; Brian McAllister Linn, *The Philippine War, 1899–1902* (Lawrence: University Press of Kansas), 5–6; Charles G. Dawes, *A Journal of the McKinley Years*, ed. Bascom N. Timmons (La Grange, IL: The Towers, 1950), 158, 188 (first quotation); "Coast Defenses: Major General Miles' Views on an All-Important Subject," *Evening Star*, April 16, 1898; Miles to Alger, April 18, 1898, Miles Collection, USAMHI; Journal, April 20, 1898, Long Papers, Massachusetts Historical Society; "McKinley's Administration, Gen. S's experiences in" file," box 93, Schofield Papers, LC; "Memorandum for the President," April 20, 1898, box 44, ibid.; Miles to Alger, March 18, 1898, Alger Papers, Clements Library; Miles to Alger, April 26, 1898, Miles Collection, USAMHI; Autobiography, 87–89, Corbin Papers, LC (second and third quotations).

11. Diary, May 15, June 17, 1898, box 52, Cortelyou Papers, LC; Lewis L. Gould, *The Spanish-American War and President McKinley* (Lawrence: University Press of Kansas, 1982), 55–62; Trask, *War with Spain*, 194–422.

12. William Roscoe Thayer, *The Life and Letters of John Hay*, 2 vols. (Boston: Houghton Mifflin, 1915), 2:337 (first quotation); Paul Carlson, *"Pecos Bill": A Military Biography of William R. Shafter* (College Station: Texas A&M University Press, 1989), 163; Richard Harding Davis, "The Battle of San Juan," *Scribner's Magazine* 24 (November 1898): 395–397; Trask, *War with Spain*, 234–365, 326–335; "The Yellow Fever Epidemic," *New York Times*, July 30, 1898 (second quotation); Vincent J. Cirillo, *Bullets and Bacilli: The Spanish-American War and Military Medicine* (New Brunswick: Rutgers University Press, 2003), 31–35, 92–100.

13. Memoirs, chap. 7, p. 10, box 380, Pershing Papers, LC; Cosmas, *Army for Empire*, 144; Richard Harding Davis, "The Porto Rico Campaign," *Scribner's Magazine* 24 (November 1898): 515 (first quotation); Alger to Miles, May 26, 1898, Alger Papers, Clements Library; "Gen. Miles Places Blame," *New York Times*, August 24, 1898 (reprinting the *Star* interview); "Gen. Miles on the Stand," *New York Times*, December 24, 1898; SD 221, pt. 7, 56th Cong., 1st sess., serial 3865, 3240–3264 (second quotation 3256), 3795–3798; "The President's Commission," *ANJ* 36 (January 14, 1899): 470–471 (third quotation). The *New York Times* declined to print the most offensive sections of Eagan's testimony. "Eagan Denounces Miles as a Liar," *New York Times*, January 13, 1899.

14. "The Case of General Eagan," *ANJ*, 36 (January 21, 1899): 489; "Eagan's Case and the Lack of Discipline in the Army," *New York Times*, January 22, 1899; Cosmas, *Army for Empire*, 287–294; Washington Chauncey Ford, ed., *Letters of Henry Adams* (*1892–1918*) (Boston: Houghton Mifflin Co., 1938), 215; SD 221, 56th Cong., 1st sess., pt. 1, serial 3859, 153–168 (quotation 166); Dodge to Boynton, March 28, 1899, roll 6, series 1, McKinley Papers, LC; SD 270, 56th Cong., 1st sess., pt. 2, serial 3871, 924. Eagan was forced to resign from the army.

15. Wooster, *Miles*, 237–241; Cosmas, *Army for Empire*, 305–308; Morison, ed., *Letters of Roosevelt* 3:96, 98, 219; Root to Miles, December 19, 21, 1901, box 19, Root Papers, LC; Miles to Root, December 20, 1901, ibid.; "The President Sternly Rebukes Gen. Miles," *New York Times*, December 22, 1901; "Army and Navy Papers Against Secretary Root," ibid., December 29, 1901.

16. Miles to SW, February 14, 1902, Miles Collection, USAMHI; HD 518, 57th Cong., 1st sess., serial 4361, 2 (first quotation); Miles to Church, March 26, 1902, box 2, Church Papers, LC; "Extract of Statement from Lieut. Gen. Nelson A. Miles before the Committee on Military Affairs," box 1A, Corbin Papers, LC; "Miles May be Retired," *New-York Tribune*, March 21, 1902; "Gen. Miles's Testimony," *New York Times*, March 25, 1902 (second and third quotations); "The Staff Plan Urged," *New-York Tribune*, April 12, 1902; Ford, ed., *Letters of Henry Adams*, 380; Morison, ed., *Letters of Roosevelt* 3:247; "Gen. Miles's Retirement," *New York Times*, April 19, 1902 (fourth quotation); Wooster, *Miles*, 242–248.

17. Weigley, *History of the U.S. Army*, 317–318; *CRec* 34:66–69, 79–85, 96–125, 1435, 1625, 1558, 1627, 1641–1643,1662–1669, 1713–1731; *Statutes* 30:979–980; 31:748–758; David Krueger, "The Red Cross, the Daughters of the American Revolution, and the Origins of the Army Nurse Corps in the Spanish-American War," *Journal of Military History* 83 (April 2019): 432.

18. Jerry Cooper, *The Rise of the National Guard: The Evolution of the American Militia, 1865–1920* (Lincoln: University of Nebraska Press, 1997), 105, 108–111; WDAR, 1902, serial 4443, 34–40; *MPP* 10:448, 539–540; *Statutes* 32:775–780; James Parker, "The New Militia Act of 1903," *North American Review* 77 (August 1903): 278–287; "For 'A Well-Regulated Militia,'" *New York Times*, January 30, 1902; "The Militia Bill," January 22, 1903.

19. Cosmas, *Army for Empire*, 313; *MPP* 10:446, 539; Weigley, *History of the U.S. Army*, 314–320; WDAR, 1902, serial 4443, 42–49 (first quotation 42–43); *CRec* 36:503 (second quotation), 540–541; *Statutes* 32:830–831 (remaining quotations); "The General Staff," *New York Times*, January 9, 1903; WDAR, 1903, serial 4628, 3; Wooster, *Miles*, 242–248.

20. WDAR, 1895, 4, 80–89, 224 (quotations); WDAR, 1902, serial 4443, 30; WDAR, 1902, serial 4451, 202; WDAR, 1903, serial 4628, 2, 35–36.

21. *The Statistical History of the United States: From Colonial Times to the Present* (New York: Basic Books, 1976), 8, 1114–1115; *Correspondence Relating to the War With Spain, Including the Insurrection in the Philippine Islands and the China Relief Expedition*, 2 vols. (1902, rpt. Washington, D.C.: Center of Military History, 1993), 1:162–163 (quotations); Jack C. Lane, *Armed Progressive: General Leonard Wood* (San Rafael, CA: Presidio Press, 1978), 55–113; Howard Gillette Jr., "The Military

Occupation of Cuba, 1899–1902: Workshop for American Progressivism," *American Quarterly* 25 (October 1973): 410–425; Marial Iglesas Utset, *A Cultural History of Cuba During the U.S. Occupation, 1898–1902*, trans. Russ Davidson (Chapel Hill: University of North Carolina Press, 2011), 18–25, 37–38, 72–73, 127–150; James Herman Pruitt II, "Leonard Wood and the American Empire" (Ph.D. diss., Texas A&M University, 2011), 331. Naval expenses from 1895 to 1903 had increased even more rapidly, from 8.8% to 16.9% of all federal spending.

22. *MPP* 10:448 (first quotation); *Correspondence Relating to the War With Spain* 2:676–678 (second quotation); Linn, *Philippine War*, 27–33, 125–126, 134–135, 325–327; Brian M. Linn, "The US Army and Nation Building and Pacification in the Philippines," in *Armed Diplomacy: Two Centuries of American Campaigning* (Fort Leavenworth, KS: Combat Studies Institute Press, 2003), 79.

23. Rudyard Kipling, "The White Man's Burden," *McClure's Magazine* 12 (February 1899): 4–5 (first quotation); Linn, *Philippine War*, 202–224; *Correspondence Relating to the War With Spain* 2:858–859 (second quotation); WDAR, 1903, serial 4630, 143.

24. Linn, "US Army and Nation Building," 78; Hugh Lenox Scott, *Some Memories as a Soldier* (New York: Century Company, 1928), 400 (quotation).

25. *Statistical History*, 8, 1140–1143.

Bibliography

1. Primary Sources

Manuscript Collections

Alger, Russell A. Papers. Clements Library, University of Michigan. Ann Arbor.

Allen, Henry T. Papers. Library of Congress. Washington, D.C.

Anderson, Robert. Papers. Library of Congress. Washington, D.C.

Archer, James Jay. Collection. Maryland Historical Society. Baltimore.

Augur, Christopher. Papers. Illinois State Historical Library. Springfield.

Augur, Christopher. Papers. Newberry Library. Chicago.

Baird, George F. Papers. Kansas State Historical Society, Center for Historical Research. Topeka.

Baldwin, Frank D. Papers. Huntington Library. San Marino, CA.

Barney, Hiram. Collection. Huntington Library. San Marino, CA.

Bayard, George D. Papers. Missouri State Historical Society. St. Louis.

Bayard, Thomas F. Papers. Library of Congress, Washington, D.C.

Belknap, William W. Papers. Library of Congress. Washington, D.C.

Bell, John. Collection. Library of Congress. Washington, D.C.

Benham-McNeil Family Papers. Library of Congress. Washington, D.C.

Bliss, Tasker H. Collection. United States Army Military History Institute. Carlisle Barracks, PA.

Bradley, Luther, Papers. U.S. Army Military History Institute. Carlisle Barracks, PA.

Breckinridge Family Papers. Library of Congress. Washington, D.C.

Brincklé, John R. Papers. Library of Congress. Washington, D.C.

Brodhead, Daniel. Letterbook. Historical Society of Pennsylvania. Philadelphia.

Brooke, John R. Papers. Historical Society of Pennsylvania. Philadelphia.

Brooks, William T. H. Papers. U.S. Army Military History Institute. Carlisle Barracks, PA.

Brown, Jacob. Papers. Clements Library. University of Michigan. Ann Arbor.

Brown, Jacob. Papers. Library of Congress. Washington, D.C.

Bryan, Guy M. Papers. Dolph Briscoe Center for American History. University of Texas. Austin.

Buchanan, Robert C. Papers. Maryland Historical Society. Baltimore.

Burr, Edward. Papers. Library of Congress. Washington, D.C.

Cameron, Simon. Papers. Historical Society of Dauphin County [Harrisburg, PA] (microfilm, Library of Congress)

Cameron, Simon. Papers. Library of Congress. Washington, D.C.

Carlton, Caleb H. Papers. Library of Congress. Washington, D.C.
Chandler, Zachariah. Papers. Library of Congress. Washington, D.C.
Chapman Papers. Dolph Briscoe Center for American History. University of Texas. Austin.
Church, William C. Papers. Library of Congress. Washington, D.C.
Churchill, Sylvester. Journals. Library of Congress. Washington, D.C.
Cleveland, Grover. Papers. Library of Congress. Washington, D.C.
Comstock, Cyrus B. Papers. Library of Congress. Washington, D.C.
Corbin, Henry C. Papers. Library of Congress. Washington, D.C.
Cortelyou, George B. Papers. Library of Congress. Washington, D.C.
Crawford, William H. Collection. Library of Congress. Washington, D.C.
Crook, George. Papers. Hayes Library. Fremont, Ohio.
Church, William Conant. Papers. Library of Congress. Washington, D.C.
Dearborn, Henry. Miscellaneous Manuscripts Collection. Library of Congress. Washington, D.C.
Desha, Joseph and John R. Papers. Library of Congress. Washington, D.C.
Draper, John W. Papers. Library of Congress. Washington, D.C.
Draper Manuscripts in the State Historical Society of Wisconsin (microfilm, Library of Congress)
Dunn Family Papers. Dolph Briscoe Center for American History. University of Texas. Austin.
Early, Jubal. Papers. Library of Congress. Washington, D.C.
Eustis, William. Papers. Library of Congress. Washington, D.C.
Ewing, Thomas. Family Papers. Library of Congress. Washington, D.C.
Foster, John Watson. Papers. Library of Congress. Washington, D.C.
French, Benjamin B. Family Papers. Library of Congress. Washington, D.C.
Fynn, John. Papers. U.S. Army Military History Institute. Carlisle Barracks, PA.
Garfield, James A. Papers. Library of Congress. Washington, D.C.
Gatewood, Charles B. Collection. Arizona Historical Society. Tucson.
Gibbon, John. Papers. Maryland Historical Society. Baltimore.
Gibson-Getty-McClure Family Papers. Library of Congress. Washington, D.C.
Giddings, Joshua R. and George Julian Papers. Library of Congress. Washington, D.C.
Graham, William M. Papers. United States Army Military History Institute. Carlisle Barracks, PA.
Grant, Ulysses S. Papers. Library of Congress. Washington, D.C.
Green, Duff. Papers. Southern Historical Collection. University of North Carolina (microfilm, Library of Congress)
Greene, Francis V. Papers. New York Public Library. New York.
Grierson, Benjamin H. Papers. Illinois State Historical Library. Springfield.
Halleck, Henry. Papers. Library of Congress. Washington, D.C.
Hammond, James Henry. Papers. Library of Congress. Washington, D.C.
Hardie, James A. Papers. Library of Congress. Washington, D.C.
Harmar, Josiah. Papers. Clements Library. University of Michigan. Ann Arbor.
Harmar, Josiah. Papers. Library of Congress. Washington, D.C.

Harper, Robert Goodloe. Papers. Library of Congress. Washington, D.C.
Harrison, William Henry. Papers. Library Congress. Washington, D.C.
Hartz, Edward L. Papers. Library of Congress. Washington, D.C.
Hatch, John Porter. Papers. Library of Congress. Washington, D.C.
Heintzelman, Samuel Peter. Papers. Library of Congress. Washington, D.C.
Hitchcock, Ethan Allen. Papers. Library of Congress. Washington, D.C.
Howard, Oliver O. Papers. Bowdoin College. Brunswick, ME.
Hoxie, Vinnie Ream and Richard L. Papers. Library of Congress. Washington, D.C.
Huggins, Eli Lundy. Papers. Bancroft Library. University of California. Berkeley.
Humphreys, Andrew. Papers. Historical Society of Pennsylvania. Philadelphia.
Innes, Harry. Papers. Library of Congress. Washington, D.C.
Jackson, Andrew. Papers. Library of Congress. Washington, D.C.
Jefferson, Thomas. Papers. Library of Congress. Washington, D.C.
Jesup, Thomas. Papers. Library of Congress. Washington, D.C.
Jesup, Thomas. Papers. U.S. Army Military History Institute. Carlisle Barracks, PA.
Jesup, Thomas S. Papers. Clements Library. University of Michigan. Ann Arbor.
Johnson, Andrew. Papers. Library of Congress. Washington, D.C.
Johnson, Richard M. Papers. Library of Congress. Washington, D.C.
Kautz, August V. Papers. Library of Congress. Washington, D.C.
King, Benjamin. Papers. Library of Congress. Washington, D.C.
Kingsburg, Jacob. Papers. Library of Congress. Washington, D.C.
Knapp, Obadiah H. Papers. Dolph Briscoe Center for American History. University of Texas. Austin.
Lamont, Daniel. Papers. Library of Congress. Washington, D.C.
Lawson, Thomas. Papers. Library of Congress. Washington, D.C.
Legion of the United States Papers. U.S. Army Military History Institute. Carlisle Barracks, PA.
Lincoln, Abraham. Papers. Library of Congress. Washington, D.C.
Logan Family Papers. Library of Congress. Washington, D.C.
Long, John. Papers. Massachusetts Historical Society. Boston.
Lowndes, William. Papers. Library of Congress. Washington, D.C.
Mackenzie, Ranald. Papers. U.S. Army Military History Institute. Carlisle Barracks, PA.
Madison, James. Papers. Library of Congress. Washington, D.C.
Maginnis, Martin. Papers. Montana Historical Society. Helena.
McCarthy, Michael B. Journals. Library of Congress. Washington, D.C.
McClellan, George B., Sr. Papers. Library of Congress. Washington, D.C.
McFarland, Alexander B. Papers. Library of Congress. Washington, D.C.
McHenry, James. Papers. Clements Library. University of Michigan. Ann Arbor.
McKinley, William. Papers. Library of Congress. Washington, D.C.
McLane, Louis. Papers. Library of Congress. Washington, D.C.
McPherson, James B. Papers. Library of Congress. Washington, D.C.
Meade, George. Papers. Historical Society of Pennsylvania. Philadelphia.
Meigs, Montgomery C. Papers. Library of Congress. Washington, D.C.
Miles, Nelson A. Collection. U.S. Army Military History Institute, Carlisle Barracks, PA.

Miles, Nelson A. Papers. Library of Congress. Washington, D.C.
Miles, Sherman. Manuscripts. Copy in author's possession.
Mordecai, Alfred. Papers. Library of Congress. Washington, D.C.
Morgan, Christopher. Papers. Library of Congress. Washington, D.C.
Myer, Albert James. Papers. Library of Congress. Washington, D.C.
Myer, Albert James. U.S. Army Signal Corps Museum Collection. Library of Congress. Washington, D.C.
Nicholas, Wilson Cary. Papers. Library of Congress. Washington, D.C.
Northwest Territory Collection. Clements Library. University of Michigan. Ann Arbor.
Nourse, Charles J. Photocopies. U.S. Army Military History Institute. Carlisle Barracks, PA.
Ord, E. O. C. Papers. Bancroft Library. University of California. Berkeley.
Ord Family Papers. Georgetown University Library. Special Collections. Washington, D.C.
Partridge, Alden. Papers. Library of Congress. Washington, D.C.
Paulding, Grace and William. Memoirs. U.S. Army Military History Institute. Carlisle Barracks, PA.
Pennypacker, Galusha. Papers. Historical Society of Pennsylvania. Philadelphia.
Pershing, John J. Papers. Library of Congress. Washington, D.C.
Peters, DeWitt C. Papers. Bancroft Library. University of California. Berkeley.
Philpot-Randall Family Papers. Maryland Historical Society. Baltimore.
Poinsett, Joel. Papers. Historical Society of Pennsylvania. Philadelphia.
Porter, David D. Family Papers. Library of Congress. Washington, D.C.
Preble, Edward. Papers. Library of Congress. Washington, D.C.
Proctor, Redfield. Papers. Proctor Free Library. Proctor, Vermont.
Randall-Bache Collection. U.S. Army Military History Institute. Carlisle Barracks, PA.
Rhodes, Charles D. Diary. Library of Congress. Washington, D.C.
Rockwell, Almon. Papers. Library of Congress. Washington, D.C.
Root, Elihu. Papers. Library of Congress. Washington, D.C.
Schofield, John. Papers. Library of Congress. Washington, D.C.
Schofield, John. Papers. United States Military Academy Library. West Point, New York.
Schureman, James W. Papers. Library of Congress. Washington, D.C.
Scott, Winfield. Papers. Clements Library. University of Michigan. Ann Arbor.
Seward, William. Papers. Rush Rhees Library. University of Rochester, NY.
Shelby Family Papers. Library of Congress. Washington, D.C.
Sheridan, Philip. Papers. Library of Congress. Washington, D.C.
Sherman, William T. Papers. Library of Congress. Washington, D.C.
Smith, Persifor. Papers. Historical Society of Pennsylvania. Philadelphia.
Smith, William Loughton. Papers. Library of Congress. Washington, D.C.
Stanley, David S. Diary. Dolph Briscoe Center for American History. University of Texas. Austin.
Stanton, Edwin M. Papers. Library of Congress. Washington, D.C.
Starr, Samuel H. Papers. Missouri State Historical Society. St. Louis.

Sumner Family Papers. Library of Congress. Washington, D.C.
Talbot, Theodore. Papers. Library of Congress. Washington, D.C.
Taylor, Zachary. Papers. Library of Congress. Washington, D.C.
Tazewell, Henry. Papers. Library of Congress. Washington, D.C.
Thayer, Sylvanius. Papers. United States Military Academy Library. West Point, NY.
Towson, Sophie. Correspondence. Maryland Historical Society. Baltimore.
Van Deventer, Christopher. Papers. Clements Library. University of Michigan. Ann Arbor.
Warfield, William H. Diary. Maryland Historical Society. Baltimore.
Washburne, E. B. Papers. Library of Congress. Washington, D.C.
Wayne, Anthony. Manuscripts. Historical Society of Pennsylvania. Philadelphia.
Wilkins, James C. Papers. Dolph Briscoe Center for American History. University of Texas. Austin.
Williams, David R. Papers. Library of Congress. Washington, D.C.
Williamson, Robert S. Papers. Library of Congress. Washington, D.C.
Wilson, Henry. Papers. Library of Congress. Washington, D.C.
Wood, Leonard. Papers. Library of Congress. Washington, D.C.
Wool, John E. Papers. Library of Congress. Washington, D.C.
Wool, John E. Papers. New York State Library, Albany.
Young, Nathaniel. Papers. Library of Congress. Washington, D.C.

National Archives and Records Administration. Washington, D.C.

RECORD GROUP 29. RECORDS OF THE BUREAU OF THE CENSUS.
Seventh Census of the United States, 1850. M432.
Eighth Census of the United States, 1860. M653.
Ninth Census of the United States, 1870. M593.
Tenth Census of the United States, 1880. T9.

RECORD GROUP 46. SENATE MILITARY AFFAIRS COMMITTEE.

RECORD GROUP 48. RECORDS OF THE OFFICE OF THE SECRETARY OF THE INTERIOR.
Interior Department Territorial Papers: Wyoming, 1870–1890. M204.

RECORD GROUP 59. GENERAL RECORDS OF THE DEPARTMENT OF STATE.
Despatches from United States Ministers in Hawaii, 1843–1930. T30.
Diplomatic Instructions of the Department of States: Hawaii, 1801–1906. M77.
State Department Territorial Papers: Montana, 1864–1872. M356.

RECORD GROUP 75. RECORDS OF THE BUREAU OF INDIAN AFFAIRS.
Letters Received by the Office of Indian Affairs, 1824–1880. M234.
Letters Sent by the Secretary of War Relating to Indian Affairs, 1800–1824. M15.

RECORD GROUP 77. RECORDS OF THE OFFICE OF THE CHIEF OF ENGINEERS.
Board on River and Harbor Improvements. Entry 53.
Civil Works Map File.

Correspondence of Topographical Officer Stationed in Washington. Entry 306.
Letters, Reports, and Statements Sent to the Secretary of War and Congress. Entry 8.
Letters and Reports of Joseph G. Totten. Entry 146.
Letters Received by the Topographical Bureau of the War Department, 1824–1865. M506.
Letters Received, 1826–1866. Entry 18.
Letters Sent, Board of Engineers, 1869–1887. Entry 464.
Letters Sent by the Office of the Chief of Engineers Relating to Internal Improvements, 1824–1830. M65.
Letters Sent by the Topographical Bureau of the War Department and by Successor Divisions in the Office of the Chief of Engineers, 1829–1870. M66.
Papers of Col. John N. Macomb, Office of the Chief Engineer. Entry 153.
Published Maps Series.
Reports on Internal Improvements, 1823–1839. Entry 250.
War Department Map Collection.

Record Group 92. Records of the Office of the Quartermaster General.
Copies of Annual Reports of Quartermaster Officers, 1863. Entry 1127.
General William Myers, Letters Sent. Entry 381.
Letters Received, 1819–1870. Entry 20.
Letters Received from the Secretary of War. Entry 22.
Letters Received from the War Department, 1863–1870. Entry 27.
Letters Sent by the Office of the Quartermaster General, Main Series, 1818–1870. M745.
Letters Sent Relating to Clothing and Equipage. . . . Entry 999.
Quartermasters Consolidated File. Entry 225.

Record Group 94. Records of the Adjutant General's Office, 1780s–1917.
General Orders and Circulars of the War Department and Headquarters of the Army, 1809–1860. M1094.
Gen. James Wilkinson's Order Book. M654.
Letters Received by the Office of the Adjutant General (Main Series), 1805–1821. M566.
Letters Received by the Office of the Adjutant General (Main Series), 1822–1860. M567.
Letters Received by the Office of the Adjutant General (Main Series), 1871–1880. M666.
Letters Received by the Office of the Adjutant General (Main Series), 1881–1889. M689.
Letters Sent by the Office of the Adjutant General (Main Series), 1800–1890. M565.
Muster Rolls and Payrolls of Militia and Regular Army Organizations in the Battle of Tippecanoe, November 1811. T1085.

Reports and Correspondence Relating to the Army Investigations of the Battle of Wounded Knee and to the Sioux Campaign of 1890–1891. M983.
War Department Collection of Post-Revolutionary War Manuscripts. M904.

Record Group 105. Records of the Bureau of Refugees, Freedmen, and Abandoned Lands.
Registers and Letters Received by the Commissioner, 1865–1872. M752.

Record Group 107. Records of the Office of the Secretary of War.
Confidential and Unofficial Letters Received, 1832–1846. Entry 21.
Confidential and Unofficial Letters Sent by the Secretary of War. M7.
Contracts, 1799–1810. Entry 44.
General Correspondence, 1890–1913.
Letters Received by the Secretary of War, Main Series, 1801–1870. M221.
Letters Received by the Secretary of War, Unregistered Series, 1789–1861. M222.
Letters Sent by the Secretary of War Relating to Military Affairs, 1800–1889. M6.
Miscellaneous Letters Sent by the Secretary of War, 1800–1809. M370.
Registers of Applications for Commissions or Promotions in the Regular Army, n.d. Entry 253.
Reports on Annual Expenditures of the War Department Bureaus on Special Matters. Entry 49.
Subsistence Contracts, 1803–1812. Entry 45.

Record Group 108. Records of the Headquarters of the Army.
General Orders and Circulars of the War Department and Headquarters of the Army, 1809–1860. M1094.
Letters Received by the Headquarters of the Army, 1827–1903. M1635.
Letters Sent by the Headquarters of the Army (Main Series), 1828–1903. M857.

Record Group 153. Records of the Office of the Judge Advocate General.
Proceedings of the Court of Inquiry in the case of Johnson C. Whittaker.

Record Group 233. Records of the United States House of Representatives.
House Appropriations Committee.
House Committee on Expenditures in the War Department.
House Committee on Military Affairs.
House Docket Books.
House Records on Committee Membership.
House Ways and Means Committee.
Select Committee on the Superintendence of Civil Works by Military Officers.

Record Group 360. Records of the Continental and Confederation Congresses and the Constitutional Convention.
Papers of the Continental Congress. M247.

Record Group 393. Records of the U.S. Army Continental Commands.
Headquarters Records, Letters Received, Department of the Missouri. Entry 2601A.
Letters Sent, Department of the Columbia. Entry 704.
Letters Sent, Department of Dakota. Entry 1167.
Letters Sent, Department of the Missouri. Entry 2575.
Letters Sent, Department of the Platte. Entry 3722.
Letters Sent, Department of Texas. Entry 4867.
Letters Sent, District of North Carolina.
Letters Sent, First Military District. Entry 5408.
Letters Sent, Western Division and Department. Entry 5568.
Letters Sent, Yellowstone Command. Entry 1333.
Records of Headquarters, Army of the Southwestern Frontier, and Headquarters, Second and Seventh Military Departments, 1835–1853. M1302.
Records of the Tenth Military Department, 1846–1851. M210.

Federal Government Documents

Adjutant General's Department. *Subject Index of the General Orders of the War Department, from January 1, 1809, to December 31, 1860.* Washington, D.C.: Government Printing Office, 1886.
American State Papers: Foreign Relations. 6 vols. Washington, D.C.: Gales and Seaton, 1833–1861.
American State Papers: Indian Affairs. 2 vols. Washington, D.C.: Gales and Seaton, 1832–1834.
American State Papers: Military Affairs. 7 vols. Washington, D.C.: Gales and Seaton, 1832–1861.
American State Papers: Miscellaneous. 2 vols. Washington, D.C.: Gales and Seaton, 1834.
Annals of the Congress of the United States, 1789–1824. 42 vols. Washington, 1834–1856.
Carter, Clarence, ed. *The Territorial Papers of the United States.* 26 vols. Washington, D.C.: Government Printing Office, 1934–1969.
Congressional Globe. 46 vols. Washington, D.C., 1834–1873.
Congressional Record. 154 vols. to date. Washington, D.C., 1874-present.
Correspondence Relating to the War with Spain, Including the Insurrection in the Philippine Islands and the China Relief Expedition. 2 vols. 1902, rpt. Washington, D.C.: Center of Military History, 1993.
House Journal. 43 vols. Washington, D.C., 1789–1875.
Journals of the Continental Congress, 1774–1789. Ed. Worthington C. Ford et al., 34 vols. Washington, D.C., 1904–1937.
Kappler, Charles J., ed. *Indian Affairs: Laws and Treaties.* 7 vols. Washington, D.C.: Government Printing Office, 1903–1904.
Letters of Delegates to Congress, 1774–1789. 26 vols. Ed. Paul H. Smith. Washington, D.C.: Government Printing Office, 1976–2000.
New American State Papers: Indian Affairs. 13 vols. Ed. Thomas C. Cochran. Wilmington, DE: Scholarly Publications, 1972.

New American State Papers: Military Affairs. Ed. Benjamin Franklin Cooling. 19 vols. Wilmington, DE: Scholarly Publications, 1979.

Register of Debates in Congress. 14 vols. Washington, D.C.: Gales and Seaton, 1825–1837.

Senate Executive Journal. 1789–1875.

Senate Journal. 43 vols. Washington, D.C., 1789–1875.

"The Statistics of the Wealth and Industry of the United States. . . . compiled from the original Returns of the Ninth Census." Washington, D.C.: Government Printing Office, 1872.

Statutes at Large of the United States of America, 1789–1903. Washington, D.C., 1850–1903.

U.S. War Department. Military Secretary's Office. *Memorandum Relative to the General Officers in the Armies of the United States During the Civil War, 1861–1865.* Washington, D.C.: Government Printing Office, 1906.

U.S. War Department. *The War of the Rebellion: A Compilation of the Official Records of the Union and Confederate Armies.* 128 vols. Washington, D.C.: Government Printing Office, 1880–1901.

U.S. Congressional Serial Set

Senate Doc. 118, 15th Cong., 1st sess., serial 2. *Statement of All the Arms and Accoutrements which have been manufactured at the different Armories.*

House Doc. 11, 15th Cong., 1st sess., serial 6. *Report, in Part, of the Committee on so much of the President's message as relates to Roads, Canals, and Seminaries of Learning.*

House Doc. 17, 15th Cong., 2nd sess., serial 17. *Establishment of a National Armory on the Western Waters.*

House Doc. 148, 15th Cong., 2nd sess., serial 24. *Statements of Contacts made by the Commissary General of Subsistence, the Ordnance Department, the Commissary General of Purchase, and the Engineer Department, in the year 1818.*

House Doc. 88, 16th Cong., 1st sess., serial 36. *Report on the Military Academy at West Point.*

Senate Doc. 18, 17th Cong., 2nd sess., serial 74. *Report of the Ordnance Department on a National Armory on the Western Waters.*

House Report 103, 17th Cong., 2nd sess., serial 87. *Fortifications at Mobile Point and Dauphin Island.*

Senate Doc. 32, 18th Cong., 2nd sess., serial 109. *Examination Made by the Board of Engineers with a view to Internal Improvement.*

House Doc. 55, 18th Cong., 2nd sess., serial 115. *Report of the Commissioners to Establish a National Armory on the Western Waters.*

House Doc. 12, 19th Cong., 1st sess., serial 131. *Petition of Pendleton County, Kentucky, for a National Armory.*

House Doc. 44, 19th Cong., 1st sess., serial 133. *Resolution of Tennessee General Assembly for a National Armory.*

House Doc. 46, 19th Cong., 1st sess., serial 133. *Louisville and Portland Canal Company, Kentucky, Regarding a National Armory.*

House Doc. 88, 19th Cong., 1st sess., serial 135. *Petition of Citizens of Connellsville Regarding a National Armory.*

House Doc. 136, 19th Cong., 1st sess., serial 138. *Documents Relating to Tygart's Valley River Regarding a National Armory.*

House Doc. 156, 19th Cong., 1st sess., serial 139. *Road from Washington to New Orleans.*

House Report 35, 19th Cong., 1st sess., serial 141. *Report on Exploration of Northwest Coast.*

House Report 42, 19th Cong., 1st sess., serial 141. *Military Roads in Michigan.*

House Resolution 45, 19th Cong., 1st sess., serial 142. *Mr. Mercer's Resolutions to Provide a Fund for Internal Improvement.*

House Doc. 7. 19th Congress, 2nd sess., serial 149. *Lead Mines—Illinois and Missouri.*

House Doc. 10, 19th Cong., 2nd sess., serial 149. *Board of Engineers and the Chesapeake and Ohio Canal.*

House Doc. 59, 19th Cong., 2nd sess., serial 151. *Report and Resolutions of the Legislature of Georgia.*

House Report 98, 19th Cong., 2nd sess., serial 161. *Report of the Select Committee.*

Senate Doc. 169, 20th Cong., 1st sess., serial 166. *Lead and Lead Mines in Missouri.*

House Doc. 2, 20th Cong., 1st sess., serial 169. *Message of the President.*

House Doc. 146, 20th Cong., 1st sess., serial 172. *Correspondence—Secretary of War and General Jackson.*

House Doc. 214, 20th Cong., 1st sess., serial 173. *Memorial from Blairsville Regarding a National Armory.*

House Doc. 216, 20th Cong., 1st sess., serial 173. *Report of the James River and Kenhawa Canal Route.*

House Doc. 261, 20th Cong., 1st sess., serial 174. *Internal Improvement.*

House Doc. 277, 20th Cong., 1st sess., serial 175. *Indian Tribes, Northwest Frontier.*

House Report 141, 20th Cong., 1st sess., serial 178. *Chesapeake and Ohio Canal.*

House Doc. 192, 20th Cong., 1st sess., serial 192. *Chesapeake and Ohio Canal, Estimates of the Cost of Making a Canal from Cumberland to Georgetown.*

House Report 48, 21st Cong., 2nd sess., serial 207. *Roads Constructed by the Army.*

Senate Doc. 90, 22nd Cong., 1st sess., serial 213. *Message of the President . . . concerning the Fur Trade, and Inland Trade to Mexico.*

House Ex. Doc. 51, 22nd Cong., 1st sess., serial 217. *Letter on Surveys and Estimates for Projects.*

Senate Doc. 512, pt. 1, 23rd Cong., 1st sess., serial 244. *Correspondence on the Subject of the Emigration of Indians.*

House Report 349, 23rd Cong., 1st sess., serial 262. *Armory—Western Waters.*

House Report 474, 23rd Cong., 1st sess., serial 263. *Regulating the Indian Department.*

House Doc. 154, 23rd Cong., 2nd sess., serial 274. *Kentucky Legislature—Armory.*

House Report 4, 23rd Cong., 2nd sess., serial 276. *Topographical Engineers.*

Senate Doc. 182, 24th Cong., 1st sess., serial 281. *Expediency of Establishing a National Armory in the valley of the Mississippi.*

Senate Doc. 419, 24th Cong., 1st sess., serial 284. *Report on Employment of Topographical Engineers.*

House Doc. 181, 24th Cong., 1st sess., serial 289. *Colonel Dodge's Journal.*

House Report 297, 24th Cong., 1st sess., serial 292. *Harbors and Rivers.*

House Report 372, 24th Cong., 1st sess., serial 294. *Arsenal—North Carolina.*

House Report 373, 24th Cong., 1st sess., serial 294. *Armory on Western Waters.*

Senate Doc. 1125, 24th Cong., 2nd sess., serial 298. *Report of Surveys.*

House Doc. 13, 24th Cong., 2nd sess., serial 301. *Coast Survey.*

Senate Doc. 181, 25th Cong., 2nd sess., serial 316. *National Foundry at Havre-de-Grace, Maryland.*

Senate Doc. 231, 25th Cong., 2nd sess., serial 316. *Establish a foundry, an armory . . . , arsenals . . . and depots. . .*

Senate Doc. 310, 25th Cong., 2nd sess., serial 317. *Establishment of a National Armory at the Town of Harrison.*

Senate Doc. 356, 25th Cong., 2nd sess., serial 317. *Statement of the Officers of the Missouri Volunteers.*

House Doc. 61, 25th Cong., 2nd sess., serial 322. *Pennsylvania Armory—Fall of Beaver.*

House Doc. 78, 25th Cong., 2nd sess., serial 323. *Court of Inquiry—Operations in Florida.*

House Doc. 120, 25th Cong., 2nd sess., serial 325. *National Armory—Western Waters.*

House Doc. 268, 25th Cong., 2nd sess., serial 328. *National Foundry—Easton, Pennsylvania.*

House Doc. 278, 25th Cong., 2nd sess., serial 328. *Military road, western frontier, &c.*

House Doc. 311, 25th Cong., 2nd sess., serial 329. *Defence of the western frontier . . . furnished by Major General Gaines.*

House Doc. 312, 25th Cong., 2nd sess., serial 329. *Pennsylvania—National Foundry. Centre County.*

House Doc. 28, 25th Cong., 3rd sess., serial 345. *Correspondence, Governor of Pennsylvania.*

House Doc. 47, 25th Cong., 3rd sess., serial 346. *Armory—Kentucky.*

House Report 168, 25th Cong., 3rd sess., serial 351. *National Foundry.*

Senate Doc. 231, 26th Cong., 1st sess., serial 358. *Establishment of a Line of Military Posts from the Missouri to the Oregon or Columbia River.*

Senate Doc. 256, 26th Cong., 1st sess., serial 358. *Memorial of Edmund P. Gaines.*

Senate Doc. 379, 26th Cong., 1st sess., serial 359. *Defense of the Western Frontier.*

House Doc. 140, 26th Cong., 1st sess., serial 365. *National Foundry—Schuylkill County, Pennsylvania.*

House Doc. 144, 26th Cong., 1st sess., serial 365. *Reservation at Fort Snelling.*

House Doc. 153, 26th Cong., 1st sess., serial 366. *Militia of the United States.*

House Doc. 177, 26th Cong., 1st sess., serial 366. *National Foundry at Troy, New York.*

House Doc. 206, 26th Cong., 1st sess., serial 368. *National Defense and National Foundries.*

Senate Doc. 229, 26th Cong., 2nd sess., serial 378. *Improvement to the System of Artillery.*

House Doc. 8, 27th Cong., 1st sess., serial 397. *Pennsylvania—National Foundry. Danville.*

House Doc. 36, 27th Cong., 2nd sess., serial 402. *Alabama Legislature—National Armory at Great Falls of Tallapoosa River.*

House Doc. 149, 27th Cong., 2nd sess., serial 403. *Western Armory.*

House Doc. 207, 27th Cong., 2nd sess., serial 404. *Armory, Springfield, Massachusetts.*

House Doc. 262, 27th Cong., 2nd sess., serial 405. *Correspondence—Secretary of War and Commanding Officer in Florida.*

House Report 830, 27th Cong., 2nd sess., serial 410. *Military Posts—Council Bluffs to the Pacific Ocean.*

Senate Doc. 243, 27th Cong., 3rd sess., serial 416. *A Report on the Exploration of the Country lying between the Missouri River and the Rocky Mountains to the Line of the Kansas and Great Platte Rivers.*

House Doc. 133, 27th Cong., 3rd sess., serial 421. *Site for a Western Armory.*

House Doc. 219, 27th Cong., 3rd sess., serial 425. *Right of President to withhold papers—frauds on Indians.*

Senate Doc. 206, 28th Cong., 1st sess., serial 434. *Naval Depot and National Armory at Vicksburg, Mississippi.*

House Doc. 33, 28th Cong., 1st sess., serial 441. *Western Armory and Naval Depot and Dock-Yard.*

House Doc. 119, 28th Cong., 1st sess., serial 442. *Naval Depot and Armory at Natchez and Adams County, Mississippi.*

House Doc. 225, 28th Cong., 1st sess., serial 443. *United States Troops in Rhode Island.*

House Report 77, 28th Cong., 1st sess., serial 445. *Remounting the Second Regiment Dragoons.*

House Report 441, 28th Cong., 1st sess., serial 446. *Armory at Massac, Illinois.*

House Report 455, 28th Cong., 1st sess., serial 446. *National Foundries.*

House Report 546, 28th Cong., 1st sess., serial 447. *Interference of the Executive in the Affairs of Rhode Island.*

Senate Doc. 85, 28th Cong., 1st sess., serial 451. *Report on National Defense, by Lieutenant Halleck.*

House Doc. 166, 28th Cong., 2nd sess., serial 467. *Report of the Exploring Expedition to the Rocky Mountains in the Year 1842, and to Oregon and North California in the Years 1843–44.*

House Report 27, 28th Cong., 2nd sess., serial 468. *National Foundries.*

Senate Doc. 337, 29th Cong., 1st sess., serial 476. *Information of the existing relations between the United States and Mexico.*

Senate Doc. 378, 29th Cong., 1st sess., serial 477. *Calling of Volunteers or Militia into the Service of the United States . . . without legal authority.*

Senate Doc. 402, 29th Cong., 1st sess., serial 477. *Letter from Major General Gaines to the War Department, in relation to calls made by him for volunteers and militia.*

House Report 576, 29th Cong., 1st sess., serial 490. *Lieutenant M. Thomas.*

Senate Ex. Doc. 7, 30th Cong., 1st sess., serial 505. Emory, William H. *Notes of a Military Reconnaissance, from Fort Leavenworth, in Missouri, to San Diego, in California, including parts of the Arkansas, Del Norte, and Gila Rivers.*

Senate Ex. Doc. 33, 30th Cong., 1st sess., serial 507. *Court Martial in the Trial of Lieutenant Colonel Fremont.*
Senate Report 226, 30th Cong., 1st sess., serial 512. *Report on Fremont Expedition.*
House Ex. Doc. 8, 30th Cong., 1st sess., serial 515. *Message of the President of the United States.*
House Ex. Doc. 60, 30th Cong., 1st sess., serial 520. *Mexican War.*
House Ex. Doc. 70, 30th Cong., 1st sess., serial 521. *New Mexico and California.*
Senate Ex. Doc. 31, 30th Cong., 2nd sess., serial 531. *Commodore Stockton's Despatches, Relating to the Military and Naval Operations in California.*
Senate Report 276, 30th Cong., 2nd sess., serial 535. *Report of Committee on Military Affairs.*
House Ex. Doc. 7, 30th Cong., 2nd sess., serial 538. *Finances. Letter from the Secretary of the Treasury.*
Senate Ex. Doc. 52, 31st Cong., 1st sess., serial 561. *Formation of a State Government in California.*
Senate Ex. Doc. 64, 31st Cong., 1st sess., serial 562. *Reconnaissances of Routes from San Antonio to El Paso.*
House Ex. Doc. 17, 31st Cong., 1st sess., serial 573. *California and New Mexico.*
House Ex. Doc. 66, 31st Cong., 1st sess., serial 577. *Claims of Texas to the Territory of New Mexico.*
Senate Ex. Doc. 1, 32nd Cong., 1st sess., serial 613. *Annual Report of the Secretary of the Interior.*
House Report 169, 32nd Cong., 1st sess., serial 656. *National Armories.*
Senate Ex. Doc. 1, 33rd Cong., 1st sess., serial 690. *Annual Report of the Secretary of the Interior.*
Senate Ex. Doc. 29, 33rd Cong., 1st sess., serial 695. *Railroad from the Mississippi River to the Pacific Ocean.*
House Misc. Doc. 76, 33rd Cong., 1st sess., serial 741. *Superintendents of National Armories.*
House Report 191, 33rd Cong., 1st sess., serial 743. *National Armories.*
Senate Ex. Doc. 50, 33rd Cong., 2nd sess., serial 752. *Fort Leavenworth.*
Senate Ex. Doc. 58, 33rd Cong., 2nd sess., serial 782. *Fort Leavenworth.*
House Ex. Doc. 50, 33rd Cong., 2nd sess., serial 783. *Delaware Indians.*
Senate Ex. Doc. 76, 34th Cong., 1st sess., serial 822. *Explorations in the Dacota Country in the year 1855.*
Senate Ex. Doc. 91, 34th Cong., 1st sess., serial 823. *Grattan Massacre.*
Senate Ex. Doc. 97, 34th Cong., 1st sess., serial 823. *Instructions sent to military officers in Kansas.*
Senate Ex. Doc. 96, 34th Cong., 1st sess., serial 827. *Statistical Report on the Sickness and Mortality in the Army.*
House Ex. Doc. 93, 34th Cong., 1st sess., serial 858. *Indian Hostilities in Oregon and Washington.*
Senate Ex. Doc. 34, 34th Cong., 3rd. sess., serial 880. *Pay and emoluments of Lieutenant General Scott.*
Senate Ex. Doc. 36, 34th Cong., 3rd sess., serial 880. *Letter on Proposed Niagara River Survey.*

Senate Ex. Doc. 1, 35th Cong., Special Senate Session 1, serial 916. *Report of Captain George B. McClellan, One of the Officers Sent to the Seat of War in Europe, 1855 and 1856.*

Senate Ex. Doc. 11, pt. 1, 35th Cong., 1st sess., serial 919. *Commissioner of Indian Affairs, Annual Report.*

Senate Ex. Doc. 17, 35th Cong., 1st sess., serial 923. *Correspondence of John W. Geary.*

House Ex. Doc. 45, 35th Cong., 1st sess., serial 955. *Expenses of the Indian Wars in Washington and Oregon Territories.*

House Ex. Doc. 88, 35th Cong., 1st sess., serial 956. *Correspondence Between the Late Secretary of War and General Wool.*

Senate Ex. Doc. 1, pt. 1, 35th Cong., 2nd sess., serial 974. *Annual Report of the Secretary of the Interior.*

Senate Report 283, 36th Cong., 1st sess., serial 1040. *Amount Due the Choctaw Indians.*

House Ex. Doc. 52, 36th Cong., 1st sess., serial 1050. *Difficulties on Southwestern Frontier.*

House Ex. Doc. 69, 36th Cong., 1st sess., serial 1051. *Indian Hostilities in New Mexico.*

House Ex. Doc. 81, 36th Cong., 1st sess., serial 1056. *Troubles on Texas Frontier.*

House Ex. Doc. 98, 36th Cong., 1st sess., serial 1057. *Correspondence with General Harney.*

House Ex. Doc. 65, 36th Cong., 1st sess., serial 1059. *Affairs in Oregon.*

House Report 648, 36th Cong., 1st sess., serial 1071. *Covote Investigation.*

House Ex. Doc. 24, 36th Cong., 2nd sess., serial 1097. *Indian Disturbances in the Territory of New Mexico.*

House Ex. Doc. 92, 37th Cong., 2nd sess., serial 1135. *Military and Naval Defenses.*

House Report 2, 37th Cong., 2nd sess., serials 1142–1143. *Government Contracts.*

Senate Ex. Doc. 27, 39th Cong., 1st sess., serial 1238. *Reports of the Assistant Commissioners of the Freedmen's Bureau.*

House Ex. Doc. 70, 39th Cong., 1st sess., serial 1256. *Wagon Road from Niobrara to Virginia City.*

House Report 30, 39th Cong., 1st sess., serial 1273. *Report of the Joint Committee on Reconstruction.*

Senate Ex. Doc. 26, 39th Cong., 2nd sess., serial 1277. *Sand Creek Massacre.*

Senate Report 156, 39th Cong., 2nd sess., serial 1279. *Condition of the Indian Tribes.*

House Ex. Doc. 23, 39th Cong., 2nd sess., serial 1288. *Protection Across the Continent.*

House Ex. Doc. 71, 39th Cong., 2nd sess., serial 1293. *Massacre of troops near Fort Phil Kearney.*

Senate Ex. Doc. 13, 40th Cong., 1st sess., serial 1308. *Origin and Progress of Indian Hostilities.*

House Ex. Doc. 20, 40th Cong., 1st sess., serial 1311. *Reconstruction.*

Senate Ex. Doc. 74, 40th Cong., 2nd sess., serial 1317. *Expense of Maintaining the Military Establishment in the Territories of New Mexico and Arizona.*

Senate Ex. Doc. 77, 40th Cong., 2nd sess., serial 1317. *Report of Brevet Brig. Gen. W. F. Raynolds on the exploration of the Yellowstone.*

House Ex. Doc. 1, 40th Cong., 2nd sess., serial 1326. *Annual Report of the Secretary of the Interior.*

House Ex. Doc. 57, 40th Cong., 2nd sess., serial 1330. *Removal of Hon. E. M. Stanton and Others.*
House Ex. Doc. 97, 40th Cong., 2nd sess., serial 1337. *Report of Indian Peace Commissioners.*
House Ex. Doc. 342, 40th Cong., 2nd sess., serial 1346. *General Orders—Reconstruction.*
Senate Ex. Doc. 13, 40th Cong., 3rd sess., serial 1360. *Battle of the Washita River.*
House Ex. Doc. 1, 41st Cong., 2nd sess., serial 1414. *Annual Report of the Secretary of the Interior.*
House Ex. Doc. 72, 41st Cong., 2nd sess., serial 1417. *James Belger.*
House Ex. Doc. 185, 41st Cong., 2nd sess., serial 1418. *Expedition against Piegan Indians.*
House Ex. Doc. 240, 41st Cong., 2nd sess., serial 1425. *Difficulties with Indian Tribes.*
House Ex. Doc. 269, 41st Cong., 2nd sess., serial 1426. *Piegan Indians.*
House Report 22, 42nd Cong., 2nd sess., serial 1529. *Affairs in the Late Insurrectionary States.*
House Ex. Doc. 1, pt. 1, 42nd Cong., 3rd sess., serial 1560. *Annual Report of the Secretary of the Interior.*
House Ex. Doc. 1, pt. 5, 43rd Cong., 1st sess., serial 1601. *Annual Report of the Secretary of the Interior.*
House Report 384, 43rd Cong., 1st sess., serial 1624. *Reduction of the Military Establishment.*
Senate Ex. Doc 5, 43rd Cong., 2nd sess., serial 1629. *Reports and Recommendations of Generals Pope and Ord Relative to the Ravages of Grasshoppers.*
House Ex. Doc. 1, pt. 1, 43rd Cong., 2nd sess., serial 1634. *Papers Related to the Foreign Relations of the United States.*
House Ex. Doc. 1, pt. 5, 44th Cong., 1st sess., serial 1680. *Annual Report of the Secretary of the Interior.*
House Misc. Doc. 56, 45th Cong., 2nd sess., serial 1808. *Reorganization of the Army.*
House Misc. Doc. 64, 45th Cong., 2nd sess., serial 1820. *Testimony Taken by the Committee on Military Affairs in Relation to the Texas Border Troubles.*
Senate Report 555, 45th Cong., 3rd sess., serial 1837. *Burnside Report.*
Senate Ex. Doc. 196, 47th Cong., 1st sess., serial 1992. *Appropriations and Expenditures for Public Buildings, Rivers and Harbors, Forts, Arsenals, Armories, and other Public Works.*
House Ex. Doc. 49, 49th Cong., 1st sess., serial 2395. *Report of the Board on Fortifications.*
Senate Ex. Doc. 97, 49th Cong., 2nd sess., serial 2448. *Report of Colonel Carrington on the Massacre near Fort Philip Kearney.*
House Report 1061, 51st Cong., 1st sess., serial 2810. *Desertions from the Army.*
Senate Ex. Doc. 7, 53rd Cong., 3rd sess., serial 3276. *Report on the Chicago Strike.*
House Doc. 353, 54th Cong., 2nd sess., serial 3550. *Annual Report of the American Historical Association, 1896.*
House Doc. 244, 55th Cong., 3rd sess., serial 3812. *Relief of People in the Yukon River Country.*
Senate Doc. 221, pts. 1 and 7, 56th Cong., 1st sess., serials 3859, 3865. *Report of the*

Commission Appointed by the President to Investigate the Conduct of the War Department in the War with Spain.

Senate Doc. 270, 56th Cong., 1st sess., serials 3870, 3871, 3872. *Food Furnished by Subsistence Department to Troops in the Field.*

House Doc. 605, 57th Cong., 1st sess., serial 4377. *Mountain Meadows Massacre.*

Senate Doc. 209, 57th Cong., 2nd sess., serial 4430. *Federal Aid in Domestic Disturbances, 1787–1903.*

House Doc. 439, pt. 3, 57th Cong., 2nd sess., serial 4534. *Reports of the Chief of Engineers and Officers of the Corps of Engineers.*

Senate Doc. 129, 61st Cong., 1st sess., serial 5568. *Precedents: Decisions on Points of Order with Phraseology in the United States Senate.*

War Department, Annual Reports

1828 Senate Doc. 1, 20th Cong., 2nd sess., serial 181.
1838 Senate Doc. 1, 25th Cong., 3rd sess., serial 338.
1839 House Doc. 2, 26th Cong., 1st sess., serial 363.
1840 Senate Doc. 1, 26th Cong., 2nd sess., serial 375.
1841 Senate Doc. 1, 27th Cong., 1st sess., serial 395.
1842 Senate Doc. 1, 27th Cong., 2nd sess., serial 413.
1843 Senate Doc. 1, 28th Cong., 1st sess., serial 431.
1844 Senate Doc. 1, 28th Cong., 2nd sess., serial 449.
1845 Senate Doc. 1, 29th Cong., 1st sess., serial 470.
1846 Senate Doc. 1, 29th Cong., 2nd sess., serial 493.
1847 Senate Doc. 1, 30th Cong., 1st sess., serial 503.
1848 House Doc. 1, 30th Cong., 2nd sess., serial 537.
1849 House Ex. Doc. 5, 31st Cong., 1st sess., serial 569.
1850 Senate Ex. Doc. 1, pt. 2, 31st Cong., 2nd sess., serial 587.
1851 Senate Ex. Doc. 1, 32nd Cong., 1st sess., serial 611.
1852 Senate Ex. Doc. 1, 32nd Cong., 2nd sess., serial 659.
1853 Senate Ex. Doc. 1, 33rd Cong., 1st sess., serial 691.
1854 Senate Ex. Doc. 1, 33rd Cong., 2nd sess., serial 747.
1855 Senate Ex. Doc. 1, 34th Cong., 1st sess., serial 811.
1856 Senate Ex. Doc. 5, 34th Cong., 3rd sess., serial 876.
1857 Senate Ex. Doc. 11, 35th Cong., 1st sess., serial 920.
1858 Senate Ex. Doc. 1, pt. 2, 35th Cong., 2nd sess., serial 975.
1859 Senate Ex. Doc. 2, 36th Cong., 1st sess., serial 1024.
1860 Senate Ex. Doc. 1, 36th Cong., 2nd sess., serial 1079.
1861 Senate Ex. Doc. 1, 37th Cong., 2nd sess., serial 1118.
1862 House Ex. Doc. 1, pt. 4, 37th Cong., 3rd sess., serial 1159.
1863 House Ex. Doc. 1, pt. 5, 38th Cong., 1st sess., serial 1184.
1864 House Ex. Doc. 38th Cong., 2nd sess., serial 1230.
1865 House Ex. Doc. 1, 39th Cong., 1st sess., serials 1249–1252.
1866 House Ex. Doc. 1, 39th Cong., 2nd sess., serial 1285.
1867 House Ex. Doc. 1, 40th Cong., 2nd sess., serial 1324.
1868 House Ex. Doc. 1, 40th Cong., 3rd sess., serial 1367.

1869 House Ex. Doc. 1, pt. 2, 41st Cong., 2nd sess., serials 1412–1413.
1870 House Ex. Doc. 1, pt. 2, 41st Cong., 3rd sess., serial 1446.
1871 House Ex. Doc. 1, pt. 2, 42nd Cong., 2nd sess., serial 1503.
1872 House Ex. Doc. 1, pt. 2, 42nd Cong., 3rd sess., serial 1558.
1873 House Ex. Doc. 1, pt. 2, 43rd Cong., 1st sess., serial 1597.
1874 House Ex. Doc. 1, pt. 2, 43rd Cong., 2nd sess., serial 1635.
1875 House Ex. Doc. 1, pt. 2, 44th Cong., 1st sess., serial 1674.
1876 House Ex. Doc. 1, pt. 2, 44th Cong., 2nd sess., serials 1742, 1745.
1877 House Ex. Doc. 1, pt. 2, 45th Cong., 2nd sess., serial 1794.
1878 House Ex. Doc. 1, pt. 2, 45th Cong., 3rd sess., serial 1843.
1879 House Ex. Doc. 1, pt. 2, 46th Cong., 2nd sess., serial 1903.
1880 House Ex. Doc. 1, pt. 2, 46th Cong., 3rd sess., serial 1952.
1881 House Ex. Doc. 1, pt. 2, 47th Cong., 1st sess., serial 2010.
1882 House Ex. Doc. 1, pt. 2, 47th Cong., 2nd sess., serial 2091.
1883 House Ex. Doc. 1, pt. 2, 48th Cong., 1st sess., serial 2182.
1884 House Ex. Doc. 1, pt. 2, 48th Cong., 2nd sess., serial 2277.
1885 House Ex. Doc. 1, pt. 2, 49th Cong., 1st sess., serial 2369.
1886 House Ex. Doc. 1, pt. 2, 49th Cong., 2nd sess., serial 2461.
1887 House Ex. Doc. 1, pt. 2, 50th Cong., 1st sess., serial 2533.
1888 House Ex. Doc. 1, pt. 2, 50th Cong., 2nd sess., serial 2628.
1889 House Ex. Doc. 1, pt. 2, 51st Cong., 1st sess., serial 2715.
1890 House Ex. Doc. 1, pt. 2, 51st Cong., 2nd sess., serial 2831.
1891 House Ex. Doc. 1, pt. 2, 52nd Cong., 1st sess., serial 2921.
1892 House Ex. Doc. 1, pt. 2, 52nd Cong., 2nd sess., serial 2930.
1893 House Ex. Doc. 1, pt. 2, 53rd Cong., 2nd sess., serial 3198.
1894 House Ex. Doc. 1, pt. 2, 53rd Cong., 3rd sess., serial 3295.
1895 House Doc. 2, 54th Cong., 1st sess., serial 3370.
1896 House Doc. 2, 54th Cong., 1st sess., serial 3478.
1897 House Doc. 2, 55th Cong., 2nd sess., serial 3630.
1898 House Doc. 2, 55th Cong., 3rd sess., serials 3744–3745.
1899 House Doc. 2, 56th Cong., 1st sess., serials 3899–3903.
1900 House Doc. 2, 56th Cong., 2nd sess., serials 4070–4076.
1901 House Doc. 2, 57th Cong., 1st sess., serials 4269, 4271, 4273.
1902 House Doc. 2, 57th Cong., 2nd sess., serials 4443, 4451.
1903 House Doc. 2, 58th Cong., 2nd sess., serials 4628, 4630, 4631.

Newspapers and Military Periodicals
Advocate of Peace (Boston)
Albany Argus
Albany Evening Journal
Albany Register
Alta California (San Francisco)
American Citizen (New York)
American Mercury (Hartford, CT)
American Railroad Journal (New York)

The Argus & Greenleaf's New Daily Advertiser (New York)
Arkansas Intelligencer (Van Buren)
Arizona Daily Miner (Prescott)
Army and Navy Chronicle
Army and Navy Journal
Aurora General Advertiser (Philadelphia)
Balance and State Journal (Albany, NY)
Baltimore Sun
Bangor Daily Whig & Courier
Bismarck Tribune
Boston Gazette
Boston Patriot
Californian (San Francisco)
California Star and Californian (San Francisco)
Centinel of Freedom (Newark)
Chicago Tribune
Christian Advocate and Journal and Zion's Herald (New York)
Christian Secretary (Hartford, CT)
Christian Watchman (Boston)
Cincinnati Commercial
City of Washington Gazette
Cleveland Daily Herald
Columbian Centinel (Boston)
Columbian Herald (Charleston, SC)
Columbian Patriot (Middlebury, VT)
Commercial Gazette (Boston)
The Constitution (Middleton, CT)
Courier-Journal (Louisville, KY)
The Crisis: Dedicated to the Support of Democratic Principles (Richmond)
Daily Age (Philadelphia)
Daily Arkansas Gazette (Little Rock)
Daily Bulletin (San Francisco)
Daily Globe (Washington)
Daily Missouri Republican (St. Louis)
Daily National Intelligencer (Washington)
Daily National Journal (Washington)
Daily Ohio Statesman (Columbus)
Daily Picayune (New Orleans)
Daily Sentinel (Raleigh)
Daily State Register (Des Moines)
Dakota Republican (Vermillion)
Evening Bulletin (San Francisco)
Evening Star (Washington)
Evening Telegraph (Boston)
Extra Globe (Washington)

Fayetteville Observer (NC)
Federal Gazette (Philadelphia)
Freedom's Champion (Atchison City, KS)
Georgia Telegraph (Macon)
Harper's Weekly
Hartford Daily Courant (Connecticut)
The Huntress (Washington)
Independent Chronicle (Boston)
Independent Gazeteer (Philadelphia)
Indianapolis Daily Sentinel
Inter-Ocean (Chicago)
The Liberator (Boston)
Log Cabin (New York)
Louisville Public Advertiser
The Mammoth (Hopedale Community, MA)
Maryland Journal (Baltimore)
Military and Naval Magazine of the United States
Milwaukee Sentinel
The Mississippian (Vicksburg)
Natchez Daily Courier
National Era (Washington)
National Gazette and Literary Register (Washington)
National Register
Newark Advocate
New London Bee (CT)
New Orleans Commercial Bulletin
New Orleans Republican
New Yorker
New York Evangelist
New York Herald
New York Journal
New York Spectator
New York Times
New-York Tribune
Niles' Register (Baltimore, Washington, Philadelphia)
North American and United States Gazette (Philadelphia)
North Carolina Journal (Halifax)
North Carolina Standard (Raleigh)
Ohio State Journal (Columbus)
Ohio Statesman (Columbus)
Oregon Statesman (Salem)
Pennsylvania Docket
People's Friend and Daily Advertiser (New York)
Philadelphia Aurora
Philadelphia Daily Age

Petersburg Index
Philadelphia Freeman's Journal
Philadelphia Inquirer
Philadelphia Magazine and Weekly Repertory
Pittsburgh Daily Post
Placer Times (Sacramento, CA)
Public Ledger (Philadelphia)
Raleigh Register and North Carolina Gazette
Republican or, Anti-Democrat (Baltimore)
Richmond Daily Enquirer and Examiner
Richmond Dispatch
Richmond Enquirer
San Antonio Daily Express
Southwestern Christian Advocate (New Orleans)
South-Western American (Shreveport, LA)
St. Louis Enquirer
Subterranean, United with the Workingmen's Advocate (New York)
The Sun (New York)
Telegraph (Columbia, SC)
Telegraph and Texas Register (Houston)
Texas Democrat (Austin)
Texas State Gazette (Austin)
United States Telegraph (Washington)
Virginia Free Press (Charleston)
Virginia Independent Chronicle (Richmond)
Washington Union
Washington Post
Weekly National Intelligencer (Washington)
Worcester Magazine . . . Containing Politicks, Miscellanies, Poetry, and News

Internet Resources

"Adams Family Papers: An Electronic Archive." Massachusetts Historical Society. www.masshist.org/digitaladams/archive.

"The American Presidency Project." University of California, Santa Barbara. www.presidency.ucsb.edu.

The Articles of Confederation and Perpetual Union. The Avalon Project: Documents in Law, History, and Diplomacy. Yale Law School. http://avalon.law.yale.edu/18th_century/contcong_07–12–76.asp.

Blackstone's Commentaries on the Laws of England. The Avalon Project: Documents in Law, History, and Diplomacy. Yale Law School. http://avalon.law.yale.edu/subject_menus/blackstone.asp.

The Documentary History of the Ratification of the Constitution Digital Edition. Ed. John P. Kaminski, Gaspare J. Saladino, Richard Leffer, Charles H. Schoenleber, and Margaret A. Hogan. Charlottesville: University of Virginia Press, 2009. http://rotunda.upress.virginia.edu/founders/RNCN.html.

"Draft Constitution for Virginia 1776." The Avalon Project: Documents in Law, History, and Diplomacy. Yale Law School. http://avalon.law.yale.edu/18th_century/jeffcons.asp.

Founders Online. Correspondence and Other Writings of Six Major Shapers of the United States. National Archives and Records Administration. www.founders.archives.gov.

Freedmen & Southern Society Project. www.freedmen.umd.edu/index.html.

Kurland, Philip B., and Ralph Lerner, eds. *The Founders' Constitution*. Online edition http://press-pubs.uchicago.edu/founders.

Marshall, John. *The Life of George Washington: Special Edition for Schools*. Ed. Robert Faulkner and Paul Carrese. Indianapolis: Liberty Fund, 2000. Online Library of Liberty. http://oll.libertyfund.org/titles/marshall-the-life-of-george-washington.

Naval History and Heritage Command. "Documentary Histories: Spanish-American War." www.history.navy.mil/research/publications/documentary-histories/united-states-navy-s.html.

Oberg, Barbara, and J. Jefferson Looney, eds. *The Papers of Thomas Jefferson Digital Edition*. Charlottesville: University of Virginia Press, Rotunda, 2008. www.upress.virginia.edu/content/papers-thomas-jefferson-digital-edition.

"Papers of the War Department, 1784 to 1800." Center for History and New Media. George Mason University. http://wardepartmentpapers.org.

"Printed Ephemera: Three Centuries of Broadsides and Other Printed Ephemera." Library of Congress. www.loc.gov/collections/broadsides-and-other-printed-ephemera.

Ramsay, David. *The History of the American Revolution in Two Volumes*. Indianapolis: Liberty Fund, 1990. Online Library of Liberty. http://oll.libertyfund.org/titles/ramsay-the-history-of-the-american-revolution-2-vols.

"Wood to the Texas Senate." Texas State Library and Archives Commission. www.tsl.state.tx.us/governors/earlystate/wood-2–1.html.

Books

Abbott, W. W., ed. *The Papers of George Washington: Retirement Series*. 4 vols. Charlottesville: University of Virginia Press, 1998–1999.

Abel, Annie H., ed. *The Official Correspondence of James S. Calhoun*. Washington, D.C.: Government Printing Office, 1915.

Adams, Charles Francis, ed. *Memoirs of John Q. Adams*. 12 vols. Philadelphia: J. B. Lippincott, 1874–1877.

———. *The Works of John Adams, Second President of the United States*. 10 vols. Boston: Little, Brown, 1850–1856.

Adams, Henry. *The Education of Henry Adams: An Autobiography*. Boston: Houghton & Mifflin Co., 1918.

Adams, Henry, ed. *The Writings of Albert Gallatin*. 3 vols. Philadelphia: J. B. Lippincott, 1879.

Adjutant General's Office. *Chronological List of Actions, &c., with Indians, from January 15, 1837 to January 1891*. 1891; rpt. The Old Army Press, 1979.

Alger, Russell A. *The Spanish-American War*. New York: Harper and Bros., 1901.

Allart, Linda, and David W. Hill, eds. *The Journals and Miscellaneous Notebooks of Ralph Waldo Emerson.* Vol. 15. Cambridge: Belknap Press of Harvard University Press, 1982.

Ames, Seth, ed. *Works of Fisher Ames, with a Selection from his Speeches and Correspondence.* Boston: Little, Brown and Co., 1854.

Anderson, Gary, and Alan R. Woolworth. *Through Dakota Eyes: Narrative Accounts of the Minnesota Indian War of 1862.* St. Paul: Minnesota Historical Society Press, 1988.

An Artillery Officer in the Mexican War, 1846–7: Letters of Robert Anderson. New York: Knickerbocker Press, 1911.

Atwater, Caleb. *Remarks made on a Tour to Prairie du Chien; thence to Washington City, in 1829.* Columbus, OH: Isaac N. Whiting, 1831.

Ballentine, George. *Autobiography of an English Soldier in the United States Army.* 2 vols. London: Hurst and Blackett, 1853.

Bandel, Eugene. *Frontier Life in the Army, 1854–1861.* Ed. Ralph P. Bieber. Glendale, CA: Arthur H. Clark Co., 1932.

Barnes, Thurlow Weed. *Memoir of Thurlow Weed.* 2 vols. Boston: Houghton, Mifflin and Co., 1884.

Basler, Roy P. *The Collected Works of Abraham Lincoln.* 9 vols. New Brunswick: Rutgers University Press, 1953–1955.

Bassett, John Spencer, ed. *Correspondence of Andrew Jackson.* 7 vols. 1926–1933; rpt. New York: Kraus Reprint, 1969.

Benet, Stephen B. *A Collection of Annual Reports and other Important Papers, Relating to the Ordnance Department.* 3 vols. Washington, D.C.: Government Printing Office, 1880.

Benton, Thomas Hart. *Thirty Years' View; or, a History of the Working of the American Government for Thirty Years, from 1820 to 1850.* 2 vols. New York: D. Appleton and Co., 1858.

Berlin, Ira, ed. *Freedom: A Documentary History of Emancipation, 1861–1867.* Series II. *The Black Military Experience.* Cambridge: Cambridge University Press, 1982.

Bigelow, John. *Retrospections of an Active Life.* 5 vols. New York: Baker Taylor & Co., 1909–1913.

Blassingame, John W., ed. *Frederick Douglass Papers*, Series I. *Speeches, Debates, and Interviews.* Volume 3, *1855–63.* New Haven: Yale University Press, 1985.

———, ed. *Slave Testimony: Two Centuries of Letters, Speeches, Interviews, and Autobiographies.* Baton Rouge: Louisiana State University Press, 1977.

Bourke, John G. *On the Border with Crook.* 1891; rpt. Lincoln: University of Nebraska Press, 1971.

Boyd, Mrs. Orsemus Bronson. *Cavalry Life in Tent and Field.* 1894; rpt. Lincoln: University of Nebraska Press, 1982.

Brockway, Beman. *Fifty Years in Journalism, Embracing Recollections and Personal Experiences with an Autobiography.* Waterton, NY: Daily Times Printing and Publishing House, 1891.

Brown, Everett S., ed. *William Plumer's Memorandum of Proceedings in the United States Senate, 1803–1807.* New York: Macmillan Co., 1923.

Browne, J. Ross. *Report of the Debates of the Convention of California, on the Formation of the State Constitution.* Washington, D.C.: John T. Towers, 1850.

Burnett, Edward C., ed. *Letters of Members of the Continental Congress.* 8 vols. Washington, D.C.: Carnegie Institution of Washington, 1921–1936.

Burrows, J. M. D. *Fifty Years in Iowa.* Davenport, Iowa: Glass & Co., 1888.

Burton, Clarence M., ed. *Michigan Pioneer and Historical Collections.* 2d ed. 40 vols. Lansing, MI, 1877–1929.

Cappon, Lester J. *The Adams-Jefferson Letters: The Complete Correspondence between Thomas Jefferson and Abigail and John Adams.* Chapel Hill: University of North Carolina Press, 1959.

Carnegie, Andrew. *Triumphant Democracy; or, Fifty Years' March of the Republic.* London: Sampson Low, Marston, Searle, & Rivington, 1886.

Carter, Robert G. *On the Border with Mackenzie.* 1935; rpt. Austin: Texas State Historical Association, 2007.

Cook, Frederick, and George S. Conover. *Journals of the Military Expedition of Major General John Sullivan Against the Six Nations of Indians in 1779.* Auburn, NY: Knapp, Peck, & Thompson, 1887.

Cooke, Philip St. George. *Scenes and Adventures in the Army; or, Romance of Military Life.* 1857; rpt. New York: Arno Press, 1973.

A Collection of Annual Reports and other Important Papers, Relating to the Ordnance Department . . . Prepared under the direction of Brig. Gen. Stephen V. Benét. 4 vols. Washington, D.C.: Government Printing Office, 1878–1890.

Correspondence of James K. Polk. 13 vols. to date. Knoxville: University of Tennessee Press, 1969–.

Correspondence of John Sedgwick, Major-General. 2 vols. Printed for Carl and Ellen Battelle Stoeckel, 1902–1903.

Crane, Charles J. *Experiences of a Colonel of Infantry.* New York: Knickerbocker Press, 1923.

Cruikshank, Ernest A. *The Correspondence of Lieut. Governor John Graves Simcoe.* 5 vols. Toronto: Ontario Historical Society, 1923–1926.

Cruse, Thomas. *Apache Days and After.* Caldwell, ID: Caxton Printers, 1941.

Cullen, Charles T., and Leslie Tobias, eds. *The Papers of John Marshall.* Vol. 4: *Correspondence and Papers, January 1799-October 1800.* Chapel Hill: University of North Carolina Press, 2015.

Cunningham, Noble E., ed. *Circular Letters of Congressmen to Their Constituents, 1789–1829.* 3 vols. Chapel Hill: University of North Carolina Press, 1978.

Dallas, George M., ed. *Life and Writings of Alexander James Dallas.* Philadelphia: J. B. Lippincott, 1871.

Davis, Charles Belmont, ed. *Adventures and Letters of Richard Harding Davis.* New York: Charles Scribner's Sons, 1917.

Dawes, Charles G. *A Journal of the McKinley Years.* Ed. Bascom N. Timmons. La Grange, IL: The Towers, 1950.

Dearborn, H. A. S. *Letters on the Internal Improvements and Commerce of the West.* Boston: H. P. Lewis, 1839.

Diary of Gideon Welles, Secretary of the Navy Under Lincoln and Johnson. 3 vols. Boston: Houghton & Mifflin, 1911.

Dippie, Brian W., ed. *Nomad: George A. Custer in Turf, Field and Farm.* Austin: University of Texas Press, 1980.

Documentary History of the First Federal Congress of the United States of America, March 4, 1789–March 3, 1791. 17 vols. Baltimore: Johns Hopkins University Press, 1972–2004.

Dodge, Grenville M. *Personal Recollections of President Abraham Lincoln, General Ulysses S. Grant, and General William T. Sherman.* Council Bluffs, IA: Monarch Printing Co., 1914.

Duncan, Russell, ed. *Blue-Eyed Child of Fortune: The Civil War Letters of Colonel Robert Gould Shaw.* Athens: University of Georgia Press, 1999.

The Education of Henry Adams: An Autobiography. Boston: Houghton Mifflin Co., 1918.

Elliott, Jonathan, ed. *Debates in the Several State Conventions on the Adoption of the Federal Constitution.* 5 vols. Washington, D.C.: n.p., 1836.

Ellsworth, Henry L. *Washington Irving on the Prairie; or, A Narrative of a Tour of the Southwest in the Year 1832.* New York: American Book Co., 1937.

Emerson, Ralph Waldo. *Essays & Lectures.* New York: Library of America, 1983.

Esarey, Logan, ed. *Governors Messages and Letters: Messages and Letters of William Henry Harrison.* 2 vols. Indianapolis: Indiana Historical Commission, 1922.

Explorer on the Northern Plains: Lieutenant Gouverneur K. Warren's Preliminary Report of Explorations in Nebraska and Dakota, in the Years 1855–'56–'57. Office of the Chief of Engineers: Government Printing Office, 1982.

Farrand, Max, ed. *The Records of the Federal Convention of 1787.* 4 vols. New Haven: Yale University Press, 1966.

The Federalist, with Letters of "Brutus." Ed. Terence Ball. Cambridge: Cambridge University Press, 2003.

Ferrell, Robert H., ed. *Monterrey is Ours! The Mexican War Letters of Lieutenant Dana, 1845–1847.* Lexington: University Press of Kentucky, 1990.

Fitzpatrick, John C., ed. *Writings of George Washington.* 39 vols. 1931–44; rpt. Westport, CT: Greenwood Press, 1970.

Flores, Dan L., ed. *Jefferson & Southwestern Exploration: The Freeman and Custis Accounts of the Red River Expedition of 1806.* Norman: University of Oklahoma Press, 1984.

Ford, Washington Chauncey, ed. *Letters of Henry Adams (1892–1918).* Boston: Houghton Mifflin Co., 1938.

Foreman, Grant, ed. *A Traveler in Indian Territory: The Journal of Ethan Allen Hitchcock, Late Major-General in the United States Army.* 1930; rpt. Norman: University of Oklahoma Press, 1996.

Fuller, Harlin M., and LeRoy R. Hafen, eds. *The Journal of Captain John R. Bell: Official Journalist for the Stephen H. Long Expedition into the Rocky Mountains, 1820.* Glendale, CA: Arthur H. Clark Co., 1973.

Fulton, Maurice Garland, ed. *Diary and Letters of Josiah Gregg.* 2 vols. Norman: University of Oklahoma Press, 1941.

Furber, George C. *The Twelve Months Volunteer; or, Journal of a Private in the Tennessee Regiment of Cavalry, in the Campaign, in Mexico, 1846–7.* Cincinnati: J. A. & U. P. James, 1850.

Gammel, H. P. N., comp. *The Laws of Texas, 1822–1897.* Austin: Gammel Book Co., 1898.

George, Henry. *Social Problems.* Chicago: Belford, Clarke & Co., 1883.

Gibbon, John. *Adventures on the Western Frontier.* Ed. Alan and Maureen Gaff. Bloomington: Indiana University Press, 2002.

Giddings, Luther. *Sketches of the Campaign in Mexico by an Officer of the First Ohio Volunteers.* New York: Putnam, 1853.

Glisan, R[odney]. *Journal of Army Life.* San Francisco: A. L. Bancroft and Co., 1874.

Gordon, George H. *A War Diary of Events in the War of the Great Rebellion: 1863–1865.* Boston: James R. Osgood and Co., 1882.

Grant, Ulysses S. *Memoirs and Selected Letters.* New York: Library of America, 1990.

Gurowski, Adam. *Diary.* Volume One. Boston: Lee and Shepard, 1862. Volume Two: New York: Carleton, 1864. Volume Three. Washington, D.C.: W. H. & O. H. Morrison, 1866.

Hackett, Mary A., et al., eds. *The Papers of James Madison: Secretary of State Series.* Vol. 8. Charlottesville: University of Virginia Press, 2007.

Hamilton, Alexander, James Madison, and John Jay. *The Federalist Papers.* With an introduction and commentary by Garry Wills. New York: Bantam Press, 1982.

Hamilton, J. G. de Roulhac, ed. *The Correspondence of Jonathan Worth.* 2 vols. Raleigh: Edward and Broughton, 1909.

Hamilton, Stanislaus M., ed. *The Writings of James Monroe.* 7 vols. New York: G. P. Putnam's Sons, 1898–1903.

Hamlin, Percy Gatling, ed. *The Making of a Soldier: Letters of General R. S. Ewell.* Richmond: Whitter & Shepperson, 1935.

Hammond, Otis G., ed. *The Utah Expedition, 1857–1858: Letters of Capt. Jesse A. Gove, 10th Inf., U.S. A., of Concord, N. H., to Mrs. Gove, and Special Correspondence of the New York Herald.* Concord: New Hampshire Historical Society, 1928.

Harris, Theodore D., ed. *Black Frontiersman: The Memoirs of Henry O. Flipper.* Fort Worth: Texas Christian University Press, 1997.

Henry, W. S. *Campaign Sketches of the War with Mexico.* New York: Harper & Brothers, 1847.

Hildreth, James. *Dragoon Campaigns to the Rocky Mountains, by a Dragoon.* 1836; rpt. New York: Arno Press, 1973.

Hitchcock, Ethan Allen. *Fifty Years in Camp and Field.* Ed. W. A. Croffut. New York: G. P. Putnam's Sons, 1909.

Hoffman, Charles F. *A Winter in the West.* 1835; rpt. Ann Arbor: University Microfilms, 1966.

Holzer, Harold, and Sara Vaughn Gabbard, eds. *1865: America Makes War and Peace in Lincoln's Final Year.* Carbondale: Southern Illinois University Press, 2015.

Howe, M. A. DeWolfe, ed. *Home Letters of General Sherman.* New York: Charles Scribner's Sons, 1909.

Hutchinson, William T., et al., eds. *The Papers of James Madison: Congressional Series.* 17 vols. Chicago and Charlottesville: University of Chicago Press and University Press of Virginia, 1962–1991.

Hutton, Paul Andrew, ed. *The Custer Reader.* Lincoln: University of Nebraska Press, 1992.

Irving, Washington. *The Adventures of Captain Bonneville, U.S.A., in the Rocky Mountains and the Far West.* Ed. Edgeley W. Todd. Norman: University of Oklahoma Press, 1961.

———. *A Tour on the Prairies.* Ed. John Francis McDermott. Norman: University of Oklahoma Press, 1956.

Jackson, Donald, and Mary Lee Spence, eds. *The Expeditions of John Charles Frémont.* 3 vols. Urbana: University of Illinois Press, 1970.

James, Edwin, comp. *Account of an Expedition from Pittsburgh to the Rocky Mountains, Performed in the Years 1819, 1820.* 3 vols. London: Longman, Hurst, Rees, Orme, and Brown, 1823

———, comp. *General Description of the country traversed by the Exploring Expedition, extracted from a report of Major Long to the Hon J. C. Calhoun, Secretary of War, dated Philadelphia, January 20th, 1821 in Account of an Expedition from Pittsburgh to the Rocky Mountains.* 2 vols. Ann Arbor: University Microfilms, 1966.

Jameson, J. Franklin, ed. *Correspondence of John C. Calhoun.* American Historical Association, *Annual Report*, 1899. Washington, D.C.: Government Printing Office, 1900.

Journal of the Constitutional Convention of the State of Illinois, Convened at Springfield, January 7, 1862. Springfield: Charles H. Lanphier, 1862.

Journal of the Convention Assembled at the City of Austin on the 4th of July 1845 for the Purpose of Framing a Constitution for the State of Texas. 1845; rpt. Austin: Shoal Creek Publishers, 1974.

A Journal of the Honourable House of Representatives at a General Court of the Commonwealth of Massachusetts . . . October 13–October 14, 1784. Boston [n.p.], 1784.

Keyes, E. D. *Fifty Years' Observations of Men and Events, Civil and Military.* New York: Charles Scribner's Sons, 1884.

Knopf, R. C., ed. *Anthony Wayne: A Name in Arms.* Pittsburgh: University of Pittsburgh Press, 1960.

———. *Campaign into the Wilderness: The Wayne-Knox-Pickering-McHenry Correspondence.* 5 vols. Columbus: Anthony Wayne Parkway Board, Ohio State Museum, 1955.

Kohn, Richard H., ed. *Anglo-American Antimilitary Tracts, 1697–1830.* New York: Arno Press, 1979.

Lamb, R. *An Original and Authentic Journal of Occurrences During the Late American War.* Dublin: Wilkinson & Courtney, 1809.

Lane, Lydia. *I Married a Soldier; or, Old Days in the Old Army.* 1893; rpt. Albuquerque: Horn and Wallace, 1964.

Latrobe, Charles J. *The Rambler in North America.* 2 vols. Second Edition. London: R. B. Seeley and W. Burnside, 1836.

Levenson, J. C., et al., eds. *The Letters of Henry Adams.* 6 vols. Cambridge: Belknap Press of Harvard University, 1982–1988.

Lowe, Percival Greene. *Five Years a Dragoon ('49 to '54) and other Adventures on the Great Plains.* Norman: University of Oklahoma Press, 1965.

Lumpkin, Wilson. *The Removal of the Cherokee Indians from Georgia. . . .* 2 vols. New York: Dodd, Mead & Co., 1907.

MacKinnon, William P., ed. *At Sword's Point*, Part I: *A Documentary History of the Utah War to 1858.* Norman, OK: Arthur H. Clark Co., 2008.

Maclay, Edgar S., ed. *Journal of William Maclay, United States Senator from Pennsylvania, 1789–1791.* New York: D. A. Appleton and Co., 1890.

Marquis, Thomas B., interpreter. *A Warrior Who Fought Custer.* Minneapolis: Midwest Co., 1931.

Marshall, J. T. *The Miles Expedition of 1874–1875: An Eyewitness Account of the Red River War.* Ed. Lonnie J. White. Austin: Encino Press, 1971.

Mayo, Robert. *Army and navy pension laws and bounty land laws of the United States: including sundry resolutions of Congress, from 1776 to 1852 . . .* Washington, D.C.: J. T. Towers, 1852.

———. *Army and navy pension laws and bounty land laws of the United States: including sundry resolutions of Congress, from 1776 to 1861 . . .* 4th ed. Washington, D.C.: W. H. & O. H. Morrison, 1861.

McClellan, George B. *McClellan's Own Story: The War for the Union, the Soldiers Who Fought It, the Civilians Who Directed It, and His Relations to It and to Them.* New York: Charles L. Webster & Co., 1887.

McConnell, H. H. *Five Years a Cavalryman: Or, Sketches of Regular Army Life on the Texas Frontier, 1866–1871.* 1889; rpt. Norman: University of Oklahoma Press, 1996.

McPherson, Edward. *The Political History of the United States during the Period of Reconstruction.* Washington, D.C.: Philp & Solomons, 1871.

———. *Political Manual for 1868: Including a Classified Summary of the Important Executive, Legislative, and Politico-Military Facts of the Period from April 1, 1867 to July 15, 1868.* Washington, D.C.: Philp & Solomons, 1868.

Meade, George Gordon, ed. *The Life and Letters of George Gordon Meade, Major-General United States Army.* 2 vols. New York: Charles Scribner's Sons, 1913.

Memoirs of Lieut.-General Scott, Written by Himself. New York: Sheldon and Co., 1864.

Miles, Nelson A. *Military Europe: A Narrative of Personal Observation and Personal Experience.* New York: Doubleday and McClure, 1898.

———. *Personal Recollections and Observations of General Nelson A. Miles . . .* 1896; rpt. Lincoln: University of Nebraska Press, 1996.

Miller, Darlis, ed. *Above a Common Soldier: Frank and Mary Clarke in the American West and Civil War.* Revised Edition. Albuquerque: University of New Mexico Press, 1997.

Morison, Elting E., ed. *The Letters of Theodore Roosevelt.* 8 vols. Cambridge: Harvard University Press, 1951–1954.

Moser, Harold D., ed. *The Papers of Daniel Webster: Correspondence* Vol. 5. Lebanon, NH: Dartmouth College Press, 1982.

Motte, Jacob R. *Journey into the Wilderness: An Army Surgeon's Account of Life in Camp and Field during the Creek and Seminole Wars, 1836–1838.* Ed. James F. Sunderman. Gainesville: University of Florida Press, 1953.

Murray, Charles Augustus. *Travels in North America during the Years 1834, 1835, & 1836.* 2 vols. New York: Harper and Brothers, 1839.

Nevins, Allen, ed. *The Diary of John Quincy Adams, 1794–1845: American diplomacy, and political, social, and intellectual life, from Washington to Polk.* New York, F. Ungar, 1951.

———, and Martin Hosley Thomas, eds. *The Diary of George Templeton Strong.* 4 vols. New York: Macmillan Co., 1952.

Oates, Stephen, ed. *Rip Ford's Texas.* Austin: University of Texas Press, 1963.

[O'Connor, Thomas]. *Impartial and Correct History of the War between the United States of America and Great Britain.* New York: John Low, 1815.

Official Letters of the Military and Naval Officers of the United States during the War with Great Britain in the Years 1812, 13, 14, & 15. With Some Additional Letters and Documents Elucidating the History of that Period. Washington, D.C.: Way & Gideon, 1823.

Oliphant, Laurence. *Minnesota and the Far West.* Edinburgh: William Blackwood and Sons, 1855.

Overfield, Lord J., II, comp. *The Little Big Horn 1876: The Official Communications, Documents and Reports; With Rosters of the Officers and Troops of the Campaign.* 1967; rpt. Lincoln: University of Nebraska Press, 1990.

The Papers of John C. Calhoun. 28 vols. Columbia: University of South Carolina Press, 1959–2003.

The Papers of Henry Clay. 10 vols. Lexington: University of Kentucky Press, 1959–1991.

The Papers of Jefferson Davis. 14 vols. Baton Rouge: Louisiana State University Prcss, 1971–2015.

The Papers of Andrew Jackson. 10 vols. to date. Knoxville: University of Tennessee Press, 1980–.

The Papers of Thomas Jefferson. 44 vols. to date. Princeton: Princeton University Press, 1950–.

The Papers of Andrew Johnson. 16 vols. Knoxville: University of Tennessee Press, 1967–2000.

The Papers of George Washington: Presidential Series. 21 vols. Charlottesville: University of Virginia Press, 1987–2020.

[Peck, John James]. *The Sign of the Eagle: A View of Mexico—1830 to 1850.* San Diego: Copley Press, 1970.

Personal Memoirs of P. H. Sheridan, General United States Army. 2 vols. New York: Charles L. Webster & Co., 1888.

Price, George A. *The Necessity for Closer Relations between The Army and The People and The Best Method to Accomplish The Result.* New York: G. P. Putnam's Sons, published for the Military Service Institution, 1885.

Proceedings of the Great Indian Peace Commission of 1867–1868. Washington, D.C.: Institute for the Development of Indian Law, 1975.

Prucha, Francis Paul, ed. *Army Life on the Western Frontier: Selections from the Official Reports Made Between 1826 and 1845 by Colonel George Croghan.* Norman: University of Oklahoma Press, 1958.

Quaife, Milo M., ed. *The Diary of James K. Polk During His Presidency, 1845–1849.* 4 vols. 1910; rpt. New York: Kraus, 1970.

Quincy, Josiah. *The Journals of Major Samuel Shaw, the First American Consul at Canton.* Boston: W. Crosby and H. P. Nichols, 1847.

Ramsey, David. *The Life of George Washington.* London: Luke Hanford & Sons, 1807.

Randall, James G., ed. *The Diary of Orville Hickman Browning.* 2 vols. Springfield: Illinois State Historical Library, 1933.

[Redfield, William]. *Sketch of the Geographical Rout[e] of a Great Railway. . . .* 2nd ed. New York: G. & C. & H. Carvill, 1830.

Redkey, Edwin S. *A Grand Army of Black Men: Letters from African-American Soldiers in the Union Army, 1861–1865.* Cambridge: Cambridge University Press, 1992.

Reminiscences of Chicago During the Great Fire. Chicago: Lakeside Press, 1915.

Richardson, James D. *A Compilation of the Messages and Papers of the Presidents, 1789–1908.* 10 vols. Bureau of National Literature and Arts, 1908.

Roberts, Madge Thornall, ed. *The Personal Correspondence of Sam Houston.* 4 vols. Denton: University of North Texas Press, 1996–2001.

Robinson, Charles. *The Kansas Conflict.* New York: Harper & Brothers, 1892.

Robinson, Charles M., III, ed. *The Diaries of John Gregory Bourke.* 5 vols. to date. Denton: University of North Texas Press, 2003–.

Rodenbough, Theo F. *From Everglade to Canyon with the Second United States Cavalry.* 1875; rpt. Norman: University of Oklahoma Press, 2000.

Roe, Frances M. A. *Army Letters from an Officer's Wife, 1871–1888.* New York: D. Appleton, 1909.

Russell, William Howard. *My Diary North and South.* Boston: T. O. H. P. Burnham, 1863.

Rutland, Robert A., et al., eds. *The Papers of James Madison: Presidential Series.* 10 vols. Charlottesville: University of Virginia Press, 1984–2020.

Ruxton, George F. *Adventures in Mexico and the Rocky Mountains.* London: John Murray, 1847.

Savage, John. *Our Living Representative Men. From Official and Original Sources.* Philadelphia: Childs & Peterson, 1860.

Schafer, Joseph, ed. and trans. *Intimate Letters of Carl Schurz, 1841–1869.* Madison: State Historical Society of Wisconsin, 1928.

Schmitt, Martin F., ed. *General George Crook: His Autobiography.* Revised Edition. Norman: University of Oklahoma Press, 1986.

Schofield, John M. *Forty-six Years in the Army.* 1897; rpt. Norman: University of Oklahoma Press, 1998.

Schoonover, Thomas D., ed. and trans. *Mexican Lobby: Matías Romero in Washington, 1861–1867.* Lexington: University Press of Kentucky, 1986.

Scott, Henry L. *Military Dictionary: Comprising Technical Definitions; Information on Raising and Keeping Troops; Actual Service, Including Makeshifts and Improved Matériel; and Law, Government, Regulation, and Administration Relating to Land Forces.* New York: D. Van Nostrand, 1861.

Scott, Hugh Lenox. *Some Memories of a Soldier.* New York: Century Company, 1928.

Seager, Robert, II, and Doris D. Maguire, eds. *Letters and Papers of Alfred Thayer Mahan.* 3 vols. Annapolis: Naval Institute Press, 1975.

Sears, Stephen W., ed. *The Civil War Papers of George B. McClellan: Selected Correspondence, 1860–1865.* New York: Ticknor and Fields, 1989.

Sheridan, P. H. *Report of an Exploration of Parts of Wyoming, Idaho, and Montana in August and September, 1882.* Washington, D.C.: Government Printing Office, 1882.

Sherman, William Tecumseh. *Memoirs.* New York: Library of America, 1990.

Showman, Richard K., ed. *The Papers of Nathanael Greene.* 13 vols. Chapel Hill: University of North Carolina Press, 1976–2005.

Simon, John Y. *The Papers of Ulysses S. Grant.* 31 vols. Carbondale: Southern Illinois University Press, 1967–2009.

———, ed. *The Personal Memoirs of Julia Dent Grant.* New York: G. P. Putnam's Sons, 1975.

Simpson, Brooks D., LeRoy P. Graf, and John Muldowny, eds. *Advice After Appomattox: Letters to Andrew Johnson, 1865–1866.* Knoxville: University of Tennessee Press, 1987.

Smith, Dwight L., ed. *From Greene Ville to Fallen Timbers: A Journal of the Wayne Campaign, July 28-September 14, 1794.* Indiana Historical Society Publications 16, no. 3. Indianapolis: Indiana Historical Society, 1952.

Smith, M[ichael]. *A Complete History of the Late American War with Great Britain and Her Allies.* 6th ed. Lexington, KY: F. Bradford, 1816.

Smith, Thomas T., et al., eds. *The Reminiscences of Major General Zenas R. Bliss, 1854–1876: From the Texas Frontier to the Civil War and Back Again.* Austin: Texas State Historical Association, 2007.

Smith, William Henry. *The St Clair Papers: The Life and Public Service of Arthur St. Clair*, 2 vols. Cincinnati: Robert Clarke, 1882.

[Stearns, Charles]. *The National Armories: A Review of the System of Superintendency, Civil and Military, Particularly with Reference to Economy, and General Management, of the Springfield Armory*, 2d ed. Springfield: G. W. Wilson's Steam Power Presses, 1852.

Story, Joseph. *Commentaries on the Constitution of the United States . . .* Boston: Hilliard, Gray and Co., 1833.

Strong, Henry W. *My Frontier Days & Indian Fights on the Plains of Texas.* N.p. N.d.

Summerhayes, Martha. *Vanished Arizona: Recollections of the Army Life of a New England Woman.* 1911; rpt. Lincoln: University of Nebraska Press, 1979.

Sumner, Charles. *Addresses on War.* Boston: Ginn & Company, 1904.

Sumner, William H. *An Inquiry into the Importance of the Militia to a Free Commonwealth . . .* Boston: Cummings and Hilliard, 1823.

Supplement to the Official Records of the Union and Confederate Armies. 100 vols. Wilmington, NC: Broadfoot Publishing, 1994–2001.

Syrett, Harold C., ed. *The Papers of Alexander Hamilton.* 26 vols. New York: Columbia University Press, 1962–1987.

Taylor, Joe F., ed. *The Indian Campaign on the Staked Plains, 1874–1875: Military Correspondence from War Department Adjutant General's Office, File 1815–1874.* Canyon, TX: Panhandle-Plains Historical Society, 1962.

Taylor, Robert J., et al., eds. *The Papers of John Adams.* Vol. 4. Cambridge: Harvard University Press, 1983.

Thayer, William Roscoe. *The Life and Letters of John Hay.* 2 vols. Boston: Houghton Mifflin, 1915.

Thompson, Jerry, ed. *Fifty Miles and a Fight: Major Samuel Peter Heintzelman's Journal of Texas and the Cortina War.* Austin: Texas State Historical Association, 1998.

Thornbrough, Gayle, ed. *Outpost on the Wabash, 1787–1791: Letters of Brigadier General Joseph Harmar and Major John Francis Hamtramck and other Letters and Documents from the Harmar Papers in the William L. Clements Library.* Indianapolis: Indiana Historical Society, 1957.

Thorndyke, Rachel Sherman, ed. *The Sherman Letters: Correspondence between General and Senator Sherman from 1837 to 1891.* New York: Charles Scribner's Sons, 1894.

Thorpe, T[homas] B[angs]. *Our Army at Monterey. . . .* Philadelphia: Carey and Hart, 1847.

Ticknor, George. *Life, Letters, and Journals.* 2 vols. Boston: Houghton Mifflin Co., 1909.

Tone, William Theobald Wolfe. *Essay on the Necessity of Improving our National Forces.* New York: Kirk and Mercein, 1819.

Upton, Emory. *The Armies of Asia and Europe: Embracing Official Reports of the Armies of Japan, China, India, Persia, Italy, Russia, Austria, Germany, France, and England.* New York: D. Appleton, 1878.

———. *The Military Policy of the United States.* Washington, D.C.: Government Printing Office, 1904.

Van Tyne, C. H., ed. *The Letters of Daniel Webster, From Documents Owned Principally by the New Hampshire Historical Society.* New York: McClure, Phillips & Co., 1902.

Vielé, Theresa Griffin. *Following the Drum: A Glimpse of Frontier Life.* 1858; rpt. Lincoln: University of Nebraska Press, 1984.

Wallace, Ernest, ed. *Ranald S. Mackenzie's Official Correspondence Relating to Texas, 1871–1873.* Lubbock: West Texas Museum Association, 1967.

Wallace, Lew. *Autobiography.* 2 vols. New York: Harper and Brothers, 1906.

Warren, Mercy Otis. *The Blockheads: or, The Affrighted Officers. A Farce.* Boston: n.p., 1776.

Wayland, Francis. *Report to the Corporation of Brown University on Changes in the System of Collegiate Education.* Providence: George H. Whitney, 1850.

Weems, M. L., and P[eter] Horry. *The Life of Gen. Francis Marion, a Celebrated Partisan Officer in the Revolutionary War.* 1809?; rpt. Philadelphia: Joseph Allen, 1833.

Whiting, Daniel P. *A Soldier's Life: Memoirs of a Veteran of 30 Years of Soldiering, Seminole Warfare in Florida, the Mexican War, Mormon Territory and the West.* Ed. Murphy Givens. Corpus Christi, TX: Nueces Press, 2011.

Wilhelm, Paul. *Travels in North America, 1822–1824.* Ed. Savoie Lottinville. Norman: University of Oklahoma Press, 1973.

Williams, Charles Richard, ed. *Diary and Letters of Rutherford Birchard Hayes.* 5 vols. Columbus: Ohio State Archaeological and Historical Society, 1922.

Wilson, George, comp. *Twentieth Annual Report of the Corporation of the Chamber of Commerce of the State of New York, for the Year 1877–78.* New York: Press of the Chamber of Commerce, 1878.

Wilson, Thomas. *The Biography of the Principal American Military and Naval Heroes: Comprehending Details of their Achievements during the Revolutionary and Late Wars.* 2 vols. New York: John Low, 1817–1819.

Winfrey, Dorman, and James M. Day, eds. *Texas Indian Papers.* 4 vols. Austin: Texas State Library, 1959–1961.

Wood, William C., ed. *Select British Documents of the Canadian War of 1812.* 3 vols. 1920–1928; rpt. New York: Greenwood Press, 1968.

Wooster, Robert, ed. *Recollections of Western Texas, Descriptive and Narrative, including an Indian Campaign, 1852–55, Interspersed with Illustrative Anecdotes, by Two of the U.S. Mounted Rifles.* Lubbock: Texas Tech University Press, 2001.

Articles

Abert, J. J. "Internal Improvement by Government—Pacific Railroad." *DeBow's Review* 12 (April 1852): 402–406.

Anderson, George S. "A Plan to Save the Forests: Forest Preservation by Military Control." *Century Illustrated Magazine* 49 (February 1895): 626–635.

"Army of the United States." *North American Review* 23 (October 1826): 245–274.

"Army Reduction." *Galaxy: A Magazine of Entertaining Reading* 21 (February 21, 1876): 260.

Bacon, Alexander S. "Is Our Army Degenerate?" *Forum* (March 1899): 11–24.

Beaumont, Eugene B. "Over the Border with Mackenzie." *United Service* 12 (March 1885): 281–288.

Benjamin, Anna North. "Women as Army Nurses: The American Woman in Action." *Frank Leslie's Popular Monthly* 48 (September 1899): 547–552.

Bland, Thomas A. "Abolish the Army." *Council Fire* 1 (December 1878): 189; 2 (January 1879): 5–6; 2 (March 1879): 36.

[Bragg, Braxton]. "Notes on Our Army." *Southern Literary Messenger* 10 (February 1844): 86–88.

Buecker, Thomas R., ed. "Letters of Caroline Frey Winne from Sidney Barracks and Fort McPherson, Nebraska, 1874–1878." *Nebraska History* 62 (Spring 1981): 1–46.

Campbell, W. A. "The Reorganization of Our Army." *United Service* 11 (April 1894): 305–316.

Carter, Robert G. "A Raid into Mexico." *Outing* 12 (April 1888): 1–9.

[Cass, Lewis]. "Removal of the Indians." *North American Review* 30 (January 1830): 62–121.

Childs, Ebenezer. "Recollections of Wisconsin Since 1820." *Report and Collections of the State Historical Society of Wisconsin* 4: 153–195.

"Coeur d'Alene Owners and Miners." *Locomotive Fireman's Magazine* 16 (September 1892): 780.

Connelley, William E., ed. "Journal of the Santa Fe Trail." *Mississippi Valley Historical Review* 12 (June 1925): 72–98; 12 (September 1925): 227–255.

Conover, Cheryl, ed. "Kentuckian in 'King Andrew's' Court: The Letters of John Waller Barry, Washington, D.C., 1831–1835." *Register of the Kentucky Historical Society* 89 (Spring 1983): 168–198.

Crabshaw, Timothy [pseud.]. "The Militia Muster: In a Letter to a Friend." *The Port Folio* (November 1817): 395–399.

Crimmins, Martin L., ed. "Freeman's Report on the Eighth Military Department." *Southwestern Historical Quarterly* 51 (July 1947): 54–58; 51 (October 1947): 167–174; 51 (January 1948): 252–258; 51 (April 1948): 350–357; 52 (July 1948): 100–108; 52 (October 1948): 227–233; 52 (January 1949): 349–353; 52 (April 1949): 444–447; 53 (July 1949): 71–77; 53 (October 1949): 202–208; 53 (January 1950): 308–319; 53 (April 1950): 443–73; 54 (October 1950): 204–218.

"Criticism—For the Port Folio." *The Port Folio*, New Series 8, no. 6 (December 1812): 551–552.

Davis, Richard Harding. "The Battle of San Juan." *Scribner's Magazine* 24 (October 1898): 387–403.

———. "The Porto Rico Campaign." *Scribner's Magazine* 24 (November 1898): 515–527.

"Democratic Candidates for the Presidency." *American Whig Review* 15 (April 1852): 311–316.

Dodge, Richard I. "The Enlisted Soldier." *Journal of the Military Service Institution of the United States* 8 (September 1887): 259–318.

Franklin, W. B. "National Defense." *North American Review* 137 (November 1883): 594–604.

Frémont, John Charles. "The Conquest of California." *Century Illustrated Magazine* 6 (April 1891): 917–928.

Fry, James B. "Origins and Progress of the Military Service Institution of the United States." *Journal of the Military Service Institution of the United States* 1 (May 1879): 20–32.

Gaines, Edmund P. "Military Importance of Railroads." *American Magazine of Useful and Entertaining Knowledge* 2 (March 1836): 283–284.

Garfield, James. "The Army of the United States." *North American Review* 126 (March-April 1878): 193–216; (May-June 1878): 442–465.

"General Gossip of Authors and Writers." *Current Literature: A Magazine of Contemporary Records* 29 (August 1900): 147–151.

Greene, F. V. "Our Defenceless Coasts." *Scribner's Magazine* 1 (January 1887): 51–66.

Griffin, Eugene. "Our Sea-Coast Defenses." *North American Review* 147 (July 1888): 64–75.

Henderson, Alfred J., and J. B. Duncan. "A Morgan County Volunteer in the Mexican War." *Journal of the Illinois State Historical Society* 41 (December 1948): 383–401.

Hosea, Lewis M. "The Regular Brigade of the Army of the Cumberland." In *Sketches of War History, 1861–1865: Papers Prepared for the Commandery of the State of Ohio, Military Order of the Loyal Legion of the United States*, ed. W. H. Chamberlin, A. M. Van Dyke, and George A. Thayer. Vol. 5, 329–360. Cincinnati: Robert Clarke Co., 1903.

Howard, Oliver O. "A Plea for the Army." *Forum* 23 (August 1897): 643–652.

[Hunt, Edward B.]. "Army Attack and National Defense." *American Whig Review* 4 (August 1846): 146–160.

Hull, John. "The Army Appropriation Bill." *Forum* 25 (May 1898): 396–402.

"Internal Improvements." *North American Review* 24 (January 1827): 1–22.

Kipling, Rudyard. "The White Man's Burden." *McClure's Magazine* 12 (February 1899): 4–5.

Knopf, Richard C., ed. "A Surgeon's Mate at Fort Defiance: The Journal of Joseph Gardner Andrews for the year 1795." *Ohio Historical Quarterly* 66 (nos. 1, 2, and 3, 1957): 57–86, 159–186, 238–268.

Kobbe, Gustav. "A Painter of the Western Frontier." *Cosmopolitan: A Monthly Illustrated Magazine* 31 (October 1901): 563–564.

McClellan, George B. "Army Organization." *Harper's New Monthly Magazine* Part I: 48 (April 1874): 670–680; Part II: 49 (June 1874): 101–111; Part III: 49 (August 1874): 401–411.

———. "The Regular Army of the United States." *Harper's New Monthly Magazine* 55 (October 1877): 774–782.

McDonough, James Lee, and William T. Alderson, eds. "Republican Politics and the Impeachment of Andrew Johnson." *Tennessee Historical Quarterly* 26 (Summer 1967): 177–183.

McPherson, Elizabeth G. ed. "Unpublished Letters from North Carolinians to Washington." *North Carolina Historical Review* 12 (April 1935): 149–172.

Miles, Nelson A. "The Lesson of the Recent Strikes." *North American Review* 159 (August 1894): 180–206.

Muir, John. "Yellowstone National Park." *Atlantic Monthly* 81 (April 1898): 509–522.

Olson, Gary D., ed. "Relief for Nebraska Grasshopper Victims: The Official Journal of Lieutenant Theodore E. True." *Nebraska History* 48 (Summer 1967): 119–140.

Parker, James. "The New Militia Act of 1903." *North American Review* 77 (August 1903): 278–287.

"The Park Grab." *Forest and Stream* 19 (January 4, 1883): 441.

"The Park Monopolists Checked." *Forest and Stream* 19 (January 11, 1883): 461–464.

Pearcy, Matthew T., ed. "Andrew Atkinson Humphreys' Seminole War Field Journal." *Florida Historical Quarterly* 85 (Fall 2006): 197–230.

Peck, Robert Morris. "Recollections of Early Times in Kansas Territory, from the Standpoint of a Regular Cavalryman." *Transactions of the Kansas State Historical Society* 8 (1903–4): 484–507.

"Poganuc People, and Other Novels." *Atlantic Monthly* 42 (October 1878): 430–437.

Pope, John. "The Second Battle of Bull Run." *Battles and Leaders of the Civil War* 2 (1885–1887): 449–494.

Reeve, Frank D., ed. "Puritan and Apache: A Diary." *New Mexico Historical Review* 23 (October 1948): 269–301.

Ruggles, George D. "The Proposed Increase of the Army." *North American Review* 159 (December 1894): 728–735.

Salter, William, ed. "Letters of Henry Dodge to General George W. Jones." *Annals of Iowa*, 3rd series, 3 (October 1897): 220–223.

Sampson, W. T. "Outline of a Scheme for the Naval Defense of the Coast." *Proceedings of the United States Naval Institute* 15 (no. 2, 1889): 169–232.

Sargent, Charles S. "The Care of the National Forest-reservations." *Garden and Forest: A Journal of Horticulture, Landscape Art and Forestry* 6 (August 23, 1893): 351–352.

Schindler, Harold. "The Bear River Massacre: New Historical Evidence." *Utah Historical Quarterly* 67 (Fall 1999): 300–308.

Schofield, J. M., and B. S. Alexander. "Documents: Pearl Harbor, 1873." *American Historical Review* 30 (April 1925): 560–565.

"Shall the U.S. Army be Increased?" *Chautauquan: A Weekly Newsmagazine* 20 (December 1894): 353.

Smalley, H. A. "A Defenceless Sea-Board." *North American Review* 138 (March 1884): 233–245.

Stacey, C. P., ed. "A Private Report of General Winfield Scott on the Border Situation in 1839." *Canadian Historical Review* 21 (December 1940): 407–414.

Sumner, E[dwin] V. "American Practice and Foreign Theory." *Journal of the U.S. Cavalry Association* 3 (June 1890): 141–150.

"Unpublished Letter of General Washington." *The Port Folio*, New Series 2, no. 6 (December 1812): 604–609.

Van der Zee, Jacob, ed. "Captain Edwin V. Sumner's Dragoon Expedition in the Territory of Iowa in the Summer of 1845." *Iowa Journal of History and Politics* 11 (April 1913): 258–267.

Wallace, William. "The Army and the Civil Power." *Journal of the Military Service Institution of the United States* 17 (March 1895): 235–266.

Wells, Henry P. "The Defense of Our Sea-Ports." *Harper's New Monthly Magazine* 71 (November 1885): 927–937.

Wetmore, W. Boecum. "The National Guard Bill in Congress." *United Service: A Quarterly Review of Military and Naval Affairs* 6 (March 1882): 337–343.

Wharton, Clifton. "The Expedition of Major Clifton Wharton in 1844." *Collections of the Kansas State Historical Society* 16 (1925): 272–305.

Whittaker, F[rederick]. "The American Army." *Galaxy: A Magazine of Entertaining Reading* 24 (September 1877): 390–399.

Williams, G. Mott, ed. "Letters of General Thomas Williams, 1862." *American Historical Review* 14 (January 1909): 304–328.

"Winthrop Sargent's Diary while with General Arthur St. Clair's Expedition Against the Indians." *Ohio Archaeological and Historical Society Publications* 33 (1924): 237–273.

Woodhull, A. A. "The Enlisted Soldier." *Journal of the Military Service Institution of the United States* 8 (March 1887): 18–68.

2. Secondary Sources

Books

Adams, George Rollie. *General William S. Harney: Prince of Dragoons.* Lincoln: University of Nebraska Press, 2001.

Adams, Kevin. *Class and Race in the Frontier Army: Military Life in the West, 1870–1890.* Norman: University of Oklahoma Press, 2009.

Allen, Robert S. *His Majesty's Indian Allies: British Indian Policy in the Defence of Canada, 1774–1815.* Toronto: Dundurn Press, 1992.

Anderson, Fred, and Andrew Cayton. *The Dominion of War: Empire and Liberty in North America, 1500–2000.* New York: Viking Penguin, 2005.

Anderson, Gary Clayton. *The Conquest of Texas: Ethnic Cleansing in the Promised Land, 1820–1875.* Norman: University of Oklahoma Press, 2005.

———. *Ethnic Cleansing and the Indian: The Crime That Should Haunt America.* Norman: University of Oklahoma Press, 2014.

———. *Kinsmen of Another Kind: Dakota-White Relations in the Upper Mississippi Valley, 1650–1862.* St. Paul: Minnesota Historical Society Press, 1984.

Angevine, Robert G. *The Railroad and the State: War, Politics, and Technology in Nineteenth Century America.* Palo Alto: Stanford University Press, 2004.

Ash, Stephen V. *A Massacre in Memphis: The Race Riot that Shook the Nation One Year after the Civil War.* New York: Hill and Wang, 2013.

Athearn, Robert G. *Forts of the Upper Missouri.* Lincoln: University of Nebraska Press, 1967.

Bailey, John W. *Pacifying the Plains: General Alfred Terry and the Decline of the Sioux, 1866–1890.* Westport, CT: Greenwood Press, 1979.

Baker, Jean H. *James Buchanan.* New York: Henry Holt, 2004.

Ball, Durwood. *Army Regulars on the Western Frontier, 1848–1861.* Norman: University of Oklahoma Press, 2001.

Balogh, Brian. *A Government Out of Sight: The Mystery of National Authority in Nineteenth-Century America.* Cambridge: Cambridge University Press, 2009.

Banks, William C., and Stephen Dycus. *Soldiers on the Home Front: The Domestic Role of the American Military.* Cambridge: Harvard University Press, 2016.

Barbuto, Richard V. *Niagara 1814: America Invades Canada.* Lawrence: University Press of Kansas, 2000.

Barksdale, Kevin T. *The Lost State of Franklin: America's First Secession.* Lexington: University Press of Kentucky, 2009.

Bartlett, Richard A. *Great Surveys of the American West.* Norman: University of Oklahoma Press, 1962.

Bauer, K. Jack. *The Mexican War, 1846–1848.* New York: Macmillan, 1974.

———. *Zachary Taylor: Soldier, Planter, Statesman of the Old Southwest.* Baton Rouge: Louisiana State University Press, 1985.

Bearss, Ed, and Arrell M. Gibson. *Fort Smith: Little Gibraltar on the Arkansas.* Norman: University of Oklahoma Press, 1969.

Beck, Paul N. *The First Sioux War: The Grattan Fight and Blue Water Creek, 1854–1856.* Lanham, MD: University Press of America, 2004.

Bell, Roger. *Last Among Equals: Hawaiian Statehood and American Politics.* Honolulu: University of Hawaii Press, 1984.

Bensel, Richard Franklin. *Yankee Leviathan: The Origins of Central State Authority in America, 1859–1877.* Cambridge: Cambridge University Press, 1990.

Bergeron, Paul H. *Andrew Johnson's Civil War and Reconstruction.* Knoxville: University of Tennessee Press, 2011.

———. *The Presidency of James K. Polk.* Lawrence: University Press of Kansas, 1987.

Bergmann, William H. *The American National State and the Early West.* Cambridge: Cambridge University Press, 2012.

Bigler, David T., and Will Bagley. *The Mormon Rebellion: America's First Civil War, 1857–1858.* Norman: University of Oklahoma Press, 2011.

Birtle, Andrew J. *U.S. Army Counterinsurgency and Contingency Operations Doctrine, 1860–1941.* Washington, D.C.: Center of Military History, 2001.

Blackhawk, Ned. *Violence over the Land: Indians and Empires in the Early American West.* Cambridge: Harvard University Press, 2006.

Bradley, Mark. *The Army and Reconstruction, 1865–1877.* Washington, D.C.: Center of Military History, 2015.

———. *Bluecoats and Tar Heels: Soldiers and Civilians in Reconstruction North Carolina.* Lexington: University Press of Kentucky. 2009.

Brandes, Stuart D. *Warhogs: A History of War Profits in America.* Lexington: University Press of Kentucky, 1997.

Bray, Kingsley M. *Crazy Horse: A Lakota Life.* Norman: University of Oklahoma Press, 2006.

Brereton, T. R. *Educating the U.S. Army: Arthur L. Wagner and Reform, 1875–1905.* Lincoln: University of Nebraska Press, 2000.

Browning, Robert. *Two If By Sea: The Development of American Coastal Defense Policy.* Westport, CT: Greenwood Press, 1983.

Burstein, Andrew. *The Passions of Andrew Jackson.* New York: Alfred A. Knopf, 2003.

———, and Nancy Isenberg. *Madison and Jefferson.* New York: Random House, 2010.

Budd, Richard M. *Serving Two Masters: The Development of American Military Chaplaincy.* Lincoln: University of Nebraska Press, 2002.

Byler, Charles A. *Civil-Military Relations on the Frontier and Beyond, 1865–1917.* Westport, CT: Praeger Security International, 2006.

Calloway, Colin G. *The American Revolution in Indian Country: Crisis and Diversity in Native American Communities.* Cambridge: Cambridge University Press, 1995.

Carlson, Paul. *"Pecos Bill": A Military Biography of William R. Shafter.* College Station: Texas A&M University Press, 1989.

Carp, E. Wayne. *To Starve the Army at Pleasure: Continental Army Administration and American Political Culture, 1775–1783.* Chapel Hill: University of North Carolina Press, 1984.

Casdorph, Paul D. *Confederate General R. S. Ewell: Robert E. Lee's Hesitant Commander.* Lexington: University Press of Kentucky, 2015.

Cashion, Ty. *A Texas Frontier: The Clear Fork Country and Fort Griffin, 1849–1887.* Norman: University of Oklahoma Press, 1996.

Castel, Albert E. *The Presidency of Andrew Johnson.* Lawrence: Regents Press of Kansas, 1963.

Cayton, Andrew R. L. *The Frontier Republic: Ideology and Politics in the Ohio Country, 1780–1825.* Kent, OH: Kent State University Press, 1986.

Chaffin, Tom. *Pathfinder: John Charles Frémont and the Course of American Empire.* Norman: University of Oklahoma Press, 2002.

Chalfant, William Y. *Cheyennes and Horse Soldiers: The 1857 Expedition and the Battle of Solomon's Fork.* Norman: University of Oklahoma Press, 1989.

Chaput, Erik J. *The People's Martyr: Thomas Wilson Dorr and His 1842 Rhode Island Rebellion.* Lawrence: University Press of Kansas, 2013.

Chernow, Ron. *Alexander Hamilton.* New York: Penguin Books, 2010.

———. *Washington: A Life.* New York: Penguin Books, 2010.

Cherrington, Ernest H. *The Evolution of Prohibition in the United States of America.* Watersville, OH: American Issue Press, 1920.

Cirillo, Vincent J. *Bullets and Bacilli: The Spanish-American War and Military Medicine.* New Brunswick: Rutgers University Press, 2003.

Clark, J. P. *Preparing for War: The Emergence of the Modern U.S. Army, 1815–1917.* Cambridge: Harvard University Press, 2017.

Clary, David A. *Fortress America: The Corps of Engineers, Hampton Roads, and United States Coastal Defense.* Charlottesville: University Press of Virginia, 1990.

Coakley, Robert W. *The Role of Federal Military Forces in Domestic Disorders, 1789–1878.* Washington, D.C.: Center of Military History, 1988.

Coffman, Edward M. *The Old Army: A Portrait of the American Army in Peacetime, 1784–1898.* New York: Oxford University Press, 1986.

Collins, Charles. *Apache Nightmare: The Battle at Cibecue Creek.* Norman: University of Oklahoma Press, 1999.

Connelly, Donald B. *John M. Schofield and the Politics of Generalship.* Chapel Hill: University of North Carolina Press, 2006.

Cooper, Jerry. *The Army and Civil Disorder: Federal Military Intervention in Labor Disputes, 1877–1900.* Westport, CT: Greenwood Press, 1980.

———. *The Rise of the National Guard: The Evolution of the American Militia, 1865–1920.* Lincoln: University of Nebraska Press, 1997.

Cooper, William J. *Jefferson Davis: American.* New York: Alfred A. Knopf, 2000.

Cosmas, Graham A. *An Army for Empire: The United States Army in the Spanish-American War.* Columbia: University of Missouri Press, 1971.

Cornell, Saul. *The Other Founders: Anti-Federalism and the Dissenting Tradition in America, 1788–1828.* Chapel Hill: University of North Carolina Press, 1999.

Cothran, Boyd. *Remembering the Modoc War: Redemptive Violence and the Making of American Innocence.* Chapel Hill: University of North Carolina Press, 2014.

Coulter, E. Merton. *Georgia: A Short History.* Chapel Hill: University of North Carolina Press, 1947.

Cowdrey, Albert E. *A City for the Nation: The Army Engineers and the Building of Washington, D.C., 1790–1967.* Washington, D.C.: Historical Division, Office of the Chief of Engineers, 1979.

Cozzens, Peter. *General John Pope: A Life for the Nation.* Urbana: University of Illinois Press, 2000.

Crackel, Theodore J. *Mr. Jefferson's Army: Political and Social Reform of the Military Establishment, 1801–1809.* New York: New York University Press, 1987.

Crapol, Edward P. *John Tyler: The Accidental President.* Chapel Hill: University of North Carolina Press, 2006.

Cress, Lawrence. *Citizens in Arms: The Army and the Militia in American Society to the War of 1812.* Chapel Hill: University of North Carolina Press, 1982.

Cunliffe, Marcus. *Soldiers & Civilians: The Martial Spirit in America, 1775–1865.* Boston: Little, Brown, 1968.

Cusick, James G. *The Other War of 1812: The Patriot War and the American Invasion of Spanish East Florida.* Gainesville: University Press of Florida, 2003.

Cutler, Donald L. *"Hang Them All": George Wright and the Plateau Indian War.* Norman: University of Oklahoma Press, 2016.

Cutrer, Thomas W. *Ben McCulloch and the Frontier Military Tradition.* Chapel Hill: University of North Carolina Press, 1993.

———. *Theater of a Separate War: The Civil War West of the Mississippi River, 1861–1865.* Chapel Hill: University of North Carolina Press, 2017.

Davis, William. *Jefferson Davis: The Man and His Hour.* New York: HarperCollins, 1991.

Dawson, Joseph G., III. *Army Generals and Reconstruction Louisiana, 1862–1877.* Baton Rouge: Louisiana State University Press, 1982.

———. *Doniphan's Epic March: The First Missouri Volunteers in the Mexican War.* Lawrence: University Press of Kansas, 1999.

Dobak, William A. *Fort Riley and Its Neighbors: Military Money and Economic Growth, 1853–1895.* Norman: University of Oklahoma Press, 1998.

———, and Thomas D. Phillips. *The Black Regulars, 1866–1898.* Norman: University of Oklahoma Press, 2001.

Donald, David. *Lincoln.* New York: Simon & Schuster, 1995.

Doubler, Michael D. *Civilian in Peace, Soldier in War: The Army National Guard, 1636–2000.* Lawrence: University Press of Kansas, 2003.

Dowd, Gregory Evans. *A Spirited Resistance: The North American Indian Struggle for Unity, 1745–1816.* Baltimore: Johns Hopkins University Press, 1992.

Downs, Gregory P. *After Appomattox: Military Occupation and the Ends of War.* Cambridge: Harvard University Press, 2015.

Dunlay, Tom. *Wolves for the Blue Soldiers: Indian Scouts and Auxiliaries with the United States Army, 1860–90.* Lincoln: University of Nebraska Press, 1982.

Edling, Max M. *A Hercules in the Cradle: War, Money, and the American States, 1783–1867.* Chicago: University of Chicago Press, 2014.

———. *A Revolution in Favor of Government: Origins of the U.S. Constitution and the Making of the American State.* New York: Oxford University Press, 2003.

Eicher, John H., and David J. Eicher. *Civil War High Commands.* Palo Alto: Stanford University Press, 2002.

Eisenhower, John S. D. *Agent of Destiny: The Life and Times of General Winfield Scott.* 1997; rpt. Norman: University of Oklahoma Press, 1999.

———. *So Far from God: The U.S. War with Mexico, 1846–1848.* 1989; rpt. Norman: University of Oklahoma Press, 2000.

Ellisor, John T. *The Second Creek War: Interethnic Conflict and Collusion on a Collapsing Frontier.* Lincoln: University of Nebraska Press, 2010.

Emerson, William K. *Marksmanship in the U.S. Army: A History of Medals, Shooting Programs, and Training.* Norman: University of Oklahoma Press, 2004.

Farley, James J. *Making Arms in the Machine Age: Philadelphia's Frankford Arsenal, 1816–1870.* University Park: Pennsylvania University Press, 1994.

Faust, Drew Gilpin. *This Republic of Suffering: Death and the American Civil War.* New York: Random House, 2008.

Ferling, John. *Almost a Miracle: The American Victory in the War of Independence.* New York: Oxford University Press, 2007.

———. *John Adams: A Life.* Knoxville: University of Tennessee Press, 1992.

———. *A Leap in the Dark: The Struggle to Create the American Republic.* New York: Oxford University Press, 2003.

———. *A Wilderness of Miseries: War and Warriors in Early America.* Westport, CT: Greenwood Publishing, 1980.

Fitzpatrick, David J. *Emory Upton: Misunderstood Reformer.* Norman: University of Oklahoma Press, 2017.

Foos, Paul. *A Short, Offhand, Killing Affair: Soldiers and Social Conflict during the Mexican-American War.* Chapel Hill: University of North Carolina Press, 2002.

Frazer, Robert W. *Forts and Supplies: The Role of the Army in the Economy of the Southwest, 1846–1861.* Albuquerque: University of New Mexico Press, 1983.

Frazier, Donald S. *Blood and Treasure: Confederate Empire in the Southwest.* College Station: Texas A&M University Press, 1995.

Frey, Sylvia R. *The British Soldier in America: A Social History of Military Life in the Revolutionary Period.* Austin: University of Texas Press, 1981.

Gaff, Alan D. *Bayonets in the Wilderness: Anthony Wayne's Legion in the Old Northwest.* Norman: University of Oklahoma Press, 2004.

Gallagher, Gary. *The Union War.* Cambridge: Harvard University Press, 2011.

Giesberg, Judith. *Army at Home: Women and the Civil War on the Northern Home Front.* Chapel Hill: University of North Carolina Press, 2009.

Gillett, Mary C. *The Army Medical Department, 1818–1865.* Washington, D.C.: Center of Military History, 1987.

———. *The Army Medical Department, 1865–1917.* Washington, D.C.: Center of Military History, 1995.

Gillette, William. *Retreat from Reconstruction, 1869–1879.* Baton Rouge: Louisiana State University Press, 1979.

Glasson, William H. *Federal Military Pensions in the United States.* Ed. David Kinley. New York: Oxford University Press, 1918.

Goetzmann, William H. *Army Exploration in the American West, 1803–1863.* New Haven: Yale University Press, 1959.

Gordon, Lesley J. *General George E. Pickett in Life and Legend.* Chapel Hill: University of North Carolina Press, 2002.

Gorenfeld, Will, and John Gorenfeld. *Kearny's Dragoons Out West: The Birth of the U.S. Cavalry.* Norman: University of Oklahoma Press, 2016.

Gould, Lewis L. *The Spanish-American War and President McKinley.* Lawrence: University Press of Kansas, 1982.

Greene, Jerome A. *American Carnage: Wounded Knee, 1890.* Norman: University of Oklahoma Press, 2014.

———. *Fort Randall on the Missouri, 1856–1892.* Pierre: South Dakota State Historical Society, 2005.

———. *Morning Star Dawn: The Powder River Expedition and the Northern Cheyennes, 1876.* Norman: University of Oklahoma Press, 2003.

———. *Nez Perce Summer, 1877: The U.S. Army and the Nee-Mee-Poo Crisis.* Helena: Montana Historical Society Press, 2000.

———. *Washita: The U.S. Army and the Southern Cheyennes, 1867–1869.* Norman: University of Oklahoma Press, 2004.

Grenier, John. *The First Way of War: American War Making on the Frontier, 1607–1814.* Cambridge: Cambridge University Press, 2005.

Grivas, Theodore. *Military Governments in California, 1846–1850.* Glendale, CA: Arthur H. Clark, 1963.

Gump, James O. *The Dust Rose Like Smoke: The Subjugation of the Zulu and the Sioux.* Lincoln: University of Nebraska Press, 1994.

Hagan, Kenneth J. *This People's Navy: The Making of American Seapower.* New York: Free Press, 1991.

Hall, John W. *Uncommon Defense: Indian Allies in the Black Hawk War.* Cambridge: Harvard University Press, 2009.

Hämäläinen, Pekka. *The Comanche Empire.* New Haven: Yale University Press, 2008.

Hampton, H. Duane. *How the U.S. Cavalry Saved Our National Parks.* Bloomington: Indiana University Press, 1971.

Hattaway, Herman, and Archer Jones. *How the North Won: A Military History of the Civil War.* Urbana: University of Illinois Press, 1983.

Hedren, Paul L. *Fort Laramie and the Great Sioux War.* 1988; rpt. Norman: University of Oklahoma Press, 1998.

———. *Powder River: Disastrous Opening of the Great Sioux War.* Norman: University of Oklahoma Press, 2016.

———. Preface and Introduction to *Campaigning with King: Charles King, Chronicler of the Old Army*, by Don Russell. Lincoln: University of Nebraska Press, 1991.

Heidler, David S., and Jeanne T. Heidler. *Old Hickory's War: Andrew Jackson and the Quest for Empire.* Baton Rouge: Louisiana State University Press, 2003.

Heitman, Francis B. *Historical Register and Dictionary of the United States Army, from its Organization, September 29, 1789, to March 2, 1903.* 2 vols. 1903; rpt. Urbana: University of Illinois Press, 1965.

Hendrickson, David C. *Peace Pact: The Lost World of the American Founding.* Lawrence: University Press of Kansas, 2003.

Herrera, Ricardo A. *For Liberty and the Republic: The American Citizen as Soldier, 1775–1861.* New York: New York University Press, 2015.

Herring, George C. *From Colony to Superpower: U.S. Foreign Relations since 1776.* New York: Oxford University Press, 2008.

Hickey, Donald R. *The War of 1812: A Forgotten Conflict.* Urbana: University of Illinois Press, 1989.

Hill, Forest G. *Roads, Rails and Waterways: The Army Engineers and Early Transportation.* Norman: University of Oklahoma Press, 1957.

Hinckley, Ted C. *The Americanization of Alaska, 1867–1897.* Palo Alto, CA: Pacific Books Publishers, 1972.

Hinderaker, Eric. *Elusive Empires: Constructing Colonialism in the Ohio Valley, 1673–1800.* Cambridge: Cambridge University Press, 1997.

Historical Statistics of the United States, Earliest Times to the Present. Millennial Edition. 5 vols. Cambridge: Cambridge University Press, 2006.

History of the U.S. Army Corps of Engineers. Alexandria, VA: Office of History, Headquarters, U.S. Army Corps of Engineers, 1998.

Hoagland, Alison K. *Army Architecture in the West: Forts Laramie, Bridger, and D. A. Russell, 1849–1912.* Norman: University of Oklahoma Press, 2004.

Hoganson, Kristin L. *Fighting for American Manhood: How Gender Politics Provoked the Spanish-American and Philippine-American Wars.* New Haven: Yale University Press, 1998.

Hoke, Donald R. *Ingenious Yankees: The Rise of the American System of Manufactures in the Private Sector.* New York: Columbia University Press, 1990.

Holt, Michael F. *By One Vote: The Disputed Presidential Election of 1876.* Lawrence: University Press of Kansas, 2008.

———. *The Rise and Fall of the American Whig Party: Jacksonian Politics and the Onset of the Civil War.* New York: Oxford University Press, 1999.

Hope, Ian C. *A Scientific Way of War: Antebellum Military Science, West Point, and the Origins of American Military Thought.* Lincoln: University of Nebraska Press, 2015.

Horsman, Reginald. *Race and Manifest Destiny: The Origins of American Racial Anglo-Saxonism.* Cambridge: Harvard University Press, 1981.

Hounshell, David A. *From the American System to Mass Production, 1800–1932: The Development of Manufacturing Technology in the United States.* Baltimore: Johns Hopkins University Press, 1984.

Howarth, Stephen. *To Shining Sea: A History of the United States Navy, 1775–1991.* New York: Random House, 1991.

Howe, Daniel Walker. *What Hath God Wrought: The Transformation of America, 1815–1848.* New York: Oxford University Press, 2007.

Hoxie, Frederick E. *Parading through History: The Making of the Crow Nation in America, 1805–1935.* Cambridge: Cambridge University Press, 1995.

Hsieh, Wayne Wei-siang. *West Pointers and the Civil War: The Old Army in War and Peace.* Chapel Hill: University of North Carolina Press, 2009.

Huntington, Samuel P. *The Soldier and the State: The Theory and Politics of Civil-Military Relations.* Cambridge: Belknap Press of Harvard University Press, 1957.

Hutton, Paul Andrew. *The Apache Wars: The Hunt for Geronimo, the Apache Kid, and the Captive Boy Who Started the Longest War in American History.* New York: Crown, 2016.

———. *Phil Sheridan and His Army.* Lincoln: University of Nebraska Press, 1985.

Isenberg, Andrew C. *The Destruction of the Bison, 1750–1920.* Cambridge: Cambridge University Press, 2000.

Isenberg, Nancy. *Fallen Founder: The Life of Aaron Burr.* New York: Viking Penguin, 2007.

Jackson, Donald. *Custer's Gold: The United States Cavalry Expedition of 1874.* 1966; rpt. Lincoln: University of Nebraska Press, 1972.

Jackson, W. Turrentine. *Wagon Roads West: A Study of Federal Road Surveys and Construction in the Trans-Mississippi West, 1846–1869.* New Haven: Yale University Press, 1963.

Jacobs, James Ripley. *The Beginning of the U.S. Army, 1783–1812.* Princeton: Princeton University Press, 1947.

Jennings, Nathan A. *Riding for the Lone Star: Frontier Cavalry and the Texas Way of War, 1822–1865.* Denton: University of North Texas Press, 2016.

Jensen, Laura. *Patriots, Settlers, and the Origins of American Social Policy.* Cambridge: Cambridge University Press, 2003.

John, Richard R. *Spreading the News: The American Postal System from Franklin to Morse.* Cambridge: Harvard University Press, 1995.

Johnson, Mark W. *That Body of Brave Men: The U.S. Regular Infantry and the Civil War in the West.* New York: Da Capo Press, 2003.

Johnson, Timothy D. *A Gallant Little Army: The Mexico City Campaign.* Lawrence: University Press of Kansas, 2007.

———. *Winfield Scott: The Quest for Military Glory.* Lawrence: University Press of Kansas, 1998.

Jones, Landon Y. *William Clark and the Shaping of the West.* New York: Hill and Wang, 2004.

Jordan, Brian Matthew. *Marching Home: Union Veterans and Their Unending Civil War.* New York: W. W. Norton, 2015.

Josephy, Alvin M., Jr. *The Civil War in the American West.* New York: Alfred A. Knopf, 1991.

Jung, Patrick J. *The Black Hawk War of 1832.* Norman: University of Oklahoma Press, 2007.

Keller, Morton. *Affairs of State: Public Life in Late Nineteenth Century America.* Cambridge: Harvard University Press, 1977.

Kemble C. Robert, *Image of the Army Officer in America: Background for Current Views.* Westport, CT: Greenwood Press, 1972.

Kenner, Charles L. *Black and White Together: Buffalo Soldiers and Officers of the Ninth Cavalry, 1867–1898.* Norman: University of Oklahoma Press, 1999.

Kieffer, Chester. *Maligned General: The Biography of Thomas Sidney Jesup.* San Rafael, CA: Presidio Press, 1979.

Kime, Wayne R. *Colonel Richard Irving Dodge: The Life and Times of a Career Army Officer.* Norman: University of Oklahoma Press, 2006.

Kiser, William S. *Coast-to-Coast Empire: Manifest Destiny and the New Mexico Borderlands.* Norman: University of Oklahoma Press, 2018.

———. *Dragoons in Apacheland: Conquest and Resistance in Southern New Mexico, 1846–1861.* Norman: University of Oklahoma Press, 2012.

Knouff, Gregory T. *The Soldiers' Revolution: Pennsylvanians in Arms and the Forging of Early American Identity.* University Park: Pennsylvania State University Press, 2004.

Kohn, Richard H. *Eagle and Sword: The Federalists and the Creation of the Military Establishment in America, 1782–1802.* New York: Free Press, 1975.

———, ed. *The United States Military Under the Constitution of the United States, 1789–1989.* New York: New York University Press, 1991.

Koistinen, Paul A. C. *Beating Plowshares into Swords: The Political Economy of American Warfare, 1607–1865.* Lawrence: University Press of Kansas, 1996.

———. *Mobilizing for War: The Political Economy of American Warfare, 1865–1919.* Lawrence: University Press of Kansas, 1997.

Korda, Michael. *Clouds of Glory: The Life and Legend of Robert E. Lee.* New York: HarperCollins, 2014.

Kreidberg, Marvin A., and Merton G. Henry. *History of Military Mobilization in the United States, 1775–1945.* Washington, D.C.: Department of the Army, 1955.

Lahti, Janne. *Cultural Construction of Empire: The U.S. Army in Arizona and New Mexico.* Lincoln: University of Nebraska Press, 2012.

———. *Wars for Empire: Apaches, the United States, and the Southwest Borderlands.* Norman: University of Oklahoma Press, 2017.

Lamar, Howard. *Dakota Territory: A Study of Frontier Politics, 1861–1889.* New Haven: Yale University Press, 1956.

———. *The Far Southwest, 1846–1912: A Territorial History.* New Haven: Yale University Press, 1966.

Lamb, Roger. *An Original and Authentic Journal of Occurrences During the Late American War.* New York: New York Times, 1968.

Lane, Jack C. *Armed Progressive: General Leonard Wood.* San Rafael, CA: Presidio Press, 1978.

Lang, Andrew F. *In the Wake of War: Military Occupation, Emancipation, and Civil War America.* Baton Rouge: Louisiana State University Press, 2017.

Larson, John Lauritz. *Internal Improvement: National Public Works and the Promise of Popular Government in the Early United States.* Chapel Hill: University of North Carolina Press, 2001.

Larson, Robert W. *Red Cloud: Warrior-Statesman of the Lakota Sioux.* Norman: University of Oklahoma Press, 1997.

Laumer, Frank. *Dade's Last Command.* Gainesville: University Press of Florida, 1993.

Laurie, Clayton D., and Ronald H. Cole. *The Role of Federal Military Forces in Domestic Disorders, 1877–1900.* Washington, D.C.: Center of Military History, 1997.

Leckie, Shirley A. *Elizabeth Bacon Custer and the Making of a Myth.* Norman: University of Oklahoma Press, 1993.

Leiker, James N. *Racial Borders: Black Soldiers along the Rio Grande.* College Station: Texas A&M University Press, 2002.

Lessoff, Alan. *The Nation and Its City: Politics, "Corruption," and Progress in Washington, D.C., 1861–1902.* Baltimore: Johns Hopkins University Press, 1994.

Levinson, Irving W. *War within War: Mexican Guerrillas, Domestic Elites, and the United States of America, 1846–1848.* Fort Worth: Texas Christian University Press, 2005.

Lewis, James E. *The Burr Conspiracy: Uncovering the Story of an Early American Crisis.* Princeton: Princeton University Press, 2017.

Linn, Brian McAllister. *The Echo of Battle: The Army's Way of War.* Cambridge: Harvard University Press, 2007.

———. *The Philippine War, 1899–1902.* Lawrence: University Press of Kansas, 2000.

Lowery, Charles D. *James Barbour, A Jeffersonian Republican.* University: University of Alabama Press, 1984.

Lubetkin, M. John. *Jay Cooke's Gamble: The Northern Pacific Railroad, the Sioux, and the Panic of 1873.* Norman: University of Oklahoma Press, 2006.

Magid, Paul. *The Gray Fox: George Crook and the Indian Wars.* Norman: University of Oklahoma Press, 2015.

Mahon, John K. *History of the Militia and the National Guard.* New York: Macmillan, 1983.

———. *History of the Second Seminole War.* Gainesville: University of Florida Press, 1967.

Main, Jackson Turner. *Political Parties before the Constitution.* Chapel Hill: University of North Carolina Press, 1973.

Malone, Laurence J. *Opening the West: Federal Internal Improvements Before 1860.* Westport, CT: Greenwood Press, 1998.

Marszalek, John F. *Assault at West Point: The Court-Martial of Johnson Whittaker.* 1972; New York: Collier Books, 1994.

———. *Sherman: A Soldier's Passion for Order.* New York: Free Press, 1993.

Martin, James Kirby, and Mark Edward Lender. *A Respectable Army: The Military Origins of the Republic, 1763–1789.* Arlington Heights, IL: Harlan Davison, 1982.

May, Robert E. *Manifest Destiny's Underworld: Filibustering in Antebellum America.* Chapel Hill: University of North Carolina Press, 2002. Kindle Edition.

McCaffrey, James M. *The Army in Transformation, 1790–1860.* Westport, CT: Greenwood Press, 2006.

———. *Army of Manifest Destiny: The American Soldier in the Mexican War, 1846–1848.* New York: New York University Press, 1992.

McConnell, Stuart. *Glorious Contentment: The Grand Army of the Republic, 1865–1900.* Chapel Hill: University of North Carolina Press, 1992.

McCullough, Matthew. *The Cross of War: Christian Nationalism and U.S. Expansion in the Spanish-American War.* Madison: University of Wisconsin Press, 2014.

McDonald, Forrest. *We the People: The Economic Origins of the Constitution.* Chicago: University of Chicago Press, 1958.

McDonough, James Lee. *William Tecumseh Sherman: In the Service of My Country, A Life.* New York: W. W. Norton, 2016.

McInnis, Verity. *Women of Empire: Nineteenth-Century Army Officers' Wives in India and the U.S. West.* Norman: University of Oklahoma Press, 2017.

McKitrick, Eric L. *Andrew Johnson and Reconstruction.* Chicago: University of Chicago Press, 1960.

McPherson, James M. *Battle Cry of Freedom: The Civil War Era.* New York: Oxford University Press, 1988.

McWhiney, Grady. *Braxton Bragg and Confederate Defeat.* New York: Columbia University Press, 1969.

Meyer, David R. *Networked Machinists: High-Technology Industries in Antebellum America.* Baltimore: Johns Hopkins University Press, 2006.

———. *The Roots of American Industrialization.* Baltimore: Johns Hopkins University Press, 2003.

Meyerson, Harvey. *Nature's Army: When Soldiers Fought for Yosemite.* Lawrence: University Press of Kansas, 2001.

Michno, Gregory F. *Depredation and Deceit: The Making of the Jicarilla and Ute Wars in New Mexico.* Norman: University of Oklahoma Press, 2017.

Miller, Darlis A. *Soldiers and Settlers: Military Supply in the Southwest, 1861–1885.* Albuquerque: University of New Mexico Press, 1989.

Missall, John, and Mary Lou Missall. *The Seminole Wars: America's Longest Indian Conflict.* Gainesville: University Press of Florida, 2004.

Moneyhon, Carl. *Texas after the Civil War: The Struggle of Reconstruction.* College Station: Texas A&M University Press, 2004.

Morris, John D. *Sword of the Border: Major General Jacob Jennings Brown, 1775–1828.* Kent, OH: Kent State University Press, 2000.

Morrison, James L., Jr. *"The Best School in the World": West Point, the Pre-Civil War Years, 1833–1866.* Kent, OH: Kent State University Press, 1986.

Moten, Matthew. *The Delafield Commission and the American Military Profession.* College Station: Texas A&M University Press, 2000.

Mullis, Tony R. *Peacekeeping on the Plains: Army Operations in Bleeding Kansas.* Columbia: University of Missouri Press, 2004.

Murphy, Douglas A. *Two Armies on the Rio Grande: The First Campaign of the US-Mexican War.* College Station: Texas A&M University Press, 2015.

Nacy, Michele J. *Members of the Regiment: Army Officers' Wives on the Western Frontier, 1890.* Westport, CT: Greenwood Press, 2000.

Nelson, Paul David. *Anthony Wayne: Soldier of the Early Republic.* Bloomington: Indiana University Press, 1985.

Ness, George T., Jr. *The Regular Army on the Eve of the Civil War.* Baltimore: Toomey Press, 1990.

Newell, Clayton R., and Charles R. Shrader. *Of Duty Well and Faithfully Done: A History of the Regular Army in the Civil War.* Lincoln: University of Nebraska Press, 2011.

Nichols, Roger L. *General Henry Atkinson: A Western Military Career.* Norman: University of Oklahoma Press, 1965.

Nichols, Roy F. *Franklin Pierce: Young Hickory of the Granite Hills.* Philadelphia: University of Pennsylvania Press, 1958.

Nielson, Jonathan M. *Armed Forces on a Northern Frontier: The Military in Alaska's History, 1867–1987.* New York: Greenwood Press, 1988.

Niven, John. *John C. Calhoun and the Price of Union: A Biography.* Baton Rouge: Louisiana State University Press, 1993.

———. *Martin Van Buren: The Romantic Age of American Politics.* New York: Oxford University Press, 1983.

Oliva, Leo E. *Soldiers on the Santa Fe Trail.* Norman: University of Oklahoma Press, 1967.

Onuf, Peter S. *Jefferson's Empire: The Language of American Nationhood.* Charlottesville: University Press of Virginia, 2000.

———. *The Mind of Thomas Jefferson.* Charlottesville: University of Virginia Press, 2007.

Orren, Karen, and Stephen Skowronek. *The Search for American Political Development.* Cambridge: Cambridge University Press, 2004.

Ostler, Jeffrey. *The Plains Sioux and U.S. Colonialism from Lewis and Clark to Wounded Knee.* Cambridge: Cambridge University Press, 2004.

Paludan, Philip Shaw. *A People's Contest: The Union and Civil War, 1861–1865.* New York: Harper and Row, 1988.

Parks, Joseph Howard. *General Edmund Kirby Smith, C. S. A.* Baton Rouge: Louisiana State University Press, 1954.

Paul, R. Eli. *Blue Water Creek and the First Sioux War, 1854–1856.* Norman: University of Oklahoma Press, 2004.

Peskin, Allan. *Winfield Scott and the Profession of Arms.* Kent, OH: Kent State University Press, 2004.

Peskin, Lawrence A. *Manufacturing Revolution: The Intellectual Origins of Early American Industry.* Baltimore: Johns Hopkins University Press, 2003.

Peterson, Norma Louis. *The Presidencies of William Henry Harrison and John Tyler.* Lawrence: University Press of Kansas, 1989.

Pinheiro, John C. *Manifest Ambition: James K. Polk and Civil-Military Relations during the Mexican War.* Westport, CT: Praeger Security International, 2007.

Prucha, Francis Paul. *American Indian Policy in the Formative Years: The Indian Trade and Intercourse Acts, 1790–1834.* 1962; rpt. Lincoln: University of Nebraska Press, 1970.

———. *Broadax and Bayonet: The Role of the United States Army in the Development of the Northwest, 1815–1860.* 1953; rpt. Lincoln: University of Nebraska Press, 1967.

———. *The Great Father: The United States Government and the American Indians.* Abridged Edition. Lincoln: University of Nebraska Press, 1986.

———. *The Sword of the Republic: The United States Army on the Frontier, 1783–1846.* London: Macmillan Co., 1969.

Quimby, Robert S. *The U.S. Army in the War of 1812: An Operational and Command Study.* East Lansing: Michigan State University Press, 1997.

Raines, Rebecca Robbins. *Getting the Message Through: A Branch History of the U.S. Army Signal Corps.* Washington, D.C.: Center of Military History, 1996.

Remini, Robert V. *Andrew Jackson & His Indian Wars.* New York: Viking Penguin, 2001.

———. *Andrew Jackson and the Course of American Democracy, 1833–1845.* New York: Harper and Row, 1984.
———. *Andrew Jackson and the Course of American Empire, 1767–1821.* New York: Harper and Row, 1977.
———. *Andrew Jackson and the Course of American Freedom, 1822–1832.* New York: Harper and Row, 1981.
———. *The Battle of New Orleans.* New York: Viking, 1999.
Resch, John. *Suffering Soldiers: Revolutionary War Veterans, Moral Sentiment, and Political Culture in the Early Republic.* Amherst: University of Massachusetts Press, 2000.
Richardson, Heather Cox. *West from Appomattox: The Reconstruction of America after the Civil War.* New Haven: Yale University Press, 2007.
Richter, William L. *The Army in Texas during Reconstruction, 1865–1870.* College Station: Texas A&M University Press, 1987.
Rippy, J. Fred. *Joel R. Poinsett: Versatile American.* Durham: Duke University Press, 1935.
Risch, Erna. *Quartermaster Support of the Army: A History of the Corps, 1775–1939.* Washington, D.C.: Center of Military History, 1989.
Robinson, Charles M., III. *Bad Hand: A Biography of General Ranald S. Mackenzie.* Austin: State House Press, 1993.
———. *The Fall of a Black Army Officer: Racism and the Myth of Henry O. Flipper.* Norman: University of Oklahoma Press, 2008.
———. *A Good Year to Die: The Story of the Great Sioux War.* Norman: University of Oklahoma Press, 1995.
Rowe, Mary Ellen. *Bulwark of the Republic: The American Militia in the Antebellum West.* Westport, CT: Praeger, 2003.
Royster, Charles. *A Revolutionary People at War: The Continental Army and American Character, 1775–1783.* 1979, rpt. New York: W.W. Norton, 1981.
Samet, Elizabeth. *Willing Obedience: Citizens, Soldiers, and the Progress of Consent in America, 1776–1898.* Palo Alto: Stanford University Press, 2003.
Satz, Ronald N. *American Indian Policy in the Jacksonian Era.* Lincoln: University of Nebraska Press, 1976.
Sawislak, Karen. *Smoldering City: Chicagoans and the Great Fire, 1871–1874.* Chicago: University of Chicago Press, 1995.
Schlicke, Carl P. *General George Wright: Guardian of the Pacific Coast.* Norman: University of Oklahoma Press, 1988.
Schubert, Frank N., ed. *The Nation-Builders: A Sesquicentennial History of the Corps of Topographical Engineers.* Washington, D.C.: Government Printing Office, 1989.
Scott, Pamela. *Capital Engineers: The U.S. Army Corps of Engineers in the Development of Washington, D.C., 1790–2004.* Alexandria, VA: U.S. Army Corps of Engineers, Office of History, 2005.
Secoy, Raymond. *Changing Military Patterns on the Great Plains (17th Century through Early 19th Century).* Locust Valley, NY: J. J. Augustin, 1953.
Sellers, Charles. *The Market Revolution: Jacksonian America, 1815–1846.* New York: Oxford University Press, 1991.

Shallat, Todd. *Structures in the Stream: Water, Science, and the Rise of the U.S. Army Corps of Engineers.* Austin: University of Texas Press, 1994.

Shy, John A. *A People Numerous and Armed: Reflections on the Military Struggle for American Independence.* New York: Oxford University Press, 1976.

Silver, James W. *Edmund Pendleton Gaines: Frontier General.* Baton Rouge: Louisiana State University Press, 1949.

Simpson, Brooks D. *Let Us Have Peace: Ulysses S. Grant and the Politics of War and Reconstruction, 1861–1868.* Chapel Hill: University of North Carolina Press, 1991.

Skaggs, David Curtis, and Larry L. Nelson, eds. *The Sixty Years' War for the Great Lakes, 1754–1814.* East Lansing: Michigan State University Press, 2001.

Skeen, C. Edward. *Citizen Soldiers in the War of 1812.* Lexington: University Press of Kentucky, 1999.

———. *1816: America Rising.* Lexington: University Press of Kentucky, 2003.

———. *John Armstrong, Jr., 1758–1843: A Biography.* Syracuse: Syracuse University Press, 1981.

Skelton, William B. *An American Profession of Arms: The Army Officer Corps, 1784–1861.* Lawrence: University Press of Kansas, 1992.

Skocpol, Theda. *Protecting Soldiers and Mothers: The Political Origins of Social Policy in the United States.* Cambridge: Belknap Press of Harvard University Press, 1995.

Skowronek, Stephen. *Building a New American State: The Expansion of National Administrative Capacities, 1877–1920.* Cambridge: Cambridge University Press, 1982.

Slaughter, Thomas P. *The Whiskey Rebellion: Frontier Epilogue to the American Revolution.* New York: Oxford University Press, 1986.

Smith, Carl. *Urban Disorder and the Shape of Relief: The Great Chicago Fire, the Haymarket Bomb, and the Model Town of Pullman.* Chicago: University of Chicago Press, 1995.

Smith, Jean Edward. *Grant.* New York: Simon & Schuster, 2001.

Smith, Mark A. *Engineering Security: The Corps of Engineers and Third System Defense Policy, 1815–1861.* Tuscaloosa: University of Alabama Press, 2009.

Smith, Merritt Roe. *Harpers Ferry Armory and the New Technology: The Challenge of Change.* Ithaca, NY: Cornell University Press, 1977.

Smith, Sherry L. *Sagebrush Soldier: Private William Earl Smith's View of the Sioux War of 1876.* Norman: University of Oklahoma Press, 1989.

———. *The View from Officers' Row: Army Perceptions of Western Indians.* Tucson: University of Arizona Press, 1990.

Smith, Thomas T. *The U.S. Army and the Texas Frontier Economy, 1845–1900.* College Station: Texas A&M University Press, 1999.

Spring, Matthew H. *With Zeal and Bayonets Only: The British Army on Campaign in North America, 1775–1783.* Norman: University of Oklahoma Press, 2008.

Stagg, J. C. A. *Mr. Madison's War: Politics, Diplomacy, and Warfare in the Early American Republic, 1783–1830.* Princeton: Princeton University Press, 1983.

Stallard, Patricia Y. *Glittering Misery: Dependents of the Indian Fighting Army.* Fort Collins and San Rafael, CO: Old Army Press and Presidio Press, 1978.

Starkey, Armstrong. *European and Native American Warfare, 1675–1815.* Norman: University of Oklahoma Press, 1998.

The Statistical History of the United States: From Colonial Times to the Present. New York: Basic Books, 1976.

Stevenson, Joan Nabseth. *Deliverance from the Little Big Horn: Doctor Henry Porter and Custer's Seventh Cavalry.* Norman: University of Oklahoma Press, 2014.

Stoltz, Joseph E. *A Bloodless Victory: The Battle of New Orleans in History and Memory.* Baltimore: Johns Hopkins University Press, 2017. Kindle e-book.

Stuart, Reginald C. *Civil-Military Relations During the War of 1812.* Santa Barbara: Praeger, 2009.

———. *War and American Thought: From the Revolution to the Monroe Doctrine.* Kent, OH: Kent State University Press, 1982.

Summers, Mark W. *The Plundering Generation: Corruption and the Crisis of the Union, 1849–1861.* New York: Oxford University Press, 1987.

Sword, Wiley. *President Washington's Indian War: The Struggle for the Old Northwest, 1790–1795.* Norman: University of Oklahoma Press, 1985.

Tate, Michael L. *The Frontier Army in the Settlement of the West.* Norman: University of Oklahoma Press, 1999.

———. *Indians and Emigrants: Encounters on the Overland Trails.* Norman: University of Oklahoma Press, 2006.

Taylor, Alan S. *The Civil War of 1812: American Citizens, British Subjects, Irish Rebels, & Indian Allies.* New York: Alfred A. Knopf, 2010.

Thian, Raphael P. *Notes Illustrating the Military Geography of the United States, 1813–1880.* Ed. John M. Carroll. Austin: University of Texas Press, 1979.

Thomas, Emory M. *Robert E. Lee: A Biography.* New York: W. W. Norton, 1997.

Thompson, Jerry. *Civil War to the Bloody End: The Life and Times of Major General Samuel P. Heintzelman.* College Station: Texas A&M University Press, 2006.

———. *Cortina: Defending the Mexican Name in Texas.* College Station: Texas A&M University Press, 2007.

Thornton, Russell. *American Indian Holocaust and Survival: A Population History since 1492.* Norman: University of Oklahoma Press, 1987.

Trask, David F. *The War with Spain in 1898.* New York: Macmillan, 1981.

Trefousse, Hans L. *Impeachment of a President: Andrew Johnson, the Blacks, and Reconstruction.* Knoxville: University of Tennessee Press, 1975.

Trennert, Robert A., Jr. *Alternative to Extinction: Federal Indian Policy and the Beginnings of the Reservation System, 1846–51.* Philadelphia: Temple University Press, 1975.

Twitchell, Ralph Emerson. *The History of the Military Occupation of the Territory of New Mexico from 1846 to 1851 by the Government of the United States.* Denver: Smith-Brooks Co., 1909.

Unruh, John D., Jr. *The Plains Across: The Overland Emigrants and the Trans-Mississippi West, 1840–60.* Champaign: University of Illinois Press, 1979.

Utley, Robert M. *Cavalier in Buckskin: George Armstrong Custer and the Western Military Frontier.* Norman: University of Oklahoma Press, 1988.

———. *The Commanders: Civil War Generals Who Shaped the American West.* Norman: University of Oklahoma Press, 2018.

———. *Frontier Regulars: The United States Army and the Indian, 1866–1891.* 1973; rpt. Lincoln: University of Nebraska Press, 1984.

———. *Frontiersmen in Blue: The United States Army and the Indian, 1848–1865.* 1967; rpt. Lincoln: University of Nebraska Press, 1981.

———. *The Lance and the Shield: The Life and Times of Sitting Bull.* New York: Henry Holt, 1993.

———. *The Last Days of the Sioux Nation.* New Haven: Yale University Press, 1963.

———, and Barry Mackintosh. *The Department of Everything Else: Highlights of Interior Department History.* Washington, D.C.: Government Printing Office, 1988.

Utset, Marial Iglesias. *A Cultural History of Cuba During the U.S. Occupation, 1898–1902.* Trans. Russ Davidson. Chapel Hill: University of North Carolina Press, 2011.

Van De Logt, Mark. *War Party in Blue: Pawnee Indian Scouts in the United States.* Norman: University of Oklahoma Press, 2010.

Wade, Richard C. *The Urban Frontier: The Rise of Western Cities, 1790–1830.* Cambridge: Harvard University Press, 1959.

Walling, Karl-Friedrich. *Republican Empire: Alexander Hamilton on War and Free Government.* Lawrence: University Press of Kansas, 1999.

Watson, Samuel J. *Jackson's Sword: The Army Officer Corps on the American Frontier, 1810–1821.* Lawrence: University Press of Kansas, 2012.

———. *Peacekeepers and Conquerors: The Army Officer Corps on the American Frontier, 1821–1846.* Lawrence: University Press of Kansas, 2013.

Watts, Steven. *The Republic Reborn: War and the Making of Liberal America, 1790–1820.* Baltimore: Johns Hopkins University Press, 1987.

Waugh, Joan. *U.S. Grant: American Hero, American Myth.* Chapel Hill: University of North Carolina Press, 2009.

Weber, David. *The Mexican Frontier, 1821–1846: The American Southwest under Mexico.* Albuquerque: University of New Mexico Press, 1982.

Weigley, Russell F. *The American Way of War: A History of United States Military Strategy and Policy.* New York: Macmillan Press, 1973.

———. *History of the United States Army.* Enlarged Edition. Bloomington: Indiana University Press, 1984.

Wert, Jeffry D. *Cavalryman of the Lost Cause: A Biography of J. E. B. Stuart.* New York: Simon & Schuster, 2008.

West, Elliott. *Contested Plains: Indians, Goldseekers, and the Rush to Colorado.* Lawrence: University Press of Kansas, 1998.

Wettemann, Robert P., Jr. *Privilege vs. Equality: Civil-Military Relations in the Jacksonian Era, 1815–1845.* Santa Barbara: Greenwood Press, 2009.

White, Richard. *The Republic for Which It Stands: The United States during Reconstruction and the Gilded Age, 1865–1896.* New York: Oxford University Press, 2017.

———, and Anthony McGinnis. *Counting Coup and Cutting Horses: Intertribal Warfare on the Northern Plains, 1738–1889.* Evergreen, CO: Cordillera Press, 1990.

Wickett, Murray R. *Contested Territory: Whites, Native Americans, and African Americans in Oklahoma, 1865–1907*. Baton Rouge: Louisiana State University Press, 2000.

Williams, T. Harry. *P. G. T. Beauregard: Napoleon in Gray*. Baton Rouge: Louisiana State University Press, 1955.

Wilson, James Harrison. *The Life of John A. Rawlins: Lawyer, Assistant Adjutant-General, Chief of Staff, Major General of Volunteers, and Secretary of War*. New York: Neale Publishing Co., 1916.

Wilson, Major T. *The Presidency of Martin Van Buren*. Lawrence: University Press of Kansas, 1984.

Wilson, Mark. *The Business of Civil War: Military Mobilization and the State, 1861–1865*. Baltimore: Johns Hopkins University Press, 2006.

Wiltse, Charles M. *Calhoun: Nationalist, 1782–1828*. Indianapolis: Bobbs Merrill, 1944.

Winders, Richard Bruce. *Mr. Polk's Army: The American Military Experience in the Mexican War*. College Station: Texas A&M University Press, 1997.

Wood, Gordon S. *Empire of Liberty: A History of the Early Republic, 1789–1815*. New York: Oxford University Press, 2009.

Woodman, Lyman L. *Duty Station Northwest: The U.S. Army in Alaska and Western Canada, 1867–1987*. 3 vols. Anchorage: Alaska Historical Society, 1996–1999.

Wooster, Robert. *The American Military Frontiers: The United States Army in the West, 1783–1900*. Albuquerque: University of New Mexico Press, 2009.

———. *Frontier Crossroads: Fort Davis and the West*. College Station: Texas A&M University Press, 2006.

———. *The Military and United States Indian Policy, 1865–1903*. New Haven: Yale University Press, 1988.

———. *Nelson A. Miles and the Twilight of the Frontier Army*. Lincoln: University of Nebraska Press, 1993.

———. *Soldiers, Sutlers, and Settlers: Garrison Life on the Texas Frontier*. College Station: Texas A&M University Press, 1987.

Wright, James E. *The Galena Lead District: Federal Policy and Practice, 1824–1847*. Madison: State Historical Society of Wisconsin, 1966.

Wright, Robert K., and Morris J. MacGregor, Jr. *Soldier-Statesmen of the Constitution*. Washington, D.C.: Center of Military History, 1987.

Articles and Book Chapters

Adler, William D. "State Capacity and Bureaucratic Autonomy in the Early United States: The Case of the Army Corps of Topographical Engineers." *Studies in American Political Development* 26 (October 2012): 107–124.

———, and Andrew J. Polsky. "Building the New American Nation: Economic Development, Public Goods, and the Early U.S. Army." *Political Science Quarterly* 125 (March 2010): 87–110.

Arndt, Jochen S. "The Highly Effective First Mississippi Volunteer Regiment in the Mexican War, 1846–1848." *Journal of Mississippi History* 69 (2007): 63–78.

Atherton, Lewis. "Western Foodstuffs in the Army Provisions Trade." *Agricultural History* 14 (October 1940): 161–169.

Baker, Anni P. "Daughters of Mars: Army Officers' Wives and Military Culture on the American Frontier." *Historian* 67 (Spring 2005): 20–42.

Ball, Durwood. "By Right of Conquest: Military Government in New Mexico and California." *Journal of the West* 41 (Summer 2002): 8–16.

———. "Stephen W. Kearny." In *Soldiers West: Biographies from the Military Frontier*, 2nd edition, ed. Paul Andrew Hutton and Durwood Ball, 43–71. Norman: University of Oklahoma Press, 2009.

Banks, William C. "Providing 'Supplemental Security': The Insurrection Act and the Military Role in Responding to Domestic Crises." *Journal of National Security Law & Policy* 3 (no. 1, 2009): 39–94.

Beaver, Daniel R. "The U.S. War Department in the Gaslight Era: Stephen Vincent Benét at the Ordnance Department, 1870–91." *Journal of Military History* 68 (January 2004): 105–132.

Belko, William S. "John C. Calhoun and the Creation of the Bureau of Indian Affairs: An Essay on Political Rivalry, Ideology, and Policymaking in the Early Republic." *South Carolina Historical Magazine* 105 (July 2004): 170–197.

Belohlavek, John M. "In Defense of Doughface Diplomacy: A Reevaluation of the Foreign Policy of James Buchanan." In *James Buchanan and the Coming of the Civil War*, ed. John W. Quist and Michael J. Birkner, 111–133. Gainesville: University Press of Florida, 2013.

———. "The Politics of Scandal: A Reassessment of John B. Floyd as Secretary of War, 1857–1861." *West Virginia History* 32 (April 1970): 145–160.

Beltman, Brian W. "Territorial Commands of the Army: The System Refined but not Perfected, 1815–1821." *Journal of the Early Republic* 11 (Summer 1991): 185–218.

Benton, William A. "Pennsylvania Revolutionary Officers and the Federal Constitution." *Pennsylvania History* 31 (1964): 419–435.

Birtle, Andrew J. "The Origins of the Legion of the United States." *Journal of Military History* 67 (October 2003): 1249–1262.

Blair, William. "The Use of Military Force to Protect the Gains of Reconstruction." *Civil War History* 51 (December 2005): 388–402.

Bouton, Terry. "A Road Closed: Rural Insurgency in Post-Independence Pennsylvania." *Journal of American History* 87 (December 2000): 855–887.

Braddock, Alan C. "Shooting the Beholder: Charles Schreyvogel and the Spectacle of Gun Vision." *American Art* 20 (Spring 2006): 36–59.

Brodhead, Michael J. "Of Mice and Mastodons: Contributions to the Literature of Mammalogy by Officers and Men of the United States Army in the Nineteenth Century." *Archives of Natural History* 18 (no. 3, 1991): 363–374.

Brooks, Risa A. "Integrating the Civil-Military Relations Subfield." *Annual Review of Political Science* 22 (2019): 379–398.

Brown, Richard Maxwell. "Western Violence: Structure, Values, Myth." *Western Historical Quarterly* 24 (February 1993): 4–20.

Buel, Richard, Jr. "Samson Shorn: The Impact of Revolutionary War on Estimates of the Republic's Strength." In *Arms and Independence: The Military Character of the American Revolution*, ed. Ronald Hoffman and Peter J. Albert, 144–165. Charlottesville: University Press of Virginia, 1984.

Burrows, Edwin G. "Military Experience and the Origins of Federalism and Anti-Federalism." In *Aspects of Early American Society and Politics*, ed. Jacob Jubb and Irwin Polishook, 83–92. Tarrytown, NY: Sleepy Hollow Restorations, 1924.

Caldwell, Norman W. "The Frontier Army Officer, 1794–1814." *Mid-America* 37 (April 1955): 101–128.

Campbell, John. "The Seminoles, the 'Bloodhound War' and Abolitionism, 1796–1865." *Journal of Southern History* 72 (May 2006): 259–302.

Carp, E. Wayne. "The Problem of National Defense in the Early American Republic." In *The American Revolution: Its Character and Limits*, ed. Jack P. Greene, 14–50. New York: New York University Press, 1987.

Case, Alfred A. "Abuse of Power: Andrew Jackson and the Indian Removal Act of 1830." *The Historian* 65 (Winter 2003): 1330–1353.

Cayton, Andrew R. L. "'Separate Interests' and the Nation-State: The Washington Administration and the Origins of Regionalism in the Trans-Appalachian West." *Journal of American History* 79 (June 1992): 39–67.

Citino, Robert M. "Military Histories Old and New: A Reintroduction." *American Historical Review* 112 (October 2007): 1070–1090.

Cloppersmith, Clifford P. "Indians in the Army: Professional Advocacy and the Regularization of Indian Military Service, 1889–1897." *Military History of the West* 26 (Fall 1996): 159–185.

Coleman, Aaron N. "'A Second Bounaparty?': A Reexamination of Alexander Hamilton during the Franco-American Crisis, 1796–1801." *Journal of the Early Republic* 28 (Summer 2008): 183–214.

Coles, Harry L. "From Peaceable Coercion to Balanced Forces, 1807–1815." In *Against All Enemies: Interpretations of American Military History from Colonial Times to the Present*, ed. Kenneth J. Hagan and William R. Roberts, 71–89. Westport, CT: Greenwood Press, 1986.

Conway, Stephen. "'The Great Mischief Complain'd of': Reflections on the Misconduct of British Soldiers in the Revolutionary War." *William and Mary Quarterly* 47 (July 1990): 370–390.

Cowdrey, Albert E. "Pioneering Environmental Law: The Army Corps of Engineers and the Refuse Act." *Pacific Historical Review* 44 (August 1975): 331–349.

Cox, John, and LaWanda Cox. "General O. O. Howard and the 'Misrepresented Bureau.'" *Journal of Southern History* 19 (November 1953): 427–456.

Crackel, Theodore J. "The Military Academy in the Context of Jeffersonian Reform." In *Thomas Jefferson's Military Academy: Founding West Point*, ed. Robert M. S. McDonald, 99–117. Charlottesville: University of Virginia Press, 2004.

Craig, Stephen C. "Medicine for the Military: George M. Sternberg on the Kansas Plains, 1866–1870." *Kansas History* 21 (Autumn 1998): 188–206.

Cress, Lawrence Delbert. "Reassessing American Military Requirements, 1783–1807." In *Against All Enemies: Interpretations of American Military History from Colonial Times to the Present*, ed. Kenneth J. Hagan and William R. Roberts, 49–69. Westport, CT: Greenwood Press, 1986.

Cutrer, Thomas W. "'A Lion in Her Path': Texas, New Mexico, and the United States Army, 1850." *Military History of the West* 34 (2004): 75–80.

Davies, Thomas M. Jr. "Assessments During the Mexican War: An Exercise in Futility." *New Mexico Historical Review* 41 (Summer 1966): 197–216.

Dawson, Joseph G., III. "American Civil-Military Relations and Military Government: The Service of Colonel Alexander Doniphan in the Mexican War," *Armed Forces and Society* 22 (Summer 1996): 555–572.

———. "Leaders for Manifest Destiny: American Volunteer Colonels Serving in the U.S.-War," *American Nineteenth Century History* 7 (June 2006): 253–280.

———. "The US Army in the South: Reconstruction as National Building." In *Armed Diplomacy: Two Centuries of American Campaigning*, 39–64. Fort Leavenworth, KS: Combat Studies Institute Press, 2003.

DeLay, Brian. "The Wider World of the Handsome Man: Southern Plains Indians Invade Mexico, 1830–1848." *Journal of the Early Republic* 27 (Spring 2007): 83–113.

Dobak, William A. "The Army and the Buffalo: A Demur." *Western Historical Quarterly* 26 (Summer 1995): 197–202.

Downs, Gregory P. "Three Faces of Sovereignty: Governing Confederate, Mexican, and Indian Texas in the Civil War Era." In *Civil War Wests: Testing the Limits of the United States.* Ed. Adam Arenson and Andrew R. Graybill, 118–138. Berkeley: University of California Press, 2015.

Eid, Leroy V. "American Indian Military Leadership: St. Clair's Defeat." *Journal of Military History* 57 (January 1993): 71–88.

———. "'A Kind of Running Fight': Indian Battlefield Tactics in the Late Eighteenth Century." *Western Pennsylvania Historical Magazine* 71 (1988): 147–171.

Ericson, David F. "The United States Military, State Development, and Slavery in the Early Republic." *Studies in American Political Development* 31 (April 2017): 130–148.

Eyal, Yonatan. "Young America and the Transformation of the Democratic Party." *Civil War History* 51 (September 2005): 245–268.

Feaver, Peter D. "Civil-Military Relations." *Annual Review of Political Science* 2 (1999): 211–241.

Fitzgerald, Michael S. "'Nature Unsubdued': Diplomacy, Expansion and the American Military Buildup of 1815–1816." *Mid-America* 77 (Winter 1995): 5–32.

———. "Rejecting Calhoun's Expansible Army Plan: The Army Reduction Act of 1821." *War in History* 3 (April 1996): 161–185.

Flaherty, Jane. "'The Exhausted Condition of the Treasury' on the Eve of the Civil War." *Civil War History* 55 (June 2009): 244–277.

Fleischman, Richard K., and Thomas N. Tyson. "Developing Expertise: Two Episodes in Early Nineteenth Century U.S. Management Accounting History." *Business and Economic History* 26 (Winter 1997): 365–380.

Flores, Dan. "Bison Ecology and Bison Diplomacy: The Southern Plains from 1800 to 1850." *Journal of American History* 78 (September 1991): 465–485.

Foreman, Sidney. "The United States Military Philosophical Society, 1802–1813." *William and Mary Quarterly* 2 (July 1945): 273–285.

Gallagher, Gary. "A Question of Loyalty." *Civil War Times* 52 (October 2013): 30–37.

Gallagher, Mary A. Y. "Reinterpreting the 'Very Trifling Mutiny' at Philadelphia in June 1783." *Pennsylvania Magazine of History and Biography* 119 (1995): 3–35.

Gibbs, William E. "Diaz' Executive Agents and United States Foreign Policy." *Journal of Interamerican Studies and World Affairs* 20 (May 1978): 165–190.

Gillette, Howard, Jr. "The Military Occupation of Cuba, 1899–1902: Workshop for American Progressivism." *American Quarterly* 25 (October 1973): 410–425.

Gough, Robert. "Officering the American Army, 1798." *William and Mary Quarterly* 43 (July 1986): 460–471.

Grandstaff, Mark R. "Preserving the 'Habits and Usages of War': William Tecumseh Sherman, Professional Reform, and the U.S. Army Officer Corps, 1865–1881, Revisited." *Journal of Military History* 62 (July 1998): 521–545.

Gratton, Brian. "Race or Politics? Henry Cabot Lodge and the Origins of the Immigration Restriction Movement in the United States." *Journal of Policy History* 30 (January 2018): 128–157.

Grippaldi, Richard N. "The Politics of Appointment in the Jacksonian Army: The (Non)Transfer of Ethan Allen Hitchcock to the Regiment of Dragoons, 1833." *Army History* 70 (Winter 2009): 26–35.

Hardy, William E. "South of the Border: Ulysses S. Grant and the French Intervention." *Civil War History* 54 (March 2008): 63–86.

Hauptman, Lawrence M. "General John E. Wool in Cherokee Country, 1836–1837: A Reinterpretation." *Georgia Historical Quarterly* 85 (Spring 2001): 1–26.

Hedren, Paul L. "Charles King." In *Soldiers West: Biographies from the Military Frontier*, 2nd edition, ed. Paul Andrew Hutton and Durwood Ball, 358–380. Norman: University of Oklahoma Press, 2009.

Heidler, Jeanne T. "'Embarrassing Situation': David E. Twiggs and the Surrender of United States Forces in Texas, 1861." *Military History of the Southwest* 21 (Fall 1991): 157–172.

Herrera, Ricardo A. "Self-Governance and the American Citizen as Soldier, 1775–1861." *Journal of Military History* 65 (January 2001): 21–52.

Higginbotham, Don. "War and State Formation in Revolutionary America." In *Empire and Nation: The American Revolution in the Atlantic World*, ed. Elija J. Gould and Peter S. Onuf, 54–71. Baltimore: Johns Hopkins University Press, 2005.

Hirsch, Adam. "The Collision of Military Cultures in Seventeenth-Century New England." *Journal of American History* 74 (March 1988): 1187–1212.

Holmes, Alice D. "'And I Was Always With Him': The Life of Jane Thorpy, Army Laundress." *Journal of Arizona History* 38 (Summer 1997): 177–190.

Holt, Marilyn Irvin. "Joined Forces: Robert Campbell and John Dougherty as Military Entrepreneurs." *Western Historical Quarterly* 30 (Summer 1999): 183–202.

Hoskin, Keith W., and Richard H. Macve. "The Genesis of Accountability: The West Point Connections." *Accounting, Organizations, and Society* 13 (1988): 37–73.

———. "Reappraising the Genesis of Managerialism: A Re-examination of the Role of Accounting in the Springfield Armory, 1815–1845." *Accounting, Auditing & Accountability Journal* 7, no. 2 (1994): 4–29.

Hyman, Harold. "Ulysses S. Grant I, Emperor of America? Some Civil-Military Continuities and Strains of the Civil War and Reconstruction." In *The United*

States Military under the Constitution of the United States, 1789–1989, ed. Richard H. Kohn, 175–192. New York: New York University Press, 1991.

Jackson, Donald. "Jefferson, Meriwether Lewis, and the Reduction of the United States Army." *Proceedings of the American Philosophical Society* 124 (June 1980): 91–96.

Jennings, Nathan A. "Texas Ranger Auxiliaries: Double-Edged Sword of the Campaign for Northern Mexico, 1846–1848." *Small Wars & Insurgencies* 26, no. 2 (2015): 313–334.

John, Richard R. "Rethinking the Early American State." *Polity* 40 (July 2008): 332–339.

———. "Ruling Passions: Political Economy in Nineteenth-Century America." *Journal of Policy History* 18 (January 2006): 1–20.

———. "The State *Is* Back In: What Now?" *Journal of the Early Republic* 38 (Spring 2018): 105–118.

Johnson, Mark W. "Emory Upton's Twenty-Six: Desertion and Divided Loyalty of U.S. Army Soldiers, 1860–1861." *Journal of Military History* 81 (July 2017): 747–774.

Johnson, Russell L. "'The Great Injustice': Social Status and the Distribution of Military Pensions after the Civil War." *Journal of the Gilded Age and Progressive Era* 10 (April 2011): 137–160.

Jordan, Weymouth T., Jr., John D. Chapala, and Shan C. Sutton. "'Notorious as the Noonday Sun': Capt. Alexander Welch Reynolds and the New Mexico Territory, 1849–1859." *New Mexico Historical Review* 75 (October 2000): 456–508.

Kanon, Thomas. "'A Slow, Laborious Slaughter': The Battle of Horseshoe Bend." *Tennessee Historical Quarterly* 58 (Spring 1999): 2–15.

Karr, Ronald Dale. "'Why Should You Be So Ferocious?': The Violence of the Pequot War." *Journal of American History* 85 (December 1998): 876–909.

Karsten, Peter. "The 'New' American Military History: A Map of the Territory, Explored and Unexplored." *American Quarterly* 36 (Summer 1984): 389–418.

Katznelson, Ira. "Flexible Capacity: The Military and Early American Statebuilding." In *Shaped by War and Trade: International Influences on American Political Development*, ed. Ira Katznelson and Martin Shefter, 58–71. Princeton: Princeton University Press, 2002.

Kaufman, Scott, and John A. Soares Jr. "'Sagacious beyond Praise?' Winfield Scott and Anglo-American–Canadian Border Diplomacy, 1837–1860." *Diplomatic History* 30 (January 2006): 57–82.

Kenner, Charles. "Guardians in Blue: The United States Cavalry and the Growth of the Texas Range Cattle Industry." *Journal of the West* 34 (January 1995): 46–54.

King, Darwin L., Kathleen M. Premo, and Carl J. Case. "Historical Influences on Modern Cost Accounting Practices." *Academy of Accounting and Financial Studies Journal* 13 (September 2009): 21–32.

Klyza, Christopher McGrory. "The United States Army, Natural Resources, and Political Development in the Nineteenth Century." *Polity* 35 (Fall 2002): 1–28.

Kohn, Richard H. "The Constitution and National Security: The Intent of the Framers." In *The United States Military under the Constitution of the United*

States, 1789–1989, ed. Richard H. Kohn, 61–94. New York: New York University Press, 1991.

———. "Inside the History of the Newburgh Conspiracy: America and the Coup d'Etat." *William and Mary Quarterly* 27 (April 1970): 187–220.

Krueger, David. "The Red Cross, the Daughters of the American Revolution, and the Origins of the Army Nurse Corps in the Spanish-American War." *Journal of Military History* 83 (April 2019): 409–434.

Larson, John Lauritz. "'Bind the Republic Together': The National Union and the Struggle for a System of Internal Improvements." *Journal of American History* 74 (September 1987): 363–387.

Laurie, Clayton D. "Filling the Breech: Military Aid to Civil Power in the Trans-Mississippi West." *Western Historical Quarterly* 25 (Summer 1994): 149–162.

Learned, Henry Barrett. "The Establishment of the Secretaryship of the Interior." *American Historical Review* 16 (July 1911): 751–773.

Lee, Wayne E. "Early American Ways of War: A New Reconnaissance, 1600–1815." *The Historical Journal* 44 (March 2001): 269–289.

———. "Fortify, Fight, or Flee: Tuscarora and Cherokee Defensive Warfare and Military Culture Adaptation." *Journal of Military History* 68 (July 2004): 713–770.

———. "Peace Chiefs and Blood Revenge: Patterns of Restraint in Native American Warfare, 1500–1800." *Journal of Military History* 71 (July 2007): 701–741.

Levinson, Irving W. "A New Paradigm for an Old Conflict: The Mexico-United States War." *Journal of Military History* 73 (April 2009): 393–416.

———. "Occupation and Stability Dilemmas of the Mexican War: Origins and Solutions." In *Armed Diplomacy: Two Centuries of American Campaigning*, 1–16. Fort Leavenworth, KS: Combat Studies Institute Press, 2003.

Lewis, James E. "A Tornado on the Horizon: The Jefferson Administration, the Retrocession Crisis, and the Louisiana Purchase." In *Empires of the Imagination: Transatlantic Histories of the Louisiana Purchase*, ed. Peter J. Kasor and François Weil, 117–140. Charlottesville: University of Virginia Press, 2009.

Linn, Brian M. "*The American Way of War* Revisited." *Journal of Military History* 66 (April 2002): 501–530.

———. "The Long Twilight of the Frontier Army." *Western Historical Quarterly* 27 (Summer 1996): 141–167.

———. "The US Army and Nation Building and Pacification in the Philippines." In *Armed Diplomacy: Two Centuries of American Campaigning*, 77–90. Fort Leavenworth, KS: Combat Studies Institute Press, 2003.

Lisowski, Lori A. "The Future of West Point: Senate Debate on the Military Academy During the Civil War." *Civil War History* 34 (March 1988): 5–21.

Lookingbill, Brad. "The Killing Fields of Wounded Knee." *Reviews in American History* 33 (September 2005): 379–386.

Maass, John. "'Humanity Mourns over Such a Site': The Army's Disaster at Terre aux Boeufs, 1809." *Army History* 85 (Fall 2012): 6–23.

MacKinnon, William P. "And the War Came: James Buchanan, the Utah Expedition, and the Decision to Intervene." *Utah Historical Quarterly* 76 (Winter 2008): 22–37.

———. "The Buchanan Spoils System and the Utah Expedition: Careers of W. M. F. Magraw and John M. Hockaday." *Utah Historical Quarterly* 31 (Spring 1963): 127–150.

———. "Epilogue to the Utah War: Impact and Legacy." *Journal of Mormon History* 29 (Fall 2003): 186–248.

———. "The Gap in the Buchanan Revival: The Utah Expedition of 1857–58." *Utah Historical Quarterly* 45 (Winter 1977): 36–46.

———. "Hammering Utah, Squeezing Mexico, and Coveting Cuba: James Buchanan's White House Intrigues." *Utah Historical Quarterly* 80 (no. 2, 2012): 132–151.

———. "Prelude to Armageddon: James Buchanan, Brigham Young, and a President's Initiation to Bloodshed." In *James Buchanan and the Coming of the Civil War*, ed. John W. Quist and Michael J. Birkner, 46–85. Gainesville: University Press of Florida, 2013.

May, Robert E. "Young American Males and Filibustering in the Age of Manifest Destiny: The United States Army as a Cultural Mirror." *Journal of American History* 78 (December 1991): 857–886.

Mayer, David N. "'Necessary and Proper': West Point and Thomas Jefferson's Constitutionalism." In *Thomas Jefferson's Military Academy: Founding West Point*. Ed. Robert M. S. McDonald, 54–76. Charlottesville: University of Virginia Press, 2004.

McCaslin, Richard B. "United States Regulars in Gray: Edward Ingraham and Company A, 1st Regular Confederate Cavalry." *Southwestern Historical Quarterly* 118 (July 2014): 25–45.

McGovern, Rory M. "The School of Experience: George W. Goethals and the U.S. Army, 1876–1907." *Journal of Military History* 81 (April 2017): 395–424.

McKenna, Marian C. "Above the Blue Line: Policing the Frontier in the Canadian and American West, 1870–1900." In *The Borderlands of the American and Canadian Wests: Essays on Regional History of the Forty-ninth Parallel*, ed. Sterling Evans, 81–106. Lincoln: University of Nebraska Press, 2006.

McNitt, Frank. "Navajo Campaigns and the Occupation of New Mexico, 1847–1848." *New Mexico Historical Review* 43 (July 1968): 173–194.

Menard, Andrew. "Striking a Line through the Great American Desert." *Journal of American Studies* 45 (May 2011): 267–280.

Metcalf, Brandon J. "The Nauvoo Legion and the Prevention of the Utah War." *Utah Historical Quarterly* 72 (Fall 2004): 300–321.

Miller, Craig E. "'Give the Book to Clemens.'" *American History* 34 (April 1999): 40–47.

Morris, Richard B. "Andrew Jackson, Strikebreaker." *American Historical Review* 55 (June 1949): 54–68.

Morrison, James L., Jr. "Military Education and Strategic Thought, 1846–1861." In *Against All Enemies: Interpretations of American Military History from Colonial Times to the Present*, ed. Kenneth J. Hagan and William R. Roberts, 113–131. Westport, CT: Greenwood Press, 1986.

Morrison, W. B. "Fort Towson." *Chronicles of Oklahoma* 8 (June 1930): 226–232.

Morsman, Jenry. "Securing America: Jefferson's Fluid Plans for the Western Perimeter." In *Across the Continent: Jefferson, Lewis and Clark, and the Making of America*, ed. Douglas Seefeldt, Jeffrey L. Hantman, and Peter S. Onuf, 46–61. Charlottesville: University of Virginia Press, 2005.

Murphy, William J., Jr. "John Adams: The Politics of the Additional Army, 1798–1800." *New England Quarterly* 52 (June 1979): 234–249.

Nelson, Harold B. "Military Roads for War and Peace, 1791–1836." *Military Affairs* 19 (Spring 1955): 1–14.

Nelson, Paul D. "General Charles Scott, the Kentucky Mounted Volunteers, and the Northwest Indian Wars, 1784–1794." *Journal of the Early Republic* 6 (Fall 1986): 219–251.

Newell, Clayton R., and Charles R. Shrader. "The U.S. Army's Transition to Peace, 1865–66." *Journal of Military History* 77 ((July 2013): 867–894.

Nichols, Roger L. "Soldiers as Farmers: Army Agriculture in the Missouri Valley, 1818–1827." *Agricultural History* 44 (April 1970): 213–222.

Nicklason, Fred. "The Civil War Contracts Committee." *Civil War History* 17 (September 1971): 232–244.

O'Brien, Greg. "The Conqueror Meets the Unconquered: Negotiating Cultural Boundaries on the Post-Revolutionary Southern Frontier." *Journal of Southern History* 67 (February 2001): 39–72.

O'Connell, Charles F., Jr. "The Corps of Engineers and the Rise of Modern Management, 1827–1856." In *Military Enterprise and Technological Change: Perspectives on the American Experience*, ed. Merritt Roe Smith, 87–116. Cambridge: MIT Press, 1985.

Oliva, Leo E. "The Army and the Fur Trade." *Journal of the West* 26 (October 1987): 21–26.

Oman, Kerry R. "The Beginning of the End: The Indian Peace Commission of 1867–1868." *Great Plains Quarterly* 22 (Winter 2002): 35–51.

Onuf, Peter S., and Jeffrey L. Hantman. "Introduction." In *Across the Continent: Jefferson, Lewis and Clark, and the Making of America*, ed. Douglas Seefeldt, Jeffrey L. Hantman, and Peter S. Onuf. Charlottesville: University of Virginia Press, 2005.

Ott, Jennifer. "'Ruining' the Rivers in the Snake Country: The Hudson's Bay Company Fur Desert Policy." *Oregon Historical Quarterly* 104 (Summer 2004): 166–195.

Parrish, Charles E., and Leland R. Johnson. "Engineering the Kentucky River: A Disastrous Debut." *Register of the Kentucky Historical Society* 95 (Autumn 1997): 369–394.

Pearcy, Matthew T. "Science, Politics and Bureaucracy: Andrew A. Humphreys and the Office of Pacific Railroad Explorations and Surveys." *Military History of the West* 38 (2008): 85–114.

Polsky, Andrew J., and William D. Adler. "The State in a Blue Uniform." *Polity* 40 (July 2008): 348–354.

Ponko, Vincent, Jr. "The Military Explorers of the American West, 1838–1860." In

North American Exploration, ed. John Logan Allen, 332–411. Lincoln: University of Nebraska Press, 1997.

Posey, John Thornton. "Rascality Revisited: In Defense of General James Wilkinson." *Filson Club History Quarterly* 74 (Fall 2000): 309–352.

Price, Catherine. "Lakotas and Euroamericans: Contrasted Concepts of 'Chieftainship' and Decision-Making Authority." *Ethnohistory* 41 (Summer 1994): 447–463.

Prucha, Francis Paul. "Andrew Jackson's Indian Policy: A Reassessment." *Journal of American History* 56 (December 1969): 527–539.

Ranson, Edward. "Nelson A. Miles as Commanding General., 1895–1903." *Military Affairs* 39 (Winter 1966): 179–200.

Resch, John, and Walter Sargent. "Changing Meanings of the American Revolution: An Overview, 1789–2006." In *War & Society in the American Revolution: Mobilizing and Home Fronts*. Ed. John Resch and Walter Sargent, 291–299. DeKalb: Northern Illinois Press, 2007.

Reuss, Martin. "Andrew A. Humphreys and the Development of Hydraulic Engineering: Politics and Technology in the Army Corps of Engineers, 1850–1950." *Technology and Culture* 26 (January 1985): 1–33.

Rives, Timothy. "Grant, Babcock, and the Whiskey Ring." *Prologue* 32 (Fall 2000): 142–153.

Robinson, Charles M., III. "Don't Ruin a Good Story with the Facts: An Analysis of Henry Flipper's Account of his Court-Martial in *Black Frontiersman*." *Southwestern Historical Quarterly* 111 (July 2007): 51–71.

Rosenberg, Nathan. "Technological Change in the Machine Tool Industry, 1840–1910." *Journal of Economic History* 23 (December 1963): 414–443.

Royster, Charles. "Founding a Nation in Blood: Military Conflict and American Nationality." In *Arms and Independence: The Military Character of the American Revolution*, ed. Ronald Hoffman and Peter J. Albert, 25–49. Charlottesville: University Press of Virginia, 1984.

Rusche, Timothy M. "Treachery Within the United States Army." *Pennsylvania History* 65 (Autumn 1998): 478–491.

Russell, Peter. "Redcoats in the Wilderness: British Officers and Irregular Warfare in Europe and America, 1740 to 1760." *William and Mary Quarterly*, 3rd Series, 35 (October 1978): 629–650.

Rust, Thomas C. "Settlers, Soldiers, and Scoundrels: Economic Tension in a Frontier Military Town." *Military History of the West* 31 (Fall 2001): 117–138.

Schindler, Harold. "The Bear River Massacre: New Historical Evidence." *Utah Historical Quarterly* 67 (October 1999): 300–308.

Seidule, James Tyrus. "'Treason is Treason': Civil War Memory at West Point, 1861–1902." *Journal of Military History* 76 (April 2012): 427–452.

Skeen, C. Edward. "Calhoun, Crawford, and the Politics of Retrenchment." *South Carolina Historical Magazine* 73 (July 1972): 141–155.

———, and Richard H. Kohn. "The Newburgh Conspiracy Reconsidered." *William and Mary Quarterly* 31 (April 1974): 273–298.

Skelton, William B. "The Army in the Age of the Common Man, 1815–1845." In *Against All Enemies: Interpretations of American Military History from Colonial*

Times to the Present, ed. Kenneth J. Hagan and William R. Roberts, 91–112. Westport, CT: Greenwood Press, 1986.

———. "The Commanding General and the Problem of Command in the United States Army, 1821–1841." *Military Affairs* 34 (December 1970): 117–122.

———. "The Confederation's Regulars: A Social Profile of Enlisted Service in America's First Standing Army." *William and Mary Quarterly* 46 (October 1989): 770–785.

———. "High Army Leadership in the Era of the War of 1812: The Making and Remaking of the Officer Corps." *William and Mary Quarterly*, 3rd ser., 51 (April 1994): 253–274.

———. "Officers and Politicians: The Origins of Army Politics in the United States before the Civil War." *Armed Forces and Society* 6 (Fall 1979): 22–48.

———. "Social Roots of the American Military Profession: The Officer Corps of America's First Peacetime Army, 1784–1789." *Journal of Military History* 54 (October 1990): 435–452.

Slap, Andrew L. "'The Strong Arm of the Military Power of the United States': The Chicago Fire, the Constitution, and Reconstruction." *Civil War History* 47 (June 2001): 146–163.

Smith, Carlton. "Congressional Attitudes towards Military Preparedness during the Monroe Administration." *Military Affairs* 40 (February 1976): 22–25.

Smith, Mark A. "The Politics of Military Professionalism: The Engineer Company and the Political Activities of the Antebellum U.S. Army Corps of Engineers." *Journal of Military History* 80 (April 2016): 355–387.

Smith, Merritt Roe. "Army Ordnance and the 'American System' of Manufacturing, 1815–1861." In *Military Enterprise and Technological Change: Perspectives on the American Experience*, ed. Merritt Roe Smith, 39–86. Cambridge: MIT Press, 1985.

———. "Industry, Technology, and the 'Labor Question' in 19th Century America: Seeking Synthesis." *Technology and Culture* 32 (July 1991): 555–570.

———. "Introduction." In *Military Enterprise and Technological Change: Perspectives on the American Experience*, ed. Merritt Roe Smith, 1–37. Cambridge: MIT Press, 1985.

———. "Two Cultures in Conflict: Soldiers and Civilians at Harpers Ferry, VA." In *Soldiers and Civilians: The U.S. Army and the American People*, ed. Gerry D. Ryan and Timothy K. Nenninger, 81–90. Washington, D.C.: National Archives and Records Administration, 1987.

Smith, Sherry L. "Lost Soldiers: Re-searching the Army in the American West." *Western Historical Quarterly* 29 (Summer 1998): 149–164.

Smith, Thomas T. "The U.S. Army and the Alamo, 1846–1877." *Southwestern Historical Quarterly*118 (January 2015): 263–285.

———. "West Point and the Indian Wars, 1802–1891." *Military History of the West* 24 (Spring 1994): 24–56.

Smits, David D. "'Fighting Fire with Fire': The Frontier Army's Use of Indian Scouts and Allies in the Trans-Mississippi Campaigns, 1860–1890." *American Indian Culture and Research Journal* 22, no. 1 (1998): 73–116.

———. "The Frontier Army and the Destruction of the Buffalo, 1865–1883." *Western Historical Quarterly* 25 (Autumn 1995): 312–338.

———. "More on the Army and the Buffalo." *Western Historical Quarterly* 26 (Summer 1995): 203–208.

Sparrow, Bartholomew H. "American Political Development, State-Building, and the 'Security State': Reviving a Research Agenda." *Polity* 40 (July 2008): 355–367.

Spiller, Roger J. "Calhoun's Expansible Army: The History of a Military Idea." *South Atlantic Quarterly* 79 (Spring 1980): 189–203.

Stagg, J. C. A. "Enlisted Men in the United States Army, 1812–1815: A Preliminary Survey." *William and Mary Quarterly*, 3rd Series, 43 (October 1986): 615–645.

———. "James Madison and George Mathews: The East Florida Revolution of 1812 Reconsidered." *Diplomatic History* 30 (January 2006): 23–55.

———. "Soldiers in Peace and War: Comparative Perspectives on the Recruitment of the United States Army, 1802–1815." *William and Mary Quarterly*, 3rd Series, 57 (January 2000): 79–120.

———. "United States Army Officers in the War of 1812: A Statistical and Behavioral Portrait." *Journal of Military History* 76 (October 2012): 1001–1034.

Swagerty, William R. "'The Leviathan of the North': American Perceptions of the Hudson's Bay Company, 1816–1846." *Oregon Historical Quarterly* 104 (Winter 2003): 478–517.

Thornton, Russell. "Cherokee Population Losses during the Trail of Tears: A New Perspective and a New Estimate." *Ethnohistory* 31 (Fall 1984): 289–300.

Tidball, Eugene C. "A Subaltern's First Experiences in the Old Army." *Civil War History* 45 (September 1999): 197–222.

Trefousse, Hans L. "Civil Warriors in Memory and Memoir: Grant and Sherman Remember." *Georgia Historical Quarterly* 75 (Fall 1991): 542–556.

Utley, Robert M. "The Frontier and the American Military Tradition." In *The American Military on the Frontier: Proceedings of the 7th Military History Symposium*, ed. James P. Tate. Washington, D.C.: Office of Air Force History, 1978.

Vargas, Mark A. "The Military Justice System and the Use of Illegal Punishments as Causes of Desertion in the U.S. Army, 1821–1835." *Journal of Military History* 55 (January 1991): 1–19.

———. "The Progressive Agent of Mischief: The Whiskey Ration and Temperance in the United States Army." *The Historian* 67 (Summer 2005): 199–216.

Volpe, Vernon L. "The Origins of the Frémont Expeditions: John J. Abert and the Scientific Exploration of the Trans-Mississippi West," *The Historian* 62 (August 2000): 244–262.

Wade, Arthur P. "The Military Command Structure: The Great Plains, 1853–1891." *Journal of the West* 15 (July 1976): 5–22.

Waghelstein, John D. "Preparing the U.S. Army for the Wrong War, Educational and Doctrinal Failure, 1865–91." *Small Wars and Insurgencies* 10 (Spring 1999): 1–33.

———. "The United States Army's First War—War in the Northwest Territory, 1790–1795." *Small Wars and Insurgencies* 12 (Summer 2001): 1–18.

Wagoner, Jennings L., Jr., and Christine Coalwell McDonald. "Mr. Jefferson's

Academy." In *Thomas Jefferson's Military Academy: Founding West Point*, ed. Robert M. S. McDonald, 118–153. Charlottesville: University of Virginia Press, 2004.

Wainwright, Nicholas B. "The Life and Death of Major Thomas Biddle." *Pennsylvania Magazine of History and Biography* 104 (July 1980): 326–344.

Walraven, Bill, and Margorie K. Walraven. "The 'Sabine Chute': The U.S. Army and the Texas Revolution." *Southwestern Historical Quarterly* 107 (April 2004): 573–601.

Warren, Jason W. "Liberty Paradox: The Failure of the Military System in Mid-Seventeenth-Century New England." In *Drawdown: The American Way of Postwar*, ed. Jason W. Warren, 52–72. New York: New York University Press, 2016.

Watson, Samuel J. "The Army Secures the Mississippi Valley: Officers, Filibusters, and Spain, 1793–1798." *Southern Studies: An Interdisciplinary Journal* 20 (Winter 2013–14): 33–63.

———. "Conquerors, Peacekeepers, or Both? The U.S. Army and West Florida, 1810–1811, a New Perspective." *Florida Historical Quarterly* 92 (Fall 2013): 69–105.

———. "Continuity in Civil-Military Relations and Expertise: The U.S. Army during the Decade before the Civil War." *Journal of Military History* 75 (January 2011): 221–250.

———. "Developing 'Republican Machines': West Point and the Struggle to Render the Officer Corps Safe for America, 1802–1833." In *Thomas Jefferson's Military Academy: Founding West Point*, ed. Robert M. S. McDonald, 154–181. Charlottesville: University of Virginia Press, 2004.

———. "Flexible Gender Roles during the Market Revolution: Family, Friendship, Marriage, and Marriage, and Masculinity among U.S. Army Officers, 1815–1846." *Journal of Social History* 29 (Fall 1995): 81–106.

———. "How the Army Became Accepted: West Point Socialization, Military Accountability, and the Nation-State During the Jacksonian Era." *American Nineteenth Century History* 7 (June 2006): 219–251.

———. "James Monroe and American Military Policy: A Lifetime of Connection and Advocacy for a Standing Army." *Virginia Magazine of History and Biography* 128 (March 2020): 2–43.

———. "Knowledge, Interest, and the Limits of Military Professionalism: The Discourse on American Coastal Defense, 1815–1860." *War in History* 5 (July 1998): 280–307.

———. "Military Learning and Adaptation Shaped by Social Context: The U.S. Army and Its 'Indian Wars,' 1790–1890." *Journal of Military History* 82 (April 2018): 373–438.

———. "Surprisingly Professional: Trajectories in Army Officer Corps Drawdowns, 1783–1848." In *Drawdown: The American Way of Postwar*, ed. Jason W. Warren, 73–106. New York: New York University Press, 2016.

———. "Trusting to 'the Chapter of Accidents': Contingency, Necessity, and Self-Constraint in Jeffersonian National Security Policy." *Journal of Military History* 76 (October 2012): 973–1000.

———. "United States Army Officers Fight the 'Patriot War': Responses to Filibustering on the Canadian Border, 1837–1839." *Journal of the Early Republic* 18 (Fall 1998): 485–519.

Watt, Robert N. "'Horses Worn to Mere Shadows': The Ninth U.S. Cavalry's Campaign against the Apaches in New Mexico Territory, 1879–1881." *New Mexico Historical Review* 86 (Spring 2011): 197–222.

———. "A Reevaluation of Colonel Benjamin Grierson's Trans-Pecos Campaigns against Victorio, July–August 1880." *Southwestern Historical Quarterly* 118 (January 2015): 241–262.

———. "Victorio's Military and Political Leadership of the Warm Springs Apaches." *War in History* 18 (November 2011): 457–494.

Wettemann, Robert P., Jr. "A Part or Apart: The Alleged Isolation of Antebellum U.S. Army Officers." *American Nineteenth Century History* 7 (June 2006): 193–217.

White, Bruce. "The American Indian as Soldier, 1890–1909." *Canadian Review of American Studies* 7 (no. 1, 1976): 15–25.

White, Richard. "The Winning of the West: The Expansion of the Western Sioux in the Eighteenth and Nineteenth Centuries." *Journal of American History* 65 (September 1978): 319–343.

Williams, T. Harry. "The Attack Upon West Point During the Civil War." *Mississippi Valley Historical Review* 25 (March 1939): 491–504.

Wilson, Mark R. "The Politics of Procurement: Military Origins of Bureaucratic Autonomy." *Journal of Policy History* 18 (January 2006): 44–73.

Wilson, R. C. "The Great Custer Battle of 1903." *Mankind: The Magazine of Popular History* 5 no. 5 (1976): 52–59.

Wood, Cynthia A. "The Lieutenants and the Lady: The Trials of Elizabeth Easton Morton." *Journal of Arizona History* 40 (Summer 1990): 157–180.

Wooster, Robert. "The Army and the Politics of Expansion: Texas and the Southwestern Borderlands, 1870–1886." *Southwestern Historical Quarterly* 93 (October 1989): 151–168.

———. "'A Difficult and Forlorn Country': The Military Looks at the Southwest, 1850–1881." *Arizona and the West* 28 (Winter 1986): 339–356.

———. "Fort Davis and the Close of a Military Frontier." *Southwestern Historical Quarterly* 105 (October 2006): 173–192.

———. "The Frontier Army and the Occupation of the West, 1865–1900." In *Armed Diplomacy: Two Centuries of American Campaigning*, 65–76. Fort Leavenworth, KS: Combat Studies Institute Press, 2003.

———. "John M. Schofield and the 'Multipurpose' Army." *American Nineteenth Century History* 7 (June 2006): 173–191.

———. "'The Whole Company Have Done It:' The U.S. Army and the Fort Davis Murder of 1860." *Journal of the West* 32 (April 1993): 19–28.

Young, Tommy R., II. "The United States Army and the Institution of Slavery in Louisiana, 1803–1835." *Louisiana Studies* 13 (Fall 1974): 201–222.

Zogbaum, Rufus Fairchild. "The Regulars in the Civil War." *North American Review* 167 (July 1898): 16–26.

Dissertations, Internet Resources, and Unpublished Materials

Adams, Francis R. "An Annotated Edition of the Personal Letters of Robert E. Lee, April 1885-April 1861." Ph.D. diss., University of Maryland, 1955.

Ball, Durwood. "The Regulars Return: The U.S. Army's Protection of Lincoln's Journey in February 1861." Paper presented at the Society for Military History Conference, Louisville, Kentucky, April 2018.

Childress, David T. "The Army in Transition: The United States Army, 1815–1846." Ph.D. diss., Mississippi State University, 1974.

Cox, J. Wendel. "A World Together, A World Apart: The United States and the Arikaras, 1803–1851." Ph.D. diss., University of Minnesota, 1998.

Fitzgerald, Michael S. "Europe and the United States Defense Establishment: American Military Policy and Strategy, 1815–1821." Ph.D. diss., Purdue University, 1990.

Gooden, Randall Scott. "The Completion of a Revolution: West Virginia from Statehood through Reconstruction." Ph.D. diss., West Virginia University, 1995.

Hamburger, Kenneth Earl. "The Technology, Doctrine, and Politics of U.S. Coast Defenses, 1880–1945: A Case Study in U.S. Defense Planning." Ph.D. diss., Duke University, 1986.

Hinton, Harwood Perry. "The Military Career of John Ellis Wool., 1812–1863." Ph.D. diss., University of Wisconsin, 1963.

Johnston, Louis, and Samuel Williamson. "What Was the GDP Worth Then?" Measuring Worth. https://measuringworth.com/datasets/usgdp.

Kershner, William. "Sylvanius Thayer: A Biography." Ph.D. diss., West Virginia University, 1976.

Lain, Bobby Dave. "North of Fifty-Three: Army, Treasury Department, and Navy Administration of Alaska, 1867–1884." Ph.D. diss., University of Texas, 1974.

Lewis, Monte Ross. "Chickasaw Removal: Betrayal of the Beloved Warriors, 1794–1844." Ph.D. diss., North Texas State University, 1981.

Miller, Cynthia Allen. "The U.S. Army Logistics Complex: A Case Study of the Northern Frontier." Ph.D. diss., Syracuse University, 1991.

Molloy, Peter Michael. "Technical Education and the Young Republic: West Point as America's Ecole Polytechnique, 1802–1833." Ph.D. diss., Brown University, 1975.

Nedergaard, Robert Eric. "Duty, Honor, Country, and Race: The Failure of Desegregation at West Point in the Nineteenth Century." Ph.D. diss., Arizona State University, 2007.

Nelson, Marion Christina. "Power in Motion: Western Success Stories of the Jeffersonian Republic." Ph.D. diss., University of Pennsylvania, 2006.

O'Donnell, Charles F. "The United States Army and the Origins of Modern Management, 1818–1860." Ph.D. diss., Ohio State University, 1982.

Officer, Lawrence H., and Samuel Williamson. "Explaining the Measures of Worth." www.measuringworth.com/explaining_measures_of_worth.php.

Pruitt, James Herman, II. "Leonard Wood and the American Empire." Ph.D. diss., Texas A&M University, 2011.

Shallat, Todd Arkin. "Structures in the Stream: A History of Water, Science, and the

Civil Activities of the U.S. Army Corps of Engineers, 1700–1861." Ph.D. diss., Carnegie-Mellon University, 1986.

Smith, Thomas Ty. "Slave-Owning U. S. Army Officers in Texas, 1850, 1860," August 24, 2020. Unpublished copy in author's possession.

Steinhauer, Dale Richard. "'Sogers': Enlisted Men in the U.S. Army, 1815–1860." Ph.D. diss., University of North Carolina, 1992.

Swails, Thomas W. "John McAllister Schofield: Military Diplomat." MA thesis, University of Hawaii, 1966.

Thoreau, Henry David. "Resistance to Civil Government," *Aesthetic Papers*, ed. Elizabeth P. Peabody. Putnam, 1849. http://commons.digitalthoreau.org/civil/resistance-to-civil-government/rcg-1-14.

United States Senate. "The Civil War Senate Reacts to Secession." www.senate.gov/artandhistory/history/common/expulsion_cases/CivilWarExpulsion.htm.

Watson, Samuel J. "Militarily Effective But Politically Contingent: Evaluating U.S. Army Pacification Efforts on the Northwestern Trans-Mississippi Frontier, 1820–1846." Paper presented at the annual meeting of the Society for Military History Conference, Ogden, Utah, April 2008.

———. "Professionalism, Social Attitudes, and Civil-Military Accountability in the U.S. Army Officer Corps, 1815–1846." Ph.D. diss., Rice University, 1996.

Williamson, Samuel. "Seven Ways to Compute the Relative Value of a U.S. Dollar Amount—1774 to Present." www.measuringworth.com/calculators/uscompare.

Young, Tommy R., II. "The United States Army in the South, 1789–1835." Ph.D. diss., Louisiana State University, 1973.

Index